11TH EDITION

ESSENTIALS OF CRIMINAL JUSTICE

LARRY J. SIEGEL
University of Massachusetts, Lowell

JOHN L. WORRALL
University of Texas at Dallas

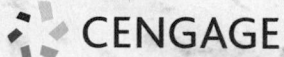

CENGAGE

Australia • Brazil • Mexico • Singapore • United Kingdom • United States

Essentials of Criminal Justice, **Eleventh Edition**
Larry J. Siegel and John L. Worrall

Senior Product Director: Marta Lee-Perriard

Product Team Manager: Carolyn Henderson Meier

Senior Content Developer: Shelley Murphy

Product Assistant: Megan Nauer

Senior Marketing Manager: Mark Linton

Senior Content Project Manager: Christy Frame

Production Service and Compositor: MPS Limited

Photo Development Editor: Kim Adams Fox

Photo Researcher: Anjali Kambli, Lumina Datamatics Ltd.

Text Researcher: Aruna Sekar, Lumina Datamatics Ltd.

Copy Editor: Lunaea Weatherstone

Senior Art Director: Helen Bruno

Text and Cover Designer: Lisa Buckley

Cover Image: flag: iStockPhoto.com/scottjay; stars: Joseph Sohm/Shutterstock.com

For product information and technology assistance, contact us at **Cengage Customer & Sales Support, 1-800-354-9706.**

For permission to use material from this text or product, submit all requests online at **www.cengage.com/permissions.** Further permissions questions can be e-mailed to **permissionrequest@cengage.com.**

Library of Congress Control Number: 2017938036

Student Edition:
ISBN: 978-1-337-55777-1

Loose-leaf Edition:
ISBN: 978-1-337-62011-6

Cengage
20 Channel Center Street
Boston, MA 02210
USA

Cengage is a leading provider of customized learning solutions with employees residing in nearly 40 different countries and sales in more than 125 countries around the world. Find your local representative at **www.cengage.com.**

Cengage products are represented in Canada by Nelson Education, Ltd.

To learn more about Cengage platforms and services, visit **www.cengage.com.** To register or access your online learning solution or purchase materials for your course, visit **www.cengagebrain.com.**

Printed in the United States of America
Print Number: 01   Print Year: 2017

This book is dedicated to
my children, Eric, Julie, Rachel, and Andrew;
my grandchildren, Jack, Brooke, and Kayla Jean;
my sons-in-law, Jason Macy and Patrick Stephens;
and my wife, partner, and best friend, Therese J. Libby.
L. J. S.

This book is dedicated to my wife, Sabrina. Thank
you for your continued love and support.
J. L. W.

About the Authors

LARRY J. SIEGEL was born in the Bronx. While living on Jerome Avenue and attending City College of New York in the 1960s, he was swept up in the social and political currents of the time. He became intrigued with the influence contemporary culture had on individual behavior: Did people shape society, or did society shape people? He applied his interest in social forces and human behavior to the study of crime and justice. Graduating from college in 1968, he was accepted into the first class of the newly opened program in criminal justice at the State University of New York at Albany, where he earned both his MA and PhD degrees. Dr. Siegel began  his teaching career at Northeastern University, where he was a faculty member for nine years. He also held teaching positions at the University of Nebraska–Omaha and Saint Anselm College in New Hampshire before being appointed a full professor in the School of Criminology and Justice Studies at the University of Massachusetts–Lowell. Dr. Siegel retired from full-time classroom teaching in 2015 and now teaches exclusively online. He has written extensively in the area of crime and justice, including books on juvenile law, delinquency, criminology, criminal justice, corrections, and criminal procedure. He is a court-certified expert on police conduct and has testified in numerous legal cases. The father of four and grandfather of three, Larry Siegel and his wife, Terry, now reside in Naples, Florida, with their two dogs, Watson and Cody.

JOHN L. WORRALL is Professor of Criminology at the University of Texas at Dallas. A Seattle native, he received a BA, double majoring in psychology and law and justice, from Central Washington University in 1994. Both his MA (criminal justice) and PhD (political science) were received from Washington State University,  where he graduated in 1999. From 1999 to 2006, he was a member of the criminal justice faculty at California State University, San Bernardino. He joined UTD in Fall 2006. Dr. Worrall has published articles and book chapters on topics ranging from legal issues in policing to crime measurement. He is the author of *Crime Control in America: What Works?* (3rd ed., Pearson) and *Criminal Procedure: From First Contact to Appeal* (5th ed., Pearson); coauthor of several texts, including most recently, with Jennifer L. Moore, *Criminal Law and Procedure* (Pearson, 2014); and editor of the journal *Police Quarterly*.

Brief Contents

Contents

PART 2 The Police and Law Enforcement 79

9 Punishment and Sentencing 214

PART 4 Corrections and Alternative Sanctions 241

10 Community Sentences: Probation, Intermediate Sanctions, and Restorative Justice 242

PART 5 Contemporary Issues in American Criminal Justice 327

Preface

Empowered by case law and legislation, the criminal justice system routinely processes millions of cases involving fraud, theft, violence, drug trafficking, and other crimes. Some are the products of vast conspiracies; others are one-time offenses by first time offenders. The vast majority fall somewhere between each of these extremes. How does the criminal justice system, which costs billions of dollars and involves millions of people, operate? What are its most recent trends and policies? How effective are its efforts to control crime? What efforts are being made to improve its efficiency? We have written the eleventh edition of *Essentials of Criminal Justice* in an attempt to help answer these questions in a concise, forthright, and objective manner.

Goals and Objectives

Because the study of criminal justice is a dynamic, ever-changing field of scientific inquiry, and because the concepts and processes of justice are constantly evolving, we have updated *Essentials of Criminal Justice* to reflect the most critical legal cases, research studies, and policy initiatives that have taken place during the past few years. *Essentials of Criminal Justice* lays a foundation for the study of criminal justice by analyzing and describing the agencies of justice and the procedures they use to identify and treat criminal offenders. It covers what most experts believe are the crucial issues in criminal justice and analyzes their impact on the justice system. This edition focuses on critical policy issues in the criminal justice system, including efforts to control and contain terrorism.

The primary goals and objectives of the eleventh edition remain the same as they have been for the previous ten:

1. Provide students with a thorough knowledge of the criminal justice system.
2. Be as readable and interesting as possible.
3. Be objective and unbiased.
4. Describe current methods of social control and analyze their strengths and weaknesses.

Every attempt has been made to make the presentation of material interesting, balanced, and objective. No single political or theoretical position dominates the text; we try to be as objective as possible. Accordingly, we have included the many diverse views that are represented within criminal justice and that characterize its interdisciplinary nature.

Organization of the Text

Essentials of Criminal Justice is a brief introduction to criminal justice. Despite its clear, concise nature, we have made every effort to ensure that the book is informative, complete, interesting, well organized, and impartial as well as stimulating and thought-provoking.

Part One gives the student a basic introduction to crime, law, and justice. Chapter 1 covers the agencies of justice, outlines the formal justice process, and introduces the concept of the informal justice system, which involves discretion, deal making, and plea bargains. Chapter 1 also examines the major perspectives on justice and shows how they shape justice policy. Chapter 2 discusses the nature and extent of crime and victimization: How is crime measured? Where and when does it occur? Who commits crime? Who are its victims? What social factors influence the crime rate? Chapter 3 provides a discussion of criminal law and its relationship to criminal justice. It covers the legal definition of crime, the types of defenses available to those charged with having committed a crime, as well as issues in constitutional procedural law.

Part Two offers an overview of law enforcement. Three chapters cover the history and development of police departments, the functions of police in modern society, issues in policing, and the police and the rule of law. Special emphasis is placed on community policing and crime prevention, technology and policing, and changes in police procedures.

Part Three is devoted to the court process, from pretrial indictment to the sentencing of criminal offenders. In this section, individual chapters focus on the organization of the court system and the roles of its major participants (judge, prosecutor, and defense attorney), pretrial procedures, the criminal trial, and sentencing. The topics explored include bail, court reorganization, sentencing, and capital punishment.

Part Four focuses on the correctional system, including probation and the intermediate sanctions of house arrest, intensive supervision, and electronic monitoring. Although the traditional correctional system of jails, prisons, community-based corrections, and parole is discussed at length, there is also a focus on restorative justice programs. Such issues as the crisis of overcrowding in prisons and jails, house arrest, correctional workers, super-maximum-security prisons, and parole effectiveness are discussed.

Part Five explores current issues in justice. One chapter deals with the problem of juveniles who break the law by considering what should be done with them and how they should be treated. Information is also provided on the development of juvenile justice, on waiving youth to the adult court, and on the death penalty for children. Chapter 14 focuses on some of the critical issues currently facing the justice system: terrorism, corporate crime, environmental crime, and cybercrime. It illustrates the dynamic nature of the justice process and the fact that the problems it faces are constantly evolving.

Key Changes in the Eleventh Edition

In addition to thoroughly updating and revising each chapter, we have included coverage of the hottest topics in criminal justice today, including but not limited to the following:

- High-profile police shootings
- Recent terror attacks
- Marijuana legalization
- Police technology, including body cameras and automated license plate recognition
- Prison downsizing
- Historic reductions in the use of capital punishment

- Privatization of prosecution and probation
- Data on police shootings

Chapter-by-chapter changes include:

Chapter 1: A new part opener features the Orlando nightclub shooting, the worst terror attack in the United States since 9/11. Chapter 1 starts with the story of Dylann Roof, the man convicted of killing nine people at the Emanuel African Methodist Episcopal Church in Charleston, South Carolina. Learning objectives were revised and content was updated with the latest data and research where appropriate. A new section on evidence-based justice is included, as is a new boxed feature called Focus on Effectiveness, which looks at a focused deterrence strategy in the city of New Orleans. The chapter wraps up with a new Ethical Reflection and writing challenge examining the possible unanticipated consequences of recreational marijuana legalization.

Chapter 2: A new chapter opening story features the ongoing heroin epidemic. Crime and victimization sections have been updated with the latest data. Learning objectives have been revised, and the chapter has been considerably streamlined. A new Contemporary Issues in Criminal Justice box features recent research on the relationship between immigration and crime. A new concept summary appears toward the end of the criminological theory section, summarizing the various explanations for criminality. A new Ethical Reflection and writing challenge appear at the end of the chapter. They explore the ethical implications and issues associated with the alleged "fudging" of crime statistics.

Chapter 3: Chapter 3 now opens with a new story about the recreational marijuana industry. The "Criminal Defenses" section has been extensively revised and reorganized (including new sections on the law enforcement defense and changing criminal defenses). "The Evolution of Criminal Law" section has also been revised, with new discussions of redefining rape and legislative changes to address the ongoing threat of terrorism. A new Contemporary Issues in Criminal Justice box summarizes research on how capable people are of using guns in self-defense. A new Ethical Reflection at the end of the chapter features the question of whether a *mens rea* requirement should be grafted onto all federal crimes.

Chapter 4: A new part opener features the so-called Ferguson effect on policing (i.e., have officers "backed off" in their activities as a result of high-profile police shootings and strained police–community relationships). A new chapter opening story features the 2016 surge in ambush-style police killings. Police agency data have been updated throughout. An expanded Criminal Justice and Technology box showcases the most recent research on police body-worn cameras. A section has also been added on the President's Task Force on Twenty-First Century Policing, and the "Technology and Law Enforcement" section toward the end of the chapter has been extensively expanded and revised.

Chapter 5: A new chapter opening story discusses the role of predictive analytics in modern law enforcement. A new Criminal Justice and Technology box covers automated license plate recognition technology. Two new Focus on Effectiveness boxes are included, one with the latest research on the deterrent effect of police patrol and another on the efficacy of controversial "stop, question, and frisk" or SQF practices. The latest data and research are also included throughout the chapter.

Chapter 6: A new chapter opening story features results from a recent Pew Research Center poll of 8,000 police officers. Police demographic data and court cases are updated throughout. A new Contemporary Issues in Criminal Justice box delves deeper into the sources of data used to estimate the number of police shootings each year. Also added is a new Criminal Justice and Technology box on through-wall radar devices, particularly their Fourth Amendment implications. Finally, a Focus on Effectiveness box features recent research on suspects' cognitive impairment following Taser use.

Chapter 7: The Part 3 opening story now features Supreme Court Justice Antonin Scalia's death in 2016. A new Chapter 7 opening story discusses the issue of private prosecution, specifically some small jurisdictions' decisions to outsource the prosecution function. A new Contemporary Issues in Criminal Justice box introduces defense attorneys who represent America's most despised criminals. A Focus on Effectiveness box features the Queens (New York) Treatment Court, and a new Ethical Reflection feature at the end of the chapter asks students to evaluate cases of prosecutorial misconduct.

Chapter 8: The chapter opens with a new story on police officers on trial for murder. Why are so few charged? And of those charged, why are so few convicted? Chapter 8 also features a new Focus on Effectiveness box that examines the relative effectiveness of various pretrial release mechanisms.

Chapter 9: A new chapter opening story features the recent decline in capital punishment in the United States. A new Ethical Reflection exercise at the end of the chapter considers the advantages and disadvantages of victim impact statements in the criminal court process. Throughout the chapter, sentencing statistics (including death penalty information) are updated, as is research on all aspects of punishment and sentencing.

Chapter 10: A new part opening story discusses the privatization of probation, and a new Chapter 10 opening story features the issue of American exceptionalism in its use of probation. A new Criminal Justice and Technology box features recent research revealing an apparent surge in the use of electronic monitoring. The chapter-ending Ethical Reflection feature has been revised to more fully tie into chapter content. Research and data on community sentences are updated throughout the chapter, as well.

Chapter 11: Learning Objectives and the order of the chapter have been extensively revised. A new Contemporary Issues in Criminal Justice box features research on whether prison downsizing leads to increases in crime. Jail and prison inmate statistics have been updated with the latest research.

Chapter 12: A new chapter opening story features the controversial case of Orville Lee Wollard who was sentenced to 20 years in prison for firing a warning shot. Learning objectives have been revised, as has the section on faith-based treatment. A new Contemporary Issues in Criminal Justice box discusses proposed changes to solitary confinement. The "Improving Chances on Reentry" section has been updated with the latest research.

Chapter 13: A new part opening story features alleged Russian hacking in the 2016 presidential election. The chapter opening story explores how recent research on adolescent development has generated concern about our nation's treatment of young people in the juvenile justice system. A new Focus on Effectiveness box features anti-bullying programming and research. Juvenile justice-related data and research have been updated throughout the chapter.

Chapter 14: A new chapter opening story features the 2015 terror attack in San Bernardino, California. The terrorism section has been reorganized, overhauled, and updated. Learning objectives and various chapter sections have been rearranged to improve flow. Recent examples of corporate enterprise crime are provided, one of them being Volkswagen's guilty plea in connection with emissions cheating. The latest data on transnational organized crimes groups is presented, as well.

Boxed Features

Focus on Effectiveness A new Focus on Effectiveness feature is added. Appearing as boxes in various places throughout the book, these have the intent of identifying quality research in criminal justice policy and teaching students to be critical thinkers about what works and doesn't work in the field—and also showcasing the best recent research on what works.

Contemporary Issues in Criminal Justice boxed features, highlighting evidence-based criminal justice policies and practices, help students think critically about current justice issues. For example, a Contemporary Issues box in Chapter 3 reviews the issues surrounding defensive gun use, another in Chapter 6 looks at data sources used to estimate the incidence of police shootings, and, in Chapter 11, another Contemporary Issues box looks at whether prison downsizing has implications for crime.

Criminal Justice and Technology boxes review some of the more recent technological advances that can aid the justice system. In Chapter 4, for example, recent research on the efficacy of body-worn cameras is showcased. A box in Chapter 10 looks at the apparent surge in electronic offender monitoring.

The very popular **Careers in Criminal Justice** boxes have been updated with information on the latest career paths in criminal justice. These boxes contain detailed information on salaries, educational requirements, future prospects, and potential pitfalls in each career area.

Other Important Chapter Features

Every chapter of *Essentials of Criminal Justice* also contains learning tools to enhance student mastery of the material.

- **Learning Objectives.** Each chapter begins with a list of key learning objectives. These objectives are then revisited in the **Summary**, where they are directly tied to the material covered in the text. The learning objectives are also integrated throughout in the text margins, signaling where the learning objective is addressed within the chapter.

- **RealityCheck.** One of the goals of this book is to expose some of the myths that persist about crime, criminals, and the criminal justice system. Is the crime rate really out of control? Are unemployed people more likely than others to commit crime? Do detectives solve the most serious crimes? Does incarceration really work? Does the death penalty deter people from committing murder? Making it clear what is true and what is merely legend is one of the greatest challenges for instructors teaching the first course in criminal justice. The **RealityCheck** feature in *Essentials of Criminal Justice* meets that challenge head on. Its purpose is to separate myth from reality and thereby inform students of the incorrect notions, perceptions, and biases they bring to class as a result of what they see on television or read in fiction and on the Internet.
- **WebApps.** Throughout the book are a variety of Web links that help students do further research and reading on the Internet. Some of these are links to websites containing information that can enrich the textual material.
- **Ethical Reflection Writing Challenges.** Each chapter presents a writing assignment that challenges students to solve an ethical dilemma they may someday confront while working within the justice system. They require students to reflect back on and incorporate chapter material in their answers.
- **Review Questions**
- **Running Marginal Glossary of Key Terms**

Ancillaries

For the Instructor

INSTRUCTOR'S RESOURCE MANUAL Includes learning objectives, key terms, a detailed chapter outline, a chapter summary, lesson plans, discussion topics, student activities, "What If" scenarios, media tools, and sample syllabi. The learning objectives are correlated with the discussion topics, student activities, and media tools.

DOWNLOADABLE TEST BANK The enhanced test bank includes a combination of multiple choice, true/false, completion, essay, and critical thinking formats, with a full answer key. The test bank is coded to the learning objectives that appear in the main text, and identifies where in the text (by section) the answer appears. Finally, each question in the test bank has been carefully reviewed by experienced criminal justice instructors for quality, accuracy, and content coverage so instructors can be sure they are working with an assessment and grading resource of the highest caliber.

CENGAGE LEARNING TESTING POWERED BY COGNERO, the accompanying assessment tool, is a flexible, online system that allows you to import, edit, and manipulate test bank content from the text's test bank or elsewhere, including your own favorite test questions, create ideal assessments with your choice of 15 question types (including true/false, multiple choice, opinion scale/likert, and essay), create multiple test versions in an instant using drop-down menus and familiar, intuitive tools that take you through content creation and management with ease, and deliver tests from your LMS, your classroom, or wherever you want—plus, import and export content into other systems as needed.

ONLINE POWERPOINT LECTURES Helping you make your lectures more engaging while effectively reaching your visually oriented students, these handy Microsoft PowerPoint® slides outline the chapters of the main text in a classroom-ready presentation. The PowerPoint® slides reflect the content and organization of the new edition of the text and feature some additional examples and real world cases for application and discussion.

For the Student

MINDTAP FOR CRIMINAL JUSTICE The most applied learning experience available, MindTap is dedicated to preparing students to make the kinds of reasoned decisions they will have to make as criminal justice professionals faced with real-world challenges. Available for virtually every criminal justice course, MindTap offers customizable content, course analytics, an e-reader, and more—all within your current learning management system. With its rich array of assets—video cases, interactive visual summaries, decision-making scenarios, quizzes, and writing skill builders—MindTap is perfectly suited to today's criminal justice students, engaging them, guiding them toward mastery of basic concepts, and advancing their critical thinking abilities.

Acknowledgments

Thanks to our terrific product manager, Carolyn Henderson Meier, who does it all for us all the time. (She is our unnamed co-author.) Plenty of credit for getting this book out must also go to the marvelous Shelley Murphy, content developer extraordinaire, to whom we can never give enough praise no matter how hard we try. Special thanks to our outstanding production manager, Christy Frame; to our wonderful and professional project manager, Lori Hazzard at MPS Limited; to the precise and knowledgeable copy editor, Lunaea Weatherstone, who did a thorough and professional job; and to the ever-creative photo researcher, Kim Adams Fox and Lumina Datamatics, who brought the book to life with colorful imagery. And of course, we are totally in debt to our incredible marketing manager, the astonishing Mark Linton. This skilled team's efforts have resulted in an exceptional new edition.

Larry Siegel
Naples, Florida

John Worrall
Dallas, Texas

ESSENTIALS OF **CRIMINAL JUSTICE**

The Nature of Crime, Law, and Criminal Justice

On June 12, 2016, American-born Omar Mateen, 29, of Fort Pierce, Florida, entered the Pulse nightclub in Orlando at 2:00 a.m. on a Sunday. Using a Sig Sauer MCX assault rifle, he started firing into the crowded gay night spot, killing 49 people and wounding 53 others. Prior to the attack, Mateen used a number of Facebook accounts to post vows of vengeance for American airstrikes in Iraq and Syria. He even called 911 in the midst of his shooting spree to pledge allegiance to Islamic State of Iraq and the Levant (ISIL). After a three-hour standoff, police forcibly entered the club with an armored vehicle, then used stun grenades to gain the upper hand. Mateen was shot and killed shortly thereafter. The incident became the deadliest mass shooting in the United States and the worst terror attack since September 11, 2001.

Mateen's parents were Afghan, and he was raised as a Muslim. Starting in 2006, he trained to be a prison guard for the Florida Department of Corrections. While a probationary employee, Mateen was terminated for allegedly joking about bringing a gun to school. He then unsuccessfully pursued a career in law enforcement, failing to become a state trooper. After that, he secured a position as a security guard with G4S Secure Solutions. The company reported that two screenings revealed no issues, but his ex-wife claimed he was "mentally unstable and mentally ill." Mateen became a "person of interest" to the Federal Bureau of Investigation (FBI) once in 2013 and again in 2014 after making comments about supposed connections he had with known terrorists. G4S subsequently fired him. Mateen continued, however, to hold firearms and security licenses at the time of the nightclub shooting.

Terrorist attacks on US soil are particularly difficult to predict and prevent. Hindsight almost always reveals warning signs, but there are limits to what the government can do early on. Should Mateen have been arrested after he became a person of interest? If so, what would be the basis for his detention? What crimes could he have been charged with? As an alternative, should authorities have tapped his phone? Probed his computer? Would *those* actions have been legal? If no formal actions could have been taken, then what makes one person more inclined than another to commit a terrible crime? Is there a set of common traits or predispositions that exist beforehand? Are people socialized into deviant behavior?

To help answer these questions, Part 1 of this text covers the basic issues and concepts of crime, law, and criminal justice. Chapter 1 covers the justice process and the organizations that are entrusted with conducting its operations: the police, courts, and corrections. It provides an overview of the justice system and sets out its most important agencies, processes, and concepts. Chapter 2 looks at the nature and extent of crime, and attempts to determine why people commit crimes such as sexual assault. Chapter 3 covers the criminal law, analyzing both its substantive and procedural components, including the legal definition of a crime.

Chapter 1 **Crime and Criminal Justice**

Chapter 2 **The Nature of Crime and Victimization**

Chapter 3 **Criminal Law: Substance and Procedure**

1

Crime and Criminal Justice

On the evening of June 17, 2015, Dylann Roof, 21, entered the Emanuel African Methodist Episcopal Church in Charleston, South Carolina, and killed nine people, including the senior pastor, with a .45-caliber semiautomatic handgun. Three other victims survived. The morning after the shooting, which happened during a Bible study, police arrested Roof in Shelby, North Carolina, 245 miles away. He promptly confessed the killings, hoping to ignite a race war.[1] Three days after the attack, authorities discovered a website called *The Last Rhodesian*, which was owned by Roof. The site contained photos of Roof posing with white supremacist and neo-Nazi symbols. In a manifesto also published on the site, he claimed to have formed his white supremacist views after the 2012 shooting of Trayvon Martin in Florida.

Roof was charged in both federal and state court, becoming the first person in history to face the death penalty at both levels. In federal court, he was indicted on 33 charges, including nine counts of using a firearm to commit murder. On July 31, 2015, he pleaded not guilty to the federal charges at the urging of his lawyer, as it was not clear at the time whether federal prosecutors would seek the death penalty. His trial began on December 7, 2016. The jury heard Roof's jailhouse confession, wherein he chuckled after he admitted to killing the people at the church. It also viewed security camera footage, including a haunting image of Roof leaving the church, gun in hand. The trial concluded after about a week, and after two short hours of deliberation, the jury found Roof guilty on all 33 counts.

Roof insisted on representing himself during the sentencing phase. He denied having any psychological issues, nor did he call any witnesses or present any evidence. He said, "I felt like I had to do it, and I still feel like I had to do it." After three hours of deliberation, the jury returned a death sentence. Melvin Graham, whose sister, Cynthia Hurd, died in the attack, welcomed the outcome: "It's a hard thing to know that someone is going to lose their life, but when you look at the totality of what happened, it's hard to say that person deserves to live when nine others don't."[2] Members of Roof's family, who were mostly silent throughout the proceedings, said in a statement they would "struggle as long as we live to understand why he committed this horrible attack, which caused so much pain to so many good people."[3]

LEARNING OBJECTIVES

LO1 Discuss the formation of the criminal justice system in America

LO2 Examine the basic component agencies of the criminal justice system

LO3 Recognize the size and scope of the contemporary justice system

LO4 Trace the formal criminal justice process

LO5 Articulate what is meant by the term *criminal justice assembly line*

LO6 Examine the informal criminal justice system

LO7 Describe the "wedding cake" model of justice

LO8 Discuss the various perspectives on justice

LO9 Discuss the ethical issues that arise in criminal justice

criminal justice system The law enforcement, court, and correctional agencies that work together to effect the apprehension, prosecution, and control of criminal offenders. They are charged with maintaining order, enforcing the law, identifying transgressors, bringing the guilty to justice, and treating criminal behavior.

Cases ranging from Dylann Roof's infamous Charleston church shooting all the way down to the most petty of property crimes are handled and processed by the **criminal justice system**. Defined as the system of law enforcement, adjudication, and correction that is directly involved in the apprehension, prosecution, and control of those charged with criminal offenses, this loosely organized collection of agencies is responsible for, among other matters, protecting the public, maintaining order, enforcing the law, identifying transgressors, bringing the guilty to justice, and treating criminal behavior. The public depends on this vast system not only to protect them from evildoers and to bring justice to their lives but also to maintain order and protect the fabric of society.

This textbook serves as an introduction to the study of criminal justice. This area of research and scholarship includes describing, analyzing, and explaining the behavior of those agencies authorized by law and statute to dispense justice—police departments, courts, and correctional agencies—and helping these institutions identify effective and efficient methods of crime control.

Myth vs. Reality

As we engage in this study of crime and justice, a unifying theme is exposing, analyzing, and setting straight some of the myths and legends that have grown up about the justice system. Many people form opinions about criminal justice from the media, which often leads to false impressions and unrealized expectations. In the movies and on TV, it takes police about an hour to catch even the most wily criminal. Shootouts and car chases are routine, and every criminal defendant receives a lengthy trial in front of an attentive jury. Journalists and the media as a whole help perpetuate these myths by routinely featuring stories exposing brutal cops and violent prisons. How true are these images of justice? How can we separate myth from reality? Throughout this textbook, we will confront such myths and legends in an attempt to sort the facts from the fiction.

This chapter introduces some basic issues, beginning with a discussion of the history of crime in America and the development of criminal justice. The major organizations and **criminal justice processes** of the criminal justice system are then introduced as an overview of how the system functions. Because there is no single view of the underlying goals that help shape criminal justice, the varying perspectives on what criminal justice really is, or should be, are set out in some detail.

criminal justice process The decision-making points, from the initial investigation or arrest by police to the eventual release of the offender and his or her reentry into society; the various sequential criminal justice stages through which the offender passes.

Developing the Criminal Justice System

LO1 Discuss the formation of the criminal justice system in America

During the nineteenth century, America experienced a surge in violent behavior. You have all seen movie westerns featuring bad men such as Jesse James, Billy the Kid, and Butch Cassidy and the Sundance Kid. These outlaws were not merely media legends; they actually robbed trains, rustled cattle, and engaged in western land wars. Bringing them to justice were such legendary lawmen as Wyatt Earp (famed for his part in the "Gunfight at the O.K. Corral"), Bat Masterson, and Pat Garrett (who shot and killed Billy the Kid).

On the East Coast, large and deadly urban gangs such as the North End Gang, Dead Rabbits, Plug Uglies, and Hudson Dusters set up operations in cities such as New York and Boston. Responding to a public outcry over rising crime rates in the United States and abroad, the first criminal justice agencies began to appear. The emergence of criminal gangs and groups in the nineteenth century and a general sense of lawlessness spurred development of formal agencies of criminal justice. In 1829, the first police agency, the London Metropolitan Police, was developed to keep the peace and identify criminal suspects. In the United States, the first police agencies were created in Boston (1838), New York (1844), and Philadelphia (1854). The penitentiary, or prison, was created to provide nonphysical correctional treatment for convicted offenders; these were considered "liberal" innovations that replaced corporal or capital punishment.

WEB APP 1.1 Wyatt Earp was one of the most colorful characters in the old West. Read about him at **http://www.wyattearp.net**. To learn more about Earp, read this article by his friend and fellow lawman Bat Masterson: **http://www.legendsofamerica.com/we-earpbymasterson.html**. Do you find it amazing that only 150 years ago the West was wild, and gunfights took place on city streets?

During the first century of their existence, these fledgling agencies of justice rarely worked together in a systematic fashion. Not until 1919, with the creation of the Chicago Crime Commission (a professional association funded by private contributions) did the work of the criminal justice system began to be recognized.[4] This organization acted as a citizens' advocate group and kept track of the activities of local justice agencies. The commission still carries out its work today.

In 1931, President Herbert Hoover appointed the National Commission on Law Observance and Enforcement, which is commonly known today as the Wickersham Commission. This national study group made a detailed analysis of the US justice system and helped usher in the era of treatment and rehabilitation. The final report found that thousands of rules and regulations governed the system and made it difficult for justice personnel to keep track of the system's legal and administrative complexity.[5]

The Modern Era of Justice

The modern era of criminal justice can be traced to a series of research projects begun in the 1950s under the sponsorship of the American Bar Foundation (ABF).[6] Originally designed to provide in-depth analysis of the organization, administration, and operation of criminal justice agencies, the ABF project discovered that the justice system contained many procedures that had been hidden from the public view. The research focus then shifted to an examination of these previously obscure processes and their interrelationship—investigation, arrest, prosecution, and plea negotiations. It became apparent that justice professionals used a great deal of personal choice in decision making, and showing how this discretion was used became a prime focus of the research effort. For the first time, the term *criminal justice system* began to be used, reflecting a view that justice agencies could be connected in an intricate yet often unobserved network of decision-making processes.

Federal Involvement in Criminal Justice

In 1967, the President's Commission on Law Enforcement and Administration of Justice (the Crime Commission), which had been appointed by President Lyndon Johnson, published its final report entitled, *The Challenge of Crime in a Free Society.*[7] This group of practitioners, educators, and attorneys was given the responsibility of creating a comprehensive view of the criminal justice process and recommending reforms. In 1968, Congress passed the Safe Streets and Crime Control Act, providing for the expenditure of federal funds for state and local crime control efforts and launching a massive campaign to restructure the justice system.[8] It funded the National Institute of Law Enforcement and Criminal Justice (NILECJ), which encouraged research and development in criminal justice. Renamed the National Institute of Justice (NIJ) in 1979, the institute has continued its mission as a major source of funding for the implementation and evaluation of innovative experimental and demonstration projects in the criminal justice system.[9]

The Safe Streets Act provided funding for the Law Enforcement Assistance Administration (LEAA), which granted hundreds of millions of dollars in aid to local and state justice agencies. Throughout its 14-year history, the LEAA provided the majority of federal funds to states for criminal justice activities. On April 15, 1982, the program came to an end when Congress terminated its funding. However, the federal government continues to fund innovation in the criminal justice system through the National Institute of Justice (NIJ) and the Bureau of Justice Assistance (BJA).

Evidence-Based Justice: A Scientific Evolution

With continued funding from federal agencies such as the National Institute of Justice, the Office of Juvenile Justice and Delinquency Prevention, and the Bureau of Justice Statistics—as well as from private sources such as the Pew Charitable Trusts and the Annie E. Casey Foundation—the study of criminal justice has embraced careful research analysis to support public policy initiatives. Although programs, policies, and

Law Enforcement Assistance Administration (LEAA) Funded by the federal government's Safe Streets Act, this agency provided technical assistance and hundreds of millions of dollars in aid to local and state justice agencies between 1969 and 1982.

procedures may have been shaped by political goals in the past, a mature justice system now relies more on the scientific collection of data to determine whether programs work and what policies should be adopted. According to this "What Works" movement,[10] empirical evidence, carefully gathered using scientific methods, must be collected and analyzed in order to determine whether criminal justice programs work and whether they actually reduce crime rates and offender recidivism. Programs must now undergo rigorous review to ensure that they achieve their stated goals and have a real and measurable effect on behavior. **Evidence-based justice** efforts have a few unifying principles:[11]

- *Target audience.* Programs must be reaching the right audience. A drug treatment program that is used with groups of college students caught smoking pot may look successful, but can it work with hard-core substance abusers? It is important for programs to work with high-risk offenders who have the greatest probability of recidivating. Targeting low-risk offenders may make programs look good, but it really proves little because the client group might not have repeated their criminal offenses even if left untreated.
- *Randomized experiments.* Whenever possible, random experiments are conducted. For example, two groups of drug users are randomly selected, the first group is placed in the special treatment program, and the other is treated in a traditional fashion, such as being put in prison. If the recidivism rates of the experimental group are superior, we have strong evidence that the novel treatment method really works. Although it is sometimes difficult to select subjects randomly, other methods (e.g., matching subjects on key characteristics such as age, race, gender, and prior record) can be substituted.
- *Intervening factors.* Evidence-based programming must consider intervening factors that enhance or impede program success. A community-based crime prevention program that is used in a high-income neighborhood may be met with general approval and prove effective in reducing local problems, such as kids drinking at night in the local park. But will the program work in a high-crime area where well-armed gangs frighten residents? Conversely, a program that is deemed a failure with a group of at-risk kids living in an inner-city neighborhood may work quite well with at-risk youngsters living in a rural environment.
- *Measurement of success.* Evidence-based programs must develop realistic measures of success. For example, a treatment may seem to work, but careful analysis might reveal that the effect quickly wears off; long-term measures of program effectiveness are needed. Program retention must also be considered. A program for teens may seem to work because those who complete the program are less likely to commit crime in the future. But before success is declared and the program is adopted on a national level, research must closely evaluate such issues as the dropout rate: Are potential failures removed before the program is completed in order to ensure overall success (and continued funding)? And what about selectivity? Is the program open to everyone, including repeat offenders, or is it limited to people who are considered to have the greatest potential for success?
- *Cost-effectiveness.* Programs may work, but the cost may be too high. In an era of tight budgets, program effectiveness must be balanced with cost. It is not enough for a program to be effective; it must also prove to be efficient.

Scientific research is now being used to dispute commonly held beliefs that may be misleading and erroneous. For example, the track record of school-based drug education programs has proven to be spotty at best: the evidence shows that the best intentions do not necessarily result in the best practice.[12] Throughout the text, we will highlight programs that have passed careful, evidence-based evaluations *and* some that have failed to stand up to such scrutiny. Many of these are discussed in a new boxed feature that appears in various places throughout this edition. Focus on Effectiveness looks at successful crime prevention programs and encourages the reader to think critically about the importance of research in informing criminal justice decision making.

The New Orleans Group Violence Reduction Strategy

The New Orleans Group Violence Reduction Strategy (GVRS) relied on multi-agency partnering and comprehensive problem solving to address citywide patterns of gang-related violence. The strategy began with a partnership between law enforcement officials and researchers who conducted a number of homicide incident reviews and gang audits to determine which groups were most prone to violence across different sectors of the city. Once proper targets were identified, a series of "offender notification" sessions were held. In these, officials delivered antiviolence messages to known gang offenders who were either incarcerated or on probation or parole. More than 150 individuals received such messages and were told to communicate to other gang members that continued violence would lead to stiff penalties. They were also told to relay the message that if any one gang member murdered or shot someone, the whole gang would come under scrutiny. Social services (e.g., employment assistance) were also provided to those individuals who wanted them.

Effects on Crime/Recidivism

Researchers who evaluated the New Orleans GVRS found that the city experienced a significant reduction in homicide that was above and beyond changes observed in comparably violent cities. The greatest reductions occurred for gang homicides, young black male homicides, and overall firearms violence. In short, the GVRS was deemed successful.

Thinking Critically About Research

How did researchers come to declare the New Orleans strategy a success? Did they compare crimes before and after the notification sessions?

Not quite. Such a simple approach would fail to account for reductions that could have occurred regardless of the GVRS. Rather, the researchers conducted a two-part evaluation that attempted to *rule out* other possible explanations for the crime reductions they witnessed. First, they identified comparably violent cities, then tracked changes in those cities against those observed in New Orleans. Second, they looked at multiple outcome measures in New Orleans and analyzed data from several points before and after the GVRS. This second approach to research accounted for unexpected trends in the data (e.g., upticks in summer months) *and* compared outcomes the GVRS was deemed likely to affect, such as gang-involved homicides, with other unrelated outcomes that were disconnected with GVRS, such as homicides with no gang involvement.

QUESTIONS

1. Why is it important, when evaluating a crime prevention strategy, to analyze data at several points before *and* after an intervention like the GVRS?
2. If you were tasked with evaluating a crime prevention program in your city, would you analyze data from other cities, too? Why or why not?

Source: Nicholas Corsaro and Robin S. Engel, "Most Challenging of Contexts: Assessing the Impact of Focused Deterrence on Serious Violence in New Orleans," *Criminology and Public Policy* 14 (2015): 471–505.

The Contemporary Criminal Justice System

The criminal justice system is society's instrument of social control. Some behaviors are considered so dangerous that they must either be strictly controlled or prohibited outright, and some people are so destructive that they must be monitored or even confined. The agencies of justice are tasked with preventing or deterring outlawed behavior by apprehending, adjudicating, and sanctioning lawbreakers. Society maintains other forms of informal social control, such as parental and school discipline, but these are designed to deal with moral, not legal, misbehavior. Only the criminal justice system maintains the power to control crime and punish those who violate the law.

Contemporary criminal justice agencies are political entities whose structure and function are lodged within the legislative, judicial, and executive branches of the government. They typically can be divided into three main components (Figure 1.1): law enforcement agencies, which investigate crimes and apprehend suspects; court agencies, in which charges are brought, indictments submitted, trials conducted, and sentences formulated; and correctional agencies, which are charged with monitoring, treating, and rehabilitating convicted offenders.

Because of its varied and complex mission, the contemporary criminal justice system in the United States is monumental in size. At last count, local governments funded half (or $132 billion) of all direct justice system—police protection, all judicial and legal services, and corrections—expenses in the United States. State government spending accounted for 31 percent (or $86 billion), and federal funding accounted for 19 percent (or $56 billion).[13]

These expenses are high because there are now more than 15,000 local, state, and county law enforcement agencies, employing nearly 1.1 million people.[14] Of these,

LO2 Examine the basic component agencies of the criminal justice system

LO3 Recognize the size and scope of the contemporary justice system

social control The control of an individual's behavior by social and institutional forces in society.

Police	Courts	Corrections
Police departments are those public agencies created to maintain order, enforce the criminal law, provide emergency services, keep traffic on streets and highways moving freely, and develop a sense of community safety. Police officers work actively with the community to prevent criminal behavior; they help divert members of special needs populations, such as juveniles, alcoholics, and drug addicts, from the criminal justice system; they participate in specialized units such as a drug prevention task force or antirape unit; they cooperate with public prosecutors to initiate investigations into organized crime and drug trafficking; they resolve neighborhood and family conflicts; and they provide emergency services, such as preserving civil order during strikes and political demonstrations.	The criminal courthouse is the scene of the trial process. Here the criminal responsibility of defendants accused of violating the law is determined. Ideally, the court is expected to convict and sentence those found guilty of crimes, while ensuring that the innocent are freed without any consequence or burden. The court system is formally required to seek the truth, to obtain justice for the individual brought before its tribunals, and to maintain the integrity of the government's rule of law. The main actors in the court process are the judge, whose responsibilities include overseeing the legality of the trial process, and the prosecutor and the defense attorney, who are the opponents in what is known as the adversary system. These two parties oppose each other in a hotly disputed contest —the criminal trial—in accordance with rules of law and procedure.	In the broadest sense, correctional agencies include community supervision or probation, various types of incarceration (including jails, houses of correction, and state prisons), and parole programs for both juvenile and adult offenders. These programs range from the lowest security, such as probation in the community with minimum supervision, to the highest security, such as 24-hour lockdown in an ultra-maximum security prison. Corrections ordinarily represent the postadjudicatory care given to offenders when a sentence is imposed by the court and the offender is placed in the hands of the correctional agency.

FIGURE 1.1 Components of the Criminal Justice System

REALITYCHECK

Myth or Reality?

At its core, the justice system is designed to protect the public from people who cannot abide by or obey the law.

REALITY. The justice system dispenses formal social control. It is made up of a group of government agencies empowered to control and punish people who violate the criminal law.

What behaviors that are currently illegal would you decriminalize and make legal? Conversely, what behaviors that are now legal do you believe should be criminalized?

725,000 are full-time sworn law enforcement officers, and the remainder are part-time officers and civilian employees. The federal government employs an additional 120,000 sworn law enforcement personnel.[15] The criminal justice system consists of nearly 17,000 courts, more than 8,000 prosecutorial agencies, about 6,000 correctional institutions, and more than 3,500 probation and parole departments.

The system is massive because it must process, treat, and care for millions of people. Although the crime rate has declined substantially, nearly 11 million people are still being arrested each year, or about 3,300 per 100,000 people.[16] While there has also been a recent decline in the number of cases brought to state courts, about 96 million cases are still being heard each year, including about 20 million that involve criminal matters and 2 million juvenile offenders.[17]

Considering the massive proportions of this system, it is not surprising that almost 7 million people are under some form of correctional supervision, including more than 2 million men and women in the nation's jails and prisons and an additional 4.75 million adult men and women being supervised in the community while on probation or parole.[18] The size of this massive correctional system is reflected in its cost. States spend about $50 billion per year on corrections. The mean state corrections expenditure per inmate is more than $28,000 per year; one-quarter of states spend $40,000 or more.[19]

The Formal Criminal Justice Process

Another way of understanding criminal justice is to view it as a process that takes an offender through a series of decision points beginning with arrest and concluding with reentry into society. During this process, key decision makers resolve whether to maintain the offender in the system or discharge the suspect without further action. This decision making is often a matter of individual discretion based on a variety of factors and perceptions. Legal factors, including the seriousness of the charges, available evidence, and the suspect's prior record, are usually considered legitimate influences on decision making. The fact that such extralegal factors as the suspect's race, gender, class, and age may also influence decision outcomes is troubling. Some critics believe that a suspect's race, class, and gender largely determine the direction a case will take, whereas supporters argue that the system is relatively fair and unbiased.[20]

In reality, few cases actually are processed through the entire formal justice system. Most are handled informally and with dispatch. The system of justice has been roundly criticized for its "backroom deals" and bargain justice. Although informality and deal making are in fact the rule, the concept of the formal justice process is important because it implies that every criminal defendant charged with a serious crime is entitled to a full range of constitutional rights under law.

A comprehensive view of the formal criminal process normally includes the following:

1. *Initial contact.* In most instances, an offender's initial contact with the criminal justice system takes place as a result of a police action:

   - Patrol officers observe a person acting suspiciously, conclude the suspect is under the influence of drugs, and take her into custody.
   - Police officers are contacted by a victim who reports a robbery; they respond by going to the scene of the crime and apprehending a suspect.
   - An informer tells police about some ongoing criminal activity in order to receive favorable treatment.
   - Responding to a request by the mayor or other political figure, the local department may initiate an investigation into an ongoing criminal enterprise such as gambling, prostitution, or drug trafficking.
   - A person walks into the police station and confesses to committing a crime—for example, killing his wife after an altercation.

2. *Investigation.* The purpose of the criminal investigation is to gather sufficient evidence to identify a suspect and support a legal arrest. An investigation can take only

REALITYCHECK
Myth or Reality?

According to the statute of limitations concept, if a murder isn't solved in 10 years, the killer can no longer be brought to justice.

MYTH. A statute of limitations is designed to restrict the maximum time after an event that legal proceedings may be initiated; after the period of time is exhausted, legal proceedings can no longer be brought. However, in the United States, there is no statute of limitations for first-degree murder.

Should the statute of limitations be waived for other crimes such as child sexual abuse?

Jim McReynolds (second from right) from the Philadelphia Police Department collects evidence at the Mount Carmel Cemetery in February 2017. More than 100 headstones were vandalized at the Jewish cemetery less than a week after similar vandalism occurred in Missouri.

AP Images/Jacqueline Larma

in-presence requirement With a few exceptions, in order to make an arrest in a misdemeanor, a police officer must have witnessed the crime personally.

nolle prosequi The term used when a prosecutor decides to drop a case after a complaint has been formally made. Reasons for a *nolle prosequi* include evidence insufficiency, reluctance of witnesses to testify, police error, and office policy.

grand jury A type of jury responsible for investigating alleged crimes, examining evidence, and issuing indictments.

true bill of indictment A written statement charging a defendant with the commission of a crime, drawn up by a prosecuting attorney and considered by a grand jury. If the grand jury finds sufficient evidence to support the indictment, it will issue a true bill of indictment.

information Charging document filed by the prosecution that forms the basis of the preliminary hearing.

probable cause hearing Term used in some jurisdictions for a preliminary hearing to show cause to bring a case to trial.

a few minutes, as in the case where a police officer sees a crime in progress and can apprehend the suspect quickly. Or it can take many years and involve hundreds of law enforcement agents. Dennis Rader, the notorious BTK ("Bind, Torture, Kill") serial killer, began his murderous streak in 1974 and was finally apprehended in 2005 after an investigation that lasted more than 30 years.[21]

3. *Arrest.* An arrest is considered legal when all of the following conditions exist: (1) the police officer believes there is sufficient evidence, referred to as *probable cause,* that a crime is being or has been committed, and the suspect is the person who committed it; (2) the officer deprives the individual of freedom; and (3) the suspect believes that he is now in the custody of the police and has lost his liberty. The police officer is not required to use the word "arrest" or any similar term to initiate an arrest, nor does the officer have to bring the suspect to the police station. To make an arrest in a misdemeanor, the officer must have witnessed the crime personally, a provision known as the **in-presence requirement**. Some jurisdictions have passed laws allowing misdemeanor arrests based on victim complaints in cases involving child abuse or domestic abuse. Arrests can also be made when a magistrate, presented with sufficient evidence by police and prosecutors, issues a warrant authorizing the arrest of the suspect.

4. *Custody.* After an arrest and while the suspect is being detained, the police may want to search for evidence, conduct an interrogation, or even encourage a confession. Witnesses may be brought to view the suspect in a lineup or in a one-on-one confrontation. Because these procedures are so crucial and can have a great impact at trial, the US Supreme Court has granted suspects in police custody protection from the unconstitutional abuse of police power, such as illegal searches and intimidating interrogations.

5. *Charging.* If the arresting officers or their superiors believe that sufficient evidence exists to charge a person with a crime, the case will be turned over to the prosecutor's office. The prosecutor's decision to charge the suspect with a specific criminal act involves many factors, including evidence sufficiency, crime seriousness, case pressure, and political issues, as well as personal factors such as a prosecutor's own specific interests and biases. After conducting a preliminary investigation of its legal merits, prosecutors may decide to take no further action in a case; this is referred to as a *nolle prosequi*.

6. *Preliminary hearing/grand jury.* The US Constitution mandates that before a trial can take place, the government must first prove probable cause that the accused committed the crime for which he is being charged. In about half the states and in the federal system, this determination is made by a **grand jury** in a closed hearing. If the prosecution presents sufficient evidence, the grand jury will issue a **true bill of indictment**, which specifies the exact charges on which the accused must stand trial. In the remaining states, the prosecution will file a charging document (usually called an **information**) before a lower trial court, which then conducts an open hearing on the merits of the case. During this procedure, sometimes referred to as a **probable cause hearing**, the defendant and the defendant's attorney may appear and dispute the prosecutor's charges. The suspect will be called to stand trial if the presiding magistrate or judge accepts the prosecutor's evidence as factual and sufficient.

7. *Arraignment.* Before the trial begins, the defendant will be arraigned, or brought before the court that will hear the case. At this time, formal charges are read, the defendant is informed of his constitutional rights (e.g., the right to be represented by legal counsel), an initial plea (not guilty or guilty) is entered, a trial date set, and bail issues are considered.

8. *Bail/detention.* Bail is a money bond levied to ensure the return of a criminal defendant for trial, allowing the defendant to remain in the community prior to trial. Defendants who do not show up for trial forfeit their bail. Those people who cannot afford to put up bail or who cannot borrow sufficient funds for it will remain in state custody prior to trial. In most instances, this means an extended stay in a county jail or house of correction. If they are stable members of the community

and have committed nonviolent crimes, defendants may be released on their own recognizance (promise to the court), without bail.

9. *Plea bargaining.* After an arraignment, or even before, the defense and prosecution will discuss a possible guilty plea in exchange for the prosecution reducing or dropping some of the charges or agreeing to a request for a more lenient sentence. Almost 90 percent of all cases end in a plea bargain, rather than a criminal trial.

10. *Trial/adjudication.* If an agreement cannot be reached or if the prosecution does not want to arrange a negotiated settlement of the case, a criminal trial will be held before a judge (bench trial) or jury, who will decide whether the prosecution's evidence against the defendant is sufficient beyond a reasonable doubt to prove guilt. If a jury cannot reach a decision—that is, if it is deadlocked—the case is left unresolved, leaving the prosecution to decide whether it should be retried at a later date.

11. *Sentencing/disposition.* After a criminal trial, if the accused has been found guilty as charged, he will be returned to court for sentencing. Possible sentencing dispositions include a fine, probation, some form of community-based corrections, a period of incarceration in a penal institution, or, in rare instances, the death penalty.

12. *Appeal/postconviction remedies.* After conviction, the defense can ask the trial judge to set aside the jury's verdict because the jury has made a mistake of law—for example, by misinterpreting the judge's instructions or convicting on a charge that was not supported by the evidence. Failing that, an appeal may be filed if, after conviction, the defendant believes that his constitutional rights were violated by errors in the trial process. Appellate courts review such issues as whether evidence was used properly, the judge conducted the trial in an approved fashion, jury selection was properly done, and the attorneys in the case acted appropriately. If the court rules that the appeal has merit, it can hold that the defendant be given a new trial or, in some instances, order his or her outright release.

13. *Correctional treatment.* After sentencing, the offender is placed within the jurisdiction of state or federal correctional authorities. The offender may serve a probationary term, be placed in a community correctional facility, serve a term in a county jail, or be housed in a prison. During this stage of the criminal justice process, the offender may be asked to participate in rehabilitation programs designed to help him make a successful readjustment to society.

14. *Release.* Upon completion of the sentence and period of correction, the offender will be free to return to society. Most inmates do not serve the full term of their sentence but are freed through an early-release mechanism, such as parole or pardon or by earning time off for good behavior. Offenders sentenced to community supervision simply finish their term and resume their lives in the community.

15. *Postrelease.* After termination of their correctional treatment, offenders may be asked to spend some time in a community correctional center, which acts as a bridge between a secure treatment facility and absolute freedom. Offenders may find that their conviction has cost them some personal privileges, such as the right to hold certain kinds of employment. These privileges may be restored by court order after the offenders prove their trustworthiness and willingness to adjust to society's rules.

The Criminal Justice Assembly Line

To justice expert Herbert Packer, the image that this process evokes is an assembly line conveyor belt down which moves an endless stream of cases, never stopping.[22] According to this view, each of the 15 stages is actually a *decision point* through which cases flow. At the investigatory stage, police must decide whether to pursue the case or terminate involvement because there is insufficient evidence to identify a suspect, the case is considered trivial, the victim decides not to press charges, and so on. At the bail stage, a decision must be made whether to set bail so high that the defendant remains in custody, to set a reasonable bail, or to release the defendant on his or her own recognizance without requiring any bail at all. Each of these decisions can have a critical effect on the defendant, the justice system, and society. If an error is made, an innocent person may suffer or a dangerous individual may be released to continue to prey upon society.

AP Images/Matt Rourke

Rafael Robb, a former economics professor at the University of Pennsylvania, confessed in 2007 to involuntary manslaughter in connection with the bludgeoning death of his wife, Ellen Robb. He was sentenced to 5 to 10 years in prison and was released in 2017. Ellen's family won a $124 million wrongful death judgement against Robb, but will probably have a hard time collecting the money.

LO5 Articulate what is meant by the term *criminal justice assembly line*

Figure 1.2 illustrates the approximate number of felony offenders removed from the criminal justice system at each stage of the process. As the figure shows, most people who commit crime escape detection, and of those who do not, relatively few are bound over for trial, convicted, and eventually sentenced to prison. About 30 percent of people arrested on felony charges are eventually convicted in criminal court; however, nearly a third of those convicted on felony charges are sentenced to probation and released

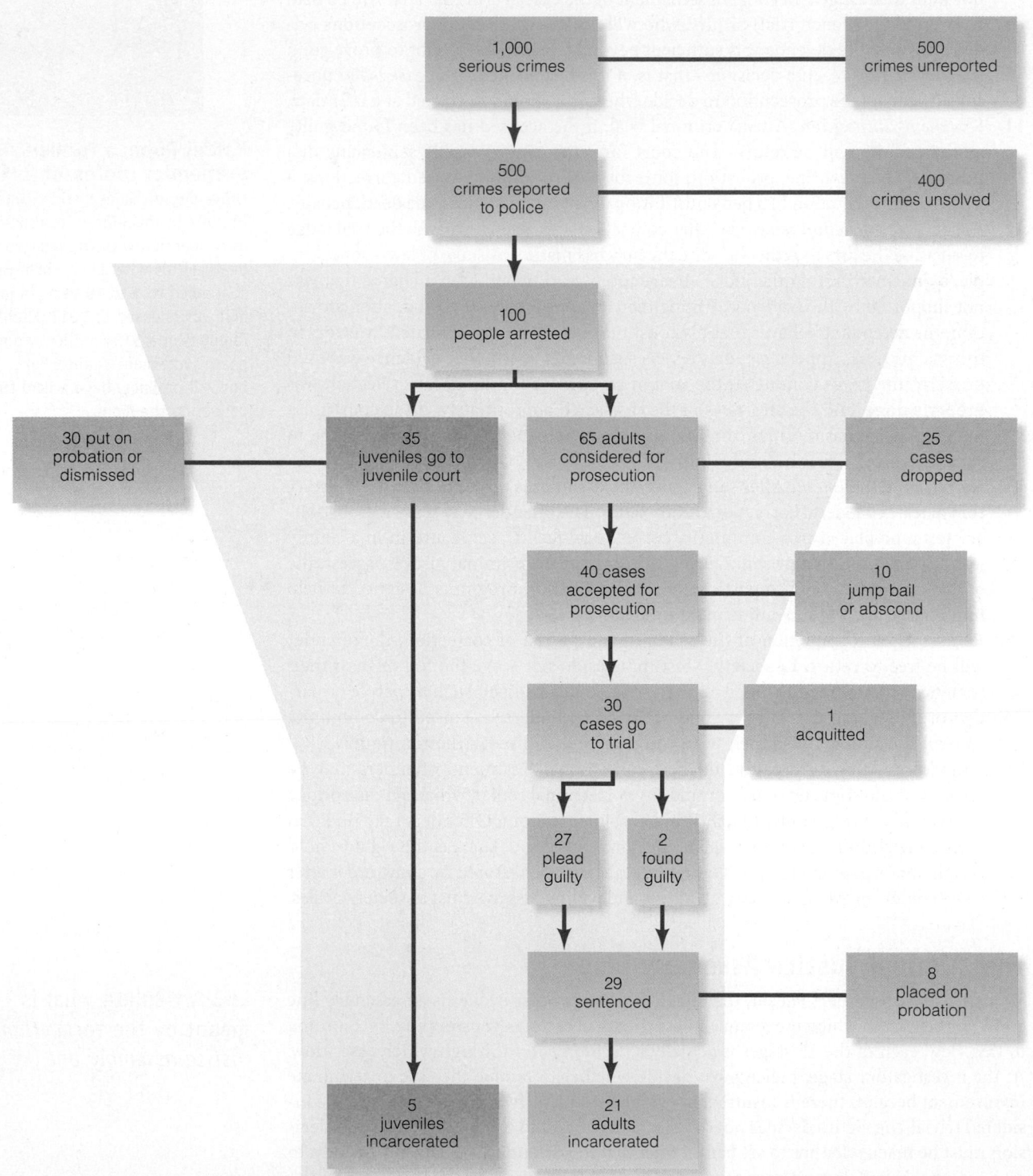

FIGURE 1.2 Criminal Justice Funnel

Sources: Brian Reaves, Felony Defendants in Large Urban Counties, 2009, Statistical Tables (Washington, DC: Bureau of Justice Statistics, 2013) http://www.bjs.gov/content/pub/pdf/fdluc09.pdf; Matthew R. Durose, Donald J. Farole, Jr., Sean P. Rosenmerkel, Felony Sentences in State Courts, 2006—Statistical Tables (Washington, DC: Bureau of Justice Statistics, 2009) http://www.bjs.gov/content/pub/pdf/fssc06st.pdf.

The System: Agencies of Crime Control	The Process
1. Police	1. Contact 2. Investigation 3. Arrest 4. Custody
2. Prosecution and defense	5. Complaint/charging 6. Grand jury/preliminary hearing 7. Arraignment 8. Bail/detention 9. Plea negotiations
3. Court	10. Adjudication 11. Disposition 12. Appeal/postconviction remedies
4. Corrections	13. Correction 14. Release 15. Postrelease

back into the community without doing time in prison.[23] For every 1,000 crimes, about 20 people are sent to prison.

In actual practice, many suspects are released before trial because of a procedural error, evidence problems, or other reasons that result in a case dismissal by the prosecutor. Although most cases that go to trial end in a conviction, others are dismissed by the presiding judge because of a witness or a complainant's failure to appear or procedural irregularities. Thus, the justice process can be viewed as a funnel that holds many cases at its mouth and relatively few at its end. Concept Summary 1.1 shows the interrelationship of the component agencies of the criminal justice system and the criminal justice process.

The Informal Criminal Justice Process

The traditional model of the criminal justice system depicts the legal process as a series of decision points through which cases flow. Each stage of the system, beginning with investigation and arrest and ending after a sentence has been served, is defined by time-honored administrative procedures and controlled by the rule of law. This "ideal" model of justice still merits concern and attention, but assuming that the system works this way for every case is overly simplistic. Although a few cases exhibit the full array of procedures, many are settled in an informal pattern of cooperation between the major actors in the justice process. For example, police may be willing to make a deal with a suspect in order to gain his cooperation, and the prosecutor may bargain with the defense attorney to gain a plea of guilty as charged in return for a promise of leniency. Law enforcement agents and court officers are allowed tremendous discretion in deciding whether to make an arrest, bring formal charges, handle a case informally, substitute charges, and so on. Crowded courts operate in a spirit of getting the matter settled quickly and cleanly, rather than engaging in long, drawn-out criminal proceedings with an uncertain outcome.

Whereas the traditional model regards the justice process as an adversarial proceeding in which the prosecution and defense are combatants, most criminal cases are actually cooperative ventures in which both the prosecution and defense get together to work out a deal; this is often referred to as the **courtroom work group**.[24] Made up of the prosecutor, defense attorney, judge, and other court personnel, the courtroom work group helps streamline the process of justice through the extensive use of deal making and plea negotiation. Rather than looking to provide a spirited defense or prosecution, cooperation rather than conflict between prosecutor and defense attorney appears to be

LO6 Examine the informal criminal justice system

LO7 Describe the "wedding cake" model of justice

courtroom work group The phrase used to indicate that all parties in the adversary process work together cooperatively to settle cases with the least amount of effort and conflict.

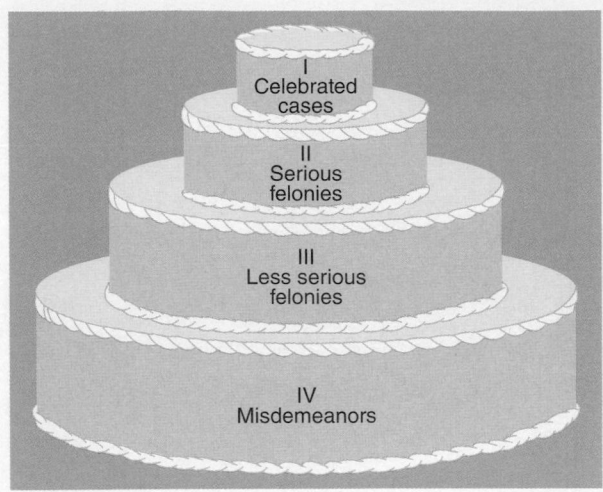

FIGURE 1.3 The Criminal Justice "Wedding Cake"

Source: Based on Samuel Walker, Sense and Nonsense About Crime, Drugs, and Communities (Belmont, CA: Cengage, 2010).

the norm. The adversarial process is only called into play in a few widely publicized criminal cases involving rape or murder. Consequently, upward of 80 percent of all felony cases and over 90 percent of misdemeanors are settled without trial.

The "Wedding Cake" Model of Justice

Samuel Walker, a justice historian and scholar, has come up with a rather creative way of describing this informal justice process: he compares it to a four-layer wedding cake, as depicted in Figure 1.3.[25]

LEVEL I The first layer of Walker's model is made up of celebrated cases involving the wealthy and famous, such as O. J. Simpson, or the not-so-powerful who victimize a famous person—such as Jared Lee Loughner, who shot Congresswoman Gabrielle Giffords. Other cases fall into the first layer because they are widely reported in the media and become the subject of widespread media interest. Still other cases fall into the first level because they involve a large number of victims, such as when James Holmes killed 12 people at a movie theater in Aurora, Colorado, on July 20, 2012. Other cases fall into the first tier because they involve the theft of a great deal of money—such as the multibillion-dollar Ponzi scheme perpetrated by Bernard Madoff, who was sentenced to 150 years in prison for his crimes.

Cases in the first layer of the criminal justice wedding cake usually receive the full array of criminal justice procedures, including competent defense attorneys, expert witnesses, jury trials, and elaborate appeals. Because of the media focus on Level I cases and the Hollywood treatment they receive, the public is given the impression that most criminals are sober, intelligent people who receive the full range of procedural rights afforded by the justice system and that most victims are members of the upper classes, a patently false impression.

LEVEL II The second layer contains serious felonies—rapes, robberies, and burglaries. Police, prosecutors, and judges all agree that these cases are worthy of the full attention of the justice system. The factors placing them in the Level II category include the following:

- They are committed by experienced, repeat offenders.
- The amount of money stolen in a burglary or larceny is significant.

Former New England Patriots tight end Aaron Hernandez stands when asked to do so by defense attorney Jose Baez, as Baez makes closing arguments in the trial for Hernandez at Suffolk Superior Court on April 6, 2017, in Boston. Hernandez was on trial for the July 2012 killings of Daniel de Abreu and Safiro Furtado, whom he encountered in a Boston nightclub. The former NFL player was found guilty. Five days later, he was found hanged in his prison cell, an apparent suicide.

- Violent acts are committed by a stranger who uses a weapon.
- Robberies involve large amounts of money taken by a weapon-wielding criminal.

Offenders in Level II cases quite often receive a full jury trial and, if convicted, can look forward to a prison sentence.

LEVEL III Although they can also be felonies, crimes that fall in the third layer of the wedding cake are less serious offenses, are committed by young or first-time offenders, or involve people who knew each other or were otherwise related, such as a domestic abuse case or a drunken brawl involving people in a "love triangle." Level III crimes may be dealt with by an outright dismissal, a plea bargain, a reduction in charges, or, most commonly, a probationary sentence.

LEVEL IV The fourth layer of the cake is made up of the millions of misdemeanors— disorderly conduct, shoplifting, public drunkenness, and minor assault—that are handled by the lower criminal courts in assembly-line fashion. Few defendants insist on exercising their constitutional rights, because the delay would cost them valuable time and money; punishment is typically a fine or probation.[26]

The wedding cake model of informal justice is an intriguing alternative to the traditional criminal justice flowchart. Criminal justice officials handle individual cases quite differently, yet particular types or classes of cases are handled with a high degree of consistency in every legal jurisdiction. For example, police and prosecutors in Los Angeles and Boston will handle the murder of a prominent citizen in a similar fashion. They will also deal with the death of an unemployed street person killed in a brawl in a similar manner. The wedding cake model is useful because it illustrates that public opinion about criminal justice is often formed on the basis of what happened in an atypical case.

Perspectives on Justice

Even though several decades have passed since the field of criminal justice began to be the subject of serious academic study, significant debate continues over the actual meaning of *criminal justice* and how the problem of crime control should be approached. After decades of effort in research and policy analysis, it is clear that criminal justice is far from a unified field. Practitioners, academics, and commentators alike have expressed irreconcilable differences concerning its goals, purpose, and direction. Considering the complexity of criminal justice, it is not surprising that no single perspective or philosophy dominates the field. What are the dominant views of the criminal justice system today? What is the role of the justice system, and how should it approach its tasks? The different perspectives on criminal justice are discussed next.

Crime Control Perspective

People who hold the **crime control perspective** believe that the proper role of the justice system is to prevent crime through the judicious use of criminal sanctions. Because the public is outraged by violent crimes, it demands an efficient justice system that hands out tough sanctions to those who choose to violate the law.[27] If the justice system were allowed to operate in an effective manner, unhampered by legal controls, potential criminals would be deterred from violating the law. Those who did commit a crime would be apprehended, tried, and punished so that they would never dare commit a crime again. Crime rates trend upward, the argument goes, when criminals do not sufficiently fear apprehension and punishment. If the efficiency of the system could be increased, and the criminal law could be toughened, crime rates would eventually decline. Effective law enforcement, strict mandatory punishment, incarceration of dangerous criminals, and the judicious use of capital punishment are the keys to reducing crime rates. Crime control may be expensive, but reducing the pain inflicted by criminal activity is well worth the price: if punishments were swift, certain, and severe, few would be tempted to break the law.

LO8 Discuss the various perspectives on justice

crime control perspective A model of criminal justice that emphasizes the control of dangerous offenders and the protection of society. Its advocates call for harsh punishments as a deterrent to crime and support availability of the death penalty.

Crime control advocates do not want legal technicalities to help the guilty go free and tie the hands of justice. They lobby for the abolition of legal restrictions on a police officer's ability to search for evidence and interrogate suspects. They want law enforcement officers to be able to profile people at an airport in order to identify terrorists, even if it means singling out individuals because of their gender, race, or ethnic origin. They are angry at judges who let obviously guilty people go free because a law enforcement officer made an unintentional procedural error.

Following are the key positions of the crime control perspective:

- The purpose of the justice system is to deter crime through the application of punishment.
- The more efficient the system, the greater its effectiveness.
- The justice system is not equipped to treat people but rather to investigate crimes, apprehend suspects, and punish the guilty.

Rehabilitation Perspective

rehabilitation perspective The view that the primary purpose of criminal justice is helping to care for people who cannot manage themselves. Crime is an expression of frustration and anger created by social inequality and can be controlled by giving people the means to improve their lifestyle through conventional endeavors.

Advocates of the rehabilitation perspective view crime as an expression of frustration and anger created by social inequality. They see the justice system as a means of caring for and treating people who have been the victims of this inequity. According to this view, crime can be controlled by giving people the means to improve their lifestyle and helping them overcome any personal and or psychological problems caused by their life circumstances.

The rehabilitation concept assumes that people are at the mercy of social, economic, and interpersonal conditions and interactions. Criminals themselves are the victims of racism, poverty, strain, blocked opportunities, alienation, family disruption, and other social problems. Violent killers such as James Holmes seem mentally and emotionally unstable. Others live in socially disorganized neighborhoods that are incapable of providing proper education, health care, or civil services. Society must help them in order to compensate for their social problems; proper treatment may prevent their crimes.

Rehabilitation advocates scoff at the notion that crime can be deterred by the threat of punishment alone. Research shows that experienced criminals perceive less risk and more reward from crime, and they are therefore unaffected by the threat of punishments.[28] Even some novice criminals are not easily deterred: they are not well informed about the actual risks of sanctions and believe that crime may actually pay.[29]

Instead of punishment and deterrence, rehabilitation advocates believe that government treatment-oriented programs can help reduce crime on both a societal (macro) and individual (micro) level. On the macro or societal level, rehabilitation efforts are aimed at preventing crimes before they occur. If legitimate opportunities are provided by job training, family counseling, educational services, and crisis intervention, crime rates decline. On a micro or individual level, rehabilitation efforts are aimed at known offenders who have already violated the law. The best way to reduce crime and recidivism (repeat offending) rates is to help offenders adopt prosocial changes in attitudes and improve cognitive thinking patterns through intensive one-on-one counseling.[30] Although the public may want to "get tough" on crime, many are willing to make exceptions, for example, by advocating leniency for younger offenders.[31]

Following are the key provisions of the rehabilitation model:

- In the long run, it is better to treat than to punish.
- Criminals are society's victims.
- Helping others is part of the American culture.
- Convicted criminals can be successfully treated within the confines of the justice system.

Due Process Perspective

due process perspective Due process provides the basic rights of a defendant in criminal proceedings and the requirements for a fair trial.

According to the due process perspective, the justice system should be dedicated to providing fair and equitable treatment to those accused of crime.[32] This means providing impartial hearings, competent legal counsel, evenhanded treatment, and

The due process clause guarantees fairness for all those who come before the law. Sometimes determining what is fair and just can be challenging. Here, Benjamin Carr, stepfather of Eric Garner, leaves the district attorney's office after a grand jury's decision not to indict the officer accused of putting the unarmed Garner in a fatal chokehold after he was arrested for selling cigarettes. The chokehold was applied despite Garner crying out "I can't breathe". Supporters of Garner's family and others have questioned whether due process—both for the family and the officers—is possible in a case that's sparked nationwide protests on excessive force and accusations by NYPD officers and union officials that the officers involved were being railroaded.

reasonable sanctions to ensure that no one suffers from racial, religious, or ethnic discrimination and that their basic constitutional rights are respected.

Those who advocate the due process orientation are quick to point out that the justice system remains an adversarial process that pits the forces of an all-powerful state against those of a solitary individual accused of a crime. If concern for justice and fairness did not exist, the defendant who lacked resources could easily be overwhelmed; miscarriages of justice are all too common. Numerous criminal convictions have been overturned because newly developed DNA evidence later showed that the accused could not have committed the crimes; many of the falsely convicted spend years in prison before their release. Evidence also shows that many innocent people have been executed for crimes they did not commit. Because such mistakes can happen, even the most apparently guilty offender deserves all the protection the justice system can offer.

The key positions advocated by due process supporters include the following:

- Every person deserves her or his full array of constitutional rights and privileges.
- Preserving the democratic ideals of American society takes precedence over the need to punish the guilty.
- Because of potential errors, decisions made within the justice system must be carefully scrutinized.
- Steps must be taken to treat all defendants fairly regardless of their sex, socioeconomic status, race, religion, or ethnicity.

Nonintervention Perspective

Supporters of the nonintervention perspective believe that justice agencies should limit their involvement with criminal defendants. They believe that regardless of whether intervention is designed to punish people or to treat them, the ultimate effect of any involvement is harmful and will have long-term negative consequences. Once involved with the justice system, criminal defendants develop a permanent record that follows them for the rest of their lives. They may be watched and kept under surveillance. Bearing an official label disrupts their personal and family life and harms their own self-image; they may view themselves as bad, evil, outcasts, troublemakers, or crazy. Official labels then may promote rather than reduce the continuity in antisocial activities.[33] When people are given less stigmatized forms of punishment, such as probation, they are less likely to become repeat offenders.[34]

nonintervention perspective A view of criminal justice that emphasizes the least intrusive treatment possible. Among its central policies are decarceration, diversion, and decriminalization. In other words, less is better.

Noninterventionists worry that contemporary technology will reduce the privacy of American citizens, especially those convicted of crime who now have a permanent and public record. Take for instance the effort to monitor former sex offenders by requiring them to be placed on Web-based sex offender registration lists. Sex offender registration laws are now used in all 50 states. They appeal to politicians who may be swayed by media crusades against child molesters and appease the public's desire to "do something" about child predators. However, research shows that sex offender registration does not reduce the number of rearrests for sex offenses, nor does it have any demonstrable effect on the time between when sex offenders were released from prison and the time they were rearrested for any new offense, such as a drug offense, theft, or another sex offense.[35]

Fearing the harmful effects of stigma and labels, noninterventionists have tried to place limitations on the government's ability to control people's lives. They have called for the **decriminalization** (reduction of penalties) and **legalization** (lawful and non-criminal) of nonserious victimless crimes, such as the possession of small amounts of marijuana. Noninterventionists have sponsored the removal of nonviolent offenders from the nation's correctional system, a policy referred to as **deinstitutionalization**. They support the placement of first offenders who commit minor crimes in informal, community-based treatment programs, a process referred to as **pretrial diversion**.

Noninterventionists fear that efforts to help or treat offenders may actually stigmatize them beyond the scope of their actual offense; this is referred to as **widening the net of justice**. Their efforts have resulted in rulings stating that these laws can be damaging to the reputation and the future of offenders who have not been given an opportunity to defend themselves from the charge that they are chronic criminal sex offenders.[36] As a group, noninterventionist initiatives have been implemented to help people avoid the stigma associated with contact with the criminal justice system.

The key elements of the nonintervention perspective include the following:

- The justice process stigmatizes offenders.
- Stigma locks people into a criminal way of life.
- Less is better. Decriminalize, divert, and deinstitutionalize whenever possible.

Equal Justice Perspective

According to those who take the equal justice perspective, the greatest challenge facing the American criminal justice system is its capability to dispense fair and equal justice to those who come before the law. It is unfair for police to issue a summons to one person for a traffic violation while letting a second offender off with a warning, or to have two people commit the same crime but receive different sentences or punishments. Unequal and inconsistent treatment produces disrespect for the system, suspiciousness, and frustration; it also increases the likelihood of recidivism. Therefore, law violators should be evaluated on the basis of their current behavior, not on what they have done in the past (they have already paid for that behavior) or on what they may do in the future (because future behavior cannot be accurately predicted). The treatment of criminal offenders must be based solely on their present behavior: punishment must be equitably administered and based on "just deserts."

The equal justice perspective has had considerable influence in molding the nation's sentencing policy. There has been an ongoing effort to reduce discretion and to guarantee that every offender convicted of a particular crime receives equal punishment. A number of initiatives have been designed to achieve this result, including mandatory sentences requiring that all people convicted of a crime receive the same prison sentence.

Following are the key elements of the equal justice perspective:

- People should receive equal treatment for equal crimes.
- Decision making in the justice system must be standardized and structured by rules and regulations.
- Whenever possible, individual discretion must be reduced and controlled.
- Inconsistent treatment produces disrespect for the system.

---

decriminalization Reducing the penalty for a criminal act but not actually legalizing it.

legalization The removal of all criminal penalties from a previously outlawed act.

deinstitutionalization The policy of removing as many offenders as possible from secure confinement and treating them in the community.

pretrial diversion A program that provides nonpunitive, community-based alternatives to more intrusive forms of punishment such as jail or prison.

widening the net of justice The view that programs designed to divert offenders from the justice system actually enmesh them further in the process by substituting more intrusive treatment programs for less intrusive punishment-oriented outcomes.

equal justice perspective The view that all people should be treated equally before the law. Equality may best be achieved through individual discretion in the justice process.

Restorative Justice Perspective

According to the concept of restorative justice, the criminal justice system should promote a peaceful and just society; the justice system should aim for peacemaking, not punishment.[37] Advocates of the restorative justice perspective view the efforts of the state to punish and control as encouraging crime rather than discouraging it. The violent, punishing acts of the state are not dissimilar to the violent acts of individuals.[38] Therefore, mutual aid rather than coercive punishment is the key to a harmonious society. Without the capacity to restore damaged social relations, society's response to crime has been almost exclusively punitive.

According to restorative justice, resolution of the conflict between criminal and victim should take place in the community in which it originated, not in some far-off prison. Under these conditions, the victim has a chance to tell his story, and the offender can directly communicate his need for social reintegration and treatment. The goal is to enable the offender to appreciate the damage he has caused, to make amends, and to be reintegrated into society.

Restorative justice programs are devised to reflect these principles. For example, police officers sometimes use mediation techniques to settle disputes, rather than resorting to formal arrest.[39] Mediation and conflict-resolution programs are common features in many communities and are being used in efforts to resolve harmful human interactions ranging from domestic violence to hate crimes.[40] Financial and community service restitution programs have been in operation for more than two decades as an alternative to imprisonment.

The most important elements of the restorative justice model are the following:

- Offenders should be reintegrated into society.
- Coercive punishments are self-defeating.
- The justice system must become more humane.

Perspectives in Perspective

Advocates of each view have attempted to promote their vision of what justice is all about and how it should be enforced. During the past few decades, the crime control and equal justice models have dominated. Laws have been toughened and the rights of the accused curtailed, the prison population has grown, and the death penalty has been employed against convicted murderers. Because the crime rate has been dropping, these policies seem to be effective; they may be questioned if crime rates once again begin to rise. There are signs they are already being questioned due to costs. Many states have closed prisons and reduced the number of persons behind bars, citing skyrocketing corrections costs.

At the same time, efforts to rehabilitate offenders, to provide them with elements of due process, and to give them the least intrusive treatment have not been abandoned. Police, courts, and correctional agencies supply a wide range of treatment and rehabilitation programs to offenders in all stages of the criminal justice system. Whenever possible, those accused of crime are treated informally in nonrestrictive, community-based programs, and the effects of stigma are guarded against. Although the legal rights of offenders are being closely scrutinized by the courts, the basic constitutional rights of the accused remain inviolate. Guardians of the process have made sure that defendants are allowed the maximum protection possible under the law. For example, criminal defendants have been awarded the right to competent legal counsel at trial; merely having a lawyer to defend them is not considered sufficient legal protection.

In sum, understanding the justice system today requires analyzing a variety of occupational roles, institutional processes, legal rules, and administrative doctrines. Each predominant view of criminal justice provides a vantage point for understanding and interpreting these rather complex issues. No single view is *the* right or correct one. Each individual must choose the perspective that best fits his or her own ideas and judgment—or propose a different view that combines elements of all the perspectives or expresses the individual's own view in a new and unique way.

restorative justice perspective
A view of criminal justice that advocates peaceful solutions and mediation rather than coercive punishments.

REALITYCHECK

Myth or Reality?

Justice tends to be objective rather than subjective; agents of the justice system put their personal feelings aside in the course of their duties.

MYTH. Agents of the justice system have varied and differing perspectives on what justice is all about and how they should approach their role and duties.

Some police officers, court officers, and correctional personnel practice a "law and order" orientation, whereas others are more interested in helping and treating offenders. What other professions maintain competing values and viewpoints?

A plain clothes California Highway Patrol detective, who had been marching with anti-police demonstrators, aims his gun at protestors after some in the crowd identified him and his partner during an arrest in Oakland, California. Chief Avery Browne, commander of the California Highway Patrol's Golden Gate Division, said two plainclothes CHP detectives were surrounded by up to 50 demonstrators who ignored orders to back off, despite one of the officers first taking out his baton and identifying himself as police. Is it ethical for police officers to go undercover in such a volatile situation or does that compromise the political process and the public right to demonstrate against government practices they find objectionable?

Noah Berger/Reuters

LO9 Discuss the ethical issues that arise in criminal justice

Ethics in Criminal Justice

The general public and criminal justice professionals are also concerned with the application of ethics in the criminal justice system.[41] Both would like every police officer on the street, every district attorney in court, and every correctional administrator in prison to be able to discern what is right, proper, and moral; to be committed to ethical standards; and to apply equal and fair justice. These demands are difficult because justice system personnel are often forced to work in an environment where moral ambiguity is the norm. Should a police officer be forced to arrest, a prosecutor charge, and a correctional official punish a woman who for many years was the victim of domestic abuse and who in desperation retaliated against her abusive spouse? Who is the victim here, and who is the aggressor? What about the parent who attacks the man who has sexually abused her young child? Should she be prosecuted as a felon? But what happens if the parent mistakenly attacks and injures the wrong person? Can a clear line be drawn between righteous retribution and vigilante justice? As students of justice, we are concerned with identifying the behavioral standards that should govern each of the elements of justice. If these can be identified, is it possible to find ways to apply these standards to police, court, and correctional agencies around the nation?

Ethics in criminal justice is an especially important topic today because of the power granted to those who control the justice system. We rely on the justice system to exert power over people's lives and to be society's instrument of social control, so we grant the system and its agents the authority to deny people their personal liberty on a routine basis. A police officer's ability to arrest and use force, a judge's power to sentence, and a correctional administrator's ability to punish an inmate give them considerable personal power that must be governed by ethical considerations. Without ethical decision making, individual civil rights may suffer and personal liberties guaranteed by the US Constitution may be trampled upon. The need for an ethical criminal justice system is further enhanced by cyber-age advances in recordkeeping and data recording. Agents of the criminal justice system now have immediate access to our most personal information, ranging from arrest records to medical history. Issues of privacy and confidentiality, which can have enormous economic, social, and political consequences, are now more critical than ever.

Ethical issues transcend all elements of the justice system. Yet each branch has specific issues that shape its ethical standards, as we will see in the following sections.

Ethics and Law Enforcement

Ethical behavior is particularly important in law enforcement because, quite simply, police officers have the authority to deprive people of their liberty. And, in carrying out their daily activities, they also have the right to use physical and even deadly force.

Depriving people of liberty and using force are not the only police behaviors that require ethical consideration. Police officers exercise considerable discretion when they choose whom to investigate, how far the investigation should go, and how much effort they should spend on a case. They also sometimes are asked to walk a fine line between legal and illegal behavior when they are searching for evidence or interrogating a suspect—for example, claiming a hidden item was actually in "plain view" or that a suspect's confession was freely given when in reality the officer used threats and coercion. In carrying out their duties, police officers must be responsive to the public's demand for protection, while at the same time remaining sensitive to the rights and liberties of those they must deter and/or control. In this capacity, they serve as the interface between the power of the state and the citizens it governs. This duality creates many ethical dilemmas. Consider the following:

- Should law enforcement agents target groups whom they suspect are heavily involved in crime and violence, or does this lead to racial/ethnic profiling? Is it unethical for a security agent to pay closer attention to a young Arab male getting on an airline flight than she pays to a well-groomed American soldier from upstate New York? Don't forget that clean-cut Tim McVeigh, who grew up in rural Pendleton, New York, and spent more than three years in the army, went on to become the Oklahoma City bomber. How can police officers balance their need to protect public security with the ethical requirement that they safeguard citizens' legal rights?
- What limits should be placed on the use of technology? Should law enforcement agencies be allowed to use tracking devices to monitor movements, take facial scans, listen in on cell phones, or hack into computers in order to keep watch on potential criminals and terrorists? Does the end justify the means?
- Should police officers tell the truth even if it means that a guilty person goes free? For example, a police officer stops a car for a traffic violation and searches it illegally. He finds a weapon used in a particularly heinous shooting in which three children were killed. Would it be ethical for the officer to lie on the witness stand and say the gun was resting on the car seat in plain sight (thereby rendering its seizure legal and proper)? Or should he tell the truth and risk having the charges dismissed, leaving the offender free to kill again?

Andrew Burton/Getty Images

Police officers eat a meal at Junior's restaurant in Brooklyn. Should police officers frequently patronize the same restaurant even if they are barred by policy from receiving discounted meals or free drinks?

WEB APP
1.5
What help is available to law enforcement officers in making ethical decisions? Various national organizations have produced model codes of conduct that can serve as behavioral guides. One well-known document created by the International Association of Chiefs of Police (IACP) says, in part, "As a law enforcement officer, my fundamental duty is to serve mankind; to safeguard lives and property; to protect the innocent against deception, the weak against oppression or intimidation, and the peaceful against violence or disorder; and to respect the constitutional rights of all men to liberty, equality, and justice." To learn more, visit their website at **http://www.theiacp.org**.

Ethics and the Courts

Ethical concerns do not stop with an arrest. As an officer of the court and the "people's attorney," the prosecutor must seek justice for all parties in a criminal matter and should not merely be targeting a conviction. To be fair, prosecutors must share evidence with the defense, must not use scare tactics or intimidation, and must represent the public interest. It is inexcusable and illegal for prosecutors to suppress critical evidence, a practice that might mean the guilty walked free and the innocent were convicted.

Prosecutorial ethics are tested when the dual roles of prosecutors cause them to experience role conflict. On the one hand, a prosecutor represents the people and has an obligation to present evidence, uphold the law, and obtain convictions as vigorously as possible. In the adversary system, it is the prosecutor who takes the side of victims and on whom the victims rely for justice. Because of overcrowded court dockets and limited resources, prosecutors more often than not seek plea deals, granting more lenient sentences in exchange for an admission of guilt. This can create an ethical dilemma: is justice being served when a guilty party is allowed to escape the full extent of the law in order to maintain efficiency in the justice process?

But as a fair and impartial officer of the court, the prosecutor must oversee the investigation of crime and make sure that all aspects of the investigation meet constitutional standards. If, during the investigation, it appears that the police have violated the constitutional rights of suspects—for example, by extracting an illegal confession or conducting an illegal search—then the prosecutor has an ethical obligation to take whatever action is necessary and appropriate to remedy legal or technical errors, even if it means rejecting a case in which the defendant's rights have been violated. Moreover, the canon of legal ethics in most states forbids the prosecutor from pursuing charges when there is no probable cause and mandates that all evidence that might mitigate guilt or reduce the punishment be turned over to the defense.

DEFENSE ATTORNEY As an officer of the court, along with the judge, prosecutors, and other trial participants, the defense attorney seeks to uncover the basic facts and elements of the criminal act. In this dual capacity of being both a defensive advocate and an officer of the court, the attorney is often confronted with conflicting obligations to his client and profession. Suppose a client confides that she is planning to commit a crime. What are the defense attorney's ethical responsibilities in this case? Obviously, the attorney would have to counsel the client to obey the law; if the attorney assisted the client in engaging in illegal behavior, the attorney would be subject to charges of unprofessional conduct and even criminal liability.

What about the situation where an attorney knows that his or her client is guilty because the client admitted as much during pretrial conferences? Should the defense lawyer still try for an acquittal? What is said privately before trial, even at a plea discussion, is never admissible during trial. An attorney would be accused of incompetence if she or he did not try to raise reasonable doubt in every case. The attorney's job is not to decide whether the client committed the offense but to provide a vigorous defense and ensure that the client is not convicted unless the prosecution can prove its case beyond a reasonable doubt. And it is impossible to make the prosecution meet its burden without aggressively challenging the evidence, even if the defender believes the client committed the crime.

Ethics and Corrections

Ethical issues do not disappear after a defendant has been convicted. The ethical issues in punishment are too vast to discuss here, but they include the following:

- Is it fair and ethical to execute a criminal? Can capital punishment ever be considered a moral choice? While lethal injections are supposed to be pain free, recent botched executions show that there is no guarantee of a painless death. No matter how it is implemented, does the death penalty violate the Constitution's ban on cruel and unusual punishment?

- Should people be given different punishments for the same criminal law violation? Is it fair and just when some convicted murderers and rapists receive probation for their crimes while others are sentenced to prison for the same offense?
- Is it fair to grant leniency to criminals who agree to testify against their coconspirator and therefore allow them to benefit from their perfidy, while others, who are not given the opportunity to "squeal," are forced to bear the full brunt of the law?
- Should some criminal inmates be granted early release because they can persuade the parole board that they have been rehabilitated, while others, who are not as glib, convincing, or well spoken, are forced to serve their entire sentence behind bars?
- Should technology be used to monitor offenders in the community? Is it ethical to track a probationer's movements with a Global Positioning System (GPS) unit attached to an ankle bracelet she is required to wear at all times? Should her Internet use and computer downloads be monitored?

Ethics are also challenged by the discretion afforded to correctional workers and administrators. Discretion is involved when a correctional officer decides whether to report an inmate for disorderly conduct, which might jeopardize his or her parole. And although the Supreme Court has issued many rulings related to prisoners' rights, no justices are at the scene of the prison to make sure that their mandates are carried out reliably and consistently.

Correctional officers have significant coercive power over offenders. They are under a legal and professional obligation not to use unnecessary force or take advantage of inmate powerlessness. Examples of abuse include an officer who beats an inmate or a staff member who coerces sex from an inmate. The possibility that these abuses of power will be perpetrated exists because of the powerlessness of the offender relative to the correctional professional.

Ethical considerations transcend all elements of the justice system. Making ethical decisions is an increasingly important task in a society that is becoming more diverse, pluralistic, and complex every day.

ETHICALREFLECTION

The onus is on everyone to "know" the criminal law. Ignorance is no defense; *you* are responsible for knowing when your behavior runs afoul of the law. The problem is there are a lot of laws. A *lot*. There are over 5,000 criminal laws at the federal level alone. Add to that the penal codes from 50 different states and the result is a bewildering array of legal provisions that not even seasoned lawyers and judges can keep track of. The law also continues to change, usually by growing. Every year sees thousands of new laws go into effect. Experts call this overcriminalization, and whether you like it or not, it creates a costly enforcement problem.

Fixing the overcriminalization problem is a priority for liberals and conservatives alike. In 2013, the Judiciary Committee of the Republican-controlled US House of Representatives created an "Overcriminalization Task Force." The National Association of Criminal Defense Attorneys (NACDL) claimed that "our nation's addiction to criminalization backlogs our judiciary, overflows our prisons, and forces innocent individuals to plead guilty not because they actually are, but because exercising their constitutional right to a trial is prohibitively expensive…" Others call overcriminalization a "national plague," noting that "when more and more behaviors are criminalized, there are more and more occasions for police, who embody the state's monopoly on legitimate violence, and who fully participate in humanity's flaws, to make mistakes."

Think back to this chapter's section on the "nonintervention" perspective on justice. As you will recall, one approach to nonintervention is decriminalization. Decriminalization, though, may present problems. Is it ethical, for example, to remove criminal penalties for certain offenses? What unanticipated consequences could manifest?

Writing Challenge: Several states have legalized recreational use of marijuana. As of this writing, such laws remain in conflict with federal law. This is an obvious problem. Should the federal government defer to the states in this instance? Or should it aggressively enforce its antidrug laws? Indeed, there are many other objections to the legalization of marijuana besides the federal/state legal conflict. What are they? Write an essay that answers the question, "What are the possible downsides of marijuana decriminalization?"

A suggested starting point is to read research pertaining to Colorado's legalization experience. A report by the Colorado Department of Public Safety called *Marijuana Legalization in Colorado: Early Findings* can be found at https://cdpsdocs.state.co.us/ors/docs/reports/2016-SB13-283-Rpt.pdf. A report by the Drug Policy Alliance called "So Far, So Good: What We Know About Marijuana Legalization in Colorado, Washington, Alaska, Oregon and Washington, DC" may help as well. It can be found at http://www.drugpolicy.org/sites/default/files/Marijuana_Legalization_Status_Report_101316.pdf.

SUMMARY

LO1 *Discuss the formation of the criminal justice system in America* There was little in the way of a formal criminal justice system until the nineteenth century when the first police agencies were created. The term criminal justice system became prominent around 1967, when the President's Commission on Law Enforcement and the Administration of Justice began a nationwide study of the nation's crime problem.

LO2 *Examine the basic component agencies of the criminal justice system* The term criminal justice refers to both the agencies that dispense justice and the process in which justice is carried out. It is assumed that these agencies work in concert to protect society and dispense fair and equal justice. On an ideal level, the criminal justice system functions as a cooperative effort among the primary agencies—police, courts, and corrections. All too often, however, these agencies act independently from one another.

LO3 *Recognize the size and scope of the contemporary justice system* The contemporary criminal justice system in the United States is monumental in size. It now costs federal, state, and local governments more than $270 billion per year for civil and criminal justice. The system is massive because it must process, treat, and care for millions of people.

LO4 *Trace the formal criminal justice process* The criminal justice process consists of the actual steps the offender takes from the initial investigation through trial, sentencing, and appeal. The justice process contains 15 stages, each of which is a decision point through which cases flow. Each of these decisions can have a critical effect on the defendant, the justice system, and society.

LO5 *Articulate what is meant by the term criminal justice assembly line* Some experts believe that the justice system processes cases in a routine, ritualized manner resembling an assembly line. Because justice is often dispensed in a hasty fashion, an innocent person may suffer a false accusation while a dangerous individual may be released to continue to prey upon society. The system acts as a "funnel": most people who commit crime escape detection, and of those who do not, relatively few are bound over for trial, convicted, and eventually sentenced to prison.

LO6 *Examine the informal criminal justice system* A great deal of the criminal justice process is informal, involving deal making and plea bargaining. Rather than engage in the adversarial process, prosecution and defense work together to settle cases efficiently. Bargains and informal negotiations are more common than formal trials.

LO7 *Describe the "wedding cake" model of justice* There are significant differences in the way each case is treated. Criminal acts that are very serious or notorious may receive the full complement of criminal justice processes, from arrest to trial. However, less serious cases are often settled when a bargain is reached between the prosecution and the defense.

LO8 *Discuss the various perspectives on justice* The role of the criminal justice system can be interpreted in many ways. People who study the field or work in its agencies bring their own ideas and feelings to bear when they try to decide on the right course of action to take or recommend. Thus, a number of different perspectives on criminal justice exist today, ranging from the most conservative (crime control) to the most liberal (restorative justice).

LO9 *Discuss the ethical issues that arise in criminal justice* Determining what is fair and just and balancing it with the need to protect the public can be difficult. The police, courts system, and correctional agencies face ethical issues ranging from ethnic and racial profiling to the use of the death penalty.

KEY TERMS

criminal justice system, p. 6

criminal justice process, p. 6

Law Enforcement Assistance Administration (LEAA), p. 7

evidence-based justice, p. 8

social control, p. 9

in-presence requirement, p. 12

nolle prosequi, p. 12

grand jury, p. 12

true bill of indictment, p. 12

information, p. 12

probable cause hearing, p. 12

courtroom work group, p. 15

crime control perspective, p. 17

rehabilitation perspective, p. 18

due process perspective, p. 18

nonintervention perspective, p. 19

decriminalization, p. 20

legalization, p. 20

deinstitutionalization, p. 20

pretrial diversion, p. 20

widening the net of justice, p. 20

equal justice perspective, p. 20

restorative justice perspective, p. 21

REVIEW QUESTIONS

1. Can a single standard of ethics be applied to all criminal justice agencies? Or is the world too complex to legislate morality and ethics?

2. Describe the differences between the formal and informal justice systems. Is it fair to treat some offenders informally?

3. What are the layers of the criminal justice "wedding cake"? Give an example of a crime for each layer.

4. What are the basic elements of each model or perspective on justice? Which best represents your own point of view?

5. How would each perspective on criminal justice consider the use of the death penalty as a punishment for first-degree murder?

6. What amendments to the Constitution are most important for the administration of justice?

2 The Nature of Crime and Victimization

Since 2000, the rate of drug overdoses in America has increased 137 percent. Deaths from opioids (including heroin and pain relievers like hydrocodone) have increased over 200 percent.[1] In several states, more people now die each year from opioid overdoses than liver disease, suicide, or even car accidents.[2] Drug overdoses are now the leading cause of injury deaths in the United States.

Much of the trend is being driven by heroin, a highly addictive, illegal drug which, like opium and morphine, is derived from the seed pod of certain poppy plants. Once the go-to drug for inner-city junkies, heroin continues to reach an ever-wider audience. It is more popular among wealthy people and women than it was in the past. Increasingly, users are young and white, and most live outside urban centers.[3] Numerous celebrities have died with the drug in their system, such as Philip Seymour Hoffman in 2014.

Why the surge? Experts attribute it to the law of unintended consequences. In the 1980s, doctors began to prescribe opioids with wild abandon. By 2004, 2.4 million people were using prescription painkillers. Law enforcement, policymakers, and even the drug companies began to take note. Purdue Pharma, OxyContin's manufacturer, reconfigured their drug so it could not be snorted. In 2014, Vicodin and other hydrocodone-based drugs joined the Drug Enforcement Administration (DEA) list of Schedule II drugs, prompting tighter regulations. Drug cartels saw this as an opportunity and starting moving huge volumes of heroin into the United States. Heroin seizures at the Mexican border have increased more than fivefold in recent years.[4]

Heroin is also exceptionally cheap. Legally purchased opiate pain medications cost on the order of $1 per milligram for the uninsured; one pill costs about $60. By contrast, a single dose of heroin can cost between $5 and $10, less than a pack of cigarettes or a 6-pack of beer. Prices do vary by region, but they remain quite low across the board. The law of supply and demand explains the affordable pricing; the market is awash with cheap heroin from Mexico. And with marijuana decriminalization catching on in the United States, opium poppies are becoming more profitable to grow than cannabis.[5] This combined with the price and relative difficulty of security prescription pills further fuels America's heroin addiction.

Illegal drug abuse is but one of the many difficult problems our justice system confronts on a daily basis. Unfortunately, crime in America is a

LEARNING OBJECTIVES

LO1 Discuss how crime is defined

LO2 Explain the methods used to measure crime

LO3 Discuss the strengths and weaknesses of crime measures

LO4 Sketch the trends in the crime rate

LO5 Summarize the factors that influence crime rates

LO6 Weigh the various crime patterns

LO7 Discuss the concept of the criminal career

LO8 Describe the characteristics of crime victims

LO9 Differentiate among the various views of crime causation

constantly moving target, not unlike a game of whack-a-mole. One problem rears its head, is beat down to some extent, then another pops up somewhere else at a later time. First it was cocaine in the 1980s, followed promptly by the crack epidemic, then methamphetamine at the turn of the century. Now it's heroin. Who knows what the future has in store?

Where do most crimes occur, and what are the patterns and trends in the crime rate? To answer these and similar questions, elaborate methods of crime data collection have been devised. These sources of crime data are essential to get an accurate reading on the nature and extent of crime as well as the nature of crime trends and patterns. Without this data, it is impossible to create crime-control policies and assess their effectiveness.

This chapter reviews some basic questions about crime addressed by criminal justice professionals: How is crime defined? How is crime measured? How much crime is there, and what are its trends and patterns? Why do people commit crime? How many people become victims of crime, and under what circumstances does victimization take place?

How Is Crime Defined?

LO1 Discuss how crime is defined

The justice system revolves around crime and the control of crime. Although for most of us the concept of "crime" seems rather simple—a violation of criminal law—the question remains: why are some acts considered a violation of the law, while others, seemingly more serious, are considered legal and noncriminal? There are three views of how and why some behaviors become illegal and are considered crimes whereas others remain noncriminal.

Consensus View

consensus view of crime The majority of citizens in a society share common ideals and work toward a common good. Crimes are acts that are outlawed because they conflict with the rules of the majority and are harmful to society.

According to what is known as the consensus view of crime, crimes are behaviors that are essentially harmful to a majority of citizens living in society and therefore have been controlled or prohibited by the existing criminal law. Using this definition, criminal law is a set of rules, codified by state authorities, that express the norms, goals, and values of the *vast majority of society*. The definition implies that criminal law and the behaviors it defines as crimes represent the *consensus* of public opinion and that there is general agreement about which behaviors society needs to control and which should be beyond state regulation.

The consensus view rests on the assumption that criminal law has a social control function—restraining those who might otherwise engage in antisocial behavior. Criminal law works to control behaviors that are inherently destructive and dangerous in order to maintain the existing social fabric and ensure the peaceful functioning of society.

Conflict View

conflict view of crime The law is controlled by the rich and powerful who shape its content to ensure their continued economic domination of society. The criminal justice system is an instrument of social and economic repression.

According to the conflict view of crime, the content of criminal law, and consequently the definition of crime, are shaped and controlled by the ongoing class struggle between the rich and poor, the haves and have-nots. According to this view, criminal law is created and enforced by the ruling class as a mechanism for controlling dissatisfied, have-not members of society. The law is the instrument that enables the wealthy to maintain their position of power and control the behavior of those who oppose their ideas and values or who might rebel against the unequal distribution of wealth.[6]

Interactionist View

interactionist view of crime Criminal law reflects the values of people who use their social and political power to shape the legal system.

moral entrepreneurs People who wage moral crusades to control criminal law so that it reflects their own personal values.

According to the interactionist view of crime, the criminal law is structured to reflect the preferences and opinions of people who hold social power and use their influence to shape the legal process.[7] These so-called moral entrepreneurs wage campaigns (moral crusades) to control behaviors they view as immoral and wrong (such as abortion) or, conversely, to legalize behaviors they consider harmless social eccentricities (such as smoking marijuana). In essence, they dedicate themselves to molding the law to reflect their own worldviews. According to the interactionist view, then, many crimes are not inherently evil or immoral

Don Blankenship, center, leaves the federal courthouse with his attorneys after the verdict in his trial in Charleston, West Virginia. The former Massey Energy CEO was convicted of a misdemeanor count connected to a deadly coal mine explosion and acquitted of more serious charges. A federal jury convicted Blankenship of conspiring to willfully violate mine safety standards. He was sentenced to a year in prison for his role in the worst mine disaster in the past 40 years.

acts but are illegal because they are in conflict with social norms. So, for example, it is perfectly legal to purchase liquor, even though 18 million Americans have alcohol problems and more people die from the effects of alcoholism every year than any other cause.[8]

DEFINING CRIME Although these views of crime differ, they generally agree on four points: (1) criminal law defines crime; (2) the definition of crime is constantly changing and evolving; (3) social forces mold the definition of crimes; and (4) criminal law has a social control function. Therefore, as used here, **crime** is defined as follows:

> Crime is a violation of social rules of conduct, interpreted and expressed by a written criminal code, created by people holding social and political power. Its content may be influenced by prevailing public sentiments, historically developed moral beliefs, and the need to protect public safety. Individuals who violate these rules may be subject to sanctions administered by state authority, which include social stigma and loss of status, freedom, and, on occasion, their lives.

How Is Crime Measured?

In addition to understanding how an act becomes a crime, it is important for criminal justice scholars to measure the nature, extent, and trends in the crime rate. They use a variety of techniques to study crime and its consequences. Three principal types of crime data have been developed—official data, victim data, and self-report data—each having particular strengths and weaknesses. The following sections review these methods in some detail and what they tell us about the crime problem in the United States and abroad.

Official Crime Data: The Uniform Crime Reports (UCR)

The Federal Bureau of Investigation (FBI) **Uniform Crime Reports (UCR)** is the best-known and most widely cited source of criminal records. The UCR includes crimes reported to local law enforcement departments and the number of arrests made by police agencies.[9] Data from the UCR are published in an annual volume called *Crime in the United States* and serves as the nation's **official crime statistics**. The FBI receives and compiles records from more than 17,000 police departments serving a majority of the US population.

The FBI tallies and annually publishes the number of reported offenses by city, county, standard metropolitan statistical area, and geographical division of the United States for the most serious crimes. These **Part I crimes** are **murder and nonnegligent manslaughter**, **forcible rape**, **robbery**, **aggravated assault**, **burglary**, **larceny**, **motor vehicle theft**, and **arson**.

crime A violation of societal rules of behavior as interpreted and expressed by a criminal legal code created by people holding social and political power. Individuals who violate these rules are subject to sanctions by state authority, social stigma, and loss of status.

LO2 Explain the methods used to measure crime

Uniform Crime Reports (UCR) The FBI's yearly publication of where, when, and how much serious crime occurred in the prior year.

official crime statistics Compiled by the FBI in its Uniform Crime Reports, these are a tally of serious crimes reported to police agencies each year.

Part I crimes The eight crimes for which, because of their seriousness and frequency, the FBI reports their incidence in its annual Uniform Crime Reports. The Part I crimes are murder and nonnegligent manslaughter, forcible rape, robbery, aggravated assault, burglary, larceny, motor vehicle theft, and arson.

murder and nonnegligent manslaughter The willful (nonnegligent) killing of one human being by another.

forcible rape Under common law, the carnal knowledge of a female forcibly and against her will. Many states have made rape a gender-neutral crime. The FBI has created a new definition of rape for its UCR program: "The penetration, no matter how slight, of the vagina or anus with any body part or object, or oral penetration by a sex organ of another person, without the consent of the victim."

robbery The taking or attempting to take anything of value from the care, custody, or control of a person or persons by force or threat of force or violence and/or by putting the victim in fear.

aggravated assault An unlawful attack by one person upon another, accompanied by the use of a weapon, for the purpose of inflicting severe or aggravated bodily injury.

burglary The unlawful entry of a structure to commit a felony or a theft.

larceny The unlawful taking, carrying, leading, or riding away of property from the possession or constructive possession of another.

motor vehicle theft The theft of a motor vehicle.

arson Any willful or malicious burning or attempting to burn, with or without intent to defraud, a dwelling house, public building, motor vehicle or aircraft, or personal property of another.

Part II crimes All other crimes except the eight Part I crimes. The FBI records all arrests made for Part II crimes, including race, gender, and age information.

In addition to Part I crimes, the UCR also collects data on the number and characteristics (age, race, and gender) of individuals who have been arrested for committing a crime. Included in the arrest data are both people who have committed Part I crimes and people who have been arrested for all other crimes, known collectively as **Part II crimes**. This latter group includes such criminal acts as sex crimes, drug trafficking, and vandalism.

COMPILING THE UNIFORM CRIME REPORTS The methods used to compile the UCR are quite complex. Each month, law enforcement agencies report the number of Part I crimes reported by victims, by officers who discovered the infractions, or by other sources. Whenever criminal complaints are found through investigation to be unfounded or false, they are eliminated from the actual count. However, the number of actual offenses known is reported to the FBI whether or not anyone is arrested for the crime, the stolen property is recovered, or prosecution ensues.

In addition, each month, law enforcement agencies also report how many crimes were cleared. Crimes are cleared in two ways: (1) when at least one person is arrested, charged, and turned over to the court for prosecution; or (2) by exceptional means, when some element beyond police control precludes the physical arrest of an offender (e.g., the offender leaves the country). Data on the number of clearances involving the arrest of only juvenile offenders, data on the value of property stolen and recovered in connection with Part I offenses, and detailed information pertaining to criminal homicide are also reported. Nationwide, slightly less than 50 percent of violent crimes and 20 percent of property crimes are cleared.

Violent crimes are more likely to be solved than property crimes because police devote more resources to these more serious acts, witnesses (including the victim) are frequently available to identify offenders, and, in many instances, the victim and offender were previously acquainted.

The UCR uses three methods to express crime data: (1) the number of crimes reported to the police and arrests made are expressed as raw figures; (2) year over year percentage changes in the number of crimes are computed; and (3) the crime rate per 100,000 people is calculated. The following equation is used:

$$\frac{\text{Number of Repeated Crimes}}{\text{Total US Population}} \times 100,000 = \text{Rate per } 100,000$$

So, in 2015, the most recent year for which UCR data were available as of this writing, there were 15,696 murders, a 10.8 percent increase from 2013. The murder rate was 4.9 per 100,000 people.[10]

HOW ACCURATE IS THE UCR? The UCR's accuracy has long been suspect. Many serious crimes are not reported to police and therefore are not counted by the UCR. The reasons for not reporting vary:

- Victims consider the crime trivial or unimportant and choose not to call the police.
- Some victims fail to report because they do not trust the police or have little confidence in their ability to solve crime. Cities in which people believe the police can help them are more likely to report crime.[11]
- People without property insurance believe it is useless to report theft.
- Victims fear reprisals from an offender's friends or family.
- Victims have "dirty hands" and are involved in illegal activities themselves, so they do not want to get involved with the police.

Because of these and other factors, less than half of all criminal incidents are reported to the police.

The way a police department records and reports criminal activity also affects the validity of UCR statistics. Some departments may define crimes loosely—reporting a trespass as a burglary or an assault on a woman as an attempted rape—whereas others pay strict attention to FBI guidelines. Some make systematic errors in UCR reporting, for example, counting an arrest only after a formal booking procedure, even though the UCR requires arrests to be counted when the suspect is released without a formal charge.

REALITYCHECK

Myth or Reality?

Most people report their criminal victimizations to police.

MYTH. Less than half of all criminal incidents are reported to police.

Have you been the victim of crime? Did you report it to the police? If not, why?

These reporting practices may help explain interjurisdictional differences in crime. There may also be differences between the way states define a crime and the definition used in the UCR program. Because many jurisdictions have broadened their classification of rape to include all forms of sexual assault, the FBI has followed suit, changing in 2012 the definition used in the UCR to "The penetration, no matter how slight, of the vagina or anus with any body part or object, or oral penetration by a sex organ of another person, without the consent of the victim."

Some critics take issue with the way the FBI records data and counts crimes. According to the "Hierarchy Rule," in a multiple-offense incident, only the most serious crime is counted. So if an armed bank robber commits a robbery, assaults a patron as he flees, steals a car to get away, and damages property during a police chase, only the robbery is reported because it is the most serious offense.

Although these issues are troubling, the UCR continues to be one of the most widely used sources of criminal statistics. Because the UCR is collected in a careful and systematic way, it is considered a highly reliable indicator of crime patterns and trends. That is, even if reporting problems compromise computing the exact number of crimes committed in a single year, measurement of year-to-year change should be accurate because measurement problems are stable over time.

NIBRS: THE FUTURE OF CRIME DATA Clearly there must be a more reliable source for crime statistics than the UCR as it stands today. Beginning in 1982, a five-year redesign effort was undertaken to provide more comprehensive and detailed crime statistics. The effort resulted in the National Incident-Based Reporting System (NIBRS), a program that collects data on each reported crime incident. Instead of submitting statements of the kinds of crime that individual citizens report to the police and summary statements of resulting arrests, NIBRS requires local police agencies to provide at least a brief account of each incident and arrest, including the incident, victim, and offender information.

In addition to common-law crimes such as rape and murder, NIBRS reporting provides information on most of the criminal justice issues facing law enforcement today— terrorism, white-collar crime, assaults on law enforcement officers, offenses in which weapons were involved, drug/narcotic offenses, hate crimes, domestic and familial abuse (including elder abuse), juvenile crime, gang-related crime, parental abduction, organized crime, and pornography, as well as arrest data related to driving under the influence. In addition, NIBRS reporting captures whether the offender was suspected of using drugs/narcotics or alcohol during or shortly before the incident and whether the offender used computer equipment to perpetrate the crime; this makes it possible to develop a national database on the nature of crime, victims, and criminals.

In 2015, the most recent year for which data were available as of this writing, 6,648 law enforcement agencies, representing more than 96 million inhabitants, submitted NIBRS data. NIBRS is slated to replace the UCR by January 1, 2021.[12]

National Incident-Based Reporting System (NIBRS) Program that requires local police agencies to provide a brief account of each incident and arrest within 22 crime patterns, including incident, victim, and offender information.

National Crime Victimization Survey (NCVS)

Because many victims do not report their experiences to the police, the UCR cannot measure all the annual criminal activity. To address the nonreporting issue, the federal government sponsors the National Crime Victimization Survey (NCVS), a comprehensive, nationwide survey of victimization conducted annually by the US Census Bureau for the Bureau of Justice Statistics (BJS).

In the most recent survey, 95,760 households and 163,880 persons age 12 or older were interviewed for the NCVS.[13] People are surveyed twice a year, so each interview covers a six-month period, households stay in the sample for three years, and new households are rotated into the sample on an ongoing basis. The NCVS collects information on crimes suffered by individuals and households, whether or not those crimes were reported to law enforcement. It estimates the proportion of each crime type reported to law enforcement and summarizes the reasons that victims give for reporting or not reporting.

There have been numerous methodological changes to the survey over the past decades, including a new sampling method, a change in the method of handling first-time

National Crime Victimization Survey (NCVS) A national survey of approximately 90,000 households, used to estimate the frequency of crime victimization, as well as characteristics of victims.

interviews with households, and a change in the method of interviewing: computer-assisted personal interviewing (CAPI) replaced paper and pencil interviewing (PAPI).

Through this massive and complex survey, the NCVS provides information about victims (age, sex, race, ethnicity, marital status, income, and educational level), offenders (sex, race, approximate age, and victim–offender relationship), and crimes (time and place of occurrence, use of weapons, nature of injury, and economic consequences). Questions also cover the experiences of victims with the criminal justice system, self-protective measures used by victims, and possible substance abuse by offenders.

The greatest advantage of the NCVS over official data sources such as the UCR is that it can estimate the total amount of annual crimes, not just those that are reported to police. As a result, the NCVS provides a more nearly complete picture of the nation's crime problem.

Because of the care with which the samples are drawn and the high completion rate, NCVS data is considered a relatively unbiased, valid estimate of all victimizations for the target crimes included in the survey. Yet, like the UCR, the NCVS may suffer from methodological problems. As a result, its findings must be interpreted with caution. Some of the potential problems include the following:

- Victims may overreport as a consequence of their misinterpretation of events; for example, a lost wallet may be reported as stolen, or an open door may be viewed as a burglary attempt.
- Victims may underreport because they are embarrassed about reporting crime to interviewers, fear getting in trouble, or simply forget an incident.
- There may be an inability to record the personal criminal activity of those interviewed, such as drug use or gambling; murder is not included for obvious reasons.
- Sampling errors may produce a group of respondents that does not represent the nation as a whole.
- A faulty question format may invalidate responses; some groups, such as adolescents, may be particularly susceptible to error due to question format.
- For some crimes, such as rape, the number of people reporting victimization is quite small so that even a slight year-to-year change can produce significant results.

Self-Report Surveys

self-report surveys A research approach that requires subjects to reveal their own participation in delinquent or criminal acts.

Self-report surveys, the third source of crime data, ask subjects to describe their past and current criminal activities, including whether they have ever been involved in substance abuse, theft, and/or violence; how often they engage in these activities; what specific kinds of drugs they took; and whether they acted alone or in groups. It is assumed that respondents will be willing to describe their illegal activities accurately because self-report surveys are typically administered in groups, anonymously and unsigned. The idea is to measure crimes that would neither be reported to the police nor show up in victim surveys, such as using cocaine. The capability of self-reports to get at these "dark figures of crime" makes it possible to track the incidence of criminal acts that are not reflected in official statistics.

Most self-report studies are administered among middle school and high school youth. Because school attendance is universal in the United States, a school-based self-report survey represents a cross-section of the community. However, self-reports are not restricted to youth crime. They are also used to examine the offense histories of prison inmates, drug users, and other segments of the population.

Although they are widely used, how valid are self-reports? Is it reasonable to expect people to candidly admit illegal acts? They have nothing to gain, and the ones who would be taking the greatest risk are the ones with official records, who may be engaging in the most criminality. Some people may exaggerate their criminal acts, forget some of them, or be confused about what is being asked. Response rate is also critical. Even if 90 percent of a school population voluntarily participates in a self-report survey, researchers can never be sure whether the few who refuse to participate or are absent that day account for a significant portion of the school's population of persistent, high-rate offenders. It is also unlikely that the most serious chronic offenders in the teenage population are the most willing to cooperate with university-based criminologists administering self-report tests.[14]

The Pros and Cons of the Crime Data Sources

Are the various sources of crime data compatible? Each has strengths and weaknesses. The FBI survey is carefully tallied and contains data on the number of murders and people arrested—information that the other data sources lack. However, this survey omits the many crimes that victims choose not to report to police, and it is subject to the reporting caprices of individual police departments.

The NCVS contains unreported crime and important information on the personal characteristics of victims, but the data consist of estimates made from relatively limited samples of the total US population, so that even narrow fluctuations in the rates of some crimes can have a major impact on findings. It also relies on personal recollections that may be inaccurate. Furthermore, the NCVS does not include data on important crime patterns, including murder and drug abuse.

Self-report surveys can provide information on the personal characteristics of offenders that is not available from any other source, such as their attitudes, values, beliefs, and psychological profiles. Yet, at their core, self-reports rely on the honesty of criminal offenders and drug abusers, a population not generally known for accuracy and integrity.

Despite these differences, the data sources seem more compatible than first believed. Although their tallies of crimes are certainly not in sync, the crime patterns and trends they record are often similar.[15] All three sources generally agree about the personal characteristics of serious criminals (such as age and gender) and about where and when crime occurs (such as urban areas, nighttime, and summer months).

L03 Discuss the strengths and weaknesses of crime measures

Crime Trends

Crime is not new to this century.[16] Studies have indicated that a gradual increase in the crime rate, especially in violent crime, occurred from 1830 to 1860. Following the Civil War, this rate increased significantly for about 15 years. Then, from 1880 up to the time of World War I, with the possible exception of the years immediately preceding and following the war, the number of reported crimes decreased. After a period of readjustment, the crime rate steadily declined until the Depression (about 1930), when another crime wave was recorded.

L04 Sketch the trends in the crime rate

Trends in the Uniform Crime Reports

As measured by the UCR, crime rates increased gradually following the 1930s until the 1960s, when the growth rate became much greater. The homicide rate, which had actually declined from the 1930s to the 1960s, also began a sharp increase that continued through the 1980s. Crime rates peaked in 1991, when the UCR recorded almost 15 million crimes in a single year. Since then, the number of crimes has mostly been in decline, with a recent uptick in 2015; about 9.2 million crimes were reported in 2015, a drop of more than 5 million reported crimes since the 1991 peak, and this decline occurred despite a boost of more than 50 million people in the general population.[17]

In 2015, the estimated number of violent offenses increased 3.9 percent compared to 2014. More disturbing still, murder and nonnegligent manslaughter increased nearly 11 percent from 2014 to 2015. It remains to be seen whether the trend will continue. And be reminded that crime is still very much down over the long term. Indeed, property crime decreased by 3.4 percent from 2014 to 2015.

Trends in the Victimization Data

According to the latest NCVS survey, US residents aged 12 or older experienced about 20 million violent and property victimizations.[18] Like the UCR data, NCVS data show that criminal victimizations have declined significantly during the past 30 years (Figure 2.1). In 1973, an estimated 44 million victimizations were recorded, far higher than today; since 1993, the rate of violent victimization has declined about 80 percent.

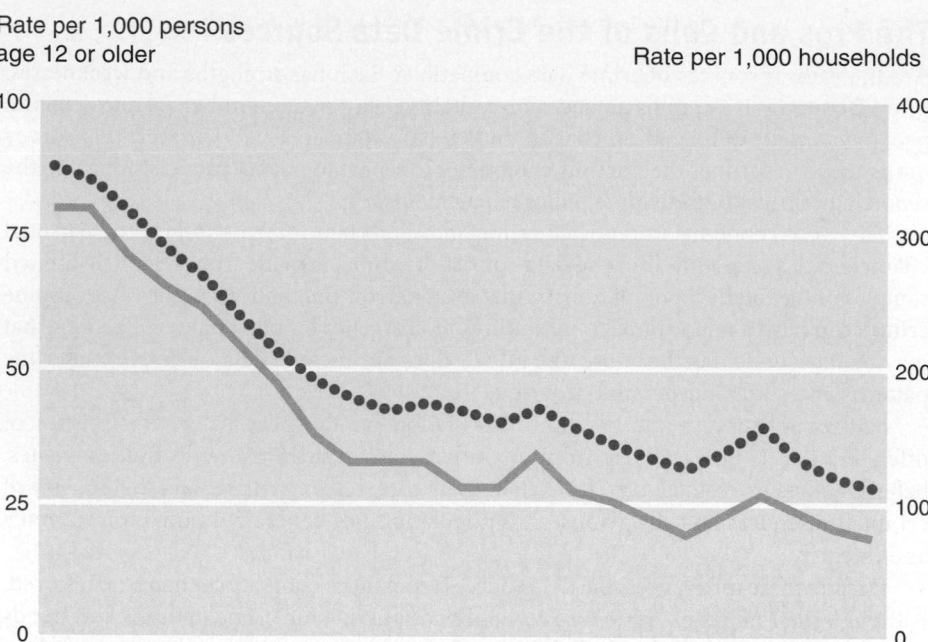

Rate per 1,000 persons
age 12 or older

Rate per 1,000 households

FIGURE 2.1 Violent and Property Victimization

Source: Jennifer L. Truman and Rachel E. Morgan, *Criminal Victimization*, 2015 (Washington, DC: Bureau of Justice Statistics, 2016).

Interestingly, the most recent NCVS results tell a different story than the Uniform Crime Reports, at least with respect to violent crime. Note in Figure 2.1 violent victimizations were lower in 2015 compared to 2014. This finding is at odds with the FBI's reporting of an increase in crime from 2014 to 2015. Clearly, victimization reporting trends do not move in lockstep with official statistics. According to the latest NCVS data, however, the decline from 2014 to 2015, though evident, was not statistical significant.[19]

Self-Report Trends

One important source of longitudinal self-report data is the Monitoring the Future (MTF) study that researchers at the University of Michigan Institute for Social Research (ISR) have been conducting annually since 1978. This national survey, which typically involves between 40,000 and 50,000 high school students, is one of the most important sources of trends in self-report data.[20]

The MTF survey shows that a surprising number of teenagers report involvement in serious criminal behavior (see Table 2.1). About 10 percent reported hurting someone badly enough that the victim needed medical care (6.4 percent said they did it more than once). About 22 percent reported stealing something worth less than $50, and another 7 percent stole something worth more than $50; over 20 percent reported shoplifting one or more times.

If the MTF data are accurate, the crime problem is much greater than official statistics would lead us to believe. According to the US Department of Education, there are about 15 million public school students in grades 9 through 12.[21] About 1.3 percent of high school students said they had used force to steal (which is the legal definition of a robbery). At this rate, high school students alone commit nearly 200,000 robberies per year. In comparison, the UCR now tallies about 325,000 yearly robberies for *all* age groups.[22] There is a clear discrepancy, then, between crimes reported to police and those disclosed in surveys such as Monitoring the Future.

The factors that help explain the upward and downward movement in crime rates, as we have experienced for the past two decades, are discussed in Exhibit 2.1.

TABLE 2.1 Monitoring the Future Survey of Criminal Activity of High School Seniors

Type of Delinquency	STUDENTS WHO Engaged in Offenses, %	
	Committed at Least Once	Committed More Than Once
Set fire on purpose	1.3	0.7
Damaged school property	3.9	3.8
Damaged work property	1.4	1.3
Auto theft	1.9	1.9
Auto part theft	1.1	1.3
Break and enter	10.3	10.7
Theft, less than $50	11.0	11.1
Theft, more than $50	3.7	3.7
Shoplift	9.2	13.0
Gang or group fight	7.1	7.2
Hurt someone badly enough to require medical care	6.4	3.9
Used force or a weapon to steal	1.3	1.4
Hit teacher or supervisor	1.1	1.3
Participated in serious fight	7.0	4.2

Source: Lloyd D. Johnson, Jerald G. Bachman, and Patrick M. O'Malley, *Monitoring the Future, 2012* (Ann Arbor: Institute for Social Research, 2014), pp. 115–118, http://www.monitoringthefuture.org/datavolumes/2012/2012dv.pdf (accessed March 25, 2016).

EXHIBIT 2.1 Factors that Influence Crime Trends

Crime experts have identified a variety of social, economic, personal, and demographic factors that influence crime rate trends. Although crime experts are still uncertain about how these factors impact the trends, directional change seems to be associated with changes in crime rates.

Age Structure

As a general rule, the crime rate follows the proportion of teens in the population: more kids, more crime! Crime rates skyrocketed in the 1960s when the baby boomers became teens and the 13- to 19-year-old population grew rapidly. Crime rate drops since 1993 can be explained in part by an aging society: the elderly commit relatively few crimes.

Immigration

Immigration has a suppressor effect on crime. Research shows that immigrants are less crime prone than the general population, so that as the number of immigrants increases, per capita crime rates decline. During the past two decades, cities with the largest increases in immigration have experienced the largest decreases in crime rates, especially homicides and robberies. This issue is further explored in the accompanying Contemporary Issues in Criminal Justice box.

Unemployment

The general public believes that crime rates increase as the economy turns down and unemployment rises. However, there is little correlation between these indicators of economic prosperity and crime rates. Unemployed people do not suddenly join gangs or commit armed robberies. Criminals are usually unemployed or underemployed and therefore not affected by short-term economic conditions.

Abortion

Evidence exists that the recent drop in the crime rate is linked to the availability of legalized abortion. In 1973, *Roe v. Wade* legalized abortion nationwide, and the drop in crime rate began approximately 18 years later, in 1991. Crime rates began to decline when the first groups of potential offenders affected by the abortion decision began reaching the peak age of criminal activity. It is possible that the link between crime rates and abortion is the result of two mechanisms: (1) selective abortion on the part of women most at risk to have children who would engage in criminal activity, and (2) improved child-rearing or environmental circumstances caused by better maternal, familial, or fetal care because women are having fewer children.

Gun Availability

As recent events show, the association between guns and crime is quite controversial. Those who advocate for the right to own guns claim that the recent spate of mass shootings have occurred at a time when gun control laws have restricted purchases, a fact which proves that criminals will obtain guns while honest citizens are restricted from carrying weapons for self-protection. Gun control advocates claim that the availability of firearms may influence the crime rate: as the number of guns in the population increases, so do violent crime rates.

Mental Health Treatment Availability

The recent spate of mass killings highlights the fact that the availability of mental health treatment may be linked to violent crime rates. Take for example mass shootings such as the Newtown massacre in 2012 in which the perpetrator, Adam Lanza, is believed to have suffered from mental illness. If more treatment becomes available for people like Lanza, incidents of mass shootings may be prevented.

Gangs

Another factor that affects crime rates is the explosive growth in teenage gangs. Surveys indicate that about 800,000 gang members reside in

(Continued)

EXHIBIT 2.1 Factors that Influence Crime Trends *(Continued)*

the United States. Data collected by the National Youth Gang Center show that gang members are responsible for a large proportion of all violent offenses committed during the adolescent years. Boys who are members of gangs are far more likely to possess guns than non-gang members; criminal activity increases when kids join gangs.

Drug Use

Some experts tie increases in the violent crime rate between 1985 and 1993 to the crack epidemic, which swept the nation's largest cities, and to drug-trafficking gangs that fought over drug turf. These well-armed gangs did not hesitate to use violence to control territory, intimidate rivals, and increase market share. As the crack epidemic subsided, so too did the violence rates in New York City and other metropolitan areas where crack use was rampant. A sudden increase in drug use, on the other hand, may be a harbinger of future increases in the crime rate, especially if guns are easily obtained and fall into the hands of gang members.

Media

Some experts argue that violent media can influence the direction of crime rates. As the availability of media with a violent theme skyrocketed with the introduction of home video players, DVDs, cable TV, computer and video games, and so on, so too did teen violence rates. Efforts to curb violence on TV may help account for a declining crime rate.

Medical Technology

Some crime experts believe that the presence and quality of health care can have a significant impact on murder rates. Murder rates might be up to five

times higher than they are today without medical breakthroughs in treating victims of violence developed over the past 40 years. The big breakthrough occurred in the 1970s when technology that had been developed to treat injured soldiers in Vietnam was applied to trauma care in the nation's hospitals. Since then, fluctuations in the murder rate can be linked to the level and availability of emergency medical services.

Justice Policy

Some law enforcement experts have suggested that a reduction in crime rates may be attributed to adding large numbers of police officers and using them in aggressive police practices that target "quality of life" crimes such as panhandling, graffiti, petty drug dealing, and loitering. It is also possible that tough laws imposing lengthy prison terms on drug dealers and repeat offenders can affect crime rates.

Sources: Bianca Bersani, "A Game of Catch-Up? The Offending Experience of Second-Generation Immigrants," *Crime and Delinquency* 60 (2014): 60–84; David Weisburd, Cody Telep, and Brian Lawton, "Could Innovations in Policing Have Contributed to the New York City Crime Drop Even in a Period of Declining Police Strength? The Case of Stop, Question and Frisk as a Hot Spots Policing Strategy," *Justice Quarterly* 31 (2014): 129–153; Richard Rosenfeld and Robert Fornango, "The Impact of Police Stops on Precinct Robbery and Burglary Rates in New York City, 2003–2010," *Justice Quarterly* 31 (2014): 96–122; Patricia L. McCall, Kenneth Land, Cindy Brooks Dollar, and Karen F. Parker, "The Age Structure-Crime Rate Relationship: Solving a Long-Standing Puzzle," *Journal of Quantitative Criminology* 29 (2013): 167–190; Tim Wadsworth, "Is Immigration Responsible for the Crime Drop? An Assessment of the Influence of Immigration on Changes in Violent Crime Between 1990 and 2000," *Social Science Quarterly* 91 (2010): 531–553.

 CONTEMPORARY ISSUES IN CRIMINAL JUSTICE

Immigration and Crime

Some critics call for tough new laws limiting immigration and/or strictly enforcing deportation laws because they believe that immigrants are prone to crime and represent a social threat. How true are their perceptions? Not very true, according to the American Immigration Council, whose research found that on the national level, US-born men ages 18 to 39 are five times more likely to be incarcerated than their foreign-born peers. Though the number of illegal immigrants in the country doubled between 1994 and 2004, violent crime declined by nearly 35 percent and property crimes by 25 percent over the same period. The declines also occurred in border cities where the immigration influx was largest.

In one of the most recent studies on the subject, Bianca Bersani and her colleagues found that first-generation immigrants (individuals born outside the United States) were less likely to commit serious crimes than their US-born counterparts. They were also less likely to become chronic offenders. These findings stand in stark contrast to common perceptions that immigrants are disproportionately responsible for fluctuations in America's crime trends.

Also interesting is a finding from the study that second-generation immigrants (individuals born in the United States who have at least one foreign-born parent) offend at similar rates to their native counterparts. What explains this phenomenon? According to Bersani and her colleagues, "the

finding that first-generation immigrants desist from crime at an earlier age compared to their peers may suggest that they are more easily deterred from further crime following criminal justice sanctions." In contrast, context (particularly neighborhood disadvantage) went a long way toward explaining delinquency in second-generation immigrants. In this way, second-generation immigrants were really no different from their native-born counterparts; faced with the same circumstances that predispose people toward breaking the law, both groups fared similarly.

CRITICAL THINKING

1. What fuels perceptions that immigrants are responsible for a disproportionate amount of criminal activity?

2. Does research on "immigrants" allow us to draw conclusions about illegal immigration and crime? Why or why not?

Sources: Walter Ewing, Daniel E. Martinez, and Ruben Rumbaut, *The Criminalization of Immigration in the United States* (Washington, DC: American Immigration Council, 2015), https://www.americanimmigrationcouncil.org/research/criminalization-immigration-united-states (accessed April 2017); Bianca E. Bersani, Thomas A. Loughran, and Alex R. Piquero, "Comparing Patterns and Predictors of Immigrant Offending Among a Sample of Adjudicated Youth," *Journal of Youth and Adolescence* 10 (2013).

Crime Patterns

By studying crime data, experts can determine whether stable patterns appear in the crime rate, which may help us better understand where crime occurs, who commits crime, and why they violate the law. What are these enduring and stable patterns?

Ecological Patterns

Distinct ecological patterns appear in the crime rate:

- Rural and suburban areas have much lower crime rates than large metropolitan centers, suggesting that urban problems—overcrowding, poverty, social inequality, narcotics use, and racial conflict—are related to crime rates.
- Crime rates are highest in the summer months, probably because people spend so much time outdoors and are less likely to secure their homes, and because schools are closed, which provides young people with greater opportunity for criminal activity.
- Crime rates are also related to the region of the country. The West and South usually have significantly higher rates than the Midwest and New England regions.

WEB APP 2.1 To read Donohue and Levitt's famous study of abortion and crime, go to **http://pricetheory.uchicago.edu /levitt/Papers/DonohueLevitt TheImpactOfLegalized2001.pdf**. Do you agree with their findings? Is there a problem with their reasoning? How about this: crime rates for all people of all ages have declined, not just those for people who became teens 18 years after *Roe v. Wade*.

LO6 Weigh the various crime patterns

Gender Patterns

Male crime rates are much higher than those of females. The most recent UCR arrest statistics indicate that males account for about 80 percent of all arrests for serious violent crimes and more than 60 percent of the arrests for serious property crimes.[23] Murder arrests occur at a ratio of approximately eight males to one female.

Even though gender differences in the crime rate have persisted over time, there seems little question that females are now involved in serious criminal activities and that there are more similarities than differences between male and female offenders.[24] UCR arrest data show that over the past decade, while male arrest rates have declined by 25 percent, female arrest rates have been more stable, declining by 12 percent.[25]

A number of views have been put forward to explain the gender differences in crime rates:

- Males are stronger and better able to commit violent crime.
- Hormonal differences make males more aggressive.
- Females are socialized to be less aggressive than males and consequently develop moral values that strongly discourage antisocial behavior.[26]
- Females have better verbal skills and use them to diffuse conflict.
- Males are granted greater personal freedom and therefore have more opportunities to commit crime. Females are subject to greater parental control.

Racial Patterns

Official crime data indicate that members of minority groups are involved in a disproportionate share of criminal activity. African Americans make up about 13 percent of the general population, yet they account for about 36 percent of arrests for Part I violent crime and for 28 percent of property crime arrests.[27] They also are responsible

AP Images/The Capital Times, Mike DeVries

Because women are committing a significant share of crime, corrections departments are developing programs designed to help female offenders behind bars. Here Wensdae Rauls (left) of Milwaukee, and Linda Miles of Reedsburg, participate in a meditation class held in the gym at the Dane County Jail in Madison, Wisconsin. The stress management and relaxation class that incorporates basic yoga poses is offered to female inmates at the jail.

The treatment of African Americans by police has become a significant national concern. Some high profile cases involving the police shooting of unarmed black men have left the relationship between police and the African American community in tatters. Can anything be done to repair the damage? Here a police officer questions three African Americans stopped on suspicion in Santa Ana, California. Is it possible that the African American crime rate is more a function of police profiling than actual participation in crime? What are your thoughts on this controversial issue?

Marmaduke St. John/Alamy Stock Photo

WEB APP 2.2 Read about the factors related to female crime and delinquency at **http://www.ojjdp.gov/pubs/238276.pdf.** What biological and social differences help explain differences in crime?

racial profiling The practice of police targeting minority groups because of a belief that they are more likely to be engaged in criminal activity.

racial threat hypothesis The view that the percentage of minorities in the population shapes the level of police activity.

for a disproportionate number of Part II arrests (except for alcohol-related arrests, which involve primarily white offenders).

Self-report studies using large samples also show that about 30 percent of black males have experienced at least one arrest by age 18 (versus about 22 percent for white males), and by age 23 almost half of all black males have been arrested (versus about 38 percent for white males).[28]

INSTITUTIONAL RACISM Racial differences in the crime rate may be a function of racism practiced in the criminal justice system by police, court, and correctional institutions. According to this view, police are more likely to arrest racial minorities because of discriminatory arrest and search practices.[29] Institutional bias creates a vicious cycle because they are targeted more frequently, young black men are more likely to possess a criminal record, and having a criminal record is associated with repeat stops and searches.[30] This view is so prevalent that the term **racial profiling** has been used to describe the practice of stopping and searching African Americans without probable cause or reasonable suspicion. Numerous studies find that minority citizens are more likely to be stopped and searched than a member of the white majority, especially if they seem "out of place," that is, driving in a white neighborhood.[31]

According to what is known as the **racial threat hypothesis**, as the percentage of minorities in the population increases, so too does the amount of social control that police direct at minority group members.[32] Police are more likely to aggressively patrol minority neighborhoods; suspect, search, and arrest minority group members; and make arrests for minor infractions, helping to raise the minority crime rate.[33] The result is a stepped-up effort to control and punish minority citizens, which segregates minorities from the economic mainstream and reinforces their physical and social isolation.[34]

Social Class Patterns

Although short-term economic trends do not seem to influence crime rates, the official data clearly indicate that crime rates are highest in deprived, inner-city areas. As the level of poverty and social disorganization in an area increases, neighborhood crime rates increase as well. Why are lower-class neighborhoods more likely than affluent communities to be afflicted by crime?

- Communities that lack economic and social opportunities also produce high levels of stress and strain, and residents may then turn to criminal behavior to relieve their frustration.[35]

- Family life is disrupted, and law-violating youth groups and gangs thrive in a climate where adult supervision has been undermined.[36]
- Socially disorganized neighborhoods lack the ability to exert social control over their residents. Lack of informal social control significantly increases the likelihood that residents will engage in criminality.
- Crime rates are high in deteriorated areas where the disadvantaged and the affluent live in close proximity. In these neighborhoods, social differences are magnified, and less affluent residents experience a feeling of relative deprivation that results in a higher crime rate.[37]
- People living in lower-class neighborhoods experience poverty, dilapidated housing, poor schools, broken families, drugs, and street gangs. Deteriorating neighborhoods attract law violators (this is known as the broken windows hypothesis).

An alternative explanation for these findings is that the relationship between official crime and social class is a function of law enforcement practices, not actual criminal behavior patterns. Police may devote more resources to poor areas, and consequently apprehension rates may be higher there. Similarly, police may be more likely to formally arrest and prosecute citizens of lower socioeconomic class than those in the middle and upper classes, which may account for the lower class's overrepresentation in official statistics and the prison population.[38]

Age Patterns

Official statistics tell us that young people are arrested at a rate disproportionate to their numbers in the population; victim surveys generate similar findings for crimes in which assailant age can be determined. As a general rule, the peak age for property crime is believed to be 16 and for violence 18. In contrast, the elderly are particularly resistant to the temptations of crime; elderly males age 65 and over are arrested predominantly for alcohol-related matters (public drunkenness and drunk driving), and elderly females are arrested mostly for larceny (shoplifting). The elderly crime rate has remained stable for the past 20 years.

When violence rates surged in the 1980s, the increase was due almost entirely to young people; the adult violence rate remained stable. How can the age–crime relationship be explained?

- Young people are part of a youth culture that favors risk taking, short-run hedonism, and other behaviors that may involve them in law violation. The high-risk lifestyle of most youths ends as they mature and become involved in forming a family and a career.[39]
- Adolescents are psychologically immature and are therefore unlikely to appreciate the wrongfulness or destructive consequences of their antisocial acts.
- Youths have limited financial resources and may resort to theft and drug dealing for income.
- Young people have the energy, strength, and physical skill needed to commit crime, and all of these erode with age.[40]
- Adolescents are aware that the juvenile justice system is not as punitive as the adult court system and are therefore more likely to risk committing criminal acts.

Recently, the arrest rate for young people has plummeted. Arrests for those 18 and under is declining at a much faster pace than the decline experienced by those over 18. If this trend continues, the age–crime association will have to someday be reevaluated.

Career Patterns: The Chronic Offender

Chronic offenders commit crime at a very early age, maintain a high rate of criminal violations throughout their lifetime, and are immune to both the ravages of age and the punishments of the justice system. They are responsible for a significant portion of all

relative deprivation The view that extreme social and economic differences among people living in the same community exacerbate criminal activity.

broken windows hypothesis The view that deteriorated communities serve as a magnet for criminals and attract criminal activity.

REALITY CHECK
Myth or Reality?
High unemployment causes crime rates to increase.

MYTH. Crime rates may actually decline during an economic downturn.

Does it seem possible that one of your relatives or family members would suddenly become a criminal or rob a bank just because they got laid off from their job during a recession?

LO7 Discuss the concept of the criminal career

serious criminal behavior. The chronic offender is one who has serious and persistent brushes with the law, who is building a career in crime, and whose behavior may be excessively violent and destructive.

The concept of the chronic offender is most closely associated with the research efforts of Marvin Wolfgang and his associates at the University of Pennsylvania. In 1972, Wolfgang, Robert Figlio, and Thorsten Sellin published a landmark study entitled *Delinquency in a Birth Cohort*.[41] The researchers used official records to follow the criminal careers of a cohort of 9,945 boys born in Philadelphia in 1945 until they reached age 18 in 1963. Here is what they found:

- About two-thirds of the cohort (6,470) never had contact with police authorities.
- About one-third (3,475) had at least one contact with the police during their adolescence.
- Of the repeat offenders, a relatively small subgroup (627 boys) was arrested five times or more. These were the chronic offenders, who made up 6 percent of the total (600 out of 10,000).
- The chronic offenders were responsible for 5,305 arrests, or 51.9 percent of the total arrests. They committed 71 percent of the homicides, 73 percent of the rapes, 82 percent of the robberies, and 69 percent of the aggravated assaults.
- Arrest and punishment did little to deter chronic offenders. In fact, punishment was inversely related to chronicity—the stricter the sanctions they received, the more likely they were to engage in repeated criminal behavior.

Since the Philadelphia survey was carried out, a number of other independent studies, including one of a larger Philadelphia cohort of children born in 1958, have confirmed the existence of the repeat offender.[42]

Victim Patterns

In addition to information on the nature and extent of crime, the various sources of crime data, especially the NCVS, can also tell us something about crime victims. How many crime victims are there in the United States, and what are the trends and patterns in victimization? The NCVS data provide a snapshot of the social and demographic characteristics of crime victims.

GENDER Gender affects one's risk of victimization. Men are much more likely than women to be victims of robbery and aggravated assault; they are also more likely to experience theft, but the differences are less pronounced. Although women are far more likely to be victims of sexual assault, thousands of men are sexually assaulted each year.

AGE Young people face a much greater victimization risk than older persons do. Victim risk diminishes rapidly after age 25. The elderly, who are thought of as being the helpless targets of predatory criminals, are actually much safer than their grandchildren. People over age 65, who make up 14 percent of the population, account for 3 to 5 percent of violent victimizations; teens aged 12 to 17, who also make up 14 percent of the population, typically account for more than 30 percent of crime victims.[43]

INCOME The least affluent Americans tend to live in inner-city, urban neighborhood areas that are crime prone. They are by far the most likely to be victims of violent crimes, and this association occurs across all gender, racial, and age groups.

MARITAL STATUS Unmarried or never married people are victimized more often than married people or widows and widowers. These relationships are probably influenced by age, gender, and lifestyle. Unmarried people tend to be younger, and young people have the highest victim risk. Conversely, widows, who are more likely to be older women, suffer much lower victimization rates because they interact with older people, are more likely to stay home at night, and avoid dangerous public places.

RACE African Americans are victimized at a higher rate than other racial groups. While interracial theft victimization rates are more similar, blacks are still more likely to suffer violent victimizations than whites.[44] Additionally, crimes committed against blacks tend to be more serious than those committed against whites. About half of all nonfatal violence against blacks can be characterized as a serious violent crime, which includes rape or sexual assault, robbery, and aggravated assault.

Why do these discrepancies exist? One clear reason is that young black males tend to live in the largest US cities, in areas beset by alcohol and drug abuse, poverty, racial discrimination, and violence. Because they are forced to live in the most dangerous areas, their lifestyle places them in the highest at-risk population group.

ECOLOGICAL FACTORS The victim rate shows distinct ecological patterns as well:

- Most victimizations occur in large urban areas; rural and suburban victim rates are far lower.
- Most incidents occur during the evening hours (6:00 P.M. to 6:00 A.M.). More serious crimes take place after 6:00 P.M., less serious crimes before 6:00 P.M.
- The most likely site for a victimization—especially a violent crime such as rape, robbery, or aggravated assault—is an open, public area such as a street, park, or field.

VICTIM–OFFENDER RELATIONSHIPS The NCVS can tell us something about the characteristics of people who commit crime. This information is available only on criminals who actually came in contact with the victim through such crimes as rape, assault, or robbery. We know that about 42 percent of all violent crimes are committed by strangers.[45] The other half of violent crimes are committed by people who were known to the victim, including friends and acquaintances, spouses, parents, children, and siblings. Also, women seem much more likely than men to be victimized by acquaintances; a majority of female assault victims know their assailants.

REPEAT VICTIMIZATION Research shows that individuals who have had prior victimization experiences have a significantly higher chance of repeat victimization than people who have not been victims.[46] Households that have experienced victimization

New York Giants kicker Josh Brown speaks with reporters at a training camp in East Rutherford, New Jersey, in 2016. Brown was subsequently released from the team after issuing a statement in which he admitted to abusing his former wife. As of this writing, he is a free agent.

AP Images/Tom Canavan

are the ones most likely to experience it again.[47] Some combination of personal and social factors may possibly encourage victimization risk. Repeat victimizations are most likely to occur in areas with high crime rates.[48]

Causes of Crime and Victimization

LO9 Differentiate among the various views of crime causation

Although the various sources of crime statistics can tell us about the nature of crime patterns and trends, knowing why an individual commits crime in the first place is also important. Such knowledge is critical if programs are to be devised to deter or prevent crime. If, for example, people commit crime because they are poor and desperate, the key to crime prevention might be a job program and government economic aid. If, however, the root cause of crime is a poor family life marked by conflict and abuse, then providing jobs will not help lower the crime rate; family counseling and parenting skills courses are likely to be more effective.

Some criminologists view crime as a social phenomenon and study the social and economic factors that influence human behavior. Others view crime as an individual-level phenomenon and attempt to identify the cognitive and psychological processes that result in antisocial behavior. Regardless of their point of view, criminologists study crime data to identify the factors and motivations that predict crime and to assess the most effective responses to crime by various methods of law enforcement. Because a great deal of uncertainty remains about the "real" cause of crime and the most effective methods of crime prevention, some of the more popular explanations are discussed in the following sections.

Rational Choice Theory

rational choice theory People will engage in delinquent and criminal behavior after weighing the consequences and benefits of their actions. Delinquent behavior is a rational choice made by a motivated offender who perceives the chances of gain as outweighing any perceived punishment or loss.

According to rational choice theory, crime is a matter of logical decision making and personal choice. Crime is attractive because it holds the promise of great rewards without corresponding effort. It's a lot easier to steal a car than to earn the money for its purchase. The gains from robbing a bank take a lot less effort than earning the sum through a minimum-wage job.

According to this view, motivated people, after thoughtful consideration, will commit crime if they believe that it will provide immediate benefits without the threat of long-term risks.[49] Consider drug dealers as an example. If they conclude that the potential

Joshua Lott/The New York Times/Redux

Stacey Turner, right, embraces a fellow mourner at the funeral service for her daughter, Precious Land, at Lawndale Community Church in Chicago on January 25, 2017. Land, a young mother who was shot and had been in a coma since May, became Chicago's 766th murder victim of 2016.

for profits is great enough, their need for cash urgent, and the chances of apprehension minimal, they will carry out the deal. If, however, they believe that the transaction will bring them only a small profit and a large risk of apprehension and punishment, they may forgo the deal as too risky. The more often they are arrested, the less likely they are to engage in a risky deal. The decision to commit a crime is similar to a business decision made after weighing potential gains and losses.

When deciding to commit crime, potential offenders balance their perceptions of getting caught and punished against the perceived benefits of crime.[50] Benefits include not only monetary gains but also psychological rewards such as excitement and increased social status among their peers.[51] Experience may play a hand in the decision-making process. Veteran criminals may not fear some future punishment because they know firsthand that apprehension risk is actually quite low.[52] Some may be deterred in the short run but soon return to their criminal ways.[53] People who are convinced that the pains of punishment outweigh the benefits of crime may become more wary and willing to desist from a criminal career.[54] A central theme of rational choice theory is that people who believe or imagine that they will be punished for crimes in the present will avoid doing those crimes in the future; this is referred to as general deterrence.[55] Even the most committed offenders (e.g., gang members) will forgo criminal activities if they fear legal punishments.[56]

Biosocial Theory

If criminals choose crime, why do they do so? After all, millions of people live in poverty, yet most choose to live law-abiding, conventional lives. So what causes a relatively few people to select a criminal way of life? According to biosocial theory, elements of the environment (e.g., family life, community factors) interact with biological factors (e.g., diet, neurological makeup) to control and influence behavior.[57] People choose crime because of a preexisting physical condition, present at birth or soon after, that makes them predisposed to being crime prone.

Biosocial theories can be divided into three broad areas of focus: biochemical factors, neurological problems, and genetic abnormalities.

BIOCHEMICAL FACTORS Some criminologists believe that biochemical abnormality may lead to antisocial behaviors. Such biochemical factors as vitamin and mineral deficiencies, hormone imbalance, and environmental contaminants (such as the presence of lead and other metals) have been linked to antisocial behavior.[58] The influence of damaging chemical and biological contaminants may begin before birth: maternal alcohol abuse and/or smoking during gestation have long been linked to prenatal damage and subsequent antisocial behavior in adolescence.[59]

NEUROLOGICAL FACTORS Evidence now suggests that decision making may in fact be regulated and controlled by the brain.[60] Some people may engage in antisocial behaviors because some neurological impairment reduces impulse control and self-control, which then leads people to make damaging behavioral choices. For example, there appears to be a link between brain dysfunction and conduct disorder (CD), which is considered a precursor of long-term chronic offending. Children with CD lie, steal, bully other children, get into fights frequently, and break schools' and parents' rules; many are callous and lack empathy and/or guilt.[61] Adolescent boys with antisocial substance disorder (ASD) repeatedly engage in risky antisocial and drug-using behaviors. Research has linked this behavior with misfiring in particular areas of the brain and suppressed neural activity.[62]

GENETIC FACTORS Violent behavior is possibly inherited and a function of a person's genetic makeup. The genes–crime association may be either direct or indirect. According to the direct view, (1) antisocial behavior is inherited, (2) the genetic makeup of parents is passed on to children, and (3) genetic abnormality is directly linked to a variety of antisocial behaviors.[63] Although it is possible that genetic makeup is directly linked to aggression, the association may also be indirect: genes are related to some personality or physical trait linked to antisocial behavior.[64]

general deterrence The theory that crime rates are influenced and controlled by the threat of criminal punishment. If people fear being apprehended and punished, they will not risk breaking the law.

biosocial theory Human behavior is a function of the interaction of biochemical, neurological, and genetic factors with environmental stimuli.

conduct disorder (CD) A pattern of repetitive behavior in which the rights of others or social norms are violated.

psychodynamic view Criminals are driven by unconscious thought patterns, developed in early childhood, that control behaviors over the life course.

bipolar disorder A psychological condition marked by mood swings between periods of wild elation and deep depression.

social learning theory Behavior patterns are modeled and learned in interactions with others.

REALITYCHECK

Myth or Reality?

Kids who watch a lot of violence on TV are more likely to get involved in violent behavior themselves.

MYTH. Millions of kids watch violent TV shows and remain nonviolent.

The link between violent media and violent behavior is still being debated. In the meantime, should young children be prevented from watching media violence?

The association between crime and genes is by no means certain, and serious debate continues regarding the influence of genetic heritability on human behaviors such as crime.[65]

Psychological Theory

Many experts believe criminality is caused by psychological factors. There are actually a number of views on the psychological basis of crime.

PSYCHODYNAMIC THEORY According to the psychodynamic view, some people encounter problems during their early development that cause an imbalance in their personality. The most deeply disturbed are referred to as psychotics, who cannot restrain their impulsive behavior. One type of psychosis is schizophrenia, a condition marked by incoherent thought processes, a lack of insight, and hallucinations. Schizophrenic offenders may suffer from delusions and feel persecuted, worthless, and alienated. Other offenders may suffer from a wide variety of mood and behavior disorders that render them histrionic, depressed, antisocial, or narcissistic.[66] They may suffer from conduct disorders, which include long histories of antisocial behavior, or mood disorders characterized by disturbance in expressed emotions. Among the latter is bipolar disorder, in which moods alternate between periods of wild elation and deep depression.[67] Some offenders are driven by an unconscious desire to be punished for prior sins, either real or imaginary. As a result, they may violate the law or even harm their parents to gain attention.

It is possible that the link between crime and mental illness is spurious, and that, in fact, both mental illness and criminal behavior are caused by some other, independent factor:

- People who suffer from prior social problems (e.g., child abuse) may be more likely to commit criminal acts, use drugs and alcohol to cope, and also suffer mental illness; child abuse may be the cause of criminality and mental illness.
- Mentally ill people may also be more likely than the mentally sound to lack financial resources. They are thus forced to reside in deteriorated, high-crime neighborhoods, a social factor that may increase criminal behavior. Living in a stress-filled urban environment may produce symptoms of both mental illness and crime.
- The police may be more likely to arrest the mentally ill, which fosters the impression that they are crime prone.
- Due to their lifestyle, people with severe mental illness are more at risk to victimization than the mentally healthy; victimization has been linked to increased crime rates.
- Those suffering from mental illness may self-medicate by using illegal substances, a practice linked to criminal behavior.[68]

BEHAVIORAL/SOCIAL LEARNING THEORY Another psychological view, known as social learning theory, is that criminal behavior is learned through interactions with others.[69] One assumption is that people act aggressively because as children they experienced violence firsthand, either observing it at home or being a target of violent parents. Children model their behavior after the violent acts of adults. Observed and experienced violence may have an interactive effect: kids who live in high-crime neighborhoods and witness violence in the community and at home, who are the direct victims of domestic and community-based violence, are the ones most likely to commit crime.[70]

COGNITIVE THEORY Law violators may lack the ability to perform cognitive functions in a normal and orderly fashion.[71] Because they have inadequate cognitive processing, criminals perceive the world as stacked against them; they believe they have little control over the negative events in their life.[72] Some may be sensation seekers who are constantly looking for novel experiences, whereas others lack deliberation and rarely think through problems. Some may give up easily, whereas others act without thinking when they get upset.

This distorted view of the world shapes their thinking and colors their judgments. Crime is viewed as an appropriate means to satisfy their immediate personal needs,

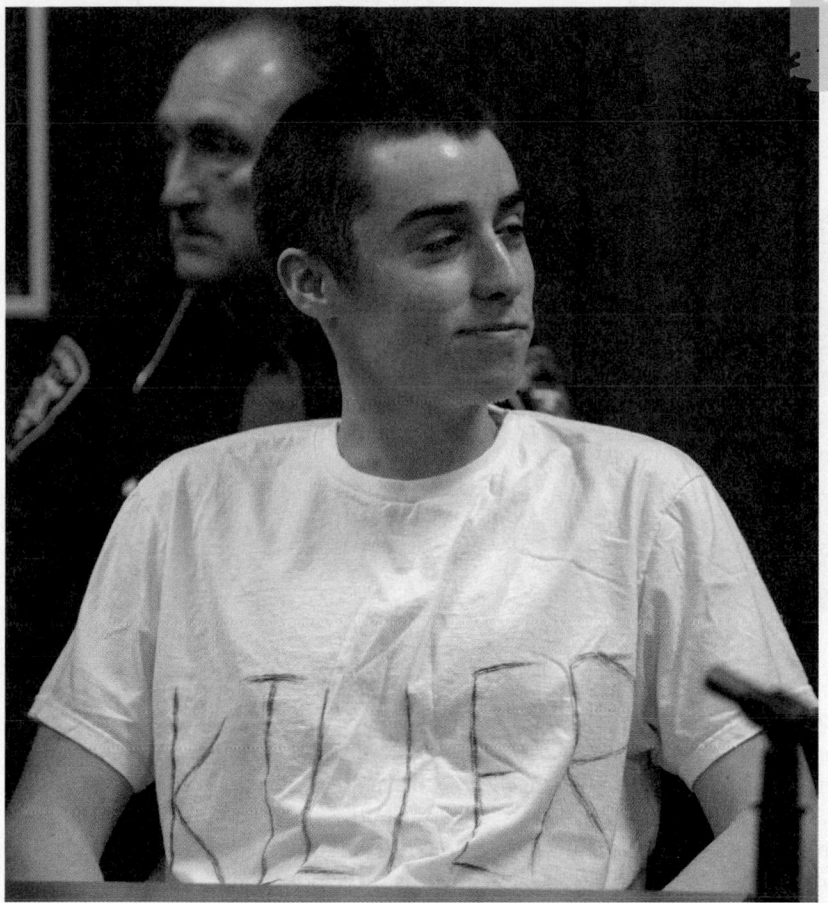

Some crimes appear to be motivated by mental illness. Here T.J. Lane smirks as he listens to the judge during a sentencing hearing on March 19, 2013, in Chardon, Ohio. Lane was given three lifetime prison sentences without the possibility of parole for opening fire in a high school cafeteria in a rampage that left three students dead and three others wounded. Lane, 18, had pleaded guilty to shooting at students at Chardon High School, east of Cleveland. Investigators have said he admitted to the shooting but said he didn't know why he did it. Before the case went to adult court last year, a juvenile court judge ruled that Lane was mentally competent to stand trial despite evidence he suffers from hallucinations, psychosis, and fantasies. Despite his mental issues, Lane was found guilty as charged, rather than incompetent or insane.

which take precedence over more distant social needs and such abstract moral concepts as "obey the law" and "respect the rights of others."[73]

PERSONALITY THEORY It is also possible that people who possess a disturbed personality structure are prone to criminal behavior. For example, people who possess an **antisocial personality** (formerly referred to as **sociopathic** or **psychopathic personality**) are believed to be dangerous, aggressive individuals who act in a callous manner. They neither learn from their mistakes nor are deterred by punishment. From an early age, they have had home lives filled with frustration, bitterness, and quarreling.[74] They exhibit low levels of guilt and anxiety, and they persistently violate the rights of others. Although they may exhibit charm and be highly intelligent, these qualities mask a disturbed personality that makes them incapable of forming enduring relationships.[75]

> **antisocial (sociopathic, psychopathic) personality**
> Individuals who are always in trouble and do not learn from either experience or punishment. They are loners who engage in frequent callous and hedonistic behaviors, are emotionally immature, and lack responsibility, judgment, and empathy.

Social Structure Theory

Another view is that the basis of crime can be found in the relationship a person has to social structures and institutions. According to **social structure theory**, the United States is a stratified society, where there are a few thousand "superrich" making more than $5 million per year, and 46 million Americans live below the poverty line, which is calculated at about $24,257 per year for a family of four.[76]

Those living in poverty face dead-end jobs, unemployment, and social failure. Because of their meager economic resources, lower-class citizens are often forced to live in poor areas marked by substandard housing, inadequate health care, renters rather than homeowners, poor educational opportunities, underemployment, and despair. Noting the universal associations among poverty, neighborhood conditions, and criminal behavior, social structure theorists suggest that antisocial behavior is a direct result of destructive social forces on human behavior.[77]

> **social structure theory** A person's position in the social structure controls his or her behavior. Those in the lowest socioeconomic tier are more likely to succumb to crime-promoting elements in their environment, whereas those in the highest tier enjoy social and economic advantages that insulate them from crime-producing forces.

AP Images/Marcio Jose Sanchez

Maria Esther Salazar, right, is visited by a friend inside her tent in "The Jungle," a homeless encampment in San Jose, California. Salazar has been arrested dozens of times and convicted of 17 felonies, almost all drug related. She had four children but raised none of them; her mother or foster parents took them in. What explains chronic criminal offending like Salazar's?

culture of poverty The crushing lifestyle of slum areas produces a culture of poverty, passed from one generation to the next, marked by apathy, cynicism, feelings of helplessness, and mistrust of social institutions, such as schools, government agencies, and the police.

The crushing burden of urban poverty results in the development of a **culture of poverty** marked by apathy, cynicism, helplessness, and distrust.[78] The culture is passed from one generation to another such that its members become part of a permanent underclass, "the truly disadvantaged."[79] In these areas, people live in constant fear and suffer social and physical incivilities—rowdy youths, trash and litter, graffiti, abandoned storefronts, burned-out buildings, littered lots, strangers, drunks, vagabonds, loiterers, prostitutes, noise, congestion, angry words, dirt, and stench. Forced to endure substandard housing and schools in deteriorated inner-city, socially disorganized neighborhoods, and cut off from conventional society, the urban poor face a constant assault on their self-image and sense of worth. And when they do seek help for their problems, they find that the social support they need to live a conventional life is absent or lacking.

Criminal acts and drug dealing provide a means of survival in an otherwise bleak existence. Those living in impoverished neighborhoods are continuously exposed to the opportunity to buy drugs and engage in antisocial acts.[80] It comes as no surprise that gangs develop in poor, deteriorated urban neighborhoods and that gang-related homicides are highest in these crowded, inner-city communities.[81] Many kids in these areas grow up hopeless and alienated, believing that they have little chance of being part of the American Dream.[82] Consequently, they become embedded in the gang culture and find it difficult to attain a more conventional lifestyle. The lack of economic opportunity makes the gang world an attractive choice for economic and social success.

A socially disorganized area is one in which institutions of social control, such as the family, commercial establishments, and schools, have broken down and can no longer carry out their expected or stated functions. Living in deteriorated, crime-ridden neighborhoods exerts a powerful influence that is often strong enough to neutralize any positive effects of a supportive family and close social ties.[83]

STRAIN THEORY Social and economic goals are common to people in all economic strata, but the ability to obtain these goals is class dependent. Most people in the United States desire wealth, material possessions, power, prestige, and other comforts.[84] Members of the lower class are unable to achieve these symbols of success through conventional means. Consequently, they feel anger, frustration, and resentment. Lower-class citizens can either accept their condition and live out their days as socially responsible, if unrewarded, citizens, or they can choose an alternative means of achieving success, such as theft, violence, or drug trafficking. Although there are other sources of strain, such as negative life experiences or losing a loved one, the strain imposed by limited opportunities may help explain why lower-class areas have such high crime rates.[85]

CULTURAL DEVIANCE THEORY Combining elements of both strain and social disorganization, cultural deviance theory holds that because of strain and social isolation, a unique lower-class culture has developed in disorganized, poverty-ridden neighborhoods. The independent subcultures maintain a unique set of values and beliefs that are in conflict with conventional social norms. Criminal behavior is an expression of conformity to lower-class subcultural values, which stress toughness, independence, and standing up to authority. These subcultural values are handed down from one generation to the next in a process called cultural transmission. Neighborhood youths who hold these values and incorporate them into their own personal code of behavior are much more likely to join gangs and violate the law than those who reject the deviant subculture.

subcultures Substrata of society that maintain a unique set of values and beliefs.

cultural transmission The passing of cultural values from one generation to the next.

Social Process Theory

Still another view, social process theory, holds that people commit crime as a result of the experiences they have while they are being socialized by the various organizations, institutions, and processes of society. People are most strongly impelled toward criminal behavior by poor family relationships, destructive peer-group relations, educational failure, and labeling by agents of the justice system. Although lower-class citizens bear the added burdens of poverty and strain, middle-class or upper-class citizens may turn to crime if their socialization is poor or destructive.

social process theory An individual's behavior is shaped by interactions with key social institutions—family, school, peer group, and the like.

The social process approach has several independent branches. The first branch, social learning theory, as discussed earlier, suggests that people learn the techniques and attitudes of crime from close and intimate relationships with criminal peers; that is, crime is a learned behavior. Kids who have delinquent friends learn both the criminal techniques and antisocial attitudes that help lock them into a delinquent way of life; therefore, the more antisocial the peer group, the more likely its members will engage in delinquency.[86]

The second branch, social control theory, maintains that everyone has the potential to become a criminal, but most people are controlled by their bonds to society. Crime occurs when the forces that bind people to society are weakened or broken. The most important version of social control theory was articulated by Travis Hirschi in his influential 1969 book, *Causes of Delinquency*.[87] Hirschi linked the onset of criminality to weakening of the ties that bind people to society. He assumes that all individuals are potential law violators, but most are kept under control because they fear that illegal behavior will damage their relationships with friends, family, neighbors, teachers, and employers. Without these social bonds, or ties, a person is free to commit criminal acts. Across all ethnic, religious, racial, and social groups, people who have a weak bond to society may fall prey to criminogenic behavior patterns.[88] People who care little for others are the ones most likely to prey upon them; the lack of social control allows people to engage in antisocial activities without shame or remorse.

social bonds The ties people have to family, peers, social institutions, and significant others.

The third branch, social reaction (labeling) theory, suggests that both crimes and criminals are subjective concepts. The difference between a forcible rape and a consensual sexual encounter often rests on what members of a jury believe and how they interpret the events that took place. The difference between an excusable act and a criminal one is a matter of interpretation. Not only are criminal acts a matter of subjective interpretation, so too are criminal identities. People who run afoul of the law are given negative labels that stigmatize them and reduce their self-image. People labeled "criminals" are assumed to be dangerous, dishonest, unstable, violent, strange, and otherwise unsound. Such labels can have long-term consequences.[89]

stigmatize To characterize or brand someone as disgraceful in order to make them feel shameful and ruin their reputation.

Once labeled deviant or criminal, a person becomes locked into a criminal way of life. It's not the quality of the act or the person that counts, but how they are labeled and treated by the rest of society.

Social Conflict Theory

Social conflict theory views the economic and political forces operating in society as the fundamental causes of criminality. The criminal law and criminal justice systems are viewed as vehicles for controlling the poor members of society. The criminal justice

social conflict theory Human behavior is shaped by interpersonal conflict, and those who maintain social power use it to further their own interests.

system is believed to help the powerful and rich impose their particular morality and standards of good behavior on the entire society, while it protects their property and physical safety from the have-nots, even though the cost may be the legal rights of the lower class. Those in power control the content and direction of the law and legal system.

Crimes are defined in a way that meets the needs of the ruling classes. Because those in power shape the content of the law, it comes as no surprise that their behavior is often exempt from legal sanctions. Those who deserve the most severe sanctions (wealthy white-collar criminals whose crimes cost society millions of dollars) usually receive lenient punishments, whereas those whose relatively minor crimes are committed out of economic necessity (petty thieves and drug dealers) receive stricter penalties, especially if they are minority group members who lack social and economic power.[90] And after they have done their time, they face a bleak future in a jobless economy in which the poor, minority group members, and those with a criminal record face high levels of unemployment.[91]

While mainstream criminologists focus on the crimes of the poor and powerless, conflict criminologists focus their attention on the law violations of the powerful. One area of concern is referred to as state (organized) crime—acts defined by law as criminal and committed by state officials, both elected or appointed, in pursuit of their jobs as government representatives. Their actions, or in some cases failure to act, amount to a violation of the criminal law they are bound by oath or duty to uphold.[92]

Developmental Theory

According to developmental theory, even as toddlers, people begin relationships and behaviors that will determine their entire life course. As children, they must learn to conform to social rules and function effectively in society. Later they are expected to begin thinking about careers, complete their schooling, leave their parents' home, enter the workforce, find permanent relationships, and eventually marry and begin their own families.[93] These transitions are expected to take place in an orderly fashion. Disruptions in life's major transitions can be destructive and ultimately promote criminality. Those who are already at risk because of socioeconomic problems or family dysfunction are the most susceptible during these awkward transitions. The cumulative impact of these disruptions sustains criminality from childhood into adulthood.

In some cases, transitions can occur too early—for example, when adolescents engage in precocious sex. In other cases, transitions may occur too late, as when a student fails to graduate on time because of bad grades or too many incompletes. Sometimes disruption of one trajectory can harm another; for example, having a baby while still a teenager is likely to disrupt educational and career development. These negative life experiences can become cumulative: as kids acquire more personal deficits, the chances of acquiring additional ones increase.[94]

Developmental theories also recognize that as people mature, the factors that influence their behavior change.[95] As people make important life transitions—from child to adolescent, from adolescent to adult, from unwed to married—the nature of social interactions also changes.[96] At first, family relations may be most influential; it comes as no shock to life course theorists when research shows that criminality runs in families and that having criminal relatives is a significant predictor of future misbehaviors.[97] In later adolescence, school and peer relations predominate; in adulthood, vocational achievement and marital relations may be the most critical influences. Some antisocial children who are in trouble throughout their adolescence manage to find stable work and maintain intact marriages as adults. These life events help them desist from crime. In contrast, less fortunate adolescents who develop arrest records and get involved with the wrong crowd may find themselves limited to menial jobs and at risk for criminal careers.

LIFE COURSE, PROPENSITY, AND TRAJECTORY There are actually three independent yet interrelated developmental views. The first, referred to as life course theory, suggests that criminal behavior is a dynamic process, influenced by individual characteristics as well as social experiences, and that the factors that cause antisocial behaviors change dramatically over a person's life span.[98] Kids who get in trouble early, especially those who are arrested early and often, may find it difficult to shake the criminal way of life as they mature.[99] While most kids age out of crime, the ability to change wilts with age as people become embedded in a criminal lifestyle. What may help a person resist a life of crime while they are still in their teens—for example, school achievement and positive family relations—may have little impact after they reach their twenties.[100] As people build up more and more social problems, they often cluster together and create a cumulative disadvantage that makes it more and more difficult to "go straight."[101]

The second view, propensity theory, suggests that human development is controlled by a "master" latent trait, such as impulsivity, intelligence level, or self-control, which remains stable and unchanging throughout a person's lifetime. As people travel through their life course, this propensity is always there, directing their behavior. Because this hidden trait is enduring, the ebb and flow of criminal behavior is shaped less by personal change and more by the impact of external forces such as opportunity. Criminality may increase upon joining a gang, a status which provides more opportunities to steal, take drugs, and attack others. In other words, the propensity to commit criminal acts is constant, but the opportunity to commit them is constantly fluctuating.

A third view, trajectory theory, suggests that subgroups within a population follow distinctively different developmental paths toward and away from a criminal career.[102] Some people may begin early in antisocial activities and demonstrate a propensity for crime, while others begin later and are influenced by life circumstances. Unlike the latent trait and life course views, trajectory theory suggests that there are different types and classes of offenders.[103]

The major views of crime causation are summarized in Concept Summary 2.1.

cumulative disadvantage The tendency of prior social problems to produce future ones that accumulate and undermine success.

propensity theory The view that a stable unchanging feature, characteristic, property, or condition, such as defective intelligence or impulsive personality, makes some people crime prone.

latent trait A hidden trait that guides human behavior.

trajectory theory The view that there are multiple independent paths to a criminal career and different types and classes of offenders.

CONCEPT SUMMARY 2.1 Concepts and Theories of Criminology

Theory	Major Premise
Choice	People commit crime when they perceive that the benefits of law violation outweigh the threat and pain of punishment.
Biochemical	Crime, especially violence, is a function of diet, vitamin intake, hormonal imbalance, or food allergies.
Neurological	Criminals and delinquents often suffer brain impairment. Attention deficit hyperactivity disorder and minimum brain dysfunction are related to antisocial behavior.
Genetic	Delinquent traits and predispositions are inherited. The criminality of parents can predict the delinquency of children.
Psychodynamic	The development of personality early in childhood influences behavior for the rest of a person's life. Criminals have weak egos and damaged personalities. They lack attachment to others.
Social structure	The conflicts and problems of urban social life and communities control the crime rate. Crime is a product of transitional neighborhoods that manifest social disorganization and value conflict.
Strain	People who adopt the goals of society but lack the means to attain them seek alternatives, such as crime. Personal-level strain produces crime.
Social learning	People learn to commit crime from exposure to antisocial behaviors. Criminal behavior depends on the person's experiences with rewards for conventional behaviors and punishments for deviant ones. Being rewarded for deviance leads to crime.
Social control	A person's bond to society prevents him or her from violating social rules. If the bond weakens, the person is free to commit crime.
Self-control	People choose to commit crime when they lack self-control. People lacking self-control will seize criminal opportunities.
Critical	People commit crime when the law, controlled by the rich and powerful, defines their behavior as illegal. The immoral actions of the powerful go unpunished.
Developmental	Early in life, people begin relationships that determine their behavior through their life course. Life transitions control the probability of offending.

The FBI's Uniform Crime Reports (UCR) program, long considered the definitive source of official crime data and trends, tells us that crime rates have mostly been in decline over the past several years. Some find it perplexing that property rates have trended downward despite a struggling economy and high unemployment. This begs an important question: should the data be trusted?

Recent research has uncovered examples of crime report manipulation in the New York City Police Department (NYCPD). For example, a study of more than a hundred retired NYPD captains and higher-ranking officers has cast doubt on the accuracy of these data. According to a survey conducted by crime experts John Eterno and Eli Silverman, these former police commanders were under intense pressure to reduce crime. To placate hard-charging commissioners such as William Bratton, some local commanders manipulated crime statistics to suggest that their efforts at crime control were working. As a consequence of the need to lower crime rates, NYPD captains and above had lower perceptions of pressure for integrity in gathering crime statistics. One reason: managers' promotions are considerably more likely to be based on crime statistics, and those seeking advancement may have used any possible means to lower crime rates. These findings were echoed in a more recent study by John Eterno, Arvind Verma, and Eli Silverman.

How did they cheat? One method was to check eBay and other websites to find prices for items that had been reported stolen that were actually lower than the value provided by the crime victim. They would then use the lower values to reduce felony grand larcenies, crimes that are in the UCR, to misdemeanor petty larcenies, which go unrecorded. Some commanders reported sending officers to crime scenes to persuade victims not to file complaints or altering crime details so they did not have to be reported to the FBI. For example, an attempted burglary must be reported, but not an illegal trespass.

Think back to this chapter's section on the Uniform Crime Reports. Although it is possible that the New York police administrators were under more pressure to reduce crime than their counterparts around the country, the fact that members of the largest police department in the United States may have fudged UCR data suggests that recent declines in crime may have been influenced by police reporting practices.

Writing Challenge: Read Eterno, Verma, and Silverman's 2016 study (available here: http://tinyurl.com/hpubscs). Summarize the study's findings. As you do, answer these questions: What factors explain reported manipulation? What factors did not explain manipulation? Also think beyond the NYPD research and speculate about the extent of the problem in other large police departments. Is the NYPD different from other agencies with respect to crime reporting? Why or why not? Also, what steps can local governments and police administrators take to ensure crime statistic manipulation does not become a serious problem?

Sources: John Eterno and Eli B. Silverman, "The NYPD's Compstat: Compare Statistics or Compose Statistics?" *International Journal of Police Science and Management* 12 (2010): 1–23; John A. Eterno, Arvind Verma, and Eli B. Silverman, "Police Manipulations of Crime Reporting: Insiders' Revelations," *Justice Quarterly* 33 (2016): 811–835.

SUMMARY

LO1 *Discuss how crime is defined* There are three independent views on how behaviors become crimes. The consensus view holds that criminal behavior is defined by laws that reflect the values and morals of a majority of citizens. The conflict view states that criminal behavior is defined in such a way that economically powerful groups can retain their control over society. The interactionist view portrays criminal behavior as a relativistic, constantly changing concept that reflects society's current moral values.

LO2 *Explain the methods used to measure crime* We get our information on crime from a number of sources, including surveys, records, interviews, and observations. One of the most important of these sources is the Uniform Crime Reports (UCR) compiled by the FBI. This national survey compiles criminal acts reported to local police. The acts are called Part I crimes (murder, rape, burglary, robbery, assault, larceny/theft, arson, and motor vehicle theft). All other crimes are referred to as Part II crimes; the FBI reports arrests for Part II crimes. The National Crime Victimization

Survey (NCVS) asks people about their experiences with crime. A third form of information is self-report surveys, which ask offenders themselves to tell about their criminal behaviors.

LO3 *Discuss the strengths and weaknesses of crime measures* The validity of the UCR has been suspect because many people fail to report crime to police due to fear, apathy, or lack of respect for law enforcement. Many crime victims also do not report criminal incidents to the police because they believe that nothing can be done or that they should not get involved. Self-reports depend on the accuracy of respondents, many of whom are drug users. While imperfect, the crime patterns found in all three data sources may be more similar than some critics believe.

LO4 *Sketch the trends in the crime rate* Crime peaked in the 1930s and declined afterward. In the 1960s, crime rates began a rapid increase for almost 30 years. Crime rates have been in a downward trend the past two decades. Even violent crimes have dropped significantly.

LO5 *Summarize the factors that influence crime rates* Changes in the crime rate have been attributed to social factors, including the age structure of society. Crime rate increases have been tied to substance abuse levels. While unemployment does not influence crime rates in the short term, long periods of economic decline may promote crime. Crime trends have been linked to abortion: crime began to decline 18 years after abortions became legal. Criminal justice policy may also have an influence on crime rates.

LO6 *Weigh the various crime patterns* Crime occurs more often in large cities during the summer and at night. Some geographic areas (the South and West) have higher crime rates than others (the Midwest and New England). Arrest data indicate that males, minorities, the poor, and the young have relatively high arrest rates. Victims of crime also tend to be poor, young, male, and members of minority groups.

LO7 *Discuss the concept of the criminal career* One of the most important findings in the crime statistics is the existence of the chronic offender. The data show that repeat, career criminals are responsible for a significant amount of all law violations. Cohort data find that career criminals begin offending early in life and, instead of aging out of crime, continue to commit crimes in adulthood.

LO8 *Describe the characteristics of crime victims* About 20 million US citizens are victims of crime each year. Data show that, as with crime, victimization has stable patterns and trends. Violent crime victims tend to be young, poor, single males living in large cities. Females are more likely than males to be victimized by someone they know. Adolescents maintain a high risk of being physically and sexually victimized.

LO9 *Differentiate among the various views of crime causation* Diverse schools of criminological theory approach the understanding of the cause of crime and its consequences. Some theories focus on the individual, whereas others view social factors as the most important element in producing crime. Developmental theories integrate variables at the social, individual, and societal levels.

KEY TERMS

consensus view of crime, p. 30

conflict view of crime, p. 30

interactionist view of crime, p. 30

moral entrepreneurs, p. 30

crime, p. 31

Uniform Crime Reports (UCR), p. 31

official crime statistics, p. 31

Part I crimes, p. 31

murder and nonnegligent manslaughter, p. 31

forcible rape, p. 31

robbery, p. 31

aggravated assault, p. 31

burglary, p. 31

larceny, p. 31

motor vehicle theft, p. 31

arson, p. 31

Part II crimes, p. 32

National Incident-Based Reporting System (NIBRS), p. 33

National Crime Victimization Survey (NCVS), p. 33

self-report surveys, p. 34

racial profiling, p. 40

racial threat hypothesis, p. 40

relative deprivation, p. 41

broken windows hypothesis, p. 41

chronic offender, p. 42

rational choice theory, p. 44

general deterrence, p. 45

biosocial theory, p. 45

conduct disorder (CD), p. 45

psychodynamic view, p. 46

bipolar disorder, p. 46

social learning theory, p. 46

antisocial (sociopathic, psychopathic) personality, p. 47

social structure theory, p. 47

culture of poverty, p. 48

subcultures, p. 49

cultural transmission, p. 49

social process theory, p. 49

social bonds, p. 49

stigmatize, p. 49

social conflict theory, p. 49

state (organized) crime, p. 50

developmental theory, p. 50

life course theory, p. 50

cumulative disadvantage, p. 51

propensity theory, p. 51

latent trait, p. 51

trajectory theory, p. 51

REVIEW QUESTIONS

1. Why are crime rates higher in the summer than during other seasons?

2. What factors account for crime rate trends?

3. What factors that are present in poverty-stricken urban areas produce high crime rates?

4. It seems logical that biological and psychological factors might explain why some people commit crime. But if crime is based on individual traits, how would we explain the fact that crime rates are higher in the West and South than the Midwest and East?

5. Considering the patterns that victimization takes, what steps should you take to avoid becoming a crime victim?

3 Criminal Law
Substance and Procedure

I s a "green rush" under way? Recreational marijuana is now legal in eight states plus the District of Columbia. Once each law is fully implemented, more than 20 percent of American adults will live in places where they can legally buy marijuana.[1] According to a recent estimate, the legal marijuana market rang up $6.7 billion in sales in 2016, a 30 percent increase from the prior year.[2] It is expected to grow to over $21 billion in a few more years.[3]

Marijuana remains illegal under federal law, however. It is considered a Schedule I drug under the Controlled Substances Act of 1970, which means it has "high potential for abuse" and "no currently accepted medical use." As of this writing, it remains to be seen what the Trump administration will do, if anything, about legal marijuana. No matter what, any change to current policy could amount to stuffing a large genie back into a small bottle.

Whether marijuana is legal or illegal doesn't seem to matter to a large swath of America. According to recent data from the National Survey on Drug Use and Health, 8.3 percent of Americans age 12 and over (22 million people) used marijuana regularly in 2015.[4] Nearly 40 million people used it at least once in the prior year. Of course, usage varies by state, but as much as one quarter of people living in states with legalized recreational marijuana report using it.

REALITYCHECK
Myth or Reality?

- A person who is convicted of a crime cannot be sued for damages also because that would be double jeopardy.

- In ancient legal codes, the standard of "an eye for an eye" was taken literally.

- Criminal law was created hundreds of years ago and rarely if ever changes.

- A murderer cannot be executed unless the state had a death penalty statute in place before his or her trial began.

- To commit crime, not only must a person engage in a harmful act, he or she must do so intentionally; unintentional acts don't count.

- People who are mentally ill cannot be found guilty of a crime.

- Under the Fourth Amendment, to search a person, the police must first obtain a warrant from a sitting judge.

- All US citizens accused of a crime have the right to be released on bail before trial.

The Washington Post/Getty Images

LEARNING OBJECTIVES

LO1 List the similarities and differences between criminal law and civil law

LO2 Summarize the historical development of the criminal law

LO3 Discuss the sources of criminal law

LO4 Identify the elements of a crime

LO5 Explain excuses and justification defenses for crime

LO6 Discuss the most recent developments in criminal law reform

LO7 Describe the role of the Bill of Rights in shaping criminal procedure

LO8 List the elements of due process of law

LO9 Explain the role the Supreme Court plays in interpreting the Constitution and shaping procedural law

The law governs almost all phases of human enterprise, including crimes, family life, property transfer, and the regulation of interpersonal conflict. And aside from being found at various levels of government (federal, state, local), it can generally be divided into four broad categories:

- *Substantive criminal law.* The branch of the law that defines crimes and their punishment. It involves such issues as the mental and physical elements of crime, crime categories, and criminal defenses. Exhibit 3.1 sets out the main goals of substantive criminal law.
- *Procedural law.* Those laws that set out the basic rules of practice in the government, including the criminal justice system. Some elements of the law of criminal procedure are the rules of evidence, the law of arrest, the law of search and seizure, questions of appeal, jury selection, and the right to counsel.
- *Civil law.* The set of rules governing relations between private parties, including both individuals and organizations (such as business enterprises and/or corporations). Civil law is used to resolve, control, and shape such personal interactions as contracts, wills and trusts, property ownership, and commerce. The element of civil law most relevant to criminal justice is torts, or the law of personal injuries.
- *Public or administrative law.* The branch of law that deals with the government and its relationships with individuals or other governments is known as public law. It governs the administration and regulation of city, county, state, and federal government agencies.

Of course, these branches of the law often overlap. In some instances, a person who has been the victim of a criminal act may also sue the perpetrator for damages in a civil tort; some crime victims may forgo criminal action and choose to file a tort claim alone. It is also possible to seek civil damages from a perpetrator even if he or she is found not guilty of the crime because the evidentiary standard in a tort action (by a preponderance of the evidence) is less than is needed for a criminal conviction (beyond a reasonable doubt).

People having conflicts with the government may find redress through the administrative law. The government has the option to pursue a legal matter through the criminal process, file a tort action, or both. White-collar crimes, including mail, wire, tax-related, or computer fraud and money-laundering violations, often involve both criminal and civil penalties, giving the government the choice of pursuing one type of action or both.

substantive criminal law A body of specific rules that declare what conduct is criminal and that prescribe the punishment to be imposed for such conduct.

criminal procedure The rules and laws that define the operation of criminal proceedings. Procedural law describes the methods that must be followed in obtaining warrants, investigating offenses, effecting lawful arrests, conducting trials, introducing evidence, sentencing convicted offenders, and reviewing cases by appellate courts.

civil law All law that is not criminal, including the law of torts (personal wrongs) and contract, property, maritime, and commercial law.

tort A personal injury or wrong for which an action for damages may be brought.

public law The branch of law that deals with the state or government and its relationships with individuals or other governments.

lex talionis Latin for "law as retaliation." From Hammurabi's ancient legal code, the belief that the purpose of the law is to provide retaliation for an offended party and that the punishment should fit the crime.

stare decisis Latin for "to stand by decided cases." The legal principle by which the decision or holding in an earlier case becomes the standard by which subsequent similar cases are judged.

EXHIBIT 3.1 The Goals of Substantive Criminal Law

- *Enforce social control.* Substantive criminal law is the main instrument of control at the disposal of an existing government. Those who hold political power use substantive criminal law to eliminate behaviors they believe pose a threat to society or challenge the government's authority.

- *Distribute retribution.* By punishing people who infringe on the rights, property, and freedom of others, the law shifts the burden of revenge from the individual to the state. Although the thought of state-sponsored retribution may be offensive to some, it is greatly preferable to a system in which injured parties or their friends and relatives would seek to redress their injuries through personal vengeance or revenge.

- *Express public opinion and morality.* Criminal law reflects public opinions and moral values. It reflects both traditional and contemporary moral values, and it may undergo change according to existing social conditions and attitudes. Criminal law is used to codify changing social values and to educate the public about what is expected of them.

- *Deter criminal behavior.* Criminal law is designed, through its application of punishment, to control, restrain, and deter illegal acts before they

actually occur. During the Middle Ages, public executions drove this point home; today, long prison sentences and an occasional execution are designed to achieve the same result.

- *Punish wrongdoing.* If the deterrent power of criminal law fails to prevent crime, the law gives the state the right to sanction or punish offenders. Those who violate criminal law are subject to physical coercion and punishment.

- *Maintain social order.* All legal systems are designed to support and maintain the boundaries of the social system they serve. The free-enterprise system is supported and sustained by criminal laws that protect property transfer and control market operations.

- *Restoration.* Victims deserve restitution or compensation for their pain and loss. Criminal law can be used to restore to victims what they have lost. Because we believe in equity and justice, it is only fair that the guilty help repair the harm they have caused others by their crimes. Punishments such as fines, forfeiture, and restitution are connected to this legal goal.

Historical Development of the Criminal Law

The roots of contemporary criminal codes can be traced to such early legal charters as the Babylonian Code of Hammurabi (2000 BCE), which rested on the concept of proportionality, *lex talionis* ("an eye for an eye"), that is still the basis of law today. Some of its provisions include the following:

- If a man puts out the eye of an equal, his eye shall be put out.
- If anyone brings an accusation of any crime before the elders and does not prove what he has charged, he shall, if it be a capital offense charged, be put to death.
- If a man knocks the teeth out of another man, his own teeth will be knocked out.
- If the slave of a freed man strikes the body of a freed man, his ear shall be cut off.[5]

The Mosaic Code of the Israelites (1200 BCE), better known today as the Ten Commandments, contains prohibitions against theft, violence, and perjury that still hold sway in the modern criminal law.

The early formal legal codes were lost during the Dark Ages (500–1000 CE). In their place, a legal system featuring monetary compensation, called *wergild* (*wer* means "worth" and refers to what the person, and therefore the crime, was worth), was developed for criminal violations. Guilt was determined by two methods: "compurgation," which involved having the accused person swear an oath of innocence while being backed up by a group of 12 to 25 oath-helpers who would attest to his or her character and claims of innocence, and "ordeal," which was based on the principle that divine forces would not allow an innocent person to be harmed.

Determining guilt by ordeal involved such measures as having the accused place his or her hand in boiling water or hold a hot iron. If the wound healed, the person was found innocent; if the wound did not heal, the accused was deemed guilty. Another ordeal, trial by combat, allowed the accused to challenge his accuser to a duel, with the outcome determining the legitimacy of the accusation.

Common Law and the Principle of *Stare Decisis*

Soon after William, Duke of Normandy, conquered England in 1066—a feat that transformed him into William the Conqueror—he sent his royal administrators to travel throughout the land, holding court in each county of his new domain. When court was in session, the royal administrator, or judge, summoned a number of citizens who would, on their oath, tell of the crimes and serious breaches of the peace that had occurred since the judge's last visit. The royal judge then decided what to do in each case, using local custom and rules of conduct as his guide in a system known as *stare decisis* (Latin for "to stand by decided cases").

The present English system of law came into existence during the reign of Henry II (1154–1189), when royal judges began to publish their decisions in local cases. This allowed judicial precedents to be established and a national law to accumulate. Other judges began to use these written decisions as a basis for their decision making, and eventually a fixed body of legal rules and principles emerged. If the new rules were successfully applied in a number of different cases, they would become precedents, which would then be commonly applied in all similar cases. This unified system evolved into a *common law* of the country that incorporated local custom and practice into a national code. Crimes that were *mala in se*, inherently evil and depraved (such as murder, burglary, and arson), and were the cornerstone of the common law, were joined by new *mala prohibitum* crimes such as embezzlement, which reflected existing social and economic conditions.

Before the American Revolution, the colonies, then under British rule, were subject to the common law. After the colonies acquired their independence, state legislatures standardized common-law crimes such as murder, burglary, arson, and rape by codifying them (putting them into statutory form in criminal codes). As in England,

LO2 Summarize the historical development of the criminal law

common law Early English law, developed by judges, that incorporated Anglo-Saxon tribal custom, feudal rules and practices, and the everyday rules of behavior of local villages. Common law became the standardized law of the land in England and eventually formed the basis of criminal law in the United States.

mala in se Refers to acts that society considers inherently evil, such as murder and rape.

mala prohibitum Crimes created by legislative bodies that reflect prevailing moral beliefs and practices.

whenever common law proved inadequate to deal with changing social and moral issues, the states and Congress supplemented it with legislative statutes, creating new elements in the various state and federal legal codes. Similarly, statutes prohibiting such offenses as identity theft have recently been passed to control human behavior unknown at the time the common law was formulated.

Sources of Criminal Law

The contemporary American legal system is codified primarily by state and federal legislatures. Each jurisdiction precisely defines crime in its legal code and sets out the appropriate punishments. However, like its English common-law roots, American criminal law is not static and is constantly evolving. A state statute based on common law may define first-degree murder as the "unlawful killing, with malice and premeditation, of one human being by another." Over time, state court decisions might help explain the meaning of the term "malice" or clarify whether "human being" refers only to someone "born and alive" or whether it can also refer to an unborn fetus (this issue is discussed in the accompanying Contemporary Issues in Criminal Justice feature).

ex post facto laws Acts that retroactively change the legal status of actions that were committed before the enactment of a law and/or change the consequences after it was enacted.

The content of the law may also be influenced by judicial decision making. A criminal offense is no longer enforceable when an appellate judge rules that the statute is

CONTEMPORARY ISSUES IN CRIMINAL JUSTICE

"Born and Alive"

Under traditional law, a person could not be charged with murder if the victim was not "born and alive." Changing social views in the United States have eroded that restriction. Today, more than two-thirds of the states have expanded their legal codes to include feticide law, which makes the killing of an unborn fetus murder.

At the federal level, the Unborn Victims of Violence Act of 2004 makes it a separate crime to harm a fetus during an assault on the mother. If the attack causes death or bodily injury to a child who is in utero at the time the conduct takes place, the penalty is the same as that for conduct had the injury or death occurred to the unborn child's mother.

State laws vary widely. A Tennessee law considers "a human embryo or fetus at any stage of gestation in utero" as a victim of such offenses as murder, voluntary manslaughter, vehicular homicide, and reckless homicide; prior to 2011, Tennessee law recognized an unborn child as a crime victim only after "viability." In a number of states, recent legislation has created a separate class of crime that increases criminal penalties when a person causes injury to a woman they know is pregnant when the injury results in miscarriage or stillbirth.

These legal changes have sparked heated debates. Those supporting penalizing the death of an unborn fetus claim that both the lives of the pregnant woman and her unborn should be explicitly protected. They assert that fetal homicide laws justly criminalize these cases and provide an opportunity to protect unborn children and their mothers. Those opposed believe that creating laws to protect a fetus could jeopardize a woman's right to choose an abortion and might create an adversarial relationship between a woman and her baby. For example, could a woman be charged with a crime for behavior during her pregnancy that might harm her unborn child, such as smoking, drinking, or using drugs? Some states have taken a middle ground. Texas law extends the protections of the entire criminal code to "an unborn child at every stage of gestation from fertilization until birth." The law does not apply to "conduct committed by the mother of the unborn child" or to "a lawful medical procedure performed by a physician or other licensed health care provider with the requisite consent."

Highlighting the controversies in this area is the case of Jennifer Jorgensen, of Miller Place, New York, who faced up to 15 years behind bars for a car crash that happened in 2008 when she was eight months pregnant. Jorgenson was driving without a seat belt when she smashed head-on into a car driven by 74-year-old Robert Kelly; both Kelly and his wife, Mary, died from their injuries. Jorgensen was originally accused of drunken driving, but at her trial, she claimed that the crash was a result of blacking out from pregnancy complications. She was acquitted of DWI and of charges related to the Kellys' deaths but was convicted of manslaughter in the death of her unborn child. Her conviction was overturned in 2015, however, because no specific New York law addressed the specific circumstances of Jorgensen's case.

CRITICAL THINKING

How do you stand on this issue? Should a person who causes the death of an unborn fetus be punished the same as someone who kills a 10-year-old child?

Source: Andrew Smith, "New York's Highest Court Tosses Manslaughter Conviction Against Jennifer Jorgensen of Sound Beach in 2008 Crash," *Newsday*, October 22, 2015, http://www.newsday.com/long-island/suffolk/new-york-s-highest-court -tosses-manslaughter-conviction-against-jennifer-jorgensen-of-sound-beach-in -2008-crash-1.10999277; News 12 Long Island, "Sentencing Rescheduled for Woman Convicted of Killing Unborn Baby," May 12, 2012, http://longisland.news12 .com/news/sentencing-rescheduled-for-woman-convicted-of-killing-unborn-baby -1.3980900; National Conference of State Legislatures, Fetal Homicide Laws, http://www.ncsl.org/research/health/fetal-homicide-state-laws.aspx. (URLs accessed April 2017.)

vague, deals with an act no longer of interest to the public, or is an unfair exercise of state control over an individual. Conversely, a judicial ruling may expand the scope of an existing criminal law, thereby allowing control over behaviors heretofore beyond its reach.

Constitutional Limits

Regardless of its source, all criminal law in the United States must conform to the rules and dictates of the Constitution.[6] Any criminal law that conflicts with the various provisions and articles of the Constitution will eventually be challenged in the appellate courts and stricken from the legal code by judicial order (or modified to adhere to constitutional principles). The Constitution has been interpreted to forbid any criminal law that violates a person's right to be treated fairly and equally; this principle is referred to as substantive due process. This means that before a new law can be created, the state must show a compelling need to protect public safety or morals.[7]

Criminal laws have been interpreted as violating constitutional principles if they are too vague or broad for their intent to be clear. A law forbidding adults to engage in "immoral behavior" could not be enforced because it does not use clear and precise language or give adequate notice as to which conduct is forbidden.[8] The Constitution also prohibits laws that make a person's status a crime. Being a heroin addict is not a crime, although laws can forbid the sale, possession, and manufacture of heroin. Finally, the Constitution limits laws that are overly cruel and/or capricious.[9]

The Constitution also forbids bills of attainder, which are legislative acts that inflict punishment without a judicial trial. This device, used by the English kings to punish rebels and seize their property, was particularly troublesome to American colonials when it was used to seize the property of people considered disloyal to the crown; hence, attainder is forbidden in the Constitution. Nor does the Constitution permit the government to pass *ex post facto laws*, which are defined as follows:

- A law that makes an action that was done before the passing of the law, and that was innocent when done, criminal and punishes such action.
- A law that makes a crime more serious after the fact than it was when first committed.
- A law that inflicts a greater punishment than was available when the crime was committed.
- A law that makes it easier to convict the offender than it was at the time the crime was committed.[10]

Crimes and Classifications

All states and the federal government have developed their own body of criminal law that defines and grades offenses, sets levels of punishment, and classifies crimes into categories. Crimes are generally grouped into three categories:

- Felonies, the most serious crimes punishable by imprisonment, such as criminal homicide, robbery, and rape, as well as crimes against property, such as burglary and larceny.
- Misdemeanors, less serious crimes punishable by a jail term, including petit (or petty) larceny, assault and battery, and the unlawful possession of marijuana.
- Violations (also called infractions), which are violations of city or town ordinances, such as traffic violations or public intoxication, punishable by a fine. Some states consider violations civil matters, whereas others classify them as crimes.

AP Images/Matthew Thayer

Steven Capobianco, who was convicted of murder and arson in the death of his pregnant ex-girlfriend, stands as he is declared guilty in his trial in Wailuku, Hawaii. After jurors found Capobianco guilty of murder, they determined the crime was especially heinous, which made it possible for the judge to sentence him to life in prison without possibility for parole.

L03 Discuss the sources of criminal law

REALITYCHECK

Myth or Reality?

Criminal law was created hundreds of years ago and rarely if ever changes.

MYTH. Criminal law changes all the time.

Can you think of acts that have been criminalized during your lifetime? What about those that have been decriminalized or legalized?

Myth or Reality?

A murderer cannot be executed unless the state had a death penalty statute in place before his or her trial began.

REALITY. The Constitution prohibits imposing a more severe punishment than that which was in place when the crime was first committed. It does not matter when the criminal was caught or when he or she was brought to trial.

A person who commits a murder in a non-death penalty state cannot be executed even if the state legalizes the death penalty before the culprit is identified, caught, and tried. Do you agree with this principle?

LO4 Identify the elements of a crime

felony A more serious offense that carries a penalty of incarceration in a state prison, usually for one year or more. Persons convicted of felony offenses lose certain rights, such as the right to vote, to hold elective office, or to maintain certain licenses.

misdemeanor A minor crime usually punished by less than one year's imprisonment in a local institution, such as a county jail.

actus reus An illegal act. The *actus reus* can be an affirmative act, such as taking money or shooting someone, or a failure to act, such as failing to take proper precautions while driving a car.

mens rea Guilty mind. The mental element of a crime or the intent to commit a criminal act.

Distinguishing between a **felony** and a **misdemeanor** is sometimes difficult. Simply put, a felony is a serious offense, and a misdemeanor is a less serious one.

The felony/misdemeanor classification has a direct effect on the way an offender is treated within the justice system. Police may arrest a felon if there is an arrest warrant issued by a court and/or probable cause that he or she committed a crime. In contrast, misdemeanants may be taken into custody only with an arrest warrant or if the police officer observed the infraction personally; this is known as the in-presence requirement. In some instances, however, police can make a misdemeanor arrest without observing its occurrence. For example, a number of jurisdictions have passed domestic violence prevention acts, which allow arrests based merely on the accusation of the injured party. These laws have been created in an effort to protect the target of the abuse from further attacks.[11]

If convicted, a person charged with a felony may be barred from certain fields of employment or some professions, such as law and medicine. A felony offender's status as an alien in the United States might also be affected, or the offender might be denied the right to hold public office, vote, or serve on a jury.[12] These and other civil liabilities exist only when a person is convicted of a felony offense, not of a misdemeanor.

The Legal Definition of a Crime

Almost all common-law crime contains both mental and physical elements. For example, to commit the crime of armed burglary, offenders must do the following things:

- Willfully enter a dwelling
- Be armed or arm themselves after entering the house, or commit an actual assault on a person who is lawfully in the house
- Knowingly and intentionally commit the crime

For the prosecutor to prove a crime occurred and that the defendant committed it, the prosecutor must show (1) that the accused engaged in the guilty act (*actus reus*, or guilty act) and (2) that the act was intentional and purposeful (*mens rea*, or guilty mind). Under common law, both the *actus reus* and the *mens rea* must be present for the act to be considered a crime. Thoughts of committing an act do not alone constitute a crime; to be considered a crime, an illegal act must occur. Let us now look more closely at these issues.

Actus Reus

The *actus reus* is a voluntary and deliberate illegal act, such as taking someone's money, burning a building, or shooting someone; an accident or involuntary act would not be considered criminal. However, even an unintentional act can be considered a crime if it is the result of negligence and/or disregard for the rights of others. A person cannot be held criminally liable for assault if while walking down the street he has a seizure and as a result his arm strikes another person in the face; his act was not voluntary and therefore not criminal. However, if this same person knew beforehand that he might have a seizure and unreasonably put himself in a position where he was likely to harm others—for instance, by driving a car—he could be criminally liable for his behavior because his actions were negligent and disregarded the rights of others.

In addition, there are occasions when the failure or omission to act can be considered a crime:

- *Failure to perform a legally required duty that is based on relationship or status.* These relationships include parent and child and husband and wife. If a husband finds his wife unconscious because she took an overdose of sleeping pills, he is obligated to save her life by seeking medical aid. If he fails to do so and she dies, he can be held responsible for her death. Parents are required to look after the welfare of their children; failure to provide adequate care can be a criminal offense.
- *Imposition by statute.* Some states have passed laws that require a person who observes an automobile accident to stop and help the other parties involved.

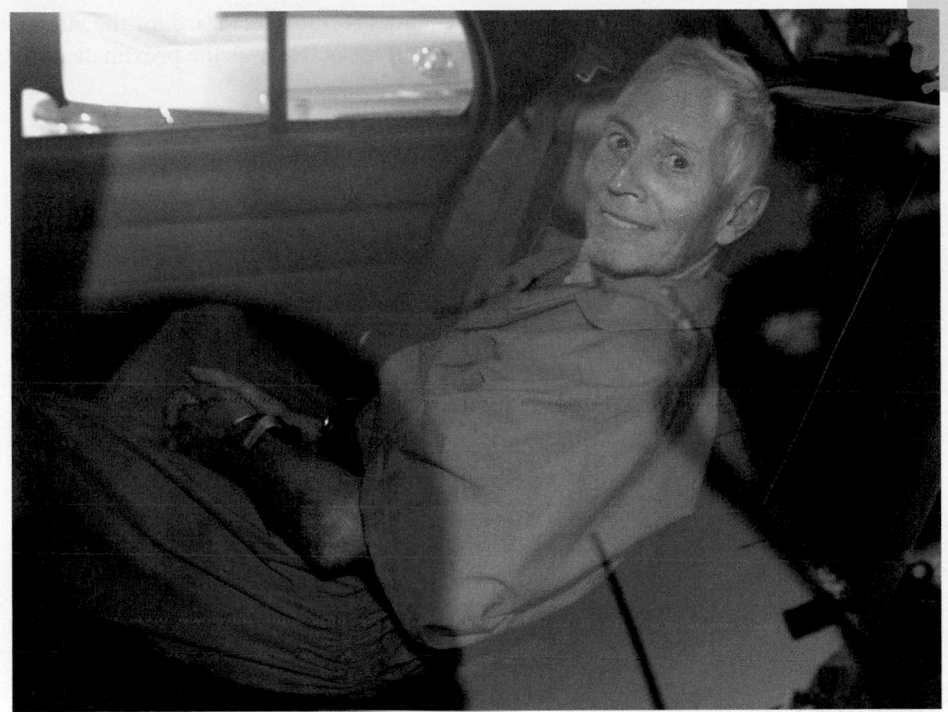

Eccentric New York real estate heir Robert Durst smiles as he is transported to jail. He was accused of shooting his friend Susan Berman in the back of the head, allegedly because she knew too much about the 1982 disappearance of Durst's wife.

- *Contractual relationship.* These relationships include lifeguard and swimmer, doctor and patient, and babysitter or au pair and child. Because lifeguards have been hired to ensure the safety of swimmers, they have a legal duty to come to the aid of drowning persons. If a lifeguard knows a swimmer is in danger and does nothing about it, and the swimmer drowns, the lifeguard can be held legally responsible for the swimmer's death.

In these cases, the duty to act is a legal and not a moral duty. The obligation arises from the relationship between the parties or from explicit legal requirements. In contrast, a private citizen who sees a person drowning is under no legal obligation to save that person. Although we may find it morally reprehensible, the private citizen could walk away and let the swimmer drown without facing legal sanctions.

Mens Rea

For an act to constitute a crime, it must be done with deliberate purpose or criminal intent. A person who enters a store with a gun with the intention of stealing money indicates by his actions the intent to commit a robbery. Criminal intent is implied if the results of a person's action, though originally unintended, are certain to occur. When Mohamed Atta and his terrorist band crashed an aircraft into the World Trade Center on September 11, 2001, they did not intend to kill any particular person in the building. Yet the law would hold that Atta, and any others conspiring with him, would be substantially certain that people in the building would be killed in the blast and that they, therefore, had the criminal intent to commit the crime of murder.

The Relationship Between *Mens Rea* and *Actus Reus*

For an act to constitute a crime, the law requires a connection be made between the *mens rea* and the *actus reus*, thereby showing that the offender's conduct was the proximate cause of the criminal act. If a man chases a woman into the street intending to assault her, and the victim is struck by a car and killed, the accused cannot claim at trial that the death was an accident caused by the inopportune passing of the motor vehicle. The law holds that the victim would never have run into the street had she not been pursued by the defendant, and that, therefore, (1) the defendant's reckless disregard for the victim's safety makes him responsible for her death, and (2) his action was the proximate cause of her death.

CRIMINAL HARM Thought alone is not a crime. For a person to be considered to have committed a crime, some act is required to prove the actor's willingness to cause harm. The nature of the harm ultimately determines what crime the person committed. If someone trips another with the intent of making the person fall down and be embarrassed in public, he has committed the crime of battery. If by some chance the victim dies from the fall, the harm caused elevates the crime to manslaughter, even if that was not the intended result.

In the crime of robbery, the *actus reus* is taking the property from the person or presence of another. To satisfy the harm requirement, the robber must acquire the victim's possessions, referred to as "asportation." The legal definition of robbery is satisfied when, even for a brief moment, possession of the property is transferred to the robber. If a robber removes a victim's wallet from his pocket and immediately tosses it over a fence when he spies a police officer approaching, the robbery is complete because even the slightest change in possession of the property is sufficient to cause harm. Nor is the value of the property a consideration; actual value is unimportant as long as the property had some value to the victim.

Ignorance and Mistake

People sometimes defend themselves by claiming either that their actions were a mistake or that they were unaware (ignorant) of the fact that their behavior was a crime. For example, they did not realize they had stepped onto private property and were guilty of trespassing.

As a general rule, ignorance of the law is no excuse. According to the great legal scholar William Blackstone, "Ignorance of the law, which everyone is bound to know, excuses no man."[13] Consequently, a defendant cannot present a legitimate defense by saying he was unaware of a criminal law, had misinterpreted the law, or believed the law to be unconstitutional.

In some instances, mistake of fact, such as taking someone else's coat that is similar to your own, may be a valid defense; an honest mistake may remove the defendant's criminal responsibility. Mistake can also be used as a defense when the government failed to make enactment of a new law public or when the offender relies on an official statement of the law that is later deemed incorrect.

Strict Liability

strict liability crimes Illegal acts whose elements do not contain the need for intent, or *mens rea*; usually, an act that endangers the public welfare, such as illegal dumping of toxic wastes.

In certain statutory offenses, known as public safety or **strict liability crimes**, *mens rea* is not essential. A person can be held responsible for such a violation independent of the existence of intent to commit the offense. Strict liability criminal statutes generally include narcotics control laws, traffic laws, health and safety regulations, sanitation laws, and other regulatory statutes. A motorist could not defend herself against a speeding ticket by claiming that she was unaware of how fast she was going and did not intend to speed, nor could a bartender claim that a juvenile to whom he sold liquor looked quite a bit older. No state of mind is generally required where a strict liability statute is violated.[14]

Criminal Defenses

L05 Explain excuses and justification defenses for crime

In 1884, two British sailors, desperate after being shipwrecked for days, made the decision to kill and eat a suffering cabin boy who was on their lifeboat. Four days later, they were rescued by a passing ship and returned to England. English authorities, wanting to end the practice of shipwreck cannibalism, tried the two men and convicted them of murder. Clemency was considered, and a reluctant Queen Victoria commuted the death sentences to six months.[15] Were the seamen justified in killing a shipmate to save their lives? If they had not done so, it is likely they all would have died. Did they act out of necessity or malice? Can there ever be a good reason to take a life? Can we ever justify killing another? Before you answer, remember that we can kill in self-defense, to prevent lethal crimes, or in times of war (more on necessity defenses later).

When people defend themselves against criminal charges, they must refute one or more of the elements of the crime of which they have been accused. Defendants may deny the *actus reus* by arguing that they were falsely accused, and the real culprit has yet to be identified, or that the act was an accident and occurred through no fault of their own. Defendants may also claim that although they did engage in the criminal act they are accused of, they lacked the *mens rea*, or mental intent, needed to be found guilty of the crime. If a person whose mental state is impaired commits a criminal act, it is possible for the person to excuse his criminal actions by claiming he lacked the capacity to form sufficient intent to be held criminally responsible. Duress, insanity, intoxication, age, and entrapment are common types of **excuse defenses**.[16]

Another type of defense is a **justification defense**. Here, the individual admits committing the criminal act but maintains that the act was justified and, given the circumstances, anyone would have acted in a similar manner; because her act was justified, she should not be held criminally liable. Among the justification defenses are consent, self-defense, necessity, and law enforcement. We will now examine some of these defenses and justifications in greater detail.

Excuse Defenses

Excuses refer to situations in which the criminal defendants admit to performing the physical act of the crime but claim they are not responsible for it because they lacked free will. It is not their fault, they claim, because they had no control over their actions; therefore, they should be "excused" from criminal responsibility.

DURESS To prove duress, defendants must show they have been forced into committing a crime in order to prevent death or serious harm to self or others. For example, a bank employee might be excused for taking bank funds if she can prove that her family was being threatened and that consequently she was acting under duress. However, there is widespread general agreement that duress is no defense for an intentional killing.

REALITYCHECK
Myth or Reality?

To commit crime, not only must a person engage in a harmful act, he or she must do so intentionally; unintentional acts don't count.

MYTH. Although most common-law crimes require intent, strict liability crimes do not have a mental requirement. Telling a police officer you did not intend to be speeding when you are stopped on the highway does not help you avoid a ticket.

Should a person on his way to a hospital emergency room be exempt from a speeding ticket? After all, he is endangering other motorists, regardless of his reason for speeding. Is there such a thing as an excuse when you violate traffic laws?

Andy Cross/Denver Post/Getty Images

James Holmes and his defense attorney Daniel King (right) sit in court for an advisement hearing at the Arapahoe County Justice Center in Centennial, Colorado, on June 4, 2013. Holmes, facing execution if convicted of killing 12 moviegoers last summer, entered a plea of not guilty by reason of insanity.

INSANITY **Insanity** is a defense to criminal prosecution in which the defendant's state of mind negates his or her criminal responsibility. A successful insanity defense results in a verdict of "not guilty by reason of insanity."[17]

Insanity is a legal category. As used in US courts, it does not necessarily mean that everyone who suffers from a form of mental illness can be excused from legal responsibility. Many people who are depressed, suffer mood disorders, or have a psychopathic personality can be found legally sane. Instead, insanity means that the defendant's state of mind at the time the crime was committed made it impossible for that person to have the necessary *mens rea* to satisfy the legal definition of a crime. A person can be undergoing treatment for a psychological disorder but still be judged legally sane if it can be proved that at the time he committed the crime, he had the capacity to understand the wrongfulness of his actions.

If a defendant uses the insanity plea, it is usually left to psychiatric testimony to prove that the person understood the wrongfulness of her actions and was therefore legally sane or, conversely, was mentally incapable of forming intent. The jury then must weigh the evidence in light of the test for sanity currently used in the jurisdiction. Such tests vary throughout the United States; the commonly used tests are listed in Exhibit 3.2.

INTOXICATION As a general rule, intoxication, which may include drunkenness or being under the influence of drugs, is not considered a defense. However, a defendant who becomes involuntarily intoxicated under duress or by mistake may be excused for crimes committed. Involuntary intoxication may also reduce the degree of the crime; a judgment may be decreased from first- to second-degree murder because the defendant uses intoxication to prove the lack of the critical element of *mens rea*.

AGE The law holds that a child is not criminally responsible for actions committed at an age that precludes a full realization of the gravity of certain types of behavior. Under common law, there is generally a conclusive presumption of incapacity for a child under age 7, a reliable presumption for a child between the ages of 7 and 14, and no presumption for a child over the age of 14. This generally means that a child under age 7 who commits

---

EXHIBIT 3.2 Various Insanity Defense Standards

The M'Naghten Rule

The M'Naghten rule, first formulated in England in 1843, defines a person as insane if at the time she committed the act she stands accused of, she was laboring under such a defect of reason, arising from a disease of the mind, that she could not tell or know the nature and quality of the act or, if she did know it, that she did not know what she was doing was wrong. In other words, she could not "tell right from wrong." The M'Naghten rule is used in the majority of the states.

The Irresistible Impulse

The irresistible impulse test was formulated in Ohio in 1834. It is used quite often in conjunction with M'Naghten and defines a person as insane if he should or did know that his actions were illegal but, because of a mental impairment, could not control his behavior. His act was a result of an uncontrollable or irresistible impulse. A person who commits a crime during a "fit of passion" would be considered insane under this test. One of the most famous cases making use of this defense occurred in 1994, when Lorena Bobbitt successfully defended herself against charges that she cut off the penis of her husband, John, after suffering abuse at his hands.

The Durham Rule

The Durham rule, or "product test," was set forth by the US Court of Appeals for the District of Columbia Circuit in 1954 and states that "an accused is not criminally responsible if his unlawful act was the product of mental disease or mental defect." It was used for some time in the state of New Hampshire.

The Insanity Defense Reform Act

The Insanity Defense Reform Act, Title 18, US Code, Section 17, was enacted by Congress in 1984 and states that a person accused of a crime can be judged not guilty by reason of insanity if "the defendant, as a result of a severe mental disease or defect, was unable to appreciate the nature and quality or the wrongfulness of his acts."

The Substantial Capacity Test

The substantial capacity test was defined by the American Law Institute in its Model Penal Code. This argues that insanity should be defined as a lack of substantial capacity to control one's behavior. Substantial capacity is defined as "the mental capacity needed to understand the wrongfulness of [an] act, or to conform … behavior to the … law." This rule combines elements of the M'Naghten rule with the concept of irresistible impulse.

a crime will not be held criminally responsible for these actions and that a child between the ages of 7 and 14 may be held responsible. These common-law rules have been changed by statute in most jurisdictions. Today, the maximum age of criminal responsibility for children ranges from 14 to 17 or 18, whereas the minimum age may be set by statute at age 7 or under age 14.[18] In addition, every jurisdiction has established a juvenile court system to deal with juvenile offenders and children in need of court and societal supervision. Thus, the mandate of the juvenile justice system is to provide for the care and protection of children under a given age, established by state statute. In certain situations, a juvenile court may transfer a more serious chronic youthful offender to the adult criminal court.

ENTRAPMENT Defendants can claim their criminal activity was justified because law enforcement agents used traps, decoys, and deception to induce criminal action; this is referred to as entrapment. It is generally legitimate for law enforcement officers to set traps for criminals by getting information about crimes from informers, undercover agents, and codefendants. Police officers are allowed to use ordinary opportunities for defendants to commit crime and to create these opportunities that involve a defendant in a crime. For example, they can pose as prostitutes or drug dealers, hang out in an area known for drug dealing and prostitution, and make an arrest if they are solicited for crime. However, entrapment occurs when the police instigate the crime, implant criminal ideas, and coerce individuals into bringing about crime. In *Sherman v. United States*, the Supreme Court found that the function of law enforcement is to prevent crime and apprehend criminals, not to implant a criminal design originating with officials of the government in the mind of an innocent person.[19]

Justification Defenses

Justifications arise in situations in which the defendants don't deny they committed a crime but claim that anyone in their situation would have acted in a similar fashion. Justification defenses deny *mens rea*: "I did a bad act, but I did it for all the right reasons."

CONSENT A person may not be convicted of a crime if the victim consented to the act in question. In other words, a rape does not occur if the victim consents to sexual relations; a larceny cannot occur if the owner voluntarily consents to the taking of property. Consent is an essential element of these crimes, and it is a valid defense where it can be proved or shown that consent existed at the time the act was committed. In some crimes, such as statutory rape, however, consent is not an element of the crime and is considered irrelevant because the state presumes that young people are not capable of providing consent.

SELF-DEFENSE Defendants may justify their actions by saying they acted in self-defense. To establish the necessary elements to constitute self-defense, the defendant must have acted under a reasonable belief that he was in danger of death or great harm and had no means of escape from the assailant.

As a general legal rule, a person defending himself may use only such force as is reasonably necessary to prevent personal harm. A person who is assaulted by another with no weapon is ordinarily not justified in hitting the assailant with a baseball bat; a person verbally threatened is not justified in striking the other party. Persons can be found guilty of murder in the first degree if, after being attacked during a brawl, they shot and killed an unarmed person in self-defense. Despite the fact that it was the victim who initiated the fray and pummeled his opponent first, the imbalance in weaponry (gun versus fist) would mitigate a finding of self-defense.[20]

To exercise the self-defense privilege, the danger to the defendant must be immediate; it is not justifiable to kill someone who threatened you with death a year ago. In addition, most jurisdictions require that the defendants prove that they sought alternative means of avoiding the danger, such as escape, retreat, or assistance from others, before they defended themselves with force.

insanity A legal defense that maintains a defendant was incapable of forming criminal intent because he or she suffers from a defect of reason or mental illness.

entrapment A criminal defense that maintains the police originated the criminal idea or initiated the criminal action.

REALITYCHECK
Myth or Reality?

It is illegal for a policewoman to dress like a prostitute, hang out on a street corner, and arrest someone who solicits her for sex; that is called entrapment.

MYTH. It is perfectly legal to arrest a suspect who approaches a provocatively dressed police officer and solicits her for sex.

What would happen if the provocatively dressed police officer made the first move? It would be entrapment if the police officer tried to convince a reluctant person to engage in a sex act for money. The criminal thought must originate with the suspect, not the police.

self-defense A legal defense in which defendants claim that their behavior was legally justified by the necessity to protect their own life and property, or that of another victim, from potential harm.

(Left) AP Images/Bill Kostroun; (Right) AP Images/Orleans Parish Sheriff

A judge sentenced 29-year-old Cardell Hayes to 25 years in prison for killing former New Orleans Saints star Will Smith and wounding Smith's wife in April 2016. Video footage showed Smith's SUV bump into Hayes's Hummer. Then, blocks later, Hayes slammed into Smith's SUV. Both men exchanged angry words before Hayes fired his handgun, killing Smith. Hayes invoked Louisiana's "stand your ground" law in his (failed) defense, claiming he thought Smith reached for his own gun.

In some instances, women (or men) kill their mates after years of abuse; this is known as battered-wife syndrome (or, in cases involving child abuse, battered-child syndrome). Although a history of battering can be used to mitigate the seriousness of the crime, a finding of not guilty most often requires the presence of imminent danger and the inability of the accused to escape from the assailant.

Most self-defense statutes require a duty to retreat before reacting to a threat with physical violence. An exception is one's own home. According to the "castle doctrine" ("every man's home is his castle"), a person is not obligated to retreat within his or her residence before fighting back. Some states, most notably Florida, now have "stand-your-ground" laws, which allow people to use force in a wide variety of circumstances and eliminate or curtail the need to retreat, even if they are not in their own home but in a public place.

Florida's law, enacted on October 1, 2005, allows the use of deadly force when a person reasonably believes it necessary to prevent the commission of a "forcible felony," including carjacking, robbery, and assault.[21] The law allows average citizens to use deadly force when they reasonably believe that their homes or vehicles have been illegally invaded. The Florida law authorizes the use of defensive force by anyone "who is not engaged in an unlawful activity and who is attacked in any other place where he or she has a right to be." Furthermore, under the law, such a person has no duty to retreat and can stand his or her ground and meet force with force. The statute also grants civil and criminal immunity to anyone found to have had such a reasonable belief.[22] The stand-your-ground law gained national prominence when George Zimmerman shot and killed Trayvon Martin and claimed he was in fear of his life. Zimmerman was found not guilty at trial when the jury supported his self-defense claims.

A common question concerns how effective people are at using guns in self-defense. This issue is examined in the accompanying Contemporary Issues in Criminal Justice box.

NECESSITY Sometimes criminal defendants, like the two sailors who killed and ate the cabin boy, argue that they acted out of "necessity." To be successful, a defense of necessity must show that considering the circumstances and conditions at the time the crime occurred, the defendant (or any reasonable person) could not have behaved in any other way. For example, a husband steals a car to take his pregnant wife to the hospital for an emergency delivery, or a hunter shoots an animal of an endangered species that was about to attack his child. The defense has been found inapplicable in cases where defendants sought to shut down nuclear power plants or abortion clinics or to destroy missile components under the belief that the action was necessary to save lives or prevent a nuclear war.

How Successfully Are Guns Used in Self-Defense?

The Second Amendment states that "a well-regulated Militia, being necessary to the security of a Free State, the right of the people to keep and bear Arms, shall not be infringed." In the landmark 2008 case *District of Columbia v. Heller*, the Supreme Court held that the Second Amendment protects an individual's right to possess a firearm for private use. It also stated that "an individual right to possess a firearm [is] unconnected with service in a militia," meaning gun ownership for self-defense (and other purposes, such as for hunting) is a constitutional right. The constitutional question is now settled, but debate continues to swirl around the question of how capable people actually *are* in using guns for self-defense.

Wayne LaPierre, head of the National Rifle Association (NRA), famously quipped that "the only way to stop a bad guy with a gun is with good guy with a gun." How true is his claim? One would think it is gospel given the recent surge in pro-gun laws. "Open carry" and "campus carry" are now familiar phrases. School teachers are legally arming themselves in some states. Prohibitions against bringing weapons to historically off-limits places, including churches, are being lifted. Access to information on who has a concealed carry permit is increasingly restricted. The list goes on.

Personal safety is now the top reason people report for owning guns, far outstripping any other reason (hunting, sport, etc.). And according to the Pew Research Center, for the first time in history Americans report that protecting gun rights is more important than controlling gun ownership. Both the shift in public opinion and changes in state firearms laws are indicative of a perception that guns can be used to deter and/or interrupt crime. Indeed, concealed carry gives people an opportunity to protect themselves from robbers and others who would do them harm. Mass shootings often occur in so-called "gun-free zones," so arming teachers *could* make would-be killers think twice. The problem is that there is little to no empirical evidence on which to base such claims. There is a wealth of research on this subject, but somehow it gets largely ignored by policymakers. Here is some of what we know with respect to defensive gun use:

- Every lethal self-defense or defense-of-life shooting is offset by approximately 34 gun murders and 78 suicides.

- In active shooter situations, it is nearly impossible for police to distinguish criminals from those coming to the rescue.

- Pete Blair and Katherine Schweit's study of 160 active shooter incidents (not mass shooting incidents but rather "an individual actively engaged in killing or attempting to kill people in a confined and populated area") in the United States found that while one in five were stopped by civilians before police arrived, in only *one case* did a "good guy with a gun" who was not a police officer or security guard interrupt the incident. The majority, interestingly, ended on the shooter's initiative.

- In a study using data from the National Crime Victimization Survey, Harvard researchers David Hemenway and Sara Solnick found that when a victim reported using a gun in self-defense, the likelihood of injury (10.9 percent) was virtually identical to the likelihood of injury had the victim taken no action at all (11 percent). Similarly, those who used guns to deter criminals had nearly as much property taken from them (34.9 percent) as did those who did not brandish guns (38.5 percent).

- The same Harvard study found that while the likelihood of injury after threatening the offender with a gun was reduced (4.1 percent), the injury rate was similar to that involving any other weapon (5.3 percent). More importantly, the likelihood of injury dropped to around 2 percent for those who hid or fled.

- Most defensive gun use occurs in the context of escalating arguments, as compared to situations in which innocent individuals are attacked and/or uninvolved bystanders rush to the rescue.

- Firearms are used more often to intimidate than they are for self-defense.

- Surveys tend to overestimate the incidence of defensive gun use, sometimes to the point of mathematical impossibility.

- The Gun Violence Archive, which attempts to catalog every publicly known incident of defensive gun use, found that guns were used defensively in just 1,886 incidents in 2016. It does not report on how many of those incidents could be classified as successful.

CRITICAL THINKING

1. Sometimes no amount of research or data can change people's minds about guns. Why is that?

2. Do you think the content of this box biased in any way? If so, how or why? (The authors *have* tried to present a neutral perspective.)

Sources: *District of Columbia v. Heller*, 554 US 570 (2008); J. Nicas and J. Palazzolo, "Pro-Gun Laws Gain Ground," *Wall Street Journal*, April 4, 2013, http://www.wsj.com/news/interactive/GUNSTATES20130404; A. Swift, "Personal Safety Top Reason Americans Own Guns Today," *Gallup*, October 28, 2013, http://www.gallup.com/poll/165605/personal-safety-top-reason-americans-own-guns-today.aspx; A. Kohut, "Despite Lower Crime Rates, Support for Gun Rights Increases," Pew Research Center, April 17, 2015, http://www.pewresearch.org/fact-tank/2015/04/17/despite-lower-crime-rates-support-for-gun-rights-increases/; C. Ingraham, "Guns in America: For Every Criminal Killed in Self-Defense, 34 Innocent People Die," *Washington Post*, June 19, 2015, https://www.washingtonpost.com/news/wonk/wp/2015/06/19/guns-in-america-for-every-criminal-killed-in-self-defense-34-innocent-people-die/; J. Holland, "Tactical Experts Destroy the NRA's Heroic Gunslinger Fantasy," *The Nation*, October 5, 2015, http://www.thenation.com/article/combat-vets-destroy-the-nras-heroic-gunslinger-fantasy/; J. P. Blair and K. W. Schweit, *A Study of Active Shooter Incidents, 2000–2013* (Washington, DC: Federal Bureau of Investigation, 2014), p. 11; D. Hemenway and S. J. Solnick, "The Epidemiology of Self-Defense Gun Use: Evidence from the National Crime Victimization Surveys, 2007–2011," *Preventive Medicine* 79 (2015): 22–27; D. Hemenway, M. Miller, and D. Azrael, "Gun Use in the United States: Results from Two National Surveys," *Injury Prevention* 6 (2000): 263–267; D. Hemenway and D. Azrael, "The Relative Frequency of Offensive and Defensive Gun Use: Results from a National Survey," *Violence and Victims* 15 (2000): 257–272; D. Hemenway, "Survey Research and Self-Defense Gun Use: An Explanation of Extreme Overestimates," *Journal of Criminal Law and Criminology* 87 (1997): 1430–1445; P. J. Cook, J. Ludwig, and D. Hemenway, "The Gun Debate's New Mythical Number: How Many Defensive Gun Uses Per Year?" *Journal of Policy Analysis and Management* 16 (1997): 463–469; Gun Violence Archive, http://www.gunviolencearchive.org/. (URLs accessed April 2017.)

LAW ENFORCEMENT Police officers, firefighters, and other first responders can use their occupation in defense of an alleged law violation committed while in the line of duty. For example, a police officer who shoots a suspect he or she believes is drawing a weapon cannot be charged with murder, even if it turns out that the suspect was unarmed. However, there are a number of exceptions to this rule. First, the action must be contained within the scope of their duties. A police officer who uses physical force while buying marijuana from a dealer would be just as criminally liable as any citizen. Second, protection from criminal liability would be limited in cases of gross negligence or malicious intent. For example, police officers could be charged with criminal assault if they used a weapon to batter a suspect they were interrogating. Police officers who drove at excessive speeds while not on emergency calls have been charged with manslaughter for causing the death of motorists.[23]

Immunity enjoyed by government agents can also sometimes spill over to private citizens who come to the aid of police or other civil servants. For example, a third party who sees a police officer grappling with a suspect and comes to the officer's aid cannot be prosecuted for assault if it later turns out that the suspect was innocent of crime. Many states have passed "Good Samaritan" laws that provide immunity from both civil and criminal actions to private citizens who, in good faith, cause injury while attempting to help someone in distress, including both private citizens and government officials.

Changing Defenses

WEB APP 3.2 Read about some unusual and creative criminal defenses here: **https://www.theblanchlawfirm.com/blog/five-of-the-most-unusual-criminal-defenses-that-actually-worked/**.

Criminal defenses are undergoing rapid change. As society becomes more aware of existing social problems that may contribute to crime, it has become commonplace for defense counsels to defend their clients by raising a variety of new defenses based on preexisting conditions or syndromes with which their clients were afflicted. Examples include "battered-woman syndrome," "Gulf War Syndrome," "child sexual abuse syndrome," "Holocaust survivor syndrome," and "adopted-child syndrome."

In using these defenses, attorneys are asking judges either to recognize a new excuse for crime or to fit these conditions into preexisting defenses. For example, a person who used lethal violence in self-defense may argue that the trauma of serving in Iraq or Afghanistan caused him to overreact to provocation. Or a victim of child abuse may use her experiences to mitigate her culpability in a crime, asking a jury to consider her background when making a death penalty decision. In some instances, exotic criminal defenses have been gender specific. Attorneys have argued that their female clients' behavior was a result of their premenstrual syndrome (PMS) and that male clients were aggressive because of an imbalance in their testosterone levels. These defenses have achieved relatively little success in the United States.[24]

Although criminal law reform may be guided by good intentions, it is sometimes difficult to put the changes into operation. Law reform may necessitate creating new enforcement agencies or severely tax existing ones. As a result, the system becomes strained, and cases are backlogged.

The Evolution of Criminal Law

LO6 Discuss the most recent developments in criminal law reform

In recent years, many states and the federal government have been examining their substantive criminal law. Because the law, in part, reflects public opinion and morality regarding various forms of behavior, what was considered criminal 40 years ago may not be considered criminal today. In some cases, states have reassessed their laws and reduced the penalties on some common practices such as public intoxication; this reduction of penalties is referred to as *decriminalization*. Such crimes, which in the past might have resulted in a prison sentence, may now be punished with a fine. In other instances, what was once considered a criminal act may be declared noncriminal or legalized. Sexual activity between consenting same-sex adults was punished as a serious felony under sodomy statutes in a number of states until the US Supreme Court ruled such statutes illegal in 2003.[25]

Creating New Crimes

In some instances, new laws have been created to conform to emerging social issues and to deal with threats to people and the environment. Some of the new crimes and legal categories created in this era of law reform are discussed next.

PHYSICIAN-ASSISTED SUICIDE Doctors helping people to end their lives became the subject of a national debate when Dr. Jack Kevorkian began practicing what he called obitiatry, helping people take their lives.[26] In an attempt to stop Kevorkian, Michigan passed a statutory ban on assisted suicide, reflecting what lawmakers believed to be prevailing public opinion; Kevorkian was convicted and imprisoned.[27] He was released on June 1, 2007, on parole due to good behavior, and died on June 3, 2011; 44 states now disallow assisted suicide either by statute or common law, including Michigan.[28]

obitiatry Helping people take their own lives.

STALKING Many states have enacted stalking statutes that prohibit and punish acts described typically as "the willful, malicious, and repeated following and harassing of another person."[29] Stalking laws were originally formulated to protect women terrorized by former husbands and boyfriends, although celebrities often are plagued by stalkers as well. In celebrity cases, these laws often apply to stalkers who are strangers or casual acquaintances of their victims. In states where there is no formal stalking statute, other offenses, such as trespassing, can be used to bring charges against a stalker.

stalking The willful, malicious, and repeated following and harassing of another person.

COMMUNITY NOTIFICATION LAWS These laws require the registration of people convicted of sex-related crimes; they were enacted in response to concern about sexual predators moving into neighborhoods. One of the best-known statutes of this kind was named after 7-year-old Megan Kanka of Hamilton Township, New Jersey, who was killed in 1994. Charged with the crime was a convicted sex offender who (unknown to the Kankas) lived across the street. On May 17, 1996, President Bill Clinton signed Megan's Law, which contained two components:

- *Sex offender registration.* Requires the states to register individuals convicted of sex crimes against children.
- *Community notification.* Compels the states to make private and personal information on registered sex offenders available to the public.

CLARIFYING RAPE Sometimes laws are changed to clarify the definition of crime and to quell public debate over the boundaries of the law. When does bad behavior cross the line into criminality, and when does it remain merely bad behavior? An example of the former can be found in changes to the law of rape. In several states, including California and Maryland, it is now considered rape if (a) the woman consents to sex, (b) the sex act begins, (c) she changes her mind during the act and tells her partner to stop, and (d) he refuses and continues. Before the legal change, such a circumstance was not considered rape but merely aggressive sex.[30]

CONTROLLING TECHNOLOGY Devices such as ATMs and cell phones have spawned a new generation of criminal acts involving theft of access numbers and software piracy. Identity theft has become a national problem, and, as a result, there has been an ongoing effort by state legislatures to change their criminal codes to make it a felony offense to send out bulk e-mail messages designed to trick consumers into revealing bank account passwords, Social Security numbers, and other personal information.[31]

PROTECTING THE ENVIRONMENT In response to the concerns of environmentalists, the federal government has passed numerous acts designed to protect the nation's well-being. The Environmental Protection Agency has successfully prosecuted significant violations of these and other new laws, including data fraud cases (e.g., private laboratories submitting false environmental data to state and federal environmental agencies); indiscriminate hazardous waste dumping that resulted in serious injuries and death; industry-wide ocean dumping by cruise ships; oil spills that caused significant damage to waterways, wetlands, and beaches; and illegal handling of hazardous substances such as pesticides and asbestos that exposed children, the poor, and other especially vulnerable groups to potentially serious illness.[32]

WEB APP 3.3 To read all about new environmental laws, go to **https://www.epa.gov /laws-regulations**. Should people who violate these laws face a prison sentence, or should such cases be handled civilly, with a fine and other penalties?

Some states, including Washington and colorado, have legalized marijuana, prompting new methods of distribution. Stephen Shearin demonstrates the use of a ZaZZZ vending machine that contains cannabis flower, hemp-oil energy drinks, and other merchandise at Seattle Caregivers, a medical marijuana dispensary, in Seattle, Washington on February 3, 2015. Vending machines selling medical marijuana opened for business in Seattle in what the company providing them billed as a first-in-the-state innovation that it expects to expand to other cities and states where pot is legal as medicine. Shearin is the president of technology company American Green Inc., which provides the machines.

David Ryder/Reuters

LEGALIZING MARIJUANA As of this writing, 28 states and the District of Columbia have legalized marijuana for medical purposes.[33] On November 6, 2012, Washington and Colorado voted to legalize possession of marijuana, up to a certain quantity. In 2015, Alaska became the third state to legalize recreational marijuana, followed shortly after by Oregon. The District of Columbia has also legalized the drug. California, Massachusetts, Maine, and Nevada joined the list in 2016.

On December 5, 2012, one day before Washington's Initiative 502 went into effect, the Seattle Police Department's "SPD Blotter" website informed city residents that people were now free to consume marijuana in the privacy of their own homes. The site also noted that for the time being officers would only issue warnings to those caught smoking weed in public. The site went on to say:

> Does this mean you should flagrantly roll up a mega-spliff and light up in the middle of the street? No. If you're smoking pot in public, officers will be giving helpful reminders to folks about the rules and regulations under I-502 (like not smoking pot in public). But the police department believes that, under state law, you may responsibly get baked, order some pizzas, and enjoy a *Lord of the Rings* marathon in the privacy of your own home, if you want to.[34]

Marijuana legalization was further touched on at in this chapter's opening story.

RESPONDING TO TERRORISM Soon after the September 11, 2001, terrorist attacks, the US government enacted several laws focused on preventing further acts of violence against the United States and creating greater flexibility in the fight to control terror activity. Most importantly, Congress passed the USA PATRIOT (an acronym for Uniting and Strengthening America by Providing Appropriate Tools Required to Intercept and Obstruct Terrorism) Act on October 26, 2001.[35] The bill, which was over 342 pages long, created new laws, and made changes to more than 15 different existing statutes. Its aim was to give sweeping new powers to domestic law enforcement and international intelligence agencies in an effort to fight terrorism, to expand the definition of terrorist activities, and to alter sanctions for violent terrorism. On March 2, 2006, Congress passed a reauthorization bill that left most of the act intact, and on March 9, President George W. Bush signed it into law. Since then, various portions of the USAPA have been extended and reauthorized.

While it is impossible to discuss every provision of this sweeping legislation here, a few of its more important elements will be examined.

THE USA PATRIOT ACT The USA PATRIOT Act expanded all four traditional tools of surveillance—wiretaps, search warrants, pen/trap orders (installing devices that record phone calls), and subpoenas. The Foreign Intelligence Surveillance Act (FISA) that allows domestic operations by intelligence agencies was also expanded. The PATRIOT Act gave greater power to the Federal Bureau of Investigation (FBI) to check and monitor phone, Internet, and computer records without first needing to demonstrate that they were being used by a suspect or target of a court order. It provided for Central Intelligence Agency (CIA) oversight of domestic intelligence gathering.

The act also centralized federal law enforcement authority within the US Department of Justice. For example, the US attorney general was given authority for investigating several federal offenses that in the past were investigated by the Secret Service and the Bureau of Alcohol, Tobacco, Firearms, and Explosives (BATF).

The act expanded the definition of *terrorism* and enabled the government to monitor more closely those people suspected of "harboring" and giving "material support" to terrorists (sections 803, 805). It increased the authority of the US attorney general to detain and deport noncitizens with little or no judicial review. The attorney general was authorized to certify that he or she has "reasonable grounds to believe" that a noncitizen endangers national security and is therefore eligible for deportation. The attorney general and secretary of state were also given the authority to designate domestic groups as terrorist organizations and deport any noncitizen who is a member.

Though many critics have called for its repeal, the PATRIOT Act was reauthorized in 2006 with a slew of provisions ensuring that the act did not violate civil rights by limiting its surveillance and wiretap authorizations.[36] More recently, President Obama extended three controversial provisions that were set to expire:

- *Lone wolf.* The government can track individuals who are not connected to a foreign power but who are thought to be affiliated with a terrorist group. This applies only to noncitizens.
- *Business records.* The government can force third parties, such as travel and telephone companies, to provide access to a suspect's records without his or her knowledge.
- *Roving wiretaps.* The government can monitor phone lines and Internet accounts that a terrorist suspect may be using, but it must first get approval from the Foreign Intelligence Surveillance Act court.[37]

THE USA FREEDOM ACT Enacted on June 2, 2015, the USA FREEDOM (an acronym for Uniting and Strengthening America by Fulfilling Rights and Ending Eavesdropping,

AP Images/John Minchillo

Crime scene investigators collect evidence from the pavement as police respond to a 2016 attack at Ohio State University in Columbus. In chillingly detailed articles in their slick online magazine *Rumiyah*, ISIL extremists exhorted English-language readers to carry out attacks with knives and vehicles. Using those very methods, Somali-born student Abdul Razak Ali Artan injured multiple people in the attack at Ohio State University. It isn't clear whether Artan ever saw or heard about the magazine's instructions, but in a Facebook post made before the attack, he said that if the US wanted Muslims to stop carrying out "lone wolf attacks," it should make peace with ISIL.

Dragnet-Collection and Online Monitoring) Act[38] restored portions of the PATRIOT Act that expired that same year. Roving wiretaps were reauthorized, as was the provision pertaining to "lone wolf" targets. The act also placed restrictions on intelligence agencies' use of bulk "metadata." This change was prompted in part by the actions of Edward Snowden, a former CIA employee who made headlines in 2013 when he leaked information about the NSA's surveillance practices.

The law in this area continues to change. As the terrorism problem evolves, and as government's ability to gather data and track the movement of people within the United States and around the world improves, continual changes will need to be made in order to balance people's civil liberties with the need to stamp out threats to the safety of innocent civilians.

LO7 Describe the role of the Bill of Rights in shaping criminal procedure

Bill of Rights The first 10 amendments to the US Constitution that spell out specific freedoms granted to citizens and limit the power of the federal government to conduct criminal prosecutions.

exclusionary rule Evidence seized in violation of the Fourth Amendment cannot be used in a court of law.

Constitutional Criminal Procedure

Although substantive criminal law primarily defines crimes, the law of criminal procedure consists of the rules and procedures that govern the pretrial processing of criminal suspects and the conduct of criminal trials. The main source of the procedural law is the body of the Constitution and the first 10 amendments, added to the Constitution on December 15, 1791, which are collectively known as the **Bill of Rights**. The purpose of these amendments is to prevent the government from usurping the personal freedoms of citizens. Arguably the most controversial of these rights is the Second Amendment, which deals with gun ownership.

The US Supreme Court's interpretation of these amendments has served as the basis for the creation of legal rights of the accused. Of primary concern are the Fourth, Fifth, Sixth, and Eighth Amendments, which limit and control the manner in which the federal government operates the justice system. In addition, the due process clause of the Fourteenth Amendment has been interpreted to apply these limits on governmental action to the state and local levels:

- The Fourth Amendment bars illegal "searches and seizures," a right especially important for the criminal justice system because it means that police officers cannot indiscriminately use their authority to investigate a possible crime or arrest a suspect. Stopping, questioning, or searching an individual without legal justification represents a serious violation of the Fourth Amendment right to personal privacy. Under the **exclusionary rule**, evidence seized in violation of the Fourth Amendment cannot be used in a court of law; it is as though it never existed.

- The Fifth Amendment limits the admissibility of confessions that have been obtained unfairly. In the 1966 landmark case *Miranda v. Arizona*, the Supreme Court held that a person accused of a crime has the right to refuse to answer questions when placed in police custody.[39] The Fifth Amendment also guarantees defendants the right to a grand jury hearing and to protection from being tried twice for the same crime (double jeopardy). Its due process clause guarantees defendants the right to fundamental fairness and the expectation of fair trials, fair hearings, and similar procedural safeguards.

- The Sixth Amendment guarantees the defendant the right to a speedy and public trial by an impartial jury, the right to be informed of the nature of the charges, and the right to confront any prosecution witnesses. It also contains the right of a defendant to be represented by an attorney—a privilege that has been extended to numerous stages of the criminal justice process, including pretrial custody, identification and lineup procedures, preliminary hearing, submission of a guilty plea, trial, sentencing, and postconviction appeal.

- According to the Eighth Amendment, "Excessive bail shall not be required, nor excessive fines imposed, nor cruel and unusual punishments inflicted." Bail is a money bond put up by the accused to attain freedom between arrest and trial. Bail is meant to ensure a trial appearance because the bail money is forfeited if the defendant misses the trial date. The Eighth Amendment does not guarantee a constitutional right to bail but, rather, prohibits the use of excessive bail, which is typically defined as an amount far greater than that imposed on similar defendants who are accused of committing similar crimes. The Eighth Amendment also forbids the use

Duties and Characteristics of the Job

- Attorneys use their experience and extensive knowledge of the law and the legal system to defend the rights of their clients and protect their best interests either in a legal setting, during a trial, or by settling their grievances in or out of court.

- They also act as legal advisors and engage in such activities as drawing up and/or interpreting a legal document or contract, and they advise clients of changes in existing laws.

- Attorneys will often choose a field of specialization such as tax law or intellectual property and typically work in firms or start their own practice.

- Some work for the federal, state, or local government; others take advantage of increasing opportunities for employment within businesses.

- Attorneys work long hours; especially if a case goes to trial; a workweek of more than 60 hours is not uncommon.

Job Outlook

- Job opportunities are expected to grow at an average rate for the next several years.

- A good academic record from a prestigious law school, as well as work experience, mobility, and additional education in a specialty field, are especially helpful.

- Jobs will be most plentiful in urban areas, where more law firms, big businesses, and government offices are typically located.

Salary

- Attorneys have a median annual salary of about $115,000 per year or about $55 per hour.

- Some partners in the largest national firms in Chicago or New York may have an annual salary in the millions.

- An attorney's salary will depend on type of employer, experience, region, and type of law being practiced. Extremely successful sole practitioners can win millions in tort actions.

Qualifications

- A bachelor's degree in a program that develops strong analytical and writing skills is recommended for preparation for law school.

- Graduating from an accredited law school and passing the bar are required.

Education and Training

- Lawyers must go to an accredited law school and pass the bar.

- Making the law review, publishing law review articles while in school, and obtaining prestigious internships can be helpful in securing coveted jobs.

- Many lawyers use their education and experience as a means of launching careers in business, politics, government, or academia.

Reality Check

- Attorneys must stay informed of the latest developments in law and often attend conferences; many states have continuing legal education (CLE) requirements that must be met.

- For certain positions, such as law school professor and positions focusing on a specialty such as patent law, further experience and education are required.

- Gaining entrance to a law school takes not only hard work and discipline but also good grades and a desirable score on the Law School Admissions Test (LSAT). Start preparing now.

- Be prepared for some long hours at work.

- Be realistic about pay. Not all lawyers start with six-figure salaries, but those hired by top metropolitan firms can expect substantial starting salaries.

- Top grads at top schools get top jobs, the bottom half of the class in the bottom-ranked schools will struggle.

Source: Bureau of Labor Statistics, *Occupational Outlook Handbook, 2015*, http://www.bls.gov/ooh/legal/lawyers.htm (accessed April 2017).

---

of cruel and unusual punishment. This prohibition protects both the accused and convicted offenders from actions regarded as unacceptable by a civilized society, including corporal punishment and torture. Capital punishment, however, is legal unless it is employed in a random, haphazard fashion or if especially cruel means of execution are used.[40] One method used to avoid "cruelty" is lethal injection. In the 2008 case *Baze and Bowling v. Rees*, the Court upheld the use of this method unless there is a "substantial risk of serious harm" that the drugs will not work effectively.[41]

- The Fourteenth Amendment is the vehicle used by the courts to apply the protection of the Bill of Rights to the states. It affirms that no state shall "deprive any person of life, liberty, or property, without due process of law." In essence, the same general constitutional restrictions applicable to the federal government can be imposed on the states.

Due Process of Law

The concept of due process, found in both the Fifth and Fourteenth Amendments, has been used to evaluate the constitutionality of legal statutes and to set standards and guidelines for fair procedures in the criminal justice system. As you may recall from Chapter 1, some criminal justice experts believe that the concept of due process is the

LO8 List the elements of due process of law

lens through which the criminal justice system must be examined. Without the application of due process, civil rights and constitutional protections are meaningless. In seeking to define the term, most legal experts believe that it refers to the essential elements of fairness under law.[42] This definition basically refers to the legal system's need for rules and regulations that protect individual rights.

Due process can actually be divided into two distinct categories, substantive and procedural. Substantive due process refers to the citizen's right to be protected from criminal laws that may be biased, discriminatory, and otherwise unfair. These laws may be vague or may apply unfairly to one group and not others. The doctrine of substantive due process holds that citizens maintain particular rights, such as freedom of speech and religion, that cannot be controlled or impeded by the government. So we as citizens have the right to criticize government policy without fear of legal retribution. In some instances, the Courts have protected rights, such as the right to marital privacy, that are not mentioned in the Constitution per se, but are considered an essential and undisputed element of American life. Based on this thinking, people have the right to buy and use contraceptives to prevent unwanted pregnancies, something that was not considered by the founding fathers![43]

Procedural due process seeks to ensure that no person will be deprived of life, liberty, or property without proper and legal criminal process. Basically, procedural due process is intended to guarantee that fundamental fairness exists in each individual case. Specific due process procedures include the following:

- Freedom from illegal searches and interrogations
- Prompt notice of charges and a formal hearing
- The right to counsel or some other representation
- The opportunity to respond to charges
- The opportunity to confront and cross-examine witnesses and accusers
- The privilege to be free from self-incrimination
- The opportunity to present one's own witnesses
- A decision made on the basis of substantial evidence and facts produced at the hearing
- A written statement of the reasons for the decision
- An appellate review procedure

Robert Wynters points to the spot where he says sheriff's deputies seized the belongings he and other homeless people had stashed for safekeeping beneath a bridge over the Truckee River on the east edge of Reno, Nevada. Wynters, 42, filed a lawsuit in US District Court accusing Washoe County of confiscating and destroying his property without prior notice or due process, in violation of his constitutional rights.

AP Images/Scott Sonner

Interpreting the Constitution

Within the context of due process, how the Supreme Court decides a specific case depends on the facts of the case, the federal and state constitutional and statutory provisions, previous court decisions, and judicial philosophy.[44] The judicial interpretation of the Constitution is not fixed but reflects what society deems fair and just at a particular time and place. The degree of loss suffered by the individual (victim or offender), balanced against the state's interests, also determines how many constitutional requirements are ordinarily applied. When the Supreme Court justices are conservative, they are less likely to create new rights and privileges and more likely to restrict civil liberties.

Take the 2009 case of *Herring v. United States*, which involved interpretation of the exclusionary rule.[45] Bennie Dean Herring had been searched after the police were informed that there was an outstanding warrant against him on a felony charge. The search turned up methamphetamine and a pistol. Soon after, it was discovered that the warrant had actually been withdrawn five months earlier and had been left in the computer system by mistake. Should the evidence be discarded because the police made an error? Or should it be allowed because they acted in good faith based on existing evidence that later proved inaccurate? The majority decision ruled that "When police mistakes leading to an unlawful search are the result of isolated negligence attenuated from the search, rather than systemic error or reckless disregard of constitutional requirements, the exclusionary rule does not apply." The Court ruled that the errors in the *Herring* case did not amount to deliberate police misconduct that should trigger the exclusionary rule.

LO9 Explain the role the Supreme Court plays in interpreting the Constitution and shaping procedural law

ETHICAL REFLECTION

A number of criminal justice reform bills have bounced around in both houses of Congress in recent years. None, though, have made sweeping changes supported by both Democrats and Republicans. Recently, a bipartisan bill to reduce sentences for nonviolent federal offenders stalled over the issue of *mens rea*. A coalition of mainly conservative lawmakers called for changes to federal law that would require a specific *mens rea* component for all federal crimes. Currently, a number of federal laws do not contain such a requirement.

Why write a specific *mens rea* component into all federal crimes? One reason concerns the sheer number of federal laws—some 5,000 federal crimes and more than 300,000 federal regulations. Proponents of *mens rea* reform claim it is impossible for anyone to fully grasp the content of that many laws. Senator Orrin Hatch (R-UT) put it this way:

> Without adequate *mens rea* protections—that is, without the requirement that a person know his conduct was wrong or unlawful—everyday citizens can be held *criminally* liable for conduct that no reasonable person would know was wrong. This is not only unfair; it is immoral. No government that purports to safeguard the liberty and the rights of its people should have power to lock individuals up for conduct they didn't know was wrong. Only when a person has acted with a guilty mind is it just, is it ethical, to brand that person a criminal and deprive him of liberty.

In other words, the notion that "ignorance is no defense" is outdated and oversimplified. It is just too easy for a well-meaning citizen to get ensnared in the legal system. Hatch then went on to describe several examples which the absence of a specific *mens rea* requirement resulted in some unfair convictions. Here is one of them:

> First is Wade Martin, an Alaskan fisherman who sold ten sea otters to a buyer he *thought* was a Native Alaskan, but who turned out not to be. Authorities charged Wade with violating the Marine Mammal Protection Act, which criminalizes the sale of sea otters to non–Native Alaskans. The fact that he *thought* the buyer was a Native Alaskan was irrelevant. Prosecutors had to prove only that the buyer was not *in fact* a Native Alaskan. The absence of a criminal intent requirement meant Wade could be convicted regardless of whether he knew what he was doing was wrong. Wade pleaded guilty to a felony charge and was ordered to pay a $1,000 fine.

Think back to this chapter's section on *mens rea*. Weigh it against Hatch's comments. Martin's case certainly highlights some absurdity in federal law, but are cases like his common?

Writing Challenge Write an essay explaining the possible unanticipated consequences of requiring specific intent for all federal crimes. Answer the following questions: Should there be a *mens rea* requirement for all crimes? Why or why not? If not all crimes, which ones? What are the implications of requiring specific *mens rea* for corporate crimes in which it is difficult to identify specific perpetrators?

Sources: Orrin Hatch, "It's Time for Criminal Justice, Mens Rea Reform," September 21, 2015, http://www.hatch.senate.gov/public/index.cfm/2015/9/hatch-it-s-time-for-criminal-justice-mens-rea-reform; M. DeBonis, "The Issue That Could Keep Congress from Passing Criminal Justice Reform," *Washington Post*, January 20, 2016, https://www.washingtonpost.com/news/powerpost/wp/2016/01/20/the-issue-that-could-keep-congress-from-passing-criminal-justice-reform/ (URLs accessed April 2017).

SUMMARY

LO1 *List the similarities and differences between criminal law and civil law* The law today can generally be divided into four broad categories. Substantive criminal law defines crimes and their punishment. Procedural criminal law sets out the basic rules of practice in the criminal justice system. Civil law governs relations between private parties, including both individuals and organizations (such as business enterprises and corporations). Administrative or public law controls the behavior of government agencies.

LO2 *Summarize the historical development of the criminal law* The roots of the criminal codes used in the United States can be traced to such early legal charters as the Babylonian Code of Hammurabi (2000 BCE) and the Mosaic Code of the Israelites (1200 BCE). In the Middle Ages, societies developed legal systems featuring monetary compensation, called wergild. After the Norman Conquest, royal judges would decide what to do in each case, using local custom and rules of conduct as a guide in a system known as stare decisis (Latin for "to stand by decided cases"). Eventually, this system evolved into a common law of the country that incorporated local custom and practice into a national code.

LO3 *Discuss the sources of criminal law* The contemporary American legal system was codified by state and federal legislatures. The content of the law may also be influenced by judicial decision making. Regardless of its source, all criminal law in the United States must conform to the rules and dictates of the Constitution.

LO4 *Identify the elements of a crime* Almost all common-law crime contains both mental and physical elements. The *actus reus* is a voluntary and deliberate illegal act, such as taking someone's money, burning a building, or shooting someone. For an act to constitute a crime, it must be done with *mens rea*, deliberate purpose or criminal intent. Certain statutory offenses exist in which *mens rea* is not essential. These offenses fall in a category known as public safety or strict liability crimes.

LO5 *Explain excuses and justification defenses for crime* When people defend themselves against criminal charges, they must refute one or more of the elements of the crime of which they have been accused. Defendants may deny the *actus reus* by arguing that they were falsely accused, and the real culprit has yet to be identified. Defendants may also claim that even though they did engage in the criminal act they are accused of, they should be excused because they lacked *mens rea*. Common excuse defenses are duress, insanity, intoxication, age, and entrapment. Common justification defenses are consent, self-defense, necessity, and law enforcement.

LO6 *Discuss the most recent developments in criminal law reform* Criminal law is constantly changing and being updated. New crimes have been created to control stalking, environmental damage, and terrorism, among other offenses. Others have been decriminalized or legalized, such as sodomy. In some cases, such as with recreational and medical marijuana, states may legalize acts that are still banned by federal law.

LO7 *Describe the role of the Bill of Rights in shaping criminal procedure* The main source of the procedural law is the body of the Constitution and the first 10 amendments—the Bill of Rights—added to the Constitution on December 15, 1791. Of primary concern are the Fourth, Fifth, Sixth, and Eighth Amendments, which limit and control the manner in which the federal government operates the justice system.

LO8 *List the elements of due process of law* The concept of due process is found in both the Fifth and Fourteenth Amendments. Due process has been used to evaluate the constitutionality of legal statutes and to set standards and guidelines for fair procedures in the criminal justice system.

LO9 *Explain the role the Supreme Court plays in interpreting the Constitution and shaping procedural law* The law of criminal procedure consists of the rules and procedures that govern the pretrial processing of criminal suspects and the conduct of criminal trials. The Supreme Court is tasked with interpreting the Constitution and setting limits on governmental behavior—for example, limiting the ability of the police in their searching, questioning, and punishing of those suspected of crime.

KEY TERMS

substantive criminal law, p. 56
criminal procedure, p. 56
civil law, p. 56
tort, p. 56
public law, p. 56
lex talionis, p. 57

stare decisis, p. 57
common law, p. 57
mala in se, p. 57
mala prohibitum, p. 57
ex post facto laws, p. 59
felony, p. 60
misdemeanor, p. 60

actus reus, p. 60
mens rea, p. 60
strict liability crimes, p. 62
excuse defenses, p. 63
justification defense, p. 63
insanity, p. 64
entrapment, p. 65

self-defense, p. 65
obitiatry, p. 69
stalking, p. 69
Bill of Rights, p. 72
exclusionary rule, p. 72

REVIEW QUESTIONS

1. What are the specific aims and purposes of criminal law? To what extent does criminal law control behavior?

2. What kinds of activities should be labeled criminal in contemporary society? Why?

3. What is a criminal act? What is a criminal state of mind? When are individuals liable for their actions?

4. Discuss the various kinds of crime classifications. To what extent or degree are they distinguishable?

5. Numerous states are revising their penal codes. Which major categories of substantive crimes do you think should be revised?

6. Entrapment is a defense used when the defendant claims he was entrapped into committing the crime. To what extent should law enforcement personnel induce the commission of an offense?

7. What legal principles can be used to justify self-defense? Given that the law seeks to prevent crime—not promote it—are such principles sound?

8. What are the minimum standards of criminal procedure required in the criminal justice system?

The Police and Law Enforcement

The August 2014 shooting in Ferguson, Missouri, of Michael Brown, left an indelible imprint on American policing. Police–minority outreach is now a high priority. Countless officers also report that now, more than ever, they act under the microscope. One Philadelphia officer said, "There's always somebody through the window with a phone recording, expecting us to do something wrong."[1] This raises an important question: has policing succumbed to a "Ferguson effect"? The answer depends on whom you ask.

Crime in some cities started to increase at about the time Michael Brown was killed. Gun violence in Baltimore increased; homicides in Milwaukee increased by 180 percent; St. Louis saw a surge in robberies. Heather MacDonald of the conservative Manhattan Institute for Policy Research authored a *Wall Street Journal* op-ed wherein she described these increases as a "new nationwide crime wave."[2] She contrasted them with the first half of 2014 (before Michael Brown was killed), a period when crime was continuing to drop. "The most plausible explanation for the current surge in lawlessness," MacDonald wrote, was "the intense agitation against American police departments" since Ferguson. Was she correct?

A year after the Michael Brown shooting, *Time* magazine spent time with police officers in Philadelphia, attempting to gain perspective on life behind the badge post-Ferguson.[3] Reporters learned from ride-alongs with on-duty cops and numerous interviews with key personnel in the department that "everything is just harder." They also found that "confrontations are more numerous, and when the blood is up, so is the risk of the very thing everyone is trying to avoid—in the tattered, volatile neighborhoods to which the rest of the world until recently paid as little attention as possible."

Richard Rosenfeld, a professor at the University of Missouri–St. Louis, notes that while crime increased in some areas following Ferguson, it did not increase everywhere.[4] And by looking closely at St. Louis, which is close to Ferguson, he found no clear evidence that homicide (or any other violent crimes) began to surge immediately following Brown's death. Indeed, homicide was increasing in St. Louis before Brown was shot, even back in 2013.

A report by the Brennan Center for Justice reached a similar conclusion. While crime has surged in some of America's cities, such accounts "have been based on a patchwork of data, typically from a very small sample of cities. Without geographically complete and historically comparable data, it is difficult to discern whether the increases these articles report are purely local anomalies, or instead part of a larger national trend."[5] Other more recent studies echo these statements; there is little to no hard scientific evidence suggesting Ferguson has taken a toll on police work.[6]

Part 2 of this text covers policing. Chapter 4 looks at the history and organization of law enforcement organizations at all levels of government. Chapter 5 discusses the role and function of policing, including patrol, investigations, and community policing. Chapter 6 tackles a number of contemporary issues in policing, among them police culture, discretion, stress fatigue, and use of force. Chapter 6 also provides an introduction to the legal environment within which the police must operate.

Chapter 4   **Police in Society: History and Organization**

Chapter 5   **The Police: Role and Function**

Chapter 6   **Issues in Policing: Professional, Social, and Legal**

4 Police in Society:
History and Organization

t was supposed to be a peaceful protest against police shootings, but it would become the deadliest day for law enforcement since September 11, 2001. On July 7, 2016, Micah Xavier Johnson ambushed and fired at police officers during an event in downtown Dallas, killing five officers and injuring seven others. A bomb squad robot killed Johnson after negotiations for his surrender failed. Days later, another attack in Baton Rouge, Louisiana, left three officers dead and another three wounded. The shooter, Gavin Long, had used social media to post ominous messages. "Zero have been successful just over simple protesting," he said. "You gotta fight back."[7] In November of the same year, a lone killer gunned down two officers in Des Moines, Iowa, as they were patrolling in their vehicles, and another man ambushed and killed a police officer in San Antonio, Texas, who was in his cruiser writing a traffic ticket.[8]

The number of police fatalities peaked in 1974 and has generally fallen since, but 2016, the most recent year for which data are available as of this writing, witnessed quite an uptick; 135 officers were killed in the line of duty, up 10 percent from the year before.[9] More disturbing was a 56 percent increase in gun deaths, and nearly one in three officers who were fatally shot in 2016 were killed in ambush-style attacks. It used to be that traffic deaths were more common than gun deaths; in 2016, traffic-related deaths were eclipsed by shooting deaths. Policing remains a relatively safe profession, though, with far more on-the-job deaths in the construction and transportation sectors.[10]

Daniel Goncalves/Redux

LEARNING OBJECTIVES

LO1 Summarize characteristics of the first law enforcement agencies

LO2 Discuss the development of law enforcement in the United States

LO3 Analyze the problems of early police agencies

LO4 Discuss how reformers attempted to create professional police agencies

LO5 Describe the major changes in law enforcement between 1970 and today

LO6 Identify the major federal law enforcement agencies

LO7 Summarize the differences among state, county, and local law enforcement

LO8 Explain the role of technology in police work

The police are the gatekeepers of the criminal justice process. They initiate contact with violators of the law and decide whether to arrest them formally and start their journey through the criminal justice system, to settle the issue in an informal way (such as by issuing a warning), or to take no action at all. The strategic position of law enforcement officers, their visibility and contact with the public, and their use of weapons and arrest power kept them in the forefront of public thought for most of the twentieth century.

This and the following two chapters evaluate the history, role, organizational issues, and procedures of police agents and agencies and discuss the legal rules that control police behavior.

LO1 Summarize characteristics of the first law enforcement agencies

The History of Police

The origin of US police agencies, like the origins of criminal law, can be traced to early English society.[11] Before the Norman Conquest in 1066 BCE, no regular English police force existed. Every person living in the villages scattered throughout the countryside was responsible for aiding neighbors and protecting the settlement from thieves and marauders. This was known as the "pledge system." People were grouped in collectives of 10 families, called **tithings**, and were entrusted with policing their own minor problems. When trouble occurred, citizens were expected to make a **hue and cry**. Ten tithings were grouped into what was called a **hundred**, whose affairs were supervised by a **constable** appointed by the local nobleman. The constable, who might be considered the first real police officer, dealt with more serious breaches of the law.[12]

Shires, which resembled the counties of today, were controlled by the **shire reeve**, who was appointed by the Crown or by a local landowner to supervise the territory and ensure that order was kept. The shire reeve, a forerunner of today's **sheriff**, soon began to pursue and apprehend law violators as part of his duties.

In the thirteenth century, the **watch system** was created to help protect property in England's larger cities and towns. Watchmen patrolled at night and helped protect the community against robberies, fires, and disturbances. They reported to the area constable, who became the primary metropolitan law enforcement agent. In larger cities, such as London, the watchmen were organized within church parishes and were usually members of the parish they protected.

In 1326, the office of **justice of the peace** was created to assist the shire reeve in controlling the county. Eventually, these justices took on judicial functions in addition to their primary role as peacekeepers. The local constable became the operational assistant to the justice of the peace, supervising the night watchmen, investigating offenses, serving summonses, executing warrants, and securing prisoners. This system helped establish the relationship between police and the judiciary, which has continued for more than 670 years.

Private Police and Thief Takers

As the eighteenth century began, rising crime rates encouraged a new form of private, paid police, who profited both legally and criminally from the lack of formal police departments. These private police agents, referred to as "thief takers," were universally corrupt, taking profits not only from catching and informing on criminals but also from receiving stolen property, theft, intimidation, perjury, and blackmail. They often relieved their prisoners of money and stolen goods and made even more income by accepting hush money, giving perjured evidence, swearing false oaths, and operating extortion rackets. Petty debtors were especially easy targets for those who combined thief taking with the keeping of alehouses and taverns. While prisoners were incarcerated, their health and safety were entirely at the whim of the thief takers, who were free to charge virtually whatever they wanted for board and other necessities. Court bailiffs who also acted as thief takers were the most passionately detested legal profiteers. They seized debtors and held them in small lockups, where they forced their victims to pay exorbitant prices for food and lodging.

tithings In medieval England, a group of 10 families who collectively dealt with minor disturbances and breaches of the peace.

hue and cry In medieval England, a call for assistance. The policy of self-help that prevailed in villages demanded that everyone respond if a citizen raised a hue and cry to get their aid.

hundred In medieval England, a group of 100 families responsible for maintaining order and trying minor offenses.

constable In medieval England, an appointed official who administered and supervised the legal affairs of a small community.

shire reeve In medieval England, the senior law enforcement figure in a county; the forerunner of today's sheriff.

sheriff The chief law enforcement officer in a county.

watch system During the Middle Ages in England, men were organized in church parishes to guard at night against disturbances and breaches of the peace under the direction of the local constable.

justice of the peace Established in 1326 England, the office was created to help the shire reeve in controlling the county; it later took on judicial functions.

The thief takers' use of violence was notorious. They went armed and were prepared to maim or kill to gain their objectives. Before he was hanged in 1725, Jack Wild, the most notorious thief taker, "had two fractures in his skull and his bald head was covered with silver plates. He had seventeen wounds in various parts of his body from swords, daggers, and gunshots, [and] … his throat had been cut in the course of his duties."[13]

Henry Fielding (famed author of *Tom Jones*), along with Saunders Welch and his brother John Fielding, sought to clean up the thief-taking system. Appointed a city magistrate in 1748, Henry Fielding operated his own group of paid police out of Bow Street in London, directing and deploying them throughout the city and its environs, deciding which cases to investigate and what streets to protect. His agents were carefully instructed on their legitimate powers and duties. Fielding's Bow Street Runners were a marked improvement over the earlier paid police because they actually had an administrative structure that improved recordkeeping and investigative procedures.

Creating Public Police

In 1829, Sir Robert Peel, England's home secretary, guided through Parliament an "Act for Improving the Police in and near the Metropolis." The Metropolitan Police Act established the first organized police force in London. Composed of more than 1,000 men, the London police force was structured along military lines; its members were known from then on as "bobbies," after its creator. They wore a distinctive uniform and were led by two magistrates, who were later given the title of commissioner. However, the ultimate responsibility for the police fell to the home secretary and consequently to the Parliament.

The early bobbies suffered from many of the same ills as their forebears. Many were corrupt, they were unsuccessful at stopping crime, and they were influenced by the wealthy. Owners of houses of ill repute, who in the past had guaranteed their undisturbed operations by bribing watchmen, now turned their attention to the bobbies. Metropolitan police administrators fought constantly to terminate cowardly, corrupt, and alcoholic officers, dismissing in the beginning about one-third of the bobbies each year.

Law Enforcement in Colonial America

Law enforcement in colonial America paralleled the British model. In the colonies, the county sheriff became the most important law enforcement agent. In addition to keeping the peace and fighting crime, sheriffs collected taxes, supervised elections, and handled a great deal of other legal business.

The colonial sheriff did not patrol or seek out crime. Instead, he reacted to citizens' complaints and investigated crimes that had occurred. His salary, related to his effectiveness, was paid on a fee system. Sheriffs received a fixed amount for every arrest made. Unfortunately, their tax-collecting chores were more lucrative than fighting crime, so law enforcement was not one of their primary concerns. In the cities, law enforcement was the province of the town marshal, who was aided, often unwillingly, by a variety of constables, night watchmen, police justices, and city council members. However, local governments had little power of administration, and enforcement of the criminal law was largely an individual or community responsibility. In rural areas in the South, slave patrols charged with recapturing escaped slaves were an early—if loathsome—form of law enforcement.[14] When these patrols apprehended runaway slaves, they administered "justice" on the spot, often with violence. In the western territories, individual initiative was encouraged by the practice of offering rewards for the capture of felons. If trouble arose, the town vigilance committee might form a posse to chase offenders. These vigilantes were called on to eradicate such social problems as theft of livestock through force or intimidation; the San Francisco Vigilance Committee actively pursued criminals in the mid-nineteenth century.

Early Police Agencies

The modern police department was born out of urban mob violence that wracked the nation's cities in the nineteenth century. Boston created the first formal US police department in 1838. New York formed its police department in 1844, and Philadelphia

LO2 Discuss the development of law enforcement in the United States

LO3 Analyze the problems of early police agencies

vigilantes Groups of citizens who tracked down wanted criminals in the Old West.

Print Collector/HIP/The Image Works

John X. Beidler, pictured here, was leader of the Montana Vigilantes, a secretive band formed to fight crime in Montana in the 1860s. He later became a stagecoach guard and a deputy US marshal. Vigilante groups like Beidler's were precursors to organized police forces in colonial America.

REALITY CHECK

Myth or Reality?

During the nineteenth century, the police were regarded as competent and professional.

MYTH. Policing in the 1800s was anything but professional. Competence often was lacking as well. It would not be until the 1900s that police departments began making major strides toward professionalism.

Is policing a profession today? What are the hallmarks of a profession?

followed in 1854. The new police departments replaced the night-watch system and relegated constables and sheriffs to serving court orders and running jails.

At first, the urban police departments inherited the functions of the institutions they replaced. For example, Boston police were charged with maintaining public health until 1853, and, in New York, the police were responsible for street sweeping until 1881. Politics dominated the departments and determined the recruitment of new officers and the promotion of supervisors. An individual with the right connections could be hired despite a lack of qualifications. Early police agencies were corrupt, brutal, and inefficient.[15] At first, police were expected to live in the area they patrolled, but as the nineteenth century drew to a close, officers left the most dangerous areas and commuted to work, thereby separating themselves from the people they were being asked to supervise and control.[16]

In the late nineteenth century, police work was highly desirable because it paid more than most other blue-collar jobs. By 1880, the average factory worker earned $450 a year, whereas a metropolitan police officer made $900 annually. For immigrant groups, having enough political clout to be appointed to the police department was an important step up the social ladder.[17] However, job security was uncertain because it depended on the local political machine staying in power.

Police work itself was primitive. There were few of even the simplest technological innovations common today, such as centralized recordkeeping. Most officers patrolled on foot, without backup or the ability to call for help. Officers were commonly taunted by local toughs and responded with force and brutality. The long-standing conflict between police and the public was born in the difficulty that untrained, unprofessional officers had in patrolling the streets of nineteenth-century US cities and in breaking up and controlling labor disputes. Police were not crime fighters as we know them today. Their main role was maintaining order, and their power was almost unchecked. The average officer had little training, no education in the law, and a minimum of supervision, yet the police became virtual judges of law and fact with the ability to exercise unlimited discretion.[18]

Police during the nineteenth century were regarded as incompetent and corrupt and were disliked by the people they served. The police role was only minimally directed at law enforcement. Its primary function was serving as the enforcement arm of the reigning political power, protecting private property, and keeping control of the ever-rising numbers of foreign immigrants.

Police agencies evolved slowly through the second half of the nineteenth century. Uniforms were introduced in 1853 in New York. The first technological breakthroughs in police operations came in the area of communications. The linking of precincts to central headquarters by telegraph began in the 1850s. In 1867, the first telegraph police boxes were installed; an officer could turn a key in a box, and his location and number would automatically register at headquarters. Additional technological advances were made in transportation. The Detroit Police Department outfitted some of its patrol officers with bicycles in 1897. By 1913, the motorcycle was being used by departments in the eastern part of the nation. The first police car was used in Akron, Ohio, in 1910, and the police wagon became popular in Cincinnati in 1912.[19] Nonpolice functions, such as care of the streets, had begun to be abandoned by police departments after the Civil War.

The control of police departments by local politicians impeded effective law enforcement and fostered an atmosphere of graft and corruption. In the nineteenth century, big-city police were still not respected by the public, were largely unsuccessful in their role as crime stoppers, and were involved in no progressive activities.

Policing in the Modern Era

The modern era of policing can be traced from the turn of the nineteenth century to the present. What are the major events that occurred during this period?

L04 Discuss how reformers attempted to create professional police agencies

The Emergence of Professionalism

In an effort to reduce police corruption, civic leaders in a number of jurisdictions created police administrative boards to reduce local officials' control over the police. These tribunals were responsible for appointing police administrators and controlling police affairs. In many instances, these measures failed because the private citizens appointed to the review boards lacked expertise in the intricacies of police work. Another reform movement was the takeover of some metropolitan police agencies by state legislators. Although police budgets were financed through local taxes, rural politicians in the state capitals usurped control of the police. New York City temporarily lost authority over its police force in 1857. It was not until the first decades of the twentieth century that cities regained control of their police forces.

The Boston police strike of 1919 heightened interest in police reform. The strike came about basically because police officers were dissatisfied with their status in society. Other professions were unionizing and increasing their standard of living, but police salaries lagged behind. The Boston police officers' organization, the Boston Social Club, voted to become a union affiliated with the American Federation of Labor. The officers went out on strike on September 9, 1919. Rioting and looting broke out, resulting in Governor Calvin Coolidge's mobilization of the state militia to take over the city. Public support turned against the police, and the strike was broken. Eventually, all the striking officers were fired and replaced by new recruits. The Boston police strike ended police unionism for decades and solidified power in the hands of reactionary, autocratic police administrators. In the aftermath of the strike, various local, state, and federal crime commissions began to investigate the extent of crime and the ability of the justice system to deal with it effectively; they then made recommendations to improve police effectiveness.[20] With the onset of the Depression, however, justice reform became a less important issue than economic revival, and little changed in the nature of policing for many years.

At about the same time, a number of nationally recognized leaders called for measures to help improve and professionalize the police. In 1893, the International Association of Chiefs of Police (IACP), a professional society, was formed. The IACP called for creating a civil service police force and for removing political influence and control. The most famous police reformer of the time was August Vollmer. While serving as police chief of Berkeley, California, Vollmer instituted university training for young officers and helped develop the School of Criminology at the University of California at Berkeley. Vollmer's disciples included O. W. Wilson, who pioneered the use of advanced training for officers and was instrumental in applying modern management and administrative techniques to policing. During this period, police professionalism was equated with an incorruptible, tough, highly trained, rule-oriented department organized along militaristic lines. The most respected department was that of Los Angeles, which emphasized the police as incorruptible crime fighters who would not question the authority of the central command.

Heritage Image Partnership Ltd/Alamy Stock Photo

Great precaution is taken to guard police headquarters in Pemberton Square during the Boston police strike of 1919. Here a cavalryman of the state guard rides a horse previously used by the mounted policemen who went on strike. The Boston police strike ended police unionism for decades and solidified power in the hands of reactionary, autocratic police administrators. In the aftermath of the strike, various local, state, and federal crime commissions began to investigate the extent of crime and the ability of the justice system to deal with it and made recommendations to improve police effectiveness.

The 1960s and Beyond

Turmoil and crisis were the hallmarks of policing during the 1960s. Throughout this decade, the Supreme Court handed down a number of decisions designed to control police operations and procedures. Police officers were now required to follow strict legal guidelines when questioning suspects, conducting searches, and wiretapping, among other duties. As the civil rights of suspects were significantly expanded, police complained that they were being "handcuffed by the courts."

Also during this time, civil unrest produced a growing tension between police and the public. African Americans, who were battling for recognition and enforcement of their rights and freedoms in the civil rights movement, found themselves confronting police lines. When riots broke out in New York, Detroit, Los Angeles, and other cities between 1964 and 1968, the spark that ignited conflict often involved the police. When students across the nation began marching in demonstrations against the Vietnam War, local police departments were called on to keep order. Police forces were ill equipped and poorly trained to deal with these social problems; it is not surprising that the 1960s were marked by a number of bloody confrontations between the police and the public.

Compounding these problems was a rapidly growing crime rate. The number of violent and property crimes increased dramatically. Drug addiction and abuse grew to be national concerns, common among all social classes. Urban police departments could not control the crime rate, and police officers resented the demands placed on them by dissatisfied citizens.

LO5 Describe the major changes in law enforcement between 1970 and today

The 1970s witnessed many structural changes in police agencies themselves. The end of the Vietnam War significantly reduced tensions between students and police. The relationship between police and minorities was still rocky, however. Local fears and distrust, combined with conservative federal policies, encouraged police departments to control what was perceived as an emerging minority group "threat."[21]

Increased federal government support for criminal justice greatly influenced police operations. During the decade, the Law Enforcement Assistance Administration (LEAA) devoted a significant portion of its funds to police agencies. Although a number of police departments used this money to purchase little-used hardware, such as antiriot gear, most of it went to supporting innovative research on police work and advanced training of police officers. Perhaps most significant, the LEAA's Law Enforcement Education Program helped thousands of officers further their college education. Hundreds of criminal justice programs were developed on college campuses around the country, providing a pool of highly educated police recruits. LEAA funds were also used to transfer technology originally developed in other fields into law enforcement. Technological innovations involving computers transformed the way police kept records, investigated crimes, and communicated with one another. State training academies improved the way police learned to deal with such issues as job stress, community conflict, and interpersonal relations. More women and minorities were recruited into police work as well. Affirmative action programs helped to slowly alter the ethnic, racial, and gender composition of US policing.

As the 1980s began, the police role seemed to be changing significantly. A number of experts acknowledged that the police were not simply crime fighters and called for police to develop a greater awareness of community issues, which resulted in the emergence of the community policing concept.[22]

Police unions, which began to grow again in the late 1960s, continued to have a great impact on departmental administration in the 1980s. Unions fought for and won increased salaries and benefits for their members. In many instances, union efforts eroded the power of the police chief to make unquestioned policy and personnel decisions. During the decade, chiefs of police commonly consulted with union leaders before making significant decisions about departmental operations.

Although police operations improved markedly during this time, police departments were also beset by problems that impeded their effectiveness. State and local budgets were cut back during the Reagan administration, and federal support for innovative police programs was severely curtailed with the demise of the LEAA.

Police–community relations continued to be a major problem. Riots and incidents of urban conflict occurred in some of the nation's largest cities.[23] They triggered persistent concern about what the police role should be, especially in inner-city neighborhoods.

The 1990s began on a sour note and ended with an air of optimism. The incident that helped change the face of American policing occurred on March 3, 1991, when Rodney King and his friend Bryant Allen were driving in Los Angeles. They refused to stop when signaled by a police car behind them but instead increased their speed; King, the driver, was apparently drunk or on drugs. When police finally stopped the car, they delivered 56 baton blows and six kicks to King in a period of two minutes, producing 11 skull fractures, brain damage, and kidney damage. They did not realize that their actions were being videotaped by an observer, who gave the tape to the media. The officers involved were eventually tried and acquitted in a suburban court by an all-white jury, a decision that set off six days of rioting.[24]

The King case prompted an era of reform. Several police experts decreed that the nation's police forces should be evaluated not on their crime-fighting ability but on their courteousness, deportment, and helpfulness. Interest was renewed in reviving an earlier style of police work featuring foot patrols and increased citizen contact. Police departments began to embrace new forms of policing that stressed cooperation with the community and problem solving. The following are some of the most notable achievements of police departments in the 1990s:

- The intellectual caliber of the police rose dramatically.
- Police began to use advanced management techniques and applied empirical data to their decision making.
- Standards of police conduct climbed. Despite well-publicized incidents of brutality, police tended to treat the public more fairly, more equitably, and more civilly than they did in the 1960s.
- Police became more diverse in race and gender.
- The work of the police became intellectually more demanding, requiring an array of new specialized knowledge about technology, forensic analysis, and crime.
- Police gradually accepted civilian review of police discipline.[25]

The President's Task Force on 21st Century Policing

On December 18, 2014, President Barack Obama signed an executive order establishing the President's Task Force on 21st Century Policing. Task force members, who included law enforcement representatives, prominent academics, and community leaders, solicited input from a variety of stakeholders and members of the public in an effort to identity the most important priorities for modern policing. The task force submitted its final report in 2015.[26] It offered a number of recommendations in six specific areas: building trust and legitimacy, policy and oversight, technology and social media, community policing and crime reduction, training and education, and officer safety and wellness. Following are some key excerpts from the task force's report:

Building Trust and Legitimacy

Law enforcement culture should embrace a guardian—rather than a warrior—mindset to build trust and legitimacy both within agencies and with the public. Toward that end, law enforcement agencies should adopt procedural justice as the guiding principle for internal and external policies and practices to guide their interactions with rank and file officers and with the citizens they serve. Law enforcement agencies should also establish a culture of transparency and accountability to build public trust and legitimacy. This is critical to ensuring decision making is understood and in accord with stated policy.

Baltimore Police Officer Edward Gillespie, of the education and training division, teaches a "Fairness and Impartiality in Policing Implicit Bias" class to in-service officers at the Baltimore Police Training Academy.

Policy and Oversight

. . . law enforcement agencies should have clear and comprehensive policies on the use of force (including training on the importance of de-escalation), mass demonstrations (including the appropriate use of equipment, particularly rifles and armored personnel carriers), consent before searches, gender identification, racial profiling, and performance measures—among others such as external and independent investigations and prosecutions of officer-involved shootings and other use of force situations and in-custody deaths. These policies should also include provisions for the collection of demographic data on all parties involved. All policies and aggregate data should be made publicly available to ensure transparency.

Technology and Social Media

Implementing new technologies can give police departments an opportunity to fully engage and educate communities in a dialogue about their expectations for transparency, accountability, and privacy

Community Policing and Crime Reduction

. . . law enforcement agencies should develop and adopt policies and strategies that reinforce the importance of community engagement in managing public safety. Law enforcement agencies should also engage in multidisciplinary, community team approaches for planning, implementing, and responding to crisis situations with complex causal factors.

Training and Education

To ensure the high quality and effectiveness of training and education, law enforcement agencies should engage community members, particularly those with special expertise, in the training process and provide leadership training to all personnel throughout their careers.

Officer Wellness and Safety

Law enforcement agencies should also promote wellness and safety at every level of the organization. For instance, every law enforcement officer should be provided with individual tactical first aid kits and training as well as anti-ballistic vests. In addition, law enforcement agencies should adopt policies that require officers to wear seat belts and bullet-proof vests and provide training to raise awareness of the consequences of failure to do so.[27]

Many of these recommendations have already been implemented—at least to some extent—in America's police departments. Ferguson brought legitimacy front and center, but law enforcement has been working for years to improve relationships with the public it serves. Likewise, a number of departments have solicited community input in their policy-making deliberations. Community policing has been popular for years. Safety and wellness have not been ignored. The question becomes, then, how much more can be done in these areas? Another question concerns the proper role of federal government intervention. The task force called for expanded federal support in each of the six areas. Is this the ideal approach?

More importantly still, will law enforcement further usher in the reforms called for by the task force? Not everyone is supportive of the task force's recommendations. In a critique of the final report, law professor Julian Cook argued that "recommendations" are not enough.[28] In his view, "meaningful reform is dependent less upon the establishment of task forces, the development of innovative ideas, and the art of persuasive argumentation than upon legislative and judicial dictates that mandate change." He pointed to a number of Supreme Court decisions in recent decades that have, in his view, eroded individual safeguards, prompting the type of "aggressive" policing the President's Task Force was assembled to address.

Policing and Law Enforcement Today

Contemporary law enforcement agencies are still undergoing transformation. An effort has been ongoing to make police "user friendly" by decentralizing police departments and making them responsive to community needs. Police and law enforcement agencies are also adapting to the changing nature of crime: they must be prepared to handle terrorism, Internet fraud schemes, and identity theft, as well as crimes like rape, robbery, and burglary.

Law enforcement duties are distributed across local, county, state, and federal jurisdictions. Approximately 477,000 sworn law enforcement officers are employed in the United States in more than 12,000 local, county, and state agencies.[29] The federal government employs another 120,000 full time law enforcement officials.[30]

Federal Law Enforcement Agencies

The federal government has a number of law enforcement agencies designed to protect the rights and privileges of US citizens; no single agency has unlimited jurisdiction, and each has been created to enforce specific laws and cope with particular situations. Federal agencies have no particular rank order or hierarchy of command or responsibility; each reports to a specific department or bureau.

Dozens of federal law enforcement agencies exist both inside and outside the cabinet-level departments. Here we focus on law enforcement agencies in two cabinet-level departments: the US Justice Department and the Department of Homeland Security.

US JUSTICE DEPARTMENT AGENCIES The US Justice Department houses four of the better-known federal law enforcement agencies.

- **Federal Bureau of Investigation (FBI)** The FBI is an investigative agency with jurisdiction over all matters in which the United States is or may be an interested party. Its jurisdiction is limited, however, to federal laws, including all federal statutes not specifically assigned to other agencies. The FBI has approximately 35,000 employees, including almost 14,000 special agents and 21,000 support personnel who perform professional, administrative, technical, clerical, craft, trade, or maintenance operations.[31] Since 9/11, the FBI has announced a reformulation of its priorities, making protecting the United States from terrorist attack its number one commitment. It is now charged with coordinating intelligence collection with the Border Patrol, the Secret Service, and the CIA. Among the agency's other activities are gathering crime statistics, running a comprehensive crime laboratory, and training local law enforcement officers.

REALITYCHECK
Myth or Reality?

Federal law enforcement agencies are housed solely within cabinet-level departments (such as the State Department).

MYTH. Law enforcement agencies exist throughout the federal government.

Many federal law enforcement agencies are not associated with a particular cabinet-level department (an example is the Postal Inspection Service). Try to identify some of the lesser-known federal law enforcement agencies.

LO6 Identify the major federal law enforcement agencies

Federal Bureau of Investigation (FBI) The arm of the US Justice Department that investigates violations of federal law, seeks to protect America from terrorist attacks, gathers crime statistics, runs a comprehensive crime laboratory, and helps train local law enforcement officers.

FBI agents and other law enforcement officials speak outside a restaurant owned by the father of Ahmad Khan Rahimi, who was arrested in connection with three bomb explosions in New York City and nearby towns in September 2016. Though no one was killed in the attacks, 31 people were wounded. Rahimi faces federal and state charges for attempted murder and use of weapons of mass destruction, among other crimes.

Drew Angerer/Getty Images News/Getty Images

Drug Enforcement Administration (DEA) The federal agency that enforces federal drug control laws.

- **Drug Enforcement Administration (DEA)** DEA agents assist local and state authorities in investigating illegal drug use and carrying out independent surveillance and enforcement activities to control the importation of narcotics. For example, DEA agents work with foreign governments in cooperative efforts aimed at destroying opium and marijuana crops at their source—hard-to-find fields tucked away in the interiors of Latin America, Asia, Europe, and Africa. Undercover DEA agents infiltrate drug rings and simulate buying narcotics to arrest drug dealers.

Bureau of Alcohol, Tobacco, Firearms, and Explosives (ATF) Federal agency with jurisdiction over the illegal sale, importation, and criminal misuse of firearms and explosives and the distribution of untaxed liquor and cigarettes.

- **Bureau of Alcohol, Tobacco, Firearms, and Explosives (ATF)** The ATF helps control sales of untaxed liquor and cigarettes and, through the Gun Control Act of 1968 and the Organized Crime Control Act of 1970, has jurisdiction over the illegal sale, importation, and criminal misuse of firearms and explosives.

US Marshals Service Federal agency whose jurisdiction includes protecting federal officials, transporting criminal defendants, and tracking down fugitives.

- **US Marshals Service** The US Marshals Service is America's oldest federal law enforcement agency and one of the most versatile. Its almost 3,700 deputy marshals and criminal investigators perform a number of functions, including judicial security, fugitive investigations, witness protection, prisoner transportation, prisoner services (the agency houses nearly 55,000 federal detainees each day), and administration of the US Justice Department's Asset Forfeiture Program.[32]

HOMELAND SECURITY AGENCIES Soon after the 9/11 attacks on the Pentagon and the World Trade Center towers in New York City, President George W. Bush proposed the creation of a new cabinet-level agency called the **Department of Homeland Security (DHS)**. On November 19, 2002, Congress passed legislation authorizing the creation of the DHS and assigned it the mission of providing intelligence analysis and infrastructure protection, strengthening the borders, improving the use of science and technology to counter weapons of mass destruction, and creating a comprehensive response and recovery division. Rather than working from the ground up, the DHS combined a number of existing agencies into a superagency that carries out a variety of missions from border security to infrastructure protection. Two of the main law enforcement agencies housed within DHS are described in some detail next.

Department of Homeland Security (DHS) Federal agency responsible for preventing terrorist attacks within the United States, reducing America's vulnerability to terrorism, and minimizing the damage and assisting in recovery from attacks that do occur.

Customs and Border Protection (CBP) Federal agency responsible for the control and protection of America's borders and ports of entry. Its first priority is keeping terrorists and their weapons out of the United States.

- **Customs and Border Protection (CBP)** After 9/11, the US Border Patrol, portions of the US Customs Service, the Immigration and Naturalization Service, and the Animal and Plant Health Inspection Service were combined into one office of Customs and Border Protection. The agency employs almost 60,000 personnel and is primarily responsible for protection of America's borders and ports of entry.[33] The largest and most visible element of CBP is the Border Patrol. Its approximately

22,000 agents combine to form one of the largest uniformed law enforcement agencies in the United States.

- **Secret Service** The US Secret Service performs two main functions. The more visible of these is protection of national leaders, notably the president but also the vice president, the president-elect, the vice president–elect, the immediate families of these individuals, former presidents and their families, visiting heads of state, and other officials. The Secret Service was first established as a law enforcement entity in 1865 and was tasked with investigating the counterfeiting of US currency. It continues this investigative function today. Since 1984, Secret Service investigative activities have been expanded to include the investigation of financial institution fraud, computer and telecommunications fraud, false identification documents, and other criminal activities.

State Law Enforcement Agencies

Unlike municipal police departments, state police were legislatively created to deal with the growing incidence of crime in nonurban areas, a consequence of the increase in population mobility and the advent of personalized mass transportation in the form of the automobile. County sheriffs—elected officials with occasionally corrupt or questionable motives—had proved ineffective in dealing with the wide-ranging criminal activities that developed during the latter half of the nineteenth century. In addition, most local police agencies were unable to protect effectively against highly mobile lawbreakers who randomly struck at cities and towns throughout a state. In response to citizens' demands for effective and efficient law enforcement, state governors began to develop plans for police agencies that would be responsible to the state, instead of being tied to local politics and possible corruption.

The Texas Rangers, created in 1835, was one of the first state police agencies formed. Essentially a military outfit that patrolled the Mexican border, it was followed by the Massachusetts State Constables in 1865 and the Arizona Rangers in 1901. The states of Connecticut (1903) and Pennsylvania (1905) formed the first truly modern state police agencies.[34]

Today, about 23 state police agencies have the same general police powers as municipal police and are territorially limited in their exercise of law enforcement regulations only by the state's boundaries. They provide investigative services to smaller communities when the need arises. The remaining state police agencies are primarily responsible for highway patrol and traffic law enforcement.

Some state police direct most of their attention to the enforcement of traffic laws. Others are restricted by legislation from becoming involved in the enforcement of certain areas of the law. For example, in some jurisdictions, state police are prohibited from becoming involved in strikes or other labor disputes, unless violence erupts.

The nation's 88,000 state police employees (about 58,000 officers and 30,000 civilians) carry out a variety of functions besides law enforcement and highway safety, including maintaining a training academy and providing emergency medical services.[35] State police crime laboratories aid local departments in investigating crime scenes and analyzing evidence. State police also provide special services and technical expertise in such areas as bomb-site analysis and homicide investigation. Some state police departments, such as California's, are involved in highly sophisticated traffic and highway safety programs, including the use of helicopters for patrol and rescue, the testing of safety devices for cars, and the conducting of postmortem examinations to determine the causes of fatal accidents.

STATE LAW ENFORCEMENT AND THE WAR ON TERROR

In the wake of the 9/11 attacks, a number of states have beefed up their intelligence-gathering capabilities and aimed them directly at homeland security. For example, the Texas Homeland Security office coordinates the resources and responses needed to prevent terrorist attacks in the Lone Star state. The state's strategic plan for homeland security prioritizes the following:

1. *Prevent.* Prevent terrorist attacks in Texas, and prevent criminal enterprises from operating successfully in Texas.

REALITYCHECK
Myth or Reality?

The core mission of the FBI is to enforce the criminal laws of the United States.

MYTH. Since 9/11, the FBI's priorities have changed. Now protection of the United States from terrorist attacks ranks near the top of its priority list.

To what extent does the FBI's decision to give priority to protection from terrorism affect its ability to fight other types of crime? Has America's law enforcement apparatus overreacted to the threat of terrorism?

Secret Service Federal agency responsible for executive protection and for investigation of counterfeiting and various forms of financial fraud.

WEB APP 4.1 Visit the Department of Homeland Security's website and examine its organizational chart at **http://www.dhs.gov /organizational-chart**. What other law enforcement agencies are part of DHS? Compare and contrast their duties with those of Customs and Border Protection and the Secret Service.

LO7 Summarize the differences among state, county, and local law enforcement

2. *Protect*. Reduce vulnerability to natural disasters, criminal and terrorist attacks, and catastrophic events.
3. *Mitigate*. Minimize the impact of terrorist and criminal attacks.
4. *Respond*. Improve the state's ability to respond to attacks and minimize damage.
5. *Recover*. Promote rapid, effective, and comprehensive recovery programs.[36]

County Law Enforcement Agencies

The county sheriff's role has evolved from that of the early English shire reeve, whose primary duty was to assist the royal judges in trying prisoners and enforcing sentences. From the time of the westward expansion in the United States until municipal departments were developed, the sheriff was often the sole legal authority over vast territories.

Today, sheriff's offices contain about 350,000 full-time employees, including about 189,000 sworn personnel.[37] The duties of a sheriff's department vary according to the size and degree of development of the county. In some jurisdictions, sheriff's offices provide basic law enforcement services such as performing routine patrols, responding to citizen calls for service, and investigating crimes.

Other standard tasks of a typical sheriff's department are serving civil process (summons and court orders), providing court security, and operating the county jail. Less commonly, sheriff's departments may serve as coroners, tax collectors, overseers of highways and bridges, custodians of the county treasury, and providers of fire, animal control, and emergency medical services. In years past, sheriff's offices also conducted executions. Typically, the law enforcement functions of a sheriff's department are restricted to unincorporated areas of a county, unless a city or town police department requests its help.

Some sheriff's departments are exclusively law enforcement oriented, some carry out court-related duties only, and some are involved solely in correctional and judicial matters and not in law enforcement. However, a majority are full-service programs that carry out judicial, correctional, and law enforcement activities. As a rule, agencies serving heavily populated areas (over 1 million) are devoted to maintaining county correctional facilities, whereas those in smaller population areas are focused on law enforcement.

COUNTY LAW ENFORCEMENT AND THE WAR ON TERROR A number of counties are now engaging in antiterror and homeland security activities. For example, the Harris County, Texas, Office of Homeland Security and Emergency Management

A woman's belongings are searched as Los Angeles County Sheriff's deputies stand guard over rail passengers at the Universal City Red Line Metro train station on December 6, 2016. Security was increased in response to federal and Los Angeles officials saying they were alerted by authorities in another country that an imminent and very specific threat had been made against the city's Red Line commuter rail system.

David McNew/Getty Images News/Getty Images

(OHSEM) is responsible for an emergency management plan that prepares for public recovery in the event of natural or manmade disasters, catastrophes, or attacks. It works in conjunction with the state, federal, and local authorities, including the city of Houston and other municipalities in the surrounding Harris County area, when required. If needed, OHSEM activates an Emergency Operations Center to allow coordination of all support agencies to provide continuity of services to the public. OHSEM is responsible for advisement, notification, and assembly of services that are in the best interest of the citizens of Harris County. They prepare and distribute information and procedures governing the same.[38]

Similarly, in Montgomery County, Maryland, the Homeland Security Department prevents, prepares for, and protects against major threats that may harm, disrupt, or destroy the community, its commerce, and institutions. Its mission is to effectively manage and coordinate the county's unified response, mitigation, and recovery from the consequences of such disasters or events should they occur. It also serves to educate the public on emergency preparedness for all hazards and conducts outreach to diverse and special populations to protect, secure, and sustain critical infrastructures to ensure the continuity of essential services.[39]

WEB APP 4.2 Go to the website for the US Justice Department's Bureau of Justice Statistics at **https://www.bjs.gov/**. Follow the "Law Enforcement" link, and determine how many law enforcement agencies exist in the United States. Is the number accurate? Why or why not?

Metropolitan Law Enforcement Agencies

Local police form the majority of the nation's authorized law enforcement personnel. Metropolitan police departments range in size from the New York City Police Department, with almost 40,000 full-time officers and 10,000 civilian employees, to rural police departments, which may consist of a single officer. At last count, nearly 12,000 local police departments nationwide had an estimated 600,000 full-time employees, including about 477,000 sworn personnel.[40] Metropolitan police departments are attracting applicants who value an exciting, well-paid job that also offers them an opportunity to provide valuable community service. Salaries in municipal police agencies are becoming more competitive.

Most TV police shows feature the crime-fighting efforts of big-city police officers, but in an overwhelming majority of departments, there are fewer than 50 officers that serve a population of fewer than 25,000. Recent data reveal that nearly three-quarters of all local police departments serve populations of fewer than 10,000 people. Around 650 such agencies employ just one sworn officer.

Municipal police officers' responsibilities are immense, and they are often forced to make split-second decisions on life-and-death matters. At the same time, they must be sensitive to the needs of citizens who are often of diverse racial and ethnic backgrounds. What's more, local police perform multiple roles, including (but not limited to) investigating crimes, identifying suspects, and making arrests (see Exhibit 4.1).

Smaller agencies can have trouble carrying out many of the same functions as their big-city counterparts; the hundreds of small police agencies in each state often provide duplicate services. Whether consolidating smaller police agencies into "superagencies" would improve services is often debated among police experts. Smaller municipal agencies can provide important specialized services that might have to be relinquished if they were combined and incorporated into larger departments. Another approach has been to maintain smaller departments but to link them via computerized information-sharing and resource-management networks.

EXHIBIT 4.1 Core Functions of Municipal Police

Law Enforcement Functions
- Identifying criminal suspects
- Investigating crimes
- Apprehending offenders and participating in their trials
- Deterring crime through patrol
- Enhancing public safety by maintaining a visible police presence

Order Maintenance Functions
- Resolving conflict and keeping the peace
- Maintaining a sense of community security and public order (i.e., peacekeeping) within the patrol area
- Keeping vehicular and pedestrian movement efficient
- Promoting civil order

Service Functions
- Aiding individuals in danger or in need of assistance
- Providing emergency medical services
- Providing public education and outreach
- Maintaining and administering police services
- Recruiting and training new police officers

private policing Crime prevention, detection, and the apprehension of criminals carried out by private organizations or individuals for commercial purposes.

METROPOLITAN LAW ENFORCEMENT AND THE WAR ON TERROR Federal and county law enforcement agencies are not alone in responding to the threat of terrorism. And, of course, nowhere is the threat of terrorism being taken more seriously than in New York City—one of the main targets of the 9/11 attacks—which has undertaken a number of antiterrorism initiatives, including the formation of its Counterterrorism Bureau.[41] Teams within the bureau have been trained to examine potential targets in the city and insulate those targets from possible attack. The city's bridges, the Empire State Building, Rockefeller Center, and the United Nations are viewed as prime targets. Bureau detectives are assigned overseas to work with the police in several foreign cities, including in Canada and Israel. Detectives have been assigned as liaisons with the FBI and with Interpol in Lyon, France. The Intelligence Division has also been revamped, and agents monitor foreign newspapers and Internet sites. The department has set up backup command centers in different parts of the city in case a terror attack puts headquarters out of operation. Several backup senior command teams have been created so that if people at the highest levels of the department are killed, individuals will already have been tapped to step into their jobs.

The Counterterrorism Bureau has assigned more than 100 city police detectives to work with FBI agents as part of a Joint Terrorist Task Force. In addition, the Intelligence Division's 700 investigators devote 35 to 40 percent of their resources to counterterrorism—up from about 2 percent before January 2002. The department also draws on the expertise of other institutions around the city. For example, medical specialists have been enlisted to monitor daily developments in the city's hospitals to detect any suspicious outbreaks of illness that might reflect a biological attack. And the police conduct joint drills with the New York Fire Department to avoid the problems in communication and coordination that marked the emergency response on September 11.

Private Policing

Supplementing local police forces is a burgeoning private security industry. Private security service, or **private policing**, has become a multibillion-dollar industry with well in excess of 10,000 firms and more than 2 million employees.[42] Even some federal police services have been privatized to cut expenses. Private police and security officials outnumber public/governmental police by a factor of three to one.[43]

Some private security firms have become billion-dollar companies. For example, G4S Security Solutions is one of the world's largest providers of security services. Among its clients are a number of Fortune 500 companies. It has several subsidiaries that work for the federal government. It has also been a contractor for National Aeronautics and Space Administration (NASA) and the US Army, and it has provided security and emergency response services to local governments—helping them guard their public transport systems, among other services. G4S has helped the US government protect nuclear reactors, guards the Trans-Alaska Pipeline System, and maintains security in closed government facilities. It also maintains a Custom Protection Officer Division, made up of highly trained uniformed security officers assigned to critical or complex facilities or situations requiring special skills in such places as government buildings, banks, and other special situations. (The Careers in Criminal Justice feature discusses a career in the private security area.)

REASONS FOR PRIVATE POLICING Private policing is so popular for the following three reasons:

- A preference for nongovernmental provision of important services, particularly crime control. Many people feel the private sector can do a more effective job than traditional government-led policing.
- The growth of mass private property, particularly large shopping malls and other properties, that attract large numbers of consumers and have little other police protection.
- A belief that government police are not capable of providing the level of service and presence that the public desires.[44]

PRIVATE AND PUBLIC POLICE COMPARED Private policing is different from public policing. Private policing is largely "client-driven," meaning that it serves the needs of those who pay the bills. And while the public police are driven by a public mandate, their primary focus is enforcement of the criminal law. Private police, in contrast, may do almost anything on behalf of their clients, some of which may have little to do with the criminal law itself. Private police are *directly* employed by a client. In contrast, public police are *indirectly* employed by taxpayers. Four additional factors distinguish private police from public police:[45]

- *Focus on loss instead of crime.* Much of private policing is concerned with loss prevention. Loss prevention includes most notably protection from theft. Major retailers employ loss prevention specialists (see accompanying Careers in Criminal Justice box) to protect their goods from being stolen. However, goods may also be "lost" through error, unethical practices, accidents, and so on. Such behaviors do not fall within the scope of the criminal law that the public police are tasked with enforcing.

  The focus on loss also removes private police from the moral dimension of the criminal law. Instead of focusing on what is right and wrong, private police are concerned solely with what their *clients* view as priorities. As Elizabeth Joh notes, "When sanctions are imposed, there may be little or no emphasis on condemning the individual wrongdoer and 'making an example' out of him or her. A bank may require an embezzler to sign a loan guarantee to pay back stolen funds, for example, rather than choose public prosecution."[46]

- *Preventive methods.* Private police are concerned almost solely with prevention. Public police also work to prevent crime, but the usual public policing method of addressing crime is reactionary; of necessity, the police usually wait for calls for service before responding. Surveillance is paramount in the private policing context, whereas public policing relies more heavily on detection of criminal acts and apprehension of suspects. Surveillance includes the use of obvious technologies such as closed-circuit television and security cameras, but private police also employ other "embedded" techniques to guard against loss and ensure compliance with expected norms of behavior. Clifford Shearing and Philip Stenning cite the example of Disneyland.[47] Every employee—and indeed, every feature, whether it be the costumed characters or the guardrails and ropes promoting a smooth flow of patrons—is there to entertain but also subtly enforce compliance with what Disney considers appropriate behavior. People who do not comply face expulsion.

- *Private justice.* Not surprisingly, private policing often employs private justice. For example, a "card counter" may be permanently banned from a casino. Another example is termination for an employee who steals from his or her employer. Private companies often have an incentive to keep matters involving loss shielded from the public eye. High-profile incidents can result in negative publicity, which can in turn affect the bottom line. Similarly, cooperation with the police in an investigation takes time away from business activity, possibly eroding profits further. Interestingly, one study found that the Macy's department store in New York City reported just over half of shoplifting incidents to the police, which again underscores the reality that private companies' priorities are often different than those of the public police.[48]

- *Private property.* The public police focus their efforts on both public and private property. Whether it be burglary from a residence, assault at a bar, or vandalism on a highway overpass, the public police make few distinctions between the types of property where the crimes occur. Private property is of course protected, such as by the US Constitution's Fourth Amendment, but the point is that public police are able to enforce and focus on crime regardless of where it occurs. In contrast, private police are concerned almost exclusively with private property.

States, on the other hand, have given private police much more latitude, exempting them from the Fourth Amendment,[49] the *Miranda* rule[50] (see Chapter 6), and the exclusionary rule[51] (also see Chapter 6). This does not mean, however, that private police have unbridled authority. In most instances, they have no more authority than the typical private citizen. As one expert put it, "Many private security guards … possess no greater legal capabilities than do ordinary citizens to forcibly detain persons who are suspected

Duties and Characteristics of the Job

- Loss prevention specialists primarily protect merchandise in retail businesses. These duties extend beyond the retail setting to include shippers, wholesalers, and other companies engaged in commerce and concerned with loss and/or theft of its products.

- Those in loss prevention provide surveillance (e.g., monitoring security camera displays) and, as appropriate, detention of shoplifters.

- Companies also use loss prevention specialists to protect them from theft by employees. The position may also perform regular inventory or "shrink" assessments, manage alarm systems, and control access to warehousing, distribution centers, and even manufacturing facilities.

Job Outlook

- Security is one of the fastest-growing professional careers worldwide.

- Opportunities exist at all levels within the security industry, and all businesses, no matter their size, need qualified personnel to address their security concerns, prevent theft, deter workplace violence, and otherwise protect themselves to ensure normal business operations.

- The Bureau of Labor Statistics estimates that employment of loss prevention specialists and other security/surveillance professionals will grow by 18 percent over the next decade.

Salary

- Entry-level positions in retail loss prevention are among the lowest paying security jobs, but the pay prospects improve as one ascends to a management position.

- Loss prevention managers make, on average around $24,000 per year. Moving into other industries, such as banking and financial services, entry-level and mid-level management positions carry a salary range of $35,000 to $100,000, depending on several factors.

Qualifications

- The qualifications for an entry-level loss prevention position are minimal. Usually just a high school diploma is required, but employees will, at a minimum, be expected to pass routine drug tests, have strong interpersonal and administrative skills, and be comfortable around computers.

- Qualifications may be stricter and increase depending upon the individual's position in the corporate hierarchy or level of risk and responsibility associated with the position.

Education and Training

- Managerial positions may require an associate's or bachelor's degree in criminal justice or a related discipline, sometimes combined with a certain amount of real-world experience.

- Some colleges and universities also offer dedicated security education degrees.

- The American Society for Industrial Security (ASIS) offers three certifications for security professionals, including those of the Certified Protection Professional (CPP), the Professional Certified Investigator (PCI), and the Physical Security Professional (PSP). These certifications require that certain knowledge and skills be demonstrated, but they also help differentiate applicants from one another, and they improve an applicant's professional credibility and earnings potential.

Reality Check

- Entry-level positions do not pay particularly well.

- Some of the most coveted positions will require specialized training and a willingness to be mobile (i.e., move to where the work is).

- The work can be dry and "routine" much of the time, punctuated by occasional moments of excitement.

Sources: Bureau of Labor Statistics, "Security Guards and Gaming Surveillance Officers," http://www.bls.gov/ooh/Protective-Service/Security-guards.htm; ASIS International, "Certified Protection Professional," https://www.asisonline.org/Certification/Board-Certifications/CPP/Pages/default.aspx (URLs accessed April 2017).

---

of or have in fact committed a crime."[52] But as time goes on and the private policing industry continues to grow, it will be interesting to see how the courts weigh in.

LO8 Explain the role of technology in police work

Technology and Law Enforcement

Budget realities demand that police leaders make the most effective use of their forces, and technology seems to be one method of increasing productivity at a relatively low cost. The introduction of technology has already been explosive. In 1964, only one city, St. Louis, had a police computer system; by 1968, 10 states and 50 cities had state-level criminal justice information systems. Today, all law enforcement organization relies on computer technology.

> **WEB APP 4.3** Visit the PoliceOne website, and navigate to the page about police body cameras at **http://www.policeone.com/police-products/body-cameras/**. Why is video becoming increasingly popular in policing? To what extent do police officers want body-worn cameras?

Law enforcement technology extends beyond computers, of course. It falls into two broad categories: hard technology and soft technology.[53] Hard technology includes new materials and equipment that police use to catch criminals and prevent crime. Body-worn cameras, featured in the accompanying Criminal Justice and Technology box fit this mold. Soft technology primarily consists of software and information systems. Innovations in this area include new crime classification techniques, system integration, and data sharing. Additional examples of hard and soft technology appear in Exhibit 4.2.

Body Cameras

Officer Joshua Jones demonstrates the activation of a body camera being worn by New York Police Department personnel in a trial program. While body camera evidence has already played a role in the disciplining of a few officers nationally, advocates are warning that the technology will not be a magic bullet for behavior or the resolution of legal disputes.

Ozier Muhammad/Redux

Several companies (e.g., Panasonic, TASER International, WatchGuard) now market body-worn cameras for police officers. More and more agencies are putting them into use. In a recent study, Lindsay Miller and Jessica Toliver of the Police Executive Research Forum sent surveys to 500 law enforcement agencies around the country to inquire about body-worn camera implementation. Of the 254 responding agencies, 63 reported using cameras. With federal funding from the Body-Worn Camera Partnership Program, even more agencies put cameras into use. If current trends are any indication, body-worn cameras will be as popular in the coming years as in-car cameras.

Why are body-worn cameras so popular all of a sudden? One reason is a federal judge's 2013 decision to order officers in specific NYPD precincts to wear body cameras after he declared the department's controversial "stop, question, and frisk" program unconstitutional. Also driving the surge in attention to body-worn cameras was the fatal 2014 shooting of an unarmed black teenager, Michael Brown, in Ferguson, Missouri. The family of Darren Wilson, the officer who shot Brown, embarked on a campaign to "…ensure that every police officer working the streets in this country wears a body camera." Brown's family was equally supportive; lawyers for the family have called on legislators across the country to require that officers wear cameras at all times. Sharing both families' sentiments, the American Civil Liberties Union (ACLU) has claimed that body-worn cameras have "…the potential to be a win-win, helping protect the public against police misconduct, and at the same time helping protect police against false accusations of abuse."

Advantages

Michael White, a professor of criminology at Arizona State University, has summarized the key advantages of body-worn cameras:

- They increase transparency, thereby improving perceptions of police legitimacy.
- Body cameras create a "civilizing effect." That is, they alter both officer and suspect behavior.
- The cameras have evidentiary value. They are useful for expeditious resolution of citizen complaints. They can also yield evidence that is useful for criminal prosecution.
- Police training can benefit from footage of actual police–citizen encounters.

Limitations

- Cameras create privacy concerns. Recordings of child victims and offenders, medical emergencies, confidential informants, and the like may create legal complications.
- Officer privacy is also an issue with cameras. A number of police unions were resistant to in-car cameras, and the same concerns have been expressed with the advent of body cameras. When, for example, can the camera be off?
- Any new technology requires policy changes and training modifications.
- Body cameras are expensive. And more than just the cost of the cameras, a number of logistical problems arise. For example, an enormous amount of video footage must be secured and stored.

The Research

British agencies were among the first to experiment with body-worn cameras. Martin Goodall reported on a study in which 300 officers in the United Kingdom voluntarily donned "head-mounted cameras." A simple pre/post comparison was performed (no control group). Among the key findings were a 10 percent reduction in violent crime in the year after the cameras were put into use, a 30 percent reduction in officer time spent on paperwork in cases involving cameras, and a 40 percent reduction in complaints.

In Strathclyde (Scotland), police put 38 body-worn cameras into use, and in Grampian (also Scotland), 18 cameras were given to officers. Evaluations of both efforts reported reductions in crime as a result of body-worn camera implementation. Some evidence of reductions in assaults on police was reported, as was evidence to suggest the public is supportive of body-worn cameras, but neither study involved a control group, and many of the pre/post comparisons were anecdotal rather than empirical.

In the first study of body-worn cameras in the United States, Tony Farrar reported on a randomized study in which each of the 54 officers in the Rialto, California, police department were assigned to wear body cameras on some shifts but not others. A total of 988 shifts over a 12-month period formed the treatment ($N = 489$) and control ($N = 499$) conditions. The study was primarily concerned with use-of-force incidents and citizen complaints. Relative to the control group, treatment group participants were involved in one-half the number of force incidents and were the targets of one-tenth the number of citizen complaints.

(Continued)

In 2012, the Mesa, Arizona, police department outfitted 50 officers with cameras. According to the department, "Officers were either assigned or volunteered to assist in evaluating the on-officer body camera system," so it appears the study did not constitute a randomized controlled trial. Nevertheless, a year-long study was completed in September 2013. Cameras were associated with reductions in complaints and stop-and-frisk searches, but increases in traffic stops and citations issued.

The Phoenix Police Department began a body camera study in 2013, funded under the Bureau of Justice Assistance SMART Policing Initiative. Following are some of the key findings:

- Cameras appeared to increase arrest activity.
- Citizen behavior was not altered by the presence of cameras.
- Complaints against officers decreased following the introduction of body-worn cameras.
- Body-worn cameras improved the processing of domestic violence cases.

CRITICAL THINKING

1. Should officers with body-worn cameras be required to announce they are wearing the devices?
2. Under what circumstances should body-worn cameras be on and off?
3. Could an officer's health or safety be put at risk with a body-worn camera? Why or why not?

Sources: L. Miller and J. Toliver, *Implementing a Body-Worn Camera Program: Recommendations and Lessons Learned* (Washington, DC: Office of Community Oriented Policing Services); Marc Santora, "Order that Police Wear Cameras Stirs Unexpected Reactions," *New York Times*, August 13, 2013, http://www.nytimes.com/2013/08/14/nyregion/order-that-police-wear-cameras-stirs-unexpected-reactions.html; Elisha Fieldstadt, "Should Every Police Officer be Outfitted with a Body Camera?," *NBC News*, November 26, 2014, http://www.nbcnews.com/storyline/michael-brown-shooting/should-every-police-officer-be-outfitted-body-camera-n256881; Jay Stanley, "Police Body-Mounted Cameras: With Right Policies in Place, a Win for All," https://www.aclu.org/technology-and-liberty/police-body-mounted-cameras-right-policies-place-win-all; Michael D. White, *Police Officer Body-Worn Cameras: Assessing the Evidence* (Washington, DC: Office of Community-Oriented Policing Services, 2014); Martin Goodall, *Guidance for the Police Use of Body-Worn Video Devices* (UK: Home Office, Police and Crime Standards Directorate), http://library.college.police.uk/docs/homeoffice/guidance-body-worn-devices.pdf; Grampian Police, *Police Body Worn Video Pilot: End Project Report* (Scotland: Grampian Police, 2010); Strathclyde Police, *Body Worn Video Camera Project – K Division: Post Implementation Review* (Scotland: Strathclyde Police, 2010); Tony Farrar, *Self-Awareness to Being Watched and Socially-Desirable Behavior: A Field Experiment on the Effect of Body-Worn Cameras and Police Use-of-Force* (Washington, DC: Police Foundation, 2013); Mesa Police Department, *On-Officer Body Camera System: Program Evaluation and Recommendations* (Mesa, AZ: Mesa Police Department), p. 1; Charles M. Katz, Mike Kurtenbach, David E. Choate, and Michael D. White, *Phoenix, Arizona, Smart Policing Initiative: Evaluating the Impact of Police Officer Body-Worn Cameras* (Washington, DC: Bureau of Justice Assistance, 2015), http://www.smartpolicinginitiative.com/sites/all/files/Phoenix%20SPI%20Spotlight%20FINAL.pdf; also see the September 2016 issue of *Police Quarterly* for additional research on the efficacy of body-worn cameras.

EXHIBIT 4.2 The Application of Hard and Soft Technology to Crime Prevention and Police

	Hard Technology	**Soft Technology**
Crime prevention	• CCTV • Street lighting • Citizen protection devices (e.g., mace, tasers) • Metal detectors • Ignition interlock systems (drunk drivers)	• Threat assessment instruments • Risk assessment instruments • Bullying ID protocol • Sex offender registration • Risk assessment prior to involuntary civil commitment • Profiling potential offenders • Facial recognition software used in conjunction with CCTV
Police	• Improved police protection devices (helmets, vests, cars, buildings) • Improved/new weapons • Less than lethal force (mobile/riot control) • Computers in squad cars • Hands-free patrol car control (Project 54) • Offender and citizen IDs via biometrics/fingerprints • Mobile data centers • Video in patrol cars	• Crime mapping (hot spots) • Crime analysis (e.g., CompStat) • Criminal history data systems enhancement • Info sharing in CJS and private sector • New technologies to monitor communications (phone, mail, Internet) to/from targeted individuals • AMBER alerts • Creation of watch lists of potential violent offenders • Gunshot location devices

Source: James Byrne and Gary Marx, "Technological Innovations in Crime Prevention and Policing: A Review of the Research on Implementation and Impact," *Cahiers Politiestudies Jaargang* 20 (2011): 17–40, at 20.

In the following subsections, we explore in more detail several of the key technological innovations that have improved law enforcement capabilities in recent years.

Identifying Criminals

Police are becoming more sophisticated in their use of computer software to identify and convict criminals. One of the most important computer-aided tasks is the identification of criminal suspects. Computers now link neighboring agencies so they can share information on cases, suspects, and warrants. On a broader jurisdictional level, the FBI implemented the National Crime Information Center in 1967. This system provides rapid collection and retrieval of data about persons wanted for crimes anywhere in the 50 states. Today, it contains records on over 12 million offenders.

In an effort to identify crime patterns and link them to suspects, many departments use computer software to conduct analysis of behavior patterns, a process called data mining.[54] By discovering patterns in crimes such as burglary, especially those involving multiple offenders, computer programs can to recognize a particular way of working a crime and thereby identify suspects most likely to fit the profile.

data mining Using computer software to conduct analysis of behavior patterns in an effort to identify crime patterns and link them to suspects.

Locating Criminals

Many technologies have also been developed for the purpose of locating criminals. Given that there are relatively few police in relation to the number of citizens, officers cannot be everywhere at the same time. Nor can they readily identify or locate criminals who do not wish to be found. One company has developed a device that can "listen" for a person hidden in the trunk of a vehicle. This is useful in the traffic stop context, when police officers are vulnerable to attack. The Enclosed Space Detection System (ESDS) has been developed for police to ascertain whether one or more persons are hidden in a vehicle. It works by detecting the motion of the vehicle caused by the shock wave produced by a beating heart.[55] Through-wall radar is a similar technology that allows law enforcement officials to know whether people are inside a structure before they enter it.[56]

Crime Scene Investigation

Traditionally, to investigate and evaluate a crime scene, detectives relied on photographic evidence and two-dimensional drawings. However, it can be difficult to visualize the positional relationships of evidence with two-dimensional tools. Now, through a combination of laser and computer technology, high-definition surveying (HDS) creates a virtual crime scene that allows investigators to maneuver every piece of evidence.

High-definition surveying gives law enforcement a complete picture of a crime scene. HDS reflects a laser light off objects in the crime scene and back to a digital sensor, creating three-dimensional spatial coordinates that are calculated and stored using algebraic equations. The HDS device projects light in a 360-degree horizontal circumference, measuring millions of points and creating a "point cloud." The data points are bounced back to the receiver, collected, converted, and used to create a virtual image of any location. The resulting data file can now be accessed from any screen.

Not only does HDS technology allow the crime scene to be preserved exactly, but the perspective can be manipulated to provide additional clues. For instance, if the crime scene is the front room of an apartment, the three-dimensional image allows the investigator to move around and examine different points of view. Or if a victim was found seated, an investigator can see and show a jury what the victim might have seen just before the crime occurred. If witnesses outside said that they looked in a living room window, an investigator can zoom around and view what the witnesses could or could not have seen through that window.

HDS technology can also limit crime scene contamination. Investigators may inadvertently touch an object at a crime scene, leaving their fingerprints, or they may move or take evidence from the scene, perhaps by picking up fibers on their shoes. Evidence is compromised if moved or disturbed from its resting place, which may contaminate the scene and undermine the case. HDS technology is a "stand-off" device, allowing investigators to approach the scene in stages by scanning from the outer perimeter and moving inward, reducing the chances of contamination. The investigative and prosecutorial value of virtual crime scenes is evident. If an HDS device is used at the scene, detectives, prosecutors, and juries can return to a crime scene in its preserved state. Showing a jury exactly what a witness could or could not have seen can be very valuable.

Crime Mapping

It is now recognized that there are geographic "hot spots" where a majority of predatory crimes are concentrated.[57] Computer mapping programs that can translate addresses into map coordinates allow departments to identify problem areas for particular crimes, such as drug dealing. Computer maps help police identify the location, time of day, and linkage among criminal events and concentrate their forces accordingly.

Crime maps offer police administrators graphic representations of where crimes are occurring in their jurisdiction. Computerized crime mapping gives the police the power to analyze and correlate a wide array of data to create immediate, detailed visuals of crime patterns. The simplest maps display crime locations or concentrations and can be used to help direct patrols to the places they are most needed. More complex maps can be used to chart trends in criminal activity, and some have even proven valuable in solving individual criminal cases. For example, a serial rapist may be caught by observing and understanding the patterns of his crime so that detectives may predict where he will strike next and stake out the area with police decoys. Instead of antiquated pin maps, computerized crime mappings let the police detect crime patterns and pathologies of related problems. It enables them to work with multiple layers of information and scenarios, and thus identify emerging hot spots of criminal activity far more successfully and target resources accordingly.

Biometrics

Biometrics is defined as automated methods of recognizing a person based on a physiological or behavioral characteristic.[58] Some biometric measures, such as fingerprint identification, have been used for years by law enforcement to identify criminals. However, recent improvements in computer technology have expanded the different types of measures that can be used for identification. Biometrics is now used to identify individuals based on voice, retina, facial features, and handwriting identification, just to name a few.

The field of biometrics is used at all levels of government, including the military and law enforcement, and is also helpful in private businesses. Financial institutions, retail shopping, and health and social fields can all use biometrics as a way to limit access to financial information or to secure Internet sites.

As opposed to current personal identification methods, such as personal identification numbers (PINs) used for bank machines and Internet transactions, biometric authenticators are unique to the user and as a result cannot be stolen and used without that individual's knowledge.

The process of recording biometric data occurs in four steps. First, the raw biometric data are captured or recorded by a video camera or a fingerprint reading device. Second, the distinguishing characteristics of the raw data are used to create a biometric template. Third, the template is changed into a mathematical representation of the biometric sample and is stored in a database. Finally, a verification process will occur when an individual attempts to gain access to a restricted site. The individual will have to present his or her fingerprint or retina to be read and then matched to the biometric sample on record. Once verification is made, the individual will have access to restricted areas. Currently, a number of programs are in effect. Immigration and Customs Enforcement has been using hand geometry systems at major US airports to check frequent international travelers. Casinos around the country have started to implement facial recognition software into their buildings so that security is notified when a known cheater enters their premises.

DNA Testing

DNA profiling, a procedure that gained national attention during the O. J. Simpson trial, allows suspects to be identified on the basis of the genetic material found in hair, blood,

biometrics Automated methods of recognizing a person based on a physiological or behavioral characteristic.

DNA profiling The identification of criminal suspects by matching DNA samples taken from their person with specimens found at the crime scene.

Cook County (Chicago) Sheriff Tom Dart, left, and Sheriff's Detective Jason Moran are photographed with three recently discovered vials of mass murderer John Wayne Gacy's blood. The sheriff's office is creating DNA profiles from the blood of Gacy and other executed killers and putting them in a national DNA database of profiles created from blood, semen, or strands of hair found at crime scenes and on the bodies of victims. They hope to find evidence that links the long-dead killers to the coldest of cold cases, as well as prompt authorities in other states to submit the DNA of their own executed inmates and possibly evidence from decades-old crime scenes to help them solve their own cases.

AP Images/M. Spencer Green

and other bodily tissues and fluids. When DNA is used as evidence in a rape trial, DNA segments are taken from the victim, the suspect, and blood and semen found on the victim. A DNA match indicates a four-billion-to-one likelihood that the suspect is the offender.

Every US state and nearly every industrialized country now maintain DNA databases of convicted offenders.[59] These databases allow comparison of crime scene DNA to samples taken at other crime scenes and to known offenders. The United States has more than 3 million samples of offenders/arrestees in its state and federal DNA databases. The United States is not alone in gathering this material: Great Britain requires that almost any violation of law enforcement results in the collection of DNA of the violator.[60]

Leading the way in the development of the most advanced forensic techniques is the Forensic Science Research and Training Center, operated by the FBI in Washington, DC, and Quantico, Virginia. The lab provides information and services to hundreds of crime labs throughout the United States. The National Institute of Justice is also sponsoring research to identify a wider variety of DNA segments for testing and is involved in developing a PCR-based DNA-profiling examination using fluorescent detection that will reduce the time required for DNA profiling.

The FBI also operates the Combined DNA Index System (CODIS), which has assisted in nearly 50,000 investigations. CODIS is a database that allows DNA taken at a crime scene to be searched electronically to find matches against samples taken from convicted offenders and from other crime scenes. Early on, the system linked evidence taken from crime scenes in Jacksonville, Florida, to ones in Washington, DC, thereby tying nine crimes to a single offender.[61] When Timothy Spence was executed in Virginia on April 27, 1994, he was the first person convicted and executed almost entirely on the basis of DNA evidence.[62] More recently, CODIS has been expanded to include a wealth of information, including profiles of individuals convicted of crimes—and even of arrestees, if state law permits.[63] Critics of this information gathering cite concerns that some arrestees are innocent and that retained data from innocent persons could be improperly used and constitute a violation of privacy and civil liberties.[64]

A recent study reported that although there is widespread knowledge about the utility of forensic evidence, it is not being adequately used by law enforcement agencies.[65] The authors found that a significant number of unsolved homicides and rapes with forensic evidence had not been submitted to laboratories for analysis. And when cases with DNA evidence make it to trial, jurors are sometimes confused by the complexities involved.[66]

Boston Globe/Getty Images

Social Media and Networking

Over the past two decades, police departments have used the Internet and particularly their websites to communicate with the public. More recently, they have jumped on the social media and social networking bandwagon. People voluntarily reveal intimate details of their lives on sites such as Facebook, something that has proven quite useful for the police. People also follow police departments on Twitter and on Nixle, a dedicated police local alert system to which anyone can sign up for free.

The Police Executive Research Forum (PERF) recently surveyed 500 police departments around the country in order to learn what, besides websites, agencies were using to stay connected with communities.[67] The study found that:

- 82 percent use Facebook
- 69 percent use Twitter
- 48 percent use YouTube
- 34 percent use LinkedIn

Facebook has proven particularly useful. For example, the Hartselle, Alabama, police department sees its Facebook page as providing an extra 1,300 sets of eyes in the community. The department, which has around 4,200 likes, used the site to identify a couple who ran up over $1,500 worth of charges on a stolen credit card.[68] After the department posted surveillance photos from a local Walmart on its Facebook page, the couple was identified by a member of the community. Other departments around the country have used Facebook to capture crooks, and not just thieves. Police in one Louisiana department successfully used Facebook as part of their effort to apprehend a suspected cop-killer.[69]

Predictive Analytics

Predictive analytics uses computer technology to predict future events based on historical data. It has been popular for years in business, but only recently has policing caught on. In policing, predictive analytics is used to predict where and when specific crimes will occur. This practice is formally known as predictive policing. A study by the RAND corporation identified four methods of predictive policing:

predictive policing Application of advanced analytics to criminal justice data for the purpose of predicting where and when crime will occur.

- *Methods for predicting crimes.* These are approaches used to forecast places and times with an increased risk of crime.
- *Methods for predicting offenders.* These approaches identify individuals at risk of offending in the future.

- *Methods for predicting perpetrators' identities.* These techniques are used to create profiles that accurately match likely offenders with specific past crimes.
- *Methods for predicting victims of crimes.* Similar to those methods that focus on offenders, crime locations, and times of heightened risk, these approaches are used to identify groups or, in some cases, individuals who are likely to become victims of crime.[70]

Is it possible to predict crime or is this just the stuff of science fiction? Few studies are available, but one published in the prestigious *Journal of the American Statistical Association* compared performance of a predictive policing algorithm with professional crime analysts.[71] Researchers in Los Angeles gave crime analysts a map of the police district and asked them to identify one precise location (approximately a half block in size) where a crime would be most likely to occur over the next 12 hours, then the computer algorithm was set up to answer the same question. The algorithm correctly predicted the location of the next crime 4.7 percent of the crime, compared to just 2.1 percent for the crime analyst.[72] Note, though, that even the algorithm was wrong nearly 95 percent of the time. Human behavior, especially criminal behavior, is hard to predict!

ETHICALREFLECTION

Think back to this chapter's section on private policing. Private policing is controversial for a number of reasons. First, there is some concern that privatization puts the profit motive ahead of more lofty concerns such as protection of public safety. Another concern is that private police could eventually replace government, or public, police. Fortunately, this looks unlikely. As one expert observed, "Private policing poses no risk of supplanting public law enforcement entirely, at least not in our lifetime, and it is far from clear to what extent the growing numbers of private security employees are actually performing functions previously carried out by public officers."[73]

More legal scrutiny will also likely result as the private security business blossoms. A number of questions remain to be answered. One important issue is whether security guards are subject to the same search and seizure standards as police officers. The US Supreme Court has repeatedly stated that purely private search activities do not violate the Fourth Amendment's prohibitions. In other words, strictly speaking, a private security guard is not bound by the constitution's search and seizure limitations (more on these in Chapter 6).

Writing Challenge Write an essay that answers the following question: might security guards be subject to Fourth Amendment requirements if they are performing services that are traditionally reserved for the police? Interestingly, the Supreme Court was confronted with a similar question in the 1964 case of *Griffin v. Maryland*, a case involving an amusement park security guard who was "deputized" by the county sheriff.[74] You may want to read the Supreme Court's decision in that case as a starting point for your research (the full case is available here: https://supreme.justia.com/cases/federal/us/378/130/case.html). And for a more recent case on whether security guards are subject to Fourth Amendment restrictions, read *United States v. Cintron*, available here: http://ca10.washburnlaw.edu/cases/2012/06/11-6316.pdf.

SUMMARY

L01 *Summarize characteristics of the first law enforcement agencies* The origin of US police agencies traces to early English society. Under the pledge system, people were grouped into tithings and were entrusted with policing their own minor problems. Ten tithings were grouped into a hundred, supervised by a constable. Ten hundreds were organized into shires overseen by the shire reeve, the precursor to the modern sheriff. Early thief takers were private police who apprehended criminals for reward payments. Henry Fielding's Bow Street Runners improved on the thief-taking system. The first organized police force was founded by Sir Robert Peel in London.

L02 *Discuss the development of law enforcement in the United States* Law enforcement in colonial America paralleled the British model. In the colonies, the county sheriff became the most important law enforcement agent. The first true US police departments were formed in Boston, New York, and Philadelphia in the early nineteenth century.

L03 *Analyze the problems of early police agencies* Early American police were viewed as being dominated by political bosses who controlled their hiring practices and policies. In the nineteenth century, big-city police were still not respected by the public, were unsuccessful in their role as crime stoppers, and were not involved in progressive activities.

L04 *Discuss how reformers attempted to create professional police agencies* Reform movements begun in the 1920s culminated in the concept of professionalism. Police professionalism was interpreted to mean tough, rule-oriented police work featuring advanced technology and hardware. The view that these measures would quickly reduce crime proved incorrect.

L05 *Describe the major changes in law enforcement between 1970 and today* The police experienced turmoil in the 1960s and 1970s, which led to reforms such as the hiring of women and members of minority groups. Questions about the effectiveness of law enforcement also led to the development of community policing. Police departments began to embrace new forms of policing that stressed cooperation with the community and problem solving.

L06 *Identify the major federal law enforcement agencies* Several major law enforcement agencies are at work in the United States. At the federal level, the FBI is the largest federal agency. Other agencies include the Drug Enforcement Administration and the US Marshals Service.

LO7 Summarize the differences among state, county, and local law enforcement Most states maintain state police who investigate crimes and patrol the roadways. County-level law enforcement, including running jails and patrolling rural areas, is provided by sheriff's departments. Local police agencies engage in patrol, investigative, and traffic functions, as well as many support activities.

LO8 Explain the role of technology in police work Most police departments rely on advanced computer-based technology to prevent and control crime, identify suspects, and collate evidence. Examples include computerized crime mapping and automated fingerprint identification systems.

KEY TERMS

tithings, p. 82

hue and cry, p. 82

hundred, p. 82

constable, p. 82

shire reeve, p. 82

sheriff, p. 82

watch system, p. 82

justice of the peace, p. 82

vigilantes, p. 83

Federal Bureau of Investigation (FBI), p. 89

Drug Enforcement Administration (DEA), p. 90

Bureau of Alcohol, Tobacco, Firearms, and Explosives (ATF), p. 90

US Marshals Service, p. 90

Department of Homeland Security (DHS), p. 90

Customs and Border Protection (CBP), p. 90

Secret Service, p. 91

private policing, p. 94

data mining, p. 99

biometrics, p. 100

DNA profiling, p. 100

predictive policing, p. 102

REVIEW QUESTIONS

1. List the problems faced by today's police departments that were also present during the early days of policing.

2. Distinguish among the duties of the state police, sheriff's departments, and local police departments.

3. Do you believe that the general public has greater respect for the police today than in the past? If so, why? If not, why not?

4. What are some of the technological advances that should help the police solve more crimes? What are the dangers of these advances?

5. Discuss the trends that will influence policing during the coming decade. What other social factors may affect police?

5

The Police
Role and Function

Human behavior is notoriously difficult to predict. Criminal behavior is even more difficult to predict. In the era of a "big data," however, it may be getting easier. A number of tech startups have begun using law enforcement data, geographic locators, and sophisticated computer algorithms to estimate where and when future crimes are likely to occur. Companies like California's PredPol claim a high degree of success with predicting crime in specific locations, but they are not seeking to replace police officers' intuition; rather, they seek to bolster intuition with information. Enter the era of predictive analytics in criminal justice.

Predictive analytics is the use of data, machine learning, and data mining to predict future outcomes based on historical data. It is a fixture in the modern business world. Sales companies use it to predict likely customers. Asset-intensive industries (such as air and rail) use it to predict equipment failures. Only recently, however, have police departments begun exploring its potential. The practice, known formally as predictive policing, involves the use of analytical techniques to identify likely targets for criminals and prevent crime.[1]

Can crime really be predicted or is this the stuff of science fiction? A recent well-designed study compared a predictive policing algorithm with the performance of professional crime analysts in Los Angeles.[2] In one part of the study researchers provided crime analysts with a map of the police district and asked them to identify one location, approximately a half block in size, where a crime would be most likely to occur within the next 12 hours. The computer algorithm was then programmed to answer the same question. Interestingly, the computer correctly predicted the location of the next crime 4.7 percent of the crime, compared to just 2.1 percent for the crime analysts. The computer algorithm was twice as effective as a professional crime analyst in predicting crime![3] The computer's performance was impressive, but over 95 percent of the time the predictions were inaccurate. This underscores just how difficult it is to predict criminal activity. It is doubtful computer predictive policing will replace police officers on the street, but it may be a valuable weapon in the law enforcement arsenal.

AP Images/Damian Dovarganes

LEARNING OBJECTIVES

LO1 Explain the organization of police departments

LO2 Articulate the complexities of the police role

LO3 Explain the limitations of patrol and methods for improving it

LO4 Summarize the investigation function

LO5 Explain what forensics is and what forensics experts do for police agencies

LO6 Discuss the concept of community-oriented policing

LO7 Discuss the concept of problem-oriented policing

LO8 Explain intelligence-led policing and the various means by which it occurs

LO9 Describe the various police support functions

The police role is extremely varied and complex. Police officers are called on to deal with increasingly difficult and unpredictable situations. The crime problem continues to evolve in response to societal developments. Whether officers engage in preventive patrol, respond to calls for service, forge relationships with citizens, or aggressively target a small list of known criminal suspects, they have to be constantly vigilant and prepared. Anything less can give criminals the upper hand, and this includes both public and political support. Without one or the other, or both, police work becomes all the more difficult.

This chapter describes the organization of police departments and their various operating branches: patrol, investigation, service, and administration. It discusses the realities and ambiguities of the police role and traces how the concept of the police mission has been changing radically. The chapter concludes with a brief overview of some of the most important administrative issues confronting today's law enforcement agencies.

The Police Organization

LO1 Explain the organization of police departments

Most municipal police departments in the United States are independent agencies within the executive branch of government, operating without specific administrative control from any higher governmental authority. Although they often cooperate and participate in mutually beneficial enterprises, such as a joint task force with state and federal law enforcement agencies, local police agencies are functionally independent organizations with unique sets of rules, policies, procedures, norms, budgets, and so on.

Most local police departments are organized in a hierarchical manner, as illustrated in Figure 5.1. Within this organizational model, each element of the department normally has its own chain of command. In a large municipal department, there may be a number of independent investigation units headed by a captain who serves as the senior administrator, a lieutenant who oversees cases and investigations and acts as liaison with other police agencies, and sergeants and inspectors who carry out fieldwork. Smaller departments may have a captain or lieutenant as head of a particular branch or unit.

Department size also affects the number of subunits. A department the size of New York's may contain several specialized investigative units, such as special victims or sex crimes, whereas many smaller departments do not employ detectives at all and rely on county or state police investigators to probe unsolved crimes. Regardless of its size, at

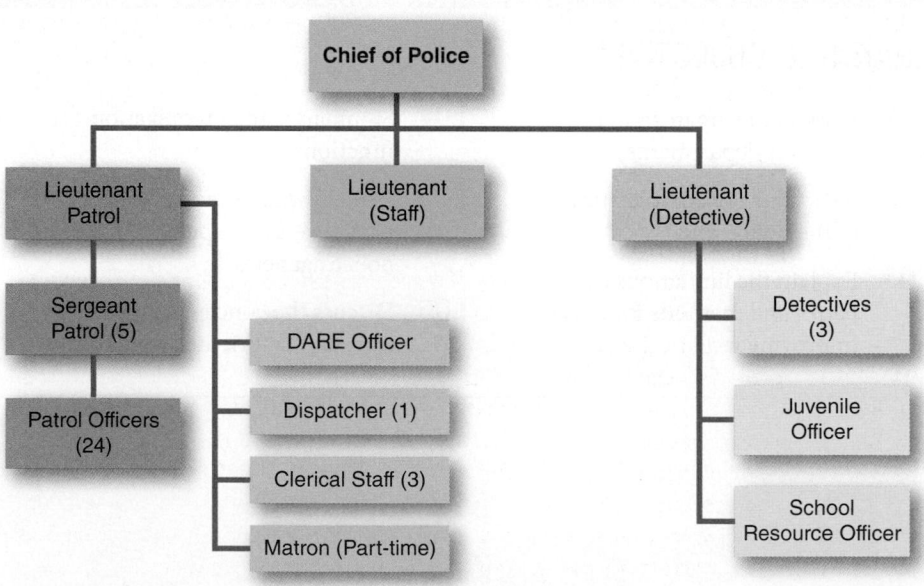

FIGURE 5.1 Vestal, New York, Police Department

Source: Town of Vestal, New York, http://www.vestalny.com/departments/police_department/organizational_chart.php (accessed April 2017).

the head of the organization is the **police chief** (sometimes called the commissioner or similar), who sets policy and has general administrative control over all the department's various operating branches.

Pros and Cons of Police Organization

The police administrative organization has both pros and cons. Because most departments are civil service organizations, administrators must rise through the ranks to get to command positions. To be promoted, they must pass a battery of tests, profiles, interviews, and so on. Most police departments employ a **time-in-rank system** for determining promotion eligibility. This means that before moving up the administrative ladder, an officer must spend a certain amount of time in the next lowest rank; a sergeant cannot become a captain without serving an appropriate amount of time as a lieutenant.

This system has both benefits and shortcomings. On the plus side, it is designed to promote stability and fairness and to limit favoritism. The chief's favorite cannot be promoted over a more experienced officer who is better qualified. Once earned, a rank can rarely be taken away or changed if new management takes over. The rank system also protects police agencies from losing talented officers trained at public expense to other departments who offer more money or other incentives.

On the downside, the rank system restricts administrative flexibility. Unlike in the private sector, where the promotion of talented people can be accelerated in the best interests of the company, the time-in-rank system prohibits rapid advancement. A police agency would probably not be able to hire a computer systems expert with a PhD and give her a command position in charge of its data-analysis section. The department would be forced to hire the expert as a civilian employee under the command of a ranking senior officer who might not be as technically proficient. Because senior administrators are promoted from within only after years of loyal service, time-in-rank may render some police agencies administratively conservative. Even when police executives adopt new programs, such as CompStat (more on this later in the chapter), they are most likely to choose those elements that confer legitimacy on existing organizations and on implementing them in ways that minimize disruption to existing organizational routines, rather than embracing truly innovative changes.[4]

The Police Role

In countless books, movies, and TV shows, the public has been presented with a view of policing that romanticizes cops as fearless crime fighters who think little of their own safety as they engage in daily high-speed chases and shootouts. How close is this portrayal of a crime fighter to real life? Not very close, according to most research. A police officer's crime-fighting efforts are only a small part of his or her overall activities. Studies of police work indicate that a significant portion of an officer's time is spent handling minor disturbances, service calls, and administrative duties. Police work, then, involves much more than catching criminals.

The most recent national survey of police contacts with civilians found that an estimated 17 percent of persons had at least one contact with police that year, and very few of them were criminals in the conventional sense of the term.[5] More than half of the contacts were for traffic-related matters, and about 30 percent were to report problems or ask for assistance, such as responding to a neighbor's complaint about music being too loud during a party or warning kids not to shoot off fireworks. These results are not surprising when Uniform Crime Report (UCR) arrest data are also considered. Each year, about 760,000 local, county, and state police officers make about 11 million arrests, or about 14 each.[6] Given an even distribution of arrests, it is evident that the average police officer makes around two arrests per month and one felony arrest per year.

These figures should be interpreted with caution because not all police officers are engaged in activities that allow them to make arrests, such as patrol or detective work. About one-third of all sworn officers in the nation's largest police departments are in

REALITYCHECK
Myth or Reality?
Police work primarily involves crime fighting.

MYTH. Crime fighting makes up only a small fraction of what police work usually entails.

Most police work entails relatively mundane tasks, such as responding to service calls and completing administrative tasks. Television programs and movies almost completely ignore this side of police work. Instead, they focus on the crime-fighting role. What are the consequences of this?

L02 Articulate the complexities of the police role

such units as communications, antiterrorism, administration, and personnel. Even if the number of arrests per officer were adjusted by one-third, it would still amount to only 9 or 10 serious crime arrests per officer per year. So even though police handle thousands of calls each year, relatively few result in an arrest for a serious crime such as a robbery or burglary; in suburban and rural areas, years may go by before a police officer arrests someone for a serious crime.

The evidence, then, shows that unlike their TV and film counterparts, the police engage in many activities that are not related to crime. Police officers function in a variety of roles ranging from dispensers of emergency medical care to keepers of the peace on school grounds. Although officers in large urban departments may be called on to handle more felony cases than those in small towns, they too will probably find that most of their daily activities are not crime related. What are some of the most important functions of police?

The Patrol Function

LO3 Explain the limitations of patrol and methods for improving it

Regardless of the policing style, uniformed patrol officers are the backbone of the police department, usually accounting for about two-thirds of a department's personnel.[7] Patrol officers are the most highly visible components of the entire criminal justice system. Patrols serve the following major purposes:

- Deter crime by maintaining a visible police presence
- Maintain public order (peacekeeping) within the patrol area
- Enable the police department to respond quickly to violations of law or other emergencies
- Identify and apprehend law violators
- Aid individuals and care for those who cannot help themselves
- Facilitate the movement of traffic and people
- Create a feeling of security in the community[8]

Patrol Activities

order maintenance (peacekeeping) The order-maintenance aspect of the police role involves peacekeeping, maintaining order and authority without the need for formal arrest, "handling the situation," and keeping things under control by using threats, persuasion, and understanding.

Most experts agree that the great bulk of patrol efforts are devoted to what has been described as order maintenance (peacekeeping): maintaining order and civility in their assigned jurisdiction.[9] Order-maintenance functions occupy the border between criminal and noncriminal behavior. The patrol officer's discretion often determines whether a noisy neighborhood dispute involves the crime of disturbing the peace or can be controlled by exercising street-corner diplomacy and sending the combatants on their way. Similarly, teenagers milling around in the shopping center parking lot may be brought in and turned over to the juvenile authorities or dispersed in a less formal and often more efficient manner.

The primary role of police seems to be "handling the situation." Police encounter many troubling incidents that need some sort of "fixing up."[10] Enforcing the law might be one tool a patrol officer uses; threat, coercion, sympathy, and understanding might be others. Most important is keeping things under control so that there are no complaints that the officer is doing nothing at all or doing too much. The real police role, then, may be as a community problem solver.

Police officers actually practice a policy of selective enforcement, concentrating on some crimes but handling the majority in an informal manner. A police officer is supposed to know when to take action and when not to, as well as whom to arrest and whom to deal with by issuing a warning or some other informal action. If a mistake is made, the officer can come under fire from peers and superiors, as well as the media and the general public.

The effectiveness of patrol has been a topic of research for several decades. One of the accompanying Focus on Effectiveness boxes summarizes the key findings in this area. The other looks at the effectiveness of stop, question, and frisk (SQF) strategies.

Does Stop, Question, and Frisk Deter Crime?

Authorized by the US Supreme Court in the 1968 *Terry v. Ohio* decision, stop, question, and frisk (SQF) has been used by police as one of many methods to control crime. When officers have reasonable suspicion that criminal activity has taken place, is taking place, or is about to take place, they can detain and question the suspect. If they also have reasonable suspicion that a suspect is armed, they can frisk him or her for weapons.

The police have used SQF with minimal controversy for several decades, but the practice received particular attention in New York City a few years back. While a total of 160,851 SQFs were recorded in 2003, the number surged to 685,000 in 2011. A successful court challenge reversed New York City's SQF practice, however, dropping the number to just 190,000 in 2013—and only 47,000 in 2014. Still, that did not stop the city's top law enforcement officer from saying, "You cannot police without [SQFs]. If you did not have it, you'd have anarchy." Throughout it all, an empirical question has persisted: does SQF deter crime?

Effects on Crime/Recidivism

To answer the question of whether SQFs actually deter crime, Weisburd and his colleagues were able to obtain data from the New York City Police Department (NYPD) which contained the exact location of all SQFs and all crime incidents in the city. The incident data included information on whether a crime was thought to have occurred after an officer responded to a call for service. Incident data are considered more inclusive than arrest data, but they are less inclusive than calls for service (a call for service may or may not amount to a crime). Weisburd and his colleagues then analyzed the relationship between SQFs and crime incidents at the street level—as opposed to, say, the neighborhood level. After a series of rigorous statistical analyses, they found that SQFs exerted a significant yet modest deterrent effect on crime.

Thinking Critically About Research

A simple approach to exploring the relationship between SQFs and crime could be to plot each over time. Indeed, Weisburd and his colleagues started by doing this. A figure in their study showed a clear upward trend in SQFs coupled with a clear decline in incidents for all of New York City during the study period. Did that show cause and effect? Of course not. Crime could have been trending downward already or other factors could have been at work. What the researchers chose to do was:

- Rule out alternative explanations
- Drill down to smaller areas (called "microplaces" in the language of social science methodology) to analyze behavior in specific areas.
- Determine whether SQF activities at one point in time reduce crime incidents at later points in time.
- Study weekly intervals of data, not months or years
- Employ a number of statistical strategies to isolate the effects of SQF on crime

Without delving into the statistical methods Weisburd and his colleagues used, suffice it to say they used a battery of approaches to determine whether there is a causal order between SQF and crime—one that could not be "explained away" by other factors. Their study is by no means the last word on the subject, but it is also backed up by a wealth of research showing that police can reduce crime by concentrating their efforts on hot spots of criminal activity.

QUESTIONS

1. Does evidence that SQF deters crime mean the strategy is preferred over other approaches?
2. What are the possible pitfalls associated with SQF?

Sources: *Terry v. Ohio*, 392 U.S. 1 (1968); David Weisburd, Alese Wooditch, Sarit Weisburd, and Sue-Ming Yang, "Do Stop, Question, and Frisk Practices Deter Crime? Evidence at Microunits of Space and Time," *Criminology and Public Policy* 15 (2016): 31–56; Anthony A. Braga, Andrew V. Papachristos, and David M. Hureau, "The Effects of Hotspots Policing on Crime: An Updated Systematic Review and Meta-Analysis," *Justice Quarterly* 31 (2014): 633–663.

Improving Patrol

In recent years, police departments have initiated a number of programs and policies in an attempt to improve patrol effectiveness. Some have proved more successful than others. Some are also more controversial than others.

PROACTIVE POLICING AND DIRECTED PATROL Although the mere presence of police may not be sufficient to deter crime, the manner in which they approach their task may make a difference. Police departments that use a proactive, aggressive law enforcement style may help reduce crime rates. Jurisdictions that encourage patrol officers to stop motor vehicles to issue citations and to aggressively arrest and detain suspicious persons also experience lower crime rates than jurisdictions that do not follow such proactive policies.[11] Departments that more actively enforce minor regulations, such as laws prohibiting disorderly conduct and traffic laws, are also more likely to experience lower felony rates.[12]

Pinpointing why **proactive policing** works so effectively is difficult. Proactive patrol efforts may help improve response time and increase the number of patrol cars that respond per crime.[13] It may have a **deterrent effect** as well: Aggressive policing increases community perception that police arrest many criminals and that most

proactive policing A police department policy that emphasizes stopping crimes before they occur, rather than reacting to crimes that have already occurred.

deterrent effect Stopping or reducing crime by convincing would-be criminals that they stand a significant risk of being apprehended and punished for their crimes.

Despite what the media might lead us to believe, police work does not always involve chasing down criminals and making arrests. The great bulk of patrol efforts are devoted to order maintenance and peacekeeping rather than to shootouts with dangerous criminals. Here Sacramento police officers Sara Butler and Mike Cooper talk with a homeless man as they hand out eviction notices to residents at a homeless tent city. Hundreds of residents living in a tent city along the American River were issued notices of eviction and were told to relocate to a nearby shelter. Their tent city was located on land belonging to the Sacramento Municipal utility District.

Justin Sullivan/Getty Images

 FOCUS ON EFFECTIVENESS

Does Patrol Deter Crime? A Look at the Evidence

A primary goal of police patrol has been to deter criminal behavior. The visible presence of patrol cars on the street and the rapid deployment of police officers to the scene of a crime are viewed as effective methods of crime control. Is this view correct?

Effects on Crime/Recidivism

The most widely heralded attempt at measuring patrol effectiveness was undertaken during the early 1970s in Kansas City, Missouri, where researchers divided 15 separate police districts into three groups: one group retained normal patrol; the second (proactive) set of districts were supplied with two to three times the normal amount of patrol forces; and the third (reactive) group had its preventive patrol eliminated, with police officers responding only when summoned by citizens to the scene of a particular crime. The Kansas City study found that these variations in patrol had little effect on the crime patterns in the 15 districts. The presence or absence of patrol officers did not seem to affect residential or business burglaries, motor vehicle thefts, larceny involving auto accessories, robberies, vandalism, or other criminal behavior, nor did their presence or absence influence citizens' attitudes toward the police, their satisfaction with police, or their fear of future criminal behavior.

Thinking Critically About Research

The Kansas City experiment gave the impression that there is little the police can do to reduce crime, but it is important to note that there were limitations associated with the research design. For example, officers sometimes entered reactive beats in order to respond promptly to calls for service. There are several other reasons why we shouldn't put too much faith in the Kansas City experiment:

- Dozens of studies are almost evenly divided on whether patrol and crime go hand in hand. Almost as many researchers have found less crime in areas with a higher police presence as have found less crime in areas with a lower police presence.

- Some studies from other countries have shown that when the police go on strike (they are usually prohibited by law from doing so in the United States), crime rates surge. This suggests that patrol certainly does something to reduce crime.

- Recent federal funding for the hiring of additional police officers has been linked to significant reductions in crime rates in cities across the country.

- When the Department of Homeland Security increases the terror threat alert level, more police are put on patrol. Researchers have found that these surges in the police presence have led to less crime.

- Increasing the size of the local police force may have other benefits for the overall effectiveness of the justice system. Adding police and bolstering resources can increase prosecution and conviction rates. Inadequate resources make it difficult to gather sufficient evidence to ensure a conviction, and prosecutors are likely to drop these cases. Adding police resources helps increase prosecutorial effectiveness.

- A recent meta-analysis and comprehensive review of the literature by Carriaga and Worrall found that there is a modest association between the police presence and crime rates.

QUESTIONS

1. What can a police agency do to improve patrol?
2. What policing methods are likely the most effective and why?

Sources: George Kelling, Tony Pate, Duane Dieckman, and Charles Brown, *The Kansas City Preventive Patrol Experiment: A Summary Report* (Washington, DC: Police Foundation, 1974); Richard C. Larson, "What Happened to Patrol Operations in Kansas City? A Review of the Kansas City Preventive Patrol Experiment," *Journal of Criminal Justice* 3 (1975): 267–297; Thomas B. Marvell and Carlisle E. Moody, "Specification Problems, Police Levels, and Crime Rates," *Criminology* 24 (1996): 609–646; Tuija Makinen and Hannu Takala, "The 1976 Police Strike in Finland," *Scandinavian Studies in Criminology* 7 (1980): 87–106; William N. Evans and Emily Owens, "COPS and Crime," *Journal of Public Economics* 91 (2007): 181–201; Government Accountability Office, *Community Policing Grants: COPS Grants Were a Modest Contributor to Declines in Crime in the 1990s* (Washington, DC: Government Accountability Office, 2005); Jonathan Klick and Alexander Tabarrok, "Using Terror Alert Levels to Estimate the Effect of Police on Crime," *Journal of Law and Economics* 48 (2005): 267–279; Joan Petersilia, Allan Abrahamse, and James Q. Wilson, "A Summary of RAND's Research on Police Performance, Community Characteristics, and Case Attrition," *Journal of Police Science and Administration* 17 (1990): 219–229; Michael L. Carriaga and John L. Worrall, "Police Levels and Crime: A Systematic Review and Meta-Analysis," *Police Journal: Theory, Practice, and Principles* 88 (2015): 315–333.

violators get caught. Criminals may think twice about committing crimes in a town that has such an active police force! Proactive policing may also help control crime because it results in conviction of more criminals. Because aggressive police arrest more suspects, there are fewer suspects left on the street to commit crime; fewer criminals produce lower crime rates.

Evidence also shows that targeting specific crimes through **directed patrol** can be successful. One aggressive patrol program, known as the Kansas City Gun Experiment, was directed at restricting the carrying of guns in high-risk places at high-risk times. Working with academics from the University of Maryland, the Kansas City Police Department focused extra patrol attention on a "hot spot" high-crime area identified by computer analysis of all gun crimes. Over a 29-week period, the gun patrol officers conducted thousands of car and pedestrian checks and traffic stops and made more than 600 arrests. Using frisks and searches, they found 29 guns; an additional 47 weapons were seized by other officers in the experimental area. In the target beat, 169 gun crimes were committed in the 29 weeks before the gun patrol, but only 86 were committed while the experiment was under way, a decrease of 49 percent.[14]

Strategies such as these have been quite a success.[15] The downturn in the violent crime rate over the past decade has been attributed to aggressive police work in large cities, such as New York, aimed at controlling or eliminating lifestyle crimes: vandalism, panhandling, and graffiti.[16] Although some commentators fear that aggressive policing will result in antagonism between proactive cops and the general public, recent research indicates that precinct-level efforts to ensure that officers are respectful of citizens helped lower the number of complaints and improved community relations.[17]

MAKING ARRESTS Can formal police action, such as an arrest, reduce crime? The evidence is mixed, but some studies suggest that contact with the police may cause some offenders to forgo repeat criminal behavior. Many first offenders will forgo criminal activity after undergoing arrest.[18] For example, an arrest for drunk driving reduces the likelihood of further driving while intoxicated.

Why do arrests deter crime? It is possible that news of increased and aggressive police arrest activity is rapidly diffused through the population and has an immediate impact on crime rates.[19] Arrests may also alter perceptions. An arrest for drunk driving may convince people that they will be rearrested if they drink and drive.[20] Consequently, as the number of arrests per capita increases, crime rates go down.

directed patrol A patrol strategy that involves concentrating police resources in areas where certain crimes are a significant problem.

REALITYCHECK
Myth or Reality?
Rapid response to 911 calls reporting a crime in progress increases the likelihood that the offender will be apprehended.

MYTH. Research shows that rapid response has almost no effect on the probability of capturing the offender. This is a fairly general assumption, however.

Are there certain types of crimes for which rapid response could work?

AP Images/Eric Risberg

San Francisco police officers investigate the scene where a high-speed car chase ended with a crash and the fatal shooting of a carjacking suspect in San Francisco. Officers shot and killed a man after he led them on a lengthy high-speed chase, crashed his truck in downtown San Francisco, and then fired a gun at good Samaritans who tried to help him, according to authorities.

RAPID RESPONSE Improving response time may be one way of increasing police efficiency. Unfortunately, however, the research fails to support such assumptions. A National Institute of Justice study examined police response times in four cities. The authors found that rapid response had virtually no effect on crime.[21] Why? One explanation is that people tend to be slow when it comes to reporting crime. For example, a person may wake up in the morning and find that his or her car was vandalized. By then the trail has gone cold, making it nearly impossible to capture the perpetrator even if the police are summoned immediately upon discovery of the crime. On the other hand, if an in-progress burglary is called in, it seems police have a better chance of apprehending the suspect if they can get to the scene quickly.[22]

BROKEN WINDOWS POLICING A critical 1982 paper by George Kelling and James Q. Wilson advocated a new approach to improving police relations in the community, an approach that has come to be known as the **broken windows model**.[23] Kelling and Wilson made three points:

broken windows model A term used to describe the role of the police as maintainers of community order and safety.

- *Neighborhood disorder creates fear.* Urban areas filled with street people, youth gangs, prostitutes, and the mentally disturbed are the ones most likely to maintain a high degree of crime.[24]
- *Neighborhoods give out crime-promoting signals.* A neighborhood filled with deteriorated housing, broken windows, and disorderly behavior gives out crime-promoting signals. Honest citizens live in fear in these areas, and predatory criminals are attracted to them.
- *Police need citizen cooperation.* If police are to reduce fear and successfully combat crime in these urban areas, they must have the cooperation, support, and assistance of the citizens.

According to the broken windows concept, a deteriorated neighborhood, whose residents are fearful, pessimistic, and despondent, is a magnet for crime. In contrast, neighborhoods where residents are civil to one another and where disorder is not tolerated send a different message: criminals are not wanted here, and criminal behavior will not be allowed. The broken windows approach holds that police administrators would be well advised to deploy their forces where they can encourage public confidence, strengthen feelings of safety, and elicit cooperation from citizens. Preserving the community, providing for public safety, and maintaining order—not crime fighting—should become the primary focus of patrol. Put another way, just as physicians and dentists practice preventive medicine and dentistry, police should help maintain an intact community structure rather than simply fighting crime.

Does it work? In one of the most rigorous tests of broken windows theory in recent years, researchers identified 34 crime-ridden areas in Lowell, Massachusetts. Half (the treatment group) received broken windows policing; the other half (the control group) received the same levels of patrol as before. Results revealed substantial reductions in crime, disorder, and calls for service in the treatment areas but not in the control areas.[25]

USING TECHNOLOGY Police departments have also relied on technology to help guide patrol efforts. The best-known program, CompStat, had its beginnings in New York City as a means of directing police efforts in a more productive way.[26] William Bratton, who had been appointed New York City police chief, wanted to revitalize the department and break through its antiquated bureaucratic structures. In 1994, he installed CompStat, a computerized system that gave local precinct commanders up-to-date information about where and when crime was occurring in their jurisdictions. Part of the CompStat program, twice-weekly "crime control strategy meetings," brought precinct commanders together with the department's top administrators who asked them to report on crime problems in their precincts and tell what they were doing to turn things around. Those involved in the strategy sessions had both detailed data and electronic pin maps that showed how crime clustered geographically in the precinct and how patrol officers were being deployed.

CompStat A program originated by the New York City police that used carefully collected and analyzed crime data to shape policy and evaluate police effectiveness.

CRIMINAL JUSTICE AND TECHNOLOGY

Automated License Plate Recognition

According to the Bureau of Justice Statistics (BJS) Law Enforcement Management and Administrative Statistics survey, approximately one in six police departments uses automated license plate recognition (ALPR). Police have used in-car cameras for years now (approximately two in three agencies do so), but license plate readers serve a different purpose. While in-car cameras are designed to reduce complaints against police and promote officer safety, license plate readers constantly scan for stolen vehicles and people of interest. One study by David Roberts and Meghann Casanova found that ALPR systems can capture upwards of 1,800 plates per minute, even if cars are moving fast. The systems are expensive, however. One unit costs between $10,000 and $22,000 per patrol car. According to Roberts and Casanova, though, ALPR benefits may outweigh the costs:

ALPR technology is a significant tool in the arsenal of law enforcement and public safety agencies. It automates a tedious, distracting, and manual process that officers regularly complete in their daily operations, and vastly improves their efficiency and effectiveness in identifying vehicles of interest among the hundreds or thousands they observe in routine patrol. Moreover, it generates a rich and enduring record of vehicle sightings, complete with time, date, and geographic location information for each observation. This data can substantially enhance the investigative capacity of law enforcement, and greatly contribute to intelligence collection and analysis functions.

Any technological advance in law enforcement is met with some resistance. ALPR systems are no exception. The American Civil Liberties Union (ACLU) has claimed the devices "have the potential to create permanent records of virtually everywhere any of us has driven, radically transforming the consequences of leaving home to pursue private life, and opening up many opportunities for abuse." In light of these concerns, the ACLU has recommended a number of rules for ALPR use, calling for no storage of data on innocent persons and use only by authorized law enforcement personnel.

Easy Fee Collection?

Vigilant Solutions, one of the largest manufacturers of ALPR technology, works with a number of law enforcement agencies in Texas. For some agencies, it has begun providing ALPR systems at no charge in exchange for receiving a portion of ticket proceeds. The "warrant redemption" program gives partner police agencies access to Vigilant's massive database of over 2.8 billion plate scans. The agencies also give Vigilant access to their outstanding court cases so the company can create a "hot list" to feed into the ALPR systems. As ALPR-equipped cruisers move about, they constantly seek vehicles on the hot list.

According to Dave Maass of the Electronic Frontier Foundation, Vigilant is also leveraging a 2015 Texas law (H.B. 121) that permits police officers to carry credit and debit card readers in their patrol cars so they can accept payment on the spot for unpaid court fines (called capias

warrants). State Representative Allen Fletcher, the bill's sponsor, defended the approach as follows:

[T]he option of making such a payment at the time of arrest could avoid contributing to already crowded jails, save time for arresting officers, and relieve minor offenders suddenly informed of an uncollected payment when pulled over for a routine moving violation from the burden of dealing with an impounded vehicle and the potential inconvenience of finding someone to supervise a child because of an unexpected arrest.

Scott Henson, author of the popular *Grits for Breakfast* criminal justice blog, sympathizes, but also expresses concern:

...here's the part that nags at me. More than ten percent of Texans at any given time have outstanding arrest warrants.... That's a lot of folks. Meanwhile, new law enforcement technology now being deployed by local agencies—specifically, hand-held and vehicle-attached license plate readers—could and [in my opinion] will facilitate agencies which deploy that [technology], using it to have their traffic-enforcement officers cherry-pick drivers with outstanding warrants instead of looking for current, real-time traffic violations. So, if more than ten percent of drivers have outstanding arrest warrants, that's a near-endless sea in which they can fish for roadside revenue generation, diverting focus from traffic safety in the pursuit of the Almighty Dollar.

Both sides present valid arguments. It will be interesting to follow what is happening in Texas.

CRITICAL THINKING

1. Is use of ALPR technology a privacy violation? Why or why not?
2. Will mobile fee collection catch on? Should it?

Sources: B. A. Reaves, *Local Police Departments, 2013: Equipment and Technology* (Washington, DC: Bureau of Justice Statistics, 2013), p. 3; L. J. Westphal, "The In-Car Camera: Value and Impact," *Police Chief*, November 9, 2004, p. 8; D. J. Roberts and M. Casanova, *Automated License Plate Recognition (ALPR) Use by Law Enforcement: Policy and Operational Guide, Summary* (Washington, DC: US Department of Justice, 2012), p. 2; American Civil Liberties Union, "You are Being Tracked," https://www.aclu.org/feature/you-are-being-tracked; Vigilant Solutions, "Guadalupe County Uses Vigilant Solutions License Plate Readers to Enforce Capias Warrants," https://www.vigilantsolutions.com/guadalupe_county_warrant_redemption_program_capias/; D. Maass, "'No Cost' License Plate Readers Are Turning Texas Police into Mobile Debt Collectors and Data Miners," Electronic Frontier Foundation, January 26, 2016, https://www.eff.org/deeplinks/2016/01/no-cost-license-plate-readers-are-turning-texas-police-mobile-debt-collectors-and; C.S.H.B. 121 Bill Analysis, http://www.legis.state.tx.us/tlodocs/84R/analysis/html/HB00121H.htm; Scott Henson, "Pragmatic Acquiescence vs. Nagging Presentiments About Roadside Ticket Collections," *Grits for Breakfast*, March 20, 2015, http://gritsforbreakfast.blogspot.com/2015/03/pragmatic-acquiescence-vs-nagging.html. (URLs accessed April 2017.)

The CompStat program required local commanders to demonstrate their intimate knowledge of crime trends and develop strategies to address them effectively. When ideas were presented by the assembled police administrators, the local commanders were required to demonstrate, in follow-up sessions, how they had incorporated the new strategies in their patrol plan. CompStat proved extremely successful and is generally credited with making a major contribution to the dramatic drop in New York City's crime rate during the past decade. See the accompanying Criminal Justice and Technology feature for a look at another technological advancement that may assist in police patrol operations.

WEB APP 5.2 Read about the CompStat process at **http://tinyurl.com/zlhkqtk**. Is the "directing and controlling" aspect of CompStat ideal? Are there any potential pitfalls associated with CompStat?

West Salem, Wisconsin, Police Chief Charles Ashbeck flies his department's new drone. Drones are finding their way into a variety of law enforcement functions, but their use remains highly restricted. Critics fear too much drone use will raise privacy concerns.

AP Images/Peter Thomson

The Investigation Function

LO4 Summarize the investigation function

Fictional detectives in movies and on television shoot first and ask questions later. When they do conduct an interrogation, they think nothing of beating a confession out of the suspect. How accurate are these portrayals? Not very. The modern criminal investigator is likely to be an experienced civil servant, trained in investigatory techniques, knowledgeable about legal rules of evidence and procedure, and at least somewhat cautious about the legal and administrative consequences of his or her actions.[27]

Investigative services can be organized in a variety of ways. In New York, each borough or district has its own detective division that supervises investigators assigned to neighborhood police precincts (stations). Local squad detectives work closely with patrol officers to provide an immediate investigative response to crimes and incidents. (In some TV shows and movies, New York City detectives are shown barking commands at patrol officers and even snapping orders at uniformed sergeants and lieutenants; in reality, both branches are considered equal, so that would never happen. A patrol sergeant is the superior officer of a junior grade detective.) New York City also maintains specialized borough squads—homicide, robbery, and special victims—to give aid to local squads and help identify suspects whose crimes may have occurred in multiple locations. Also, specialty squads help in areas such as forensics. In smaller cities, detective divisions may be organized into sections or bureaus, such as homicide, robbery, or rape.

How Do Detectives Detect?

Detectives investigate the causes of crime and attempt to identify the individuals or groups responsible for committing particular offenses. They may enter a case after patrol officers have made the initial contact, such as when a patrol car interrupts a crime in progress, and the offenders flee before they can be apprehended. Detectives can investigate a case entirely on their own, sometimes by following up on leads provided by informants. Sometimes detectives go undercover to investigate crime; a lone agent can infiltrate a criminal group or organization to gather information on future criminal activity. Undercover officers can also pose as victims to capture predatory criminals who have been conducting street robberies and muggings.[28]

In his study of investigation techniques, Martin Innes found that police detectives rely heavily on interviews and forensic evidence to flesh out a narrative of the crime, creating in a sense the "story" that sets out how, where, and why the incident took place.[29] To create their story, contemporary detectives typically use a three-pronged approach:[30]

- *Specific focus.* Interview witnesses, gather evidence, record events, and collect facts at the immediate crime scene.
- *General coverage.* (1) Canvass the neighborhood and make observations; (2) conduct interviews with friends, families, and associates; (3) contact coworkers or employers for information about victims and suspects; (4) construct victim/suspect timelines to outline their whereabouts prior to the incident.
- *Informative.* Use modern technology to collect records of cell phones and pagers, computer hard drives (pads, notebooks, desktops, and servers), diaries, notes, and documents. This approach includes data that persons of interest in the investigation use, which, in turn, tell about their lives, interactions with others, and geographic connections.

Detective work is an art as well as a science, based on experience and knowledge of human behavior gained on the job. As sociologist Robert Jackall found when he studied detectives in New York City, the investigative branch has a unique culture and operating style.

Sting Operations

Another approach to investigation, commonly referred to as a **sting operation**, involves organized groups of detectives or patrol officers working in plain clothes who deceive criminals into openly committing illegal acts or conspiring to engage in criminal activity.

To sting criminals, some jurisdictions maintain **vice squads**, patrol officers working in plain clothes who focus on crimes of public morals such as prostitution or gambling. For example, police officers may pose as prostitutes and arrest those who solicit their services.

Sting operations can be highly successful, but they are also open to criticism.[31] Covert police activities have often been criticized as violating the personal rights of citizens, while forcing officers into demeaning roles. Some studies, though, have found that police officers often perceive sting work as professionally rewarding.[32]

By its very nature, a sting involves deceit by police agents that often comes close to entrapment. Sting operations may encourage criminals to commit new crimes because they have a new source for fencing stolen goods. Innocent people may damage their

REALITYCHECK
Myth or Reality?
The more serious the crime, the more likely it is that detectives will solve it.

REALITY. Investigations of serious criminal incidents receive more attention. Consequently, they are solved at a higher rate.

Are there any unintended side effects of concentrating resources on serious crimes at the expense of less serious ones? Or are serious crimes solved for other reasons than just prioritizing them?

ZUMA Press Inc./Alamy Stock Photo

An undercover Palm Beach County (Florida) sheriff's deputy poses as a prostitute. The sting was one of several recent furtive operations by the agency intended to catch "johns" in the act. The man was not arrested and did not hire the decoy for sexual acts.

reputations by buying merchandise from a sting operation when they had no idea the items had been stolen. By putting the government into the fencing business, such operations blur the line between law enforcement and criminal activity.

Evaluating Investigations

Serious criticism has been leveled at the nation's detective forces for being bogged down in paperwork and being relatively inefficient in clearing cases. One famous study of 153 detective bureaus by the RAND Corporation, a well-known think tank, found that a great deal of a detective's time was spent in unproductive work and that investigative expertise did little to solve cases; half of all detectives could be replaced without negatively influencing crime clearance rates.[33]

Although some questions remain about the effectiveness of investigations, police detectives do make a valuable contribution to police work because their skilled interrogation and case-processing techniques are essential to eventual criminal conviction.[34] Detective work may be improved if investigators are able to spend more time on each case, allowing them to carefully collect physical evidence at the scene of the crime, identify witnesses, check departmental records, and use informants.[35] Research shows that in more serious cases, especially homicide investigations, where detectives devote a lot of attention to a single crime, the likelihood increases that they will eventually identify and arrest the culprit.[36]

Nonetheless, a majority of cases that are solved are done so when the perpetrator is identified at the scene of the crime by patrol officers. Research shows that if a crime is reported while in progress, the police have about a 33-percent chance of making an arrest; the arrest probability declines to about 10 percent if the crime is reported 1 minute later, and to 5 percent if more than 15 minutes have elapsed. As the time between the crime and the arrest grows, the chances of a conviction are also reduced, probably because the ability to recover evidence is lost. Put another way, after a crime has been completed and the investigation is put in the hands of detectives, the chances of identifying and arresting the perpetrator diminish rapidly.[37]

One reason for investigation ineffectiveness is that detectives often lack sufficient resources to carry out a lengthy ongoing probe of any but the most serious cases. Research shows the following:

- *Unsolved cases.* Almost 50 percent of burglary cases are screened out by supervisors before assignment to a detective for a follow-up investigation. Of those assigned, 75 percent are dropped after the first day of the follow-up investigation. Although robbery cases are more likely to be assigned to detectives, 75 percent of them are also dropped after one day of investigation.
- *Length of investigation.* The vast majority of cases are investigated for no more than four hours stretching over three days. An average of 11 days elapses between the initial report of a crime and suspension of the investigation.
- *Sources of information.* Early in an investigation, the focus is on the victim; as the investigation is pursued, emphasis shifts to the suspect. The most critical information for determining case outcome is the name and description of the suspect and related crime information. Victims are most often the source of information; unfortunately, witnesses, informants, and members of the police department are consulted far less often. However, when these sources are tapped, they are likely to produce useful information.
- *Effectiveness.* Preliminary investigations by patrol officers are critical. In situations where the suspect's identity is not known immediately after the crime is committed, detectives make an arrest in less than 10 percent of all cases.[38]

Improving Investigation with Technology

In Chapter 4, some technological breakthroughs that have aided crime investigation were discussed in some detail. Information technology (IT) has revolutionized police work in many areas, including communications, criminal identification, and record

REALITYCHECK

Myth or Reality?

Most crimes are solved when the perpetrator is identified at the crime scene.

REALITY. The majority of cases are solved when the perpetrator is identified early.

This is contrary to the view portrayed in the fictional media, wherein the investigators always apprehend criminals by examining trace evidence and following up on questionable leads. What other misconceptions are conveyed by programs such as *CSI* and *Law & Order*?

storage. A number of tasks that used to involve painstaking labor by individuals are now being conducted with IT. Take, for instance, searching criminal histories. Police agencies are now using a program called CopLink to facilitate this time-consuming task. CopLink integrates information from different jurisdictions into a single database that detectives can access when working on investigations.[39] The CopLink program enables investigators to search the entire database of past criminal records and computes a list of possible suspects even if only limited data are available, such as first or last name, partial license plate numbers, vehicle type, vehicle color, location of crime, and/or type of weapon used.

Another technique that is improving investigation success is the use of DNA profiling. Using DNA in support of criminal investigations has increased both in the United States and around the world. The first national DNA database—the UK National DNA Database—is regarded by many police experts as the most important development in investigative technology since the adoption of fingerprint comparison early in the previous century.[40] Still other strategies have been employed, such as the use of social networking.

Improving Investigations with Forensic Science

Investigations have improved along with advances in forensic science. The *CSI* television series and its various spin-offs have drawn attention to the developing field of forensics in police work, which uses a variety of sciences, mathematical principles, and problem-solving methods to identify perpetrators. Forensic means "pertaining to the law," and forensic scientists perform comprehensive chemical and physical analyses on evidence submitted by law enforcement agencies. Although most forensic scientists focus on criminal cases (they are sometimes referred to as criminalists), others work in the civil justice system—for example, performing handwriting comparisons to determine the validity of a signature on a will.

Today, forensic specialists can examine blood and other body fluids and tissues for the presence of alcohol, drugs, and poisons and can compare body fluids and hair for typing factors, including DNA analysis. Forensic scientists analyze trace physical evidence such as blood spatters, paint, soil, and glass to help reconstruct a crime scene and interpret how the crime was committed. In addition to forensics, investigation

L05 Explain what forensics is and what forensics experts do for police agencies

forensic science The use of scientific techniques to investigate questions of interest to the justice system and to solve crimes.

AP Images/Scott G. Winterton

A Utah medical examiner, relying in part on DNA and dental records, determined that the bones pictured here were those of 23-year-old Theresa Rose Greaves, who disappeared in 1983.

is being improved by information technology, which allows investigators to compare evidence found at the crime scene with material collected from similar crimes by other police agencies.

Forensic analyses involve the use of complex instruments and of chemical, physical, and microscopic examining techniques. In addition to analyzing crime scene investigations, forensic scientists provide testimony in a court of law when the case is brought to trial. Some forensic scientists are generalists, and others specialize in a particular scientific area, including toxicology, blood pattern analysis, crime scene investigation, impression evidence (e.g., footprints), trace evidence (e.g., hair left at a crime scene), and questioned documents. There is a forensics expert for nearly every conceivable type of evidence and criminal activity.

Community-Oriented Policing

LO6 Discuss the concept of community-oriented policing

Police agencies have been trying for several decades to gain the cooperation and respect of the communities they serve. At first, efforts at improving the relationships between police departments and the public involved programs with the general title of police–community relations (PCR). Developed at the station house and departmental levels, these initial PCR programs were designed to make citizens more aware of police activities, alert them to methods of self-protection, and improve general attitudes toward policing.

Although PCR efforts demonstrated the willingness of police agencies to cooperate with the public, some experts believed that law enforcement agencies needed to undergo a significant transformation to create meaningful partnerships with the public. In their view, community relations and crime control effectiveness cannot be the province of a few specialized units housed within a traditional police department. Instead, the core police role must be altered if community involvement is to be won and maintained. This led to the development of community-oriented policing (COP), a set of programs and strategies designed to bring police and the public closer together and create a more cooperative working environment between them.

community-oriented policing (COP) Programs and strategies designed to bring police and the public closer together and create a more cooperative working environment between them.

Implementing Community-Oriented Policing

The COP concept was originally implemented through a number of innovative demonstration projects.[41] Among the most publicized were experiments in foot patrol, which took officers out of cars and set them to walking beats in the neighborhood. Foot patrol

foot patrol Police patrols that take officers out of cars and put them on a walking beat to strengthen ties with the community.

Officer Mohamed Mohamed stops by an impromptu soccer game while fulfilling his community policing duties in Mankato, Minnesota. Mohamed, originally from Somalia, is hoping to start a more organized sports program as part of his community policing assignment in the city's Somali community.

AP Images/Pat Christman

efforts were aimed at forming a bond with community residents by acquainting them with the individual officers who patrolled their neighborhood and letting them know that police were caring and available.

The first foot patrol experiments were conducted in cities in Michigan and New Jersey. An evaluation of foot patrol indicated that although it did not bring down the crime rate, residents in areas where foot patrol was added perceived greater safety and were less afraid of crime.[42]

Since the advent of these programs, hundreds of communities have adopted innovative forms of decentralized, neighborhood-based COP models. The federal government has encouraged the growth of COP by providing billions of dollars to hire and train officers through its Office of Community Oriented Policing Services (COPS) program, which has given local departments more than $10 billion in aid since its inception.[43] Recent surveys indicate that there has been a significant increase in COP activities and that certain core programs, such as crime prevention, have become embedded in the police role.[44] COP programs have been implemented in large cities, suburban areas, and rural communities.[45]

Changing the Police Role

COP also emphasizes sharing power with local groups and individuals. A key element of the COP philosophy is that citizens must actively participate with police to fight crime. Such participation is essential because the community climate is influenced by the informal social control created by a concerned citizenry coupled with effective policing.[46] Participation might involve providing information in area-wide crime investigations or helping police reach out to troubled youths. The following are some other changes that have been linked to COP initiatives:

- *Neighborhood orientation.* To achieve the goals of COP, some police agencies have tried to decentralize, an approach sometimes referred to as **neighborhood-oriented policing (NOP)**.[47] According to this view, problem solving is best done at the neighborhood level where issues originate, not at a far-off central headquarters. Because each neighborhood has its own particular needs, police decision making must be flexible and adaptive. For example, neighborhoods undergoing change in racial composition may experience high levels of racially motivated violence and require special police initiatives to reduce tensions.[48]
- *Changing management styles.* COP also means the redesign of police departments' administration and management. Management's role must be reinterpreted to focus on the problems of the community, not on the needs of the police department. The traditional vertical police organizational chart must be altered so that top-down management gives way to bottom-up decision making. The patrol officer becomes the manager of his beat and a key decision maker.
- *Changing recruitment and training.* COP means that police departments must alter their recruitment and training requirements. Future officers must develop community-organizing and problem-solving skills, along with traditional police skills. Their training must prepare them to succeed less on their ability to make arrests or issue citations and more on their ability to solve problems effectively.

Challenges of Community-Oriented Policing

The core concepts of police work are changing as administrators recognize the limitations and realities of police work in modern society. If they are to be successful, COP strategies must be able to react effectively to some significant administrative problems.

DEFINING COMMUNITY Critics believe that COP works best in stable, affluent areas that are already characterized by a strong sense of community. The challenge of community is to reach out to all people in all neighborhoods, including young people and minorities, who may previously have been left out of the process.

neighborhood-oriented policing (NOP) Community-oriented policing efforts aimed at individual neighborhoods.

REALITYCHECK
Myth or Reality?
COP can succeed in any community if the police try hard enough.

MYTH. COP is a two-way street that requires both police efforts and community participation.

Research shows that areas already defined by a clear sense of community benefit from COP initiatives more than those that are not. Is COP thus biased toward more affluent or cohesive areas? Can COP really solve the historical problems it is intended to address?

DEFINING ROLES Police administrators must also establish the exact role of community police agents. How should they integrate their activities with those of regular patrol forces? For example, should foot patrols have primary responsibility for policing in an area, or should they coordinate their activities with officers assigned to patrol cars?

CHANGING SUPERVISOR ATTITUDES Some supervisors are wary of COP because it supports a decentralized command structure. Supervisors who learn to actively embrace COP concepts are the ones best able to encourage patrol officers to follow suit.[49]

REORIENTING POLICE VALUES Research shows that police officers who have a traditional crime control orientation are less satisfied with COP efforts than those who are public service oriented.[50] In some instances, officers holding traditional values may go as far as stigmatizing their own comrades assigned to COP; their targets often feel penalized by a lack of administrative support.[51] It is thus unlikely that COP activities can be successful unless police line officers make a firm commitment to the values of the program.[52]

REVISED TRAINING Because the COP model calls for an expansion of the police role from law enforcer to community organizer, police training must be revised to reflect this new mandate. If COP is to be adopted on a wide scale, a whole new type of police officer must be recruited and trained in a completely new way. Training must prepare officers to succeed less on their ability to make arrests or issue citations and more on their ability to solve problems, prevent crime effectively, and deal with neighborhood diversity and cultural values.[53]

REORIENTED RECRUITMENT To make COP successful, mid-level managers must be recruited and trained who are receptive to and can implement community-change strategies.[54] The selection of new recruits must be guided by a desire to find individuals with the skills and attitudes that support COP.

Community-Oriented Policing Effectiveness

Empirical evidence suggests that *some* COP efforts can reduce disorder and impact the crime rate.[55] The most successful programs give officers time to meet with local residents to talk about crime in the neighborhood and allow officers to use personal initiative to solve problems. Although not all programs work (police–community newsletters and cleanup campaigns do not seem to do much good), the overall impression has been that patrol officers can actually reduce the level of fear in the community. Where it is used, citizens seem to like COP, and those who volunteer and get involved in community crime-prevention programs report higher confidence in the police force and its ability to create a secure environment.[56]

On the other hand, there is no clear-cut evidence that COP is highly successful at reducing crime across the board. Crime rate reductions in cities that have used COP may be the result of an overall downturn in the nation's crime rate, rather than a result of COP efforts. Researchers have also found that it is difficult to change the traditional values and attitudes of police officers involved in the programs.[57]

problem-oriented policing (POP) A style of police operations that stresses proactive problem solving, rather than reactive crime fighting.

Problem-Oriented Policing

Closely associated with, yet independent from, the COP concept are the **problem-oriented policing (POP)** strategies. Traditional police models focus on responding to calls for help in the shortest possible time, dealing with the situation, and then getting on the street again as soon as possible. In contrast, POP is proactive.

POP requires police agencies to identify particular long-term community problems—street-level drug dealers, prostitution rings, gang hangouts—and develop strategies to eliminate them.[58] As with COP, police departments must rely on local residents and private resources to be problem solvers. This means that police managers must learn how to develop community resources, design efficient and cost-effective solutions to problems, and become advocates as well as agents of reform.[59]

A significant percentage of police departments are now using special units to confront specific social problems. POP models are supported by ample evidence that a great deal of urban crime is concentrated in a few hot spots.[60] A significant portion of all police calls in metropolitan areas typically radiate from a relatively few locations: bars, malls, bus depots, hotels, and certain apartment buildings.[61] By implication, concentrating police resources on these hot spots of crime could reduce crime appreciably.[62] Problem-oriented strategies are being developed that focus on specific problem areas and/or specific criminal acts. For example, a POP effort in Sarasota, Florida, which was aimed at reducing prostitution, involved intensive, focused, high-visibility patrols to discourage prostitutes and their customers; undercover work to arrest prostitutes and drug dealers; and collaboration with hotel and motel owners to identify and arrest pimps and drug dealers.[63]

Another well-known program, Operation Ceasefire, was a POP intervention aimed at reducing youth homicide and youth firearms violence in Boston. According to evaluations of the program, Ceasefire produced significant reductions in youth homicide victimization and gun assault incidents in Boston that were not experienced in other communities in New England or elsewhere in the nation.[64] The strategy was replicated in a number of cities throughout the United States, including Chicago and Phoenix.[65]

Although programs such as these seem successful, the effectiveness of any street-level problem-solving effort must be interpreted with caution.[66] It is possible that the criminals will be displaced to other, "safer" areas of the city and will return shortly after the program is declared a success and the additional police forces have been pulled from the area.[67] Nonetheless, evidence shows that merely saturating an area with police may not deter crime, but focusing efforts on a particular problem may indeed have a crime-reducing effect.

hot spots of crime Places from which a significant portion of all police calls originate. These hot spots include taverns and housing projects.

WEB APP 5.3 Read about specific POP strategies at the Center for Problem-Oriented Policing: **http://www.popcenter.org/.** What have police departments done to target difficult problems such as false burglary alarms, loud car stereos, drive-by shootings, and homeless encampments? Which of these and other problems listed under the website's "POP Guides" tab do you think is most demanding of law enforcement? Why?

Intelligence-Led Policing

Since 9/11, policing has experienced a fundamental philosophical change by combining a homeland security focus with the many advances made in the realms of COP and POP.[68] An outgrowth of this combination is intelligence-led policing (ILP), which has been described as "the collection and analysis of information to produce an intelligence end product designed to inform police decision making at both the tactical and strategic levels."[69] More simply, ILP is intended to further shift the emphasis in police work away from reactive responses and individual case investigations. It instead emphasizes information sharing, collaboration, and strategic solutions to crime problems at various levels. ILP relies heavily on the following:

- Confidential informants
- Offender interviews
- Careful analysis of crime reports and calls for service
- Suspect surveillance
- Community sources of information[70]

The British have a long history of sophisticated intelligence gathering and analysis. All 43 British constabularies, as well as the London Metropolitan Police, have had intelligence units for some time to deal with problems ranging from drugs to organized crime.[71] The UK National Drugs Intelligence Unit, created in the 1980s, gathers intelligence to aid in the enforcement of laws against drug trafficking. In 1992, the National Criminal Intelligence Service (NCIS) was formed, mainly to deal with the problem of organized crime. One of its responsibilities is to work with the chemical industry in the United Kingdom to identify and disrupt the production of synthetic drugs.

LO8 Explain intelligence-led policing and the various means by which it occurs

intelligence-led policing (ILP) The collection and analysis of information to generate an "intelligence end product" designed to inform police decision making at both the tactical and the strategic level.

In contrast, American law enforcement agencies have, until recently, had little intelligence-gathering capacity. If it occurred at all, intelligence gathering was mostly reserved for large police agencies. According to David Carter, one of the leading experts on ILP, "Early law enforcement initiatives typically had no analysis and essentially consisted of dossiers kept on individuals who were suspicious or were deemed to be threats of some sort, often based on intuitive, rather than empirical, threat criteria."[72] Current ILP initiatives attempt to compensate for this shortcoming.

ILP bears a great deal of similarity to POP. The two are somewhat different, however, in that POP puts problem identification and solution in the hands of individual street-level officers, whereas ILP emphasizes a top-down managerial approach by which administrators set priorities for crime prevention and enforcement and then pass these priorities down through the agency.[73] ILP is similar to COP in that it relies on residents as part of the intelligence-gathering process. But COP emphasizes the desires of the community, whereas ILP relies on problem identification through careful analysis of the criminal environment as a whole. ILP has even been likened to CompStat, discussed earlier in this chapter. See Table 5.1 for a summary of the differences and commonalities between CompStat and ILP.

To gain a more concrete grasp of the ILP concept, consider these examples:

- A county sheriff's office identifies narcotics control as its top priority and develops strategies accordingly. The office targets known offenders and groups, shuts down open-air drug markets and crackhouses, and participates in school-based drug awareness programs to help prevent drug use.
- A statewide agency identifies vehicle insurance fraud as a top area for enforcement. The agency targets those involved in staged accidents, identifies communities in which insurance fraud is prevalent, exposes ongoing fraudulent activity, and mounts a public education campaign.
- A police agency in a small city makes safe streets a priority. The agency focuses on directed enforcement in identified hot spots. It also targets career criminals whose apprehension will significantly reduce the number of crimes being committed. Preventive measures include enhanced patrols, improved street lighting, and crime-watch programs.[74]

TABLE 5.1 Comparison of CompStat and Intelligence-Led Policing

CompStat	Commonalities	Intelligence-Led Policing
Single jurisdiction	Both have a goal of prevention.	Multiple jurisdictions
Incident-driven	Both require the following: • Organizational flexibility • Consistent information input • A significant analytic component	Threat-driven
Street crime and burglary		Criminal enterprises and terrorism
Crime mapping		Commodity flow; trafficking and transiting logistics
Time-sensitive (24-hour feedback and response)		Strategic
Disrupt crime series (e.g., burglary ring)		Disrupt enterprises
Drives operations: • Patrol • Tactical unit • Investigators		Drives operations: • Joint terrorism task forces • Organized crime investigations • Task forces
Analysis of offender MO (*modus operandi*)		Analysis of enterprise MO (modus operandi)

Source: Office of Community-Oriented Policing Services, *Intelligence-Led Policing: The Integration of Community Policing and Law Enforcement Intelligence, Part 4* (Washington, DC: COPS Office, n.d.), p. 43.

Fusion Centers

In the spring of 2002, law enforcement executives from around the country met at a Criminal Intelligence Sharing Summit. Summit participants called for the development of a national intelligence plan that could be used to prevent future terrorist attacks like the ones that occurred on 9/11. After this meeting, the Global Justice Information Sharing Initiative and the Intelligence Working Group were formed. These groups eventually developed the National Criminal Intelligence Sharing Plan (NCISP).[75] The report outlined a number of "action steps" that could be taken to improve intelligence gathering and sharing among law enforcement agencies across the country. The NCISP sought to communicate the following:

- A model intelligence-sharing plan
- A mechanism to promote ILP
- A blueprint for law enforcement administrators to follow when enhancing or building an intelligence system
- A model for intelligence process principles and policies
- A plan that respects and protects individuals' privacy and civil rights
- A technology architecture to provide secure, seamless sharing of information among systems
- A national model for intelligence training
- An outreach plan to promote timely and credible intelligence sharing
- A plan that leverages existing systems and networks, yet allows flexibility for technology and process enhancements

As part of this process, many states and large cities have formed fusion centers. According to the National Fusion Center Guidelines, a fusion center is "an effective and efficient mechanism to exchange information and intelligence, maximize resources, streamline operations, and improve the ability to fight crime and terrorism by analyzing data from a variety of sources."[76] Often located in police departments, these centers are set up for the purpose of sharing information and intelligence within specific jurisdictions and across levels of government. Fusion centers often emphasize terrorism prevention and crime fighting with extensive use of technology. They frequently resemble a department's technological "nerve center" and are usually housed in a central location where information is collected and then shared with decision makers. Fusion centers focus on four main goals:

- Provide support for a range of law enforcement activities, including anticrime operations and terrorism prevention.

National Criminal Intelligence Sharing Plan (NCISP) A formal intelligence-sharing initiative that identifies the security and intelligence-sharing needs recognized in the wake of the 9/11 terrorist attacks.

fusion centers Mechanisms to exchange information and intelligence, maximize resources, streamline operations, and improve the ability to fight crime and terrorism by analyzing data from a variety of sources.

AP Images/Lisa Billings

Officer Jim Griffen organizes a search while manning the Communications Center at the Virginia Emergency Operations Center at State Police headquarters in Midlothian, Virginia.

- Provide help for major incident operations and support for units charged with interdiction and criminal investigations.
- Provide the means for community input, often through tip lines.
- Provide assistance to law enforcement executives so they can make informed decisions about departmental priorities.[77]

Fusion centers are intended to provide a mechanism through which government agencies, law enforcement, and the private sector can work together for the common purpose of protecting the homeland and preserving public safety. They are based on a model of collaboration. Collaboration between agencies and across levels of government has been lacking throughout history, but the events of 9/11 affirmed a need for change. The concept of fusion centers will continue to catch on, and more will probably be developed as law enforcement becomes increasingly aware of the benefits they can yield.

Support Functions

LO9 Describe the various police support functions

As the model of a typical police department indicates (refer to Figure 5.1), not all members of a department engage in what the general public regards as "real police work"—patrol, detection, and traffic control. Even in departments that embrace COP and POP, many police resources are actually devoted to support and administrative functions. There are too many tasks to mention in detail, but the most important include those discussed next.

Many police departments maintain their own personnel service, which carries out such functions as recruiting new police officers, creating exams to determine the most qualified applicants, and handling promotions and transfers. Innovative selection techniques are constantly being developed and tested. For example, the Behavioral-Personnel Assessment Device (B-PAD) requires police applicants to view video scenarios and respond as though they were officers handling the situation; reviews indicate that this procedure may be a reliable and unbiased method of choosing new recruits.[78]

internal affairs The branch of the police department that investigates charges of corruption or misconduct on the part of police officers.

Larger police departments often maintain an **internal affairs** branch charged with policing the police. Internal affairs units process citizen complaints of police corruption, investigate what may be the unnecessary use of force by police officers, and probe police participation in actual criminal activity, such as burglaries or narcotics violations. In addition, internal affairs divisions may assist police managers when disciplinary action is brought against individual officers. The internal affairs function is controversial because investigators are feared and distrusted by fellow police officers. Nonetheless, rigorous self-scrutiny is the only way police departments can earn the respect of citizens. Because of these concerns, it has become commonplace for police departments to institute citizen oversight over police practices and to establish civilian review boards that have the power to listen to complaints and conduct investigations.

Most police departments are responsible for the administration and control of their own budgets. This task includes administering payroll, purchasing equipment and services, planning budgets for future expenditures, and auditing departmental financial records.

Police departments include separate units charged with maintaining and disseminating information on wanted offenders, stolen merchandise, traffic violators, and so on. Modern data management systems enable police to use their records in a highly sophisticated fashion. For example, officers in a patrol car who spot a suspicious-looking vehicle can instantly receive a computerized rundown on whether it has been stolen. And if stolen property is recovered during an arrest, police using this sort of system can determine who reported the loss of the merchandise and arrange for its return.

In many departments, training is continuous throughout an officer's career. Training usually begins at a police academy, which may be run exclusively for larger departments or may be part of a regional training center serving smaller and varied governmental units. More than 90 percent of all police departments require preservice training, including nearly all departments in larger cities (population over 100,000). The average officer receives more than 500 hours of preservice training, including 400 hours in the classroom and the rest in field training.[79] Police in large cities often receive more than 1,400 hours of instruction divided almost evenly between classroom and field instruction.[80] Among the topics usually covered are law and civil rights, firearms handling, emergency medical care, and restraint techniques.[81]

After assuming their police duties, new recruits are assigned to field-training officers who break them in on the job. However, training does not stop here. On-the-job training is a continuous process in the modern police department and covers such areas as weapons skills, first aid, crowd control, and community relations. Some departments use roll call training, in which superior officers or outside experts address police officers at the beginning of the workday. Other departments allow police officers time off to attend annual training sessions to sharpen their skills and learn new policing techniques.

Police departments provide emergency aid to the ill, counsel youngsters, speak to school and community agencies on safety and drug abuse, and provide countless other services designed to improve citizen–police interactions.

Larger police departments maintain specialized units that help citizens protect themselves from criminal activity. They advise citizens on effective home security techniques or conduct Project ID campaigns—engraving valuables with an identifying number so that they can be returned if recovered after a burglary; police also work in schools to build positive relationships between themselves and members of the community.[82] Police agencies maintain (or have access to) forensic laboratories that enable them to identify substances to be used as evidence and to classify fingerprints.

 ## CAREERS IN CRIMINAL JUSTICE CRIME ANALYST

Duties and Characteristics of the Job

- Crime analysts engage in a number of important law enforcement support functions. Foremost, they study patterns of criminal activity and profile suspects.

- They analyze crime data (calls for service, arrests made, etc.) and often use that information to forecast the days, times, and places those crimes are most likely to occur.

- They are also called upon to provide information on demand, analyze long-term programs, and develop intelligence.

Job Outlook

- The job outlook for crime analysts is quite favorable.

- According to the International Association of Crime Analysts (IACA), the demand for qualified crime analysts has increased more than tenfold in the past 15 years. It will continue to increase even more over time as law enforcement further comes to realize the potential of sophisticated data gathering and analysis.

- Some crime analysts are involved in grant writing and may earn part of their wages from "soft money," which can make the situation unpredictable for some of them.

- Less populous cities with few police officers generally do not require dedicated or full-time crime analysts. Opportunities also exist in certain task force offices.

Salary

- Specialized knowledge is required and, as such, crime analysts tend to do fairly well in terms of compensation.

- An entry-level crime analyst can make as much as $60,000 per year. Experienced and well-educated crime analysts can make $80,000 per year or more.

- A supervising crime analyst in a large city such as Los Angeles can make close to $100,000 per year, if not more.

Qualifications

- Crime analysts are often civilian employees, which may prove desirable for those who do not want to become sworn peace officers.

- Crime analysts require knowledge of techniques and methods used in data collection, statistical analysis, report preparation, and research.

- Knowledge of numerous computer applications is also required, as is a full command of the English language for report writing and communications, familiarity with law enforcement operations, and the like.

Education and Training

- Many positions require a four-year degree, often with a concentration in criminal justice, criminology, and/or policing. Some permit a combination of work experience and education short of a four-year degree.

- Positions may or may not require any particular licensing or certification, but either can make an applicant more competitive. For example, the IACA offers a certification program. According to IACA, graduates may be more marketable and/or earn more from their employing agencies as a result of the certification.

Reality Check

- A crime analyst position requires specialized knowledge of complex computer applications and a fondness for numbers.

- Most positions are located in large police departments.

- Crime analysis is mostly a "behind the scenes" function and does not see the level of action one may encounter in a sworn position.

Sources: International Association of Crime Analysts, "What Is Crime Analysis?" http://www.iaca.net/dc_about_ca.asp; IACA, "Analyst Position Descriptions," http://www.iaca.net/resources.asp (URLs accessed April 2017).

Planning and research functions include designing programs to increase police efficiency and strategies to test program effectiveness. Police planners monitor recent technological developments and institute programs to adapt them to police services. Crime analysts support the department through the compilation and analysis of statistics to help administrators make decision as to how best allocate resources. See the accompanying Careers in Criminal Justice feature for additional information.

ETHICALREFLECTION

Consider the following hypothetical scenario:

The Middle City police force created "crime control teams"—decentralized units relieved of routine duties that were not crime related and given responsibility for controlling serious crime, apprehending offenders, conducting investigations, and increasing clearance rates on a neighborhood basis. Two team members, Officers Donald Libby and Karen Johnson, each with more than 15 years on the force, were part of a team assigned to displace gangs of local teenagers who were constantly causing problems in the neighborhood. After a few months on the job, Libby and Johnson were the target of numerous complaints related to their treatment of neighborhood youths. They were charged with roughing up neighborhood kids, slapping some of them around, and being disrespectful. In the most serious incident, they used a nightstick on a 15-year-old whom they claim had resisted arrest after they found him smoking marijuana in the park. The youth suffered a broken arm and concussion and required hospitalization. When interviewed by the internal affairs division, the officers admitted they scuffled with the boy but claimed they were "only doing their job." Besides, they argued, community leaders had demanded results, and their aggressive style had helped lower the crime rate in the area by more than 20 percent. The boy and his parents have filed suit, claiming that the amount of force used was unnecessary and violated his civil rights.

Think back to this chapter's discussion of police strategies, including the Focus on Effectiveness box devoted to stop, question, and frisk. Don't get wrapped up yet in legal issues (those are covered in the next chapter). Instead, focus on the ethics of heavy-handed approaches to law enforcement (such as SQF) vis-à-vis community engagement strategies, like community-oriented policing.

Writing Challenge: As the officers' defense attorney, write an essay outlining their defense. Again, don't worry about legal rules. How would you defend the two officers? Draw from this chapter's sections on community policing, problem solving, and other sections as needed. Also consider visiting and gathering additional information from the Office of Juvenile Justice and Delinquency Prevention's (OJJDP) Model Programs site at http://www.ojjdp.gov /mpg/ or from the National Institute of Justice, https://www.crimesolutions.gov/.

SUMMARY

LO1 *Explain the organization of police departments* Most municipal police departments in the United States are independent agencies within the executive branch of government. Typically, local police departments are organized in a hierarchical manner and employ a time-in-rank system for determining promotion eligibility.

LO2 *Articulate the complexities of the police role* A police officer's crime-fighting efforts are only a small part of his or her overall activities. Studies of police work indicate that a significant portion of an officer's time is spent handling minor disturbances, service calls, and administrative duties. The police role involves many activities that are not crime related. The primary role of police seems to be "handling the situation."

LO3 *Explain the limitations of patrol and methods for improving it* Most experts agree that the great bulk of patrol efforts are devoted to what has been described as order maintenance or peacekeeping: maintaining order and civility in the assigned jurisdiction. Evidence is mixed on the deterrent effect of patrol. Efforts to improve patrol have

included proactive policing and directed patrol, targeting specific offenses for more arrests, rapid response, broken windows policing, and increased utilization of technology, including CompStat. Of these, rapid response has proven least effective.

LO4 *Summarize the investigation function* Detectives investigate the causes of crime and attempt to identify the individuals or groups responsible for committing particular offenses. Police detectives make a valuable contribution to police work because their skilled interrogation and case-processing techniques are essential to eventual criminal conviction.

LO5 *Explain what forensics is and what forensics experts do for police agencies* Investigations have improved along with advances in forensic science. Forensic scientists perform comprehensive chemical and physical analyses on evidence submitted by law enforcement agencies.

LO6 *Discuss the concept of community-oriented policing* Community-oriented policing consists of a set of programs and strategies designed to bring police and the public closer together and create a more cooperative working environment between them. COP is now well integrated in most police departments, and empirical evidence suggests that some COP efforts can reduce disorder and crime.

LO7 Discuss the concept of problem-oriented policing Closely associated with, yet independent from, the COP concept are POP strategies. Proactive POP strategies require police agencies to identify particular long-term community problems (such as street-level drug dealers, prostitution rings, and gang hangouts) and develop strategies to eliminate them.

LO8 Explain intelligence-led policing and the various means by which it occurs ILP consists of the collection and analysis of information designed to inform police decision making at both the tactical and strategic levels. It emphasizes top-down problem solving. ILP relies on community input, but priorities are set at the department level, rather than identified by residents.

LO9 Describe the various police support functions Many police departments maintain their own personnel service, which carries out such functions as recruiting new police officers, creating exams to determine the most qualified applicants, and handling promotions and transfers. Larger police departments often maintain an internal affairs branch charged with "policing the police." Another important function of police communication is the effective and efficient dispatching of patrol cars.

KEY TERMS

police chief, p. 109

time-in-rank system, p. 109

order maintenance (peacekeeping), p. 110

proactive policing, p. 111

deterrent effect, p. 111

directed patrol, p. 113

broken windows model, p. 114

CompStat, p. 114

sting operation, p. 117

vice squads, p. 117

forensic science, p. 119

community-oriented policing (COP), p. 120

foot patrol, p. 120

neighborhood-oriented policing (NOP), p. 121

problem-oriented policing (POP), p. 122

hot spots of crime, p. 123

intelligence-led policing (ILP), p. 123

National Criminal Intelligence Sharing Plan (NCISP), p. 125

fusion centers, p. 125

internal affairs, p. 126

REVIEW QUESTIONS

1. Should the primary police role be law enforcement or community service? Explain.

2. Should a police chief be permitted to promote an officer with special skills to a supervisory position, or should all officers be forced to spend "time in rank"? Explain your answer.

3. Do the advantages of proactive policing outweigh the disadvantages? Explain.

4. Explain the concept of broken windows policing. Why might it be successful?

5. What are the problems facing investigators and forensics experts today?

6. Can the police and the community ever form a partnership to fight crime? Why or why not? Does the COP model remind you of early forms of policing? Explain.

6

Issues in Policing
PROFESSIONAL, SOCIAL, AND LEGAL

Following several high-profile police shootings of unarmed African American suspects, law enforcement is under the microscope. Protests and calls for reform have made an already difficult job even harder. What do police think of the heightened scrutiny? A recent national survey of 8,000 police officers conducted by the Pew Research Center officers some interesting insights.[1] Fatal encounters between police and African Americans (which include citizen *and* officer killings) have resulted in:

- 90 percent of officers reporting that their jobs are now harder.
- 93 percent of officers becoming more concerned about their safety.
- 76 percent of officers reporting reluctance to use force in certain situations.
- 75 percent of interactions between officers and African Americans becoming more tense than before.
- 72 percent of officers becoming less willing to engage in stop and frisk tactics.

Other findings from the survey reveal the duality of the police role. Nearly 8 in 10 officers reported receiving thanks for their service, but two-thirds reported being verbally abused during the same period. Nearly as many officers who say their jobs make them feel proud (58 percent) also say their jobs make them feel frustrated (51 percent) and callous (58 percent). And unfortunately, there are no signs that matters are improving. The survey also revealed that officers remain deeply skeptical of the protests that have followed certain deadly encounters. Only 14 percent of officers felt that the public understands the risks they face while on duty, and more officers than ever report the need for aggressive tactics in certain situations. All in all, the survey revealed that:

> Exposure to the dark side of life, coupled with the stress that officers encounter working in high-pressure situations or with hostile individuals, means that many officers may pay an emotional price for their service.[2]

REALITYCHECK
Myth or Reality?

- Male police officers believe that female police officers can perform the job just as well as they can.
- Police officers feel that no one else understands what they do for a living.
- Veteran police officers receive the most citizen complaints.
- Thousands of people are fatally shot by police each year.
- The police are not required to advise all arrestees of their *Miranda* rights.
- Some warrantless searches are permissible as long as the police have probable cause.
- Legal loopholes enable guilty criminals to go free in alarming numbers.

AP Images/Uncredited

LEARNING OBJECTIVES

LO1 Summarize demographic trends in policing

LO2 Explain how minority and female officers act and are treated

LO3 Explain police culture and personality

LO4 Identify distinct policing styles

LO5 Describe factors that affect police discretion

LO6 Discuss four major problems of policing

LO7 Distinguish between deadly and nondeadly force—and methods for controlling each

LO8 Explain the importance of less-lethal weapons

LO9 Analyze the Supreme Court's involvement with the police through its effort to control search and seizure and interrogation, and through establishment of the exclusionary rule

WEB APP 6.2 Read the report *Tired Cops: The Prevalence and Potential Consequences of Police Fatigue* at **https://www.ncjrs .gov/pdffiles1/jr000248d.pdf**. What else besides what is briefly discussed in this chapter can be done to control the problem of fatigue in law enforcement? Also visit the National Sleep Foundation site at **https://sleepfoundation.org /sleep-topics/shift-work-and-sleep**, and research the effects of shift work on sleep-related issues and fatigue.

REALITYCHECK

Myth or Reality?

Veteran police officers receive the most citizen complaints.

MYTH. Younger and less-experienced officers receive the most complaints.

Why do younger and less-experienced officers receive the most complaints? Can training solve the problem? If so, what kind of training: academy or on-the-job?

police brutality Usually involves such actions as the use of abusive language, the unnecessary use of force or coercion, threats, prodding with nightsticks, stopping and searching people to harass them, and so on.

corruption Exercising legitimate discretion for improper reasons or using illegal means to achieve approved goals.

- In California, a sheriff's deputy working alone drifts off a deserted highway and is killed instantly when his patrol car crashes into a tree.
- An officer in Florida, who has had trouble staying awake, runs a red light in her patrol car and crashes into a van driven by a deputy sheriff, injuring him severely.
- A police officer driving home from working in Ohio nods off at the wheel, begins swerving in and out of traffic, and runs off the road, striking and killing a man jogging down the sidewalk.

CONTROLLING FATIGUE What can be done to control police fatigue? One option is for administrators to make special efforts during scheduling to ensure that officers do not work too much overtime. Another is for administrators to adopt policies that place limitations on second jobs. Many officers moonlight as security guards, which may affect their on-the-job performance. A recent government report offered several other recommendations for limiting fatigue.

Violence and Brutality

Evidence shows that only a small proportion of officers are continually involved in use-of-force incidents. Why do these cops continually get involved in violent confrontations? Aggressive cops may overreact to the stress of police work and at the same time feel socially isolated. They believe that the true source of their frustration is beyond their reach, so they take their frustrations out on readily available targets: vulnerable people in their immediate environment.[90]

What kind of police officer gets involved in problem behavior? Are some officers "chronic offenders"? Research seems to show that a few officers are in fact chronic offenders who account for a significant portion of all citizen complaints. The officers receiving the bulk of complaints tend to be young and less experienced.[91] Efforts to deal with these "problem cops" are now being undertaken in police departments around the nation.

CURBING VIOLENCE Because incidents of brutality undermine efforts to build a bridge between police and the public, police departments around the United States have instituted specialized training programs to reduce them. A number of larger departments are instituting early warning systems to change the behavior of individual officers who have been identified as having performance problems. In most systems, problem officers are identified by their behavior profiles: citizen complaints, firearm discharge and use-of-force reports, civil litigation, incidents of resisting arrest, and high-speed pursuits and vehicular damage. The initial intervention generally consists of a review by the officer's immediate supervisor, who advises the officer of the sanctions he faces if problems continue; some cases are referred to counseling, training, or police psychologists. Evaluations of early warning programs indicate that they are quite successful.[92]

Some departments have developed administrative policies that emphasize limiting the use of force and containing armed offenders until specially trained backup teams are sent to take charge of the situation. Administrative policies have been found to be an effective control on use of deadly force, and their influence can be enhanced if they are clearly supported by the chief of police.[93]

Perhaps the greatest factors in controlling the use of **police brutality** are the threat of civil judgments against individual officers who use excessive force, police chiefs who ignore or condone violent behavior, and the expectations that prevail in the cities and towns in which they are employed.

Corruption

Ever since their creation, US police departments have wrestled with the problem of controlling illegal and unprofessional behavior by their officers. **Corruption** pervaded the American police when the early departments were first formed. In the nineteenth century, police officers systematically ignored violations of laws related to drinking, gambling, and prostitution in return for regular payoffs. Some actually entered into relationships with professional criminals, especially pickpockets. Illegal behavior was tolerated in return for goods or information. Police officers helped politicians gain office by allowing electoral fraud to flourish; some senior officers sold promotions to higher rank in the department.[94] Although most police officers are not corrupt, the few who are dishonest bring discredit to the entire profession.

VARIETIES OF CORRUPTION Police deviance can include a number of activities. In a general sense, it involves misuse of authority by police officers in a manner designed to yield personal gain for themselves or others.[95]

EXHIBIT 6.2 Varieties of Police Corruption

- *Internal corruption.* This corruption takes place among police officers themselves, involving both the bending of departmental rules and the outright performance of illegal acts.

- *Selective enforcement or nonenforcement.* This occurs when police abuse or exploit their discretion. If an officer frees a drug dealer in return for valuable information, that is considered a legitimate use of discretion; if the officer does so for money, that is an abuse of police power.

- *Active criminality.* This is participation by police in serious criminal behavior. Police may use their positions of trust and power to commit the very crimes they are entrusted with controlling.

- *Bribery and extortion.* This includes practices in which law enforcement roles are exploited specifically to raise money. Bribery is initiated by the citizen; extortion is initiated by the officer.

Source: Michael Johnston, *Political Corruption and Public Policy in America* (Monterey, CA: Brooks/ Cole, 1982), p. 75.

However, debate continues over whether a desire for personal gain is an essential part of corruption. Some experts argue that police misconduct also involves such issues as the unnecessary use of force, unreasonable searches, or an immoral personal life and that these should be considered just as serious as corruption motivated by economic gain.

Scholars have attempted to create typologies categorizing the forms that the abuse of police powers can take. When investigating corruption among police officers in New York City, the **Knapp Commission** classified abusers into two categories: **meat eaters** and **grass eaters**. Meat eaters aggressively misuse police power for personal gain by demanding bribes, threatening legal action, or cooperating with criminals. In contrast, grass eaters accept payoffs when their everyday duties place them in a position to "look the other way."

Other police experts have attempted to create models to better understand police corruption. It may be possible to divide police corruption into four major categories, as depicted in Exhibit 6.2.

Knapp Commission A public body that led an investigation into police corruption in New York and uncovered a widespread network of payoffs and bribes.

meat eaters A term for police officers who actively solicit bribes and vigorously engage in corrupt practices.

grass eaters A term for police officers who accept payoffs when everyday duties place them in a position to "look the other way."

CAUSES OF CORRUPTION No single explanation satisfactorily accounts for the various forms the abuse of power takes. One view holds that policing tends to attract individuals who do not have the financial means to maintain a coveted middle-class lifestyle. As they develop the cynical, authoritarian police personality, accepting graft seems an all-too-easy method of achieving financial security. A second view is that the wide discretion police enjoy, coupled with low visibility among the public and their own supervisors, makes them likely candidates for corruption. A third perspective holds that corruption is a function of society's ambivalence toward many forms of vice-related criminal behavior that police officers are sworn to control. Unenforceable laws governing moral standards promote corruption because they create large groups with an interest in undermining law enforcement. These include consumers who do not want to be deprived of their chosen form of recreation—people who gamble, want to drink after the legal closing hour, or patronize prostitutes.

CONTROL OF CORRUPTION How can police misconduct be controlled? One approach is to strengthen the internal administrative review process in police departments. A strong and well-supported internal affairs division has been linked to lowered corruption rates.[96] Another approach, instituted by then New York Commissioner Patrick Murphy in the wake of the Knapp Commission, is the accountability system. This holds that supervisors at each level are directly accountable for the illegal behaviors of the

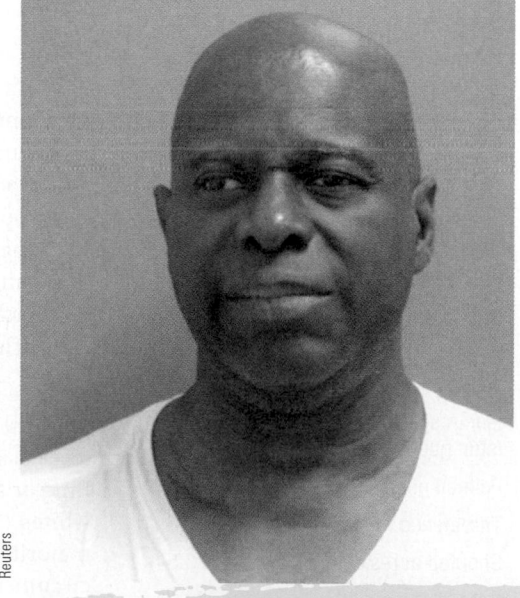

Reuters

Chicago police officer Lowell Houser, 57, was charged with first-degree murder for killing a man when he was off duty. Houser allegedly got into an argument with Jose Nieves as he was moving into a house in northwest Chicago. Nieves was unarmed.

LO7 Distinguish between deadly and nondeadly force—and methods for controlling each

deadly force Force that is likely to cause death or bodily harm.

suicide by cop A form of suicide in which a person acts in an aggressive manner with police officers in order to induce them to shoot to kill.

TABLE 6.1 Police Response in Encounters with Citizens in Which Use of Force Was Reported

Types of Force Used or Threatened by Police	Percent
Pushed or grabbed	53.5
Kicked or hit	12.6
Sprayed chemical/pepper spray	4.9
Electroshock weapon (stun gun)	4.1
Pointed gun	25.6
Threatened force	76.6
Shouted at resident	75.5
Cursed at resident	39.1
Number (in thousands)	**547**

Source: Christine Eith and Matthew R. Durose, *Contacts Between Police and the Public, 2008* (Bureau of Justice Statistics, 2011), p. 13, https://www.bjs.gov/content/pub/pdf/cpp08.pdf. Percentages do not sum to 100 because some people reported, in cases where force was used, that officers used more than one type of force.

officers under them. Consequently, a commander can be demoted or forced to resign if someone under his or her command is found guilty of corruption.[97] Close scrutiny by a department, however, can lower officer morale and create the impression that the officers' own supervisors distrust them.

Another approach is to create outside review boards or special prosecutors, such as the Mollen Commission in New York and the Christopher Commission in Los Angeles, to investigate reported incidents of corruption. However, outside investigators and special prosecutors are often limited by their lack of intimate knowledge of day-to-day operations. As a result, they depend on the testimony of a few officers who are willing to cooperate, either to save themselves from prosecution or because they have a compelling moral commitment. Outside evaluators also face the problem of the blue curtain, which is quickly drawn when police officers feel their department is under scrutiny.

Some jurisdictions have even developed review boards that monitor police behavior and tactics and investigate civilian complaints. Although police agencies in some communities have embraced citizen reviews, others find them troublesome. Departmental opposition is most likely when oversight procedures represent outside interference, oversight staff lack experience with and understanding of police work, and/or oversight processes are unfair. Despite serious reservations about citizen oversight, many law enforcement administrators have identified positive outcomes from having a review board in place. These include improving community relations, enhancing an agency's ability to police itself, and (most important) improving an agency's policies and procedures. Citizen oversight bodies can recommend changes in the way the department conducts its internal investigations into alleged misconduct and can also suggest ways to improve department policies governing officer behavior.[98]

Use of Force

How much force is being used by the police in the United States today? Despite some highly publicized incidents that get a lot of media attention, research reveals that the use of force is not very common. A national survey on police contacts with civilians, sponsored by the federal government, sheds some light on this issue.[99] The following are among the survey's most important findings:

- An estimated 17 percent of US residents age 16 or older had a face-to-face contact with a police officer.
- Contact between police and the public was more common among males, whites, and younger residents.
- Overall, about 9 out of 10 persons who had contact with police felt officers acted properly.
- An estimated 1.4 percent of people stopped by police had force used or threatened against them during their most recent contact.
- Blacks and Hispanics were two to three more times likely than whites to be searched during traffic stops.[100]

The data indicate that (1) relatively few contacts with police and the public involve physical force, but (2) there seem to be race and ethnic differences in the rate at which force is applied. As Table 6.1 shows, half of the force incidents involved more than scuffling or shouting. And even though African Americans (82 percent) were less likely than whites (91 percent) to feel that the police acted properly during a contact, the great majority of citizens of all races considered police behavior to be appropriate given the circumstances of the contact.

Deadly Force

As it is commonly used, the term **deadly force** refers to the actions of a police officer who shoots and kills a suspect who flees from arrest, assaults a victim, or attacks an officer.[101] The justification for the use of deadly force can be traced to English common

AP Images/Uncredited

Types of force

Verbal control commands

↓

Control holds (e.g., escort, pain-compliance holds)

↓

Chemical incapacitants (e.g., OC, CS)

↓

CED (e.g., Taser)

↓

Strikes/punches

↓

Chemical/kinetic hybrids (e.g., pepper filled projectiles)

↓

Baton/impact weapons

↓

Incapacitation holds (e.g., neck restraints)

↓

Kinetic weapons or munitions (e.g., beanbag projectile)

↓

Firearms

FIGURE 6.1 Relative Ranking of Force Types

Source: Adapted from Michael R. Smith, Robert J. Kaminski, Geoffrey P. Alpert, Lorie A. Fridell, John MacDonald, and Bruce Kubu, *A Multi-Method Evaluation of Police Use of Force Outcomes: Final Report to the National Institute of Justice* (Washington, DC: National Institute of Justice, 2010), Table 3-13, p. 3-22, https://www.ncjrs.gov/pdffiles1/nij/grants/231176.pdf.

law, in which almost every criminal offense was a felony and bore the death penalty. The use of deadly force in the course of arresting a felon was considered expedient, saving the state the trouble of conducting a trial (the "fleeing-felon rule").[102]

Although the entertainment media depict hero cops in a constant stream of deadly shootouts in which scores of bad guys are killed, the actual number of people killed by the police each year is usually around 400, although that number is disputed by some (see accompanying Contemporary Issues in Criminal Justice box).[103] And some of these shootings may even be precipitated by the target as a form of suicide.[104] This tragic event has become so common that the term **suicide by cop** has been coined to denote victim-precipitated killings by police.[105]

CONTROLLING DEADLY FORCE Because the police use of deadly force is such a serious issue, ongoing efforts have been made to control it. One of the most difficult issues in controlling the problem was the continued use of the fleeing-felon rule in a number of states. In 1985, the Supreme Court outlawed the indiscriminate use of deadly force with its decision in *Tennessee v. Garner*. In this case, the Court ruled that the use of deadly force against apparently unarmed and nondangerous fleeing felons is an illegal seizure of their person under the Fourth Amendment. Deadly force may not be used unless it is necessary to prevent an escape, and the officer has probable cause to believe that the suspect poses a significant threat of death or serious injury to the officer or others. The majority opinion stated that where the suspect poses no immediate threat to the officer and no threat to others, the harm resulting from failing to apprehend the suspect does not justify the use of deadly force to do so: "A police officer may not seize an unarmed, nondangerous suspect by shooting him dead."[106]

Individual state jurisdictions still control police shooting policy. Some states have adopted statutory policies that restrict the police use of violence. Others have upgraded training in the use of force. So-called "force continuums" have been adopted by a number of police departments, but they are gradually giving way to an "objective reasonableness" standard, which is discussed further in the nondeadly force section below. Also see Figure 6.1 for a "ranking" of types of force, from least to most serious.

Another way to control police shootings is through internal review and policy making by police administrative review boards. For example, since 1972, the New York City Police Department has conducted an internal investigation any time an officer's

Getting at the Dark Figure of Police Shootings

As you know by now, there is a dark figure of crime in America. Every data source we covered in Chapter 2 is limited: official data don't include those who fail to report crime, some people fail to fully disclose their experiences in victimization surveys, and self-reports require that people tell the truth. Crime continues to evolve, too, and data collection instruments often fail to keep pace. What you may *not* know is that there is also a dark figure of police shootings. How often do police shoot and injure or kill? Surprisingly, data are in short supply, and they suffer from the same limitations as our best crime data.

The Bureau of Justice Statistics (BJS) collects data on contacts between the police and the public, including information about use-of-force, but the most recent survey is from 2008. Cuts to federal funding for research, even federal government research, have made it difficult to collect current data. BJS also collects data on homicide trends in the United States, including information on justifiable killings. It is possible to extract from those data some estimates for the incidence of police shootings. We used the same data to arrive at our estimate of approximately 400 justifiable police homicides each year. Our estimate is just that: an *estimate*. Available data are simply inadequate.

In a February 2015 speech, not long after Ferguson, FBI Director James Comey expressed dismay over the lack of police shooting data:

> Not long after riots broke out in Ferguson late last summer, I asked my staff to tell me how many people shot by police were African-American in this country. I wanted to see trends. I wanted to see information. They couldn't give it to me, and it wasn't their fault. Demographic data regarding officer-involved shootings is not consistently reported to us through our Uniform Crime Reporting Program. Because reporting is voluntary, our data is incomplete and therefore, in the aggregate, unreliable.

Geoffrey Alpert, a University of South Carolina professor and police force expert, is also frustrated by the lack of data: "How can we address concerns about 'use of force,' and how can we address concerns about officer-involved shootings if we do not have a reliable grasp on the demographics and circumstances of those incidents?" David Klinger and his colleagues also lamented the "paltry" state of data on police shootings: "How often do American police officers use deadly force against citizens? And what is the role of citizen race in the deadly force picture? Unfortunately, neither question can be answered satisfactorily because existing national data on police use of deadly force have critical limitations…"

Some agencies are very forthcoming with their use-of-force data, others not so much. How transparent a police department is depends largely on where it is located, who is leading it, and even what the legal requirements are. In Dallas, for example, an "open data portal" publishes detailed information on police shootings going back to 2003, including the names and demographic characteristics of the officers and suspects involved. Texas recently enacted legislation requiring all agencies in the state to do more or less the same. The state's attorney general now publishes police shooting data on its website.

Strangely enough, the best data we have are generated by the media. Crowdsourcing is also becoming a popular method of measuring police shootings. Following is a quick summary of the more well-known alternatives to official reporting.

Washington Post

The *Washington Post* maintains a comprehensive listing of police shootings going back to 2015. The database, which is based on news reports, public records, Internet searches, and original reporting, reported 990 fatal police shootings in 2015 and 963 in 2016. That is more than double the federal government's estimate. Unfortunately, the *Post*'s data do not go back before 2015.

Deadspin

The website *Deadspin* claims to be compiling information on every police-involved shooting in America, going back to at least 2011. The site set up an open submission form so members of the public could submit reports. This crowdsourcing approach is designed to cast as wide a net as possible. It is not clear if data are still being collected, but between August 20, 2014, and December 7, 2015, 2,181 fatal police shootings were reported.

Fatal Encounters

The website *Fatal Encounters*, maintained by D. Brian Burghart, the editor and publisher of the *Reno News & Review*, uses several data sources to count police shootings. Paid researchers tally shootings from such sites as *Killed By Police* and *The Homicide Report*, published by the *Los Angeles Times*. Public records requests are also submitted, and the site also relies on crowdsourcing. As of early 2017, the site has cataloged more than 18,000 records of people killed by police, going back to January 1, 2000.

Whose numbers should be believed? It is tough to say. At least the future holds a measure of promise. On December 18, 2014, President Barack Obama signed into law the Death in Custody Reporting Act of 2013. The law requires states that receive certain federal justice-related funds report to the US attorney general on a quarterly basis information concerning "the death of any person who is detained, arrested, en route to incarceration, or incarcerated in state or local facilities or a boot camp prison."

Sources: Dallas OpenData, https://www.dallasopendata.com/; Attorney General of Texas, "Police Office Involved Shooting Reports," https://www.texasattorneygeneral .gov/cj/peace-officer-involved-shooting-report; G.P. Alpert, "Toward a National Database of Officer-Involved Shootings," *Criminology and Public Policy* 15 (2016): 237–242, p. 239; D. Klinger, R. Rosenfeld, D. Isom, and M. Deckard, "Race, Crime, and the Micro-Ecology of Deadly Force," *Criminology and Public Policy* 15 (2016): 193–222, at 194; *Washington Post*, "Fatal Force," https://www.washingtonpost.com /graphics/national/police-shootings-2016/; *Deadspin*, http://deadspin.com/deadspin -police-shooting-database-update-were-still-go-1627414202; *Fatal Encounters*, http://www.fatalencounters.org/. (URLs accessed April 2017.)

weapon is discharged (within the exception of training situations). Several dispositions are possible. These can range from a conclusion that the shooting was in accordance with law and policy, all the way to termination and even criminal prosecution (if the prosecutor feels criminal charges are merited). The review board approach is controversial because it can mean that the department recommends that one of its own officers be turned over for criminal prosecution.[107]

Kristine Biggs Johnson breaks down as her attorney, Bob Sykes, plays a YouTube video from a law enforcement dash camera when she was shot in the eye. She filed a lawsuit against a Morgan County Sheriff's (Utah) deputy for improper use of deadly force against her. The shooting was deemed unjustified by Davis County Attorney Troy Rawlings, but no charges were filed against the deputy.

Nondeadly Force

Nondeadly force is force that is unlikely to cause death or significant bodily harm. Nondeadly force can range from the use of handcuffs and suspect compliance techniques to rubber bullets and stun guns. Officers resort to nondeadly force in a number of circumstances. They may begin with verbal commands and then escalate the force used when confronted with a resistant suspect. Researchers have found that the crime in question is strongly linked to the type of nondeadly force used and that officers are also influenced by past experience, the presence of other officers, and the presence and behavior of bystanders.[108] And even though nondeadly force is used more often than deadly force, it is still relatively rare—and at the lower end of the severity scale (e.g., grabbed by officer instead of hit). Researchers have estimated that police use or threaten to use nondeadly force in only 1.7 percent of all contacts and 20 percent of all arrests.[109]

nondeadly force Force that is unlikely to cause death or significant bodily harm.

CONTROLLING NONDEADLY FORCE In *Graham v. Connor*, the Supreme Court ruled that issues related to nondeadly force must be judged from the standpoint of a reasonable officer (formally called "objective reasonableness").[110] For example, say an officer is approached in a threatening manner by someone wielding a knife. The assailant fails to stop when warned and is killed by the officer, but it turns out later that the shooting victim was deaf and could not hear the officer's command. The officer would not be held liable if, at the time of the incident, he had no way of knowing the person's disability.

L08 Explain the importance of less-lethal weapons

Less-Lethal Weapons

In the past few years, about a thousand local police forces have started using so-called less-lethal weapons to subdue certain suspects. By far the most popular are Tasers, which deliver electric shocks with long wire tentacles, producing intense muscle spasms. Other technologies include guns that shoot giant nets, guns that shoot rubber bullets, and lights that can temporarily blind a suspect, among many others.

Research suggests less-lethal weapons may help reduce police use of force.[111] They may also reduce suspect resistance, but they can be limited in certain situations, such as when suspects are under the influence of drugs or are in very close proximity (e.g., less than three feet) to officers.[112] See the accompanying Focus on Effectiveness box for another possible limitation of Taser use.

less-lethal weapons Weapons designed to disable or immobilize rather than kill criminal suspects.

Tasers and Cognitive Impairment

Suspects who are subjected to "custodial interrogation" must be advised of the familiar *Miranda* rights ("you have the right to remain silent," etc.). *Miranda* rights, which stem from the US Supreme Court's 1966 decision in *Miranda v. Arizona*, are intended to protect people from incriminating themselves, which is an important Fifth Amendment privilege. Recently, some have expressed concern that Taser exposure may affect suspects' willingness to share information with the police. They assume that a person who is "tased" during an altercation with officers could have his or her cognitive abilities impaired. Such an assumption indeed has merit. After all, Tasers cause uncontrollable muscle contractions that result in immediate loss of neuromuscular control. Why would the brain not also be affected?

In a creative study, Robert Kane and Michael White solicited student volunteers and randomly assigned them to four different groups. In one group, subjects were tased with no other intervention on the researchers' part. In another group, participants vigorously punched a heavy bag for 30 seconds before being tased. The exertion was used to simulate physical altercations with police officers. The participants in the remaining two groups served as controls and were not tased. All participants then completed a number of cognitive tests. Interestingly, Kane and White found that Taser exposure led to "short-term auditory recall" problems. Also, tased individuals temporarily had trouble assimilating new information through the auditory process. The effects lasted approximately 60 seconds after Taser exposure.

Effects on Crime/Recidivism

Would Taser exposure have any effect on crime? Perhaps not directly, but the Taser could conceivably create a loophole that makes it difficult for prosecutors to secure convictions. Assume, for example, that a suspect is tased, arrested, and then interrogated. Even if the police advise the individual of his *Miranda* rights, what if he decides to waive those rights and offers up an incriminating statement? Would he have made that statement but for the Taser? Perhaps not. In looking at existing case law, only a handful of suspects have challenged their confessions on the grounds that they had been tased and were not in full control of their faculties, but none have succeeded thus far.

Thinking Critically About Research

The Kane and White study is important because it was an experiment. Experiments (with random assignment to treatment and control conditions) are exceptionally rare in criminal justice. They are even less common when they involve controversial activities like shocking participants with Tasers! The researchers had to jump through a number of hoops to secure permission from their university's Institutional Review Board, which is designed to ensure that human subjects are protected from potentially harmful research projects.

QUESTIONS

1. Do Tasers open a potential loophole in the criminal process?
2. What other potential loopholes exist?

Sources: *Miranda v. Arizona*, 384 US 436 (1966); Robert J. Kane and Michael D. White, "Taser Exposure and Cognitive Impairment: Implications for Valid *Miranda* Waivers and the Timing of Police Custodial Interrogations," *Criminology and Public Policy* 15 (2016): 79–107.

WEB APP 6.3 Visit the National Institute of Justice's website on the Taser at **https://www.nij .gov/topics/technology/less-lethal /pages/conducted-energy-devices .aspx**. Carefully read the section on "Safety of Conducted Energy Devices." Write an essay that answers the following question: Are Tasers safe? Be sure to explain what "weight" should be assigned to reporting from the National Institute of Justice relative to other organizations, such as Taser International, the device's manufacturer.

LO9 Analyze the Supreme Court's involvement with the police through its effort to control search and seizure and interrogation, and through establishment of the exclusionary rule

Police Searches and Interrogations

The police are charged with preventing crime and, when crime does occur, with investigating the case, identifying the culprit, and making an arrest. To carry out these tasks, police officers need to be able to search for evidence, to seize items such as guns and drugs, and to question suspects, witnesses, and victims, because at trial, they must provide prosecutors with sufficient evidence to prove guilt "beyond a reasonable doubt." This requirement means that soon after a crime is committed, they must make every effort to gather physical evidence, obtain confessions, and take witness statements that will stand up in court. Police officers also realize that evidence such as the testimony of a witness or a coconspirator may evaporate before the trial begins. Then the outcome of the case may depend on some piece of physical evidence or a suspect's statement taken early in the investigation.

The need for police officers to gather evidence can conflict with the constitutional rights of citizens. For example, although police might prefer a free hand to search homes and cars for evidence, the Fourth Amendment restricts police activities by limiting searches and seizures to those deemed "reasonable." Likewise, when police want to vigorously interrogate a suspect, they must honor the Fifth Amendment's prohibition against forcing people to incriminate themselves. The following sections address some key areas in which police operations have been restricted or curtailed by the courts.

Interrogation and Confessions

After an arrest is made, police want to interrogate suspects, hoping they will confess to the crime, name coconspirators, or make incriminating statements that can be used against them in court. But the Fifth Amendment guarantees people the right to be free from self-incrimination. The courts have used this phrase to prohibit law enforcement agents from using physical or psychological coercion while interrogating suspects to get them to confess or give information. Confessions obtained from defendants through coercion, force, trickery, or promises of leniency are inadmissible because their trustworthiness is questionable.

THE *MIRANDA* WARNING In 1966, in the case of *Miranda v. Arizona*, the Supreme Court created objective standards for questioning by police after a defendant has been taken into custody.[113] Custody occurs when a person is not free to walk away, such as when an individual is arrested. The Court maintained that before the police can question a person who has been arrested or is in custody, they must inform the individual of his or her Fifth Amendment right to be free from self-incrimination. This is accomplished by the police issuing what is known as the *Miranda* warning, which informs the suspect of the following:

- He has the right to remain silent.
- If he makes a statement, it can be used against him in court.
- He has the right to consult an attorney and to have the attorney present at the time of the interrogation.
- If he cannot afford an attorney, one will be appointed by the state.

If the defendant is not given the *Miranda* warning before the investigation, the evidence obtained from the interrogation cannot be admitted at trial. An accused person can waive his or her *Miranda* rights at any time. For the waiver to be effective, however, the state must first show that the defendant was aware of all the *Miranda* rights and must then prove that the waiver was made with the full knowledge of constitutional rights. People who cannot understand the *Miranda* warning because of their age, mental handicaps, or language problems cannot be legally questioned without their attorney present; if they *can* understand their rights and then waive them, they may be questioned.[114] The Supreme Court has decided a number of *Miranda*-related cases over the years. The key cases are summarized in Exhibit 6.3.

Miranda is now a police (and a prime-time television) institution. It is not surprising that today police administrators who in the past might have been wary of the restrictions forced by *Miranda* now actually favor its use.[115] Yet in spite of its acceptance, critics have called the *Miranda* decision incomprehensible and difficult to administer. How can one tell when a confession is truly voluntary or when it has been produced by pressure and coercion? Aren't all police interrogations essentially coercive?[116] To ensure that *Miranda* rules are being followed, many departments now routinely videotape interrogations.[117] Nonetheless, the *Miranda* decision continues to be an important one.

Search and Seizure

When conducting investigations, police officers want to collect evidence, seize it, and carry it away. They may want to enter a suspect's home; look for evidence of a crime, such as bloody clothes, drugs, missing money, or a weapon; seize the evidence; and store it in the evidence room so it can later be used at trial. The manner in which police may seize evidence is governed by the search-and-seizure requirements of the Fourth Amendment of the US Constitution, which was designed by the framers to protect a criminal suspect from unreasonable searches and seizures. Under normal circumstances, no search or seizure undertaken without a search warrant is lawful.

A search warrant is a court order authorizing and directing the police to search a designated place for evidence of a crime. To obtain a search warrant, the following procedural requirements must be met: (1) the police officer must request the warrant from the court; (2) the officer must submit an affidavit establishing the proper grounds for the warrant; and (3) the affidavit must state the place to be searched and the property to be seized.

Miranda warning The requirement that police officers inform suspects subjected to custodial interrogation that they have a constitutional right to remain silent, that their statements can later be used against them in court, that they can have an attorney present to help them, and that the state will pay for an attorney if they cannot afford to hire one.

REALITYCHECK
Myth or Reality?

The police are not required to advise all arrestees of their *Miranda* rights.

REALITY. *Miranda* rights need be read only when custody (such as arrest) is coupled with interrogation.

Police departments may adopt more restrictive policies, however, requiring *Miranda* warnings any time a person is arrested. Should the *Miranda* warnings be read every time a person is arrested?

search warrant An order issued by a judge, directing officers to conduct a search of specified premises for specified objects or persons and bring them before the court.

EXHIBIT 6.3 Important *Miranda*-Related Decisions over the Years

Fare v. Michael C. **(1978)** The *Miranda* warning applies only to the right to have an attorney present. The suspect cannot demand to speak to a priest, a probation officer, or any other official.[118]

New York v. Quarles **(1984)** A suspect can be questioned in the field without a *Miranda* warning if the information the police seek is needed to protect public safety. For example, in an emergency, suspects can be asked where they hid their weapons.[119] This is known as the public safety doctrine.

Oregon v. Elstad **(1985)** Admissions made in the absence of *Miranda* warnings are not admissible at trial, but post-*Miranda* voluntary statements (those made after the warnings are read) are admissible. A post-*Miranda* voluntary statement is admissible even if an initial incriminating statement was made in the absence of *Miranda* warnings.[120]

Colorado v. Connelly **(1986)** The admissions of mentally impaired defendants can be admitted in evidence as long as the police acted properly, and there is a preponderance of evidence that the defendants understood the meaning of *Miranda*.[121]

Moran v. Burbine **(1986)** An attorney's request to see the defendant does not affect the validity of the defendant's waiver of the right to counsel. Police misinformation to an attorney does not affect waiver of *Miranda* rights.[122] For example, a suspect's statements may be used if they are given voluntarily, even though his family has hired an attorney and the statements were made before the attorney arrived. Only the suspect can request an attorney, not his friends or family.

Colorado v. Spring **(1987)** Suspects need not be aware of all the possible outcomes of waiving their rights for the *Miranda* warning to be considered properly given.[123]

Minnick v. Mississippi **(1990)** When counsel is requested, interrogation must cease and cannot be resumed until an attorney is present.[124]

Arizona v. Fulminante **(1991)** The erroneous admission of a coerced confession at trial can be ruled a harmless error that would not automatically result in overturning a conviction.[125]

Davis v. United States **(1994)** A suspect who makes an ambiguous reference to an attorney during questioning, such as "Maybe I should talk to an attorney," is not protected under *Miranda*. The police may continue their questioning.[126]

Chavez v. Martinez **(2003)** Failure to give a suspect a *Miranda* warning is not illegal unless the case becomes a criminal issue.[127]

United States v. Patane **(2004)** A voluntary statement given in the absence of a *Miranda* warning can be used to obtain evidence that can be used at trial. Failure to give the warning does not make seizure of evidence illegal per se.[128]

Missouri v. Seibert **(2004)** *Miranda* warnings must be given before interrogation begins. The accused in this case was interrogated and confessed in the absence of *Miranda* warnings. *Miranda* rights were then read, at which point the accused "re-confessed." The pre-*Miranda* questioning was improper.[129]

Maryland v. Shatzer **(2010)** *Miranda* protections do not apply if a suspect is released from police custody for at least 14 days and then questioned. However, if the suspect is rearrested, then *Miranda* warnings must be read.[130]

Florida v. Powell **(2010)** The *Miranda* warnings do not require that the suspect be advised that he or she has the right to have an attorney present during questioning. It is sufficient to advise the suspect that he or she has the right to talk with a lawyer before questioning and to consult a lawyer at any time during questioning.[131]

Berghuis v. Thompkins **(2010)** Unless a suspect asserts his or her *Miranda* rights, any subsequent voluntary statements given after the warnings are admissible in court. Simply remaining silent does not imply that a suspect has invoked *Miranda* protection.[132]

J.D.B. v. North Carolina **(2011)** Children may be more prone to confessing to crimes they did not commit, and this needs to be taken into consideration in deciding whether a police interrogation is also custodial. In other words, the suspect's age factors into the *Miranda* custody analysis.[133]

Howes v. Fields **(2012)** A prisoner questioned about events that occurred prior to his or her incarceration is not considered "in custody" for *Miranda* purposes. In this case, Fields, the inmate, was free to walk away from questioning and go back to his cell.[134]

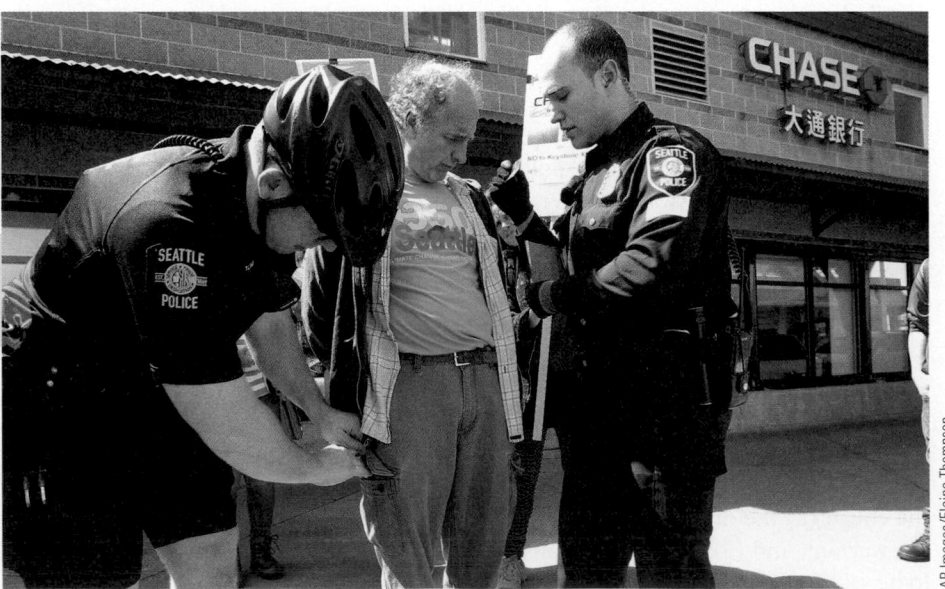

Protester Peter Weston is searched by police after being arrested for declining to leave a demonstration in Seattle on May 8, 2017. Climate activists opposed to oil pipeline projects demonstrated at several JPMorgan Chase bank locations, calling on the bank not to do business with TransCanada, the company pushing for the Keystone XL oil pipeline.

AP Images/Elaine Thompson

CRIMINAL JUSTICE AND TECHNOLOGY

Through-Wall Radar

Back in 2001, the US Supreme Court decided on the role of thermal imaging (heat sensing) devices in law enforcement. The case, *Kyllo v. United States*, involved a man who had been growing marijuana in his home. Police used a handheld thermal imager to detect heat escaping Kyllo's house. The scan showed that the roof over the garage and one side of the house was relatively warm compared to the rest of the home—and much warmer than neighboring homes. Based on that and other information, a search warrant was obtained. More than 100 marijuana plants and growing equipment were found. Kyllo sought to have the evidence excluded from his trial, arguing that police use of a thermal imager without a warrant was itself a search and therefore in violation of the Fourth Amendment. The Supreme Court agreed. Now law enforcement officials must first secure a search warrant before being able to conduct thermal imager scans.

Fast forward to the present. A new technology, through-wall radar, can reveal even more detail than thermal imagers. Although thermal imagers reveal only escaping heat and cannot see *inside* buildings, through-wall radar permits police to learn where and how many people are inside a building, at distances of up to 50 feet. The handheld Range-R, manufactured by CyTerra Corporation, looks a lot like an ordinary stud finder. It is designed to be held up against the wall outside a room of interest, then, like a finely tuned motion detector, it sends radio waves through the wall designed to detect the smallest of human movements, even a person's breathing. Importantly, it does not show a *picture* of what is inside, only information on a digital readout about how many people are inside and how far away they are.

The benefits of through-wall radar are obvious; knowing who, if anyone, is behind closed doors can go a long way toward protecting officer safety and needless loss of life. CyTerra says its device is "[d]esigned to increase situation awareness in urban environments [and] provides its users with vital intelligence necessary to safely undertake a variety of law enforcement and search and rescue operations." Of course, though, through-wall radar raises constitutional concerns. If thermal imager use constitutes a search, then why would

the same rule not apply to through-wall radar? Indeed, this issue came up in a recent federal court case. Officers used a through-wall radar device, but the court decided not to reverse Steven Denson's conviction for firearm-related offenses because it concluded the officers had other information to believe their man was hiding inside the home. Nevertheless, the court took care to emphasize that through-wall radar will face additional legal challenges:

> It's obvious to us and everyone else in this case that the government's warrantless use of such a powerful tool to search inside homes poses grave Fourth Amendment questions. New technologies bring with them not only new opportunities for law enforcement to catch criminals but also new risks for abuse and new ways to invade constitutional rights.... Unlawful searches can give rise not only to civil claims but may require the suppression of evidence in criminal proceedings. We have little doubt that the radar device deployed here will soon generate many questions for this court and others along both of these axes.

Denson petitioned the Supreme Court for review, but it denied certiorari. For the time being, the Tenth Circuit's decision officers the only guidance in this interesting area of Fourth Amendment jurisprudence.

CRITICAL THINKING
1. Should through-wall radar be used more often in policing?
2. What other technological advances in law enforcement raise Fourth Amendment questions? Why?

Sources: *Kyllo v. United States*, 533 US 27 (2001); Brad Heath, "New Police Radars Can 'See' Inside Homes," *USA Today*, January 20, 2015, http://www.usatoday.com /story/news/2015/01/19/police-radar-see-through-walls/22007615/; L3 Communications CyTerra, *Range-R*, http://www.cyterra.com/products/ranger.htm; *United States v. Denson*, 775 F.3d 1214 (Tenth Cir. 2014). (URLs accessed April 2017.)

A warrant cannot be issued unless the presiding magistrate is presented with sufficient evidence to conclude that an offense has been or is being committed and that the suspect is the one who committed the offense; this is referred to as the **probable cause** requirement. In other words, the presiding judge must conclude from the facts presented by the police that there is probable cause a crime has been committed and that the person or place to be searched is materially involved in that crime; there must be solid evidence of criminal involvement.

Searches must also be reasonable under the circumstances of the crime. Police would not be able to get a warrant to search a suspect's desk drawer for a missing piano! Nor could police obtain a warrant that allows them to tear down the walls of a person's house because it is suspected that they contain drugs. A search is considered unreasonable when it exceeds the scope of police authority or is highly invasive of personal privacy, even if it reveals incriminating evidence. For more on the privacy issue, see the accompanying Criminal Justice and Technology box.

probable cause The evidentiary criterion necessary to sustain an arrest or the issuance of an arrest or search warrant; less than absolute certainty or "beyond a reasonable doubt," but greater than mere suspicion or "hunch."

WARRANTLESS SEARCHES To make it easier for police to conduct investigations and to protect public safety, the Supreme Court has ruled that under certain circumstances, a valid search may be conducted without a search warrant. The six major exceptions are:

- *Search incident to a valid arrest.* A warrantless search is valid if it is made incident to a lawful arrest. The reason for this exception is that the arresting officer must

Myth or Reality?

Some warrantless searches are permissible as long as the police have probable cause.

REALITY. Certain types of warrantless searches are permissible, but not all of them. For example, it is never permissible for an officer, with probable cause but no warrant, to enter a private residence in the absence of exigent circumstances.

Has the Supreme Court created enough exceptions to the Fourth Amendment warrant requirement? Why or why not?

stop and frisk The situation when police officers who are suspicious of an individual run their hands lightly over the suspect's outer garments to determine whether the person is carrying a concealed weapon. Also called a patdown or threshold inquiry, a stop and frisk is intended to stop short of any activity that could be considered a violation of Fourth Amendment rights.

have the power to disarm the accused, protect himself or herself, preserve the evidence of the crime, and prevent the accused from escaping from custody. Because the search is lawful, the officer retains what he or she finds if it is connected with a crime. The officer is permitted to search only the defendant's person and the areas in the defendant's immediate physical surroundings that are under his or her control.[135] Interestingly, the Supreme Court recently decided that officers *cannot*, without a warrant, search digital information on a cell phone following a person's arrest.[136]

- *Stop and frisk.* In the landmark *Terry v. Ohio* decision, the Supreme Court held that police officers can perform a **stop and frisk** when they have reasonable suspicion to believe criminal activity is afoot. For example, say the individual is seen lurking outside a closed store and peering through the windows. In such a case, the officer has a right to stop and question the individual and, if the officer has reason to believe that the person is carrying a concealed weapon, may frisk the subject—that is, pat down the person's outer clothing for the purpose of finding a concealed weapon. If an illegal weapon is found, then an arrest can be made and a search incident to the arrest performed.[137] Would it be legal to pat down a person merely because that person is standing in a high-crime neighborhood? Probably not. The Supreme Court suggests that an officer would need more suspicion—for example, if the person ran away when he spotted the police approaching.[138]

- *Automobile search.* An automobile may be searched without a warrant if there is probable cause to believe the car was involved in a crime.[139] Because automobiles are inherently mobile, there is a significant chance that evidence will be lost if the search is not conducted immediately; also, people should not expect as much privacy in their cars as in their homes.[140] Police officers who have legitimately stopped an automobile and who have probable cause to believe that contraband is concealed somewhere inside it may conduct a warrantless search of the vehicle that is as thorough as a magistrate could authorize by warrant.

Because traffic stops can be dangerous, the Court has ruled that if a police officer perceives danger during a routine traffic stop, he can order the driver and passengers from the car without suspicion and conduct a limited search of their persons to ensure police officer safety.[141] Police officers can search the car and passengers after a traffic stop, as long as the search is reasonable and related to officer safety.[142] Usually, the search must be limited to the area under the driver's control or reach. Also, if someone in the vehicle is arrested, officers can only then search the vehicle for objects related to the offense of arrest, as the Supreme Court announced in *Arizona v. Gant.*[143]

- *Consent search.* In a consent search, individuals waive their constitutional rights; therefore, neither a warrant nor probable cause need exist. For a consent search to be legal, the consent must be given voluntarily; threat or compulsion invalidates the search.[144] Although it has been held that voluntary consent is required, it has also been maintained that the police are under no obligation to inform individuals of their right to refuse the search.[145]

- *Plain-view search.* Even when an object is in a house or other areas involving an expectation of privacy, the object can be freely inspected if it can be seen by the general public. If a police officer looks through a fence and sees marijuana growing in a suspect's fields, no search warrant is needed for the property to be seized. The articles are considered to be in plain view, and therefore a search warrant need not be obtained to seize them.[146]

- *Exigent circumstances.* The Supreme Court has identified a number of exigent, or emergency, circumstances in which a search warrant might normally have been required, but because of some immediate emergency, police officers can search suspects and places without benefit of a warrant. These circumstances include hot pursuit, danger of escape, threats to evidence, and threats to others. In each situation, officers must have probable cause.[147] For example, as the Supreme Court recently decided in *Kentucky v. King*, it is constitutionally permissible for officers to forcibly enter a residence if they have probable cause that evidence is being destroyed within.[148] They can also use deadly force to terminate car chases that pose grave public safety risks, as was decided in 2014.[149]

The Exclusionary Rule

The **exclusionary rule** provides that all evidence obtained by unreasonable searches and seizures is inadmissible in criminal trials. Similarly, it excludes the use of illegal confessions under Fifth Amendment prohibitions.

After police agencies were created in the mid-nineteenth century, evidence obtained by unreasonable searches and seizures was admitted by state and federal governments in criminal trials. The only criteria for admissibility were whether the evidence was incriminating and whether it would help the judge or jury reach a verdict. Then, in 1914, the US Supreme Court established the exclusionary rule in the case of *Weeks v. United States*, when it ruled that evidence obtained by unreasonable search and seizure must be excluded from a federal criminal trial.[150] In 1961, the Supreme Court made the exclusionary rule applicable to state courts in the landmark decision of *Mapp v. Ohio*.[151]

CONTROVERSY AND CURRENT STATUS When the exclusionary rule applies, valuable evidence may not be usable at trial because the police made an error or failed to obtain a proper warrant. This means that guilty defendants can go free when the police make mistakes, intentional or otherwise. What's more, because courts frequently decide in many types of cases (particularly those involving victimless offenses, such as gambling and drug use) that certain evidence should be excluded, the rule is believed to result in excessive court delays and to affect plea-bargaining negotiations negatively. In fact, however, the rule appears to result in relatively few case dismissals. Research efforts show that prosecutions are lost because of suppression rulings less than 1 percent of the time.[152]

Over time, the Supreme Court has been diminishing the scope of the exclusionary rule. For example, evidence is admissible in court if the police officers acted in good faith by first obtaining court approval for their search, even if the warrant they received was deficient or faulty.[153] This has come to be known as the **good faith exception**.

exclusionary rule Evidence seized in violation of the Fourth Amendment cannot be used in a court of law.

good faith exception The principle that evidence may be used in a criminal trial, even though the search warrant used to obtain it is technically faulty, if the police acted in good faith and to the best of their ability when they sought to obtain it from a judge.

ETHICAL REFLECTION

Think back to this chapter's section on less-lethal weapons. As Tasers have found their way into mainstream law enforcement use, researchers have been drawn to the question of whether they present an effective alternative to conventional use-of-force measures. This research has yielded a wide range of conclusions, ranging from very supportive to very critical. Staunch advocates of Tasers include the manufacturer and much of the law enforcement community. Critics include most notably human rights organization Amnesty International. It has been especially critical of Taser deaths. Most research findings fall somewhere between these extremes.

For example, research has shown that Tasers are more effective at incapacitating suspects than pepper spray. And as Eugene Paoline and his colleagues found, Taser use reduces officer injury compared to other force measures.[154] Dozens of studies have also concluded that Tasers pose minimal risk of death or serious injury, but much of the research has been conducted in laboratory settings on animals and healthy human volunteers. In response to this limitation, Michael White and Justin Ready compared news reports of fatal and nonfatal Taser incidents. They found that suspect drug use, mental illness, and continued resistance were associated with Taser deaths, but they concluded that more research is necessary if we are ever to know for sure.[155] In the meantime, they suggest the development of model policy guidelines because of potential unanticipated consequences associated with Taser use.

Writing Challenge Write an essay that lays out a set of guidelines for proper Taser use. When should Tasers be used? When should they *not* be used? Consult the links at the following URL for a wealth of information and suggestions: http://www.aele.org/law/Digests/ECWarticles.html.

SUMMARY

LO1 *Summarize demographic trends in policing* US police departments have made a concerted effort to attract women and minority police officers, and today about 11 percent of all officers are female and about 23 percent are racial minorities.

LO2 *Explain how minority and female officers act and are treated* Minority police officers now seem as self-assured as white officers. They may even be more willing to use their authority to take official action than white officers. Studies of policewomen indicate that they are still struggling for acceptance, believe that they do not receive equal credit for their job performance, and report that it is common for them to be sexually harassed by their coworkers. African American women, who account for less than 5 percent of police officers, occupy a unique status. They often incur the hostility of both white women and African American men, who feel threatened that these officers will take their place.

LO3 *Explain police culture and personality* Experts have found that the experience of becoming a police officer and the nature of the job itself cause most officers to band together in a police subculture characterized by cynicism, clannishness, secrecy, and insulation from others in society—the blue curtain. The police officer's working personality is shaped by constant exposure to danger and the need to use force and authority to defuse and control threatening situations.

LO4 *Identify distinct policing styles* Four styles of police work seem to fit the current behavior patterns of most police agents: the crime fighter, the social agent, the law enforcer, and the watchman.

LO5 *Describe factors that affect police discretion* The majority of police officers use a high degree of personal discretion in carrying out daily tasks, a phenomenon sometimes referred to as "low-visibility decision making" in criminal justice. Several factors contribute to discretionary decision making: legal factors, environmental factors, departmental factors, peer factors, situational factors, and extralegal factors.

LO6 *Discuss four major problems of policing* Police officers experience tremendous stress. Fatigue is also a problem in modern police agencies; officers often work long hours and can become overly tired from performance of their duties. Because incidents of brutality undermine efforts to build a bridge between police and the public, police departments around the United States have instituted specialized training programs to reduce it. Ever since their creation, US police departments have wrestled with the problem of controlling illegal and unprofessional behavior by their officers.

LO7 *Distinguish between deadly and nondeadly force— and methods for controlling each* Police officers are empowered to use force in the pursuit of their daily tasks. The term deadly force refers to the actions of a police officer who shoots and kills a suspect who flees from arrest, assaults a victim, or attacks an officer. Nondeadly force is that which is unlikely to cause death or significant bodily harm. Because the police use of force is such a serious issue, ongoing efforts have been made to control its use. Methods used to control police force include adhering to important court decisions and formulating appropriate policies.

LO8 *Explain the importance of less-lethal weapons* Less-lethal weapons give police officers an opportunity to subdue certain suspects without the need for lethal force. The Taser is the most popular less-lethal weapon in use today.

LO9 *Analyze the Supreme Court's involvement with the police through its effort to control search and seizure and interrogation, and through establishment of the exclusionary rule* The need for police officers to gather evidence can conflict with the constitutional rights of citizens. In the 1966 case of *Miranda v. Arizona*, the Supreme Court created objective standards for questioning by police after a defendant has been taken into custody. Under normal circumstances, no search or seizure undertaken without a search warrant is lawful. The Supreme Court has also ruled that under certain circumstances, a valid search may be conducted without a search warrant. The exclusionary rule provides that all evidence obtained by unreasonable searches and seizures is inadmissible in criminal trials.

KEY TERMS

REVIEW QUESTIONS

1. Should male and female officers have the same duties in a police department? Explain your reasoning.

2. How can education enhance the effectiveness of police officers?

3. Do you think that an officer's working the street will eventually produce a cynical personality and distrust for civilians? Explain.

4. A police officer orders an unarmed person running away from a burglary to stop; the suspect keeps running and is shot and killed by the officer. Has the officer committed murder? Explain.

5. Would you like to live in a society that abolished police discretion and used a full enforcement policy? Why or why not?

6. Should illegally seized evidence be excluded from trial, even though it is conclusive proof of a person's criminal acts? Might there be another way to deal with police violation of the Fourth Amendment—for example, making them pay a fine?

7. Have criminals been given too many rights by the courts? Should courts be more concerned with the rights of victims or the rights of offenders? Have the police been "handcuffed" and prevented from doing their job in the most efficient manner?

Courts and Adjudication

On February 13, 2016, US Supreme Court Justice Antonin Scalia died of natural causes at a resort outside Marfa, Texas. He was 79. Appointed to the Court by President Ronald Reagan in 1986, Scalia was known for his wit and intellect, both of which came through in caustic legal opinions. He was conservative but also somewhat unpredictable. Some of his opinions sided squarely with criminal defendants when he felt government power was too overreaching. For example, in *Maryland v. King*, a case which permitted police to take and analyze DNA cheek swabs from arrestees as part of the normal booking procedure, Scalia wrote: "I doubt that the proud men who wrote the charter of our liberties would have been so eager to open their mouths for royal inspection."

Scalia was also an "originalist," meaning he interpreted the Constitution as it was originally written. He defined originalism in this way: "The Constitution that I interpret and apply is not living but dead, or as I prefer to call it, enduring. It means today not what current society, much less the court, thinks it ought to mean, but what it meant when it was adopted."[1] Scalia would also let it be known, in a particularly eloquent manner, when he felt an issue and/or case was "beneath" the Supreme Court. This came out loud and clear in his dissent in *PGA Tour, Inc. v. Martin*, a case in which the Court decided whether a disabled professional golfer could use a motorized cart during play:

> It has been rendered the solemn duty of the Supreme Court of the United States, laid upon it by Congress in pursuance of the Federal Government's power "[t]o regulate Commerce with foreign Nations, and among the several States," to decide What Is Golf. I am sure that the Framers of the Constitution, aware of the 1457 edict of King James II of Scotland prohibiting golf because it interfered with the practice of archery, fully expected that sooner or later the paths of golf and government, the law and the links, would once again cross, and that the judges of this august Court would some day have to wrestle with that age-old jurisprudential question, for which their years of study in the law have so well prepared them: Is someone riding around a golf course from shot to shot really a golfer?

Part 3 of this text covers courts and adjudication. Chapter 7 provides an introduction to the court system as well as the roles of the prosecution and the defense. Chapter 8 covers pretrial and trial procedures. Pretrial topics include bail, charging the defendant, plea bargaining, and diversion. The trial section of Chapter 8 summarizes the trial process and the legal rights defendants enjoy. Chapter 9 looks at punishment and sentencing. The chapter begins with the history and goals of punishment, and then it moves into specific types of sentences. Chapter 9 wraps up with a review of capital punishment and the controversies surrounding it.

Oakland Tribune/Getty Images

7 Courts, Prosecution, and the Defense

Prosecutors are powerful actors in the criminal process. They enjoy enormous discretion in deciding whether to bring charges against criminal suspects. Like policing, prosecution is mostly a "public," or government function. Police officers are "commissioned" by the states in which they work; prosecutors are typically county employees authorized to practice law in their respective states. But as we discussed back in Chapter 4, law enforcement is increasingly becoming privatized. Police officers can't be everywhere, so businesses, communities, and other stakeholders have taken it upon themselves to pay for their own security. There are signs that prosecution might be headed in the same direction.

Most large jurisdictions have both the financial means and the work-load to justify employment for several full-time government prosecutors. In smaller jurisdictions, however, it is often cost prohibitive to hire and retain such employees. How, then, do these less populous areas ensure they will have prosecutors to bring cases against suspected criminals? Many have started to outsource prosecution through a system of competitive bidding. The process goes like this: A local government will issue a request for proposals, or RFP, asking local attorneys to submit proposals to assume prosecution functions. Once they are received, each proposal is reviewed to evaluate issues of experience, qualifications, and of course cost. Ideally, the best and most cost-effective proposal will be granted the contract.

There are benefits and drawbacks to this approach. On the one hand, it is not that outsourcing fully turns prosecution over to the private sector. The attorneys who bid must be authorized to practice law in the jurisdiction seeking proposals. Moreover, it is quite common for local governments to outsource services, both in and out of criminal justice. On the other hand, could financial motives take precedence over promoting justice? Critics of outsourcing prosecution answer with a resounding "yes." In a recent study

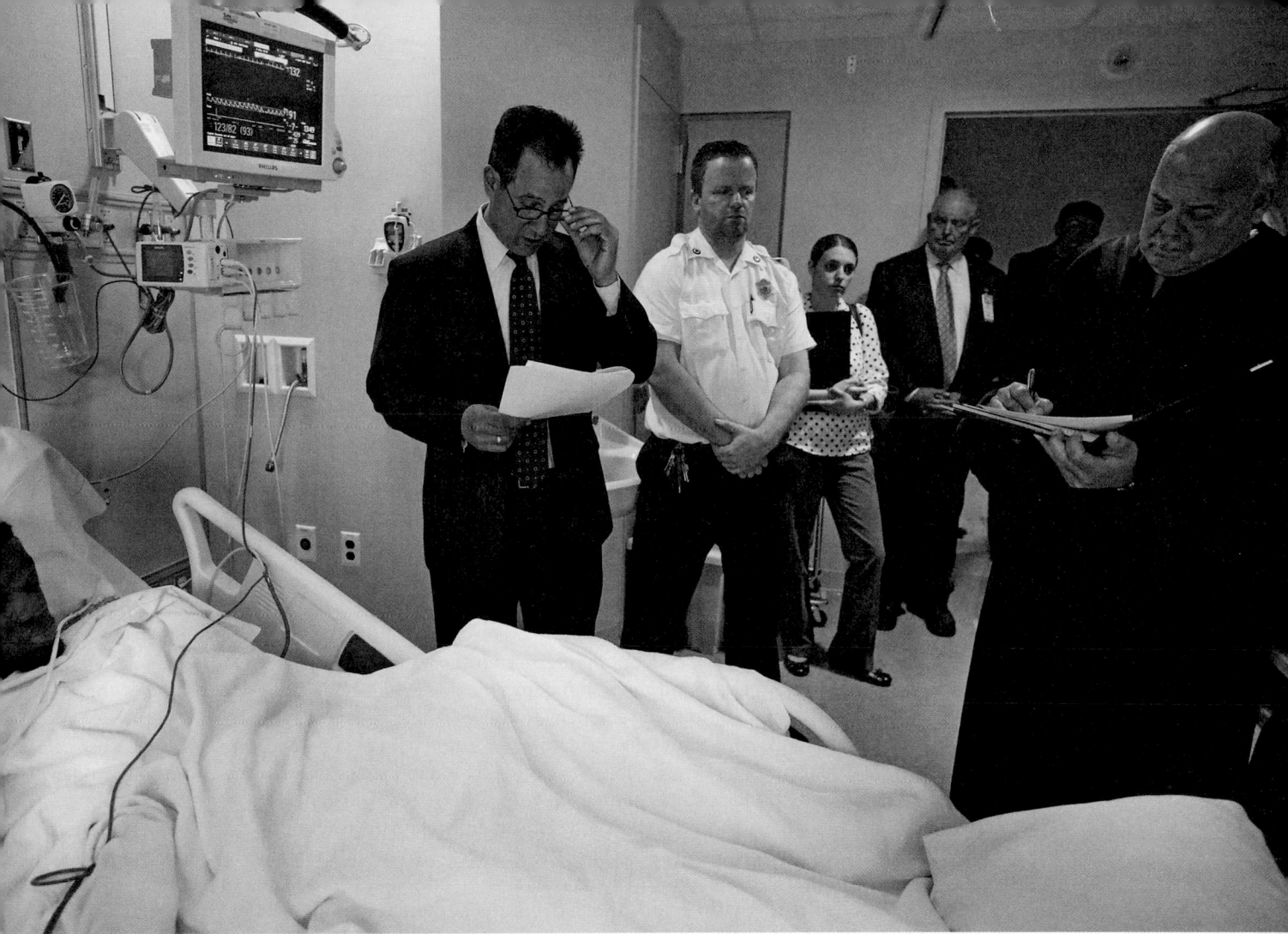

AP Images/David L. Ryan

LEARNING OBJECTIVES

LO1 Describe the varying structures of state court systems

LO2 Describe the federal court system

LO3 Summarize the selection procedure for and duties of the trial judge

LO4 Explain the role of the prosecutor

LO5 Describe prosecutorial discretion, and summarize its pros and cons

LO6 Identify the role of the defense attorney in the justice process

LO7 Discuss the different forms of indigent defense

LO8 Summarize the pros and cons of private attorneys

LO9 Evaluate the expanding role of technology in the court process

of the competitive bidding process for prosecution, law professor Maybell Romero cited this concern:

> While "[e]fficiency gains are the major reason that governments enter into privatization agreements,"...the use of outsourced prosecution services, particularly those hired through an RFP/competitive bidding process is dangerous, subjecting the hired prosecutors to much of the same political pressure as elected officials while also generating unusual and outsized pressures to prioritize budgets and fine/fee generation.[2]

Questions of how efficiently use government resources and ensure justice are not easily answered. Whether it is for prosecution, defense, the judiciary, or even court structure, people have a wide range of ideas for how best to promote fair and cost-effective criminal justice operations. This chapter considers a number of such proposals, beginning with the courts.

The criminal court is the setting in which many of the most important decisions in the criminal justice system are made. Eyewitness identification, bail, trial, plea negotiations, and sentencing all involve court decisions. The criminal court is a complex social agency with many independent but interrelated subsystems: administrator, prosecutor, defense attorney, judge, and probation department. The entire process—from filing of the initial complaint to final sentencing of the defendant—is governed by precise rules of law designed to ensure fairness. However, in today's crowded court system, such abstract goals are often impossible to achieve. The nation's court system is chronically underfunded, and recent economic downturns have not helped matters.

These constraints have a significant impact on the way courts carry out justice. Quite often, the US court system is the scene of accommodation and "working things out," rather than an arena for a vigorous criminal defense. Plea negotiations and other nonjudicial alternatives, such as diversion, are far more common than the formal trial process. Consequently, US criminal justice can be selective. Discretion accompanies defendants through every step of the process, determining what will happen to them and how their cases will be resolved. "Discretion" means that two people committing similar crimes may receive highly dissimilar treatment. Most people convicted of homicide receive a prison sentence, but about 5 percent receive probation as a sole sentence; indeed, more murderers get probation than the death penalty.[3]

In this chapter, we examine the structure and function of the court system. The US court system has evolved over the years into an intricately balanced legal process. To carry out this complex process, each state maintains its own state court organization and structure, and the federal court has an independent trial court system. These are described next.

State Courts

L01 Describe the varying structures of state court systems

Every state maintains its own court system. States are free to create as many courts as they wish, to name courts what they like (in New York, felony courts are known as supreme courts!), and to establish specialized courts that handle a single type of legal matter, such as drug courts and domestic courts. Consequently, no two court organizations are exactly alike. State courts handle a wide variety of cases and regulate numerous personal behaviors ranging from homicide to property maintenance.

Courts of Limited Jurisdiction

state courts of limited jurisdiction Courts that have jurisdiction over misdemeanors and conduct preliminary investigations of felony charges.

Depending on the jurisdiction in which they are located, **state courts of limited jurisdiction** are known by a variety of names—municipal courts, county courts, district courts, and metropolitan courts, to mention just a few. They are known as courts of limited jurisdiction because they are restricted to hearing minor or less serious civil and criminal cases.

Usually, courts of limited jurisdiction handle misdemeanor criminal infractions, violations of municipal ordinances, traffic violations, and civil suits where the damages involve less than a certain amount of money (usually $1,000 or less). In criminal matters, they hear cases involving misdemeanors such as shoplifting, disorderly conduct, and simple assault. Their sanctioning power is also limited. In criminal matters, punishments may be limited to fines, community sentencing, or incarceration in the county jail for up to a year. In addition to their trial work, limited jurisdiction courts conduct arraignments, preliminary hearings, and bail hearings in felony cases (before they are transferred to superior courts).

The nation's approximately 13,500 independent courts of limited jurisdiction are the ones most often accused of providing assembly-line justice. Because the matters they decide involve minor personal confrontations and conflicts—family disputes, divorces, landlord–tenant conflicts, barroom brawls—the rule of the day is "handling the situation" and resolving the dispute.

SPECIALIZED COURTS A growing phenomenon in the United States is the creation of specialty courts that focus on one type of criminal act, such as drug courts and mental health courts.[4] All cases within the jurisdiction that involve this particular type of crime

---

FOCUS ON EFFECTIVENESS

The Queens (New York) Treatment Court

The Queens Treatment Court (QTC) is a drug court designed for first-time nonviolent drug offenders. Participants who meet eligibility requirements are typically given the option, in the form of a plea agreement, to either join the QTC program or receive felony probation (cases could also go to trial if no plea agreement is reached). The court seeks to reduce recidivism by providing a range of services, including treatment, to offenders who are arrested in Queens County, New York. The mission of the QTC is "to provide offenders with the tools necessary for long-term sobriety, using court-supervised treatment and case management services as an alternative to incarceration."

The QTC uses a postplea adjudication model. This means defendants start by pleading guilty to a drug charge. They also agree to serve out a term of incarceration if they fail out of the drug treatment program. Participation runs for 12 months, divided into three treatment phases. Each phase requires four consecutive sanctionless months before participants can move to the next phase. All participants appear in drug court each week at the start of the program, with gradual phase-out of court appearances in later stages of treatment. Treatment is individually tailored to the needs of each defendant.

Effects on Crime/Recidivism

Researchers compared QTC participants to similar defendants who had been arrested before the court was in operation. Formal steps (known as propensity score matching) were taken to ensure comparability of the treatment (those individuals who went through the QTC program) and control (offenders who would have been eligible for the QTC program were it around at the time of their arrests). Recidivism data were collected from the New York State Division of Criminal Justice Services. The researchers then tracked both treatment and control group members over time. They found that after one year, only 10 percent of QTC participants had a new arrest compared to 31 percent in the control group. After two years, the difference was 18 percent for the treatment group, 42 percent for the control group. Indeed, according to CrimeSolutions.gov, "the QTC program produced one

of the largest recidivism impacts of any drug court nationwide that has been evaluated…"

Thinking Critically About Research

The researchers who evaluated the QTC could not use an experimental research design, as doing so would raise serious ethical questions. In other words, it would not be fair to randomly assign participants to treatment and control conditions (why should some people benefit from treatment and others not benefit?). They *did*, however, conduct a rigorous quasi-experimental design that ensured comparability of treatment and control groups. Also, they evaluated a large sample of individuals *and* tracked their behavior over time. Finally, recall that offenders who refuse to participate likely receive several years of felony probation or take their chances at trial. This means there was minimal potential in the study for what researchers call a "selection effect," or the idea that those who volunteer to participate are the most likely to succeed anyway. QTC participants arguably chose treatment to avoid harsh penalties, not because they were amenable to treatment in the first place.

QUESTIONS

1. Should specialized courts require up-front guilty pleas for participation? Is such a plea a strong motivator for completion?
2. Is it fair for prosecutors to present plea agreements similar to those used in the QTC? In other words, is it fair to offer defendants an opportunity to participate in treatment or face a felony probation sentence?

Source: CrimeSolutions.gov, "Program Profile: Queens (NY) Treatment Court," https://www.crimesolutions.gov/ProgramDetails.aspx?ID=93 (accessed February 2017); Michael Rempel, Dana Fox-Kralstein, Amanda Cissner, Robyn Cohen, Melissa Labriola, Donald Farole, Ann Bader, and Michael Magnani, *The New York State Adult Court Evaluation: Policies, Participants, and Impacts* (New York: Center for Court Innovation, 2003).

Specialized Courts

Drug Courts

The drug court movement began in Florida to address the growing problem of prison overcrowding due in large part to an influx of drug-involved offenders. Drug courts were created to have primary jurisdiction over cases involving substance abuse and drug trafficking. The aim is to place nonviolent first offenders into intensive treatment programs rather than in jail or prison. Today, nearly 3,000 drug courts operate across the United States. Drug courts address the overlap between the public health threats of drug abuse and crime: crimes are often drug-related, and drug abusers are frequently involved with the criminal justice system. Drug courts provide an ideal setting to address these problems by linking the justice system with health services and drug treatment providers, while easing the burden on the already over-taxed correctional system.

Mental Health Courts

Based largely on the organization of drug courts, mental health courts focus their attention on mental health treatment to help people with emotional problems reduce their chances of reoffending. By focusing on the need for treatment, along with providing supervision and support from the community, mental health courts provide a venue for those dealing with mental health issues to avoid the trauma of jail or prison, where they will have little if any access to treatment.

Community Courts

Community courts are also becoming popular. Rather than targeting specific types of problems such as drugs or mental health, these courts take a more generalized focus. The main concern with community courts is providing "accessible justice" for residents who cannot easily get to downtown court-houses and focusing on quality-of-life offenses that may not be seen as top priority in traditional criminal courts. Community courts often have several on-site services available, as well. The first community court was Manhattan's Midtown Community Court.

Domestic Violence Courts

Several jurisdictions across the country have created their own domestic vio-lence courts. Brian Ostrom described domestic violence courts in this way: They "seek to coordinate with medical, social service, and treatment pro-viders and establish special procedures and alternative sentencing options to promote effective outcomes. Success necessitates systemwide collabora-tion and the ongoing commitment of judges, health care professionals, the police, prosecution, and citizens who witness violent acts." Today, some 300 domestic violence courts are in operation nationwide. Given how new they are, however, not many of them have been evaluated.

Gun Courts

Rhode Island created the nation's first gun court in 1994. Unlike some of the other specialized courts, this gun court was concerned mainly with mini-mizing delay and ensuring that gun offenders received the toughest penalties the law allows. Other gun courts emphasize educating defendants about gun violence and safety. Many such courts have focused their efforts on juvenile gun offenders.

Other Specialized Courts

There are specialized courts for many different types of crime and social prob-lems. In addition to targeting the preceding crimes, specialized courts have been formed to deal with everything from homelessness and sex offenses to parole reentry and teen bullying. We have moved well beyond the world of the traditional limited jurisdiction court. Limited jurisdiction courts still exist, but these are often being supplanted by courts whose jurisdiction is not only limited but also very narrow.

CRITICAL THINKING

1. Do you believe that specialized courts are needed for other types of crimes, such as sex offenses?
2. Should a judge preside over a specialized court, or should it be administered by treatment personnel?

Sources: US Department of Justice, "Drug Courts," http://www.ncjrs.gov/pdffiles1 /nij/238527.pdf; Shelli Rossman et al., *Criminal Justice Interventions for Offenders with Mental Illness: Evaluation of Mental Health Courts in Bronx and Brooklyn, New York* (Washington, DC: US Department of Justice, National Institute of Justice, 2012); Brian J. Ostrom, "Domestic Violence Courts: Editorial Introduction," *Criminology and Public Policy* 3 (2003): 105–108; Office of Juvenile Justice and Delinquency Prevention, "Gun Court—Providence, RI, Profile No. 37," http://www.ojjdp.gov/pubs /gun_violence/profile37.html; Greg Berman, John Feinblatt, and Sarah Glazer, *Good Courts: The Case for Problem-Solving Justice* (New York: New Press, 2005) (URLs accessed April 2017).

---

are funneled to the specialty court, where presumably they will be resolved promptly. Examples of such courts are featured in the accompanying Contemporary Issues in Criminal Justice box. Also see the accompanying Focus on Effectiveness box for a dis-cussion of the Queens (New York) Treatment Court.

What makes specialized courts different from traditional courts? According to the Center for Court Innovation, specialized courts have these six features:

- *Outcomes are elevated above process.* The main concern is reducing recidivism.
- *Judicial monitoring is critical.* Judges closely monitor offenders.
- *Informed decision making is necessary.* Judges hand down sentences with more infor-mation about offenders' backgrounds than may be available in traditional sentencing contexts.
- *Collaboration.* Specialized courts typically collaborate with other public and private agencies, many of which are housed in the courthouse.

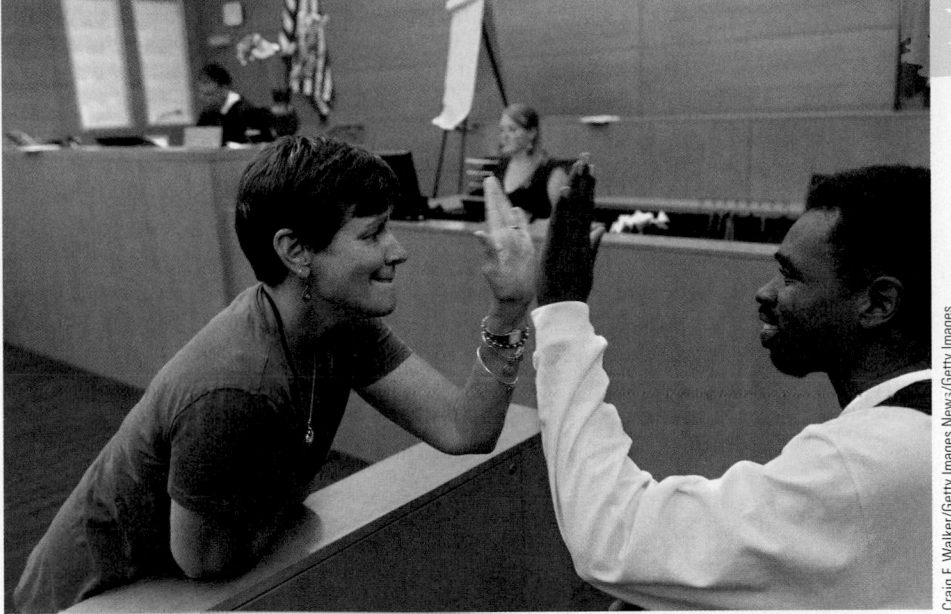

George Brady gets a high five from Shari Lewinski, program administrator of behavioral health courts, in Denver, Colorado. George, a client in Denver's Court to Community program, was commended by Judge Johnny Barajas for keeping all his appointments for the second week in a row. The Court to Community program is a jail diversion initiative designed to help keep people with mental illness out of jail.

- *Nontraditional roles.* Specialized court personnel often assume different roles. For example, prosecutors in specialized courts are more interested in helping defendants than in seeing that they are convicted or punished.
- *Systemic change.* Specialized courts try to change the way the criminal justice system works.[5]

Courts of General Jurisdiction

Approximately 2,000 courts of general jurisdiction exist in the United States; they are variously called felony, superior, supreme, county, and circuit courts. Courts of general jurisdiction handle the more serious felony cases, such as murder, rape, and robbery, and civil cases where damages are over a specified amount, such as $10,000. Courts of general jurisdiction may also be responsible for reviewing cases on appeal from courts of limited jurisdiction.

Courts of general jurisdiction are typically organized in judicial districts or circuits, based on a political division such as a county or a group of counties. They then receive cases from the various limited courts located within the county or jurisdiction. Some general courts separate criminal and civil cases so that some specialize in civil matters while others maintain a caseload that is exclusively criminal.

State court systems now handle about 94 million new cases each year, a number that has decreased more than 10 percent in the past decade. The great majority of these cases are traffic related, and about 20 million involve some form of criminal conduct.[6]

Appellate Courts

If defendants believe that the procedures used were in violation of their constitutional rights, they may ask an appellate court to review the trial process. Appellate courts do not try cases; they review the procedures of the case to determine whether an error was made by judicial authorities. In some instances, defendants can file an appeal if they believe that the law they were tried under was in violation of constitutional standards (e.g., the crime they were charged with—say, "being a public nuisance"—was vague and ill defined) or if the procedures used in the case contravened principles of due process and equal protection or were in direct opposition to a constitutional guarantee (e.g., they were denied the right to have competent legal representation).

It is the role of the appellate court to decide whether the trial judge made a legal error that influenced the outcome of the case, thereby denying the defendant a fair trial.

courts of general jurisdiction State or federal courts that have jurisdiction over felony offenses and more serious civil cases (i.e., cases involving more than a dollar amount set by the legislature).

appellate court A court that reconsiders a case that has already been tried to determine whether the measures used complied with accepted rules of criminal procedure and were in accordance with constitutional doctrines.

Judicial error can include admitting into evidence illegally seized material, improperly charging a jury, allowing a prosecutor to ask witnesses improper questions, and so on. If, upon review, the appellate court decides that an error has been made, it can order a new trial or even allow the defendant to go free.

State criminal appeals are heard in one of the appellate courts in the 50 states and the District of Columbia. Each state has at least one **court of last resort**, usually called a state supreme court, which reviews issues of law and fact appealed from the trial courts; a few states have two high courts, one for civil appeals and the other for criminal cases.

Many people believe that criminal appeals clog the nation's court system because so many convicted criminals try to "beat the rap" on a technicality. In fact, criminal appeals represent a small percentage of the total number of cases processed by the nation's appellate courts. All types of appeals, including criminal ones, continue to inundate the courts, so most courts are having problems processing cases expeditiously.

Figure 7.1 illustrates the interrelationship of appellate and trial courts in a model state court structure. Each state's court organization, of course, may vary from this

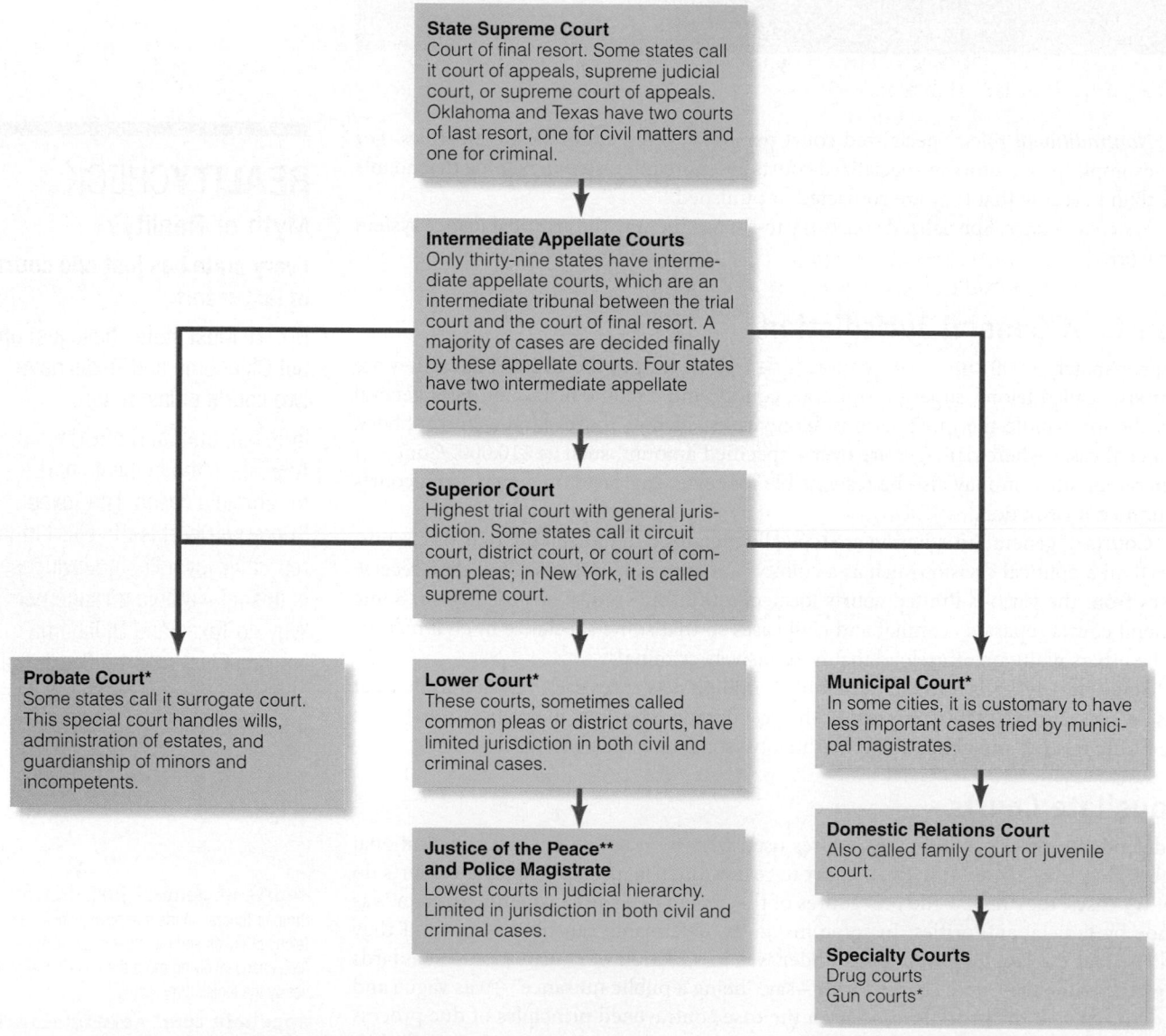

State Supreme Court
Court of final resort. Some states call it court of appeals, supreme judicial court, or supreme court of appeals. Oklahoma and Texas have two courts of last resort, one for civil matters and one for criminal.

Intermediate Appellate Courts
Only thirty-nine states have intermediate appellate courts, which are an intermediate tribunal between the trial court and the court of final resort. A majority of cases are decided finally by these appellate courts. Four states have two intermediate appellate courts.

Superior Court
Highest trial court with general jurisdiction. Some states call it circuit court, district court, or court of common pleas; in New York, it is called supreme court.

Probate Court*
Some states call it surrogate court. This special court handles wills, administration of estates, and guardianship of minors and incompetents.

Lower Court*
These courts, sometimes called common pleas or district courts, have limited jurisdiction in both civil and criminal cases.

Municipal Court*
In some cities, it is customary to have less important cases tried by municipal magistrates.

Justice of the Peace
and Police Magistrate**
Lowest courts in judicial hierarchy. Limited in jurisdiction in both civil and criminal cases.

Domestic Relations Court
Also called family court or juvenile court.

Specialty Courts
Drug courts
Gun courts*

FIGURE 7.1 Model of a State Judicial System

*Courts of special jurisdiction, such as probate, family, and juvenile courts, and the so-called inferior courts, such as common pleas and municipal courts, may be separate courts or part of the trial court of general jurisdiction.
**Justices of the peace do not exist in all states. Where they do exist, their jurisdictions vary greatly from state to state.
Source: American Bar Association, Law and the Courts (Chicago: ABA, 1974), p. 20; Bureau of Justice Statistics, State Court Organization–1998 (Washington, DC: Department of Justice, 2000).

standard pattern. Although most states have a tiered court organization (lower, upper, and appellate courts), all vary in the way they delegate responsibility to a particular court system, and some have consolidated their courts into a single, unified system.

Federal Courts

The legal basis for an independent federal court system is contained in Article 3, Section 1, of the US Constitution, which provides that "the judicial power of the United States shall be vested in one Supreme Court, and in such inferior courts as Congress may from time to time ordain and establish." The important clauses in Article 3 indicate that the federal courts have jurisdiction over the laws of the United States and over treaties and cases involving admiralty and maritime jurisdiction, as well as over controversies between two or more states and citizens of different states.[7] This complex language generally means that state courts have jurisdiction over most common-law crimes but that the federal system maintains jurisdiction over violations of federal criminal statutes, civil suits between citizens of different states, and suits between a citizen and an agency of the federal government.

Within this authority, the federal government has established a three-tiered hierarchy of court jurisdiction that, in order of ascendancy, consists of the (1) US district courts, (2) US courts of appeals (circuit courts), and (3) the US Supreme Court (see Figure 7.2).

US District Courts

The US district courts serve as the trial courts of the federal system and were organized by Congress in the Judicial Act of 1789. Today, 94 independent courts are in operation. Originally, each state was allowed one court; as the population grew, however, so did the need for courts, so now some states have multiple jurisdictions.

WEB APP 7.1 Visit the Court Statistics Project website and examine the court system structure in the state in which you reside at **http://www.courtstatistics.org/other-pages/state_court_structure_charts.aspx**. Compare and contrast your state's court system structure with that of a neighboring state.

LO2 Describe the federal court system

Supreme Court	**United States Supreme Court**
Appellate Courts	**US Courts of Appeals** 12 Regional Circuit Courts of Appeals 1 US Court of Appeals for the Federal Circuit
Trial Courts	**US District Courts** 94 judicial districts US Bankruptcy Courts **US Court of International Trade** **US Court of Federal Claims**
Federal Courts and other entities outside the Judicial Branch	**Military Courts (trial and appellate)** **Court of Veterans Appeals** **US Tax Court** **Federal administrative agencies and boards**

FIGURE 7.2 The Federal Judicial System

US district courts have jurisdiction over cases involving violations of federal laws, including civil rights abuses, interstate transportation of stolen vehicles, and kidnappings. They may also hear cases on questions involving citizenship and the rights of aliens. The jurisdiction of the US district court will occasionally overlap that of state courts. Citizens who reside in separate states and are involved in litigation of an amount in excess of $10,000 may choose to have their cases heard in either of the states or in the federal district court. Finally, federal district courts hear cases where one state sues a resident (or firm) in another state, where one state sues another, or where the federal government is a party in a suit.

US Courts of Appeals

There are 13 judicial circuits, each with a court of appeals. Each circuit's court of appeals (formally called the "Court of Appeals for the [number] Circuit") is empowered to review federal and state appellate court cases on substantive and procedural issues involving rights guaranteed by the Constitution. Circuit courts do not actually retry cases, nor do they determine whether the facts brought out during trial support conviction or dismissal. Instead, they analyze judicial interpretations of the law, such as the charge (or instructions) to the jury, and reflect on the constitutional issues involved in each case they hear.

Although federal court criminal cases make up only a small percentage of appellate cases, they are still of concern to the judiciary. Steps have been taken to make appealing more difficult. The US Supreme Court has tried to limit the number of appeals being filed by prison inmates, which often represent a significant number of cases appealed in the federal criminal justice system.

The US Supreme Court

The Supreme Court is the nation's highest appellate body and the court of last resort for all cases tried in the various federal and state courts. The Court is composed of nine members appointed for lifetime terms by the president, with the approval of Congress. The Court has discretion over most of the cases it will consider and may choose to hear only those it deems important, appropriate, and worthy of its attention. The Court chooses some 300 of the 5,000 cases appealed each year, and only about 100 of these receive full opinions.

writ of certiorari An order of a superior court requesting that the record of an inferior court (or administrative body) be brought forward for review or inspection.

When the Supreme Court decides to hear a case, it grants a writ of certiorari, requesting a transcript of the proceedings of the case for review. At least four of the nine justices sitting on the Court must vote to grant the writ of certiorari even before the case can be considered for review. More than 90 percent of the cases heard by the Court are brought by petition for a writ of certiorari. The Court has original jurisdiction for the remaining cases (e.g., those involving disputes between the states).

landmark decision A decision handed down by the US Supreme Court that becomes the law of the land and serves as a precedent for resolving similar legal issues.

When the Supreme Court rules on a case, usually by majority decision (at least five votes), its rule becomes a precedent, or landmark decision, that must be honored by all lower courts. If, for example, the Court grants a particular litigant the right to counsel at a police lineup, all similarly situated clients must be given the same right.

SUPREME COURT PROCEDURE After the Supreme Court decides to hear a case, it reviews written arguments (referred to as legal briefs) outlining the case and the points of law to be considered. After the written material is reviewed, attorneys for each side in the case are allowed 30 minutes to present an oral argument before the court members. Then the justices normally meet in what is known as a "case conference" to discuss the case and vote to reach a decision (see Figure 7.3).

In reaching a decision, the Supreme Court reevaluates and reinterprets state statutes, the US Constitution, and previous case decisions. On the basis of its review of the case, the Court either affirms or reverses the decision of the lower court. When

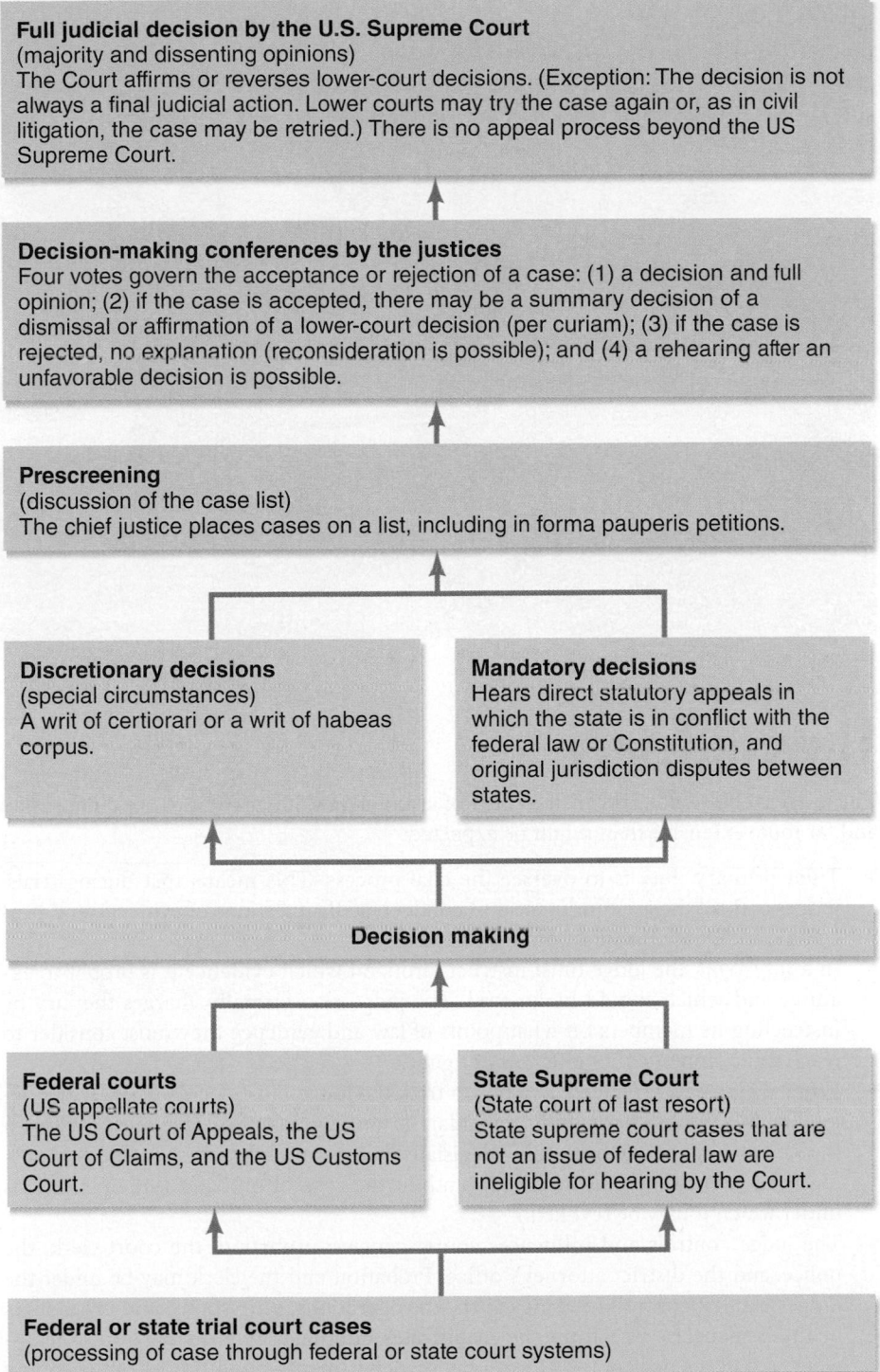

Full judicial decision by the U.S. Supreme Court
(majority and dissenting opinions)
The Court affirms or reverses lower-court decisions. (Exception: The decision is not always a final judicial action. Lower courts may try the case again or, as in civil litigation, the case may be retried.) There is no appeal process beyond the US Supreme Court.

Decision-making conferences by the justices
Four votes govern the acceptance or rejection of a case: (1) a decision and full opinion; (2) if the case is accepted, there may be a summary decision of a dismissal or affirmation of a lower-court decision (per curiam); (3) if the case is rejected, no explanation (reconsideration is possible); and (4) a rehearing after an unfavorable decision is possible.

Prescreening
(discussion of the case list)
The chief justice places cases on a list, including in forma pauperis petitions.

Discretionary decisions
(special circumstances)
A writ of certiorari or a writ of habeas corpus.

Mandatory decisions
Hears direct statutory appeals in which the state is in conflict with the federal law or Constitution, and original jurisdiction disputes between states.

Decision making

Federal courts
(US appellate courts)
The US Court of Appeals, the US Court of Claims, and the US Customs Court.

State Supreme Court
(State court of last resort)
State supreme court cases that are not an issue of federal law are ineligible for hearing by the Court.

Federal or state trial court cases
(processing of case through federal or state court systems)

FIGURE 7.3 Tracing the Course of a Case to the US Supreme Court

the justices reach a decision, and in the event that the Court's decision is split, the chief justice of the Court assigns a member of the majority group to write the opinion. Another justice normally writes a dissent, or minority, opinion; a single opinion may be written if the decision is unanimous. When the case is finished, it is submitted to the public and becomes the law of the land. The decision represents the legal precedents that add to the existing body of law on a given subject, change it, and guide its future development.

Faith and Freedom Coalition chairman Ralph Reed speaks during a rally in front of the US Supreme Court on April 19, 2017. The Court was hearing oral arguments in *Trinity Lutheran Church v. Comer*, a case about a religious preschool that was rejected from a state program that provides reimbursement grants to purchase rubberized surface material for children's playgrounds.

Mark Wilson/Getty Images News/Getty Images

The Judiciary

The judge is the senior officer in a court of criminal law. Judges' duties are quite varied and far more extensive than might be expected:

- Their primary duty is to oversee the trial process. This means that during trials, judges control the appropriateness of conduct, settle questions of evidence and procedure, and guide the questioning of witnesses.
- In a **jury trial**, the judge must instruct jurors on which evidence it is proper to examine and which should be ignored. The judge also formally charges the jury by instructing its members on what points of law and evidence they must consider to reach a decision of either guilty or not guilty.
- When a jury trial is waived, in a bench trial, the judge must decide whether the defendant is guilty as charged. If a defendant is found guilty, the judge must decide on the sentence (in some cases, this is legislatively determined), which includes choosing the type of sentence, its length, and, in the case of probation, the conditions under which it may be revoked.
- The judge controls and influences court agencies: probation, the court clerk, the police, and the district attorney's office. Probation and the clerk may be under the judge's explicit control. In some courts, the operations, philosophy, and procedures of these agencies are within the magistrate's administrative domain. In others— where a state agency controls the probation department—the attitudes of the county or district court judge greatly influence the way a probation department is run and how its decisions are made.

While carrying out their duties, judges must be wary of the legal controls placed on the trial process by the appellate court system. If an error is made, the judge's decision may be reversed, causing (at the very least) personal embarrassment. Some experts believe that fear of reversal may shape judicial decision making, but research shows that judges may be more independent than previously believed.

Of course, judges do not wield their power in isolation. They work together with prosecutors and defense attorneys, whose work is featured shortly. They are also assisted by a number of courtroom personnel, including clerks, court administrators, security personnel, court reporters, and other support staff. See Exhibit 7.1 for additional details.

jury trial The process of deciding a case by a group of persons selected and sworn in to serve as jurors at a criminal trial, often as a 6- or 12-person jury.

US Supreme Court Associate Justice Anthony Kennedy administers the judicial oath to Judge Neil Gorsuch as his wife, Marie Louise Gorsuch, holds a bible and President Donald Trump looks on. The ceremony took place in the Rose Garden at the White House on April 10, 2017. Earlier in the day Gorsuch, 49, was sworn in as the 113th Associate Justice in a private ceremony at the Supreme Court.

The Asahi Shimbun/Getty Images

EXHIBIT 7.1 Court Staff

The most visible courtroom personnel include the judge, the prosecutor, and the defense attorney. However, many other important court personnel and staff persons are involved as well. The typical large jurisdiction probably has a mix of the following personnel working in the courtroom or courthouse at any given time.

Clerk Court clerks are responsible for a wide range of duties. Their main responsibilities include maintaining court records; receiving, processing, and maintaining judgments; issuing process, such as summonses, subpoenas, and wage garnishments; preserving the court seal; swearing in witnesses, jurors, and grand jurors; collecting fees and fines; handling inquiries from attorneys and other parties; and printing and distributing opinions of the court.

Court Administrator There are two general types of court administrators. The first is a state employee. In each state, these individuals are part of the state administrative office of the court, which is usually under the direction of the state supreme court. Court administrators help develop and implement policies and services for the judicial branch throughout the state. They also conduct research and determine whether judicial needs are identified and incorporated into long-term plans. They establish priorities for the courts, address financial problems and budgeting issues, and manage the use of technology within a state's judicial branch. The second type of court administrator is a local court administrator. These individuals manage the daily operations of the court, usually under the direction of the presiding judge. They provide administrative support for court programs, help the court establish new programs and evaluate them, and manage purchasing and accounts payable, among other responsibilities.

Court Security The marshal or bailiff for the court is responsible for courthouse security. In some states, such as California, court security is provided by sheriff's deputies who screen people entering the building, provide security during trials, and transport suspects to court from jail. Depending on the jurisdiction, court security personnel may take on additional responsibilities, including some investigation, bond supervising, community service monitoring, and making arrests as needed.

Legal Staff The larger and more powerful the court, the more likely it will have a variety of legal staff. These personnel can include legal counsel (prosecutors and defense attorneys), staff attorneys, research attorneys, and law clerks. Law clerks are not to be confused with court clerks. Unlike court clerks, law clerks are often recent law school graduates who assist judges with researching issues before the courts and with writing opinions. US Supreme Court law clerks are the cream of the crop, having graduated from many of the nation's top law schools.

Judicial Support Staff A judge's support staff may include executive assistants, administrative assistants, secretaries, or a mix of all three. Support staff members edit and type judicial opinions, create and arrange files, coordinate meetings, coordinate travel arrangements, answer telephone and e-mail inquiries, mail correspondence, and serve as an intermediary between the judge and other outside parties.

Court Reporter The court reporter records judicial proceedings word for word. See the Careers in Criminal Justice feature in Chapter 8 for more on court reporters.

Jury Staff Many courts have dedicated jury personnel who maintain and review lists of prospective jurors. They may also determine who is eligible to serve, determine the number of jurors needed, issue summonses for jury service, and handle requests by jurors for dismissal, exemption, or disqualification. These individuals may also meet with prospective jurors to explain the process, tell them where to go, and dismiss them from service at the end of the day.

Other Officers Many courts have representatives on site from other criminal justice agencies. Juvenile court officers may be present who are vested with the authority to take charge of children who come under the jurisdiction of the juvenile or family court. Representatives from probation may assist judges by performing presentence investigations that can be used during sentencing. In some states, the probation department is part of the judiciary and is thus more closely connected with the court than probation departments in other states.

The Judge and the Justice System

Judicial attitudes and philosophy have a major impact on how the justice system operates. Judicial attitudes may extend way beyond the courtroom. Police policies may be directly influenced by the judge, whose sentencing discretion affects the arrest process. If a local judge usually imposes minimal sentences—such as a fine—for a particular offense, the police may be reluctant to arrest offenders for that crime, knowing that doing so will basically be a waste of time. Similarly, if a judge is known to have a liberal attitude toward police discretion, the local department may be more inclined to engage in practices that border on entrapment or to pursue cases through easily obtained wiretaps. However, a magistrate oriented toward strict use of due process guarantees would stifle such activities by dismissing all cases involving apparent police abuses of personal freedoms.

The district attorney's office may also be sensitive to judicial attitudes. The district attorney might forgo indictments in cases that the presiding magistrate expressly considers trivial or quasi-criminal and in which the judge has been known to take only token action, such as the prosecution of pornographers.

Finally, the judge considers requests by prosecutors for leniency (or severity) in sentencing. The judge's reaction to these requests is important if the police and the district attorney are to honor the bargains they may have made with defendants to secure information, cooperation, or guilty pleas. When police tell informers that they will try to convince the judge to go easy on them to secure required information, they will often discuss the terms of the promised leniency with representatives of the court. If a judge ignores police demands, the department's bargaining power is severely diminished, and communication within the criminal justice system is impaired.

Judicial Qualifications and Selection

Judicial qualifications and selection vary between the federal and state levels. In general, the federal level has fewer formal qualifications and more informal qualifications. The opposite is often true at the state level.

FEDERAL LEVEL Federal judges are appointed by the president with the advice and consent of the Senate. Senate confirmation of federal judiciary appointees, especially those chosen to serve on the US Supreme Court, can be a contentious process. One exception to this process exists for the appointment of a **US magistrate judge**. Magistrate judges are federal trial judges appointed by district court judges who preside over various civil cases with the consent of the parties and over certain misdemeanor cases.

Interestingly, there are almost no formal qualifications for federal judges. The Constitution and federal law are silent on judicial qualifications. Potential federal judges do not have to pass any exams or even be a lawyer for that matter. Even so, positions in the federal judiciary are very prestigious and sought after. They thus attract highly qualified, seasoned attorneys.

STATE LEVEL The qualifications for appointment to one of the existing 30,000 judgeships vary from state to state and court to court. Most often, the potential judge must be a resident of the state, licensed to practice law, a member of the state bar association, and at least 25 years and less than 70 years of age. However, a significant degree of diversity exists in the basic qualifications, depending on the level of court jurisdiction. Although almost every state requires judges to have a law degree if they are to serve on appellate courts or courts of general jurisdiction, it is not uncommon for municipal or town court judges to lack a legal background, even though they have the power to incarcerate criminal defendants for petty crimes such as vandalism.

Many methods are used to select judges, depending on the level of court jurisdiction. In some jurisdictions, judges are appointed officials, most often appointed by the state

L03 Summarize the selection procedure for and duties of the trial judge

US magistrate judge A federal trial judge who is appointed by a district court judge and who presides over various civil cases with the consent of the parties and over certain misdemeanor cases.

REALITYCHECK

Myth or Reality?

There are almost no formal qualifications for federal judges.

REALITY. It is true that there are almost no formal qualifications for federal judges.

There are no exams, no age requirements, and no requirements that a federal judge be a US citizen. There is not even a law degree requirement! Even so, the federal judiciary attracts highly qualified people. Why do you suppose there are almost no formal qualifications for federal judges?

governor. In some states, in an effort to remove politics from judicial appointments, the governor's recommendations must be confirmed by the state senate, the governor's council, a special confirmation committee, an executive council elected by the state assembly, or an elected review board. Some states employ a judicial nominating commission that submits names to the governor for approval.

Another form of judicial selection is popular election. Judges may run as members of the Republican, Democratic, or other parties, or without party affiliation. Although this practice is used in a majority of states, each state sets its own terms of appointment. In some states, judges are elected to 15-year terms and in others to 4-year terms.[8] See Figure 7.4 for a map of judicial selection methods by state.

The state of Missouri pioneered a nonpartisan method of selecting judges. This **Missouri Plan** is now used in some manner in the majority of states. The plan consists of three parts:

1. A judicial nominating commission selects and nominates potential candidates for the bench. In Missouri, the judicial commission is composed of the chief justice of the state supreme court, three lawyers elected by the Missouri bar (the organization of all lawyers licensed in this state), and three citizens selected by the governor.
2. An elected official (usually from the executive branch, such as the governor) makes appointments from the list submitted by the commission.
3. Subsequent nonpartisan and noncompetitive elections take place, in which incumbent judges run on their records and voters can choose either to retain or to dismiss them.[9]

The quality of the judiciary is a concern. Although merit plans, screening committees, and popular elections are designed to ensure a competent judiciary, it has often been charged that many judicial appointments are made to pay off political debts or to reward cronies and loyal friends. Also not uncommon are charges that those who want to be nominated for judgeships are required to make significant political contributions.

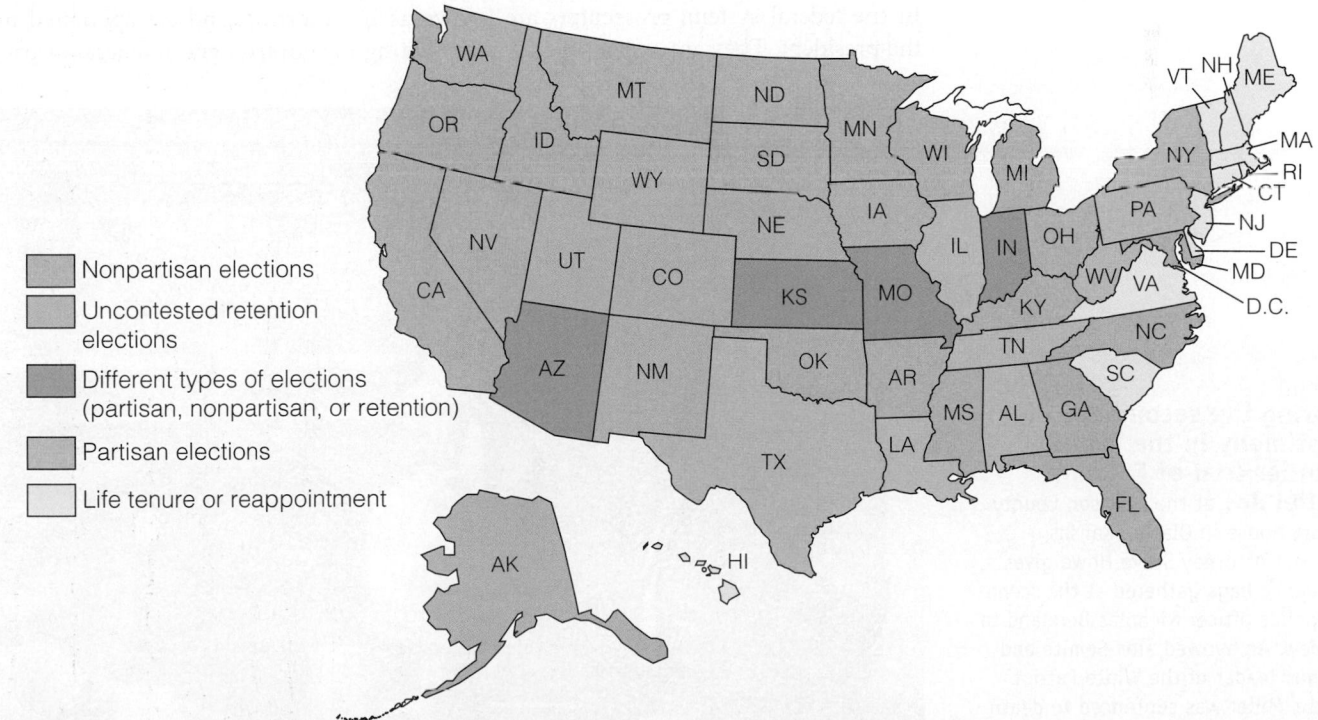

FIGURE 7.4 Selection Methods by State for General Jurisdiction Trial Court Judges

Legend:
- Nonpartisan elections
- Uncontested retention elections
- Different types of elections (partisan, nonpartisan, or retention)
- Partisan elections
- Life tenure or reappointment

Source: American Bar Association, http://www.americanbar.org/content/dam/aba/migrated/leadership/fact_sheet.authcheckdam.pdf.

prosecutor Representative of the state (executive branch) in criminal proceedings; advocate for the state's case—the charge—in the adversary trial. Examples include the attorney general of the United States, US attorneys, the attorneys general of the states, district attorneys, and police prosecutors.

REALITY CHECK

Myth or Reality?

Elected state judges can be affiliated with a political party.

REALITY. This is not true in all states, but some states permit partisan judicial elections. This means a judge can run as a Democrat, a Republican, an independent, or a member of any other political party.

Should judges be allowed to run on political platforms? Why or why not?

The Prosecutor

Depending on the level of government and the jurisdiction in which he or she functions, the prosecutor may be known as a district attorney, county attorney, state's attorney, or US attorney. Whatever the title, the prosecutor is the people's attorney, who is responsible for representing the public in criminal matters. The prosecutor participates in investigations both before and after arrest, prepares legal documents, participates in obtaining arrest or search warrants, and decides whether to charge a suspect and, if so, with which offense. The prosecutor argues the state's case at trial, advises the police, participates in plea negotiations, and makes sentencing recommendations.

Because they are the chief law enforcement officers of a particular jurisdiction, their jurisdiction spans the entire justice system process from the time when search and arrest warrants are issued or a grand jury is impaneled to the final sentencing decision and appeal. Following are some of the general duties of a prosecutor:

- Provides advice to law enforcement officers during investigation to determine whether criminal charges should be filed
- Represents the state in plea negotiations, pretrial motions, and bail hearings during the pretrial stage
- Represents the state at hearings, criminal trials, and appeals
- Acts as legal advisor to county commissioners and other elected officials

In addition to these duties, local jurisdictions may create specific programs directed by local prosecutors. One example is career-criminal prosecution programs, which involve identifying dangerous adult and juvenile offenders who commit a high number of crimes, so that prosecutors can target them for swift prosecution. Many jurisdictions have developed protection programs so that victims of domestic violence can obtain temporary court orders (and, after a hearing, more long-term court orders) protecting them from an abusive spouse; research indicates that protection orders can reduce the incidence of repeat violence.[10]

Types of Prosecutors

In the federal system, prosecutors are known as US attorneys and are appointed by the president. They are responsible for representing the government in federal district

During the second day of testimony in the capital murder trial of F. Glenn Miller Jr., at the Johnson County Court House in Olathe, Kansas, District Attorney Steve Howe gives evidence bags gathered at the scene to police officer Nicholas Berkland to review. An avowed anti-Semite and former leader of the White Patriot Party, Miller was sentenced to death for the April 2014 slayings of three people at two suburban Kansas City Jewish centers.

AP Images/Joe Ledford

courts. The chief prosecutor is usually an administrator, and assistants normally handle the actual preparation and trial work. Federal prosecutors are professional civil service employees with reasonable salaries and job security.

On the state and county levels, the attorney general and the district attorney, respectively, are the chief prosecutorial officers. Again, the bulk of the criminal prosecution and staff work is performed by scores of full- and part-time attorneys, police investigators, and clerical personnel. Most attorneys who work for prosecutors at the state and county levels are political appointees who earn low salaries, handle many cases, and (in some jurisdictions) maintain private law practices. Many young lawyers take these staff positions to gain the trial experience that will qualify them for better opportunities.

In urban jurisdictions, the structure of the district attorney's office is often specialized, with separate divisions for felonies, misdemeanors, and trial and appeal assignments. In rural offices, chief prosecutors handle many of the criminal cases themselves. Where assistant prosecutors are employed, they often work part time, have limited professional opportunities, and depend on the political patronage of chief prosecutors for their positions.

The personnel practices, organizational structures, and political atmosphere of many prosecutors' offices often restrict their effectiveness in investigating and prosecuting criminal offenses. For many years, prosecutors have been criticized for bargaining justice away, using their positions as stepping-stones to higher political office, and often failing to investigate or simply dismissing criminal cases. Lately, however,

CAREERS IN CRIMINAL JUSTICE PARALEGAL

Duties and Characteristics of the Job

- Paralegals assist lawyers by conducting much of the preparation for trials.

- A paralegal's exact duties vary according to the needs of the office for which he or she works. However, a paralegal's work typically includes assisting with or carrying out client interviews, drafting legal documents, reviewing pertinent case law, summarizing legal proceedings, and doing some standard office work.

- Paralegals do much of the same work as a lawyer but within definite limits. For example, paralegals cannot advise on legal issues.

- Although most paralegals have general legal knowledge, it is becoming more common, especially for long-term or career paralegals, to choose a field of specialization.

Job Outlook

- The paralegal profession is expected to grow rapidly in the near future for several reasons, most prominently the fact that some organizations need legal expertise but do not want the extra expense of hiring a lawyer.

- Opportunities for advancement are available in larger offices, especially in urban areas.

- Ultimately, many paralegals use their knowledge and skills to earn a law degree and become a lawyer or judge. They can also move on to better-paying careers where legal experience is useful, such as insurance claims adjuster.

Salary

- The median (half earn above the amount, half earn below it) annual salary for paralegals is $48,800

- The lowest 10 percent earned less than $30,600, but the top 10 percent earned almost $80,000.

- The best paid paralegals work for the federal government.

Qualifications

- Much of a paralegal's work is focused on conducting legal research, so skills that aid this process are critical.

- There is something of a political aspect to gaining this position because in some areas, one must be elected or appointed to it.

Education and Training

- A bachelor's degree with an emphasis on writing, analytical, and research skills is necessary.

- Because much of this research can now be done using computer programs, databases, and the Internet, up-to-date computer skills confer a distinct advantage.

- Most paralegals enter their profession with training from a two-year paralegal program approved by the American Bar Association. However, it is possible for people with a liberal arts degree to enter the field by working in legal offices and learning skills on the job.

Reality Check

- Relevant educational experience and certification are useful for gaining employment.

- Paralegal work involves a great deal of behind-the-scenes office work and research, so applicants need to be comfortable with both.

- Jobs with the most potential for upward mobility will be found in urban settings.

- Paralegals must always keep up with changes in the law in their areas of specialization.

Sources: Bureau of Labor Statistics, US Department of Labor, "Paralegals and Legal Assistants," *Occupational Outlook Handbook*, http://www.bls.gov/ooh/Legal/Paralegals -and-legal-assistants.htm; *Princeton Review*, "A Day in the Life of a Paralegal," http:// www.princetonreview.com/careers/105/paralegal (URLs accessed April 2017).

the prosecutor's public image has improved. Violations of federal laws, such as white-collar crime, drug peddling, and corruption, are being more aggressively investigated by the 94 US attorneys and the nearly 2,000 assistant US attorneys. Aggressive federal prosecutors have also made extraordinary progress in the war against insider trading and securities fraud on Wall Street. There have been a number of highly publicized indictments alleging that some corporate managers abused their power to loot company assets.

Today, about 2,400 state court prosecutors' offices are in operation, which employ about 79,000 attorneys, investigators, and support staff to handle felony cases in the state trial courts.[11] Usually, the most active prosecutors are employed in larger counties with populations of more than 500,000.

Prosecutors, like other justice system professionals, are now confronting issues related to cyber crime and terrorism and the use of technology both to commit crimes and to solve them after they occur. According to the most recent federal survey of prosecutors:

- At least two-thirds of state court prosecutors had litigated a computer-related crime such as credit card fraud (80 percent), identity theft (69 percent), or transmission of child pornography (67 percent).
- About one-quarter (24 percent) of the offices participated in a state or local task force for homeland security; one-third reported that an office member attended training on homeland security issues.
- Most prosecutors (95 percent) relied on state-operated forensic laboratories to perform DNA analysis, with about a third (34 percent) also using privately operated DNA labs.[12]

Prosecutorial Discretion

L05 Describe prosecutorial discretion, and summarize its pros and cons

The prosecutor decides whether to bring a case to trial or to dismiss it outright. Even if the prosecutor decides to pursue a case, the charges may later be dropped if conditions are not favorable for a conviction; this is referred to as *nolle prosequi*.

The courts have protected the prosecutor's right to exercise discretion over processing of legal cases, maintaining that prosecutorial decision making can be controlled or overturned only if a defendant can prove that the prosecutor let discrimination guide his or her decision making.[13] Even in felony cases, the prosecutor ordinarily exercises much discretion in deciding whether to charge the accused with a crime.[14] After a police investigation, the prosecutor may be asked to review the sufficiency of the evidence to determine whether a criminal complaint should be filed. In some jurisdictions, this may involve presenting the evidence at a preliminary hearing. In other cases, the prosecutor may decide to seek a criminal complaint through the grand jury or other information procedure.

Without question, prosecutors exercise a great deal of discretion in even the most serious cases. In a now classic study, Barbara Boland examined the flow of felony cases through three jurisdictions in the United States: Golden, Colorado; the borough of Manhattan in New York City; and Salt Lake City, Utah.[15] Although procedures were different in the three districts, prosecutors used their discretion to dismiss a high percentage of the cases before trial. When cases were forwarded for trial, very few defendants were actually acquitted, indicating that the prosecutorial discretion was exercised to screen out the weakest cases. In addition, of those cases accepted for prosecution, a high percentage ended with the defendant pleading guilty. All the evidences here point to the conclusion that prosecutorial discretion is used to reduce potential trial cases to a minimum.

The prosecutor may also play a limited role in exercising discretion in minor offenses. This role may consist of simply consulting with the police after their investigation results in a complaint being filed against the accused. In such instances, the decision to charge a person with a crime may be left primarily to the discretion of the law enforcement agency. The prosecutor may decide to enter this type of case after an arrest has been made and a complaint filed with the court, and then subsequently determine whether to adjust the matter or proceed to trial.

Factors Influencing Prosecutorial Discretion

Research indicates that a wide variety of factors influence prosecutorial discretion in invoking criminal sanction. These include legal issues, victim issues, extralegal issues, and resource issues.

LEGAL ISSUES Legal issues can include the characteristics of the justice system, the crime, the criminal, and the victim. The quality of police work and the amount and relevance of the evidence the police gather are critical legal variables that a prosecutor considers in deciding whether to bring a case forward to trial.[16] A defendant who is a known drug user, has a long history of criminal offending, and caused the victim extensive physical injuries is more likely to be prosecuted than one who is a first offender, does not use drugs, and did not seriously injure the victim.[17] Crime seriousness certainly influences discretion, too. As might be expected, prosecutors are much more likely to use their discretion in minor incidents than in more serious ones.

VICTIM ISSUES In some instances, the victim's behavior may influence charging decisions. Some victims may become reluctant to press charges, especially if the offender is a parent or spouse. Domestic violence cases are often difficult to prosecute. Some victims are unlikely to encourage or work with prosecutors even after the police get involved. Victim cooperation is a key factor in the decision to prosecute cases: the odds of a case being prosecuted are seven times greater when victims are considered cooperative.[18]

EXTRALEGAL ISSUES Extralegal factors include the offender's race, gender, and ethnic background. Of course, due process considerations demand that these personal characteristics have no bearing on the use of prosecutorial discretion. Nonetheless, some research efforts have found that the race of the offender or victim influences prosecutorial discretion; others show that decisions are relatively unbiased.[19] Proving racial influence is difficult. To establish bias, a defendant must produce credible evidence that similarly situated defendants of other races could have been prosecuted but were not.

RESOURCE ISSUES Resource issues that influence prosecutorial discretion include the availability of treatment and detention facilities, the size of caseloads, and the number of prosecutors available. In some drug cases, prosecutors may decline to bring the case to trial because preparing it for prosecution would demand costly forensic analysis, expert witnesses, and forensic accountants.[20] Some research efforts have concluded that the availability of resources may be a more critical factor in shaping prosecutorial discretion than either legal or extralegal factors. In a world of tight government budgets, a prosecutor's office may be forced to accept plea bargains simply because it lacks the resources and personnel to bring many cases to trial.[21]

The Pros and Cons of Prosecutorial Discretion

Regardless of its source, the proper exercise of prosecutorial discretion can improve the criminal justice process by preventing the rigid implementation of criminal law. Discretion allows the prosecutor to consider alternative decisions and humanize the operation of the criminal justice system. If prosecutors had little or no discretion, they would be forced to prosecute all cases brought to their attention. As Judge Charles Breitel put it, "If every policeman, every prosecutor, every court, and every postsentence agency performed his or its responsibility in strict accordance with rules of law, precisely and narrowly laid down, the criminal law would be ordered but intolerable."[22]

On the other side, too much discretion can lead to abuses that result in the abandonment of law. Prosecutors are political creatures. Although they are charged with serving the people, they also must keep their reputations in mind; losing too many high-profile cases may jeopardize their chances of reelection. They therefore may be unwilling to prosecute cases where the odds of conviction are low; they are worried about convictability.[23]

REALITYCHECK

Myth or Reality?

Prosecutors base their charging decisions solely on legal factors, such as the seriousness of the offense.

MYTH. Limited resources, along with several other extralegal factors, shape prosecutorial decision making.

Resource concerns are all the more important in this day and age. News accounts of courts strapped for money and prosecutors dropping charges against some suspects to save precious resources seem all too common. In what other ways are resource constraints likely to affect the administration of justice?

Prosecutorial Ethics

Although the prosecutor's primary duty is to enforce criminal law, the fundamental obligation is to seek justice. If the prosecutor discovers facts suggesting that the accused is innocent, he or she must bring this information to the attention of the court.

In carrying out their stated duties, prosecutors are sometimes caught in an ethical conundrum. They are compelled by their supervisors to do everything possible to obtain a guilty verdict, while acting as public officials concerned to ensure that justice is done. Sometimes this conflict can lead to prosecutorial misconduct. According to some legal authorities, unethical prosecutorial behavior is often motivated by the desire to obtain a conviction and by the fact that such misbehavior is rarely punished by the courts.[24] Some prosecutors may conceal evidence, misrepresent evidence, or influence juries by impugning the character of opposing witnesses. Even where a court may instruct a jury to ignore certain evidence, a prosecutor may attempt to sway the jury or the judge by simply mentioning the tainted evidence.

Prosecutorial Misconduct

Because prosecutorial misconduct is a serious matter, the courts have reviewed such prosecutorial behavior as making disruptive statements in court, failing to adhere to sentence recommendations pursuant to a plea bargain, making public statements harmful to the state's case that are not constitutionally protected under the First Amendment, and withholding evidence that might exonerate a defendant.

Courts have also been more concerned about prosecutors who use their discretion in a vindictive manner to punish defendants who exercise their legal rights. Three cases illustrate controls placed on "vindictive" prosecutors:

- *North Carolina v. Pearce.* In this case, the US Supreme Court held that a judge in a retrial cannot impose a sentence more severe than that originally imposed. In other words, a prosecutor cannot seek a stricter sentence for a defendant who succeeds in getting her first conviction set aside.[25]
- *Blackledge v. Perry.* The Supreme Court found that imposing a penalty on a defendant for having successfully pursued a statutory right of appeal is a violation of due process of law and amounts to prosecutorial vindictiveness.[26]
- *Bordenkircher v. Hayes.* In this case, the Court allowed the prosecutor to carry out threats of increased charges made during plea negotiations when the defendant refused to plead guilty to the original charge.[27]

These decisions provide the framework for the "prosecutorial vindictiveness" doctrine: due process of law may be violated if the prosecutor retaliates against a defendant, and there is proof of actual vindictiveness. The prosecutor's legitimate exercise of discretion must be balanced against the defendant's legal rights.

The Defense Attorney

The defense attorney is the counterpart of the prosecuting attorney in the criminal process. The accused has a constitutional right to counsel, and when the defendant cannot afford an attorney, the state must provide one. The accused may obtain counsel from the private bar if he can afford to do so; if the defendant is indigent, private counsel or a **public defender** may be assigned by the court (see the discussion on the defense of the indigent later in this chapter).

The Role of the Criminal Defense Attorney

The defense counsel is an attorney as well as an officer of the court. As an attorney, the defense counsel is obligated to uphold the integrity of the legal profession and to observe the requirements of the American Bar Association's Code of Professional Responsibility in the defense of a client.

Defense attorneys are viewed as the prime movers in what is essentially an **adversarial procedure**: the procedure used to determine truth in the adjudication of

public defender An attorney usually employed (at no cost to the accused) by the government to represent poor persons accused of a crime.

adversarial procedure The process of publicly pitting the prosecution and the defense against one another in pursuit of the truth.

LO6 Identify the role of the defense attorney in the justice process

guilt, in which the defense (advocate for the accused) is pitted against the prosecution (advocate for the state), with the judge acting as arbiter of the legal rules. Under the adversary system, the burden is on the state to prove the charges beyond a reasonable doubt. The defense uses all means at its disposal to refute the state's case. This system of having the two parties publicly debate, though imperfect, is thought to be the most effective method of arriving at the truth in a criminal case.

As a member of the legal profession, however, the defense counsel must be aware of his or her role as an officer of the court. The defense counsel is obligated to uphold the integrity of the legal profession and to rely on constitutional ideals of fair play and professional ethics to provide adequate representation for a client.

The Right to Counsel

The Sixth Amendment to the US Constitution allows for provision of counsel at trial. But what about the indigent criminal defendant who cannot afford to retain an attorney?

In the 1963 landmark case of *Gideon v. Wainwright*, the US Supreme Court took the first major step on the issue of right to counsel by holding that state courts must provide counsel to indigent defendants in felony prosecutions.[28] Almost 10 years later, in the 1972 case of *Argersinger v. Hamlin*, the Court extended the obligation to provide counsel to all criminal cases where the penalty includes imprisonment—regardless of whether the offense is a felony or a misdemeanor.[29] These two major decisions are related to the Sixth Amendment right to counsel as it applies to the presentation of a defense at the trial stages of the criminal justice system.

In numerous Supreme Court decisions since *Gideon v. Wainwright* (see Exhibit 7.2), the states have been required to provide counsel for indigent defendants at virtually all other stages of the criminal justice process, beginning with arrest and concluding with the defendant's release from the system. Today, the Sixth Amendment right to counsel and the Fifth and Fourteenth Amendments' guarantee of due process of law have been judicially interpreted together to provide the defendant with counsel by the state in all types of criminal proceedings.

Areas remain in the criminal justice system where the courts have not required that the assistance of counsel be provided for the accused. These include pre-indictment lineups; booking procedures, including the taking of fingerprints and other forms of identification; grand jury investigations; appeals beyond the first review; disciplinary proceedings in correctional institutions; and revocation hearings after release. Nevertheless, the general rule of thumb is that no person can be deprived of freedom or lose a "liberty interest" without representation by counsel.

Sixth Amendment The US constitutional amendment containing various criminal trial rights, such as the right to public trial, the right to trial by jury, and the right to confrontation of witnesses.

Gideon v. Wainwright The 1963 US Supreme Court case that granted counsel to indigent defendants in felony prosecutions.

Defense attorney Teresa Mann presents an argument to Fulton County Superior Court Judge Jerry Baxter during the Atlanta Public Schools test-cheating trial in Fulton County Superior Court. Several educators were convicted on April 1, 2015, of racketeering and other lesser offenses for inflating test scores of children in struggling schools. Nine of them were sentenced to prison.

AP Images/Kent D. Johnson

EXHIBIT 7.2 Important *Gideon*-Related Decisions over the Years

Douglas v. California (1963) The Fourteenth Amendment guarantees the defendant the right to counsel during his or her first mandatory appeal.[30]

In re Gault (1967) Juveniles enjoy the right to counsel in adjudicatory hearings.[31]

Coleman v. Alabama (1970) The preliminary hearing is a "critical stage," meaning that the defendant enjoys the right to counsel at it.[32]

Argersinger v. Hamlin (1972) The Sixth Amendment right to counsel extends to those accused of committing misdemeanors.[33]

Morrissey v. Brewer (1972) There is no right to counsel in parole revocation hearings.[34]

Gagnon v. Scarpelli (1973) There is no right to counsel in probation revocation hearings.[35]

Ross v. Moffitt (1974) There is no right to counsel provided for the second, discretionary appeal.[36]

Scott v. Illinois (1979) If there is no possibility of confinement, the Sixth Amendment right to counsel does not apply.[37]

Morris v. Slappy (1983) The Sixth Amendment does not require a "meaningful" relationship between the defendant and his or her attorney.[38]

Wheat v. United States (1988) A trial court can deny the defendant's choice of counsel if the attorney's representation carries with it the strong possibility of a conflict of interest.[39]

United States v. Monsanto (1989) It is not unconstitutional for a court to seize a defendant's assets such that it forces him or her to rely on a public defender.[40]

United States v. Gonzalez-Lopez (2006) A convicted defendant has the automatic right to a new trial when a trial judge mistakenly refuses to allow the defendant's paid attorney to represent him.[41]

Rothgery v. Gillespie County (2008) The right to counsel attaches at the initial appearance, shortly after arrest.[42]

LO7 Discuss the different forms of indigent defense

assigned counsel A lawyer appointed by the court to represent a defendant in a criminal case because the person is too poor to hire counsel.

contract system (attorney) Providing counsel to indigent offenders by having attorneys under contract to the county handle all (or some) such cases.

Legal Services for the Indigent

To satisfy the constitutional requirements that indigent defendants be provided with the assistance of counsel at various stages of the criminal process, the federal government and the states have had to evaluate and expand criminal defense services. Today, about 3,000 state and local agencies are providing indigent legal services in the United States.

Providing legal services for the indigent offender is a huge and costly undertaking. Although most states have a formal set of rules to signify who is an indigent, and many require indigents to repay the state for at least part of their legal services (known as "recoupment"), indigent legal services still cost over $1.5 billion annually.

Programs providing counsel assistance to indigent defendants can be divided into three major categories: public defender systems, assigned counsel systems, and contract systems (attorney) (see Exhibit 7.3). Other approaches to the delivery of legal services include the use of mixed systems, such as representation by both the public defender and the private bar, law school clinical programs, and prepaid legal services.

EXHIBIT 7.3 The Forms of Indigent Defense

Public Defender A salaried staff of full-time or part-time attorneys render indigent criminal defense services through a public or private nonprofit organization, or as direct government-paid employees. The first public defender program in the United States opened in 1913 in Los Angeles. Public defenders can be part of a statewide agency, county government, the judiciary, or an independent nonprofit organization or other institution.

Assigned Counsel The appointment is from a list of private bar members who accept cases on a judge-by-judge, court-by-court, or case-by-case basis. This may include an administrative component and a set of rules and guidelines governing the appointment and processing of cases handled by the private bar members. There are two main types of assigned counsel systems. In the first, which makes up about 75 percent of all assigned counsel systems, the presiding judge appoints attorneys on a case-by-case basis; this is referred to as an ad hoc assigned counsel system. The second type is referred to as a coordinated assigned counsel system, in which an administrator oversees the appointment of counsel and sets up guidelines for the administration of indigent legal services. The fees awarded to assigned counsels can vary widely, depending on the nature of the case. Restructuring the attorney fee system is undoubtedly needed to maintain fair standards for the payment of such legal services.

Contract Systems Nonsalaried private attorneys, bar associations, law firms, consortiums or groups of attorneys, or nonprofit corporations contract with a funding source to provide court-appointed representation in a jurisdiction. In some instances, an attorney is given a set amount of money and is required to handle all cases assigned. In other jurisdictions, contract lawyers agree to provide legal representation for a set number of cases at a fixed fee. A third system involves representation at an estimated cost per case until the dollar amount of the contract is reached. At that point, the contract may be renegotiated, but the lawyers are not obligated to take new cases.

Source: Carol J. DeFrances, *State-Funded Indigent Defense Services, 1999* (Washington, DC: Bureau of Justice Statistics, 2001).

Although many jurisdictions have a combination of these programs, statewide public defender programs vary widely and are complicated.[43]

In general, the attorney list/assigned counsel system is used in less populated areas, where case flow is minimal, and a full-time public defender is not needed. Public defenders are usually found in larger urban areas with high case flow rates. So although a proportionately larger area of the country is served by the assigned counsel system, a significant proportion of criminal defendants are represented by public defenders.

The Private Bar

Although most criminal defendants are represented by publicly supported lawyers, there are also private attorneys who specialize in criminal practice. Because most lawyers are not prepared in law school for criminal work, their skill often results from their experience in the trial courts. Some nationally known criminal defense attorneys represent defendants for large fees in celebrated and widely publicized cases, but this occurs rather infrequently. Some also represent high-profile offenders accused of committing heinous crimes (see the accompanying Contemporary Issues in Criminal Justice box for more on this).

Besides this limited group of well-known criminal lawyers, some lawyers and law firms serve as house counsel for such professional criminals as narcotics dealers, gamblers, prostitutes, and even big-time burglars. These lawyers, however, constitute a very small percentage of the private bar practicing criminal law.

LO8 Summarize the pros and cons of private attorneys

CONTEMPORARY ISSUES IN CRIMINAL JUSTICE

Defending the Despised

Miriam Conrad, head of Boston's Federal Public Defender Office, was the lead defense attorney for Dzhokhar Tsarnaev, the man convicted and sentenced to die in connection with the Boston Marathon bombing on April 15, 2013. She has been called a terrorist sympathizer, an enemy combatant, and America's "most reviled lawyer." Why? In addition to defending Tsarnaev, she has represented a number of other infamous criminals, including shoe bomber Richard Reid, who is locked up in a "supermax" prison in Florence, Colorado, and Rezwan Ferdaus, who is serving 17 years in prison for plotting to bomb the Pentagon and US Capitol with remote control aircraft. Conrad, a former newspaper reporter turned attorney, takes a measure of delight in defending high-profile suspects. "There are very few clients I've had who I didn't like," she said. "If you scratch the surface, many have had difficult lives, and as their lawyer, I sort of see them whole, not just as a person charged with a crime."

Judy Clarke, another lawyer who served on the Tsarnaev defense team, has also defended her share of America's most despised criminals, including the Unabomber, Ted Kaczynski, Eric Rudolph, the man who detonated a bomb at the 1996 Olympics in Atlanta, and Jared Loughner, who shot former Representative Gabrielle Giffords and 18 others outside a supermarket in Arizona in 2011. All three men received life in prison rather than the death penalty. Clarke, who strongly believes people are not born evil, is known for spending hundreds of hours getting to know her clients—all to put on the best defense possible. She has even been called "St. Judy" because of her devotion to her clients. Clarke is also vehemently opposed to the death penalty, believing society should not legalize killing. This motivates her work and helps explain how she has succeeded on several occasions in sparing her clients the death penalty. Many defense attorneys clamor for the spotlight but not Clarke.

David Hoose, another prominent defense attorney, drew attention for his role in representing Kristen Gilbert, a veteran hospital nurse who killed four patients by overdosing them with drugs. She, like several of Clarke's clients, was also sentenced to a long prison term rather than executed. Attorneys Craig Weintraub and Jay Schlachet represented Ariel Castro, who was sentenced to life in prison plus 1,000 years for kidnapping, rape, and murder. He, too, was able to avoid the death penalty, but he later committed suicide in prison. Like many of their colleagues, Weintraub and Schlachet are opposed to the death penalty: "We saved him from potentially lethal injection and 20 years on death row, which would have cost the taxpayers and the community millions and millions of dollars, and we spared the women the anguish and 'revictimization' of events."

Most of the criminals these attorneys represent cannot afford counsel, much less attorneys with such successful records. Sometimes, anti–death penalty groups help foot the bill. Other times the defense attorneys serve as court-appointed counsel and work for a rate similar to that of others tasked with representing lower-profile defendants. Rarely are they in it for fame and fortune.

CRITICAL THINKING

1. Should those accused of the most heinous crimes be represented by the likes of Judy Clarke and Miriam Conrad? Does it matter whether the death penalty is in play in a particular case?
2. What about those accused of less serious offenses who cannot afford representation? Do they get the same zealous defense?
3. What, if any, inequities are perpetuated by the current system we have in place?

Sources: Henry Gass, "An 'All-Star Team' to Defend Accused Boston Bomber Tsarnaev," *Christian Science Monitor*, January 2, 2015, http://www.csmonitor.com/USA/Justice/2015/0102/An-all-star-team-to-defend-accused-Boston-bomber-Tsarnaev; P. R. Keefe, "The Worst of the Worst," *The New Yorker*, September 14, 2015, http://www.newyorker.com/magazine/2015/09/14/the-worst-of-the-worst; C. Wolff, "CJN Interview with Ariel Castro's Lawyers Craig Weintraub and Jaye Schlachet," *Cleveland Jewish News*, August 17, 2013, https://tinyurl.com/hwt3jpq. (URLs accessed April 2017).

A large number of criminal defendants are represented by lawyers who often accept many cases for small fees. These lawyers may belong to small law firms or work alone, but a sizable portion of their practice involves representing those accused of crime. Other private practitioners occasionally take on criminal matters as part of their general practice. A lawyer whose practice involves a substantial proportion of criminal cases is often considered a specialist in the field. And there is little question that having a preeminent private attorney can help clients achieve a favorable outcome (a "not guilty" verdict).

Does the Type of Lawyer Matter?

Do criminal defendants who hire their own private lawyers do better in court than those who depend on legal representatives provided by the state? Is one type of defense attorney for the indigent better than another?

Although there are some advantages to private counsel, national surveys indicate that state-appointed attorneys do quite well in court. According to data compiled by the federal government:

- Conviction rates for indigent defendants and for those with their own lawyers were about the same in federal and state courts. About 90 percent of the federal defendants and 75 percent of the defendants in the most populous counties were found guilty regardless of which type of attorneys represented them.
- Of those found guilty, however, those represented by publicly financed attorneys were incarcerated at a higher rate than those defendants who paid for their own legal representation.
- On average, sentence lengths for defendants sent to jail or prison were shorter for those with publicly financed attorneys than for those who hired counsel. In federal district court, those with publicly financed attorneys were given just under five years on average, and those with private attorneys just over five years. In large state courts, those with publicly financed attorneys were sentenced to an average of two and a half years, and those with private attorneys to three years.[44]

The Competence of Defense Attorneys

Inadequacy of counsel may occur in a variety of instances. The attorney may refuse to meet regularly with the client, fail to cross-examine key government witnesses, or fail to investigate the case properly. A defendant's plea of guilty may be based on poor advice,

Attorney Stephen Diaco listens to testimony during the penalty phase in the case against three Adams and Diaco lawyers accused of orchestrating a DUI setup. They had a paralegal lure the plaintiff in a lawsuit against one of their clients into driving drunk and then getting caught. Diaco and the two other attorneys were barred from ever practicing law again in Florida.

AP Images/Douglas R. Clifford

where the attorney may misjudge the admissibility of evidence. When co-defendants have separate counsel, conflicts of interest between the defense attorneys may arise. On an appellate level, the lawyer may decline to file a brief, instead relying on a brief submitted for one of the co-appellants.

The US Supreme Court defined the concept of attorney competence in the 1984 case of *Strickland v. Washington*.[45] The case established the two-pronged test for determining effectiveness of counsel:

1. The defendant must show that the counsel's performance was deficient and that such serious errors were made as to essentially eliminate the presence of counsel guaranteed by the Sixth Amendment.
2. The defendant must also show that the deficient performance prejudiced the case to such an extent that the defendant was deprived of a fair trial.

Determining whether defense counsel is ineffective is a subjective decision. The Supreme Court has ruled that an attorney can be effective even when he admits a client's guilt before the trial is over, as long as doing so is part of a reasonable defense strategy, such as gaining sympathy from the jury.[46] For a defense attorney to be considered incompetent, he or she would have to miss filings, fail to follow normal trial procedure, and/or fail to use defense tactics that the average attorney would be sure to follow, such as using expert witnesses or mentioning past behaviors that might mitigate guilt.

Court Administration

In addition to qualified personnel, there is a need for efficient management of the judiciary system. The need for efficient management techniques in an ever-expanding criminal court system has led to the recognition that improving court administration is one way to relieve court congestion. Management goals include improving the organization and scheduling of cases, devising methods to allocate court resources efficiently, administering fines and monies due to the court, preparing budgets, and overseeing personnel.

The federal courts have led the way in creating and organizing court administration. In 1939, Congress passed the Administrative Office Act, which established the Administrative Office of the United States Courts. Its director was charged with gathering statistics on the work of the federal courts and preparing the judicial budget for approval by the Conference of Senior Circuit Judges. One clause of the act created a judicial council with general supervisory responsibilities for the district and circuit courts.

Unlike the federal government, the states have experienced slow and uneven growth in the development and application of court management principles. The first state to establish an administrative office was North Dakota in 1927. Today, all states employ some form of central administration.

Using Technology in Court Management

In most jurisdictions today, centralized court administrative services perform numerous functions with the help of computers that free the judiciary to fulfill their roles as arbiters of justice. Rapid retrieval and organization of data are used for such functions as these:

- Maintaining case histories and statistical reporting
- Monitoring and scheduling cases
- Preparing documents
- Indexing cases
- Issuing summonses
- Notifying witnesses, attorneys, and others of required appearances
- Selecting and notifying jurors
- Preparing and administering budgets and payrolls

REALITYCHECK
Myth or Reality?
Privately retained defense attorneys are more effective than court-appointed defense attorneys.

MYTH. Research reveals that public defenders and court-appointed attorneys perform similarly on average.

No clear evidence exists that having an expensive, privately retained attorney markedly increases one's chance of acquittal. What does this say about privately retained defense attorneys? What about court-appointed attorneys?

LO9 Evaluate the expanding role of technology in the court process

Computer technology is also being applied in the courts in such areas as videotaped testimonies, new court reporting devices, information systems, and data processing systems to handle such functions as court docketing and jury management. In 1968, only 10 states had state-level automated information systems; today, all states employ such systems for a variety of tasks and duties. Other developing areas of court technology include the following.[47]

COMMUNICATIONS Court jurisdictions are cooperating with police departments in the installation of communications gear that makes it possible to arraign defendants over closed-circuit television while they are in police custody. Closed-circuit television has been used for judicial conferences and scheduling meetings. Some courts are using voice-activated cameras to record all testimony during trials; these are the sole means of keeping trial records.

VIDEOCONFERENCING About 400 courts across the country have videoconferencing capabilities. It is now being employed for juvenile detention hearings, expert witness testimony at trial, oral arguments on appeal, and parole hearings. More than 150 courts use two-way live, televised remote linkups for first appearance and arraignment. Defendants typically appear from a special location in the jail where they can see and hear, and be seen and heard by, the presiding magistrate.

EVIDENCE PRESENTATION High-tech courtrooms are now equipped for real-time transcription and translation, audio-video preservation of the court record, remote witness participation, computer graphics displays, monitor screens for jurors, and computers for counsel and judge.

CASE MANAGEMENT In the 1970s, municipal courts installed tracking systems, which used databases to manage court data. These older systems were limited and could not process the complex interrelationships that pervade information about persons, cases, time, and financial matters in court cases. Contemporary relational databases now provide the flexibility to handle complex case management.

INTERNET UTILIZATION The Internet has found its way into the court system. In the federal system, J-Net is the judiciary's intranet website. J-Net makes it easier for judges and court personnel to find important information in a timely fashion.

AP Images/Gary C. Knapp

Technology will become ever more present in the courtrooms of the future. The courtroom featured here contains monitor screens throughout, including one in front of each juror. Courts like this one rely on computer technology and the Internet to bring together witnesses, lawyers, judges, and the jury.

INFORMATION SHARING Technology has been harnessed to make it easier for courts to share information within and between states. This helps cut down on costs and accelerates the criminal justice process.

The computer cannot replace the judge, but it can be used to help speed up the trial process by identifying backlogs and bottlenecks that can be eradicated with intelligent managerial techniques. Just as a manager must know the type and quantity of goods on hand in a warehouse, so an administrative judge must have available information about those entering the judge's domain, what happens to them after they are in it, and how they fare after judgment has been rendered.

ETHICAL REFLECTION

As we discussed earlier in this chapter, prosecutors sometimes go "too far" in their efforts to secure convictions against criminals. For example, a prosecutor may engage in selective or unfair prosecution, such as by targeting one person for personal reasons rather than making a decision based on the evidence. Prosecutors have also been known to engage in what is known as pretextual prosecution. This occurs when a prosecutor who lacks evidence to charge a particular person with one crime instead charges the individual with a lesser, unrelated offense. The key here is "unrelated." If, for example, a prosecutor lacks evidence to charge someone with first-degree murder and instead pursues second-degree murder charges, such a decision is perfectly acceptable. In contrast, if a prosecutor lacks evidence to charge a person with racketeering and instead charges the individual with a violation of the Federal Meat Inspection Act, this is a pretextual prosecution.[48]

In extreme cases, prosecutors have been known to fabricate evidence, use false statements at trial, withhold potentially favorable evidence from the defense (a violation of due process), influence witnesses, renege on plea agreements, and so on. What can be done? On the one hand, prosecutors cannot be sued for their decisions on whether to press charges or for how they act. Even in the most egregious of cases of flagrant misconduct, a prosecutor cannot be held liable for his or her actions during the judicial stage of a case.[49] This is known as absolute immunity. On the other hand, although prosecutors cannot be sued for misconduct, they can be punished by their superiors and state bar association disciplinary boards for misconduct that is too severe.

Writing Challenge Visit the Marshall Project's Prosecutorial Misconduct page here: https://www.themarshallproject.org/records/1-prosecutorial-misconduct. Read one of the "Marshall Project Originals" stories linked on that page and write a report about the case. Answer the following questions: What did the prosecutor do wrong, if anything? What else went wrong in the case? Who was most responsible for the miscarriage of justice detailed in the story? What criminal justice reforms could or should be undertaken to eliminate these sorts of issues?

SUMMARY

LO1 *Describe the varying structures of state court systems* State courts handle a wide variety of cases and regulate numerous personal behaviors ranging from homicide to property maintenance. Courts of limited jurisdiction are restricted in the types of cases they may hear. Courts of general jurisdiction handle the more serious felony cases (such as murder, rape, and robbery) and civil cases in which damages are over a specified amount, such as $10,000. Appellate courts do not try cases; they review the procedures of the case to determine whether an error was made by judicial authorities.

LO2 *Describe the federal court system* The federal government has established a three-tiered hierarchy of court jurisdiction that, in order of ascendancy, consists of the US district courts, the US courts of appeals (circuit courts), and the US Supreme Court.

LO3 *Summarize the selection procedure for and duties of the trial judge* The judge is the senior officer in a court of

criminal law. His or her primary duty is to oversee the trial process. The qualifications for appointment to one of the existing 30,000 judgeships vary between the federal and state level—and from state to state. Most typically, the potential judge must be a resident of the state, must be licensed to practice law, must be a member of the state bar association, and must be at least 25 years of age and less than 70 years of age. Selection methods vary, too, and include election, appointment, and combinations of each.

LO4 *Explain the role of the prosecutor* In the federal system, prosecutors are known as US attorneys and are appointed by the president. On the state and county levels, the attorney general and the district attorney, respectively, are the chief prosecutorial officers. Whatever the title, the prosecutor is the people's attorney, who is responsible for representing the public in criminal matters. Even if the prosecutor decides to pursue a case, the charges may later be dropped if conditions are not favorable for a conviction, in a process called nolle prosequi.

LO5 *Describe prosecutorial discretion, and summarize its pros and cons* Regardless of its source, the proper exercise of prosecutorial discretion can improve the criminal justice process by preventing the rigid implementation of criminal law. Although the prosecutor's primary duty is to enforce criminal law, his or her fundamental obligation as an attorney is to seek justice, as well as to convict those who are guilty.

LO6 *Identify the role of the defense attorney in the justice process* The defense attorney is the counterpart of the prosecuting attorney in the criminal justice process. In the 1963 landmark case of *Gideon v. Wainwright*, the Supreme Court took the first major step on the issue of right to counsel by holding that state courts must provide indigent defendants in felony prosecutions with private counsel or a public defender.

LO7 *Discuss the different forms of indigent defense* To satisfy the constitutional requirements that indigent defendants be provided with the assistance of counsel at various stages of the criminal process, the federal government and the states have had to provide indigent defense services. Most criminal defendants are represented by publicly supported lawyers (e.g., public defenders), but many private attorneys also specialize in criminal practice.

LO8 *Summarize the pros and cons of private attorneys* Even though there are some advantages to private counsel, national surveys indicate that state-appointed attorneys do quite well in court. The *Strickland v. Washington* case established the two-pronged test for determining effectiveness of counsel.

LO9 *Evaluate the expanding role of technology in the court process* Technology is important to the administration and management of courts. High-tech courtrooms are equipped for real-time transcription and translation, audio-video preservation of the court record, remote witness participation, computer graphics displays, monitor screens for jurors, and computers for counsel and judge. Contemporary relational databases provide the flexibility to handle complex case management.

KEY TERMS

state courts of limited jurisdiction, p. 160

courts of general jurisdiction, p. 163

appellate court, p. 163

court of last resort, p. 164

writ of certiorari, p. 166

landmark decision, p. 166

jury trial, p. 168

US magistrate judge, p. 170

Missouri Plan, p. 171

prosecutor, p. 172

public defender, p. 176

adversarial procedure, p. 176

Sixth Amendment, p. 177

Gideon v. Wainwright, p. 177

assigned counsel, p. 178

contract system (attorney), p. 178

REVIEW QUESTIONS

1. Specialized courts (such as drug courts) are popping up all over the country. What is your assessment of this trend? Why do you feel this way?

2. Should defense attorneys cooperate with a prosecutor if it means their clients will go to jail?

3. Should a prosecutor have absolute discretion over which cases to proceed on and which to drop?

4. Should clients be made aware of an attorney's track record in court?

5. Does the assigned counsel system present an inherent conflict of interest, inasmuch as attorneys are hired and paid by the institution they are to oppose?

6. Should victims play a role in the application of prosecutorial discretion? Before you answer, consider how that system might harm some defendants and benefit others.

8 Pretrial and Trial Procedures

About 17 officers are charged with murder or manslaughter each year.[1] That number may be increasing in light of recent high-profile police shootings of unarmed minority suspects, such as the 2014 death of Laquan McDonald in Chicago, whose case resulted in first-degree murder charges against officer Jason Van Dyke (see photo).[2] Nevertheless, it is still highly unusual to see police officers charged with serious crimes. Why? According to criminologist Philip Stinson, "To charge an officer in a fatal shooting, it takes something so egregious, so over that top that it cannot be explained in any rational way. It also has to be a case that prosecutors are willing to hang their reputations on."[3] Prosecutors make the same point; most will only bring charges if the evidence can clearly disprove an officer's story that he was defending himself. So, for example, if a video clearly depicts an officer shooting a person in the back, murder or manslaughter charges are likely.

If police officers are rarely charged in cases involving questionable killings, how many are *convicted*? Fewer still. Indeed, any prosecutor tasked with putting a police officer on trial for murder faces an uphill climb. Why? Are juries reluctant to treat police officers in the same was as ordinary criminals? Johnny Baer, a prosecutor in Pennsylvania, seems to think so: "People want and are willing to give police officers the benefit of the doubt, when they're in uniform, and they're making split-second decisions, in very difficult environments."[4] As another prosecutor put it, "To get [jurors] to buy into a story where the officers is the bad guy goes fundamentally against everything they believe."[5] Thus, despite public outcries over questionable shootings, people may harbor deep-seated hesitancies to convict officers of serious crimes.

Legal standards also make it difficult to convict police officers in people's deaths. Officers are authorized—and indeed expected—to use force in certain situations. This is not the case with ordinary citizens. Also, the question of whether too much force was used in a particular case is often complicated, and there are no objective standards that work perfectly across all scenarios. Juries need to weigh each individual case differently—and they often have to think

AP Images/Charles Rex Arbogast

Jason Van Dyke, the Chicago police officer charged with murdering Laquan McDonald, leaves Cook County Criminal Court.

LEARNING OBJECTIVES

LO1 Summarize the bail process

LO2 Discuss the main issues associated with bail

LO3 Differentiate between the two main mechanisms for charging defendants (grand jury indictment and prosecutor's information)

LO4 Summarize the pleas available to a criminal defendant

LO5 Explain the issues involved in plea bargaining

LO6 Describe the plea-bargaining process

LO7 Explain the purpose of pretrial diversion

LO8 Explain the legal rights of the accused at trial

LO9 Summarize the trial process

Which Bail Release Mechanism Is Most Effective?

Relatively few researchers have tried to determine which bail release mechanism is most effective. This oversight is important. If, for example, surety bail is the most effective, then this suggests the bail industry is more effective than the government in ensuring defendants appear in court. On the flipside, if the government is more effective in managing pretrial release, then perhaps we don't need commercial bail. Or what if some other approach is more effective? Are defendants who post the full amount of bail more likely to show up for their court dates?

Effects on Crime/Recidivism

In one of the early studies, researchers at the Bureau of Justice Statistics (BJS) attempted to answer these questions. They investigated several of the types of bail we discuss in this chapter: recognance, surety bond, deposit bond, full cash bond, conditional release, and unsecured bonds. They also added two other types: property bond and emergency release. With a property bond, the defendant posts property valued in the amount of his/her bail with the court. Failure to appear results in forfeiture of the property. Emergency release refers, simply, releasing the defendant prior to trial because of exceptional circumstances. An example is jail overcrowding.

Surety bond is most common. Does that mean it is most effective, though? According to BJS researchers, the probability of being charged with pretrial misconduct was highest for unsecured bond and for emergency release. It was lowest for property bonds. Deposit bonds came next, followed by surety bonds. In looking specifically at failures to appear, the researchers found that emergency release was the least favorable approach. If emergency release was excluded, the percentage of those who failed to appear varied between 17 and 28 percent for each release mechanism, so the moral of the story was there was no clear and obvious winner.

A more recent study of pretrial release in Dallas reached some different conclusions. In that study, researchers at the University of Texas at Dallas compared the efficacy of four different pretrial release mechanisms. The terms they used were:

- *Attorney bond.* Texas law permits attorneys in some locations throughout the state to post bonds for individuals seeking pretrial release.

- *Cash bond.* Defendant posts full amount of bail with the court. If he or she fails to appear, the full amount is forfeited.

- *Commercial bond.* This is surety bail. A bonding agent posts bail in exchange for a fee, usually 10 percent.

- *Pretrial bond.* Reserved for low-risk defendants, this approach has the defendant pay a modest fee to the county in exchange for release. He or she is then held accountable to the county's Pretrial Services

Division but is not formally supervised. It is close to release on recognizance but not identical.

The researchers found that defendants released via commercial bond were the least likely to abscond. This finding held up even as the researchers controlled for other factors likely to influence whether a defendant would appear (such as criminal history, age, indigent status). The least effective approach, according to the study, was pretrial bond. The findings were not without controversy. With pretrial services coming in last, Dallas County was not painted in the most favorable light. Officials explained the finding as a result of understaffing. On the other hand, the bail industry applauded the results. Drew Campbell, spokesman for Dallas County's bail bond companies, said his constituents felt "vindicated by the study's results but also want to continue to work with the county to improve the system."

Thinking Critically About Research

Which release mechanism is most effective, then? The answer is not completely clear. It depends on where and when the study is conducted. It depends on who is compared to whom. It depends on which release mechanisms are in place in one location relative to the other. The bail system in the United States contains a patchwork of release mechanisms, so it will not be completely clear anytime soon which approach is most effective.

No study could ever offer the "last word" on what pretrial release mechanism is preferred; however, if one's concern is with a specific jurisdiction, then a study that carefully matches defendants with one another (on such factors as prior record, demographic makeup, etc.), assigns them to various forms of pretrial release, and then follows enough of them over time could reveal important insights.

QUESTIONS

1. Should private for-profit companies be involved in the bail process?
2. For what types of offenders and offenses should bail be denied?
3. What constitutes excessive bail?

Sources: T. H. Cohen and B. A. Reaves, *Pretrial Release of Felony Defendants in State Courts* (Washington, DC: Bureau of Justice Statistics, 2007), p. 10; R. G. Morris, *Research Report: Pretrial Release Mechanisms in Dallas County, Texas* (Richardson, TX: University of Texas at Dallas), https://www.utdallas.edu/epps/ccjs/dl/Dallas%20 Pretrial%20Release%20Report%20-FINAL%20Jan%202013c.pdf; K. Krause, "New Study Shows a Quarter of Dallas County Criminal Defendants Fail to Show up for Court," *Dallas Morning News*, January 13, 2013, http://www.dallasnews.com/news/community -news/dallas/headlines/20130113-new-study-shows-a-quarter-of-dallas-county -criminal-defendants-fail-to-show-up-for-court.ece (URLs accessed April 2017).

release on recognizance (ROR)
A nonmonetary condition for the pretrial release of an accused individual; an alternative to monetary bail that is granted after the court determines that the accused has ties in the community, has no prior record of default, and is likely to appear at subsequent proceedings.

- *Surety bail.* The defendant pays a percentage of the bond, usually 10 percent, to a bonding agent who posts the full bail. The fee paid to the bonding agent is not returned to the defendant if he or she appears in court. The bonding agent is liable for the full amount of the bond should the defendant fail to appear. Bonding agents often require posting collateral to cover the full bail amount. This is the most common form of bail.
- *Conditional bail.* The defendant is released after promising to obey some specified conditions in lieu of cash, such as attending a treatment program before trial.
- *Unsecured bond.* The defendant is released with no immediate requirement of payment. However, if the defendant fails to appear, he or she is liable for the full amount.
- *Release on recognizance.* According to the **release on recognizance (ROR)** concept, eligible defendants are released without bail upon their promise to return for trial.

Bail Issues

Whether a defendant can be expected to appear for his or her trial is a key issue in determining bail. Bail cannot be used to punish an accused, nor can it be denied or revoked at the whim of the court. Nonetheless, for the following reasons, critics argue that monetary bail is one of the most objectionable aspects of the criminal justice system:

- It is discriminatory because it works against the poor.
- It is costly because the government must pay to detain those offenders who cannot make bail but who would otherwise remain in the community.
- It is unfair because a higher proportion of detainees receive longer sentences than people released on bail.
- It is dehumanizing because innocent people who cannot make bail suffer in the nation's deteriorated jail system.

There is also the problem of racial and ethnic disparity in the bail process. Some research efforts show that the decision whether to grant bail may be racially or ethnically biased; black and Latino defendants receive less favorable treatment than whites charged with similar offenses.[9] Although these results are troubling, it is often difficult to gauge racial/ethnic disparity in the bail process because differences in income, community ties, family support, and criminal record, rather than judicial bias, may account for any observed differences in the bail process. Despite these drawbacks, the bail system remains in place to ensure that defendants return for trial and that the truly dangerous can be kept in secure confinement pending their court proceedings.

BONDSMEN AND BOUNTY HUNTERS When bailees abscond before trial, bondsmen routinely hire skip tracers, enforcement agents, or bounty hunters to track them down. Each year a large network of full-time bail enforcement agents catch thousands of fugitives in the United States. Although organizations such as the National Institute of Bail Enforcement attempt to provide training, some untrained and/or unprofessional bounty hunters may use brutal tactics that can end in tragedy. Consequently, efforts have been made to reform and even eliminate money bail and reduce the importance of bonding agents.

PRETRIAL DETENTION CONDITIONS The criminal defendant who is not eligible for bail or ROR is subject to pretrial detention in the local county jail. The jail has long been a trouble spot for the criminal justice system. Conditions tend to be poor, and rehabilitation is a low priority. Hundreds of jails are overcrowded, and many are under court orders to reduce their populations and improve conditions.

LO2 Discuss the main issues associated with bail

WEB APP 8.1 Visit the website of the Fugitive Recovery Network, an organization devoted to supporting the bail bond industry, at **http://fugitiverecovery.com/**. From there click on "Bail Bond Laws," click on the map of the United States, then read the laws in the state where you reside (not all states may be available). What are the limits on fugitive recovery, according to state law?

AP Images/Drew Godleski

Aaron Kennedy, left, and Jim Elliott, bail enforcement agents from Salt lake City, look over paperwork while trying to track down a man who jumped bail and had a warrant out for his arrest. Kennedy and Elliott were contracted by a bail bond company.

What happens to people who do not get bail or who cannot afford to put up bail money? Traditionally, these individuals are more likely to be convicted and then to get longer prison sentences than those who commit similar crimes but who were released on bail. A federally sponsored study of case processing in the nation's largest counties found that about 63 percent of all defendants granted bail were convicted; in contrast, 78 percent of detainees were convicted.[10] Detainees are also more likely than releasees to be convicted of a felony offense and, therefore, are eligible for a long prison sentence instead of the much shorter term of incarceration given misdemeanants.

BAIL REFORM Critics believe that the bail system is discriminatory because defendants who are financially well off can make bail, whereas indigent defendants languish in pretrial detention in the county jail—and then get convicted at higher rates. This has led to a number of bail-related reforms. The first such reform program was pioneered by the Vera Institute of Justice in an experiment called the Manhattan Bail Project, which began in 1961 with the cooperation of the New York City criminal courts and local law students.[11] The project found that if the court had sufficient background information about the defendant, it could make a reasonably good judgment about whether the accused would return to court. When release decisions were based on such information as the nature of the offense, family ties, and employment record, most defendants who were released on their own recognizance returned to court. The results of the Vera Institute's initial operation showed a default rate of less than 0.7 percent.

The success of ROR programs in the early 1960s resulted in bail reforms that culminated with the enactment of the federal Bail Reform Act of 1966, the first change in federal bail laws since 1789.[12] This legislation sought to ensure that release would be granted in all noncapital cases in which there was sufficient reason to believe that the defendant would return to court. The law clearly established the presumption of ROR that must be overcome before money bail is required, authorized 10 percent deposit bail, introduced the concept of conditional release, and stressed the philosophy that release should be under the least restrictive conditions necessary to ensure court appearance.

During the 1970s and early 1980s, the pretrial release movement was hampered by public pressure over pretrial increases in crime. As a result, the more recent federal legislation, the Bail Reform Act of 1984, mandated that no defendants will be kept in pretrial detention simply because they cannot afford money bail, established the presumption for ROR in all cases in which a person is bailable, and formalized restrictive preventive detention provisions (explained later in this chapter). The 1984 act required that community safety, as well as the risk of flight, be considered in the release decision. Consequently, such criminal justice factors as the seriousness of the charged offense, the weight of the evidence, the sentence that may be imposed upon conviction, court appearance history, and prior convictions are likely to influence the release decisions of the federal court.

PREVENTIVE DETENTION Bail reform acts have made it easier for some people to secure pretrial release, but they have also helped keep defendants who are considered dangerous behind bars before trial without the possibility of bail—a practice known as preventive detention. These laws require that certain dangerous defendants be confined before trial for their own protection and that of the community. Preventive detention is an important manifestation of the crime control perspective on justice because it favors the use of incapacitation to control the future behavior of suspected criminals. Critics, however, are concerned that preventive detention amounts to punishment before trial.

The most striking use of preventive detention can be found in the federal Bail Reform Act of 1984.[13] Although the act does contain provisions for ROR, it also allows judges to order preventive detention if they determine "that no condition or combination of conditions will reasonably assure the appearance of the person as required and the safety of any other person and the community."[14]

REALITYCHECK

Myth or Reality?

A significant percentage of those released on bail never show up for their scheduled court dates.

MYTH. Research suggests otherwise. The Manhattan Bail Project found that less than 1 percent of those released default.

Official statistics tell a similar story; relatively few people released before their trial dates reoffend, get arrested, or fail to show up when they are required to do so. Could the same be expected with ROR programs?

A number of state jurisdictions have incorporated elements of preventive detention into their bail systems. Although most of the restrictions do not constitute outright preventive detention, they serve to narrow the scope of bail eligibility. These provisions include three main features: (1) exclusion of certain crimes from bail eligibility, (2) definition of bail to include appearance in court and community safety, and (3) the limitations on right to bail for those previously convicted.

PRETRIAL SERVICES In our overburdened court system, determining which defendants can safely be released on bail pending trial is critical.[15] In many jurisdictions, specialized pretrial services help courts deal with this problem. Hundreds of pretrial bail programs have been established in rural, suburban, and urban jurisdictions; they are typically operated in probation departments, court offices, and local jails, and through independent county contractors. These programs provide a number of critical services:

- Gathering and verifying information about arrestees—including criminal history, current status in the criminal justice system, address, employment, and drug and alcohol use history—which judicial officers can then take into account in making release/detention decisions.
- Assessing each arrestee's likelihood of failure to appear and chances of being rearrested.
- Monitoring released defendants' compliance with conditions of release designed to minimize pretrial crime, including curfews, orders restricting contact with alleged victims and possible witnesses, home confinement, and drug and alcohol testing.
- Providing direct "intensive" supervision for some categories of defendants by using program staff and collaborating with the police, other agencies, and community organizations.

Some pretrial services programs are now being aimed at special needs. One type focuses on defendants suffering from mental illness; almost three-quarters of pretrial services programs now inquire about mental health status and treatment as a regular part of their interview, and about one-quarter report having implemented special supervision procedures for defendants with mental illness. Another area of concern is domestic violence. About one-quarter of all pretrial programs have developed special risk-assessment procedures for defendants charged with domestic violence offenses, and about one-third have implemented special procedures to supervise defendants charged with domestic violence offenses.

Charging the Defendant

Charging a defendant with a crime is a process that varies somewhat, depending on whether it occurs via a grand jury or a preliminary hearing.

The Indictment Process and the Grand Jury

The grand jury was an early development of the English common law. Under the Magna Carta (1215), no freeman could be seized and imprisoned unless he had been judged by his peers. To determine fairly who was eligible to be tried, a group of freemen from the district where the crime was committed would be brought together to examine the facts of the case and determine whether the charges had merit. Thus, the grand jury was created as a check against arbitrary prosecution by a judge who might be a puppet of the government.

The concept of the grand jury was brought to the American colonies by early settlers and later incorporated into the Fifth Amendment of the US Constitution, which states that "no person shall be held to answer for a capital, or otherwise infamous crime, unless on presentment or indictment of a grand jury." What is the role of the grand jury today? First, the grand jury has the power to act as an independent investigating body. In this capacity, it examines the possibility of criminal activity within its jurisdiction.

LO3 Differentiate between the two main mechanisms for charging defendants (grand jury indictment and prosecutor's information)

WEB APP 8.2 Visit the National Center for State Courts' Grand Jury Resource Guide page at **http://www.ncsc.org/Topics/Jury /Grand-Juries/Resource-Guide .aspx.** Click on "State Links" and read about grand jury procedure in your state.

These investigative efforts may be directed toward general rather than individual criminal conduct, for example, organized crime or insider trading. After an investigation is completed, a report called a **presentment** is issued. The presentment contains not only information concerning the findings of the grand jury but also, usually, a recommendation of indictment.

The grand jury's second and better-known role is to act as the community's conscience in determining whether the accusation of the state (the prosecution) justifies a trial. The grand jury relies on the testimony of witnesses called by the prosecution through its subpoena power. After examining the evidence and the testimony of witnesses, the grand jury decides whether probable cause exists for prosecution. If it does, an **indictment**, or true bill, is affirmed. If the grand jury fails to find probable cause, a **no bill** (meaning that the indictment is ignored) is passed. In some states, a prosecutor can present evidence to a different grand jury if a no bill is returned; in other states, this action is prohibited by statute.

CRITIQUING THE GRAND JURY The grand jury usually meets at the request of the prosecution, and hearings are closed and secret. Neither the defense attorney nor the defendant is allowed to attend, and grand jury hearings are not open to the public. The prosecuting attorney presents the charges and calls witnesses who testify under oath to support the indictment. This process has been criticized as being a "rubber stamp" for the prosecution because the presentation of evidence is shaped by the district attorney, who is not required by law to reveal information that might exonerate the accused.[16] An alternative is to open the grand jury room to the defense and hold the government to the same types of constitutional safeguards to protect defendants that are now used at trial.[17]

The Information Process and the Preliminary Hearing

In about half the states, a prosecutor's **information** is the charging mechanism of choice. When a person is charged in this fashion, a **preliminary hearing** is necessary. The purposes of the preliminary hearing and the grand jury hearing are the same—to establish whether probable cause is sufficient to merit a trial. The procedures differ between the two, however.

The preliminary hearing is conducted before a magistrate or lower-court judge and, unlike the grand jury hearing, is open to the public unless the defendant requests otherwise. Present at the preliminary hearing are the prosecuting attorney, the defendant, and the defendant's counsel, if one has already been retained. The prosecution presents its

Tulsa Police Officer Betty Shelby arrives at the Tulsa County Courthouse on May 11, 2017, for her manslaughter trial in the shooting death of Terence Crutcher. Dash cam and helicopter video footage never provided a clear image of the circumstances surround the shooting. Shelby was ultimately acquitted after eight hours of jury deliberations.

evidence and witnesses to the judge. The defendant or the defense counsel then has the right to cross-examine witnesses and to challenge the prosecutor's evidence.

After hearing the evidence, the judge decides whether there is sufficient probable cause to believe that the defendant committed the alleged crime. If so, the defendant is bound over for trial, and the prosecuting attorney's information (described earlier; it is similar to an indictment) is filed with the superior court, usually within 15 days. If the judge does not find sufficient probable cause, the charges are dismissed, and the defendant is released from custody.

A unique aspect of the preliminary hearing is the defendant's right to waive the proceeding, a procedure that has advantages (and disadvantages) for both the prosecutor and the defendant. For the prosecutor, waiver helps avoid the need to reveal evidence to the defense before trial. Defense attorneys may waive the preliminary hearing for three possible reasons: (1) when the defendant has already decided to plead guilty, (2) to speed the criminal justice process, and/or (3) to avoid the negative publicity that might result from the hearing. On the other hand, a preliminary hearing may have some advantage for the defendant who believes that it will result in a dismissal of the charges. In addition, the preliminary hearing gives the defense an opportunity to learn what evidence the prosecution has. Figure 8.1 outlines the significant differences between the grand jury and the preliminary hearing processes.

Arraignment

After an indictment or information is filed following a grand jury or preliminary hearing, an arraignment takes place before the court that will try the case. At the arraignment, the judge informs the defendant of the charges against him or her and appoints counsel if one has not yet been retained. According to the Sixth Amendment of the US Constitution, the accused has the right to be informed of the nature and cause of the accusation. Thus, the judge at the arraignment must make sure that the defendant clearly understands the charges.

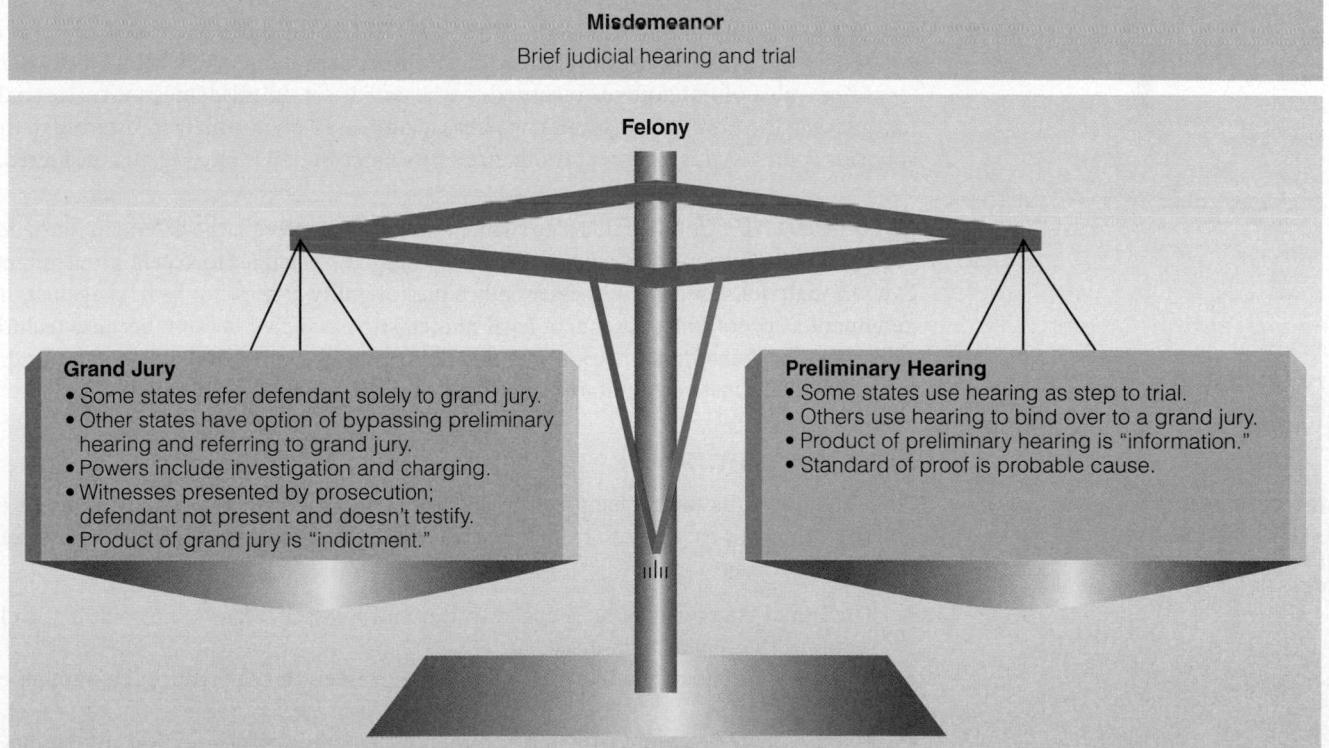

Misdemeanor
Brief judicial hearing and trial

Felony

Grand Jury
- Some states refer defendant solely to grand jury.
- Other states have option of bypassing preliminary hearing and referring to grand jury.
- Powers include investigation and charging.
- Witnesses presented by prosecution; defendant not present and doesn't testify.
- Product of grand jury is "indictment."

Preliminary Hearing
- Some states use hearing as step to trial.
- Others use hearing to bind over to a grand jury.
- Product of preliminary hearing is "information."
- Standard of proof is probable cause.

FIGURE 8.1 Charging the Defendant with a Crime
Note the difference between the grand jury and the preliminary hearing.

After the charges are read and explained, the defendant is asked to enter a plea. If a plea of not guilty or not guilty by reason of insanity is entered, a trial date is set. When the defendant pleads guilty or *nolo contendere*, a date for sentencing is arranged. The magistrate then either sets bail or releases the defendant on personal recognizance.

LO4 Summarize the pleas available to a criminal defendant

The Plea

Ordinarily, a defendant in a criminal trial will enter one of three pleas: guilty, not guilty, or *nolo contendere*.

GUILTY Most defendants appearing before the courts plead guilty prior to the trial stage. A guilty plea has several consequences. It functions not only as an admission of guilt but also as a surrender of the entire array of constitutional rights designed to protect a criminal defendant against unjustified conviction, including the right to remain silent, the right to confront witnesses against him or her, the right to a trial by jury, and the right to have an alleged offense proven beyond a reasonable doubt. After a plea is made, it cannot be rescinded or withdrawn after sentencing, even if there is a change in the law that might have made conviction more problematic.[18]

As a result, judges must follow certain procedures when accepting a plea of guilty. First, the judge must clearly state to the defendant the constitutional guarantees that he or she automatically waives by entering this plea. Second, the judge must believe that the facts of the case establish a basis for the plea and that the plea is made voluntarily. Third, the defendant must be informed of the right to counsel during the pleading process. In many felony cases, the judge will insist on the presence of defense counsel. Finally, the judge must inform the defendant of the possible sentencing outcomes, including the maximum sentence that can be imposed.

After a guilty plea has been entered, a sentencing date is arranged. In a majority of states, a guilty plea may be withdrawn and replaced with a not-guilty plea at any time prior to sentencing, if good cause is shown.

NOT GUILTY At the arraignment or before the trial, a not-guilty plea is entered in one of two ways: (1) it is verbally stated by the defendant or the defense counsel, or (2) it is entered for the defendant by the court while the defendant stands mute before the bench.

After a plea of not guilty is recorded, a trial date is set. In misdemeanor cases, trials take place in the lower-court system, whereas felony cases are normally transferred to the superior court. At this time, a continuance or issuance of bail is once again considered.

NOLO CONTENDERE With this plea (which means "no contest"), the defendant does not accept or deny responsibility for the crime(s) charged but agrees to accept punishment. Even though *nolo contendere* is essentially a plea of guilty, it may not be held against the defendant as proof in a subsequent legal matter, such as a civil lawsuit, because technically there has been no admission of guilt. This plea is accepted at the discretion of the trial court and must be voluntarily and intelligently made by the defendant.

Plea Bargaining

Plea bargaining is the exchange of prosecutorial and judicial concessions for pleas of guilty. Normally, a bargain can be made between the prosecutor and the defense attorney in one of four ways:

LO5 Explain the issues involved in plea bargaining

plea bargaining Nonjudicial settlement of a case in which the defendant exchanges a guilty plea for some consideration, such as a reduced sentence.

- The initial charges may be reduced to those of a lesser offense, thus automatically reducing the sentence imposed.
- In cases where many counts are charged, the prosecutor may reduce the number of counts.
- The prosecutor may promise to recommend a lenient sentence, such as probation.
- When the charge imposed has a negative label attached (such as child molester), the prosecutor may alter the charge to a more "socially acceptable" one (such as assault) in exchange for a plea of guilty.

Strange Plea Agreements

The typical plea agreement results in a reduced charge or a favorable sentencing recommendation by the prosecutor, but some agreements can only be described as strange or at least outside the box. What follows are some examples identified by law professor and former judge Joseph Colquitt. In exchange for leniency, the defendant agrees to:

- Make a charitable contribution
- Relinquish property ownership
- Surrender a professional license
- Undergo sterilization
- Undergo surgical castration
- Enter the military
- Not pursue appeals
- Undertake a shaming punishment, such as carrying a sign that says "I stole from this store"
- Seal the records of a case
- Surrender profits from crime, such as from books written about the crime
- Be banished to another location

These are examples of what Colquitt calls "ad hoc plea bargaining." In his view, ad hoc plea bargaining takes these forms:

(1) the court may impose an extraordinary condition of probation following a guilty plea, (2) the defendant may offer or be required to perform some act as a quid pro quo for a dismissal or more lenient sentence, (3) the court may impose an unauthorized form of punishment as a substitute for a statutorily established method of punishment, (4) the state may offer some unauthorized benefit in return for a plea of guilty, or (5) the defendant may be permitted to plead guilty to an unauthorized offense, such as a "hypothetical" or nonexistent charge, a nonapplicable lesser-included offense, or a nonrelated charge.

Ad hoc plea bargaining is controversial not just because it is unusual. In some cases it can border on unethical. In one case, the prosecutor offered leniency to a drug defendant if he would surrender several thousand dollars in cash that was found during a search of his property. In another case, a defendant was afforded leniency for agreeing to forfeit interest in his vehicle.

CRITICAL THINKING

1. Are ad hoc plea bargains reasonable? Are they fair?
2. What if the tables were turned and, say, a speeding motorist offered $100 to the officer who stopped her in exchange for leniency? What would happen then?

Source: Joseph A. Colquitt, "Ad Hoc Plea Bargaining," *Tulane Law Review* 75 (2001): 695–776; Timothy Lynch, *The Case Against Plea Bargaining*, https://object.cato.org/sites/cato.org/files/serials/files/regulation/2003/10/v26n3-7.pdf (accessed April 2017).

There is little question that these methods result in lesser sentences, especially when defendants are in states whose sentencing policies limit judicial discretion. Pleading guilty to reduced charges may help replace the absence of judicial leniency.[19]

Plea bargaining is one of the most common practices in the criminal justice system and a cornerstone of the informal justice system. Today more than 90 percent of criminal convictions are the result of negotiated pleas of guilty. Even in serious felony cases, plea bargaining can be an option. And it can happen from the earliest stages of criminal charges all the way up to the "shadow of the trial," or right before a verdict is reached.[20]

See the accompanying Contemporary Issues in Criminal Justice box for more on some interesting plea agreements.

Plea bargaining is actually a relatively recent development, which took hold late in the nineteenth century. During the first 125 years after the nation's birth, the trial by jury was viewed as the fairest and most reliable method of determining the truth in a criminal matter. However, plea bargaining became more attractive at the turn of the twentieth century, when the mechanization of manufacture and transportation prompted a flood of complex civil cases; this event persuaded judges that criminal cases had to be settled quickly lest the court system break down.[21]

Pros and Cons of Plea Negotiation

Because of excessive criminal court caseloads and the personal and professional needs of the prosecution and the defense (to reach disposition of the case in the least possible time), plea bargaining has become an essential yet controversial part of the administration of justice. Proponents contend that plea bargaining actually benefits both the state and the defendant in the following ways:

- The overall costs of the criminal prosecution are reduced.
- The administrative efficiency of the courts is greatly improved.

- The prosecution can devote more time to more serious cases.
- The defendant avoids possible detention and an extended trial and may receive a reduced sentence.
- Resources can be devoted more efficiently to cases that need greater attention.[22]

Those who favor plea bargaining believe it is appropriate to enter into plea discussions when the interests of the state in the effective administration of justice will be served. Opponents of the plea-bargaining process believe that the negotiated plea should be eliminated for the following reasons:

- It encourages defendants to waive their constitutional right to trial.
- Plea bargains allow dangerous offenders to receive lenient sentences. Jesse Timmendequas, a previously convicted sex offender, was given a 10-year plea-bargained sentence for child rape. Upon his release, he raped and killed 7-year-old Megan Kanka in one of the nation's most notorious crimes.[23]
- Plea bargaining also raises the danger that an innocent person will be convicted of a crime if he or she is convinced that the lighter treatment ensured by a guilty plea is preferable to the risk of conviction and a harsher sentence following a formal trial.
- Prosecutors are given a free hand to induce or compel defendants to plea-bargain, thus circumventing the law.[24]
- It is possible that innocent persons will admit guilt if they believe that the system is biased and that they have little chance of being acquitted.
- A guilty-plea culture has developed among defense lawyers. Elements of this attitude include the belief that most of their clients are dishonest people who committed the crime with which they have been charged and that getting a "sentence discount" for them is the best and only way to go.[25]

Legal Issues in Plea Bargaining

The Supreme Court has reviewed the propriety of plea bargaining in several decisions and, while imposing limits on the practice, has upheld its continued use. The Court has ruled in several key cases that:

- Defendants are entitled to the effective assistance of counsel to protect them from pressure and influence.[26]
- Pleas must be made voluntarily and without pressure. However, a prosecutor can tell defendants that they may be facing the death penalty if they go to trial.[27]

Joseph Koetters (right), a former high school teacher accused of having sex with two students and getting one pregnant, pleads guilty and is sentenced in Los Angeles Superior Court while his attorney, Leonard Levine, listens to the terms of the plea agreement. Koetters was sentenced to a year in jail for four criminal counts and was required to register as a sex offender.

- Any promise made by the prosecutor during the plea negotiations must be kept after the defendant admits guilt in open court. A prosecutor who promises leniency in private negotiations must stick to that position in court.[28]
- Defendants must also keep their side of the bargain to receive the promised offer of leniency.[29] For example, if they agree to testify against a co-defendant, they must give evidence at trial or forfeit the bargain.
- A defendant's due process rights are not violated when a prosecutor threatens to re-indict the accused on more serious charges—for example, as a habitual offender— if the defendant does not plead guilty to a lesser offense.[30]
- Accepting a guilty plea from a defendant who maintains his or her innocence is valid.[31]
- Statements made during a plea bargain may be used under some circumstances at trial if the negotiations break down. Statements made during a plea negotiation can be used if the defendant (1) admits to a crime during the bargaining process but then (2) later testifies in open court that he or she did not do the act and (3) is innocent of the charges.[32]

Plea-Bargaining Decision Making

The plea-bargaining process is largely informal, lacking in guidelines, and discretionary. Research shows that prosecutorial discretion rather than defendant characteristics controls plea negotiations.[33] Yet studies also show that plea bargaining reflects a degree of cooperation between prosecutors and defense attorneys; in the vast majority of cases, they work together to achieve a favorable outcome.[34]

Research on plea negotiation indicates that the process is rather complex. Offender, case, and community characteristics also weigh heavily on the negotiation process.[35] Such factors as the offense, the defendant's prior record and age, and the type, strength, and admissibility of evidence are important in the plea-bargaining decision as well.[36] The attitude of the complainant is also an important factor in the decision-making process. In victimless cases, such as heroin possession, the attitude of the police is most often considered, whereas in victim related crimes, such as rape, the victim's attitude is a primary concern. Even the prosecutor's ego or political objectives can factor in. The list of factors that can affect plea agreements is practically endless.

THE ROLE OF THE DEFENSE COUNSEL Although the prosecutor formulates and offers the deal, the defense counsel—a public defender or a private attorney—is required to play an advisory role in plea negotiations. The defendant's counsel is expected to be aware of the facts of the case and familiar with the law and to advise the defendant of the alternatives available. The defense attorney is basically responsible for making certain that the accused understands the nature of the plea-bargaining process and the guilty plea. This means that the defense counsel should explain to the defendant that by pleading guilty, he is waiving certain rights that would be available if he were to go to trial. In addition, the defense attorney has the duty to keep the defendant informed of developments and discussions with the prosecutor regarding plea bargaining. While doing so, the attorney for the accused cannot misrepresent evidence or mislead the client into making a detrimental agreement. The defense counsel is not just ethically but also constitutionally required to communicate all plea-bargaining offers to a client, even if counsel believes the offers to be unacceptable.[37]

THE ROLE OF THE JUDGE The leading national legal organization, the American Bar Association, is opposed to judicial participation in plea negotiations.[38] According to ABA standards, judges should not be a party to arrangements for the determination of a sentence, whether as a result of a guilty plea or a finding of guilty based on proof. According to this view, judicial participation in plea negotiations (1) creates the impression in the mind of defendants that they cannot receive a fair trial, (2) lessens the ability of the judge to make an objective determination of the voluntary nature of the plea, (3) is inconsistent with the theory behind the use of presentence investigation reports, and (4) may induce innocent defendants to plead guilty because they are afraid to reject the disposition desired by the judge.[39] How, then, are judges involved in plea bargaining? Judges must approve plea agreements after they have been negotiated.

THE ROLE OF THE VICTIM What role should victims play in plea bargaining? Some suggest that the system today is too "victim driven" and that prosecutors too often seek approval for the plea from a victim or family member. Others maintain that the victim plays an almost secondary role in the process. In reality, the victim is not "empowered" at the pretrial stage of the criminal process. Statutes do not require that the prosecutor defer to the victim's wishes, and there are no legal consequences of ignoring the victim in a plea-bargaining decision.

Plea-Bargaining Reform

In recent years, efforts have been made to convert plea bargaining into a more visible, understandable, and fair dispositional process. Safeguards and guidelines have been developed to ensure that innocent defendants do not plead guilty under coercion. For example, the judge questions the defendant about the facts of the guilty plea before accepting the plea; the defense counsel is present and can advise the defendant of his or her rights; the prosecutor and the defense attorney openly discuss the plea; and full and frank information about the defendant and the offenses is made available at this stage of the process. In addition, judicial supervision ensures that plea bargaining is conducted in a fair manner.

NEGOTIATION OVERSIGHT Some jurisdictions have established guidelines to provide consistency in plea-bargaining cases. Guidelines define the kinds and types of cases and offenders that may be suitable for plea bargaining. Guidelines cover such aspects as avoiding overindictment and controlling unprovable indictments, reducing felonies to misdemeanors, and bargaining with defendants.[40]

BANNING PLEA BARGAINING What would happen if plea bargaining were banned outright, as its critics advocate? Numerous jurisdictions throughout the United States have experimented with bans on plea bargaining. In 1975, Alaska eliminated the practice. Honolulu has also attempted to abolish plea bargaining. Other jurisdictions, including Iowa, Arizona, Delaware, and the District of Columbia, have sought to limit the use of plea bargaining.[41] In theory, eliminating plea bargains means that prosecutors in these jurisdictions make no concessions to a defendant in exchange for a guilty plea.

In reality, however, in these and most jurisdictions, sentence-related concessions, charge-reduction concessions, and alternative methods for prosecution continue to be used in one way or another.[42] Where plea bargaining is limited or abolished, the number of trials may increase, the sentence severity may change, and more questions about the right to a speedy trial may arise. Discretion may also be shifted further up the system. Instead of spending countless hours preparing for and conducting a trial, prosecutors may dismiss more cases outright or decide not to prosecute them after initial action has been taken.

L07 Explain the purpose of pretrial diversion

diversion A noncriminal alternative to trial, usually featuring counseling, job training, and educational opportunities.

Pretrial Diversion

Another important feature in the early court process is placing offenders into noncriminal **diversion** programs before their formal trial or conviction. The first pretrial diversion programs were established more than 40 years ago to reduce the stigma created by the formal trial process. To avoid stigma and labeling, diversion programs suspend criminal proceedings so that the accused can participate in a community treatment program under court supervision. Diversion programs give the client an opportunity to do the following:

- Avoid the stigma of a criminal record
- Continue to work and support his or her family
- Continue pursuing educational goals
- Access rehabilitation services, such as anger management, while remaining in the community
- When needed, make restitution to the victim of crime or pay back the community through volunteer services

Diversion also enables the justice system to reduce costs and alleviate prison crowding. Diversion programs can take many forms. Some are run by separate, independent agencies that were originally set up with federal funds but are now being continued with county or state assistance. Others are organized as part of a police, prosecutor, or probation department's internal structure. Still others represent a joint venture between the county government and a private, nonprofit organization that carries out the treatment process.

First viewed as a panacea that could reduce court congestion and help treat minor offenders, diversion programs soon came under fire when national evaluations concluded that they are no more successful at avoiding stigma and reducing recidivism than traditional justice processing.[43] There was also the suspicion that diversion might "widen the net" of the justice system. By this, critics meant that the people placed in diversion programs were the ones most likely to have otherwise been dismissed after a brief hearing with a warning or small fine.[44] Now they were receiving more treatment than they would have if the program had not been in place. Those who would ordinarily have received a more serious sentence were not eligible for diversion anyway. Thus, rather than limiting contact with the system, the diversion programs actually increase its grasp.

Of course, not all justice experts agree with this charge, and some programs have shown great promise. Rigorous evaluations indicate that given the proper treatment, some types of offenders, such as drug offenders, who are offered a place in pretrial programs can significantly lower their rates of recidivism.[45]

WEB APP 8.3 Visit the San Francisco Pretrial Diversion Project website at **http://sfpretrial .com/**. What programs and services are available to certain defendants in lieu of trial? What defendants are eligible? Which program do you feel is most effective and why?

The Trial

The criminal trial is an open and public hearing designed to examine the facts of the case brought by the state against the accused. Criminal trials are relatively rare events (most cases are settled by a plea bargain during the pretrial stage), but they are an important and enduring fixture in the criminal justice system. By its very nature, the criminal trial is a symbol of the moral authority of the state and of the administration of objective and impartial justice.

Most formal trials are heard by a jury, although some defendants waive their constitutional right to a jury trial and request a **bench trial**, in which the judge alone renders a verdict. In this situation, which occurs daily in the lower criminal courts, the judge may initiate a number of formal or informal dispositions, including dismissing the case, finding the defendant not guilty, finding the defendant guilty and imposing a sentence, or even continuing the case indefinitely. The decision the judge makes often depends on the seriousness of the offense, the background and previous record of the defendant, and the judgment of the court about whether the case can be properly dealt with in the criminal process. The judge may simply continue the case without a finding, in which case the verdict is withheld without a finding of guilt to induce the accused to improve her behavior in the community; if the defendant's behavior does improve, the case is ordinarily closed within a specific amount of time.

This section reviews some of the institutions and processes involved in **adjudication** and trial. We begin with a discussion of the legal rights that structure the trial process.

bench trial The trial of a criminal matter by a judge only. The accused waives any constitutional right to trial by jury.

adjudication The determination of guilt or innocence; a judgment concerning criminal charges. The majority of offenders charged plead guilty; of the remainder, some cases are adjudicated by a judge and a jury, some are adjudicated by a judge without a jury, and others are dismissed.

Legal Rights During Trial

Underlying every trial are constitutional principles, complex legal procedures, rules of court, and interpretations of statutes—all designed to ensure that the accused will receive a fair trial.

THE RIGHT TO AN IMPARTIAL JUDGE Even though the Constitution does not say so, every criminal defendant enjoys the right to a trial by an impartial judge. The Supreme Court ruled as much way back in the 1927 case of *Tumey v. Ohio*. In that case, a municipal court judge was also the mayor, an executive official. What's more, he received fines and fees that he ordered against defendants who were convicted in his courtroom. The Supreme Court held that it is a violation of due process when a judge "has a direct, personal, substantial pecuniary interest in reaching a conclusion against [a defendant] in his case."[46]

What if a judge is not impartial? How can such a judge be removed? Generally, the judge will excuse himself or herself if there is a conflict of interest. Judicial codes of ethics provide the guidelines judges need to make such decisions. Some jurisdictions, however, permit peremptory removal of judges.[47] These are like the peremptory challenges used in jury selection (covered later in this chapter). When this occurs, one of the attorneys can move to have the judge removed, and another judge will come on board. Usually the peremptory removal can occur only once.

THE RIGHT TO BE COMPETENT AT TRIAL To stand trial, a criminal defendant must be considered mentally competent to understand the nature and extent of the legal proceedings. If a defendant is considered mentally incompetent, his trial must be postponed until treatment renders him capable of participating in his own defense.

Can state authorities force a mentally unfit defendant to be treated so that he can be tried? In *Riggins v. Nevada* (1992), the US Supreme Court ruled that forced treatment does not violate a defendant's due process rights if it was medically appropriate and, considering less intrusive alternatives, was essential for the defendant's own safety or the safety of others.[48]

THE RIGHT TO CONFRONT WITNESSES The Sixth Amendment states that "In all criminal prosecutions, the accused shall enjoy the right … to be confronted with the witnesses against him." The accused enjoys this right not just by being able to confront witnesses in person but by being allowed to participate in his or her trial. That is, trials

Robert Lewis Dear addresses Judge Gilbert Martinez during a court appearance in Colorado Springs. Prosecutors filed charges against Lewis in connection with a Planned Parenthood attack in which police Officer Garrett Swasey, Iraq war veteran Ke'Arre Stewart, and Jennifer Markovsky, a mother of two, were killed. On May 11, 2016, a judge declared Dear incompetent to stand trial and ordered that he be indefinitely committed to a state mental hospital.

Pool/Getty Images

cannot be conducted without the accused being afforded the right to appear in person. This right can be waived or forfeited through misconduct. The accused may choose not to show up,[49] which is constitutionally permissible, and he or she may forfeit the right to appear by acting out and causing a significant distraction in the courtroom.[50] There are also some exceptions, such as in child abuse cases, where it is felt that child victims would suffer irreparable harm by being forced to appear before their abusers.[51]

The confrontation clause is essential to a fair criminal trial because it restricts and controls the admissibility of hearsay evidence. Hearsay evidence is akin to secondhand evidence; rather than being told firsthand, it consists of information related by a second party (it is what one person hears and then says—hence the term "hearsay"). The framers of the Constitution sought face-to-face accusations in which the defendant has a right to see and cross-examine all witnesses. The idea that it is always more difficult to tell lies about people to their face than behind their back underlies the confrontation clause.

THE RIGHT TO COMPULSORY PROCESS The Sixth Amendment says, in part, that the accused shall "have compulsory process for obtaining witnesses in his favor." Compulsory process means to compel the production of witnesses via a subpoena. A subpoena is an order requiring a witness to appear in court at a specified time and place. The Supreme Court decided that compulsory process is a fundamental right in the case of *Washington v. Texas* (1967).[52]

THE RIGHT TO AN IMPARTIAL JURY It is no accident that of all the rights guaranteed to the people by the Constitution, only the right to a jury trial in criminal cases appears in both the original Constitution (Article III, Section 2) and the Bill of Rights (the Sixth Amendment). Although they may have disagreed on many points, the framers did not question the wisdom of the jury trial.

Today, the criminal defendant has the right to choose whether the trial will be before a judge or a jury. Although the Sixth Amendment guarantees the defendant the right to a jury trial, the defendant can and often does waive this right. A substantial proportion of defendants, particularly those charged with misdemeanors, are tried before the court without a jury.

The major legal issue surrounding jury trial has been whether all defendants—those accused of misdemeanors as well as those accused of felonies—have an absolute right to a jury trial. Although the Constitution says that the right to a jury trial exists in "all criminal prosecutions," the Supreme Court has restricted this right. In *Baldwin v. New York* (1970), the Court decided that a defendant has a constitutional right to a jury trial when facing a possible prison sentence of six months or more, regardless of whether the crime committed was a felony or a misdemeanor.[53] When the possible sentence is six months or less, the accused is not entitled to a jury trial unless it is authorized by state statute. In most jurisdictions, the more serious the charge, the greater the likelihood of trial—and by jury.

THE RIGHT TO COUNSEL AT TRIAL Recall from previous chapters that the defendant has a right to counsel at numerous points in the criminal justice process. Today, state courts must provide counsel at trial to indigent defendants who face even the possibility of incarceration.[54] The threat of incarceration need not be immediate. Even if the defendant might be sentenced to probation in which a prison or jail term is suspended, or might receive any other type of sentence containing a threat of future incarceration, he or she is afforded the right to counsel at trial.[55]

What if a defendant wants to serve as his or her own attorney? As a result of a 1975 Supreme Court decision, defendants are now permitted to proceed *pro se*, or for themselves.[56] Today, when defendants ask to be permitted to represent themselves and are found competent to do so, the court normally approves their requests. However, these defendants are nearly always cautioned by the court against self-representation. When *pro se* defendants' actions are disorderly and disruptive, the court can terminate their right to represent themselves.

confrontation clause A part of the Sixth Amendment that establishes the right of a criminal defendant to see and cross-examine all the witnesses against him or her.

hearsay evidence Testimony that is not firsthand but, rather, relates information told by a second party.

compulsory process Compelling the production of witnesses via a subpoena.

REALITYCHECK
Myth or Reality?
The Sixth Amendment right to a jury trial extends to defendants in all criminal trials.

MYTH. Although the Sixth Amendment says otherwise, the Supreme Court has restricted this right to cases where the possible sentence exceeds imprisonment for six months.

There are some exceptions to the general rule that jury trials are offered when the possible punishment exceeds six months, but the fact remains that those accused of minor crimes are rarely tried before juries. Is this fair? Is it just? Before answering, consider that serious crimes (those that would merit jury trials) are the exception rather than the rule.

pro se "For oneself"; presenting one's own defense in a criminal trial; self-representation.

THE RIGHT TO A SPEEDY TRIAL The tactics employed by wary defense attorneys (pretrial motions, complex plea negotiations, delay tactics during trial), along with inefficiencies in the court process (such as the frequent granting of continuances, poor scheduling procedures, and the abuse of time by court personnel), have made delays in criminal cases a serious and constitutional issue. As the American Bar Association states in the *Standards Relating to Speedy Trial*, "Congestion in the trial courts of this country, particularly in urban centers, is currently one of the major problems of judicial administration."[57] Delays in the trial process conflict with the Sixth Amendment's guarantee of a right to a speedy trial.[58]

THE RIGHT TO A PUBLIC TRIAL The Sixth Amendment refers to a "public trial." This simply means that all trials must be open to the public. The right to a public trial is generally unrestricted. Anyone who wants to see a criminal trial can do so.

Sometimes having a trial open to the public can cause problems. In the 1966 case of *Sheppard v. Maxwell*, the courtroom was packed with people, including members of the media, for all nine weeks of the trial. Reporters handled evidence and took pictures throughout the trial. The Supreme Court eventually reversed the defendant's conviction, citing the "carnival atmosphere." The case did not lead to the exclusion of cameras from the courtroom, but some judges require that they be kept out. This is why one sometimes sees sketches of a case instead of actual photos.

Adverse pretrial publicity can prevent a defendant from getting a fair trial. The release of premature evidence by the prosecutor, extensive and critical reporting by the news media, and vivid and uncalled-for details in indictments can all prejudice a defendant's case. Press coverage can begin early in a criminal case and can even affect the outcome.

As a general rule, pretrial publicity and reporting cannot be controlled. However, judges may bar the press from some pretrial legal proceedings and hearings, such as preliminary hearings, when police officers make an arrest, or when a warrant is being served, if their presence will infringe on the defendant's right to a fair trial.[59] Other steps can be taken as well. These include changes of venue (moving the trial to another jurisdiction, where there is less press coverage and hence less contamination of the pool of potential jurors) and gag orders (restrictions on what the parties or the media can report), among others.

THE RIGHT TO BE CONVICTED BY PROOF BEYOND A REASONABLE DOUBT The standard required to convict a defendant charged with a crime at the adjudicatory stage of the criminal process is **proof beyond a reasonable doubt**. This requirement dates back to early American history, and over the years has become the accepted measure of persuasion needed by the prosecutor to convince the judge or jury of the defendant's guilt. Many twentieth-century US Supreme Court decisions have reinforced this standard by making "beyond a reasonable doubt a due process and constitutional requirement."[60] In *Brinegar v. United States* (1949), for instance, the Supreme Court stated:

> Guilt in a criminal case must be proven beyond a reasonable doubt and by evidence confined to that which long experience in the common-law tradition, to some extent embodied in the Constitution, has crystallized into rules of evidence consistent with that standard. These rules are historically grounded rights of our system, developed to safeguard men from dubious and unjust convictions with resulting forfeitures of life, liberty, and property.[61]

The reasonable doubt standard is an essential ingredient of the criminal justice process. It is the prime instrument for reducing the risk of convictions based on factual errors.[62] The underlying premise of this standard is that it is better to release a guilty person than to convict someone who is innocent. Because the defendant is presumed innocent until proven guilty, this standard forces the prosecution to overcome this presumption with the highest standard of proof. Unlike the civil law, where a mere **preponderance of the evidence** is the standard, the criminal process requires proof beyond a reasonable doubt for each element of the offense.[63] The various evidentiary standards of proof are analyzed and compared in Exhibit 8.1.

proof beyond a reasonable doubt The standard of proof needed to convict in a criminal case. The evidence offered in court does not have to amount to absolute certainty, but it should leave no reasonable doubt that the defendant committed the alleged crime.

preponderance of the evidence The level of proof in civil cases; more than half the evidence supports the allegations of one side.

EXHIBIT 8.1 Evidentiary Standards of Proof: Degrees of Certainty

Standard	Definition	Ruling
Absolute certainty	No possibility of error; 100 percent certainty	Not used in civil or criminal law
Beyond reasonable doubt; moral certainty	Conclusive and complete proof, without leaving any reasonable doubt about the innocence or guilt of the defendant; allows the defendant the benefit of any possibility of innocence	Criminal trial
Clear and convincing	Prevailing and persuasive to the trier of fact	Civil commitments, insanity defense evidence
Preponderance of the evidence	Greater weight of evidence in terms of credibility; more convincing than an opposite point of view	Civil trial
Probable cause	US constitutional standard for arrest and search warrants, requiring existence of facts sufficient to warrant that a crime has been committed	Arrest, preliminary hearing, motions
Sufficient evidence	Adequate evidence to reverse a trial court	Appellate review
Reasonable suspicion	Rational, reasonable belief that facts warrant investigation of a crime on less than probable cause	Police investigations
Less than probable cause	Mere suspicion; less than reasonable belief to conclude criminal activity exists	Prudent police investigation where safety of an officer or others is endangered

The Trial Process

The trial of a criminal case is a formal process conducted in a specific and orderly fashion in accordance with rules of criminal law, procedure, and evidence. Unlike what transpires in popular TV programs involving lawyers—where witnesses are often asked leading and prejudicial questions and where judges go far beyond their supervisory role—the modern criminal trial is a complicated and often time-consuming, technical affair. It is a structured adversarial proceeding in which both prosecution and defense follow specific procedures and argue the merits of their cases before the judge and jury. Each side seeks to present its case in the most favorable light.

LO9 Summarize the trial process

Although each jurisdiction in the United States has its own trial procedures, all jurisdictions conduct criminal trials in a generally similar fashion. The basic steps of the criminal trial, which proceed in an established order, are described in this section and outlined in Figure 8.2.

JURY SELECTION In both civil and criminal cases, jurors are selected randomly from licensing or voter registration lists within each court's jurisdiction. Few states impose qualifications on those called for jury service, although most mandate a residency requirement.[64] There is also little uniformity in the amount of time served by jurors; the

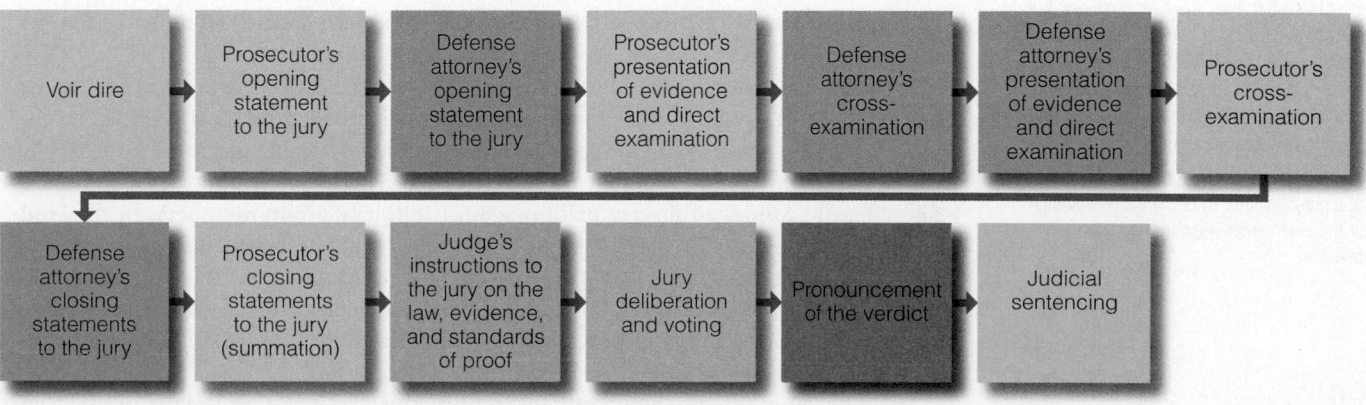

FIGURE 8.2 The Steps in a Jury Trial
Source: Marvin Zalman and Larry Siegel, *Criminal Procedure: Constitution and Society* (St. Paul, MN: West, 1991), p. 655.

term ranges from one day to months, depending on the nature of the trial. In addition, most jurisdictions prohibit convicted felons from serving on juries, as well as others exempted by statute, such as public officials, physicians, and attorneys.

The initial list of persons chosen, which is called a **venire**, or jury array, provides the state with a group of potentially capable citizens able to serve on a jury. Many states, by rule of law, review the venire to eliminate unqualified persons and to exempt those who, by reason of their professions, are not allowed to be jurors. The actual jury selection process begins with those remaining on the list.

The court clerk, who handles the administrative affairs of the court—including the processing of the complaint and other documents—randomly selects what he or she believes will be enough names to fill the required number of places on the jury. After reporting to a courtroom, the prospective jurors are first required to swear that they will truthfully answer all questions asked about their qualifications to serve. A group of 12 will be asked to sit in the jury box while the remaining group stands by.

After prospective jurors are chosen, the lengthy process of **voir dire** (from the Old French for "to tell the truth") starts. To determine their appropriateness to sit on the jury, prospective jurors are examined under oath by the government, the defense, and sometimes the judge about their backgrounds, occupations, residences, and possible knowledge of or interest in the case. A juror who acknowledges any bias for or prejudice against the defendant—if the defendant is a friend or relative, or if the juror has already formed an opinion about the case—may be removed by either the prosecution or the defense with a **challenge for cause** asking the judge to dismiss the biased juror. If the judge accepts the challenge, the juror is removed for cause and replaced with another juror from the remaining panel. Because normally no limit is placed on the number of challenges for cause that can be exercised, it often takes considerable time to select a jury, especially for controversial and highly publicized criminal cases.

Justin Ross Harris is pictured during jury selection for his trial at the Glynn County Courthouse in Brunswick, Georgia. Harris, who was accused of intentionally leaving his toddler son in a hot SUV to die, was found guilty of murder and sentenced to life in prison without the possibility of parole.

AP Images/Stephen B. Morton

venire The group called for jury duty from which jury panels are selected.

voir dire The process in which a potential jury panel is questioned by the prosecution and the defense to select jurors who are unbiased and objective.

challenge for cause A request that a prospective juror be removed because he or she is biased or has prior knowledge about a case, or for other reasons that demonstrate the individual's inability to render a fair and impartial judgment in a particular case.

peremptory challenge The dismissal of a potential juror by either the prosecution or the defense for unexplained, discretionary reasons.

Besides challenges for cause, both the prosecution and the defense are allowed **peremptory challenges**, which enable the attorneys to excuse jurors for no particular reason or for undisclosed reasons. A prosecutor might not want a bartender as a juror in a drunk-driving case, believing that a person with that occupation would be sympathetic to the accused. Or the defense attorney might excuse a male prospective juror because the attorney prefers to have a predominantly female jury. The number of peremptory challenges given to the prosecution and defense is limited by state statute and often varies by case and jurisdiction.

The peremptory challenge has been criticized by legal experts who question the fairness and propriety with which it has been used.[65] Historically, the most significant criticism was that it was used by the prosecution to exclude African Americans from serving on juries in which the defendant was also African American—a policy that seemed to allow legally condoned discrimination against minority group members. In the landmark 1986 case *Batson v. Kentucky*, the Supreme Court held that the use of peremptory challenges against potential jurors by prosecutors in criminal cases violated the US Constitution if the challenges were based solely on race.[66] Since that decision, the issue of race discrimination in the use of peremptory challenges has been raised by defendants in numerous cases.

It is becoming increasingly difficult to find impartial jurors, especially in this technological age. Heinous crimes have always been broadcast all over the news, and the result has sometimes been to contaminate the pool of prospective jurors. Now jurors are able to turn to their smartphones and seek information about *any* case. By searching the Internet and sharing information (such as on Facebook), which they are expressly forbidden to do, they often learn more about cases than is presented in court. As one article noted, this practice is "wreaking havoc on trials around the country, upending deliberations and infuriating judges."[67] Although there is no official tally of the number of cases compromised by jurors' Internet research, the number is certainly growing. For example, a Florida case involving a man accused of illegally selling prescription drugs was upended because one juror researched the case on her own and was able to discover information not presented at trial. After her actions came to light, the judge had no choice but to declare a mistrial.

OPENING STATEMENTS After the jury has been selected, and the criminal complaint has been read to the jurors by the court clerk, the prosecutor and the defense attorney may each make an opening statement about the case. The purpose of the prosecutor's statement is to acquaint the judge and jury with the particular criminal charges, to outline the facts, and to describe how the government will prove the defendant guilty beyond a reasonable doubt. The defense attorney reviews the case and indicates how the defense intends to show that the accused is not guilty.

Both sides use the opening statement to give the jury a concise overview of the evidence that is to follow. Neither attorney is allowed to make prejudicial remarks or inflammatory statements or to mention irrelevant facts. Both are free, however, to identify what they will eventually prove by way of evidence, which includes witnesses, physical evidence, and the use of expert testimony. The opening statements are important because they give both sides an opportunity to sway the jury before the trial begins.

PROSECUTION'S CASE Following the opening statements, the government begins its case by presenting evidence to the court through its witnesses. Numerous types of evidence are presented at trial (see Exhibit 8.2). Those called as witnesses—such as police officers, victims, or experts—provide testimony via direct examination. During direct examination, the prosecutor questions the witness to reveal the facts believed pertinent to the government's case. Testimony involves what the witness actually saw, heard, or touched; it does not include opinions. However, a witness's opinion can be given in certain situations, such as when describing the motion of a vehicle or indicating whether a defendant appeared to act intoxicated or insane. Witnesses may also qualify to give opinions because they are experts on a particular subject relevant to the case. For example, a psychiatrist may testify about a defendant's mental capacity at the time of the crime.

Upon completion of the prosecutor's questioning, the defense usually conducts a cross-examination of the witness. During this exchange, the defense attorney may

direct examination The questioning of one's own (prosecution or defense) witness during a trial.

cross-examination The process in which the defense and the prosecution interrogate witnesses for the other side during a trial.

EXHIBIT 8.2 Types of Evidence Presented at Trial

In general, the primary test for the admissibility of evidence in a criminal proceeding is its relevance; that is, the court must consider whether the gun, tool, or bottle has relevant evidentiary value in determining the issues in the case. Ordinarily, evidence that establishes an element of the crime is acceptable to the court. In a prosecution for possession of drugs, evidence that shows the defendant to be a known drug user might be relevant. In a prosecution for bribery, photos of the defendant receiving a package from a coconspirator would clearly be found relevant to the case. The following are the four main types of evidence:

- *Testimonial evidence.* Given by police officers, citizens, and experts, this is the most basic form of evidence. The witness must state, under oath, what he or she heard, saw, or experienced.

- *Real evidence.* Exhibits that can be taken into the jury room for review by the jury constitute real evidence. A revolver that may have been in the

defendant's control at the time of a murder, tools in the possession of a suspect charged with a burglary, and a bottle allegedly holding narcotics are examples of real, or physical, evidence. Photographs, maps, diagrams, and crime scene displays are other types of real evidence.

- *Documentary evidence.* This type of evidence includes writings, government reports, public records, business or hospital records, fingerprint identification, and DNA profiling.

- *Circumstantial evidence.* In trial proceedings, circumstantial (indirect) evidence is often inferred or indirectly used to prove a fact in question. For example, in a murder case, evidence that carpet fibers found on the body match the carpet in the defendant's home may be used at trial to link the two, even though they do not provide direct evidence that the suspect actually killed the victim.

Myth or Reality?

The death penalty deters homicide.

MYTH. Most research on this subject has shown that the death penalty does little, if anything, to deter homicide.

Why are most researchers convinced the death penalty fails to deter homicide? Clearly it is effective from a specific deterrent standpoint, but why might would-be killers not be deterred by the threat of capital punishment?

brutalization effect An outcome of capital punishment that enhances, rather than deters, the level of violence in society. The death penalty reinforces the view that violence is an appropriate response to provocation.

is used more often, in nations with a large minority population. This phenomenon has led to formulation of what is referred to as the "minority-group-threat hypothesis," which states that the use of extreme punishment is related to the regulation of groups that are racially, culturally, or ethnically different.[84] Let's look at some of the evidence:

- Homicides with male offenders and female victims are more likely to result in a death sentence than homicides involving female offenders and male victims.[85]
- Homicides involving strangers are more likely to result in a death sentence than homicides involving nonstrangers or acquaintances.
- Prosecutors are more likely to recommend the death sentence for people who kill white victims than they are in any other racial combination of victim and criminal.[86] Prosecutors are less likely to seek the death penalty if the victim is a minority group member.[87] A male minority group member killing a white female is more likely to result in the death penalty than any other race/gender combination.[88]

Ever since the death penalty was first instituted in the United States, disproportionate numbers of minorities have been executed. Charges of racial bias are supported by the disproportionate numbers of African Americans who have received the death sentence, who are currently on death row, and who have been executed. Racism was particularly blatant when the death penalty was invoked in rape cases: of those receiving the death penalty for rape, 90 percent in the South and 63 percent in the North and West were African American.[89] Today, about 42 percent of inmates on death row are African American, a number disproportionate to the minority representation in the population.[90] When a black criminal kills a white victim, the likelihood of the death penalty being invoked is far greater than when a white criminal kills a black victim.[91]

CAUSES MORE CRIME THAN IT DETERS Some critics fear that the introduction of capital punishment will encourage criminals to escalate their violent behavior, consequently putting police officers at risk. A suspect who kills someone during a botched robbery may be inclined to "fire away" upon encountering police rather than to surrender peacefully. The killer faces the death penalty already, so what does he have to lose? Geoffrey Rapp studied the effect of capital punishment on the killings of police and found that, all other things being equal, the greater the number of new inmates on death row, the greater the number of police officers killed by citizens.[92] Rapp concluded that what the death penalty seems to do is create an extremely dangerous environment for law enforcement officers because it does not deter criminals and may lull officers into a false sense of security, leading them to believe that the death penalty will deter violence directed against them and causing them to let their guard down.

The death penalty may also produce more violence than it prevents—the so-called **brutalization effect**.[93] Executions may increase murder rates because they raise the general violence level in society and because people prone to violence actually identify with the executioner, not with the target of the death penalty. When someone gets in a conflict with such violence-prone individuals or challenges their authority, these individuals may "execute" them, just as the state executes people who violate its rules.[94] Evidence shows that the brutalization effect does influence murder rates: stranger homicides increase after an execution.[95] People may be more inclined to settle conflicts with violence after a state executes a criminal—"If they can do it, why can't I?"[96]

CRUEL AND INHUMAN Abolitionists believe that executions are unnecessarily cruel and inhuman and come at a high moral and social cost. Even death by lethal injection, which is considered relatively humane by advocates, has been challenged because it may cause extreme pain and can take much longer to cause death than was originally believed.[97] Our society does not punish criminals by subjecting them to the same acts they themselves committed. Rapists are not sexually assaulted, and arsonists do not have their houses burned down. Why, then, should murderers be killed?

Robert Johnson has described the execution process as a form of torture in which the condemned are first tormented psychologically by being made to feel powerless and alone while on death row; suicide is a constant problem among those awaiting death.[98] The execution itself is a barbaric affair marked by the smell of burning flesh and stiffened bodies (though electrocution is fairly rare these days, the most recent such execution occurred in 2013). The executioners suffer from delayed stress reactions, including anxiety and a dehumanized personal identity.

MOST DEVELOPED COUNTRIES HAVE ABANDONED IT According to the Death Penalty Information Center, 141 of 195 countries have abolished the death penalty in law or practice.[99] Just since 1990, more than 45 countries have abolished the death penalty for all crimes. Even China has recently revised its criminal law to eliminate the death penalty for certain crimes. According to LiYing Li, "This signifies a leap forward in China's legal reforms and an effort by China to move closer to the international norms."[100]

IT IS EXPENSIVE Some people complain that they do not want to support "some killer in prison for 30 years." Abolitionists counter that legal appeals drive the cost of executions far higher than the cost of years of incarceration. If the money spent on the judicial process were invested, the interest would more than pay for the lifetime upkeep of death row inmates. Because of numerous appeals, the median time between conviction by a jury, sentencing by a judge, and execution can be lengthy. For example, recent data show that the average inmate sentenced to death has been on death row for almost 12 years.[101]

MORALLY WRONG The death penalty is brutal and demeaning, according to critics. They argue that even if the general public voices approval of the death penalty, "social vengeance by death is a primitive way of revenge which stands in the way of moral progress."[102] And although early religious leaders accepted the death penalty, today many (such as the Catholic Church) condemn the practice of execution.[103]

In his book *The Contradictions of American Capital Punishment*, Franklin Zimring links America's obsession with the death penalty—unique among developed nations—with its vigilante tradition, in which people on the frontier took justice into their own hands, assuming that their targets were always guilty as charged.[104] The death penalty was widely practiced against slaves, and, at one time, mass executions were a brutal and common practice to stifle any thought of escapes and/or revolts.[105]

While the debate continues, there seems to be little question that the public's support for the death penalty has weakened, and concomitantly, the number of death sentences being handed down is in sharp decline (this was covered in this chapter's opening story).[106] Whether these developments portend the demise of capital punishment remains to be seen.

Legal Issues in Capital Punishment

The constitutionality of the death penalty has been a major concern to both the nation's courts and its social scientists. In 1972, the Supreme Court in *Furman v. Georgia* decided that the discretionary imposition of the death penalty was cruel and unusual punishment under the Eighth and Fourteenth Amendments of the US Constitution.[107] The Supreme Court did not completely rule out the use of capital punishment as a penalty; rather, it objected to the arbitrary and capricious manner in which it was imposed. After *Furman*, many states changed statutes that had allowed jury discretion in imposing the death penalty. Then, in July 1976, the Supreme Court ruled on the constitutionality of five state death penalty statutes. In the first case, *Gregg v. Georgia*, the Court found valid the Georgia statute holding that a finding by the jury of at least 1 "aggravating circumstance" out of 10 is required in pronouncing the death penalty in murder cases.[108] In the *Gregg* case, the jury imposed the death penalty after finding beyond a reasonable doubt two aggravating circumstances: (1) the offender was engaged in the commission of two other capital felonies, and (2) the offender committed the offense of murder for the purpose of receiving money and other financial gains (specifically, an automobile).[109] The *Gregg* decision signaled the return of capital punishment as a sentencing option.

WEB APP 9.3 Take the Death Penalty Quiz on the Death Penalty Information Center's (DPIC) website at **http://www.deathpenaltyinfo.org/node/183**. Also visit Amnesty International's website for a list of countries that have abolished (called abolitionists) and retained (called retentionists) capital punishment at **https://www.amnesty.org/en/what-we-do/death-penalty/**. Is the United States in good company with countries that have retained the death penalty? Why or why not?

L07 Articulate the legal issues associated with capital punishment

LO3 *Identify various sentencing models* Indeterminate sentences are tailored to fit individual needs. Convicted offenders are typically given a "light" minimum sentence that must be served and a lengthy maximum sentence that is the outer boundary of the time that can be served. Determinate sentences offer a fixed term of years, the maximum set in law by the legislature, to be served by the offender sentenced to prison for a particular crime. Sentencing guidelines have been implemented to provide judges with a recommended sentence based on the seriousness of a crime and the background of an offender. Some states have passed mandatory sentence legislation (e.g., three-strikes) prohibiting people convicted of certain offenses, such as violent crimes or drug trafficking, from being placed on probation; they must serve at least some time in prison.

LO4 *Explain how sentences are imposed* In some instances, when an accused is convicted of two or more charges, the judge must decide whether to impose consecutive or concurrent sentences. When judges impose an incarceration sentence, they know and take into account the fact that the amount of time spent in prison is reduced by the implementation of "time off for good behavior."

LO5 *Summarize factors associated with sentencing decisions* State sentencing codes usually include various factors that can legitimately influence the length of prison sentences, including the severity of the offense, the offender's prior criminal record, whether the offender used violence, whether the offender used weapons, and whether the crime was committed for money. Evidence supports an association between social class and sentencing outcomes: members of

the lower class may expect to get longer prison sentences than more affluent defendants. Most research indicates that women receive more favorable outcomes the further they go in the criminal justice system. The same is often true with the elderly. Minorities also seem to receive longer sentences than Caucasians, especially those who are indigent or unemployed.

LO6 *List the arguments for and against capital punishment* Proponents of capital punishment feel that executions serve as a strong deterrent for serious crimes. They also argue that capital punishment is morally correct, is proportional to the crime, reflects public opinion, and can be implemented with little to no chance of error. Critics of capital punishment cite the potential for error and the supposed unfair use of discretion in sentencing people to death (some offenders get death sentences while others do not). They also claim that capital punishment represents misplaced vengeance and that there is not enough public support for the death penalty. Finally, critics argue the death penalty does not deter crime; that it abandons all hope for offender rehabilitation; is biased against certain demographics; amounts to immoral, cruel, and inhuman punishment; may cause crime to increase; is expensive; and has been abandoned in most developed nations.

LO7 *Articulate the legal issues associated with capital punishment* The constitutionality of the death penalty has been a major concern to both the nation's courts and its social scientists. Although the Supreme Court has upheld the death penalty for the most serious offenders, it has prohibited it as a sentence for certain crimes, notably rape—even child rape. Juveniles cannot be sentenced to death nor can the mentally retarded.

KEY TERMS

penitentiaries, p. 218

general deterrence, p. 218

specific deterrence, p. 219

incapacitation, p. 219

blameworthy, p. 220

just desert, p. 220

rehabilitation, p. 220

equity, p. 220

indeterminate sentences, p. 220

determinate sentences, p. 221

sentencing guidelines, p. 222

mandatory sentence, p. 223

concurrent sentences, p. 224

consecutive sentences, p. 224

chivalry hypothesis, p. 227

victim impact statement, p. 229

brutalization effect, p. 234

REVIEW QUESTIONS

1. Discuss the sentencing dispositions in your jurisdiction. What are the pros and cons of each?

2. Compare the various types of incarceration sentences. What are the similarities and differences? Why are many jurisdictions considering the passage of mandatory sentencing laws?

3. Discuss the issue of capital punishment. In your opinion, does it serve as a deterrent? What new rulings has the Supreme Court made on the legality of the death penalty?

4. Why does the problem of sentencing disparity exist? Do programs exist that can reduce the disparity of sentences? If so, what are they? Should all people who commit the same crime receive the same sentence? Explain.

5. Should convicted criminals be released from prison when correctional authorities are convinced they are rehabilitated? Why or why not?

AP Images/Damian Dovarganes

Corrections and Alternative Sanctions

More than a dozen states and 1,000 courts use for-profit companies to administer probation. Why? To save money. Instead of having the government absorb costs, private probation makes supervision "offender-funded." Probationers themselves pay for their supervision; no public moneys are spend on probation services. Some states in which probation is publicly-funded do require probationers to pay for part of their supervision, but fully private probation—that is, the government turning over all responsibility for offender supervision to the private sector—is a different animal.

Lately, private probation has come under fire. Probationers serviced by private, for-profit companies pay modest monthly fees for their supervision, ranging anywhere from $30 to $100 per month. These amounts may seem reasonable, but many probationers are only on probation because of failure to pay fines at sentencing. It is not uncommon in several states for judges to determine whether offenders can pay their fines at sentencing; if they cannot, a payment plan is arranged and private probation is the likely outcome. This, as Human Rights Watch, claims is a "tax on poverty."

Others have called private probation a "modern-day debtors' prison." In one case featured in the national media, a teenager, Kevin Thompson, received a traffic ticket for making an illegal left turn.[1] He was summoned to a Georgia court, but after arriving late, he was flagged for "failure to appear," so his license was suspended. He paid a fee to revoke the suspension, but then failed to file the correct paper work. Three months later, he was pulled over again and slapped with an $810 fine for driving on a suspended license. Being a low-paid tow-truck driver, Thompson was unable to pay the amount in full. The court passed his case on to Judicial Correction Services, one of the large private probation firms. He borrowed money and took extra jobs, all the while hitching rides to meet with his probation officer because he could not drive. He became unable to make the required payments in time and was sentenced to a stint in jail. Perhaps Thompson's case is an extreme example, but his experience was enough to draw the attention of the American Civil Liberties Union, which sued the county on his behalf. The case was settled.

Part 4 contains three chapters that cover the current correctional process in all its various forms. Chapter 10 surveys community-based corrections, including probation, and alternative sanctions ranging from fines to electronic monitoring and home confinement. Chapter 11 introduces the history of corrections and also reviews the various forms of secure corrections being used today. Finally, Chapter 12 looks at the prison experience, covering such topics as prison culture, sexual assault, treatment programs, and prisoners' rights. Leaving prison, parole, and the reentry process are also discussed.

10 Community Sentences

Probation, Intermediate Sanctions, and Restorative Justice

It is well known that the United States' incarceration rate stands out relative to other nations. Indeed, it is the highest in the world. What is not so well known is that America is also exceptional with its use of probation. Probation is a far more common sanction than imprisonment, so we know it will be used more often than putting people behind bars, but relative to many other countries, the US probation rate is out of step. In a recent study, "American Exceptionalism in Probation Supervision," researchers at the Robina Institute of Criminal Law and Criminal Justice compared US probation rates to those of various European nations.[2] Here is a brief summary of their findings (also see Figure 12.1):

- The average adult probation rate (1,605 per 100,000 people) in the United States is more than five times that of 40 comparison nations (297 per 100,000 people).
- Several US states have probation rates 9 to 10 times than European nations.
- Of all 50 US states, Ohio puts the most adults on probation.
- Of the European nations examined (there were almost 40 of them), Turkey puts the most adults on probation (1,212 out of 100,000), but if Turkey were a US state, it would be in 29th place relative to other states.
- The United States has around 4 million people on probation compared to only 1.5 million in all the European nations examined.
- New Hampshire was the state with the lowest adult probation rate (379 per 100,000). Interestingly, 12 European countries reported fewer than 70 probationers per 100,000 people.

We hear often of mass incarceration. We do not hear much about mass probation. Fortunately, as prison populations in the United States have leveled off and even declined in recent years, so has probation; fewer adults are on probation in the United States now than a few years ago (we will look more closely at the data later in this chapter). Even so, European countries use probation much less often than the United States does. Why? Crime rates fail to

AP Images/Rich Pedroncelli

LEARNING OBJECTIVES

LO1 Explain the concept of community sentencing

LO2 Describe the history of community sentences

LO3 Define the different types of probation sentences

LO4 List the rules of probation

LO5 Explain the organization and administration of probation services

LO6 List and discuss the elements of a probation department's duties

LO7 Discuss the legal rights of probationers

LO8 Debate the effectiveness of probation

LO9 Explain what is meant by intermediate sanctions

LO10 Define restorative justice, and discuss its merits

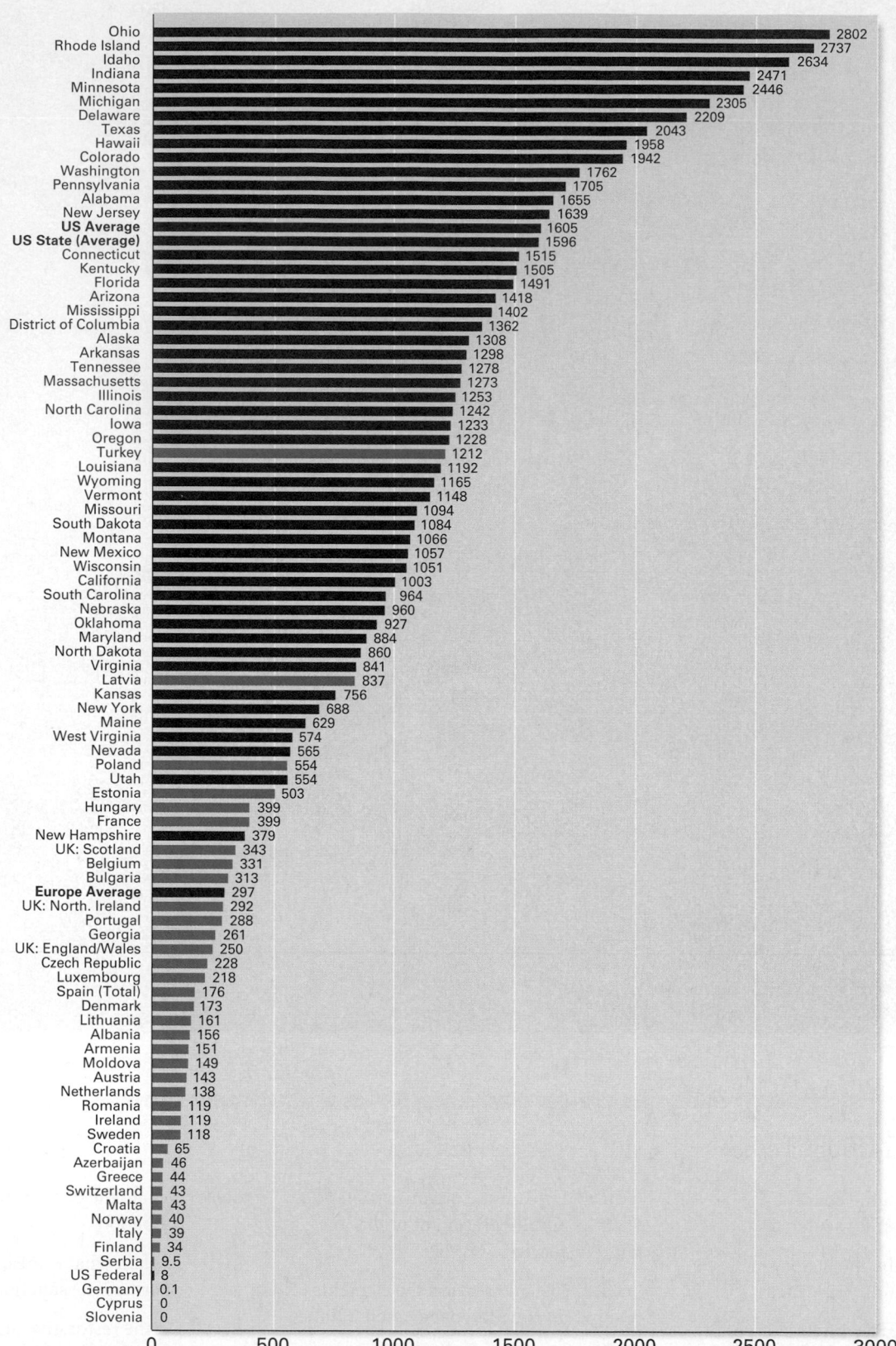

FIGURE 10.1 Probation Supervision Rates in the United States and Europe, Rates per 100,000 Adult Residents

Source: Data from Robina Institute of Criminal Law and Criminal Justice, *New Data Brief: American Exceptionalism in Probation Supervision*, February 2016, http://www.robinainstitute.org/news/new-data-brief-american-exceptionalism-probation-supervision.

offer much of an explanation. For example, according to UN statistics, the most recently recorded theft rate per 100,000 people in the United Kingdom (England and Wales) was 2,329.7, compared to 1,876.1 in the United States.[3] If crime explained probation rates, then we would expect to see a higher probation rate in the United Kingdom, but probation there is used about one-fifth as much as it is in America. France reports a similar burglary rate to that of the United States, but it uses probation a quarter as much as the United States does. What, then, explains America's exceptionalism in putting people on probation?

Community sentencing, including probation, is the most common form of correctional treatment because it makes no sense to lock up nondangerous, repentant offenders in an overcrowded and dangerous correctional system, which can turn them into hardened criminals. It may be both more effective and less costly to have them remain in the community under the supervision of a trained court officer, where they can receive treatment that will help them turn their lives around. Rehabilitation would be aided immensely if those who commit crime could be made to understand the problems their actions cause their family, friends, and community. Other reasons for the attractiveness of community sentences include:

- They are less costly than a sentence to jail or prison.
- They help the offender maintain family and community ties.
- They can be structured to maximize security and maintain public safety.
- They can be scaled in severity to correspond to the seriousness of the crime.
- They can feature restoration and reintegration rather than punishment and ostracism.
- They give convicted offenders a "second chance" that can enable them to resume a more productive lifestyle.[4]

In a tight economic environment, cost-effective programming such as probation makes economic sense. It is not surprising that a growing number of convicted offenders are being offered community sentences ranging from traditional probation to house arrest and placement in community correctional centers, simply because this approach makes both economic and practical sense. For example, when Christopher Krebs and his associates carefully compared treatment outcomes of large groups of drug-involved offenders in Florida they found that community-based drug treatment reduced the chances for a subsequent felony arrest by 22 percent. In comparison, prison- or jail-based treatment, which cost three times as much as community-based treatment, did not have similar success; inmates showed no particular improvement after attending an institutional drug treatment program.[5] Clearly community-based programs can be both practical and cost effective.

This chapter reviews these criminal sanctions. It begins by discussing the role of traditional probation as a community-based correctional practice and a brief history of community sentencing. Then it focuses on so-called alternative or intermediate sanctions, such as intensive supervision, house arrest, and electronic monitoring. Finally, the chapter turns to a discussion of the concept of restorative justice and programs based on its principles.

What Is Probation?

probation A sentence entailing the conditional release of a convicted offender into the community under the supervision of the court (in the person of a probation officer), subject to certain conditions for a specified time.

judicial reprieve The common-law practice that allowed judges to suspend punishment so that convicted offenders could seek a pardon, gather new evidence, or demonstrate that they had reformed their behavior.

recognizance The medieval practice of allowing convicted offenders to go unpunished if they agreed to refrain from any further criminal behavior.

sureties During the Middle Ages, people responsible for the behavior of an offender released before trial.

As the term is used today, probation is a criminal sentence that suspends or delays a correctional term in a prison or jail so that, instead of being incarcerated, offenders are returned to the community for a period in which they must (1) abide by certain conditions set forth by the court, and (2) be supervised by a probation officer. It is the most commonly used means of dispensing correctional treatment to convicted offenders.

The fact that probation is used so often rests on the belief that most convicted criminals are neither dangerous nor a menace to society and can be reformed if given a second chance. Probation provides offenders the opportunity to prove themselves while being closely supervised in the community by trained personnel who can help them reestablish proper forms of behavior. Even felony offenders can be successfully rehabilitated if given the proper balance of community supervision, treatment, and control. And importantly, during tough economic times, probation is a cost-effective alternative to incarceration. So it's not just petty offenders who get probation: an overwhelming majority of convicted offenders including felons also get a "second chance" via probation.[6]

The History of Probation and Community Sentencing

LO1 Explain the concept of community sentencing

Where did the idea of community supervision and control begin? During medieval times, the practice of judicial reprieve allowed judges to suspend punishment so that convicted offenders could seek a pardon, gather new evidence, or demonstrate that they had reformed their behavior. Another practice, called recognizance, enabled convicted offenders to go unpunished if they agreed to refrain from further criminal behavior. Sometimes sureties were required—these were people who made themselves responsible for the behavior of an offender after the offender's release.

John Augustus and the Creation of Probation

LO2 Describe the history of community sentences

John Augustus of Boston is usually credited with originating community sentencing.[7] As a private citizen, Augustus began in 1841 to supervise offenders released to his custody by a Boston judge. Over an 18-year period, Augustus supervised close to 2,000 convicted offenders and helped them get jobs and establish themselves in the community. Augustus had an amazingly high success rate, and few of his charges ever became involved in crime again.

In 1878, Augustus's work inspired the Massachusetts legislature to pass a law authorizing the appointment of a paid probation officer for the city of Boston. In 1880, probation was extended to other jurisdictions in Massachusetts, and by 1898, the probation movement had spread to the superior (felony) courts.[8] The Massachusetts experience was copied by Missouri (1887) and Vermont (1898) and, soon after, by most other states. In 1925, the federal government established a probation system for the US district courts. The probation concept soon became the most widely used correctional mechanism in the United States.[9]

Probation Today

Approximately 2,000 adult probation agencies are currently in operation in the United States. Slightly more than half are associated with a state-level agency, whereas the remaining agencies are organized at the county or municipal level of government. About 30 states combine probation and parole supervision into a single agency; in some jurisdictions, probation supervision is carried out by private contractors.

As Figure 10.2 shows, the adult probation population grew between 2005 and 2007 until more than 4 million people were on probation. Then, in 2008, the number of people on probation slowly began to decline, a trend that has continued until today.[10]

While growth in the probation population has ended for now, there are still almost 4 million people on probation, and more than 2 million people are placed on probation annually.

Who is on probation? Males make up three-quarters of the adult probation population. More than half of probationers are white non-Hispanic, and nearly a third are African Americans. Nearly 20 percent, or one in five, probationers are being supervised for a violent offense; nearly 60 percent of probationers are being supervised for a felony offense. Without probation, the correctional system would rapidly become even more overcrowded, overly expensive, and unmanageable.

Awarding Probation

Most probation orders involve a contract between the court and the offender in which a prison or jail term is suspended, and the probationer promises to obey a set of probation rules, or conditions mandated by the court. If the rules are violated, or if the probationer commits another criminal offense, probation may be revoked: the community sentence is terminated, and the original sentence of incarceration is enforced. Revocation is not automatic, and the presiding judge can decide to let the offender remain in the community. If an offender on probation commits a second offense that is more serious than the first, he or she may also be indicted, tried, and sentenced to a longer prison sentence based on the second offense.

Today, probationary sentences may be granted by state and federal district courts and state superior (felony) courts. In most jurisdictions, although juries can recommend probation, the presiding judge makes the final sentencing decision. Most states have attempted to shape judicial discretion by creating guidelines for granting probation, directing them to look at such factors as the manner in which the crime was carried out or whether pain was inflicted on a vulnerable victim such as a child. In contrast, probation may be recommended when defendants are youthful or when they were pressured by a codefendant into committing the crime. A recent Supreme Court case, *Gall v. United States*, held that granting a probationary sentence to a deserving defendant was not unreasonable even though the Federal Sentencing Guidelines called for a prison sentence. Gall had voluntarily withdrawn from a drug ring three years before indictments were handed down. He moved to another state, opened a business, and started a new life. The judge decided to give him a break and handed down a probation-only sentence. When the prosecution appealed, the Court held that it is appropriate for the sentencing judge to consider all the elements in the case when deciding whether a probation sentence is appropriate.[11]

More than half of all cases involve a direct sentence to probation for a fixed period of time. In many cases, the judge will formulate a prison sentence and then suspend it if the offender agrees to obey the rules of probation while living in the community (a suspended sentence). If the offender completes the probation term without further trouble, his or her sentence is considered served. Some offenders receive a split sentence in which they must first serve a jail term before being released on probation. In the remaining cases, the imposition of the sentence is suspended and the case continued without a finding until further notice.

For misdemeanors, probation usually extends for the entire period of the jail sentence, whereas felonies are more likely to warrant probationary periods that are actually shorter than the suspended prison sentences. The typical felony probation sentence is a little more than three years.[12]

Probation Eligibility

Although originally conceived as a way to provide a second chance for young offenders who committed nonserious crimes, probation today is also a means of reducing the population overload in an overcrowded and underfunded correctional system. Many serious

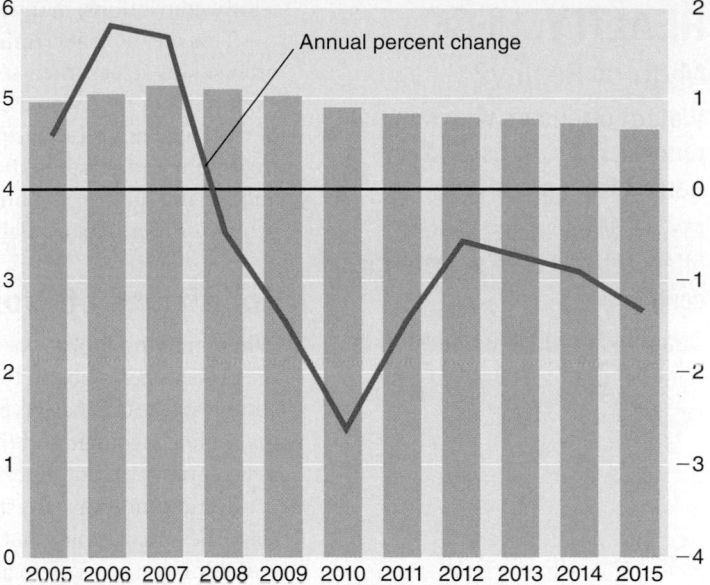

Year end population (in millions)   **Annual percent change**

Annual percent change

Note: Estimates are based on most recent data and may differ from previously published statistics. See *Methodology*.

FIGURE 10.2 Adults on Probation

Source: Danielle Kaeble and Thomas P. Bonczar, *Probation and Parole in the United States, 2015*, Bureau of Justice Statistics, 2016.

LO3 Define the different types of probation sentences

probation rules Conditions or restrictions mandated by the court that must be obeyed by a probationer.

revocation An administrative act performed by a parole authority that removes a person from parole, or a judicial order by a court removing a person from parole or probation, in response to a violation on the part of the parolee or probationer.

suspended sentence A prison term that is delayed while the defendant undergoes a period of community treatment. If the treatment is successful, the prison sentence is terminated.

LO4 List the rules of probation

WEB APP 10.1 To learn more about the administration of probation services and a variety of probation issues and programs, go to the American Probation and Parole Association website at **http://www.appa-net.org**.

LO5 Explain the organization and administration of probation services

criminal offenders are therefore given probation sentences, including people with prior felony convictions; many repeat felony offenders are given community sentences!

This means that criminal defendants may receive probation even though the current offense was at least their second conviction for a felony offense. Nor are violent criminals exempt from receiving a community sentence: about 20 percent of all people convicted of violent felonies receive probation.[13] So there are two distinct sides to probation: (1) the treatment and rehabilitation of nondangerous offenders deserving of a second chance, and (2) the supervision and control of criminals who might otherwise be incarcerated if probation were not available.

Conditions of Probation

When granting probation, the court sets down certain conditions or rules of behavior that the probationer is bound to obey. Although probation officers themselves can later set some conditions, courts have typically ruled that the most restrictive ones must be approved by the sentencing judge and that probation officers cannot require the defendant to adhere to new requirements of supervision about which he or she did not have reasonable notice.[14]

Some conditions are standard and are applied in every probation case (e.g., "Do not leave the jurisdiction"), but the sentencing judge usually has broad discretion to set specific conditions on a case-by-case basis. Sometimes an individual probationer is given specific rules related to his or her particular circumstances, such as the requirement to enroll in an anger management or drug treatment program, make a personal apology to the victim, or have no contact with his or her ex-spouse.[15] A presiding judge may not impose capricious or cruel conditions, of course, such as requiring an offender to make restitution out of proportion to the seriousness of the criminal act.[16] Judges may, however, legally impose restrictions tailored to fit the probationer's individual needs and/or to protect society from additional harm. For example, they can force sex offenders to register with state authorities and require probationers to take periodic polygraph tests to determine whether they have engaged in illegal behavior.[17] Community supervision may be revoked if probationers fail to comply with the conditions of their probation and do not obey the reasonable requests of the probation staff to meet their treatment obligations.[18]

Administration of Probation Services

Probation services are organized in a variety of ways, depending on the state and the jurisdiction in which they are located. Some states have an independent statewide probation service, and, in others, probation is controlled by local courts. Some states bifurcate the process, for example, by having a state agency monitor felony probationers and local courts supervise misdemeanants. A clear majority of states combine probation and parole supervision services in a single unit situated within the department of corrections or organized as an independent agency; about one-quarter of probationers are supervised in these joint operations. Some departments combine juvenile and adult probation departments, whereas others maintain these departments separately.

Regardless of how probation services are organized, probation officers (POs) are typically assigned to a department situated in a single court district, such as a juvenile, superior, district, or municipal court. The relationship between the department and court personnel (especially the judge) is extremely close.

In the typical department, the chief probation officer (CPO) sets policy, supervises hiring, determines training needs, and may personally discuss with or recommend sentencing to the judge. The probation staff carries out the actual monitoring and treatment of offenders.

An officer's working style is influenced by both personal values and the department's general policies and orientation toward the goals of probation.[19] Traditionally, probation officers were placed along a continuum. At one extreme, officers considered themselves "social workers" who maintained a treatment orientation with the goal of helping offenders adjust in the community, whereas at the other extreme, they considered themselves "law enforcers" who were more concerned with supervision, control, and public safety. Another group took a more balanced approach to their work, employing a blend of social work and law enforcement that is neither indulgent of antisocial attitudes and noncompliance nor authoritative and heavy-handed toward their clients.[20]

In an important study, Joel Miller surveyed thousands of active probation officers and found that they can be grouped around their engagement with clients, ranging from those most involved to those least involved.[21] Those who were most involved were concerned with emphasizing consequences of behaviors and risks of detention, monitoring behaviors, and fully enforcing rules when transgressions occur. The highly involved officers want to engage probationers with therapeutic services, family-based services, and skill-building programs, while helping them avoid risky places and activities. High engagers are willing to work with family members to help the client. In contrast, low engagers often have minimal or sporadic contact with clients and almost none with family members. They are the officers least able to help clients navigate the path to successful completion of probation orders and rules.

For more on a career as a probation officer, see the Careers in Criminal Justice feature.

 ## CAREERS IN CRIMINAL JUSTICE PROBATION OFFICER

Duties and Characteristics of the Job

- Probation officers monitor offenders' behavior through personal contact with the offenders and their families.
- Another part of the probation officer's job involves working in the courts.
- The number of cases a probation officer has depends on both the counseling needs of offenders and the risks they pose to society.
- Probation officers may find their jobs stressful because they work with convicted criminals and interact with many other individuals who may be angry, upset, or uncooperative, including family members and friends of their clients.
- Although stress makes these jobs difficult at times, the work also can be rewarding. Many probation officers gain personal satisfaction from counseling members of their community and helping them become productive citizens.

Job Outlook

- Jobs for probation officers are more plentiful in urban areas.
- There are also more jobs in states that have numerous men and women on probation.
- Employment of probation officers is projected to grow during the next few years.
- Overcrowding in prisons also has swelled the probation population as judges and prosecutors search for alternative forms of punishment, such as electronic monitoring and day reporting centers.
- Other openings will result from the need to replace workers who leave the occupation permanently, including the large number expected to retire over the next several years.

Salary

- The 90,000 probation officers in the United States earn a median annual salary of about $49,000.
- The lowest 10 percent earned less than $32,900, but the highest paid 10 percent earned more than $86,000.
- Officers and specialists who work in urban areas usually have higher earnings than those working in rural areas.

Qualifications

- Prospective probation officers must be in good physical condition and must be emotionally stable.

- Most agencies require applicants to be at least 21 years old and, for federal employment, not older than 37.
- Those convicted of felonies may not be eligible for employment in these occupations.
- Probation officers need strong writing skills due to the large number of reports they must prepare.
- Familiarity with computers is often required.
- Job candidates also should be knowledgeable about laws and regulations pertaining to corrections.

Education and Training

- Educational requirements for probation officers vary by state, but a bachelor's degree in social work or criminal justice is usually required.
- Some states require probation officers to have one year of work experience in a related field or one year of graduate study in criminal justice, social work, or psychology.
- Most probation officers must complete a training program and work as trainees for about six months. Candidates who successfully complete the training period obtain a permanent position after which they may have to pass a certification test. In addition, they may be required to work as trainees for up to one year before being offered a permanent position.
- Some probation officers specialize in a certain type of casework. For example, an officer may work only with domestic violence offenders or deal only with substance-abuse cases. Officers receive training specific to the group that they are working with so that they are better prepared to help that type of offender.
- Applicants usually must also pass written, oral, psychological, and physical examinations.

Reality Check

- Probation can be challenging, but it is also quite rewarding.
- Although an advanced degree is not a requirement, it may be the key to advancement in larger departments.
- Budget cutbacks may mean tougher cases entering community corrections rather than more expensive custodial placements.

Source: US Department of Labor, "Probation Officers and Correctional Treatment Specialists," 2015, http://www.bls.gov/ooh/community-and-social-service/probation-officers-and-correctional-treatment-specialists.htm (accessed March 2017).

presentence investigation An investigation performed by a probation officer attached to a trial court after the conviction of a defendant.

Elements of Probation

Probation officers (POs) engage in five primary tasks: presentence investigation, intake, diagnosis/risk classification, supervision, and treatment.

PRESENTENCE INVESTIGATION In the investigative stage, the supervising probation officer accumulates important information on the background and activities of the offender being considered for probation. This presentence investigation serves as the basis for sentencing and controls whether the convicted defendant will be granted community release or be sentenced to secure confinement. In the event that the offender is placed on probation, the investigation becomes useful as a tool to shape treatment and supervision efforts.

The style and content of presentence investigations may vary among jurisdictions and also among individual POs within the same jurisdiction. Some departments require voluminous reports covering every aspect of the defendant's life. Other departments require that officers stick to the basic facts, such as the defendant's age, race, sex, and previous offense record.

At the conclusion of most presentence investigations, a recommendation is made to the presiding judge that reflects the department's sentencing posture on the case at hand. This is a crucial aspect of the report because the sentencing judge usually follows the probation department's recommendation. Numerous factors may contribute to a recommendation of community treatment; among the most critical are the investigator's conclusion that the defendant is someone probation officers can work with and effectively treat. Equally important is the belief that the perspective probationer will be able to abide by both legal and institutional rules.[22]

intake The process in which a probation officer settles cases at the initial appearance before the onset of formal criminal proceedings; also, the process in which a juvenile referral is received and a decision is made to file a petition in the juvenile court, release the juvenile, or refer the juvenile elsewhere.

INTAKE Probation officers who conduct intake interviews may be looking to settle the case without the necessity of a court hearing. The probation officer will work with all parties involved in the case—offender, victim, police officer, and so on—to design an equitable resolution of the case. If the intake process is successful, the probation officer may settle the case without further court action, recommend restitution or other compensation, or recommend unofficial or informal probation. If an equitable solution cannot be found, the case is filed for a court hearing.

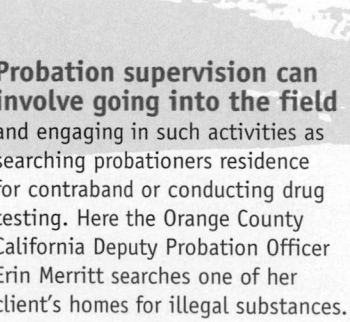

Probation supervision can involve going into the field and engaging in such activities as searching probationers residence for contraband or conducting drug testing. Here the Orange County California Deputy Probation Officer Erin Merritt searches one of her client's homes for illegal substances.

Lucy Nicholson/Reuters

DIAGNOSIS/RISK CLASSIFICATION To select appropriate treatment modes, probation officers analyze the client's character, attitudes, and behavior at various points in the probation process, from the assignment of cases to selection of treatment modalities.[23] An effective diagnosis integrates all that has been learned about the individual, organized in such a way as to facilitate the establishment of future treatment goals. Based on the risk level diagnosis, some clients may receive frequent (intensive) supervision in which they are contacted by their supervising probation officer almost every day, whereas those considered low risk are assigned to minimum monitoring.

Developing effective risk assessment has taken on greater importance because probation is now routinely employed with felons who have been convicted of violent crimes such as rape and murder.[24] A number of **risk classification** approaches are now used, but most employ such objective measures as the offender's age, employment status, drug abuse history, prior felony convictions, and number of address changes in the year prior to sentencing. Some departments are using standardized tests to predict failure and assign treatment such as the Level of Service Inventory-Revised (LSI-R).[25] Another approach, the Post-Conviction Risk Assessment (PCRA) scale, is widely used to classify probationers in the federal system and is now being evaluated to determine whether it can be employed to pinpoint risk factors that interfere with supervision of probationers and undermine effectiveness.[26]

> **risk classification** Classifying probationers so that they may receive an appropriate level of treatment and control.

Some critics have complained that the emergence of standardized diagnostic tools and tests has diminished the probationer officer's individual role in classification, thereby eliminating the human element from diagnosis and treatment.[27] To counter this argument, a number of jurisdictions are testing or have implemented advanced classification systems based on highly sophisticated methodologies. Philadelphia is now using *random forest modeling* to assess each new case and then assign the probationer to a high-, moderate-, or low-risk category.[28] The tool is a sophisticated statistical approach that considers the effects of a large number of personal, social, and legal variables with complex interactions. In 10 to 15 seconds, the tool assigns a new probationer to one of three categories. The lowest level of risk is assigned to those who are predicted to not commit any new offense in the next two years. The moderate-risk level identifies those who are likely to commit a crime, but not a serious one. The high-risk level is for those who are most likely to commit a serious crime such as murder, attempted murder, aggravated assault, rape, or arson.

Community supervision is based on the determined risk level. Probation officers who are supervising high-risk individuals are given the smallest caseloads.

SUPERVISION An important part of the probation officer's duties is monitoring clients in the community, making sure they obey their probation orders, and helping them to stay out of trouble. In some cases, this can mean giving random drug tests, monitoring the family situation, and keeping in touch with employers. Some officers have a control orientation, believe in strict supervision, and are quick to sanction offenders who violate rules. Others are more treatment oriented and question the effectiveness of punitive sanctions and strict supervision. Recent research has identified a new breed of younger probation officers who are actually more inclined to control and punish rule violators than their older counterparts. One reason for this turn to closer and more punitive supervision is the threat of litigation. Failure to supervise probationers adequately can result in the officer and the department being held legally liable for civil damages.[29]

TREATMENT Probation staff are assigned to carry out a program of therapy designed to help the client deal with the problems that are suspected of being the cause of her or his antisocial behavior. In years past, the probation staff had primary responsibility for supervision and treatment, but today's large caseloads limit opportunities for hands-on treatment; most probation treatment efforts rely on community resources.

Treatment protocols may vary according to client needs. Some of those who have a drinking problem may be asked to participate in a community-based 12-step program;

Probation departments are constantly trying out new treatment techniques. On April 9, 2015, Judge David A. Tapp, right, addresses members of the Supervision Motivation Accountable Responsibility and Treatment program, also known as SMART probation, at the Pulaski County Courthouse in Somerset, Kentucky. This group is among a handful of addicts that are participating in a special probation program overseen by Judge Tapp. The program provides medication under the brand name Vivitrol that blocks the opioid receptors in the brain. This means that opioids like prescription painkillers and heroin would have no effect on addicts, which would help them stop using the drugs.

others might spend time in a residential detoxification center. A spousal abuser may be required to enroll in an anger management program. A probation officer may work with teachers and other school officials to develop a program designed to help a young probationer reduce his or her truancy and avoid becoming a dropout.

A number of innovative techniques are now being used with probationers. One popular technique, motivational interviewing, assumes that disinterested probationers forced into treatment will lack the will to change. Motivational interviewing therefore attempts to increase probationers' awareness of their potential problems and to help them acknowledge the risks they face if they fail to change their behavior. Clients are asked to visualize a better future and learn strategies to reach their goals.[30]

Legal Rights of Probationers

What are the legal rights of probationers? How has the US Supreme Court set limits on the probation process? A number of important legal issues surround probation, one set involving the civil rights of probationers and another involving the rights of probationers during the revocation process.

LO7 Discuss the legal rights of probationers

motivational interviewing A technique that increases the probationers' awareness of their potential problems by asking them to visualize a better future and learn strategies to reach their goals.

CIVIL RIGHTS The Court has ruled that probationers have a unique status and therefore are entitled to fewer constitutional protections than other citizens.

- *Minnesota v. Murphy (1984).* The probation officer–client relationship is not confidential, as are physician–patient and attorney–client relationships. If a probationer admits to committing a crime to his or her probation supervisor, the information can be passed on to the police or district attorney. The *Murphy* decision held that a probation officer could even use trickery or psychological pressure to get information and turn it over to the police.[31]
- *Griffin v. Wisconsin (1987). Griffin* held that a probationer's home may be searched without a warrant because probation departments "have in mind the welfare of the probationer" and must "respond quickly to evidence of misconduct."[32]
- *United States v. Knights (2001).* The warrantless search of a probationer's home for the purposes of gathering criminal evidence is legal under some circumstances—for example, if (1) the search was based on a reasonable suspicion that the probationer had committed another crime while on probation, and (2) submitting to searches was part of the probation order. The government's interest in preventing crime, combined with *Knights's* diminished expectation of privacy, required only a *reasonable suspicion* to make the search fit within the protections of the Fourth Amendment.[33]

REVOCATION RIGHTS During the course of a probationary term, violating the rules or terms of probation or committing a new crime can result in probation being revoked, at which time the offender may be placed in an institution. Revocation is often a difficult decision because it conflicts with the treatment philosophy of many probation departments.

If revocation is a possibility, the offender is notified, and a formal hearing is scheduled to look into the matter. If the charges against the probationer are upheld, the offender can either be maintained on probation or have his probation revoked and be forced to serve the remainder of his sentence behind bars.

In some significant decisions, the Supreme Court provided procedural safeguards to apply at proceedings to revoke probation (and parole):

- *Mempa v. Rhay (1967).* A probationer is constitutionally entitled to counsel in a revocation-of-probation proceeding where the imposition of sentence had been suspended.[34]
- *Morrissey v. Brewer (1972). Morrissey*, a parole case, established that an informal inquiry must be held to determine whether there is probable cause that a parolee has violated the conditions of parole. If so, a formal revocation hearing is required before parole can be revoked. Because the revocation of probation and that of parole are similar, the standards in *Morrissey* are applied to the probation process as well.[35]
- *Gagnon v. Scarpelli (1973). Gagnon* established that both probationers and parolees have a constitutionally limited right to legal counsel in revocation proceedings.[36] A judge may deny counsel under some circumstances, such as when probation will be continued despite the violation.
- *Beardon v. Georgia (1983).* In *Beardon*, the Court ruled that a judge cannot revoke a defendant's probation for failure to pay a fine and/or make restitution. The state may not thereafter imprison a defendant solely because he or she lacks the resources to pay because this would be a violation of a probationer's right to equal protection.[37]
- *United States v. Granderson (1994).* The *Granderson* ruling helped clarify what can happen to a probationer whose community sentence is revoked. Granderson was eligible for a six-month prison sentence but instead was given 60 months of probation. When he tested positive for drugs, his probation was revoked. The statute he was sentenced under required that he serve one-third of his original sentence in prison. When the trial court sentenced him to 20 months, he appealed. Was his original sentence six months or 60 months? The Supreme Court found that it would be unfair to force a probationer to serve more time in prison than he would have served if originally incarcerated and ruled that the proper term should have been one-third of the six months, or two months.[38]

How Successful Is Probation?

Probation is the most commonly used alternative sentence for a number of reasons: it is humane, it helps offenders maintain community and family ties, and it is cost effective. Incarcerating an inmate typically costs over $25,000 per year, sometimes as much as $60,000 per year, whereas probation costs about $2,000 per year, and sometimes much less depending on the type of supervision used.[39]

Although unquestionably inexpensive, is probation successful? If most probation orders fail, the costs of repeated criminality would certainly outweigh the cost savings of a probation sentence. National data indicate that about 60 percent of probationers successfully complete their probationary sentence, whereas about 40 percent are rearrested, violate probation rules, or abscond. Of those who leave probation, about 15 percent find themselves behind bars.

Most revocations occur for technical violations during the first three months of the probation sentence.[40] Typically, many revocations stem from failure to attend required treatment programs that were originally created to help probationers kick their drug habits, stay out of trouble, and succeed on probation; others are absconders who leave the jurisdiction without notice.[41]

Probation may work because it is easier to treat offenders in their home environment than in a closed institution. When Christopher Krebs and his associates carefully compared treatment outcomes of large groups of drug-involved offenders in Florida, they found that institutional treatment in jail or prison cost three times as much as community-based treatment but was actually less successful; inmates showed no particular improvement after attending institutional drug treatment programs, while those on probation achieved positive results. They concluded that the use of community-based treatment can increase public safety while costing a lot less than locking up offenders.[42] Even clients with the most serious personal problems, such as mental illness, seem to do better on probation than in closed institutions.[43]

Probation officers can search a probationer's home without a warrant if they suspect foul play or criminal activity.

REALITY. Probationers have fewer expectations of privacy than the average citizen, and their home can be searched without a warrant if there is cause.

Do you think that probationers should have the same civil rights as anyone else living in the community?

L08 Debate the effectiveness of probation

How Successful Is Felony Probation?

Are probationers convicted of serious felonies more likely to recidivate than minor offenders who receive probation? Is it possible that the success of probation reflects the fact that probationers are far less dangerous and incorrigible than offenders sentenced to prison? One way to determine the real success of probation is to disaggregate felons from misdemeanants and see how the former group does on community sentencing. In a classic study, Joan Petersilia and her colleagues at the RAND Corporation, a private think tank, traced the outcomes of 1,672 men convicted of felonies who had been granted probation in Los Angeles and Alameda counties in California.[44] The crimes these probationers committed were indistinguishable from those of offenders sentenced to prison.

Petersilia found that 1,087 (65 percent) of the felony probationers were soon rearrested; of those rearrested, 853 (51 percent) were convicted; and of those convicted, 568 (34 percent) were sentenced to jail or prison. Of the probationers who had new charges filed against them, 75 percent were charged with burglary, theft, robbery, and other predatory crimes; 18 percent were convicted of serious, violent crimes.

Although the failure rate found by Petersilia seems disturbingly high, her findings still support the continued use of probation, given the fact that felons who receive probation are less likely to recidivate than felons who are sent to prison for committing similar crimes.[45] Incarcerating offenders increases the likelihood of recidivism.[46] Granting felons probation may actually produce more favorable outcomes at a much lower cost than an incarceration sentence.

Who Fails on Probation and Who Succeeds?

Who is most likely to fail on probation? Many probationers have grown up in troubled households in which family members are or have been incarcerated and/or drug abusers. Others have lived part of their lives in foster homes or state institutions and have suffered high rates of physical and sexual abuse. This sort of deprived background often makes it difficult for probationers to comply with the rules of probation and forgo criminal activity. Surveys indicate that almost 20 percent of probationers suffer from mental illness and that those with a history of instability are most likely to be rearrested.[47]

Prior record is also related to probation success: clients who have a history of criminal behavior, prior probation, and previous incarceration are the most likely to fail.[48] Also, as probation sentences have become more common, caseloads now contain significant numbers of serious repeat offenders, a group that is difficult to treat and control.[49]

In contrast, probationers who are married with children, have lived in the area for two or more years, and are adequately employed are the most likely to be successful on probation.[50] Among female probationers, those who have stable marriages, are better educated, and are employed are more likely to complete probation orders successfully than male or female probationers who are single, less educated, and unemployed.

The Future of Probation

Some critics are worried that probation is now undergoing a shift from traditional casework methods that featured diagnosis and treatment to an emphasis on risk assessment and control.[51] To improve the effectiveness of probation even more, in a process that leading expert Joan Petersilia calls "reforming, reinvesting, and restructuring," several steps appear to be necessary, including providing more financial resources and implementing quality programming for appropriate probation target groups.[52] A number of initiatives that are now ongoing or being suggested may help shape the future of probation:

- *Making probationers pay.* At least 25 states now impose some form of fee on probationers to defray the cost of community corrections. Massachusetts initiated **day fees**, which are based on the probationer's wages (the usual fee is between one and three days' wages each month).[53] Texas requires judges to impose supervision fees unless the offender is truly unable to pay; fees make up more than half the probation department's annual budget.[54]

day fees A program requiring probationers to pay some of the costs of their treatment.

- *Making probation more effective.* Legislatures are instituting policies that reward the most effective and efficient local departments. In 2008, the Arizona legislature established an incentive system that rewards departments with up to 40 percent of any cost savings in each county resulting from a reduction in probation revocations. The money can then be used to fund substance abuse treatment, community supervision services, and victim services.[55]
- *HotSpot probation.* HotSpot probation initiatives involve police officers, probation agents, neighbors, and social service professionals in community supervision teams. Using a team approach, they provide increased monitoring of offenders through home visits and drug testing. They also work with the offenders to ease reentry through offender creation of work crews that participate in community cleanups, work on vacant houses, and participate in other projects.[56]
- *Area needs.* Some experts suggest that probation caseloads be organized around area needs rather than client needs. Research shows that probationers' residences are concentrated in certain locations. As such, it might make sense to assign probation officers' cases on the basis of where they live so that they can acquire a working knowledge of community issues and develop expertise on how best to serve their clients' interests and needs.[57]
- *Specialized probation.* Some probation departments are experimenting with focused or specialized probation, in which teams of probation officers take on clients convicted of one specific type of crime, such as drug offenses or domestic violence, rather than treating a mixed bag of offenders. Focusing on specialized caseloads enables probation officers to develop specific treatment and control skills.[58] In some instances, probation officers collaborate with other social service agencies such as public health to provide a range of services to treat special needs clients.[59]
- *Private probation.* Used in at least 10 US states, including Florida, Georgia, Colorado, and Missouri, private probation involves contracting with companies that, for a fee, engage in many typical probation activities from supervision to giving periodic breathalyzer tests.[60] By utilizing private probation for low-risk offenders, state probation departments can commit more resources to high-risk offenders.[61]
- *Swift and sure punishment.* The threat of swift and sure punishment that is somewhat less than a full revocation may help reduce rule violations. Hawaii has been experimenting with a system that provides immediate punishment for any probationers found in violation of their court orders; Hawaii's HOPE program

AP Images/Bob Andres

Cortney Gunter, a probation and parole officer with the Department of Juvenile Justice, shakes hands with Georgia Governor Nathan Deal after Deal announced a proposal of a 20 percent pay raise for more than 3,300 state law enforcement officers during a news conference in Atlanta. The governor said in a statement that the demands of protecting Georgians have changed and grown, which requires better pay and better training.

is described more fully in the accompanying Focus on Effectiveness feature.[62] Delaware's Step'n Out program is designed for offenders who fail drug tests. Participants are then given drug tests once or twice a week. Continued drug use progressively leads to mandated treatment, more frequent testing, curfew, and incarceration sanctions. Those who are drug free are reclassified and move to standard community supervision.[63]

FOCUS ON EFFECTIVENESS

Hawaii HOPE

Hawaii's HOPE program is designed to keep people on probation by threatening them at a formal warning hearing with "swift and certain" punishment, rather than severe sanctions, for violating terms of probation. The program is geared to drug-involved offenders.

HOPE begins with a "warning hearing," sometimes called an "orientation hearing," in which the judge clearly lays out the program's rules and structure, and probationers are put on notice that they will be punished for violations and that a probationer's success is entirely within his or her own control.

The program requires probationers with drug conditions to undergo regular random drug tests (six times a month during the first few months) to ensure that there is a zero-tolerance approach to drug usage; those who fail a drug test are arrested immediately. Typically, the jail term is several days, servable on the weekend if the probationer is employed; sentences increase for successive violations.

HOPE differs from other programs by:

- Focusing on reducing drug use and missed appointments rather than on drug treatment and imposing drug treatment on every participant.

- Mandating drug treatment for probationers only if they continue to test positive for drug use or if they request a treatment referral. A HOPE probationer who has a third or fourth missed or "dirty" drug test may be mandated into residential treatment as an alternative to probation revocation.

- Requiring probationers to appear before a judge only when a violation is detected—in this respect, HOPE requires less treatment and fewer court resources than drug courts.

- Having probationers who are employed serve any jail time, at least initially, on a weekend so they do not jeopardize their employment.

Because only a small fraction of HOPE probationers receive mandated treatment, the program can afford to use intensive, long-term residential treatment, rather than relying primarily on outpatient drug-free counseling as do most diversion programs and drug courts.

Currently, at least 100 replications of HOPE-style models are being tested around the nation, and many correctional experts see its swift and sure punishment approach as a correctional panacea. But some respected correctional experts caution that what worked in Hawaii may have limited effect elsewhere. Some critics are concerned that the program relies on swift-and-certain sanctions and that alone may not be enough to reduce recidivism and improve people's lives

Effects on Crime/Recidivism

Careful evidence-based evaluations of the HOPE program have not yielded a clear indication of whether the program is successful. For example, here is a summary of the most recent research available as of this writing:

- Zachary Hamilton and his colleagues compared participants in a HOPE-like program in Washington State (called SAC, for "Swift and Certain") to individuals in a matched control group. Random assignment was not

possible. They found that SAC participants fared better than controls on several outcome measures, including recidivism and treatment program utilization.

- Daniel O'Connell and his colleagues conducted a randomized controlled trial to evaluate the effectiveness of HOPE-like programming in the state of Delaware, called "Decide Your Time," or DYT. They found "no discernible difference across multiple drug use, probationary, and recidivism measures…" In other words, DYT participants fared no better than those who received traditional probation.

- Pamela Lattimore and hear colleagues conducted a multisite evaluation of HOPE programming, also with random assignment of participants to treatment and control conditions. They found that HOPE supervision was not associated with reductions in arrests.

Thinking Critically About Research

What are we to make of the conflicting findings regarding HOPE? Should we put total stock in the randomized controlled trials? Perhaps, but Mark A. R. Kleiman cautions us to drill down further. For example, he notes that the comparison conditions in the three studies summarized above were "heterogeneous," meaning they were not the same across studies. Also, since there are so many HOPE-like programs in operation throughout the country, it is important to look closely at what programming is offered so that apples-to-apples comparisons can be made across studies. He notes that HOPE-like programming "is not a single, homogeneous, manualized 'program-in-a-box' that can be implemented in any jurisdiction or with any population." The moral of the story, then, is not just to examine the quality of the research design but also to look closely at the interventions and outcomes—especially when comparing the findings from multiple studies.

QUESTIONS

1. Do you agree with the Hawaii HOPE model?
2. Can warning people and punishing them be enough to turn their lives around?
3. Does it just seem too easy to be true?

Sources: Zachary Hamilton, Christopher M. Campbell, Jacqueline van Wormer, Alex Kigerl, and Brianne Posey, "Impact of Swift and Certain Sanctions: Evaluation of Washington State's Policy for Offenders on Community Supervision," *Criminology and Public Policy* 15 (2016): 1009–1072; Daniel O'Connell, John J. Brent, and Christy A. Visher, "Decide Your Time: A Randomized Trial of a Drug Testing and Graduated Sanctions Program for Probationers," *Criminology and Public Policy* 15 (2016): 1073–1102; Pamela K. Lattimore, Doris L. MacKenzie, Debbie Dawes, and Stephen Tueller, "Outcome Findings from the HOPE Demonstration Field Experiment: Is Swift, Certain, and Fair an Effective Supervision Strategy?" *Criminology and Public Policy* 15 (2016): 1103–1141; Mark A. R. Kleiman, "Swift-Certain-Fair: What Do We Know Now, and What Do We Need to Know?" *Criminology and Public Policy* 15 (2016): 1185–1193.

Probation is unquestionably undergoing dramatic changes. In many jurisdictions, traditional probation is being supplemented by **intermediate sanctions**, which are penalties that fall between traditional community supervision and confinement in jail or prison. These new correctional services are discussed in the following sections.

intermediate sanctions Punishments that fall between probation and prison ("probation plus"). Community-based sanctions, including house arrest and intensive supervision, serve as alternatives to incarceration.

Intermediate Sanctions

He may be willing to take a grenade for us, do the halftime show at the Super Bowl, and give us uptown funk, but will he do community service? Just a few days after winning the Grammy for "Best Male Pop Vocal Performance," Bruno Mars pleaded guilty to cocaine possession at a court in Las Vegas but was spared going to jail. His punishment was probation, a $2,000 fine, 200 hours of community service at a nonprofit organization, and eight hours with a drug counselor in Los Angeles.

Bruno Mars's sentence reflects the growing trend to add additional sanctions to traditional probation sentences; in his case, the sanctions were monetary fines and community service. These programs can be viewed as "probation plus" because they add restrictive penalties and conditions to traditional community service orders, which feature treatment and rehabilitation over control and restraint.[64] Here are some of the advantages of intermediate sanctions:

- They are less costly than jail or prison sentences.
- They help the offender maintain family and community ties.
- They can be structured to maximize security and maintain public safety.
- They can be scaled in severity to correspond to the seriousness of the crime.
- They can feature restoration and reintegration rather than punishment and ostracism.
- By siphoning off offenders from the secure correctional system, they reduce the need for future prison and jail construction.
- Intermediate sanctions help meet the need to develop community sentences that are fair, equitable, and proportional.[65]
- They can be designed to increase control over probationers whose serious or repeat crimes make a straight probation sentence inappropriate, yet for whom a prison sentence would be unduly harsh and counterproductive.[66]

L09 Explain what is meant by intermediate sanctions

AP Images/Jim Coe

Owen Labrie is escorted out of the Merrimack County Superior Courtroom in Concord, New Hampshire, after a judge agreed to new bail conditions. Labrie, a prep school graduate convicted of sexually assaulting a 15-year-old freshman girl as part of a game of sexual conquest called Senior Salute, will be required to use electronic monitoring via GPS.

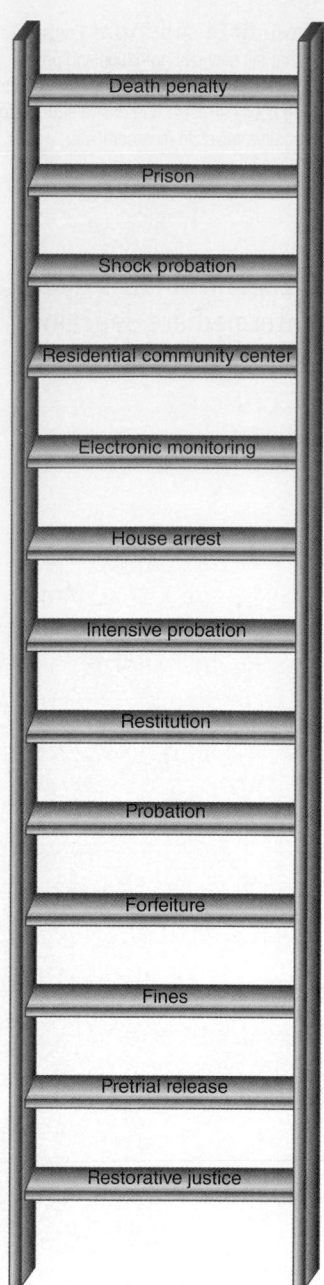

FIGURE 10.3 Punishment Ladder

Death penalty

Prison

Shock probation

Residential community center

Electronic monitoring

House arrest

Intensive probation

Restitution

Probation

Forfeiture

Fines

Pretrial release

Restorative justice

fines Money payments levied on offenders to compensate society for their misdeeds.

day fines Fines geared to the average daily income of the convicted offender in an effort to bring equity to the sentencing process.

forfeiture The seizure of personal property by the state as a civil or criminal penalty.

- Intermediate sanctions can potentially be used as halfway-back strategies for offenders who violate the conditions of their community release. Rule violators can be placed under increasingly more intensive supervision before actual incarceration is required.

Intermediate sanctions include programs that are usually administered by probation departments: intensive probation supervision, house arrest, electronic monitoring, restitution orders, shock probation or split sentences, and residential community corrections.[67] Intermediate sanctions also involve sentences that may be administered independently of probation: fines and forfeiture, pretrial programs, and pretrial and post-trial residential programs. Intermediate sanctions therefore range from the barely intrusive, such as restitution orders, to the highly restrictive, such as house arrest accompanied by electronic monitoring and a stay in a community correctional center.

As Figure 10.3 illustrates, intermediate sanctions can form the successive steps of a meaningful "ladder" of scaled punishments outside of prison, thereby restoring and equity to nonincarceration sentences.[68] Forgers may be ordered to make restitution to their victims, and rapists can be placed in a community facility and receive counseling at a local clinic. This feature of intermediate sanctions enables judges to fit the punishment to the crime without resorting to a prison sentence.

The forms of intermediate sanctions currently in use are more thoroughly discussed in the following sections.

Fines

Monetary payments, or **fines**, can be imposed on offenders as an intermediate punishment for their criminal acts. They are a direct offshoot of the early medieval practice of requiring that compensation (*wergild*) be paid to the victim and the state for criminal acts. Fines are still commonly used in Europe, where they are often the sole penalty, even in cases involving chronic offenders who commit fairly serious crimes.[69]

In the United States, fines are most commonly used in cases involving misdemeanors and lesser offenses. Fines are also frequently used in felony cases where the offender benefited financially.

Fines may be used as a sole sanction but are typically combined with other punishments, such as probation. Judges commonly levy other monetary sanctions along with fines, such as court costs, public defender fees, probation and treatment fees, and victim restitution, to increase the force of the financial punishment. However, evidence shows that many offenders fail to pay fines and that courts are negligent in their efforts to collect unpaid fees.[70]

In most jurisdictions, little guidance is given to the sentencing judge directing the imposition of the fine. Judges often have inadequate information on the offender's ability to pay, and this results in defaults and contempt charges. Because the standard sanction for nonpayment is incarceration, many offenders held in local jails are confined for nonpayment of criminal fines. Even though the US Supreme Court in *Tate v. Short* (1971) recognized that incarcerating a person who is financially unable to pay a fine discriminates against the poor, many judges continue to incarcerate offenders for noncompliance with financial orders.[71] To compensate for this disparity, some jurisdictions have experimented with **day fines** geared to an offender's net daily income. Used in Europe, day fines are designed to be equitable and fairly distributed, by being weighted by a daily-income value taken from a chart similar to an income tax table; the number of the offender's dependents is also taken into account. The day fine concept means that the severity of punishment is geared to the offender's ability to pay.[72]

Forfeiture

Another intermediate sanction with a financial basis is criminal (*in personam*) and civil (*in rem*) **forfeiture**. Both involve the seizure of goods and instrumentalities related to the commission or outcome of a criminal act. The difference is that criminal forfeiture proceedings target criminal defendants and can only follow a criminal conviction. In contrast, civil forfeiture proceedings target property used in a crime and do not require that formal criminal proceedings be initiated against a person or that the person be proved guilty of a crime.[73] Federal law provides that after arresting drug traffickers, the government may seize the boats they used to import the narcotics, the cars they used to carry the drugs overland, the warehouses in which the drugs were stored, and the homes paid for with the drug profits; on conviction, the drug dealers lose permanent ownership of these "instrumentalities" of crime.

Forfeiture is not a new sanction. During the Middle Ages, "forfeiture of estate" was a mandatory result of most felony convictions. The Crown could seize all of a felon's real and personal property. Forfeiture derived from the common-law concept of "corruption of blood," or "attaint," which prohibited a felon's family from inheriting or receiving his property or estate. The common law mandated that descendants could not inherit property from a relative who might have obtained the property illegally: "[T]he Corruption of Blood stops the Course of Regular Descent, as to Estates, over which the Criminal could have no Power, because he never enjoyed them."[74]

Forfeiture gained momentum in US law with the passage of the Racketeer Influenced and Corrupt Organization (RICO) Act and the Continuing Criminal Enterprises Act, both of which allow the seizure of any property derived from illegal enterprises or conspiracies. Although these acts were designed to apply to ongoing criminal conspiracies, such as drug or pornography rings, they are now being applied to a far-ranging series of criminal acts, including white-collar crimes. More than 100 federal statutes use forfeiture of property as a punishment.

Although law enforcement officials at first applauded the use of forfeiture as a hard-hitting way of seizing the illegal profits of drug law violators, the practice has been criticized because the government has often been overzealous in its application. For example, million-dollar yachts have been seized because someone aboard possessed a small amount of marijuana; this confiscatory practice is referred to as **zero tolerance**. This strict interpretation of the forfeiture statutes has come under fire because it is often used capriciously, the penalty is sometimes disproportionate to the crime involved, and it makes the government a "partner in crime."[75] It is also alleged that forfeiture unfairly targets a narrow range of offenders. For example, it is common for government employees involved in corruption to forfeit their pensions, but employees of public companies are exempt from such punishment.[76] There is also the issue of conflict of interest: because law enforcement agencies can use forfeited assets to supplement their budgets, they may direct their efforts to cases that promise the greatest "payoff" rather than to cases that have the highest law enforcement priority.[77]

Restitution

Another popular intermediate sanction is **restitution**, which can take the form of requiring offenders either to pay back the victims of crime (**monetary restitution**) or to serve the community to compensate for their criminal acts (**community service restitution**).[78] Restitution programs offer offenders a chance to avoid a jail or prison sentence or a lengthier probation period. The programs may help them develop a sense of allegiance to society, better work habits, and some degree of gratitude for being given a second chance. Restitution serves many other purposes, including giving the community something of value without asking it to foot the bill for an incarceration, and helping victims regain lost property and income.

If a defendant is sentenced to pay monetary restitution as part of her probation order, victim loss is determined, and a plan is developed for paying fair compensation. To avoid the situation in which a wealthy offender can fill a restitution order by merely writing a check, judges will sometimes order that compensation be paid out of income derived from a low-paid social service or public works job.

Community service orders usually require duty in a public nursing home, shelter, hospital, drug treatment unit, or works program; some young vandals may find that they must clean up the damage they caused to the school or the park. Judges and probation officers have embraced the concept of restitution because it appears to benefit

zero tolerance The practice of seizing all instrumentalities of a crime, including homes, boats, and cars. It is an extreme example of the law of forfeiture.

restitution A condition of probation in which the offender repays society or the victim of crime for the trouble and expense the offender caused.

monetary restitution A sanction requiring that convicted offenders compensate crime victims by reimbursing them for out-of-pocket losses caused by the crime. Losses can include property damage, lost wages, and medical costs.

community service restitution An alternative sanction that requires an offender to work in the community at such tasks as cleaning public parks or working with disabled children in lieu of an incarceration sentence.

Jonathan Todd Schwartz, right, former business manager for singer Alanis Morissette, looks on as his attorney Nathan Hochman addresses reporters outside a federal courthouse in Los Angeles following sentencing in Schwartz's embezzlement case. Schwartz was sentenced to six years in federal prison for stealing more than $7 million from the singer and other clients, and was ordered to pay $8.6 million in restitution.

the victim, the offender, the criminal justice system, and society.[79] Financial restitution is inexpensive to administer, helps avoid stigma, and provides some compensation for victims of crime. Helping them avoid a jail sentence can mean saving the public thousands of dollars that would have gone to maintaining them in a secure institution, frees up needed resources, and gives the community the feeling that equity has been restored to the justice system.

Does restitution work? Most reviews rate it as a qualified success. One evaluation of community service in Texas found that nearly three-fourths of offenders with community service orders met their obligations and completed community service work.[80] The Texas experience is not atypical; most restitution clients successfully complete their orders and have no subsequent contact with the justice system.[81]

Shock Probation and Split Sentencing

Shock probation and split sentences are alternative sanctions designed to allow judges to grant offenders community release only after they have sampled prison life. These sanctions are based on the premise that if offenders get a taste of incarceration sufficient to shock them into law-abiding behavior, they will be reluctant to violate the rules of probation or commit another crime.

In a number of states and in the Federal Criminal Code, a jail term can actually be a condition of probation, an arrangement known as split sentencing. About 10 percent of probationers are now given split sentences. The shock probation approach involves resentencing an offender to probation after a short prison stay. The shock comes because the offender originally received a long maximum sentence but is then eligible for release to community supervision at the discretion of the judge (usually within 90 days of incarceration).

Shock probation and split sentencing have been praised as ways to limit prison time, reintegrate the client quickly into the community, maintain family ties, and reduce prison populations and the costs of corrections.[82] An initial jail sentence probably makes offenders more receptive to the conditions of probation because it amply illustrates the problems they will face if probation is violated.

But split sentences and shock probation programs have been criticized by those who believe that even a brief period of incarceration can interfere with the purpose of probation, which is to provide the offender with nonstigmatizing, community-based treatment. Even a short-term commitment subjects probationers to the destructive effects of institutionalization, disrupts their life in the community, and stigmatizes them for having been in jail.

shock probation A sentence in which offenders serve a short prison term before they begin probation to impress them with the pains of imprisonment.

split sentences A practice that requires convicted criminals to spend a portion of their sentence behind bars and the remainder in the community.

Intensive Probation Supervision

Intensive probation supervision (IPS) programs, also referred to as intensive supervision probation, have been implemented in some form in about 40 states. IPS programs involve small caseloads of 15 to 40 clients who are kept under close watch by probation officers. IPS programs typically have three primary goals:

- *Decarceration.* Without intensive supervision, clients would normally be sent to already overcrowded prisons or jails.
- *Control.* High-risk offenders can be maintained in the community under much closer security than traditional probation efforts can provide.
- *Reintegration.* Offenders can maintain community ties and be reoriented toward a more productive life, while avoiding the pains of imprisonment.

In general, IPS programs rely on a great degree of client contact to achieve the goals of decarceration, control, and reintegration. Most programs have admissions criteria based on the nature of the offense and the offender's criminal background. Some programs exclude violent offenders; others will not take substance abusers. In contrast, some jurisdictions do not exclude offenders based on their prior criminal history.

IPS programs are used in several ways. In some states, IPS is a direct sentence imposed by a judge; in others, it is a postsentencing alternative used to divert offenders from the correctional system. A third practice is to use IPS as a case management tool to give the local probation staff flexibility in dealing with clients. Other jurisdictions use IPS in all three ways, in addition to applying it to probation violators to bring them halfway back into the community without resorting to a prison term.

EVALUATIONS OF IPS IPS programs are a mixed bag. IPS clients have a higher rearrest rate than other probationers. IPS clients may be perceived as more serious criminals who might otherwise have been incarcerated. Probation officers may also be more willing to revoke the probation of IPS clients because they believe these clients pose a greater risk to the community. Why risk the program to save a few "bad apples"? Some studies have found no differences in reoffending between intensive supervision clients and those subjected to regular supervision levels.[83]

Although these results are discouraging, other efforts do show more positive outcomes.[84] One recent evaluation conducted in probation departments in Iowa, Oklahoma, and Colorado found that reducing probation officer caseloads can reduce criminal recidivism. Reduced caseloads can lead to improved recidivism outcomes because officers are better able to identify treatment needs among their clientele, and thus better able to direct resources to those most in need.[85] Research also has found that IPS clients have better records than similar offenders who suffer incarceration.[86]

IPS seems to work better for some offenders than for others. Those with good employment records seem to do better than the underemployed or unemployed.[87] Younger offenders who commit petty crimes are the most likely to fail on IPS; ironically, people with these characteristics are the ones most likely to be included in IPS programs.[88]

IPS may also be more effective when it is combined with particular treatment modalities such as cognitive-behavioral treatment, which stresses such life skills as problem solving, social skills, negotiation skills, management of emotion, and values enhancement.[89]

House Arrest

When design guru and television personality Martha Stewart was released from prison in 2005 after serving time in an insider trading case, she was required to serve a five-month term of house arrest in which she could not leave home for more than 48 hours at a time and had to wear an electronic tracking device. Her sentence was not unique—except for the fact that her estate is so big that walking to the edges of the property put her out of range of her tracking device.

House arrest requires convicted offenders to spend extended periods of time in their own home as an alternative to an incarceration sentence. For example, persons convicted on a drunk-driving charge might be sentenced to spend between 6 P.M. Friday

intensive probation supervision (IPS) A type of intermediate sanction involving small probation caseloads and strict monitoring on a daily or weekly basis.

house arrest A form of intermediate sanction that requires the convicted offender to spend a designated amount of time per week in his or her own home—such as from 6 P.M. Friday until 8 A.M. Monday.

and 8 A.M. Monday and every weekday after 5:30 P.M. in their home for six months. According to current estimates, more than 10,000 people are under house arrest.

As with IPS programs, house arrest initiatives vary a great deal. Some are administered by probation departments, and others are simply judicial sentences monitored by surveillance officers. Some check clients 20 or more times a month, whereas others do only a few curfew checks. Some use 24-hour confinement; others allow offenders to attend work or school.

No definitive data indicate that house arrest is an effective crime deterrent, nor is there sufficient evidence to conclude that it has utility as a device to lower the recidivism rate. Existing data show that IPS recidivism rates are almost identical to a matched sample of inmates.[90] Although these findings are troublesome, the advantages of house arrest in reducing costs and overcrowding in the correctional system probably make further experimentation inevitable.

Electronic Monitoring

For house arrest to work, sentencing authorities must be assured that arrestees are actually at home during their assigned times. Random calls and visits are one way to check on compliance with house arrest orders. However, one of the more interesting developments in the criminal justice system has been the introduction of **electronic monitoring (EM)** devices to manage offender obedience to home-confinement orders.[91] Some use continuous signaling devices that are battery powered and transmit a radio signal two or more times per minute. They are placed on the offender's wrist or ankle with a tamper-resistant strap and must be worn at all times. A receiver detects the transmitter's signals and conveys a message via telephone report to a central computer when either it stops receiving the radio frequency or the signal resumes. When installed in a typical home environment, receivers can detect transmitter signals from a distance of 150 feet or more.

Electronic monitoring supporters claim EM has the benefits of relatively low cost and high security, while helping offenders avoid the pains of imprisonment in overcrowded, dangerous state facilities. Because offenders are monitored by computers, an initial investment in hardware eliminates the need for hiring many more supervisory officers to handle large numbers of clients. Due to its low cost and assumed effectiveness, EM is now being used with a wide variety of offenders, even those who have committed serious felony sex offenses.[92]

Another innovation is the field monitoring device, or "drive-by" units: probation officers use a portable device that can be handheld or used in a vehicle with a roof-mounted antenna. When within 200 to 800 feet of an offender's ankle or wrist transmitter, the portable device can detect the radio signals of the offender's transmitter.[93] These services are particularly important in domestic violence cases, where victims may not feel safe in their own home and are forced to flee to shelters.[94]

There is evidence that EM can be effective. Studies conducted in California and Florida show very positive results.[95] For example, when Kathy Padget and her associates evaluated data on more than 75,000 offenders placed on home confinement in Florida, they found that EM significantly reduces the likelihood of technical violations, reoffending, and absconding.[96] William Bales and his associates found strong empirical evidence that EM is an effective correctional strategy to divert offenders from prison and can also be used effectively as a form of postprison supervision. They conclude that the recent growth in the use of EM is beneficial and reduces threats to public safety, especially when combined with GPS tracking technology.[97] However, other studies found little evidence that EM can reduce recidivism, and, in some instances, it may have a negative effect.[98]

Global Positioning System (GPS) Monitoring

Effectively managing offenders within the community requires knowing what inmates are doing at all times and making sure they are not placing themselves in risky situations. GPS technology now enables authorities to monitor the geographic locale and conditions of release. For example, the system can be programmed to indicate a violation whenever a known sex offender approaches a school or a day care center.[99] Some GPS

electronic monitoring (EM)
Requiring convicted offenders to wear a monitoring device as part of their community sentence. Typically part of a house arrest order, this enables the probation department to ensure that offenders are complying with court-ordered limitations on their freedom.

A Surge in Electronic Offender Tracking

Electronic offender tracking is nothing new. Crude devices that used to report whether an offender left a particular location have been replaced with sophisticated GPS-tracking systems that can easily keep tabs on offenders' whereabouts at all times. And as with most technologies, it has become more accessible and cheap. This begs the question, is electronic offender tracking being used more often than it should be?

According to a recent Public Safety Performance Project study from the Pew Charitable Trusts, the answer may be yes. A 2015 survey revealed that the number of accused and convicted criminals placed on electronic monitoring increased nearly 140 percent in 10 short years, raising concerns over what many feel is an ever-widening criminal justice "net."

The Pew survey was innovative because rather than contacting local governments to ask about their supervision practices, it instead went to the companies that make and sell tracking devices. The researchers were able to survey enough companies to capture 96 percent of all electronic tracking devices sold in the past several years. And the companies are doing just fine! Some 53,000 devices were sold in 2005, but that number swelled to 125,000 in 2015.

The survey also showed that the greatest growth in electronic offender supervision occurred in the area of GPS technology; it accounted "for all of the 10-year growth in electronic tracking, more than offsetting a decline in the use of [older] RF devices," those that would simply inform authorities when a supervised individual left a particular location.

In fairness, it should be noted that electronic monitoring is still the exception when it comes to supervising released offenders. Nationally, nearly 3.8 million people were supervised in the community during 2015 (not including parole), so electronic monitoring seems to occur in just 3 to 4 percent of cases.

CRITICAL THINKING

1. Should electronic monitoring be used more or less?
2. What are the strengths and limitations of electronic monitoring? Do they differ based on the devices used?

Sources: The Pew Charitable Trusts, *Use of Electronic Offender-Tracking Devices Expands Sharply,* September 7, 2016, http://www.pewtrusts.org/en/research-and -analysis/issue-briefs/2016/09/use-of-electronic-offender-tracking-devices-expands -sharply (accessed May 2017); Danielle Kaeble and Lauren Glaze, *Correctional Populations in the United States, 2015* (Washington, DC: Bureau of Justice Statistics, 2016).

---

technology employs victim notification systems that alert the victim when the offender is approaching that person's residence. A transmitter is worn by both the offender and the victim, and a receiver is placed at both residences.

The Oklahoma Department of Corrections is now testing a GPS-based monitoring system called GeoShadow that uses GIS (geographic information system) to analyze patterns of movement of both individuals and groups within the community. GeoShadow is designed to let probation officers better assess an offender's location in the community, identify patterns that lead to problem behavior as it unfolds, and improve corrections-based GPS monitoring systems. Knowing an offender's movement patterns also helps assess treatment issues and make decisions about early intervention.[100]

See the accompanying Criminal Justice and Technology box for more on recent trends in the use of GPS (and other) tracking.

Residential Community Corrections

The most secure intermediate sanction is a sentence to a **residential community corrections (RCC)** facility. Such a facility has been defined as "a freestanding nonsecure building that is not part of a prison or jail and houses pretrial and adjudicated adults. The residents regularly depart to work, to attend school, and/or [to] participate in treatment activities and programs."[101]

Traditionally, the role of community corrections was played by the nonsecure halfway house, which was designed to reintegrate soon-to-be-paroled prison inmates into the community. Inmates spent the last few months of their sentence in the halfway house, acquiring suitable employment, building up cash reserves, obtaining an apartment, and developing a job-related wardrobe.

The traditional concept of community corrections has expanded. Today, the community correctional facility is a vehicle to provide intermediate sanctions as well as a prerelease center for those about to be paroled from the prison system. RCC has been used as a direct sentencing option for judges who believe particular offenders need a correctional alternative halfway between traditional probation and a stay in prison. Placement in an RCC center can be used as a condition of probation for offenders who need a nonsecure community facility that provides a more structured treatment environment

residential community corrections (RCC) A nonsecure facility, located in the community, that houses probationers who need a more secure environment. Typically, residents are free during the day to go to work, school, or treatment, and they return in the evening for counseling sessions and meals.

CONCEPT SUMMARY 10.1 Intermediate Sanctions

Sanction	Goal	Problems
Fines	Monetary sanction	Overburdens the poor
Forfeiture	Monetary sanction, equity	Can be overreaching
Restitution	Pay back victim	Does not reduce recidivism
Shock incarceration and split sentence	"Taste of bars" as a deterrent	Can cause labeling and stigma
Intensive probation	Small caseloads, more supervision	High failure rate
House arrest	Avoids jail	Lacks treatment possibility
Electronic monitoring	Supervision by computer	Technology-dependent, no treatment
Residential community	Less secure than prison	Expensive, high failure rate

than traditional probation. It is commonly used in the juvenile justice system for youths who need a more secure environment than can be provided by traditional probation yet are not deemed a threat to the community and do not require a secure placement.

More than 2,000 state-run community-based facilities are in use today. In addition, up to 2,500 private, nonprofit RCC programs operate in the United States. About half also house inmates who have been released from prison and use the RCC placement as a way to ease back into society. The remainder are true intermediate sanctions, including about 400 federally sponsored programs.

day reporting centers (DRCs)
Nonresidential community-based treatment programs.

DAY REPORTING CENTERS One recent development in community corrections has been the use of RCC facilities as **day reporting centers (DRCs)**.[102] These provide a single location to which a variety of clients can report for supervision and treatment. They can be used as a step up in security for probationers who have failed in the community and as a step down in security for jail or prison inmates.[103]

Evaluations show that DRCs can be successful at reducing recidivism.[104] DRCs seem to work better with certain types of offenders, such as those who are older and more experienced, than with others, such as younger offenders.[105] DRC participants with alcohol problems, criminal companions, and poor living situations are also more likely to fail. In contrast, those who receive counseling seem to do better.[106]

Concept Summary 10.1 sets out the goals and problems of the various forms of intermediate sanctions.

Restorative Justice Programs

LO10 Define restorative justice, and discuss its merits

restorative justice A view of criminal justice that advocates peaceful solutions and mediation rather than coercive punishments.

Some critics and specialists in criminal justice believe that the new alternative and intermediate sanctions add a punitive aspect to community sentencing that can hinder rehabilitation efforts. Instead, the advocates of **restorative justice** suggest a policy based on restoring the damage caused by crime and creating a system of justice that includes all the parties harmed by the criminal act: the victim, the offender, the community, and society.[107]

Restorative justice models are consistent with the thought of Australian justice expert John Braithwaite, who argues that crime control today involves shaming and stigmatizing offenders. This helps set them apart from normative society and undermines their potential for change. Instead, he calls for a policy of "reintegrative shaming." Here disapproval is limited to the offender's evil deeds. Law violators must be brought to realize that although their actions have caused harm, they are still valuable people—people who can be reaccepted by society. A critical element of reintegrative shaming occurs when the offenders themselves begin to understand and recognize their wrongdoing and shame. To be reintegrative, shaming must be brief and controlled, and it must be followed by ceremonies of forgiveness, apology, and repentance.[108] Braithwaite's work is at the core of the restorative justice movement.

The Concept of Restoration

According to the restorative view, crimes bring harm to the community in which they occur. The traditional justice system has done little to involve the community in the justice process. What has developed is a system of coercive punishments administered by bureaucrats that is inherently harmful to offenders and reduces the likelihood that they will ever again become productive members of society. This system relies on punishment, stigma, and disgrace. What is needed instead is a justice policy that repairs the harm caused by crime and involves all parties that have suffered from that harm, including the victim, the community, and the offender. Exhibit 10.1 sets out the principles of the restorative justice approach.

An important aspect of achieving these goals is that offenders must accept accountability for their actions and responsibility for the harm their actions caused. Only then can they be restored as productive members of their community. Restoration involves turning the justice system into a "healing" process rather than a distributor of retribution and revenge.

Most people involved in offender-victim relationships actually know one another or were related in some way before the criminal incident took place. Instead of treating one of the involved parties as a victim deserving sympathy and the other as a criminal deserving punishment, it is more productive to address the issues that produced the conflict between these people. Rather than taking sides and choosing whom to isolate and punish, society should try to reconcile the parties involved in conflict.[109] The effectiveness of justice ultimately depends on the stake a person has in the community (or a particular social group). If a person does not value her membership in the group, she will be unlikely to accept responsibility, show remorse, or repair the injuries caused by her actions.

EXHIBIT 10.1 Basic Principles of Restorative Justice

- Crime is an offense against human relationships.
- Victims and the community are central to justice processes.
- The first priority of justice processes is to assist victims.
- The second priority is to restore the community, to the greatest degree possible.
- The offender has a personal responsibility to victims and to the community for crimes committed.
- The offender will develop improved competency and understanding as a result of the restorative justice experience.
- Stakeholders share responsibilities for restorative justice through partnerships for action.

Source: Anne Seymour, "Restorative Justice/Community Justice," in the *National Victim Assistance Academy Textbook* (Washington, DC: National Victim Assistance Academy, 2001), updated June 2015.

WEB APP 10.2 There are many sources detailing restorative justice. A few sites that can help you learn more about this approach include the following: Restorative Justice Online, **http://www.restorativejustice.org**, and Eastern Mennonite University, Center for Justice and Peacebuilding, **http://www.emu.edu/cjp/restorative-justice/**.

Elijah Nouvelage/Reuters

Restorative justice programs can be aimed at the front end of the system as an alternative to incarceration, but can also be aimed at people already in the system. Here Manuel Zarate hugs his daughter Brittany and grandson Andrew Almodovar at the end of a "Get On the Bus" visiting day to Folsom State Prison arranged by the California Department of Corrections and Rehabilitation (CDCR) and the Center for Restorative Justice Works (CRJW) in Folsom, California. Buses with children and their caregivers traveled free of charge to two prisons, as part of an outreach program to reunite children with their incarcerated fathers.

Restoration Programs

Restoration programs try to include all the parties involved in a criminal act: the victim, the offender, and the community. Although processes differ in structure and style, they generally include the following:

- Recognition by offenders that they have caused injury to personal and social relations, and a determination and acceptance of responsibility (ideally accompanied by a statement of remorse)
- A commitment to both material reparation (e.g., monetary restitution) and symbolic reparation (e.g., an apology)
- A determination of community support and assistance for both victim and offender

The intended result of the process is to repair injuries suffered by the victim and the community, while ensuring reintegration of the offender.

Negotiation, mediation, consensus building, and peacemaking have been part of the dispute resolution process in European and Asian communities for centuries.[110] Native American people and members of Canada's First Nations have long used the type of community participation in the adjudication process (in sentencing circles, sentencing panels, and panels of elders) that restorative justice advocates are now embracing.[111]

In some Native American communities, people accused of breaking the law meet with community members, victims (if any), village elders, and agents of the justice system in a sentencing circle. All members of the circle express their feelings about the act that was committed and raise questions or concerns. The accused can express regret about his or her actions and a desire to change the harmful behavior. People may suggest ways in which the offender can make things up to the community and those who were harmed. A treatment program, such as Alcoholics Anonymous, may be suggested, if appropriate.

Restoration in Practice

Restorative justice policies and practices are now being adapted around the world. Restorative justice is being embraced on many levels in the justice system.

SCHOOLS Some schools have employed restorative justice practices to avoid more punitive measures such as expulsion in dealing with students involved in drug and alcohol abuse. Schools in Minnesota, Colorado, and elsewhere are trying to involve students in "relational rehabilitation" programs, which strive to improve offenders' relationships with key figures in the community who may have been harmed by their actions.[112]

POLICE PROGRAMS Restorative justice has also been implemented when police first encounter crime. The new community policing models can be viewed as an attempt to incorporate restorative concepts into law enforcement. Restorative justice relies on criminal justice policy makers listening to and responding to the needs of those who will be affected by their actions, and community policing relies on policies established with input and exchanges between officers and citizens.[113] The technique is also being used by police around the world. In England, police are using a format called restorative cautioning. After an arrest was made, police in England and Wales traditionally had four alternative procedures they could follow: (1) take no further action, (2) give an informal warning, (3) administer a formal police caution, or (4) decide to prosecute by sending the case to the Crown Prosecution Service. In the new restorative cautioning approach, a trained police facilitator uses a script to encourage an offender to take responsibility for repairing the harm caused by the offense. Sometimes the victim is present, in which case the meeting is called a restorative conference; usually, however, the victim is not present. Traditional cautioning, by contrast, lasts only a few minutes, requires no special training, and focuses on the officer explaining the possible consequences of future offending.[114]

PRETRIAL PROGRAMS Some jurisdictions have instituted restorative justice programs as a form of diversion from the court process. A popular restorative justice method is the family group conference, made up of the person who has committed the offense (usually a young first-time offender), members of his or her family and whomever the family invites, the victim(s) or their representative, a support person for the victim(s), a representative of the police, the mediator or manager of the process, and sometimes a social worker and/or a lawyer. The main goal of a conference is to formulate a plan about how best to deal with the offending. There are three principal components to this process:

- Ascertain whether or not the young person admits the offense; conferences only proceed if the young person does so or if the offense has been proved in the Youth Court.
- Share information among all the parties at the conference about the nature of the offense, the effects of the offense on the victims, the reasons for the offending, any prior offending by the young person, and so on.
- Decide the outcome or recommendation.

The family group conference is a meeting between those entitled to attend in a relatively informal setting. The room is usually arranged with comfortable chairs in a circle. When all are present, the meeting may open with a prayer or a blessing, depending on the customs of those involved. The coordinator then welcomes the participants, introduces each of them, and describes the purposes of the meeting. What happens next can vary, but usually the police representative then reads out the summary of the offense. The young person is asked if he or she agrees that this is what happened, and any variation is noted. If he or she does not agree, the meeting progresses no further, and the police may consider referring the case to the Youth Court for a hearing. Assuming the young person agrees, the victim or a spokesperson for the victim is then usually asked to describe what the events meant for them. Next, a general discussion of the offense and the circumstances underlying it occurs. There can be a lot of emotion expressed at this point. It is at this point, too, that the young person and his or her family may express their remorse for what has happened and make an apology to the victim, although more often this occurs later on. After everybody has discussed what the offending has meant and options for making good the damage, the professionals and the victim leave the family and the young person to meet privately to discuss what plans and recommendation they want to make to repair the damage and to prevent reoffending. The private family time can take as little as half an hour or much longer. When the family is ready, the others return, and the meeting is reconvened. This is the point at which the young person and the family usually apologize to the victim. A spokesperson for the family outlines what they propose, and all discuss the proposal. When there is agreement among all present, the details are formally recorded, and the conference concludes with the sharing of food.[115]

COURT PROGRAMS In the court system, restorative programs usually involve diverting the offender from the formal court process. Instead, these programs encourage meeting and reconciling the conflicts between offenders and victims via victim advocacy, mediation programs, and sentencing circles, in which crime victims and their families are brought together with offenders and their families in an effort to formulate a sanction that addresses the needs of each party. They can be quite effective.[116] Victims are given a chance to tell their stories, and offenders can help compensate them financially or provide some service (such as repairing damaged property).[117] Again, the goal is to enable offenders to appreciate the damage they have caused, to make amends, and to be reintegrated into society. Restorative justice has found a niche all over the world. It is even being used to resolve cases in the Middle East involving Arabs and Israelis![118]

The Challenge of Restorative Justice

Although restorative justice holds great promise, there are also some concerns.[119] One issue is whether programs reach out to all members of the community. Research indicates that entry into these programs may be tilted toward white offenders and more restrictive to minorities, a condition that negates the purpose of the restorative movement.[120]

Restorative justice programs must be especially aware of cultural and social differences, which can be found throughout America's heterogeneous society.[121] What may be considered restorative in one subculture may be considered insulting and damaging in another.[122] Similarly, so many diverse programs call themselves restorative that evaluating them is difficult. Each one may be pursuing a unique objective. In other words, no single definition of restorative justice has been arrived at.[123]

Possibly the greatest challenge to restorative justice is the difficult task of balancing the needs of offenders with those of their victims. If programs focus solely on responding to the victim's needs, they may risk ignoring the offender's needs and increasing the likelihood of reoffending. Advocates of restorative justice may falsely assume that relatively brief interludes of public shaming will change deeply rooted criminal predispositions.[124] But is it reasonable to include any form of punishment or sanction in a restorative-based program?[125]

In contrast, programs focusing on the offender may turn off victims and their advocates. Many victims do want an apology, if it is heartfelt and easy to get. But some want, even more urgently, to put the traumatic incident behind them, to retrieve stolen property being held for use at trial, and to be assured that the offender will receive treatment he is thought to need if he is not to victimize someone else. For victims such as these, restorative justice processes can seem unnecessary at best.[126]

ETHICALREFLECTION

Reflect back on the various community sanctions introduced throughout this chapter, then read this hypothetical:

Frank Fellman, the first-round draft choice of the local NFL team, was convicted for reckless endangerment. He was driving at 2 A.M. when he struck a young woman who was crossing an intersection; she suffered a broken leg. At trial, the evidence showed that the woman was legally drunk and had entered the intersection against the light. Fellman, who had a long history of battles with the law, was already under a probation order forbidding any misbehavior and imposing an 11 P.M. curfew. At a hearing, the presiding judge reminded him that he had been warned against any further violations and it had been made clear that violating the conditions of probation would not be tolerated. During the presentencing investigation, the probation department concluded that Fellman was not a danger, and his scores on the risk assessment scale used by the department found that minimum supervision probation would work in his case. Based on this evidence, the judge chose not to revoke his probation if he made restitution to the victim, surrendered his license, and wore an ankle bracelet tracking device. Because his probation was continued, Fellman would be able to attend training camp and not miss the season.

The news media got hold of the story and claimed that Fellman was being given an unfair advantage because he was an athlete. As a result of the public outcry, the judge reversed his decision and ordered Fellman to serve six months in jail. Fellman's lawyers have filed an emergency appeal, asking you, the appellate court judge, to grant him relief and suggesting (1) that the original sentence was overly harsh, and (2) the withdrawal of the house arrest order solely because of media attention was a violation of his due process rights.

Writing Challenge Write an essay on how you would deal with the case. In your paper, address whether you think Fellman should be jailed for his behavior even though his scores on a risk classification scale say otherwise. Should we trust these scales, or do they conflict with the ethical treatment of people convicted of crime? You may also want to address these issues: Is he being punished because of his status? How would the public be served by putting Fellman in jail and jeopardizing his career?

SUMMARY

LO1 *Explain the concept of community sentencing*
Community sentencing relies on the belief that the typical offender can be successfully treated while remaining in the community and, given the proper care and services, is unlikely to recidivate. A great variety of community sentences are in use now, ranging from traditional probation to house arrest and placement in community correctional centers.

LO2 *Describe the history of community sentences* The roots of community sentencing can be traced to the English common-law practice of judicial reprieve, which allowed judges to suspend punishment so that convicted offenders

could seek a pardon, gather new evidence, or demonstrate that they had reformed their behavior. John Augustus of Boston is usually credited with pioneering community sentencing in the United States when he voluntarily supervised young people convicted of crime, a practice that led to the modern probation concept.

LO3 *Define the different types of probation sentences*
Probationary sentences may be granted by state and federal district courts and state superior (felony) courts. Some are to a straight term of probation, while others involve a suspended sentence, a delayed sentence, or a mixed sentence involving a jail or prison stay.

LO4 *List the rules of probation* When granting probation, the court sets down certain conditions or rules of behavior that the probationer is bound to obey. Rules can set curfews, prohibit behaviors such as drinking and owning a gun, and/or mandate that the probationer hold a job and not leave the jurisdiction without permission. Probation may be revoked if clients fail to comply with rules and disobey reasonable requests to meet their treatment obligations.

LO5 *Explain the organization and administration of probation services* Some states have a statewide probation service, but each court jurisdiction controls its local department. Other states maintain a strong statewide authority with centralized control and administration.

LO6 *List and discuss the elements of a probation department's duties* Staff officers in probation departments are usually charged with five primary tasks: investigation, intake, diagnosis/risk classification, supervision, and treatment. As part of clients' entry into probation, an assessment is made about how much risk they pose to the community and themselves. On the basis of this assessment, offenders are assigned to a specific supervision level.

LO7 *Discuss the legal rights of probationers* The US Supreme Court has ruled that probationers have a unique status and therefore are entitled to fewer constitutional protections than other citizens. During the course of a probationary term, violating the rules or terms of probation or committing a new crime can result in probation being revoked.

LO8 *Debate the effectiveness of probation* Probation is cost-effective. Although the failure rate seems disturbingly high, even the most serious criminals who receive probation are less likely to recidivate than those who are sent to prison for committing similar crimes. Young males who are unemployed or who have a very low income, a prior criminal record, and a history of instability are most likely to be rearrested.

LO9 *Explain what is meant by intermediate sanctions* Intermediate sanctions add some other community sanction to a probation sentence, such as a fine, electronic monitoring, or house arrest. They offer effective alternatives to prisons and jails. They also have the potential to save money; although they are more expensive than traditional probation, they are far less costly than incarceration.

LO10 *Define restorative justice, and discuss its merits* Restorative programs stress healing and redemption rather than punishment and deterrence. Restoration means that offenders accept accountability for their actions and responsibility for the harm their actions caused. Restoration programs are now being used around the nation and involve mediation, sentencing circles, and similar nonpunitive treatment efforts.

KEY TERMS

probation, p. 246

judicial reprieve, p. 246

recognizance, p. 246

sureties, p. 246

probation rules, p. 247

revocation, p. 247

suspended sentence, p. 247

presentence investigation, p. 250

intake, p. 250

risk classification, p. 251

motivational interviewing, p. 252

day fees, p. 254

intermediate sanctions, p. 257

fines, p. 258

day fines, p. 258

forfeiture, p. 258

zero tolerance, p. 259

restitution, p. 259

monetary restitution, p. 259

community service restitution, p. 259

shock probation, p. 260

split sentences, p. 260

intensive probation supervision (IPS), p. 261

house arrest, p. 261

electronic monitoring (EM), p. 262

residential community corrections (RCC), p. 263

day reporting centers (DRCs), p. 264

restorative justice, p. 264

sentencing circle, p. 266

REVIEW QUESTIONS

1. What is the purpose of probation? Identify some conditions of probation, and discuss the responsibilities of the probation officer.

2. Discuss the procedures involved in probation revocation. What are the rights of the probationer? Is probation a privilege or a right?

3. Should a convicted criminal make restitution to the victim? When is restitution inappropriate? Could it be considered a bribe?

4. Should offenders be fined on the basis of the seriousness of what they did or in terms of their ability to pay?

Is it fair to base day fines on wages? Should offenders be punished more severely because they are financially successful?

5. Does house arrest involve a violation of personal freedom? Does wearing an ankle bracelet smack of "Big Brother"? Would you want the government monitoring your daily activities?

6. Do you agree that criminals can be restored through community interaction? Considering the fact that recidivism rates are so high, are traditional sanctions a waste of time, and are restorative methods the wave of the future?

Corrections
History, Institutions, and Populations

A correctional officer in New York's Attica prison was distributing mail to inmates in C Block when he became fazed by all the noise and disorder, and he ordered the inmates to quiet down. The inmates ignored the order, and one had the temerity to shout back "You shut up!" while taunting the officer with an obscene suggestion. After calm was restored and the inmates locked down, three officers went to the cell of George Williams, whom they suspected of being disrespectful. Williams, a 29-year-old African American, was serving a sentence of two to four years for robbing two jewelry stores in Manhattan and had just been transferred to Attica. He had only four months to go on his sentence and was trying to stay out of trouble; he was not even aware of what had gone on earlier. The guards ordered him to strip for a search and then marched him down the hall to an empty room where he assumed he would be asked to give a urine test. Instead, the three guards began pummeling Williams so severely that he suffered broken bones in his legs and face. Witnesses said he had been kicked up to 50 times and struck with a dozen more blows from nightsticks. Williams begged for his life and cried loudly enough that prisoners two floors below could hear his screams. Other guards were called in to join the beating.

Williams was brought to the prison infirmary, but because his injuries were so serious, he was subsequently taken to two local hospitals. All told, Williams suffered a broken shoulder, several cracked ribs, two broken legs, a severe fracture of the orbit surrounding his left eye, a large amount of blood lodged in his left maxillary sinus, and multiple cuts and bruises.

When medical personnel alerted state authorities, an investigation was conducted that led to charges of gang assault and evidence tampering against three corrections officers—Keith Swack, Sean Warner, and Matthew Rademacherbeing. Hoping to avoid a jail sentence, on March 5, 2015, the three pleaded guilty to misdemeanor charges of official misconduct.[1]

Damon winter/The New York Times/Redux

LEARNING OBJECTIVES

LO1 Explain how the first penal institutions developed in Europe and the United States

LO2 Compare the New York and Pennsylvania prison models

LO3 Chart the development of corrections from the nineteenth century to present

LO4 Explain the purposes of jails and the makeup of jail populations

LO5 Classify the different types of federal and state penal institutions

LO6 Discuss prison population trends

LO7 Summarize the varieties of alternative correctional institutions

LO8 Explain the issues surrounding private prisons

The Williams case aptly illustrates the brutality of prison life and the violence that is a routine occurrence in large maximum-security prisons. George Williams was just one of the more than 1.5 million inmates in a vast correctional system that has branches in the federal, state, and county levels of government.[2] Felons may be placed in state or federal penitentiaries (prisons), which are usually isolated, high-security structures. Misdemeanants are housed in local county jails, reformatories, or houses of correction. Juvenile offenders have their own institutions called schools, camps, ranches, or homes; these are typically nonsecure facilities that provide both confinement and rehabilitative services for young offenders and will be discussed further in Chapter 13.

The contemporary correctional system, then, encompasses a wide range of institutions ranging from nonsecure camps that house white-collar criminals to super-maximum-security institutions, such as the federal prison in Florence, Colorado, where the nation's most dangerous felons are confined.

One of the great tragedies of our time is that "correctional" institutions—whatever form they may take—do not seem to "correct," and many former inmates recidivate soon after reentering society. It can be reasonably estimated that more than half of all inmates will be back in prison within six years of their release; this means that each year, many thousands of former inmates return to prison because they failed on parole.

prisons State or federal correctional institutions for incarceration of felony offenders for terms of one year or more.

jails Places to detain people awaiting trial, to serve as a lockup for drunks and disorderly individuals, and to confine convicted misdemeanants serving sentences of less than one year.

A debate has been ongoing regarding the true role of secure corrections. Some penal experts maintain that **prisons** and **jails** should be used to keep dangerous offenders apart from society, dispensing "just deserts" for their crimes.[3] Under this model, correctional effectiveness is measured in terms of such outcomes as physical security, length of incapacitation, and inmates who return to society fearing criminal sanctions. An opposing view is that the purpose of corrections is treatment and that, when properly funded and effectively directed, correctional facilities can provide successful offender rehabilitation.[4] Numerous examples of successful treatment programs flourish in prisons. Educational programs enable inmates to get college credits, vocational training has become more sophisticated, counseling and substance abuse programs are almost universal, and every state maintains early-release and community correctional programs of some sort.

Today, the desert/incapacitation model, sometimes called the *new penology*, holds sway. Rather than administer individualized treatment, decision makers rely on actuarial tables and tests to make decisions; indeed, they seem more concerned with security and "managing" large inmate populations than with treating individual offenders.[5] Critics charge that this policy has resulted in a rapidly increasing prison population that is bereft of the human touch; defenders counter that it is effective because the crime rate declined at the same time that the number of people under lock and key began to significantly increase. Although the prison population has begun to decline, as a result of this 20-year prison boom, the United States today has the highest percentage of the population behind prison bars of any country in the Western world (458 per 100,000); in comparison, Germany has about 76 prisoners per 100,000 population, France 101, Japan 45, and India 33.[6]

Is there any point to this creation of mass incarceration in the United States? Although some experts believe it is responsible for the crime rate drop in America, others are still unsure. Police effectiveness and improving social conditions may be more important factors in lowering crime rates than the current prison boom.[7] Some, such as Ernest Drucker, go as far as to treat it as a plague on society, whose root can be traced back to the war on drugs and the unconscious desire to control the behavior of young minority males, who make up a disproportionate number of the drug offenders put behind bars.[8] In a widely read book, *The New Jim Crow*, Michelle Alexander also links the rise in the prison population to efforts by the government to marginalize young people of color at every stage of the justice system and then make it almost impossible for them to reform after their release.[9] She believes strong parallels can be drawn between what is being done today and the Jim Crow laws that created a racial caste systems of the past: racial stigma, shame, disenfranchisement, and legalized discrimination.

Even though the new penology dominates, correctional rehabilitation is still an important element of the justice system, and there are numerous opportunities for careers in such positions as corrections counselor, described in the Careers in Criminal Justice feature.

CAREERS IN CRIMINAL JUSTICE CORRECTIONS COUNSELOR

Duties and Characteristics of the Job

- The responsibility of corrections counselors is to review the situation of individual offenders and determine the most effective method of rehabilitation. They create, enact, manage, and sometimes evaluate programs designed to improve the psychosocial functions of offenders.
- Corrections counselors also provide counseling and educational sessions, survey the needs of offenders, and prepare reports for court.
- Counselors may choose a field of specialization, such as substance abuse or juvenile rehabilitation.
- They most often work in an office setting.
- Counseling can be a stressful job, given the population being served, the serious nature of inmate problems, and the pressure for immediate results.

Job Outlook

- The employment of counselors is expected to grow at a faster than average rate in the near future.
- The expansion of the prison system means that opportunities for employment as a corrections counselor are good.
- Thanks to high rates of turnover within the field, prospects for employment are very good. A corrections counselor with the proper education and training has the potential to find employment readily and to be promoted to administrative and supervisory positions. In addition, many openings will be created by the need to replace large numbers of these workers expected to retire in the coming years. For these reasons, job opportunities should be excellent for those who qualify.

Salary

- The median annual salary for correctional treatment specialists about $49,000; the highest 10 percent recently earned more than $86,000 per year.
- Higher wages tend to be found in urban areas, and those with graduate-level education are also more likely to have higher salaries and greater opportunities for advancement.

Qualifications

- Qualifications for higher-paid positions are more demanding. Education and work experience should familiarize the corrections counselor with the criminal justice system and prepare him or her for determining how to reduce a client's chances of recidivism, as well as how to deal with unwilling clients.
- The ability to speak more than one language is also an advantage.
- Personality characteristics and skills such as the desire to help others and the ability to communicate well are important.
- Because of the settings and populations counselors work with, a counselor will need to pass a background check and gain security clearance of the appropriate level.
- Some states also require certification before a corrections counselor can work in that state.

Education and Training

- Corrections counselors should have a bachelor's degree in a field such as social work, criminal justice, or psychology.
- Additional education at the master's level in these fields may be necessary to advance or to get certain positions.
- For some positions, clinical training can take the place of experience. Specialized skills such as expertise working with drug addiction or violent offenders can also lead to a higher-paying position.
- In addition to educational requirements, many entry-level jobs require some previous work experience, such as substance abuse counseling or corrections casework.

Reality Check

- Counselors should be prepared to work with needy, troubled people.
- Burnout can be a problem. It is important not to personalize the work or take it home.

Source: Bureau of Labor Statistics, *Probation Officers and Correctional Treatment Specialists Occupational Outlook Handbook*, http://www.bls.gov/ooh/community -and-social-service/probation-officers-and-correctional-treatment-specialists.htm (accessed May 2017).

In this chapter, we explore the correctional system, beginning with the history and nature of correctional institutions. Then, in Chapter 12, we will examine institutional life in some detail.

The History of Correctional Institutions

The original legal punishments were typically banishment or slavery, restitution, corporal punishment, and execution. The concept of incarcerating convicted offenders for long periods of time as a punishment for their misdeeds did not become the norm of corrections until the nineteenth century.[10]

Although the use of incarceration as a routine punishment began much later, some early European institutions were created specifically to detain and punish criminal offenders. Penal institutions were constructed in England during the tenth century to

LO1 Explain how the first penal institutions developed in Europe and the United States

hold pretrial detainees and those waiting for their sentence to be carried out.[11] During the twelfth century, King Henry II constructed a series of county jails to hold thieves and vagrants before the disposition of their sentence. In 1557, the workhouse in Brideswell was built to hold people convicted of relatively minor offenses who would work to pay off their debt to society. Those who had committed more serious offenses were held there pending execution.

Le Stinche, a prison in Florence, Italy, was used to punish offenders as early as 1301.[12] Prisoners were enclosed in separate cells, classified on the basis of gender, age, mental state, and seriousness of their crime. Furloughs and conditional release were permitted, and—perhaps for the first time—a period of incarceration replaced corporal punishment for some offenses. Although Le Stinche existed for 500 years, relatively little is known about its administration or whether this early example of incarceration was unique to Florence.

Jail conditions were deplorable because jailers ran them for personal gain. The fewer services provided, the greater their profit. Early jails were catchall institutions that held not only criminal offenders awaiting trial but also vagabonds, debtors, the mentally ill, and assorted others.

From 1776 to 1785, a growing inmate population that could no longer be transported to North America forced the English to house prisoners on **hulks**—abandoned ships anchored in harbors.

The hulks became infamous for their degrading conditions and brutal punishments but were not abandoned until 1858. The writings of John Howard, the reform-oriented sheriff of Bedfordshire, drew attention to the squalid conditions in British penal institutions. His famous book, *The State of the Prisons* (1777), condemned the lack of basic care given to English inmates awaiting trial or serving sentences.[13] Howard's efforts to create humane standards in the British penal system resulted in the Penitentiary Act, by which Parliament established a more orderly penal system, with periodic inspections, elimination of the fee system, and greater consideration for inmates.

The Origin of Corrections in the United States

Although Europe had jails and a variety of other penal facilities, correctional reform was first instituted in the United States. The first American jail was built in James City in the Virginia colony in the early seventeenth century. However, the modern American correctional system had its origin in Pennsylvania under the leadership of William Penn.

At the end of the seventeenth century, Penn revised Pennsylvania's criminal code to forbid torture and the capricious use of mutilation and physical punishment. These penalties were replaced with imprisonment at hard labor, moderate flogging, fines, and forfeiture of property. All lands and goods belonging to felons were to be used to make restitution to the victims of their crimes, with restitution being limited to twice the value of the damages. Felons who owned no property were assigned by law to the prison workhouse until the victim was compensated.

Penn ordered that a new type of institution be built to replace the widely used public forms of punishment—stocks, pillories, gallows, and branding irons. Each county was instructed to build a house of corrections similar to today's jails. County trustees or commissioners were responsible for raising money to build the jails and providing for their maintenance, although they were operated by the local sheriff. Penn's reforms remained in effect until his death in 1718, at which time the criminal penal code was changed back to open public punishment and harsh brutality.

One of the first American penal institutions was Newgate Prison, which opened in 1773 in Connecticut on the site of an abandoned copper mine and was in use until the 1820s.[14] In 1785, Castle Island prison was opened in Massachusetts and operated for about 15 years. The origin of the modern correctional system is usually traced to eighteenth-century developments.

Why did prisons develop at this time? One reason was that during this period of enlightenment, a concerted effort was made to alleviate the harsh punishments and torture that had been the norm. The interest of religious groups, such as the Quakers, in prison reform was prompted in part by humanitarian ideals. Another factor was the economic potential of prison industry, which was viewed as a valuable economic asset in times of short labor supply.[15]

In 1776, these trends led Pennsylvania once again to adopt William Penn's code, and, in 1787, a group of Quakers led by Benjamin Rush formed the Philadelphia Society for Alleviating the Miseries of Public Prisons. The aim of the society was to bring some degree of humane and orderly treatment to the growing penal system. The Quakers' influence on the legislature resulted in limiting the use of the death penalty to cases involving treason, murder, rape, or arson. Their next step was to reform the institutional system so that the prison could serve as a suitable alternative to physical punishment.

The only models of custodial institutions at that time were the local county jails that Penn had established. These facilities were designed to detain offenders, to securely incarcerate convicts awaiting other punishment, or to hold offenders who were working off their crimes. The Pennsylvania jails placed men, women, and children of all ages indiscriminately in one room. Liquor was often freely sold.

Under pressure from the Quakers to improve these conditions, the Pennsylvania legislature in 1790 called for the renovation of the prison system. The eventual result was the creation of a separate wing of Philadelphia's Walnut Street Jail to house convicted felons (except those sentenced to death). Prisoners were placed in solitary cells, where they remained in isolation and did not have the right to work.[16] Quarters that contained the solitary or separate cells were called the penitentiary house, as was already the custom in England.

The New York and Pennsylvania Systems

As the nineteenth century got under way, both the Pennsylvania and the New York prison systems were experiencing difficulties maintaining the ever-increasing numbers of convicted criminals. Initially, administrators dealt with the problem by increasing the use of pardons, relaxing prison discipline, and limiting supervision.

In 1816, New York built a new prison at Auburn, hoping to alleviate some of the overcrowding at Newgate. The Auburn Prison design became known as the congregate system because most prisoners ate and worked in groups. In 1819, construction began on a wing of solitary cells to house unruly prisoners. Three classes of prisoners were then created. One group remained continually in solitary confinement as a result of breaches of prison discipline, the second group was allowed labor as an occasional form of recreation, and the third and largest class worked together during the day and was separated only at night.

The philosophy of the Auburn prison system was crime prevention through fear of punishment and silent confinement. The worst felons were to be cut off from all contact with other prisoners, and although they were treated and fed relatively well, they had no hope of pardon to relieve their solitude or isolation. For a time, some of the worst convicts were forced to remain alone and silent during the entire day. This practice, which led to mental breakdowns, suicides, and self-mutilations, was abolished in 1823. The solution adopted at Auburn was to keep convicts in separate cells at night but allow them to work together during the day under enforced silence.

Regimentation became the standard mode of prison life. Convicts did not simply walk from place to place; instead, they went in close order and single file, each looking over the shoulder of the preceding person, faces inclined to the right, feet moving in unison. The lockstep prison shuffle was developed at Auburn and is still used in some institutions today.[17] The inmates' time was regulated by bells telling them when to wake up, work, and sleep. The system was so like the military that many of its early administrators were recruited from the armed services.

Sam Scholes/Moment/Getty Images

Pictured is death row at the Eastern State Penitentiary in Philadelphia, Pennsylvania. The prison was operational from 1829 until 1971 and used a "revolutionary" system of separate incarceration cells. When it was built, it was the largest and most expensive public structure in the world.

Walnut Street Jail An eighteenth-century institution that housed convicted criminals in Philadelphia.

penitentiary house Term used for early prisons, so named because inmates were supposed to feel penitence for their sins.

LO2 Compare the New York and Pennsylvania prison models

congregate system Prison system first used in New York that allowed inmates to engage in group activities such as work, meals, and recreation.

REALITYCHECK
Myth or Reality?
The first correctional institutions were actually considered a "liberal" reform.

REALITY. Although they might be considered a harsh form of punishment today, prisons were originally considered a humanitarian reform sponsored by religious groups.

Considering that recidivism rates are so high, should we embrace the treatment and rehabilitation elements of incarceration rather than focusing on prison as a means of dispensing punishment?

In 1818, Pennsylvania took the radical step of establishing a prison that placed each inmate in a single cell for the duration of his sentence. Classifications were abolished because each cell was intended as a miniature prison that would prevent the inmates from contaminating one another. The new Pennsylvania state prison, called the Western Penitentiary, had an unusual architectural design. It was built in a semicircle, with the cells positioned along its circumference. Built back to back, some cells faced the boundary wall, and others faced the internal area of the circle. Its inmates were kept in solitary confinement almost constantly, being allowed out for about an hour a day for exercise. In 1829, a second, similar penitentiary using the isolate system was built in Philadelphia and was called the Eastern Penitentiary.

Pennsylvania system The correctional model used in Pennsylvania that isolated inmates from one another to prevent them from planning escapes, to make them easy to manage, and to give them time to experience penitence.

Supporters of the **Pennsylvania system** believed that the penitentiary was truly a place to do penance. By removing the sinner from society and allowing the prisoner a period of isolation in which to consider the evils of crime, the Pennsylvania system reflected the influence of religion and religious philosophy on corrections. Its supporters believed that solitary confinement with in-cell labor would make work so attractive that upon release, the inmate would be well suited to resume a productive existence in society.

The Pennsylvania system eliminated the need for large numbers of guards or disciplinary measures. Isolated from one another, inmates could not plan escapes or collectively break rules. When discipline was a problem, however, the whip and the iron gag were used.

Advocates of the Auburn system believed that theirs was the cheapest and most productive way to reform prisoners and that solitary confinement as practiced in Pennsylvania was cruel and inhumane. In contrast, advocates of Pennsylvania's isolation model argued that their system was quiet, efficient, humane, and well ordered, yielding the ultimate correctional facility.[18] They considered the Auburn system a breeding place for criminal associations because it allowed inmates to get to know one another.

New York's congregate model eventually prevailed and spread throughout the United States. Many of its features are still used today. Its innovations included congregate working conditions, the use of solitary confinement to punish unruly inmates, military regimentation, and discipline. Concept Summary 11.1 describes the differences between these two prison systems.

Corrections in the Nineteenth Century

LO3 Chart the development of corrections from the nineteenth century to present

The prison of the nineteenth century was remarkably similar to that of today. The congregate system was adopted in all states except Pennsylvania. Prisons were overcrowded, and the single-cell principle was often ignored. Although the prison was viewed as an improvement over capital and corporal punishment, it quickly became the scene of depressed conditions. Inmates were treated harshly and routinely whipped and tortured. Prison brutality flourished in these institutions, which had originally been devised as a more humane correctional alternative. In these early penal institutions, brutal corporal punishment was doled out indoors where, hidden from public view, it could become even more savage.[19]

Prison industry developed and became the predominant theme around which institutions were organized. Some prisons used the **contract system**, in which officials sold the labor of inmates to private businesses. Sometimes the contractor supervised the inmates inside the prison itself. Under the **convict-lease system**, the state leased its prisoners to a business for a fixed annual fee and gave up supervision and control. Finally, some institutions had prisoners produce goods for the prison's own use.[20]

contract system The practice of correctional officials selling the labor of inmates to private businesses.

convict-lease system The practice of leasing inmates to a business for a fixed annual fee.

CONCEPT SUMMARY 11.1 Early Correctional Systems				
Prison	**Structure**	**Living Conditions**	**Activities**	**Discipline**
Auburn system	Tiered cells	Congregate	Group work	Silence, harsh punishment
Pennsylvania system	Single cells set in semicircle	Isolated	In-cell work, Bible study	Silence, harsh punishment

The development of prison industry quickly led to the abuse of inmates, who were forced to work for almost no wages, and to profiteering by dishonest administrators and business owners. During the Civil War era, prisons were major manufacturers of clothes, shoes, boots, furniture, and the like. Beginning in the 1870s, opposition by trade unions sparked restrictions on interstate commerce in prison goods. The prison, like the police department, became the scene of political intrigue and of efforts by political administrators to control the hiring of personnel and dispensing of patronage.

REFORM EFFORTS The National Congress of Penitentiary and Reformatory Discipline, held in Cincinnati in 1870, heralded a new era of prison reform. Organized by penologists Enoch Wines and Theodore Dwight, the Congress provided a forum for corrections experts from around the nation to call for the treatment, education, and training of inmates. By 1870, Zebulon Brockway, warden of the Elmira Reformatory in New York, advocated individualized treatment, the indeterminate sentence, and parole. The reformatory program initiated by Brockway included elementary education for illiterates, designated library hours, lectures by faculty members of the local Elmira College, and a group of vocational training shops. From 1888 to 1920, Elmira administrators used military-like training to discipline the inmates and organize the institution. The military organization could be seen in every aspect of the institution: schooling, manual training, sports, supervision of inmates, and even parole decisions.[21] The cost to the state of the institution's operations was to be held to a minimum.

THE DEVELOPMENT OF PAROLE In the early seventeenth century, English judges began to spare the lives of offenders by banishing them to the newly formed overseas colonies. In 1617, the Privy Counsel of the British Parliament standardized this practice by passing an order granting reprieves and stays of execution to convicts willing to be transported to the colonies. Transportation was viewed as an answer to labor shortages caused by war, disease, and the opening of new commercial markets.

In 1717, the British Parliament passed legislation embodying the concept of *property in service*, which transferred control of prisoners to a contractor or shipmaster until the expiration of their sentences. When the prisoners arrived in the colonies, their services could be resold to the highest bidder. After sale, an offender's status changed from convict to indentured servant.

Transportation quickly became the most common sentence for theft offenders. In the American colonies, property in service had to be abandoned after the revolution. Thereafter, Australia, claimed as a British colony in 1770, became the destination for most transported felons. From 1815 to 1850, large numbers of inmates were shipped to Australia to serve as indentured servants working for plantation owners, in mines, or on sheep stations.

The English Penal Servitude Act of 1853 all but ended transportation and substituted imprisonment as a punishment. Part of this act made it possible to grant a *ticket-of-leave* to those who had served a sufficient portion of their prison sentence. This form of conditional release permitted former prisoners to be at large in specified areas. The conditions of their release were written on a license that the former inmates were required to carry with them at all times. Conditions usually included sobriety, lawful behavior, and hard work. Many releasees violated these provisions, prompting criticism of the system. Eventually, members of prisoner aid societies helped supervise and care for releasees.

The concept of parole spread to the United States. As early as 1822, volunteers from the Philadelphia-based Society for Alleviating the Miseries of Public Prisons began to help offenders

This image shows the execution of a woman by electrocution in Sing Sing prison in Newburgh, New York, on April 9, 1899.

after they were released from prison. In 1851, the society appointed two agents to work with inmates discharged from Pennsylvania penal institutions. Massachusetts appointed an agent in 1845 to help released inmates obtain jobs, clothing, and transportation.

In the 1870s, using a carefully weighted screening procedure, Zebulon Brockway selected rehabilitated offenders from Elmira Reformatory for early release under the supervision of citizen volunteers known as *guardians*. The guardians met with the parolees at least once a month and submitted written reports on their progress. The parole concept spread rapidly. Ohio created the first parole agency in 1884. By 1901, as many as 20 states had created some type of parole agency. By 1927, only Florida, Mississippi, and Virginia had not established some sort of parole release. Parole had become institutionalized as the primary method of release for prison inmates, and half of all inmates released in the United States were paroled.[22]

Prisons in the Twentieth Century

The early twentieth century was a time of contrasts in the US prison system.[23] At one extreme were those who advocated reform, such as the Mutual Welfare League, led by Thomas Mott Osborne. Prison reform groups proposed better treatment for inmates, an end to harsh corporal punishment, the creation of meaningful prison industries, and educational programs. Reformers argued that prisoners should not be isolated from society and that the best elements of society—education, religion, meaningful work, and self-governance—should be brought to the prison. Osborne went so far as to spend a week in New York's notorious Sing Sing Prison to learn firsthand about its conditions.

In time, some of the more rigid prison rules gave way to liberal reform. By the mid-1930s, few prisons required inmates to wear the red-and-white-striped convict suit; nondescript gray uniforms were substituted. The code of silence ended, as did the lockstep shuffle. Prisoners were allowed "the freedom of the yard" to mingle and exercise an hour or two each day.[24] Movies and radio appeared in the 1930s. Visiting policies and mail privileges were liberalized.

A more important trend was the development of specialized prisons designed to treat particular types of offenders. In New York, for example, the prisons at Clinton and Auburn were viewed as industrial facilities for hard-core inmates, Great Meadow was an agricultural center for nondangerous offenders, and Dannemora was a facility for the criminally insane. In California, San Quentin housed inmates considered salvageable by correctional authorities, and Folsom was reserved for hard-core offenders.[25]

Prison industry also evolved. Opposition by organized labor helped put an end to the convict-lease system and forced inmate labor. By 1900, a number of states had restricted the sale of prisoner-made goods on the open market. The worldwide Great Depression, which began in 1929, prompted industry and union leaders to further pressure state legislators to reduce competition from prison industries. A series of ever more restrictive federal legislative initiatives led to the Sumners-Ashurst Act (1940), which made it a federal offense to transport interstate commerce goods made in prison for private use, regardless of the laws of the state receiving the goods.[26] The restrictions imposed by the federal government helped to severely curtail prison industry for 40 years. Private entrepreneurs shunned prison investments because they were no longer profitable. The result was inmate idleness and make-work jobs.[27]

Despite some changes and reforms, the prison in the mid-twentieth century remained a destructive total institution. Although some aspects of inmate life improved, severe discipline, harsh rules, and solitary confinement were the way of life in prison.

World Digital Library

Under the lease system, private companies would pay corrections officials for the services of inmates for farming, road construction, and other labor-intensive projects. This 1915 photo shows inmates who had been leased out to harvest timber in Florida.

Contemporary Correctional Institutions

The modern era has been a period of change and turmoil in the nation's correctional system. Three trends stand out. First, the prisoners' rights movement occurred between 1960 and 1980. After many years of indifference (the so-called "hands-off" doctrine), state and federal courts ruled in case after case that institutionalized inmates had rights to freedom of religion and speech, medical care, procedural due process, and proper living conditions. Inmates won rights unheard of in the nineteenth and early twentieth centuries. Since 1980, however, an increasingly conservative judiciary has curtailed the growth of inmate rights.

Second, violence within the correctional system became a national concern. Well-publicized riots at New York's Attica Prison and the New Mexico State Penitentiary drew attention to the potential for death and destruction that lurks in every prison. Prison rapes and killings have become commonplace. The locus of control in many prisons has shifted from the correctional staff to violent inmate gangs. In reaction, some administrators have tried to improve conditions and provide innovative programs that give inmates a voice in running the institution. Another reaction has been to tighten discipline and build new super-maximum-security prisons to control the most dangerous offenders. The problem of prison overcrowding has made efforts to improve conditions extremely difficult.

Third, the view that traditional correctional rehabilitation efforts have failed prompted many penologists to reconsider the purpose of incarcerating criminals. Between 1960 and 1980, it was common for correctional administrators to cling to the **medical model**, which viewed inmates as sick people who were suffering from some social malady that prevented them from adjusting to society. Correctional treatment could help cure them and enable them to live productive lives after they returned to the community. In the 1970s, efforts were also made to help offenders become reintegrated into society by providing them with new career opportunities that relied on work-release programs. Inmates were allowed to work outside the institution during the day and return in the evening. Some were given extended furloughs in the community. Work-release programs became a political issue when, in a famous incident, Willie Horton, a furloughed inmate from Massachusetts, raped a young woman. Criticism of the state's "liberal" furlough program helped Vice President George H. W. Bush defeat Massachusetts Governor Michael S. Dukakis for the US presidency in 1988. In the aftermath of the Horton case, a number of states, including Massachusetts, restricted their furlough policies.

medical model A correctional philosophy grounded on the belief that inmates are sick people who need treatment rather than punishment to help them reform.

Sakamaki/Redux

A guard at Eyman Prison in Florence, Arizona, keeps watch from a highly advanced control room from which he can immediately lock or open the doors on death row by using touch-screen technology.

penal harm A philosophy based on the belief that harsh treatment while serving a correctional sentence will convince offenders that crime does not pay, thereby lowering the chances of recidivism

Prisons have come to be viewed as places for control, incapacitation, and punishment, instead of sites for rehabilitation and reform. Advocates of the "no-frills," or **penal harm** movement believe that if prison is a punishing experience, would-be criminals will be deterred from committing crimes, and current inmates will be encouraged to go straight. Nonetheless, efforts to use correctional institutions as treatment facilities have not ended, and such innovations as the development of private industries on prison grounds have kept the rehabilitative ideal alive.

The pressure on correctional institutions caused by overpopulation and the burden of constantly increasing correctional costs have prompted the development of alternatives to incarceration, such as intensive probation supervision, house arrest, and electronic monitoring (refer to Chapter 10). What has developed is a dual correctional policy: keep as many nonviolent offenders out of the correctional system as possible by means of community-based programs, and incarcerate dangerous, violent offenders for long periods of time.[28] These efforts have been compromised by a growing get-tough stance in judicial and legislative sentencing policy, accented by mandatory minimum sentences for gun crimes and drug trafficking. More than 1.5 million people are still behind bars in prisons and jails despite the development of alternatives to incarceration and a two-decade-long decline in the crime rate.

The following sections review the most prominent types of correctional facilities in operation today.

Jails

LO4 Explain the purposes of jails and the makeup of jail populations

The nation's jails are institutional facilities with five primary purposes:

- Detain accused offenders who cannot make or are not eligible for bail prior to trial
- Hold convicted offenders who are awaiting sentence
- Serve as the principal institution of secure confinement for offenders convicted of misdemeanors
- Hold probationers and parolees picked up for violations and waiting for a hearing
- House felons when state prisons are overcrowded

A number of formats are used to jail offenders. About 15,000 local jurisdictions maintain short-term police or municipal lockups that house offenders for no more than 48 hours before a bail hearing can be held; thereafter, detainees are kept in the county jail.

Jail Populations and Trends

After rising for more than a decade, the number of people being held in America's more than 3,200 jails[29] began to decline in 2009, and there were about 728,000 jail inmates by 2015.[30] The jail incarceration rate—the confined population per 100,000 US residents—is now about 234 per 100,000, down from a 2007 high of 259 jail inmates per 100,000 residents. This recent downward trend in jail population may be a reflection of a declining US crime rate and greater reliance on alternatives to incarceration such as probation, electronic monitoring, and house arrest.

Who goes to jail? Although males outnumber females by a significant margin, the gap is narrowing. While the male population actually declined between 2010 and 2014, the female population increased nearly 20 percent (see Table 11.1).

Whites make up about 47 percent of the jail population, meaning that a disproportionate number of jail inmates are minority group members.[31] Disproportionate minority representation in jail may be caused, in part, by race-based disparity in sentencing practices. Research shows that black men have an increased likelihood of receiving jail sentences (as opposed to probation) compared to white men and women who commit similar crimes.[32]

Another reason may be linked to racial differences in the economy, which translates into racial differences in the ability to both personally meet bail and qualify for third-party loans (from bondsmen) in order to pay for bail. The inability to obtain bail can

TABLE 11.1 Gender Trends in Local Jail Populations

	Local jail	
	Males	**Females**
2000	550,162	70,987
2010	656,360	92,368
2014	635,500	109,100

Source: Lauren Glaze and Danielle Kaeble, *Correctional Populations in the United States, 2015,* US Department of Justice, 2016.

have long-term consequences: pretrial detainees tend to get longer prison sentences and are more likely to be incarcerated than those released on bail. The failure by minority group members to obtain bail may be the first step to subsequent overrepresentation in jail and prison.

At one time, many thousands of minor children were held in jails as runaways, truants, and so on. The number of juveniles held in adult jails has been in decline since 1995, a result of ongoing government initiatives to remove juveniles from adult facilities; nonetheless, about 4,200 minors are still being held in adult jails each day.[33]

Jail Conditions

Jails are usually a low-priority item in the criminal justice system. Because they are often administered on a county level, jail services have not been sufficiently regulated, nor has a unified national policy been developed to mandate what constitutes adequate jail conditions. Consequently, jails in some counties are physically deteriorated, holding dangerous and troubled people, many of whom suffer from emotional problems that remain untreated.

Suicide

Considering the fact that jails hold troubled people with substance abuse and mental health issues, it should come as no surprise that the percentage of jail inmates who take their own lives is higher than that of the general population. However, while jail conditions and jail suicides remain an important problem, a national survey conducted by the National Center on Institutions and Alternatives (NCIA) found a dramatic decrease in the rate of suicide in county jails during the past 20 years. The suicide rate in county jails was calculated to be 38 deaths per 100,000 inmates, which was approximately three times greater than that in the general population of the United States (at 11 deaths per 100,000 citizens), but about a 70 percent decrease from the 107 suicides per 100,000 inmates 20 years ago.[34] Why have jail suicides declined? One reason may be greater recognition of the problem and efforts to provide services to the jail population, a significant portion of whom have psychological and substance abuse problems and a history of past suicide attempts. Another possible answer may be found in the development of new-generation jails, discussed next.

New-Generation Jails

To relieve overcrowding and improve effectiveness, a jail-building boom has been under way. Many of the new jails are using modern designs referred to as "new-generation jails."[35] Traditional jails are constructed in what is referred to as the linear/intermittent surveillance model. Jails using this design are rectangular, with corridors leading to either single- or multiple-occupancy cells arranged at right angles to the corridor. Correctional officers must patrol to see into cells or housing areas, and when they are in a position to observe one cell, they cannot observe others; unobserved inmates are essentially unsupervised.

In contrast, new-generation jails allow for continuous observation of residents. There are two types: direct-supervision and indirect-supervision jails. Direct-supervision jails contain a cluster of cells surrounding a living area or "pod," which has tables, chairs, televisions, and other material. A correctional officer is stationed within the pod. The officer can observe the inmates continuously and is able to relate to them on a personal level. Placing the officer in the pod achieves an increased awareness of the behaviors and needs of the inmates. This results in a safer environment for both staff and inmates. Because interaction between inmates is constantly and closely monitored, dissension can be quickly detected before it escalates. During the day, inmates stay in the open area (dayroom) and typically are not permitted to go into their rooms except with permission of the officer in charge. The officer controls door locks to cells from the control panel. In case of trouble or if the officer leaves the station for an extended period of time, command of this panel can be switched to a panel at a remote location, known as central

Life is very slow for the more than 45 sex offenders living in one pod in the Los Angeles Twin Towers Jail. Laws concerning sexually violent predators allow authorities to keep sex offenders behind bars after they have served their time as they await civil trials that may result in their being committed to state mental hospitals. They sleep on bunk beds in a dorm type setting, but are allowed special privileges, such as newspapers to read, more television time, and additional personal items.

Carolyn Cole/Los Angeles Times/Getty Images

control. The officer usually wears a device that permits immediate communication with central control, and the area is also covered by a video camera monitored by an officer in the central control room. Indirect-supervision jails are similar in construction, but the correctional officer's station is located inside a secure room. Microphones and speakers inside the living unit permit the officer to hear and communicate with inmates.

Prisons

The prison is the final repository for the most troubled criminal offenders. Many come from distressed backgrounds and have little hope or opportunity; all too many have emotional problems and grew up in abusive households. A majority are alcohol and drug dependent at the time of their arrest. Those considered both dangerous and incorrigible may find themselves in super-maximum-security prisons, where they spend most of their days confined to their cells.

LO5 Classify the different types of federal and state penal institutions

Types of Prisons

More than 1,700 public adult correctional facilities are currently housing state prisoners. In addition, there are about 100 federal prisons and more than 100 privately run institutions.[36] Usually, prisons are organized or classified on three levels—maximum-, medium-, and minimum-security—and each has distinct characteristics.

maximum-security prisons
Correctional institutions that house dangerous felons and maintain strict security measures, high walls, and limited contact with the outside world.

MAXIMUM-SECURITY PRISONS Housing the most notorious criminals, and often the subject of films and stories, maximum-security prisons are probably the institutions most familiar to the public. Famous "max prisons" have included Sing Sing, Joliet, Attica, Walpole, and the most fearsome prison of all, the now-closed federal facility on Alcatraz Island, known as the Rock.

A typical maximum-security facility is fortress-like, surrounded by stone walls with guard towers at strategic places. These walls may be 25 feet high, and sometimes inner and outer walls divide the prison into courtyards. Barbed wire or electrified fences are used to discourage escape. High security, armed guards, and stone walls give the inmate the sense that the facility is impregnable and reassure the citizens outside that convicts will be completely incapacitated. Because they fear that violence may flair up at any minute, prison administrators have been quick to adapt the latest high-tech measures to help them maintain security, a topic covered in the Criminal Justice and Technology feature.

Technocorrections: Contemporary Correctional Technology

Technical experts have identified numerous areas of correctional management that can be aided by information technology (IT), including reception and commitment; sentence and time accounting; classification; caseload management; security; discipline; housing/bed management; medical services; grievances; programs; scheduling; investigations/gang management; property; trust accounting; visitation; release and discharge; and community supervision. Because IT can be applied in so many areas within correctional establishments, prison administrators have begun to take advantage of the potential offered by the new technologies. Following are a few examples of IT being used in prisons today.

All-in-One Drug Detection Spray

Mistral sprays are now being used and have proven effective at identifying drugs without adverse impact on the safe operation of the prison. Mistral's drug detection and identification system consists of four types of aerosol sprays and three types of test papers. Used in different combinations, the sprays and test papers can detect trace quantities of marijuana, methamphetamines, heroin, or cocaine.

Ground-Penetrating Radar

Ground-penetrating radar (GPR) can locate tunnels that inmates use to escape. GPR works almost like an old-fashioned Geiger counter, but instead of detecting metal, the system detects changes in ground composition, including voids such as those created by a tunnel.

Heartbeat Monitoring

Now it is possible to prevent escapes by monitoring inmates' heartbeats! The Advanced Vehicle Interrogation and Notification System (AVIAN) detects the presence of persons trying to escape by hiding in vehicles. Using the data from seismic sensors that are placed on the vehicle, the AVIAN reads the shock wave generated by the beating heart, which couples to any surface or object with which the body is in contact. It collects the data and analyzes it using advanced signal-processing algorithms in less than 15 seconds to detect a person hiding in a vehicle such as a large truck. The system works by accounting for all the frequencies of movement in the vehicle, such as the expansion and contraction of an engine or rain hitting the roof.

Backscatter Imaging System for Concealed Weapons

This system uses a backscatter imager to detect weapons and contraband. The primary advantage of this device over current walk-through portals is that it can detect nonmetallic as well as metallic weapons. It uses low-power x-rays equal to about five minutes of exposure to the sun at sea level. Although these x-rays penetrate clothing, they do not penetrate the body.

Body-Scanning Screening System

This is a stationary screening system to detect nonmetallic weapons and contraband in the lower body cavities. It uses simplified magnetic resonance imaging (MRI) as a noninvasive alternative to x-ray and physical body cavity searches. The stationary screening system makes use of first-generation medical MRI.

Personal Alarm Location System

It is now possible for prison employees to carry a tiny transmitter linking them with a computer in a central control room. In an emergency, they can hit an alarm button and transmit to a computer that automatically records whose distress button has been pushed. An architectural map of the facility instantly appears on screen, showing the exact location of the staff member in need of assistance.

Biometric Recognition

A new biometric system uses facial recognition by matching more than 200 individual points on the human face with a digitally stored image. The system is used to control access in buildings and rooms inside buildings. It is now available and will become much more common in the near future.

Monitoring Trouble Spots

The Correctional Operational Trend Analysis System (COTAS) is used to monitor places by predicting potential trouble spots within prisons. Knowing ahead of time where trouble might arise lets managers assign extra staff or take other actions that can prevent violence and other problems. The system manages information that lets all levels of managers monitor cross-functional operations quickly. COTAS can identify trends, patterns, and areas of concerns within specific individual institutions and statewide.

Suicide Warning System

An automated suicide warning system has been developed as a cost-effective, noninvasive approach to behavior monitoring. This radar-based system can measure an inmate's heart rate, breathing rate, and body motions without being attached to the individual. The system consists of the following:

- "Personal health status" sensors that can be enclosed in a box on the ceiling to remotely and noninvasively monitor inmates' pulse and breathing
- Network connections to remote monitors
- Software designed to interpret motion data and create a decision tree for whom to notify officers

A wall-mounted range controlled radar (RCR) system—originally designed for home security motion detectors—measures subtle motions on the body's surface caused by heart and lung activity. Alarms are activated when the system detects suspicious changes in heart rate, breathing rate, or body motion. A key feature of the device is that it is less obtrusive. Inmates are prone to tamper with or destroy monitoring devices, but a device that does not require physical contact with the prisoner could make tampering or destruction less likely. Automated monitoring technology provides continuous surveillance to supplement the visual inspections and alert officers quickly to any attempt. By installing these devices, prisons are able to reduce the number of officers needed to monitor prisoners, freeing staff for other corrections tasks.

CRITICAL THINKING

1. Some elements of technocorrections intrude on the privacy of inmates. Should the need for security outweigh an inmate's right to privacy?
2. Should probationers and parolees be monitored with modern technology? Do they deserve more privacy than incarcerated inmates?

Sources: CorrectionsOne.com, *Prison Technology*, https://www.correctionsone.com/prison-technology/; National Institute of Justice, "Predicting Trouble Spots Within Prisons," http://www.nij.gov/nij/topics/corrections/institutional/monitoring-inmates/predicting-trouble.htm; National Institute of Justice, "Suicide Watch Technologies Could Improve Monitoring, Reduce Staff Time," http://nij.gov/topics/corrections/institutional/monitoring-inmates/pages/suicide-watch.aspx; National Institute of Justice, "Detecting Drugs on Surfaces Quickly and Easily," http://nij.gov/topics/corrections/institutional/contraband/Pages/drug-detection.aspx. (URLs accessed May 2017.)

Inmates live in interior, metal-barred cells that contain their own plumbing and sanitary facilities and are locked securely either by key or by electronic device. Cells are organized in sections called blocks, and, in large prisons, a number of cell blocks make up a wing. During the day, the inmates engage in closely controlled activities: meals, workshops, education, and so on. Rule violators may be confined to their cells or spend time in solitary confinement; and working and other shared recreational activities are viewed as privileges.

The byword of the maximum-security prison is "security." Correctional workers are made aware that each inmate may be a dangerous criminal or violent, and, as a result, the utmost security must be maintained. These prisons are designed to eliminate hidden corners where people can congregate, and passages are constructed so that they can be easily blocked off to quell disturbances.

WEB APP 11.1 To read about the harsh life in a supermax prison, go to **http://www.npr.org /2012/06/21/155513749/the-grim -realities-of-life-in-supermax -prisons**. Are supermax prisons essentially damaging to inmates, and should they be abolished?

SUPER-MAXIMUM-SECURITY PRISONS Some states have constructed **super-maximum-security prisons** (supermax prisons) to house the most predatory criminals. These high-security institutions can be independent correctional centers or locked wings of existing prisons.[37] Some supermax prisons lock inmates in their cells 22 to 24 hours a day, never allowing them out unless they are shackled.[38]

The 490-bed facility in Florence, Colorado, has the most sophisticated security measures in the United States, including 168 video cameras and 1,400 electronically controlled gates. Inside the cells, all furniture is unmovable; the desk, bed, and TV stand are made of cement. All potential weapons, including soap dishes, toilet seats, and toilet handles, have been removed. The cement walls are 5,000-pound quality, and steel bars crisscross every eight inches inside the walls. Cells are angled so that inmates can see neither each other nor the outside. This cuts down on communication and denies inmates a sense of location to prevent escapes.

Despite the fact that supermax prisons such as Florence have gotten mixed reviews, they are now being used around the world.[39] Some critics believe that they infringe directly on the rights of inmates because they deprive them of such basic rights such as human contact; they also eliminate any opportunity for rehabilitation.[40] Others claim that a disproportionate number of minority group members are being held in these institutions under extremely harsh conditions.[41] Keramet Reiter argues that while supermaxes are technologically advanced, they are intentionally designed to limit all physical, human contact because they contain "the worst of the worst prisoners"—those too violent and dangerous to live in a general prison population. The unintended consequence of this draconian regime is the creation of violence. Supermaxes, she concludes, are a novel and uniquely modern form of state violence, and their legal and ethical implications should be reconsidered.[42]

Some of the most important research on supermax prisons has been conducted by Daniel Mears and his colleagues. In one study, Mears, along with Jamie Watson, found that supermax prisons may actually enhance the quality of life of inmates and consequently improve their mental health.[43] They increase privacy, reduce danger, and even provide creature comforts (such as TV sets) that are unavailable in general-population prisons. Staff report less stress and fear because they have to contend with fewer disruptive inmates.

On the other hand, Mears has found that supermax prisons also have some unintended negative consequences. Staff may have too much control over inmates—a condition that damages staff–inmate relationships. Long hours of isolation may be associated with mental illness and psychological disturbances. Supermax inmates seem to have a more difficult time readjusting upon release. A stay in a supermax prison inhibits reintegration into other prisons, communities, and families. In one study that examined data from the Florida Department of Corrections, Mears, along with William Bales, found that supermax incarceration may increase violent recidivism.[44] Mears and colleague Jennifer Castro also surveyed wardens and found that even though they seem to favor supermax prisons, they also expressed concern that the general public consider supermax institutions inhumane, that they drain limited funds from state budgets, and that they produce increases in litigation and court interventions, as well as increased recidivism and reentry failure among released inmates.[45]

MEDIUM-SECURITY PRISONS Although they are similar in appearance to maximum-security prisons, in medium-security prisons, the security and atmosphere are neither so tense nor so vigilant. Medium-security prisons are also surrounded by walls, but there may be fewer guard towers or other security precautions; visitations with personal contact may be allowed. Although most prisoners are housed in cells, individual honor rooms in medium-security prisons are used to reward those who make exemplary rehabilitation efforts. Finally, medium-security prisons promote greater treatment efforts, and the relaxed atmosphere allows freedom of movement for rehabilitation workers and other therapeutic personnel.

MINIMUM-SECURITY PRISONS Operating without armed guards or perimeter walls, minimum-security prisons usually house the most trustworthy and least violent offenders; white-collar criminals may be the most common occupants. Inmates are allowed a great deal of personal freedom. Instead of being marched to activities by guards, they are summoned by bells or loudspeaker announcements, and they assemble on their own. Work furloughs and educational releases are encouraged, and vocational training is of the highest level. Dress codes are lax, and inmates are allowed to grow beards or mustaches and to demonstrate other individual characteristics.

Minimum-security facilities may have dormitories or small private rooms for inmates. Prisoners are allowed to own personal possessions that might be deemed dangerous in a maximum-security prison, such as radios.

Minimum-security prisons have been criticized for being like "country clubs"; some federal facilities for white-collar criminals even have tennis courts and pools (they are derisively called "Club Fed"). Yet they remain prisons, and the isolation and loneliness of prison life deeply affects the inmates.

Inmate Population Trends

America's vast correctional system, with more than 2,000 public and private institutions, now contains nearly 1.6 million inmates in the state and federal prison systems.[46] As Figure 11.1 shows, after decades of sharp increases, the imprisonment rate peaked in 2009 and has since declined (save for a slight uptick in 2013). In 2015, the most recent year for which data were available at the time of this writing, the imprisonment rate for US residents of all ages was 471 sentenced prisoners per 100,000.

LO6 Discuss prison population trends

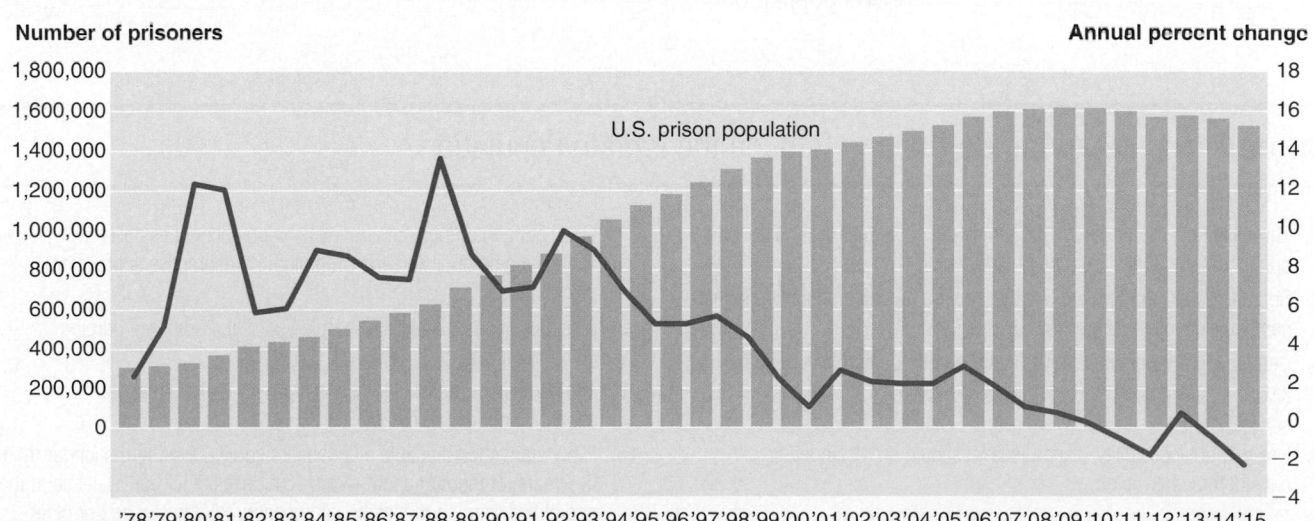

Number of prisoners — U.S. prison population — Annual percent change

'78 '79 '80 '81 '82 '83 '84 '85 '86 '87 '88 '89 '90 '91 '92 '93 '94 '95 '96 '97 '98 '99 '00 '01 '02 '03 '04 '05 '06 '07 '08 '09 '10 '11 '12 '13 '14 '15

Note: Jurisdiction refers to the legal authority of state or federal correctional officials over a prisoner, regardless of where the prisoner is held.

FIGURE 11.1 Prisoners Under the Jurisdiction of State or Federal Correctional Authorities, December 31, 1978–2015
Source: E. Ann Carson, *Prisoners in 2015*, Bureau of Justice Statistics, 2016.

Although any decline in the prison population is welcome, a disconnect remains between the significant drop in the crime rate and the more modest reduction in the imprisonment rate. What are the causes of this disjunction?

- Many people who are released from prison soon return after failing on parole and other forms of early release. Hence, a significant portion of the prison population is made up of reentries.
- Criminal legislation, including guideline-based mandatory-minimum sentencing laws, increases the chances that a convicted offender will be incarcerated and limits the availability of early release via parole.[47]
- The amount of time served in prison has increased because of such developments as truth-in-sentencing laws that require inmates to serve at least 85 percent of their sentences behind bars. Although truth-in-sentencing funding has ended, its effects are still being felt. Between 1990 and 2012, the number of inmates who maxed out their sentences in prison grew 119 percent, from fewer than 50,000 to more than 100,000. More than 40 percent of inmates maxed out their prison terms and left without supervision in Florida, Maine, Massachusetts, New Jersey, North Carolina, Ohio, Oklahoma, South Carolina, and Utah.[48]
- There is a significant association among drug use, drug arrests, and prison overcrowding.[49] The drug epidemic in the 1980s and 1990s helped swell prison populations with people serving very long sentences.

While the prison inmate population has stabilized, there are still far too many people in prison. In Exhibit 11.1, legal scholar Michael Tonry sets out a 10-point plan to reduce the prison population. Indeed, several states have adopted reforms consistent with Tonry's views. The California experience is featured in the accompanying Contemporary Issues in Criminal Justice box.

Profile of the Prison Inmate

Who makes up this population? Prison inmates are disproportionately young, male, minority group members, and poor.

RACE African Americans make up the largest portion of male inmates compared to whites and Hispanics. The black imprisonment rate is 2,228 per 100,000 US residents over 18 compared to 1,084 per 100,000 for Hispanics and 319 per 100,000 for whites.[50] Clearly, the racial disparity in the sentencing process results in similar disparity in the prison population.

EXHIBIT 11.1 What Can Be Done to Reduce the Inmate Population?

1. Three-strikes, mandatory minimum sentence, and similar sentencing enhancement laws should be abolished.
2. Sentencing enhancement laws that are not repealed should be significantly narrowed in range and severity.
3. Sentencing enhancement laws that are not repealed should authorize judges to grant another lesser sentence when it's "in the interest of justice."
4. Life-without-possibility-of-parole laws should be rescinded or considerably narrowed.
5. The use of truth-in-sentencing laws should be ended.
6. Criminal codes should be changed to set considerably lower maximum sentences that correspond more closely to the seriousness of crimes.
7. Every state that does not already have one should establish a sentencing commission and promulgate presumptive sentencing guidelines.
8. All states should establish a parole board and employ a parole guidelines system.
9. The combined rate of federal and state jail and prison populations should be cut in half by 2020.
10. Every state should enable all prisoners serving fixed terms longer than five years, or indeterminate terms, to be eligible for early release at the end of five years, and making all prisoners 35 years of age or older eligible for parole after serving three years.

Source: Michael Tonry, "Remodeling American Sentencing: A Ten-Step Blueprint for Moving Past Mass Incarceration," *Criminology and Public Policy* 13 (2014): 503–533.

Is Prison Downsizing Dangerous?

The US prison population seems to be in slow decline. Data reported in this chapter suggest as much. Not all states have seen shrinkages, but the majority have. Indeed, four states—New Jersey, New York, Rhode Island, and California—have reduced their prison populations by 20 percent. Even some Southern states, which are traditionally harsh on crime, have reduced their prison populations. Mississippi and South Carolina have reduced their prison populations by 18 and 11 percent, respectively.

What is behind the reductions? One obvious answer is the high cost of incarceration. In response, most states have adopted reforms intended to reduce mandatory minimum sentencing. For example, California voters approved initiatives in 2012 and 2016 to reduce prison populations. The 2012 initiative reformed the state's punitive three-strikes law. The 2016 initiative expanded parole eligibility and placed limits on trying juveniles as adults. Voters in the Golden State also authorized changes in the way certain offenses were classified.

At its peak in 2006, California had nearly 175,000 inmates behind bars in the state's 33 prisons. In 2008, it was ranked second in the nation in prison spending. Many of its prisons exceeded capacity by as much as 300 percent. These developments led Governor Arnold Schwarzenegger to declare a "Prison Overcrowding State of Emergency." The deplorable conditions in California's prisons prompted a three-judge panel to decide they violated the Eighth Amendment's prohibition against cruel and unusual punishment. And in 2011, the US Supreme Court, in *Brown v. Plata*, affirmed the lower court's decision and ordered California to reduce its prison capacity by 137 percent, which translated into about 33,000 inmates. In response, Governor Jerry Brown signed into law the California Public Safety Realignment Act. The act moved several felons from state prisons to state jails, changed parole rules, and reformed the way in which probation and parole technical violations were dealt with.

Some would say California did what it had to do. But what effect did realignment have on crime? Wouldn't releasing inmates, especially those convicted of serious crimes, lead to a surge in crime? These are empirical questions. In an interesting study, Jody Sundt and her colleagues compared crime trends in California to those from the population of all 50 states. The results of various statistical models revealed that realignment had no effect on crime in multiple time periods. This prompted the researchers to conclude:

> Significant reductions in the size of prison populations are possible without endangering public safety. Within just 15 months of its passage, realignment reduced the size of the total prison population by 27,527 inmates, prison crowding declined from 181 percent to 150 percent of design capacity, approximately $453 million was saved, and there was no adverse effect on the overall safety of Californians. With a mixture of jail use, community corrections, law enforcement and other preventive efforts, California counties have provided a comparable level of public safety to that previously achieved by state prisons.

In fairness, few studies have examined the effects of realignment. It is likely that more time and study are necessary before we can conclude with certainty that California's approach to reducing prison populations was successful. But other researchers, such as Magnus Lofstrom and Steven Raphael at the Public Policy Institute of California, *have* reached similar conclusions, so perhaps it is high time to get "smarter" with incarceration.

CRITICAL THINKING

1. Should other states replicate California's realignment initiative? Why or why not?
2. How should parole be reformed to reduce prison populations?
3. Will a new presidential administration resurrect tough-on-crime policies and lead to future surges in the incarcerated population?

Sources: The Sentencing Project, *Repurposing: New Beginnings for Closed Prisons*, http://www.sentencingproject.org/wp-content/uploads/2016/12/Repurposing-New-Beginnings-for-Closed-Prisons.pdf (accessed May 2017); Jody Sundt, Emily J. Salisbury, and Mark G. Harmon, "Is Downsizing Prisons Dangerous? The Effect of California's Realignment Act on Public Safety," *Criminology and Public Policy* 15 (2016): 315–341; Magnus Lofstrom and Steven Raphael, "Incarceration and Crime: Evidence from California's Public Safety Realignment Reform," *Annals of the American Academy of Political and Social Science* 664 (2016): 196–220.

Prisoners from Sacramento County await processing after arriving at the Deuel Vocational Institution in Tracy, California. Corrections officials say they are adopting new sentencing rules that aim to trim the state prison population by nearly 9,500 inmates within four years. The regulations released on March 24, 2017, include steps like reducing sentences by up to six months for earning a college degree and by up to a month each year for participating in self-help programs such as drug counseling.

AGE AND GENDER As of 2015, there were about 104,000 female inmates, or 7 percent of the total. Also, inmates tend to be relatively young. About 12 percent are under 24 years or age, and another 17 percent are aged 30 to 34. In contrast, 2 percent are aged 65 or older. Although the inmate population is generally young, long prison sentences for some crimes have created an ongoing problem of the elderly inmate, which is discussed in the Contemporary Issues in Criminal Justice feature.

OFFENSE About half of all inmates in state prisons are serving sentences for violent offenses, and about 20 percent for property offenses. Murder is the most common violent offense among state prisoners, followed by robbery and rape or sexual assault. A higher percentage of males (54 percent) are imprisoned for violent offenses than females (36 percent).

SOCIAL PROBLEMS Many inmates suffer from multiple social problems: they are undereducated, underemployed, and come from abusive homes. A significant number experienced homelessness (living on the street or in a homeless shelter) and other related social problems, including mental illness, substance abuse, and unemployment just before their incarceration.[51] For these reasons, it is not surprising when surveys show that inmates suffer from serious psychological and emotional problems, including psychosis and major depression.[52]

CONTEMPORARY ISSUES IN CRIMINAL JUSTICE

Elderly Inmates

The population of elderly prisoners in the United States has increased by more than 1,400 percent since 1981. Three decades ago, American prisons housed fewer than 9,000 prisoners age 55 and older; today, that number stands at 156,000. By 2040, the elderly prisoner population may top 400,000.

The care of the elderly is extremely expensive. Inmates over 50 are more likely to have health and mental health problems than noninstitutionalized Americans because they often come from poor backgrounds, have a greater likelihood of drug and alcohol abuse, and have more restricted access to health care. Many suffer from chronic illnesses such as hypertension, asthma or other lung disease, and arthritis. National studies find that nearly 40 percent of state inmates 55 and older have a recent history of mental health problems or disorders. It is not surprising, then, that the average cost of housing an inmate over 60 is $70,000 a year, which is about three times the average cost for other prisoners. More than $16 billion is now being spent annually caring for these aging inmates, and this amount is expected to grow dramatically as their numbers rise.

The aging of the prison population has come about from longer sentences resulting from the get-tough-on-crime measures that impose truth-in-sentencing, mandatory sentences, and three-strikes laws, as well as an increasing number of older people convicted of sex crimes and murder.

There are different adjustment rates for elderly prisoners. The longer the amount of time remaining to be served, the harder it usually is for the elderly person to deal with confinement. Background factors, such as level of education and marital status, can also affect the adjustment of the elderly. Some inmates, especially those imprisoned early in life, are more institutionally dependent than others. Some have higher morale and are more involved in programs and prison life than others. In many prisons, however, there is little programming or specialized treatment geared for elderly inmates. The elderly prisoner is vulnerable to victimization and requires special attention when it comes to medical treatment, housing, nutrition, and institutional activities.

What Can Be Done?

Some states are now contracting with private nursing homes to care for some of their elderly and disabled inmates under so-called "medical parole" programs. However, there has been resistance to this form of early release, and not all private facilities have been willing to accept elderly inmates. Connecticut has asked the commercial nursing home industry to create unique, nonsecure facilities that hold prison inmates and patients from the state mental hospital who require long-term nursing care. This way, the inmates are not sharing a room with noncriminals. Other states, including Michigan, Kentucky, and Wisconsin, are considering this approach.

CRITICAL THINKING

1. Older prisoners need more orderly conditions, safety precautions, emotional feedback, and familial support than younger prisoners. They are particularly uncomfortable in crowded conditions, tend to prefer small groups, and want time alone. Should they be housed in traditional prisons, no matter what they have done in the past?

2. Would community-based institutions be a more suitable alternative?

Sources: The Marshall Project, *Aging Inmates*, https://www.themarshallproject.org/records/251-aging-inmates; Christine Vestal, "For Aging Inmates, Care Outside Prison Walls," *Kaiser Health News*, http://khn.org/news/for-aging-inmates-care-outside-prison-walls/; B. Williams, M. Stern, J. Mellow, M. Safer, and R. B. Greifinger, "Aging in Correctional Custody: Setting a Policy Agenda for Older Prisoner Health Care," *American of Journal Public Health* 102 (2012): 1475–1481; D. J. James and L. E. Glaze, *Mental Health Problems of Prison and Jail Inmates* (Washington, DC: Bureau of Justice Statistics, 2006); Anthony A. Sterns and Greta Lax, "The Growing Wave of Older Prisoners: A National Survey of Older Prisoner Health, Mental Health and Programming," *Corrections Today* 70 (August 2008): 70–76 (URLs accessed May 2017).

Alternative Correctional Institutions

In addition to prisons and jails, a number of other correctional institutions are operating within the United States. Some have been in use for quite some time, whereas others have been developed more recently as part of innovative or experimental programs.

L07 Summarize the varieties of alternative correctional institutions

Prison Farms and Camps

Prison farms and camps are used to detain offenders. These types of facilities are found primarily in the South and the West and have been in operation since the nineteenth century. Today, more than 100 facilities (vocational training centers, ranches, and so on) exist in the nation. Prisoners on farms produce dairy products, grain, and vegetable crops that are used in the state correctional system and other governmental facilities, such as hospitals and schools. Forestry camp inmates maintain state parks, fight forest fires, and do reforestation work. Ranches, primarily a western phenomenon, employ inmates in cattle raising and horse breeding, among other activities. Road gangs repair roads and state highways.

Shock Incarceration in Boot Camps

Another correctional innovation that gained popularity in the 1980s and 1990s, the **boot camp**, housed youthful, first-time offenders in military discipline and physical training. The concept is that short periods (90 to 180 days) of high-intensity exercise and work will "shock" the inmate into going straight. Tough physical training is designed to promote responsibility and improve decision-making skills, build self-confidence, and teach socialization skills. Inmates are treated with rough intensity by drillmasters who may call them names and punish the entire group for the failure of one member.[53]

Some programs also include educational and training components, counseling sessions, and treatment for special-needs populations, whereas others devote little or no time to therapeutic activities. Some allow voluntary participation, and others allow voluntary termination.[54]

Empirical research has not supported boot camp effectiveness.[55] There is little evidence that boot camps can significantly lower recidivism rates. Because of these sketchy results, the federal government and most state correctional authorities have closed their boot camp programs, and relatively few remain in operation.[56]

boot camp A short-term militaristic correctional facility in which inmates undergo intensive physical conditioning and discipline.

Reuters

John Cook, an inmate at the State of New York Wallkill Correctional Facility, pets a retired thoroughbred on a prison farm. The Second Chances program that teaches horsemanship skills to inmates marked its 30th anniversary at the Wallkill Correctional Institute. Wallkill was the first prison to house retired racehorses, and it has served as a model for nine other correctional facilities now practicing the program.

Legal scholar Alexander Volokh has proposed a novel approach to improve prisons: create a voucher system. School vouchers have been used to allow parents to choose which school to send their children, with the aim of improving school quality by transforming students and parents into consumers. Volokh asks, what if we did the same for prisons? What if convicted criminals could choose their prison rather than being assigned by a correctional authority? Under his voucher system, prisons would compete for prisoners, with the result that prisons would adopt policies prisoners value. Prisons would become more constitutionally flexible—for example, allowing for more faith-based programs—and would also have increased freedom to offer valued benefits in exchange for the waiver of constitutional rights. As far as prison quality goes, the advantages of vouchers would plausibly include greater security, higher-quality health care, and better educational opportunities—features that prison reformers favor for their rehabilitative value. The counterarguments are threefold: (1) allowing inmates to choose their prison is either impossible or morally undesirable; (2) due to informational or other problems, prisoner choice would not succeed in improving overall prison quality; (3) prison quality might improve too much, diluting the deterrent value of prison. Although Volokh believes these counterarguments have substantial force, he believes they do not foreclose the possibility that prison choice could result in socially desirable improvements that could outweigh these disadvantages.

Writing Challenge: Reflect back on this chapter's discussion of private vs. public prisons and write an essay discussing the ethics of a prison voucher system. Are they really similar to school vouchers? If the purpose of prisons is to dispense punishment, is it ethical to allow people to choose their own penalty?

Source: Alexander Volokh, "Prison Vouchers," *University of Pennsylvania Law Review* 160 (2012): 779–863.

SUMMARY

L01 *Explain how the first penal institutions developed in Europe and the United States* Although the routine use of incarceration as a criminal punishment began in the late eighteenth and early nineteenth centuries, some early European institutions were created specifically to detain and punish criminal offenders. The "modern" American correctional system had its origins in Pennsylvania under the leadership of William Penn. Penn created Philadelphia's Walnut Street Jail, which was used to house convicted felons, except those sentenced to death. He believed inmates could be reformed through work and religious training.

L02 *Compare the New York and Pennsylvania prison models* In 1816, New York built a new prison at Auburn that used the congregate system, in which most prisoners ate and worked in groups. In contrast, Pennsylvania established a prison that placed each inmate in a single cell for the duration of his sentence. By the late nineteenth century, the congregate system was adopted in all states except Pennsylvania.

L03 *Chart the development of corrections from the nineteenth century to present* The National Congress of Penitentiary and Reformatory Discipline, held in Cincinnati in 1870, heralded a new era of prison reform. Another important trend was the development of specialized prisons designed to treat particular types of offenders. Parole, specialized prisons, and prison industries also evolved during this period. The modern era has been a period of change and turmoil in the nation's correctional system.

L04 *Explain the purposes of jails and the makeup of jail populations* The nation's jails are institutional facilities used to detain accused offenders who cannot make or are not eligible for bail prior to trial and to hold convicted offenders awaiting sentence. They serve as the principal institution of secure confinement for offenders convicted of misdemeanors.

L05 *Classify the different types of federal and state penal institutions* Maximum-security prisons housing the most notorious criminals are fortress-like, surrounded by stone walls with guard towers at strategic places. Some states have constructed super-maximum-security prisons (supermax prisons) to house the most predatory criminals. Similar in appearance to maximum-security prisons, medium-security prisons are characterized by less vigilant security provisions and a less tense atmosphere. Operating without armed guards or perimeter walls, minimum-security prisons usually house the most trustworthy and least violent offenders.

L06 *Discuss prison population trends* After years of rapid growth, the inmate population has finally stabilized. The population is still high despite the nation's crime drop, most likely because tough new criminal legislation, including mandatory sentencing laws, increased the chances that a convicted offender will be incarcerated and limited the availability for early release via parole. The recent stabilization in the prison population may be temporary; if the crime rate increases, so too will the number of inmates.

L07 *Summarize the varieties of alternative correctional institutions* In addition to prisons and jails, a number of other correctional institutions are operating within the United States. Prison farms, camps, and ranches are popular throughout the United States. Boot camps became popular in the 1980s and 1990s, but have mostly fallen out of favor in recent years. Numerous community correctional facilities called halfway houses also hold inmates just before their release.

LO8 *Explain the issues surrounding private prisons*
Privately run prisons are increasingly common throughout the United States. In some instances, a private corporation will finance and build an institution and then contract with correctional authorities to provide services for convicted criminals. Sometimes the private concern will finance and build the institution and then lease it outright to the government. There is no clear and convincing scientific evidence that private prisons perform any better or worse than government-run prisons. Nevertheless, some private service providers have been sued for perceived inadequate services.

KEY TERMS

prisons, p. 272

jails, p. 272

hulks, p. 274

Walnut Street Jail, p. 275

penitentiary house, p. 275

congregate system, p. 275

Pennsylvania system, p. 276

contract system, p. 276

convict-lease system, p. 276

medical model, p. 279

penal harm, p. 280

maximum-security prisons, p. 282

super-maximum-security prisons, p. 284

medium-security prisons, p. 285

minimum-security prisons, p. 285

boot camp, p. 289

halfway houses, p. 290

REVIEW QUESTIONS

1. Would you allow a community correctional center to be built in your neighborhood?

2. Should pretrial detainees and convicted offenders be kept in the same institution?

3. Should inmates be allowed to choose the type of prison in which they serve their sentence?

4. Should private companies be allowed to run correctional institutions?

5. What are the drawbacks to shock incarceration?

6. Should the elderly be housed in the same institutions as younger inmates?

12 Prison Life
Living in and Leaving Prison

After several prior altercations with his daughter's live-in boyfriend, 53-year-old Orville Lee Wollard reached his breaking point. He came home one day to find his daughter Sarah on the family's front porch with a black eye; the boyfriend, Austin O'Hara, was inside. Wollard grabbed his gun, pointed it at O'Hara, and told him to leave. Instead of complying, O'Hara punched a hole in the wall, smiled at Wollard, and then began advancing toward him. "It was either shoot him or fire a warning shot, but I couldn't let him have the gun," Wollard recounted.[1] He then fired a bullet into a nearby wall. No one was hurt and O'Hara left. No calls to police were made until several weeks later, when O'Hara called the police to report that Wollard had shot a gun at him. Wollard was arrested and charged with aggravated assault with a firearm.

Wollard spent a year in county jail prior to his trial, then prosecutors offered him a deal: plead guilty to a felony and be sentenced to five years' probation or let a jury decide the proper punishment. He chose the latter, pleading not guilty. At trial he was not permitted to bring up details about his prior run-ins with O'Hara; he was only permitted to say the boy was "no longer welcome." The jury ended up rejecting Wollard's self-defense claim and found him guilty. The judge—and even the officer who prepared Wollard's sentencing report— felt extenuating circumstances justified leniency (even the prosecutors felt probation was appropriate!), but the case triggered Florida's 10–20-Life gun law and Wollard was sentenced to 20 years in prison. Twenty years in prison for firing a warning shot.[2] On the day of his sentencing, Wollard expressed shock:

> I'm amazed. I'm stunned. I have spent my whole life pursuing education [and] helping the community. Then one day this person ... assaults my daughter, he threatens me. I protect myself. No one injured in this whole thing and I'm going to prison and the drug dealer's on the street. And again, with all respect to [the court], I would expect this from the former Soviet Union ... not the United States.[3]

A few years into his sentence, Wollard filed a petition for commutation of his sentence, asking the state's Board of Clemency to release him. A hearing was granted. Board members included the governor, Rick Scott, the attorney

AP Images/Loren Elliott

LEARNING OBJECTIVES

LO1 Discuss the male prison experience

LO2 Describe the inmate social code and inmate culture

LO3 Summarize the female prison experience

LO4 Discuss the different forms of correctional treatment

LO5 Describe the world of correctional officers

LO6 Discuss the causes of prison violence

LO7 Explain what is meant by prisoners' rights, and discuss some key privileges that have been granted to inmates

LO8 Discuss the parole process and the problems of prisoner reentry

general, and two other elected officials, all Republicans. Under Florida rules, the governor's vote is the most important; even if the other three board members favor release, the governor must also agree. Eighteen minutes into the commutation hearing, Governor Scott said, "I deny commutation of sentence." That was on September 30, 2015.

Wollard remains in prison to this day, but lawmakers have taken notice. As of this writing, a proposed change to Florida's 10-20-Life statute is making its way through the state legislature.[4] Sponsored by Rep. Neil Combee, a Republican, the bill would eliminate aggravated assault from the list of crimes that trigger mandatory minimums and reduce the sentence for that offense to three years. Were Wollard's case isolated, a change to the law because of one individual could be seen as unnecessary; however, according to the Florida Department of Corrections, 167 other inmates are serving 20-year sentences for aggravated assaults in which there was no intention to kill.[5]

Wollard continues to hold out hope that he will be released, but he has come to grips with the fact he may not get out of prison until he is in his 70s: "It's too late for any of that," he said. "Even if I got out tomorrow, that's nice. But the career's gone, the house is gone, everything's gone. The family's split all over the four winds of the earth." "I'm already dead," he said. "I just haven't fallen over yet."[6]

Is it ethical and fair to put a person like Wollard in prison for 20 years? Unfortunately, his trials are not unique. America relies heavily on incarceration. While the inmate population has been in recent decline, there are still about 1.5 million people in prison in the United States.[7] As a result of this policy of mass incarceration, the nation has undergone a prison-building boom: there were 568 state prisons in 1979, 957 in 1990, and there are more than 1,700 as of the most recent prison census.[8] These facilities take a variety of forms, including prisons, prison hospitals, prison farms, and boot camps; centers for reception, classification, or alcohol and drug treatment; and work release centers.[9] Not all prisons are brand new: 25 were built before 1875, 79 between 1875 and 1924, and 141 between 1925 and 1949. In fact, some of the first prisons ever constructed, such as the Concord Reformatory in Massachusetts, are still in operation.

Although most prisons are classified as medium-security, more than half of all inmates are held in large maximum-security institutions. Despite the continuous outcry by penologists against the use of fortress-like prisons, institutions holding 1,000 or more inmates still predominate.

Many of these institutions are also operating above stated capacity. Recreation and workshop space has been turned into dormitories housing 30 or more inmates in a single room. And, rather than rehabilitating their residents, penal institutions seem to exacerbate their criminal tendencies. It is popular to describe the typical prison as a "school for crime" in which young offenders are taught by older cons to become sophisticated criminals.

This chapter presents a brief review of some of the most important issues confronting the nation's troubled correctional system, including inmate life, treatment strategies, inmate legal rights, and release from prison.

L01 Discuss the male prison experience

Men Imprisoned

total institutions Regimented, dehumanizing institutions such as prison, in which inmates are kept in social isolation, cut off from the world at large.

Prisons in the United States are total institutions. This means that inmates locked within their walls are segregated from the outside world, kept under constant surveillance, and forced to obey strict official rules to avoid facing formal sanctions. Their personal possessions are taken from them, and they must conform to institutional norms of dress and personal appearance. Many human functions are strictly curtailed; heterosexual sex, friendships, family relationships, education, and participation in group activities become privileges of the past.

An inmate's first experience most often occurs in a classification or reception center, where inmates are given a series of psychological and other tests and evaluated on the basis of their personality, background, offense history, and treatment needs. On the basis of the classification they are given, they are assigned to a permanent facility. Hardcore, repeat, and violent offenders will go to the maximum-security unit; white-collar, non-dangerous offenders may qualify for a minimum-security facility; mentally disordered offenders will be held in a facility that can provide psychiatric care; and so on. Today, sophisticated classification instruments are used to maximize the effectiveness of placements, thereby cutting down on the cost of incarceration.[10] When they arrive at prison, inmates are stripped, searched, shorn, and assigned living quarters. They quickly learn what the term *total institution* really means. Inmate turned author James A. Paluch Jr. calls his cell a "cold coffin . . . leaving a chilling effect on anyone forced to live inside them."[11] Those with extremely long prison sentences—for example, life without parole— may lose hope and develop significant psychological disorders.[12]

Newcomers swiftly discover that all previous concepts of personal privacy and dignity are soon forgotten. Inmates in large, inaccessible prisons may find themselves physically cut off from families, friends, and associates. Visitors may find it difficult to travel great distances to see them; mail is censored and sometimes destroyed. And while incarcerated, inmates are forced to associate with a peer group afflicted with a disproportionate share of mental and physical problems. Various communicable diseases are commonly found, such as hepatitis C virus, HIV, and syphilis. Not surprisingly, inmate health is significantly worse than that of the general population.[13] Personal losses include the deprivation of liberty, goods and services, heterosexual relationships, autonomy, and security.[14] Inmates, even tough guys like Tommy Silverstein, may be subject to verbal and physical attack and threats, with little chance of legal redress. Overcrowded prisons are filled with young, aggressive men who are responsible for the majority of inmate-on-inmate assaults.[15]

Inmates may find that some prisoners have formed cliques, or groups, based on ethnic backgrounds or personal interests; they are also likely to encounter Mafia-like or racial terror groups that must be dealt with. Inmates may find that power in the prison is shared by correctional officers and inmate gangs; the only way to avoid being beaten and raped may be to learn how to beat and rape.

Some prisoners, especially the most vulnerable, become the target of charismatic leaders seeking to recruit them to some cause or group. Angry and embittered by their circumstances and separated from their families, these vulnerable inmates are looking for meaning and identity. Some inmates are so alienated from social life that they fall prey to radical antigovernment groups that have their own hierarchy, code of conduct, secret communication system, and collective identity.

But not all inmates are radicalized or have what it take to join radical cells. If they are weak and unable to defend themselves, new inmates may find that they are considered "punks"; if they ask a guard for help, they are labeled a "snitch." Those most likely to be targets of sexual assaults may spend their sentence in protective custody, sacrificing the "freedom of the yard" and rehabilitation services for personal protection.[16]

 **WEB APP 12.1** Read about supermax inmate Thomas Silverstein's experience in prison at **https://thomassilverstein.wordpress.com/**.

Coping in Prison

Despite all these hardships, many inmates learn to adapt to the prison routine. Each prisoner has his own method of coping. He may stay alone, become friends with another inmate, join a group, or seek the advice of treatment personnel. Inmates soon learn that their lifestyle and activities can contribute to their being victimized by more aggressive inmates. The more time they spend in closely guarded activities, the less likely they are to become the victims of violence. The more they isolate themselves from others who might protect them, the greater their vulnerability to attack. The more visitors they receive, the more likely they are to be attacked by fellow inmates jealous of their relationships with the outside world.[17]

Some learn how to fight back to prove they cannot be bullied. Older, more experienced men are better able to cope with the prison experience; younger inmates, especially juveniles sent to adult prisons, are more likely to participate in violent episodes.[18]

Men who viewed violence as an acceptable method of settling disputes before entering prison are the ones most likely to use violence while they are inmates.[19] Inmates who have a history of prearrest drug use and have been incarcerated for violent crimes are the ones most likely to get involved in assaults and drug/alcohol offenses while they are incarcerated.[20] Survival in prison may depend on one's ability to identify troubled inmates and avoid contact.

Sexual Coercion

Scott Howard, a 39-year-old federal prisoner, went to Washington to testify before a congressional committee about his experiences behind bars. During the three years he had spent in Colorado, he was repeatedly raped, assaulted, and extorted by members of a large, notorious gang. The gang was the 211 Crew, a white supremacist group whose leaders pressured him for money and demanded that he help them in an ambitious $300,000 fraud scheme; their threats soon turned into physical attacks, then sexual assaults. He was forced to perform oral sex on gang members and raped repeatedly. Having been housed in other facilities, Howard thought he knew how to keep out of trouble. He'd seen plenty of intimidation and gang-related fights at other lockups, but nothing like the atmosphere in Colorado's Fremont Prison where he had been assigned. Prisoners sporting black eyes in the lunch line were a common sight. Members of the 211 Crew commanded their own set of tables in the dining hall, known as the Four Corners, and charged weaker white inmates tribute for the privilege of living in one of "their" units. Howard told the committee, "My efforts to report were mostly fruitless—and often put me at greater risk. I spent well over a year trying to get protection by writing to officials. Because I am openly gay, officials blamed me for the attacks. They said as a homosexual I should expect to be targeted by one gang or another." On his last day as a Colorado prisoner before going to federal prison, he was put in a cell with one of the gang leaders and sexually assaulted. He eventually settled a civil-rights lawsuit against several corrections officials for $165,000.[21] Is it ethical and fair to house a vulnerable inmate such as Scott Howard in the general prison population? But then again, should someone get special housing based on their sexual orientation? If so, should there be a separate wing for gay inmates? Following this logic, should prisons be racially or ethnically segregated?

Scott Howard's experience is certainly not unique: rape and sexual coercion are customary prison behavior. Some inmates will demand regular sexual access in exchange for protection from even more violent rape and beatings. In his shocking memoir, *Fish*, T. J. Parsell writes about how he was sent to prison at age 17 for a robbery (with a toy gun). Parsell was raped on his first night by four older inmates, who then flipped a coin to decide who would "own" him for the rest of his sentence.[22]

Who are the targets of prison sexual violence? Younger inmates, gay men, and bisexual men are selected most often to be targets of sexual assaults.[23] Young males may be raped and kept as sexual slaves by older, more aggressive inmates. When these "slave holders" are released, they often sell their "prison wives" to other inmates.[24] Some inmates will request that regular sexual payments be made to them in exchange for protection from even more violent inmates who threaten rape and beatings.[25] These weaker inmates are called "punks" and put at the bottom of the inmate sexual hierarchy. Straight inmates are more likely to respect "true" homosexuals because they were gay before entering prison and are therefore "true to themselves," while punks are despised because they are weak: they did not want to have sex with other men but were too weak to resist or not brave enough to stand up to sexual predators. Even "queens," inmates who look and act like women, get more respect than punks because they chose their lifestyle and did not have it forced upon them by others.[26]

WEB APP 12.2 To read more about Scott Howard's case, go to **http://www.westword.com/2011-02-03/news/211-crew-rapes-extorts-scott-howard-colorado-prison/**. Would you advocate a policy of isolating gay men from the general prison population?

HOW COMMON IS PRISON RAPE? While stories of prison rape abound, it has proven difficult to gain an accurate picture of the frequency and prevalence of sexual assault in prison. The most recent national survey employed a sample of about 100,000 inmates ages 16 and older, asking them about nonconsensual sexual acts, abusive sexual contacts, inmate-on-inmate and staff-on-inmate victimization, and level of coercion. The survey found the following:

- An estimated 4 percent of state and federal prison inmates and 3 percent of jail inmates reported experiencing one or more incidents of sexual victimization by another inmate or facility staff in the past 12 months or since admission to the facility, if less than 12 months.
- Sexual assault rates reported by prison and jail inmates were higher among females than males, higher among whites than blacks, and higher among inmates with a college degree than those who had not completed high school.
- Some institutions had much higher rates of victimization than others.
- An estimated 1.8 percent of juveniles ages 16 to 17 held in prisons and jails reported being victimized by another inmate, compared to 2 percent of adults in prisons and 1.6 percent of adults in jails.
- Among state and federal prison inmates, an estimated 6.3 percent of those identified with serious psychological distress reported that they were sexually victimized by another inmate. In comparison, among prisoners with no indication of mental illness, 0.7 percent reported being victimized by another inmate.[27]

If 4 percent of all inmates were sexually assaulted in the past year, it means that at least 60,000 inmates were victimized. However, this data must be interpreted with caution because many victims may be reluctant to admit to being raped. Some are either too embarrassed to tell anyone or fear harassment by other inmates and further retaliation by their attackers.[28] Others may misunderstand what constitutes a "rape," not considering verbal coercion a form of sexual assault. Some refuse to report rape because they believe nothing can be done. It is not surprising that there is little consistency in estimates of inmate assault: some research efforts indicate that rape is very rare, whereas others find that nearly half of all inmates experience some form of sexual coercion.[29]

One way to avoid these problems is by surveying inmates *after* they are released from prison, thereby removing the threat of coercion that occurs while they are still behind bars. A national survey of released inmates found evidence that prison rape is still a significant problem: about 10 percent former state or local prisoners in America reported being sexually victimized at least once by an inmate or staff member in prison. Just about the same number of former inmates were victimized by staff members as they were by other inmates; any sexual contact between staff and inmate is considered nonconsensual and illegal. About half who reported sexual involvement with a prison staff member said they were offered favors or privileges in exchange, while a third said they were verbally coerced. Gay and bisexual men seemed to be by far the most frequently targeted in prison; 39 percent of gay men and 34 percent of bisexual men reported being sexually victimized by another inmate, while only 3.5 percent of heterosexual men reported incidents.[30]

It is disturbing, to say the least, that inmates are more likely to experience sexual coercion from staff than other inmates.[31] If anything, these data may underreport the problem: most inmates say they are aware of sexual coercion in prison and at least know an inmate who had been raped.[32]

To help correctional administrators better cope with this problem, Congress enacted the Prison Rape Reduction Act of 2003, which established three programs in the Department of Justice:

- A program dedicated to collecting national prison rape statistics, interpreting data, and conducting research
- A program dedicated to the dissemination of information and procedures for combating prison rape
- A program to assist in funding state programs[33]

LO2 Describe the inmate
social code and inmate
culture

inmate subculture The loosely defined
culture that pervades prisons and has its own
norms, rules, and language.

inmate social code An unwritten
code of behavior, passed from older inmates
to younger ones, that serves as a guideline
to appropriate inmate behavior within the
correctional institution.

prisonization Assimilation into the
separate culture in the prison that has its own
set of rewards and behaviors, as well as its
own norms, rules, and language. The traditional
prison culture is now being replaced by a violent
gang culture.

The Inmate Social Code

For many years, criminal justice experts maintained that inmates formed their own
world with a unique set of norms and rules, known as the **inmate subculture**.[34] A
significant aspect of the inmate subculture was a unique **inmate social code**—unwritten
guidelines that expressed the values, attitudes, and type of behavior that older
inmates demanded of younger ones. Passed on from one generation of inmates to
another, the inmate social code represented the values of interpersonal relations in
the prison.

National attention was first drawn to the inmate social code and subculture by Donald
Clemmer's classic book *The Prison Community*, in which he presented a detailed
sociological study of life in a maximum-security prison.[35] Clemmer was able to identify
a unique language, or argot, that prisoners use. He found that prisoners tend to group
themselves into cliques on the basis of such personal criteria as sexual preference, political
beliefs, and offense history. He found complex sexual relationships in prison and
concluded that many heterosexual men turn to homosexual relationships when faced
with long sentences and the loneliness of prison life.

Clemmer's most important contribution may have been his identification of the
prisonization process. This he defined as the inmate's assimilation into the existing
prison culture through acceptance of its language, sexual code, and norms of behavior.
Those who become the most "prisonized" are the least likely to reform on the outside.

Using Clemmer's work as a jumping-off point, a number of prominent sociologists
have set out to explore more fully the various roles in the prison community. The most
important principles of the dominant inmate culture are listed in Exhibit 12.1.

Although some inmates violate the code and exploit their peers, the "right guy"
is someone who uses the inmate social code as his personal behavior guide. He is always
loyal to his fellow prisoners, keeps his promises, is dependable and trustworthy,
and never interferes with inmates who are conniving against the officials.[36] The right
guy does not go around looking for a fight, but he never runs away from one; he acts
"like a man."

The effects of prisonization may be long-term and destructive. Many inmates become
hostile to the legal system, learning to use violence as a means of solving problems
and to value criminal peers.[37] For some, this change may be permanent; for others, it is
temporary, and they may revert to their "normal" life after release.

EXHIBIT 12.1 Elements of the Inmate Social Code

1. *Don't interfere with inmates' interests.* Within this area of the code are maxims related to
   serving the least amount of time in the greatest possible comfort. For example, inmates
   are warned never to betray another inmate to authorities; in other words, grievances
   must be handled personally. Other aspects of the noninterference doctrine include "Don't
   be nosy," "Don't have a loose lip," "Keep off the other inmates' backs," and "Don't put
   another inmate on the spot."
2. *Don't lose your head.* Inmates are also cautioned to refrain from arguing, quarreling,
   or engaging in other emotional displays with fellow inmates. The novice may hear such
   warnings as "Play it cool," and "Do your own time."
3. *Don't exploit inmates.* Prisoners are warned not to take advantage of one another: "Don't
   steal from cons," "Don't welsh on a debt," and "Be right."
4. *Be tough and don't lose your dignity.* Although Rule 2 forbids conflict, after it starts, an
   inmate must be prepared to deal with it effectively and thoroughly. Maxims include "Don't
   cop out," "Don't weaken," and "Be tough; be a man."
5. *Don't be a sucker.* Inmates are cautioned not to make fools of themselves or support the
   guards or prison administration over the interest of the inmates: "Be sharp."

Source: Gresham Sykes, *The Society of Captives* (Princeton, NJ: Princeton University Press, 1958).

The New Inmate Culture

The importation of outside values into the inmate
culture has had a dramatic effect on prison
life. Although the old inmate subculture may
have been harmful because its norms and values
insulated the inmate from change efforts, it also
helped create order in the institution and prevented
violence among the inmates. People who
violated the code and victimized others were
sanctioned by their peers. An understanding
developed between guards and inmate leaders:
the guards would let the inmates have things
their own way, and the inmates would not let
things get out of hand and draw the attention of
the administration.

The old system may be dying or already
dead in most institutions. The change seems to
have been precipitated by the black power movement
in the 1960s and 1970s. Black inmates were
no longer content to play a subservient role and
challenged the power of established white inmates.
As the black power movement gained

prominence, racial tension in prisons created divisions that severely altered the inmate subculture. Older, respected inmates could no longer cross racial lines to mediate disputes. Predatory inmates could victimize others without fear of retaliation. Consequently, more inmates than ever are now assigned to protective custody for their own safety.

In the new culture, African American and Latino inmates are much more cohesively organized than whites.[38] Inmates with long histories of delinquent and antisocial behaviors imported their cultural values into prison.[39]

New prison groups formed out of religious or political affiliations, such as the Black Muslims; others out of efforts to combat discrimination in prison, such as the Latino group La Nuestra Familia; or from street gangs, such as the Vice Lords or Gangster Disciples in the Illinois prison system and the Crips in California. Where white inmates have successfully organized, it is in the form of a neo-Nazi groups such as the Aryan Brotherhood. Racially homogeneous gangs arc so cohesive and powerful that they are able to replace the original inmate code with one of their own.

Women Imprisoned

LO3 Summarize the female prison experience

At the turn of the twentieth century, female inmates were viewed as morally depraved people who flouted conventional rules of female behavior. The treatment of white and African American women differed significantly. In some states, white women were placed in female-only reformatories designed to improve their deportment; black women were placed in male prisons, where they were put on chain gangs and were subject to beatings.[40]

Female Institutions

Women's prisons tend to be smaller than those housing male inmates. Although some female institutions are strictly penal, with steel bars, concrete floors, and other security measures, the majority are nonsecure institutions similar to college dormitories and group homes in the community. Women's facilities, especially those in the community, commonly offer inmates a great deal of autonomy and allow them to make decisions affecting their daily lives.

However, like men's prisons, women's prisons suffer from a lack of adequate training and of health, treatment, and educational facilities. Psychological counseling often takes the form of group sessions conducted by laypeople, such as correctional officers. Many female inmates are mothers and had custody of their children before incarceration, but little effort is made to help them develop better parenting skills. Although most female (and male) inmates have at least one child, less than a quarter actually get an annual visit. Who takes care of these children while their mothers are incarcerated? Most children of incarcerated women are placed with their father, a grandparent, another relative, or a family friend. About 10 percent wind up in foster homes or state facilities.[41]

Job-training opportunities are also an issue, but improvements have occurred in recent years. Early surveys revealed that the prison experience did little to prepare women to reenter the workforce after they completed their sentence. Gender stereotypes shaped vocational opportunities, and female inmates were typically trained for "women's roles," such as childrearing.[42] Additionally, they were not given the preparation they need to make successful adjustments in the community.[43] More recently, the picture has approved; the majority of state prisons provide vocational and educational training for female inmates, and nearly all the federal prisons do.[44] Still, female inmates face difficulty on release. One federal report noted,

> ... the majority of female offenders are economically marginalized and face substantial challenges when they return to the community after a period of incarceration. These challenges impede efforts to obtain and maintain employment.[45]

Female Inmates

Like their male counterparts, female inmates are young (most are under age 30), minority group members, unmarried, undereducated (more than half are high school dropouts), and either unemployed or underemployed. The typical woman behind bars is a poor, unskilled woman of color who has small children, has health problems, has a history of abuse, and is incarcerated for low-level drug or property offenses.[46] Recent research shows a high correlation between early experience of abuse and serving a life sentence and that women serving time are much more likely to experience abuse than male inmates.[47] It is not surprising that these conditions also produce high suicide rates in the female prison population.[48] They lack a solid employment history, are in poor physical health, and have a history of financial problems.[49]

Incarcerated women also have had a troubled family life. Significant numbers were at-risk children, products of broken homes and the welfare system; over half have received welfare at some time during their adult lives. Many have been physically or sexually abused at some point in their lives. This pattern continued in adult life: many female inmates were victims of domestic violence. It is not surprising that many display psychological problems.[50]

A significant number of female inmates report having substance abuse problems. About three-fourths have used drugs at some time in their lives, and almost half were involved with addictive drugs, such as cocaine, heroin, or PCP. The incarceration of so many women who are low criminal risks yet face a high risk of exposure to HIV (human immunodeficiency virus, which causes AIDS) and other health threats because of their prior history of drug abuse presents a significant problem. One study of incarcerated women found that one-third of the sample reported that before their arrest, they had traded sex for money or drugs; 24 percent of the women reported trading sex for money or drugs "weekly or more often."[51] Such risky behavior significantly increases the likelihood of their carrying the AIDS virus or other sexually transmitted diseases.

Prison life may be particularly harsh on African American female inmates, who suffer discrimination within the prison setting itself.[52] As Donna Hubbard Spearman, who spent 24 years in prison on drug-related offences, writes:

> African American women are already subjected by a society that places us at the bottom of the totem pole. Within the prison system, not only are we placed at the bottom of the totem pole, but we are considered less than the average inmate. We have a stigma of going back into a community where African American men are almost made martyrs and heroes when they come out of prison . . . but when we go back into our communities, we are not only unfit people, now we're unfit mothers, and it's hard to trust us.[53]

The picture that emerges of the female inmate is troubling. After a lifetime of emotional turmoil, physical and sexual abuse, and drug use, it seems improbable that

WEB APP 12.3 To read about the problems faced by women in prison, go to the ACLU website at **https://www.aclu.org/prisoners-rights/women-prison**. Should there be a difference in the way men and women are treated in prisons?

Tiffany Schipitz, center, sits with other female inmates during a Prostitution Anonymous meeting at Chicago's Cook County Jail. Schipitz, 35, says she was coerced into prostitution and stayed because of a drug addiction.

AP Images/Martha Irvine

overcrowded, underfunded correctional institutions can forge a dramatic turnaround in the behavior of at-risk female inmates. Many have lost custody of their children, a trauma that is more likely to afflict those who are already substance abusers and suffer from depression.[54] It should come as no surprise that many female inmates feel strain and conflict, which are psychological conditions related to violent episodes.[55]

SEXUAL VIOLENCE IN WOMEN'S PRISONS There are also numerous reports of female prisoners being sexually abused and exploited by male correctional workers who either use brute force or psychological coercion to gain sexual control over inmates. The national survey on sexual abuse found that almost 7 percent of female inmates report being abused by another inmate and 2 percent by a staff member.[56] Staff-on-inmate sexual misconduct covers a wide range of behaviors, from lewd remarks to voyeurism, to assault and rape. Few if any of these incidents are reported, and perpetrators rarely go to trial. Institutional workers cover for each other, and women who file complaints are offered little protection from vengeful guards.[57] Because the situation persists, more than 40 states and the District of Columbia have been forced to pass laws criminalizing some types of staff sexual misconduct in prisons. However, not all sexual liaisons in women's prisons are unwanted, and when Rebecca Trammell conducted interviews with former female inmates, she found that some inmates fight over correctional officers as the only men in their lives. The "relational violence" which may occur is similar to what is commonly described as adolescent behavior.[58]

Adapting to the Female Institution

You may have seen the TV series *Orange Is the New Black*, which tells the tale of Piper Chapman, a 30-something public relations executive who is sentenced to a year in a minimum-security women's prison in Connecticut for a crime she committed 10 years earlier. Chapman learns how to adjust to life behind bars and actually makes friends with her fellow inmates, some of whom are street-tough drug users with little education compared to her own experience at Smith College. Chapman has to endure senseless rules, frequent strip searches and head counts, and boring days. She works as an electrician and starts running on the track. Not the typical prisoner (she is white, educated, and gets family support), she nonetheless finds prison to be not as bad as she at first feared.

Orange Is the New Black may be accurate in that daily life in women's prisons differs somewhat from that in male institutions. As Piper Chapman finds, women usually do not present an immediate physical danger to staff and fellow inmates. Relatively few engage in violent behavior, and incidents of inmate-initiated sexual aggression, so common in male institutions, are rare in women's prisons.[59] Few female inmates experience the violent atmosphere common in male institutions or suffer the same racial and ethnic conflict and divisiveness.[60] However, even though female inmates may not experience the same level of violence as do male inmates, that does not mean their experience is a bed of roses. Many are forced to undergo a process of prison socialization fraught with danger and volatile situations.[61] However, female inmates seem to receive more social support from both internal sources (e.g., inmate peers, correctional staff) and external sources (e.g., families, peers)—a factor that may lessen the pains of prison life, help them adjust, and improve the social climate within female institutions.[62]

A form of adaptation to prison used by women is the make-believe family, also known as a play family. This group contains masculine and feminine figures acting as fathers and mothers; some even act as children and take on the role of brother or sister. Formalized marriages and divorces may be conducted. Sometimes one inmate plays multiple roles, such that a "sister" in one family may "marry" and become the "wife" of another inmate. It is estimated that about half of all female inmates are members of make-believe families. Some have questioned the extent to which make-believe families are still prevalent in American prisons, but by most accounts they are still common.[63]

make-believe family, also known as a play family In female institutions, the substitute family group—including faux father, mother, and siblings—created by some inmates.

Correctional Treatment

LO4 Discuss the different forms of correctional treatment

Almost every prison facility uses some mode of treatment for inmates. This may come in the form of individual or group therapy programs or educational or vocational training. Some inmates are in significant need of services, and it is often difficult to match inmates with the correct treatment assistance.[64] This section presents a number of therapeutic methods that have been used nationally in correctional settings and identifies some of their more salient features.

Individual and Group Treatment

Prison inmates typically suffer from a variety of cognitive and psychosocial deficits, such as poor emotional control, social skills, and interpersonal problem solving; these deficits are often linked to long-term substance abuse. Modern counseling programs help inmates control emotions (e.g., understanding why they feel the way they do, dealing with nervousness or anxiety, solving their problems creatively); communicate with others (e.g., understanding what people tell them, communicating clearly when they write); deal with legal concerns (e.g., keeping out of legal trouble, avoiding breaking laws); manage general life issues (e.g., finding a job, dealing with difficult coworkers, being a good parent); and develop and maintain social relationships (e.g., having good relations with others, making others happy, making others proud).[65]

To achieve these goals, correctional systems use a variety of intensive individual and group techniques, including behavior modification, aversive therapy, milieu therapy, reality therapy, transactional analysis, and responsibility therapy. Some programs use traditional techniques such as group therapy while others employ nontraditional artistic and spiritual activities, such as visual and performance arts, meditation, and yoga.[66]

ANGER MANAGEMENT Anger and lack of self-control have been linked to violent criminal behavior both in the institution and, upon release, in the community. As a result, anger management programs may be the form of group therapy most frequently offered within prison settings.[67] Anger management is often combined with other group techniques as part of drug treatment and sex offender treatment programs. Cognitive-behavioral approaches are frequently used as a means of helping inmates find ways to control their anger.

cognitive-behavioral therapy (CBT) A treatment approach that focuses on patterns of thinking and beliefs to help people become conscious of their own thoughts and behaviors so they can make positive changes.

COGNITIVE-BEHAVIORAL THERAPY (CBT) A very popular treatment approach in the correctional setting, cognitive-behavioral therapy (CBT) focuses on patterns of thinking and the beliefs, attitudes, and values that underlie thinking.[68] The therapy assumes that most people can become conscious of their own thoughts and behaviors and then make positive changes. A person's thoughts are often the result of experience, and behavior is often influenced and prompted by these thoughts. In addition, thoughts may sometimes become distorted and fail to reflect reality accurately. When used in a correctional setting, the goal of CBT is to restructure distorted thinking and perception, which in turn changes a person's behavior for the better. Characteristics of distorted thinking may include immature or developmentally arrested thoughts; poor problem solving and decision making; an inability to consider the effects of one's behavior; a hampered ability to reason and accept blame for wrongdoing; or an inability to manage feelings of anger. These distorted thinking patterns can lead to making poor decisions and engaging in antisocial behavior to solve problems. People taking part in CBT learn specific skills that can be used to solve the problems they confront all the time as well as skills they can use to achieve legitimate goals and objectives. CBT first concentrates on developing skills to recognize distorted or unrealistic thinking when it happens, and then on changing that thinking or belief to mollify or eliminate problematic behavior.

National evaluations of CBT programs in the prison setting find them highly successful. Cognitive-behavioral therapy seems to be more effective with more dangerous, hard-core offenders than with less dangerous clients. The best results occur when higher-risk offenders receive more intensive services that target criminogenic characteristics such as criminal thinking patterns, using cognitive-behavioral and social learning approaches.[69]

FAITH-BASED PROGRAMS Research has shown that inmates involved in religious programs and education do better following release than those in comparison groups but that the differences quickly erode.[70] Nonetheless, under the George W. Bush administration, faith-based rehabilitation efforts flourished.[71] In 2003, then-governor Jeb Bush dedicated the first faith-based prison in the United States, a 750-bed medium-security facility for men in Lawtey, Florida.[72]

Private institutions are also getting into the mix. In 2014, Corrections Corporation of America (CCA) announced that it now employs chaplains and program facilitators, who offer inmate residents a variety of worship services, faith-based counseling, and religious resources to address practical and spiritual needs. These professionals design and deliver a continuum of care that approaches and treats the inmate as "the total person." By addressing such social problems as addiction, education, and faith in integrative programs and therapeutic living communities, CCA clients are provided with a variety of rehabilitative opportunities.[73]

Although these programs are based on faith or spiritual principles, the study of religious texts or materials and participation in religious services or rituals are not viewed as their central focus. Instead, faith-based programs are more often involved in secular activities such as helping clients gain skills or training, building support networks, and creating a supportive relationship among staff, volunteers, and clients.[74]

Faith-based programs seem to work better with some inmates than others, and those who enter such programs with feelings of self-worth are more likely to complete the course than those with less confidence.[75]

DRUG TREATMENT Many prisons have programs designed to help inmates suffering from alcohol and substance abuse. However, the need for services is overwhelming because about 85 percent of the entire inmate population are addicted to drugs and alcohol, have a history of substance abuse, were under the influence of alcohol or other drugs at the time of their crime, committed their offense to get money to buy drugs, were incarcerated for an alcohol or drug law violation, or shared some combination of these characteristics. Despite this overwhelming need, only about 11 percent of inmates are provided with some form of services.[76]

In the face of this apparent lack of adequate substance abuse treatment, there have been efforts to aid inmates suffering from addiction. One of the first institutions to develop drug treatment, the Federal Bureau of Prisons uses cognitive-behavioral treatment as its centerpiece. This extensive program includes drug abuse education, nonresidential drug abuse treatment for short-term offenders, and the Residential Drug Abuse Program (RDAP), in which inmates live in a unit separate from the general population and experience living in a prosocial community. They participate in half-day programming and half-day work, school, or vocational activities. RDAP is typically nine months long. After they leave the institution, drug-involved inmates participate in community treatment services (CTS), which provide continuity of care for offenders placed in Residential Reentry Centers (RRCs) and on home confinement. CTS has a comprehensive network of contracted community-based treatment providers in all 50 US states that provide treatment services to RDAP participants, including treatment for mentally ill offenders and sex offenders, and crisis intervention counseling for situational depression, grief/loss, adjustment issues, and anxiety.[77]

In addition to this federal program, state institutions provide drug programs that sometimes rely on inmate self-help through 12-step groups such as Narcotics Anonymous or Alcoholics Anonymous. Others rely on traditional counseling programs such as cognitive-behavioral counseling. Another approach is to provide abusers with methadone as a substitute for heroin; some evaluations have shown this method to be effective.[78] Because substance abuse is so prevalent among correctional clients, some correctional facilities have been reformulated into **therapeutic communities** (TC) that

therapeutic communities
Institutions that rely on positive peer pressure within a highly structured social environment to create positive inmate change.

apply a psychosocial, experiential learning process and rely on positive peer pressure within a highly structured social environment. The community itself, including staff and program participants, becomes the primary method of change. They work together as members of a "family" to create a culture where community members confront each other's negative behavior and attitudes and establish an open, trusting, and safe environment. The TC approach, then, relies on mutual self-help. It also encourages personal disclosure rather than the isolation of the general prison culture.[79]

Treating substance-abusing offenders has proven difficult. Even such highly touted programs as CBT and the TC approach have yielded mixed results: some evaluations have found clients in these programs are just as likely to recidivate as those in the general population.[80] Nonetheless, success rates may be masked by the way individual programs are administered and the effectiveness of treatment delivery. For example, evidence suggests that those inmates who successfully complete TC programs have significantly lower recidivism rates than nonattendees and are more likely to seek treatment after they return to the community. In addition, when run correctly, TC programs seem effective in reducing rearrest and reincarceration rates.[81]

HIV/AIDS TREATMENT The AIDS-infected inmate has been the subject of great concern. Two groups of people at high risk of contracting HIV are intravenous drug users who share needles and males who engage in same-sex relations—two behaviors common in prison. Because drug use is common and syringes scarce, many high-risk inmates share drug paraphernalia, increasing the danger of HIV infection.[82] Although the numbers are constantly changing, the rate of HIV infection among state and federal prisoners has stabilized at around 2 percent, and there are about 25,000 HIV-infected inmates.

Correctional administrators have found it difficult to arrive at effective policies to confront AIDS. Although all state and federal jurisdictions do some AIDS testing, only the Federal Bureau of Prisons and relatively few states conduct mass screenings of all inmates. Most states test inmates only if there are significant indications that they are HIV-positive.

Most correctional systems are now training staff about AIDS. Educational programs for inmates are often inadequate because administrators are reluctant to give them information on safe sex and the proper cleaning of drug paraphernalia (both sexual relations and drug use are forbidden in prison).

Educational Programs

Besides programs stressing personal growth through individual analysis or group therapy, inmate rehabilitation is also pursued through vocational and educational training. Although these two kinds of training sometimes differ in style and content, they can also overlap when, for example, education involves practical, job-related study.

The first prison treatment programs were in fact educational. A prison school was opened at the Walnut Street Jail in 1784. Elementary courses were offered in New York's prison system in 1801 and in Pennsylvania's in 1844. An actual school system was established in Detroit's House of Corrections in 1870, and the Elmira Reformatory opened a vocational trade school in 1876. Today, most institutions provide some type of educational program. At some prisons, inmates can obtain a high school diploma or a general educational development (GED) certificate through equivalency exams. Other institutions provide an actual classroom education, usually staffed by certified teachers employed full time at the prison or by part-time teachers who also teach full time at nearby public schools.

Educational programs vary in quality and intensity. Some are full-time programs employing highly qualified and concerned educators, whereas others are part-time programs without any real goals or objectives. In some institutions, programs have been designed to circumvent the difficulties inherent in the prison structure. They encourage volunteers from the community and local schools to tutor willing and motivated inmates. Some prison administrators have arranged flexible schedules for inmate students

Educational programs are offered in most correctional facilities. Here Simone Taylor, 25, receives her high school diploma from School Board Vice President Linda Young during a graduation ceremony at Nevada's Florence McClure Women's Correctional Center. More than 70 female inmates at Nevada's only women's prison earn their high school diplomas, GEDs, and vocational certificates each year from the Clark County School District's adult education program.

and actively encourage their participation in these programs. In several states, statewide school districts serving prisons have been created. Forming such districts can make better-qualified staff available and provide the materials and resources necessary for meaningful educational programs.

Most research indicates that participation in correctional education programs has benefits both in and out of prisons. Karen Lahm found that inmates who take part in GED, high school, vocational, and/or college programs report much fewer rule violations while incarcerated than those who ignore educational opportunities.[83] Participation in prison-based education produces higher postrelease earnings and employment rates, especially for minority inmates.[84] However, the results of prison education on recidivism are a mixed bag: some studies show a positive effect, while others find little or no relationship.[85]

Vocational Programs

Every state correctional system also has some job-related services for inmates. Some have elaborate training programs inside the institution, whereas others have instituted prerelease and postrelease employment services. Inmates who hope to obtain parole need to participate in prison industry. Documenting a history of stable employment in prison is essential if parole agents are to convince prospective employers that the ex-offender is a good risk, and postrelease employment is usually required for parole eligibility.[86] A few of the more important work-related services are discussed in the following sections.

VOCATIONAL TRAINING Most institutions provide vocational training programs. On the federal level, the Federal Prison Industries, which is more commonly known as UNICOR, teaches inmates to produce goods and services for government use such as clothing and textiles, industrial products, and office furniture. UNICOR sales average about $800 million a year and yield a profit of $120 million a year—making UNICOR the most profitable line of business in the United States.[87]

Despite the promising aspects of such programs, they have also been seriously criticized. Inmates often have trouble finding skill-related, high-paying jobs upon their release. Equipment in prisons is often secondhand, obsolete, and hard to come by. Some programs are thinly disguised excuses for prison upkeep and maintenance, and unions and other groups resent the intrusion of prison labor into their markets.

WORK RELEASE To supplement programs stressing rehabilitation via in-house job training or education, more than 40 states have attempted to implement work release or furlough programs. These allow deserving inmates to leave the institution and hold regular jobs in the community.

Inmates enrolled in work release may live at the institutions at night while working in the community during the day. However, security problems (e.g., contraband may be brought in) and the usual remoteness of prisons often make this arrangement difficult. More typical is the extended work release, where prisoners are allowed to remain in the community for significant periods of time. To help inmates adjust, some states operate community-based prerelease centers where inmates live while working. Some inmates may work at their previous jobs, whereas others seek new employment.

Work release programs have proven to be a mixed bag as well. On the one hand, inmates are sometimes reluctantly received in the community and find that certain areas of employment are closed to them. Citizens are often concerned about prisoners "stealing" jobs or working for lower than normal wages; consequently, such practices are prohibited by Public Law 89-176, which controls the federal work release program. On the other hand, inmates gain many benefits from work release, including the ability to maintain work skills, maintain community ties, and make an easier transition from prison to the outside world. For those who have learned a skill in the institution, work release offers an excellent opportunity to try out a new occupation. For others, the job may be a training situation in which new skills are acquired. A number of states have reported that few work release inmates abscond while in the community.

PRIVATE PRISON ENTERPRISE The federal government helped put private industry into prisons when it approved the Free Venture Program in 1976. Seven states, including Connecticut, South Carolina, and Minnesota, were given grants to implement private industries inside prison walls.

Today, private prison industries use a number of models. One approach, the state-use model, makes the correctional system a supplier of goods and services that serves state-run institutions.[88] In another approach, the free-enterprise model, private companies set up manufacturing units on prison grounds or purchase goods made by inmates in shops owned and operated by the corrections department. In the corporate model, a semi-independent business is created on prison grounds, and its profits go to the state government and inmate laborers.

REALITYCHECK

Myth or Reality?

Despite negative publicity that "nothing works," many prison rehabilitation efforts are actually effective.

REALITY. Many prison programs have proved effective, and the "nothing works" mantra seems overstated.

How would you treat prison inmates? Should they get a free education and job training, benefits that may not be available to the average American?

POSTRELEASE PROGRAMS Vocational programming also involves helping inmates obtain jobs before they are released and keep them after they are on the outside. A number of correctional departments have set up employment services designed to ease the transition between institution and community. Employment program staff assess inmates' backgrounds to determine their abilities, interests, goals, and capabilities. They also help them create job plans essential to receiving early release (parole) and successfully reintegrating into the community. Some programs maintain community correctional placements in sheltered environments that help inmates bridge the gap between institutions and the outside world. Services include job placement, skill development, family counseling, and legal and medical assistance.

Can Rehabilitation Work?

Despite the variety and number of treatment programs in operation, questions remain about their effectiveness. In an oft-cited research effort, Robert Martinson and his associates (1975) found that a majority of treatment programs were failures, giving birth to the cry that "nothing works" in prison rehabilitation.[89] Martinson's work created considerable debate over the effectiveness of correctional treatment. Even some of the most carefully crafted treatment efforts, using the most up-to-date rehabilitation modalities (such as CBT), failed to have a positive impact on inmates returning to the community, a finding that supports the "nothing works" mantra.[90]

Treatment proponents have dismissed the "nothing works" philosophy as exaggerated and, using sophisticated data analysis techniques, have found evidence that correctional rehabilitation can be effective.[91] When Paul Gendreau and Robert Ross reviewed the published work on correctional rehabilitation programs, they found that many intervention programs reported success.[92] More recently, Mark Lipsey and Francis Cullen's comprehensive review of the studies of correctional rehabilitation found consistently positive effects on reducing recidivism. Success seems to rely on the type of treatment, its implementation, and the nature of the offenders to whom it is applied.[93]

Correctional Officers

L05 Describe the world of correctional officers

Controlling a prison is a complex task. On the one hand, a tough, high-security environment may meet the goals of punishment and control but fail to reinforce positive behavior changes. On the other hand, too liberal an administrative stance can lower staff morale and place inmates in charge of the institution. For many years, prison guards were viewed as ruthless people who enjoyed their power over inmates, fought rehabilitation efforts, were racist, and had a "lock psychosis" developed from years of counting, numbering, and checking on inmates. This view has changed in recent years. Correctional officers are now viewed as public servants who are seeking the security and financial rewards of a civil service position.[94] Most are in favor of rehabilitation efforts and do not harbor any particular animosity toward the inmates.[95]

The correctional officer has been characterized as a "people worker" who must be prepared to deal with the problems of inmates on a personal level and also as a member of a complex bureaucracy who must be able to cope with the demands of an evolving inmate population. For example, with the increasing population of older inmates, correctional officers must now be able to recognize impairment in prison, assess the effects of dementia, recognize the special needs of older prisoners, and work in geriatric housing units.[96]

What are the most significant problems faced by correctional workers today? Those forced to work in facilities that are underfunded, understaffed, and crowded report high levels of stress and impaired job performance due to understaffing and overwork. Research shows that officers at the most crowded prisons are most stressed and fearful of inmates.[97]

Another problem faced by correctional officers is probably the stress created by the duality of their role: maintainers of order and security *and* advocates of treatment and rehabilitation.[98] Eric Lambert and his associates found that the stress of the prison experience can lead to emotional exhaustion, a powerful dimension of job burnout, which if left unchecked is associated with high levels of turnover, absenteeism, and general job dissatisfaction.[99]

Although these problems are significant, correctional officers who have high levels of job satisfaction, good relations with their coworkers, and high levels of social support seem to be better able to deal with the stress of the correctional setting.[100] The most successful officers can have a sizable impact on a prisoner's ability to adjust to prison life. Correctional staff members who conduct themselves professionally and gain the respect and cooperation of the inmates are able to have a very positive influence on their later readjustment to society.[101]

For more on the work of a correctional officer, read the Careers in Criminal Justice feature.

Female Correctional Officers

Women now work side by side with male guards in almost every state, performing the same duties. Research indicates that discipline has not suffered because of the inclusion of women in the guard force. Sexual assaults have been rare, and more negative attitudes have been expressed by the female guards' male peers than by inmates. Most commentators believe that the presence of female guards can have an important beneficial effect on the self-image of inmates and can improve the guard–inmate working relationship.

Duties and Characteristics of the Job

- The primary job of a correctional officer is to supervise individuals who are serving time in prison after being convicted.

- Their duties include supervising and submitting reports on inmate behavior, maintaining order within the population by enforcing institutional rules and policies, and ensuring order in the institution by searching for contraband or settling disputes between inmates.

- Although correctional officers tend to work a standard 5-day, 40-hour work week, odds are they will work overtime on weekends, holidays, and nights as well, because jails and prisons must be staffed at all hours.

Job Outlook

- Opportunities exist for employment at the local level, but a majority of correctional officer positions are at state and federal prisons. A smaller number of jobs are available with private institutions.

- Thanks to a growing demand for correctional officers, combined with high rates of turnover within the field, prospects for employment are very good.

- A good correctional officer with the proper education and training has the potential to be promoted to correctional sergeant and to other administrative and supervisory positions.

Salary

- Median annual salary for a correctional officer is about $40,000 per year.

- The lowest 10 percent earned less than $27,830, but the top 10 percent earned more than $73,060.

- Correctional officers usually are provided with uniforms or a clothing allowance to purchase their own uniforms. Their retirement coverage entitles correctional officers to retire at age 50 after 20 years of service or at any age with 25 years of service.

Qualifications

- Exact qualifications vary depending on what level of government and what type of setting the position is in.

- A majority of correctional institutions look for several characteristics in potential employees: correctional officers should be US citizens, be at least 18 to 21 years old, and be able to pass a background check and a drug test.

- Correctional officers must also be in good physical and mental health, meet education requirements, and be able to work in a challenging environment where good judgment and quick thinking are necessary.

- Tests may be administered to judge whether an applicant meets these qualifications.

Education and Training

- Although only a high school diploma may be necessary to become a correctional officer, a bachelor's degree (especially in a field such as criminology, sociology, or criminal justice) will make career advancement easier and can greatly increase annual salary.

- After hiring and training, there may be a period of on-the-job training with an experienced officer.

- At the federal level, a bachelor's degree or three years of experience in a related occupation is necessary for employment.

- Federal corrections officers will have at least 200 hours of on-the-job training and a period of training at the Federal Bureau of Prisons.

Reality Check

- Correctional officers are forced to routinely deal with, and sometimes restrain, people who suffer from HIV, hepatitis B and C, tuberculosis, and other contagious diseases.

- Officers are in danger of physical harm from prison-made weapons.

- When conducting body or cell searches, correction officers are in danger of being jabbed or cut by a piece of contraband.

- Officers must control mentally ill inmates.

- Officers are subject to taunts and verbal harassment.

Source: Bureau of Labor Statistics, *Correctional Officers and Bailiffs*, http://www.bls.gov/ooh/Protective-Service/Correctional-officers.htm (accessed May 2017).

Ironically, female correctional officers may find that an assignment to a male institution can boost their career. Recent restrictions on male staff in female institutions, in the wake of well-publicized sex scandals, have forced administrators to assign women officers to the dormitory areas, the least desirable areas in which to work. Women officers are not similarly restricted in male-only facilities.[102]

Prison Violence

Conflict, violence, and brutality are sad but ever-present facts of institutional life. Violence can involve individual conflict: inmate versus inmate, inmate versus staff, and staff versus inmate. Nonsexual assaults may stem from an aggressor's desire to shake down the victim for money and personal favors, may be motivated by racial conflict, or may simply be used to establish power within the institution. For example, on February 1, 2017, at the James T. Vaughn Correctional Center in Smyrna, Delaware, a 19-hour standoff between inmates and law enforcement ended with the death of one correctional officer and injuries to several others.[103] The uprising began when inmates used homemade weapons to overpower prison staff, seized control of a cell block, and took three guards and a correctional counselor hostage.

Violence can also involve large groups of inmates, such as the infamous Attica riot in 1971, which claimed 39 lives, or the New Mexico State Penitentiary riot in 1980, in which the death toll was 33. More than 300 prison riots have occurred since the first one in 1774; 90 percent have occurred since 1952.[104]

What Causes Prison Violence?

There is no single explanation for either collective or individual prison violence, although theories abound.[105] However, research by Benjamin Steiner shows that factors related to prison administration, inmate population characteristics, and the racial makeup of inmates and staff can influence violence levels.[106] Some of the factors related to individual and collective violence, respectively, are discussed in some detail next.

LO6 Discuss the causes of prison violence

INDIVIDUAL VIOLENCE

- *History of prior violence.* Before they were incarcerated, many inmates were violence-prone individuals who always used force to get their own way. Some are former gang members who join inmate gangs as soon as they enter the institution.[107] In many instances, street gangs maintain prison branches that unite the inmate with his former violence-prone peers.[108] Although the association between a history of violence and aggression behind bars is significant, some recent research by Jon Sorenson and Mark Cunningham found that people convicted of murder are no more violent than other members of the inmate population. Their finding is important because it runs counter to the argument that murderers are dangerous people with a "propensity for murder." Sorenson and Cunningham's conclusion that a murder conviction is not any greater predictor of prison violence than a conviction for some other offense counters an important argument for the use of capital punishment.[109]
- *Age.* Younger inmates, those with a record of prior incarceration, and those who have suffered prearrest drug use are the ones most likely to engage in disruptive behavior in prison, especially if they are not active participants in institutional treatment programs.[110] Sadly, juvenile offenders who are sentenced to adult institutions have significantly higher violence rates than the adult inmate population.[111] Although it may be puzzling to some that inmates convicted of murder seem no more violent behind bars than the next inmate, it is possible that these may be older inmates who have learned from experience to "do their own time."[112]
- *Psychological factors.* Many inmates suffer from personality disorders. Research shows that among institutionalized offenders, psychopathy is the strongest predictor of violent recidivism and indifferent response to treatment.[113] In the crowded, dehumanizing world of the prison, it is not surprising that people with extreme psychological distress may resort to violence to dominate others.[114]
- *Prison conditions.* The prison experience itself causes people to become violent. Inhuman conditions, including overcrowding, depersonalization, and the threat of sexual assault, are violence-producing conditions.[115] Research shows that violence rates may be higher in the most run-down and unwholesome prisons.[116] Even in the most humane prisons, life is a constant put-down, and prison conditions are a threat to the inmates' sense of self-worth; violence is an expected consequence of these conditions. Violence levels are not much different between high-security and low-security prisons, suggesting that the prison experience itself, and not the level of control, produces violence.[117] The converse is also true: effective interventions can help reduce violence in even the most disruptive inmates, especially those who begin to realize that repeat violent incidents are punished by long-term stays in segregation and other negative consequences.[118]
- *Lack of dispute-resolution mechanisms.* Many prisons lack effective mechanisms for handling inmate grievances against either prison officials or other inmates fairly and equitably. Prisoners who complain about other inmates are viewed as "rats" or "snitches" and are marked for death by their enemies. Similarly, inmates' complaints

Sergeant Richard Bratz of the Delaware State Police issues a statement about the prison guards who were taken hostage by prison inmates at James T. Vaughn Correctional Center in Smyrna, Delaware, on February 2, 2017.

or lawsuits filed against the prison administration may result in their being placed in solitary confinement—"the hole."

- *Basic survival.* Inmates resort to violence to survive. The lack of physical security, the dearth of adequate mechanisms for resolving complaints, and the code of silence promote individual violence by inmates who might otherwise be effectively controlled.

COLLECTIVE VIOLENCE

- *Inmate-balance theory.* Riots and other forms of collective violence occur when prison officials make an abrupt effort to take control of the prison and limit freedoms. Crackdowns occur when officials perceive that inmate leaders have too much power and take measures to control their illicit privileges, such as gambling or stealing food.[119]
- *Administrative-control theory.* Collective violence is caused by prison mismanagement, lack of strong security, and inadequate control by prison officials. Poor management may inhibit conflict management and set the stage for violence. Repressive administrations give inmates the feeling that nothing will ever change, that they have nothing to lose, and that violence is the only means for change.

Despite these problems, both the suicide rate and the homicide rate in prisons have been in sharp decline. Although it is difficult to determine the cause of this drop in violence directed at self and others, more advanced security measures coupled with improved prison administration may be responsible.

L07 Explain what is meant by prisoners' rights, and discuss some key privileges that have been granted to inmates

hands-off doctrine The legal practice of allowing prison administrators a free hand to run the institution, even if correctional practices violate inmates' constitutional rights; ended with the onset of the prisoners' rights movement in the 1960s.

Prisoners' Rights

Before the early 1960s, it was accepted that upon conviction, an individual forfeited all rights not expressly granted by statutory law or correctional policy; in other words, inmates were civilly dead. The US Supreme Court held that convicted offenders should expect to be penalized for their misdeeds and that part of their punishment was the loss of freedoms that law-abiding citizens take for granted.

One reason why inmates lacked rights was that state and federal courts were reluctant to intervene in the administration of prisons unless the circumstances of a case clearly indicated a serious breach of the Eighth Amendment protection against cruel and unusual punishment. This judicial policy is referred to as the hands-off doctrine.

As the 1960s drew to a close, the hands-off doctrine was eroded. Federal district courts began seriously considering prisoners' claims about conditions in the various state and federal institutions and used their power to intervene on behalf of the inmates. In some ways, this concern reflected the spirit of the times, which saw the onset of the civil rights movement, and subsequently emerged in the areas of student rights, public welfare, mental institutions, juvenile court systems, and military justice.

Beginning in the late 1960s, such activist groups as the NAACP Legal Defense Fund and the ACLU's National Prison Project began to search for appropriate legal vehicles to bring prisoners' complaints before state and federal courts. The most widely used device was the federal Civil Rights Act, 42 U.S.C. 1983:

> Every person who, under color of any statute, ordinance, regulation, custom, or usage of any State or Territory subjects, or causes to be subjected, any citizen of the United States or other person within the jurisdiction thereof to the deprivation of any rights, privileges, or immunities secured by the Constitution and laws shall be liable to the party injured in an action at law, suit in equity, or other proper proceeding for redress.

The legal argument went that, as US citizens, prison inmates could sue state officials if their civil rights were violated—for example, if they were the victims of racial or religious discrimination.

The subsequent prisoners' rights crusade, stretching from 1964 to 1980, paralleled the civil rights and women's movements. Battle lines were drawn between prison officials, who hoped to maintain their power and resented interference by the courts, and inmate groups and their sympathizers, who used state and federal courts as a forum for demanding better living conditions and personal rights.

To slow down prison litigation, which had been clogging the federal courts, Congress passed the Prison Litigation Reform Act in 1996.[120] The most important provision of the act requires prisoners to exhaust all internal administrative grievance procedures before they can file a civil rights case in federal court. It also bars litigation if a prisoner has not suffered a physical injury in addition to a violation of his or her constitutional rights. There is a limitation on the number of times an appeal can be filed: If a judge decides that it is frivolous, malicious, or does not state a proper claim, it counts as a "strike." After you get three strikes, another lawsuit cannot be filed unless the inmate is willing to pay the entire court filing fee up front. The Supreme Court has upheld the provisions of the act in two cases—one dealing with a request for monetary relief and the other with allegations of excessive use of force—*Booth v. Churner* (2001) and *Porter v. Nussle* (2002), respectively, in which the Court ruled that it is constitutional to require that an inmate go through all administrative processes before a case can be brought to the courts.[121] Civil rights groups believe that these cases have a chilling effect on inmate litigation.[122]

Although the prisoners' rights movement may have slowed, it has not ended. Some of the most important substantive and procedural rights of inmates are discussed next.

Substantive Rights

Through a slow process of legal review, the courts have granted inmates a number of substantive rights that have significantly influenced the entire correctional system. The most important of these rights are discussed in the following sections.

ACCESS TO COURTS, LEGAL SERVICES, AND LEGAL MATERIALS Courts have held that inmates are entitled to have legal materials available and must be provided with assistance in drawing up and filing complaints. Inmates who help others, so-called jailhouse lawyers, cannot be interfered with or harassed by prison administrators.

FREEDOM OF THE PRESS AND OF EXPRESSION Courts have consistently ruled that only when a compelling state interest exists can prisoners' First Amendment rights be modified; correctional authorities must justify the limiting of free speech by showing that granting it would threaten institutional security. If prison administrators believe that correspondence undermines prison security, the First Amendment rights of inmates can be curtailed.[123]

substantive rights A number of civil rights that the courts, through a slow process of legal review, have established for inmates, including the rights to receive mail and medical benefits and to practice their religion.

jailhouse lawyers Inmates trained in law or otherwise educated who help other inmates prepare legal briefs and appeals.

FREEDOM OF RELIGION The Supreme Court has ruled that inmates have the right to assemble and pray in the religion of their choice, even if the religions are not mainstream, such as Wicca or Satanism.[124] There are some exceptions—for example, if religious prisoners receive favored treatment, or if religious exercise and security concerns are not properly balanced. Therefore, religious symbols and practices that interfere with institutional security can be restricted. Administrators can draw the line if responding to religious needs becomes cumbersome or impossible for reasons of cost or security.

The 2015 case of *Holt v. Hobbs* illustrates how the line between religious and institutional security can become blurred. Gregory Holt, an Arkansas inmate who had converted to the Muslim religion and changed his name to Abdul Muhammad, was denied the ability to grow the half-inch beard that his Muslim faith commanded because prison officials were afraid that contraband such as razor blades, drugs, homemade darts, and SIM cards for cell phones could be hidden in beards. After numerous appeals in lower courts, the Supreme Court took the case. Writing for the majority, Justice Samuel Alito found that Muhammad had "easily satisfied" the requirement of showing that the ban on beards burdened his religious practices. He also noted that the idea that security "would be seriously compromised by allowing an inmate to grow a half-inch beard is hard to take seriously." He went on to say, "An item of contraband would have to be very small indeed to be concealed by a half-inch beard," he wrote, "and a prisoner seeking to hide an item in such a short beard would have to find a way to prevent the item from falling out." In this case the right to religious freedom won out over the need for prison security.

MEDICAL RIGHTS In early prisons, inmates' right to medical treatment was restricted through the "exceptional circumstances doctrine." Using this policy, the courts would hear only those cases in which the circumstances revealed utter disregard for human dignity, while denying hearings to less serious cases. The cases that were allowed access to the courts usually entailed total denial of medical care.

To gain their medical rights, prisoners have resorted to class-action suits (suits brought on behalf of all individuals affected by similar circumstances—in this case, poor medical attention). In the most significant case, *Newman v. Alabama* (1972), the entire Alabama prison system's medical facilities were declared inadequate.[125] The Supreme Court cited the following factors as contributing to inadequate care: insufficient physician and nurse resources, reliance on untrained inmates for paramedical work, intentional failure in treating the sick and injured, and failure to conform to proper medical standards. The *Newman* case forced corrections departments to upgrade prison medical facilities.

It was not until 1976, in *Estelle v. Gamble*, that the Supreme Court clearly affirmed inmates' right to medical care.[126] Gamble had hurt his back in a Texas prison and filed suit because he contested the type of treatment he had received and questioned the lack of interest that prison guards had shown in his case. The Supreme Court said, "Deliberate indifference to serious medical needs of prisoners constitutes the 'unnecessary and wanton infliction of pain,' proscribed by the Eighth Amendment."[127] The *Gamble* ruling mandated that inmate health care reflect what is available to citizens in the general community. Consequently, correctional administrators must consider access, quality, and cost of health care as part of the prison regime.[128]

CRUEL AND UNUSUAL PUNISHMENT The concept of cruel and unusual punishment is founded in the Eighth Amendment of the Constitution. The term itself has not been specifically defined by the Supreme Court, but the Court has held that treatment constitutes cruel and unusual punishment when it does the following:

- Degrades the dignity of human beings[129]
- Is more severe than (is disproportional to) the offense for which it has been given[130]
- Is deliberately indifferent to a person's safety and well-being[131]
- Shocks the general conscience and is fundamentally unfair[132]
- Punishes people because of their status, such as race, religion, and mental state[133]
- Is in flagrant disregard of due process of law, such as punishment that is capriciously applied[134]

cruel and unusual punishment
Physical punishment or punishment that is far in excess of that given to people under similar circumstances and is therefore banned by the Eighth Amendment. The death penalty has so far not been considered cruel and unusual if it is administered in a fair and nondiscriminatory fashion.

State and federal courts have placed strict limits on disciplinary methods that may be considered inhumane. Corporal punishment all but ended after the practice was condemned in *Jackson v. Bishop* (1968).[135] Although the solitary confinement of disruptive inmates continues, its prolonged use under barbaric conditions has been held to be in violation of the Eighth Amendment. Courts have found that inmates placed in solitary have the right to adequate personal hygiene; to exercise, mattresses, and ventilation; and to rules specifying how they can earn their release. See the accompanying Contemporary Issues in Criminal Justice box for more on the issues associated with solitary confinement.

CONTEMPORARY ISSUES IN CRIMINAL JUSTICE

Reforming Solitary

Violent and disruptive inmates are put in solitary confinement, or "administrative segregation," presumably to protect other inmates, staff, and even themselves. According to a Yale Law School report, between 80,000 and 100,000 inmates are segregated at any given time. Solitary confinement often lasts for 23 hours each day; the inmates typically receive just one hour for exercise and showers, but they never interact physically with other inmates. Isolation cells are generally small. Inmates may or may not have a window that gives them a view outside the prison. They are generally put in full restraints before being moved anywhere. Most services (meals, medical visits, book deliveries) are received in their cells. The objective is near total isolation from staff and other inmates.

Not surprisingly, researchers have come to question the long-term psychological effects of inmate isolation. A 2011 National Institute of Justice-funded study found that inmates in solitary confinement did not experience mental health problems during a one-year period. A more recent study, however, found that inmates subjected to solitary confinement harmed themselves at rates much higher than inmates in the general population; more than half of the acts of self-harm reported occurred in the solitary confinement group, which accounted for a mere 7.3 percent of the inmates studied.

Another question concerns whether solitary confinement forces violent and disruptive inmates to change their ways. A 2016 study authored by Robert Morris at the University of Texas at Dallas found that short-term solitary confinement had no effect on the incidence, timing, or development of subsequent misconduct. Needless to say, then, the jury is still out on whether solitary confinement is harmful and/or effective, but this has not stopped critics from arguing that isolation is overused. Indeed, there is a measure of consensus among experts that prisons resort to solitary confinement more often than they should. There is also increasing consensus that reform is necessary.

What can prisons do better with their use of solitary confinement? To answer this question, a two-day colloquium was recently held by the Prisoner Reentry Institute at the John Jay College of Criminal Justice in New York City. The participants issued a 90-page report identifying 23 recommendations for improvement, some of which included:

- The only criterion for confining a person to social isolation within prison should be behavior; persons should not be confined based upon their affiliation or status.

- Separation from the general population must always provide for adequate living conditions and for meaningful routine, and periodic medical and mental health assessments.

- Prison discipline should incorporate a continuum of measures to hold incarcerated persons proportionately accountable for their behavior, and

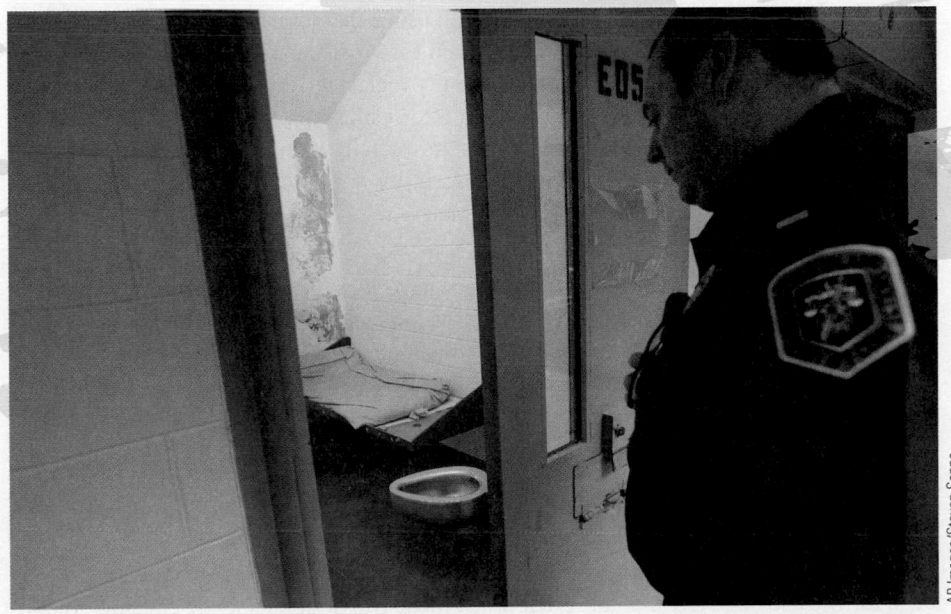

Correctional officer Lt. Joshua Macomber looks into a cell in what prison officials describe as a disciplinary confinement area rather than solitary confinement, at the Rhode Island Department of Corrections High Security Center, in Cranston. Some lawmakers in Rhode Island are pushing to curb the use of solitary confinement in state prisons. Prison officials say they already have standards limiting the use of disciplinary confinement, but some advocates say it's been used arbitrarily.

(Continued)

the use of isolated confinement should be the last resort. Alternatives to isolated confinement as punishment are desirable and should be found.

- Decisions about the use of segregation in prison for other reasons should be made by multi-disciplinary teams with a view toward improving outcomes.

- The purpose of isolated confinement must be to improve the outcome for the affected individual and to make the prison and the community safer. To that end there must be meaningful interventions designed to address the reasons for the confinement and attainable means for the individual to transition back to the general population of the prison.

Even President Barack Obama lamented the state of solitary confinement in America. In a *Washington Post* editorial, the 44th president called attention to the case of Kalief Browder, a 16-year-old from the Bronx who was accused of stealing a backpack. Prior to his trial, he spent two years in solitary. He was released in 2013, without having stood trial, and ultimately killed himself at just 22 years of age. Browder's case is an extreme example, but it is not isolated. Obama said:

> The United States is a nation of second chances, but the experience of solitary confinement too often undercuts that second chance. . . . How can we subject prisoners to unnecessary solitary confinement, knowing its effects, and then expect them to return to our communities as whole people? It doesn't make us safer. It's an affront to our common humanity.

CRITICAL THINKING

1. What is your perspective on solitary confinement? Defend your position.
2. What are the limitations of the research discussed?
3. Was the president correct in his criticism of solitary?

Sources: *Time-In-Cell: The ASCA-Liman 2014 National Survey of Administrative Segregation in Prison*, The Liman Program, Yale Law School, August 2015, https://www.law.yale.edu/system/files/area/center/liman/document/asca-liman _administrativesegregationreport.pdf; M. L. O'Keefe, K. J. Klebe, A. Stucker, K. Sturm, and W. Leggett, *One Year Longitudinal Study of the Psychological Effects of Administrative Segregation* (Washington, DC: National Institute of Justice, 2011), https:// www.ncjrs.gov/pdffiles1/nij/grants/232973.pdf; F. Kaba et al., "Solitary Confinement and Risk of Self-Harm Among Jail Inmates," *American Journal of Public Health* 104 (2014): 442–447; R. G. Morris, "Exploring the Effect of Exposure to Short-Term Solitary Confinement Among Violent Prison Inmates," *Journal of Quantitative Criminology* 32 (2016): 1–22; *Proceedings of a Colloquium to Further a National Consensus on Ending the Over-Use of Extreme Isolation in Prisons*, John Jay College of Criminal Justice, September 30–October 1, 2015, http://thecrimereport.s3.amazonaws.com /2/4a/d/3344/approaches_to_reforming_solitary.pdf; S. Handelman, "Changing the Rules for Solitary," *The Crime Report*, January 15, 2016, http://www.thecrimereport .org/news/inside-criminal-justice/2016-01-changing-the-rules-for-solitary; Barack Obama, "Why We Must Rethink Solitary Confinement," *Washington Post*, January 25, 2016, https://www.washingtonpost.com/opinions/barack-obama-why-we-must -rethink-solitary-confinement/2016/01/25/29a361f2-c384-11e5-8965 -0607e0e265ce_story.html. (URLs accessed May 2017.)

REALITY CHECK

Myth or Reality?

Inmates lose all civil rights after they enter a high-security correctional facility.

MYTH. Inmates retain many civil rights, even behind prison walls.

Should inmates maintain all civil rights, including the right to vote or to give press interviews, while in prison? Is it ethical to allow nonlawyers to help inmates prepare cases?

WEB APP 12.4 To read more about prisoners' legal rights, check out the ACLU website at **http:// www.aclu.org/prisoners-rights/**. Do you believe that incarcerated felons should lose all their legal rights?

RACIAL SEGREGATION In the 2005 case *Johnson v. California*, the Supreme Court ruled that the segregation of prison inmates based on race, in their cells or anywhere on prison grounds, is an inappropriate form of racial classification.[136] However, it left it open for lower courts to decide, using a standard of *strict scrutiny*, when segregation is inappropriate and unconstitutional. *Johnson* focused on the policy of segregating inmates upon their arrival at a prison. However, the Court's ruling seemed to suggest that if racial segregation was allowed for incoming inmates, there is a danger that it might also be used "in the dining halls, yards, and general housing areas." Segregation should only be allowed, the judges reasoned, if a prison administrator could prove that it served a compelling interest to promote prison safety. The Court recognized that "prisons are dangerous places, and the special circumstances they present may justify racial classifications in some contexts."

Because a riot occurred in Chino prison after California began to integrate prison entry centers, it is possible that future efforts to racially integrate prisons will be frustrated. State courts, even when using a strict scrutiny standard, may conclude that racial integration is just too dangerous in some instances.

OVERALL PRISON CONDITIONS Prisoners have long had the right to the minimal conditions necessary for human survival, such as food, clothing, shelter, and medical care. A number of attempts have been made to articulate reasonable standards of prison care and to make sure that officials adhere to them. Courts have held that although people are sent to prison for punishment, it does not mean that prison should be a punishing experience.[137] In the 1994 case of *Farmer v. Brennan*, the court ruled that prison officials are legally liable if, knowing that an inmate faces a serious risk of harm, they disregard that risk by failing to take measures to avoid or reduce it. Furthermore, prison officials should be able to infer the risk from the evidence at hand; they need not be warned or told.[138]

Although inmates retain the right to reasonable care, if there is a legitimate purpose for the use of governmental restrictions, those restrictions may be considered constitutional. Thus, it might be possible to restrict reading material, allow strip searches,

Inmates have the right to bring their legal issues to court. Here, Rene Lima-Marin stands in a room waiting to be searched by a guard as per procedure before returning to his cell at Kit Carson Correctional Center in Burlington, Colorado. Lima-Marin, who was sent back to prison after being mistakenly released six years earlier, said it was cruel and unusual punishment to put him back behind bars after he reformed his life and started a family. A judge in 2000 sentenced Lima-Marin to a total of 98 years in prison for multiple counts stemming from the robbery of two video stores when he was 20. In May 2017, Colorado Governor John Hickenlooper pardoned Lima-Marin, citing his rehabilitation and contributions to the community. Ironically, before Lima-Marin could walk out of prison, he was detained by Immigration and Customs Enforcement (ICE). His case is being appealed.

and prohibit inmates from receiving packages from the outside if the restrictions are legitimate security measures. If overcrowded conditions require it, inmates may be double-bunked in cells designed for a single inmate.[139]

Leaving Prison: Parole

At the expiration of their prison term, most inmates return to society and try to resume their lives. For some inmates, their reintegration into society comes by way of **parole**—the planned community release and supervision of incarcerated offenders before the expiration of their full prison sentences. Once on parole, former inmates have to live by a strict set of rules that mandate they stay out of trouble, stay drug and alcohol free, be employed, and attend counseling. Parolees are monitored by their case officers, who may administer random drug tests and use Global Positioning System (GPS) tracking devices to keep tabs on their whereabouts.[140]

In some states, parole is granted by a **parole board**, a duly constituted body of men and women who review inmate cases and determine whether offenders have reached a rehabilitative level sufficient to deal with the outside world. The board also dictates what specific parole rules parolees must obey. Most boards are independent agencies that consist of members appointed by the governor; the rest are affiliated with the Department of Corrections. A majority have the authority to make final release decisions; most require interviews with parole-eligible offenders prior to release. A majority of parole boards also set the rules of parole and are given the power to revoke parole when these rules are violated or the parolee commits another crime.[141]

In a number of jurisdictions, discretionary parole has been abandoned, and the amount of time a person must remain in prison is a predetermined percentage of the sentence, assuming there are no infractions or escape attempts. In this "mandatory parole release" approach, the inmate is released when the unserved portion of the maximum prison term equals his or her earned good time (minus time served in jail awaiting trial). In some states, sentences can be reduced by more than half with a combination of statutory and earned good time. If the conditions of their release are violated, mandatory releasees can have their good time revoked and be returned to the institution to serve the remainder of their unexpired term. The remaining inmates are released for a variety of reasons, including expiration of their term, commutation of their sentence, and court orders to relieve overcrowded prisons. The use of discretionary parole has been in steep decline, while the number of inmates released on mandatory parole has increased significantly. More

LO8 Discuss the parole process and the problems of prisoner reentry

parole The early release of a prisoner from imprisonment, subject to conditions set by a parole board.

parole board A panel of people who decide whether an offender should be released from prison on parole after serving the minimum portion of their sentence ordered by the sentencing judge.

than 850,000 people are currently on parole. However, like the prison population itself, the number of people on parole has finally stabilized, reversing years of increases upward.[142]

Is There a Legal Right to Parole?

What happens if the parole authority denies early release, but the inmate believes he is deserving of parole? Perhaps he has witnessed other inmates receiving parole who have similar institutional records. Can he question the parole board's decision via the courts? The Supreme Court answered this question in 2011 when it ruled in the consolidated cases of *Swarthout v. Cooke* and *Cate v. Clay* that there is in essence no absolute or legal right to receive parole. The Court held that while the due process clause requires fair procedures in parole hearing, both Cooke and Clay received adequate process because they were allowed an opportunity to be heard and were provided a statement of the reasons why parole was denied. However, the courts do not have the right to step in and conclude the parole board's (and governor's) decisions were faulty. If the process is fair, then the inmate must live with the outcome.[143]

Parole Effectiveness

Despite all efforts to treat, correct, and rehabilitate incarcerated offenders, many return to prison shortly after their release. Persons released from prison face a multitude of difficulties. They remain largely uneducated, unskilled, and usually without solid family support systems—then add to this the burdens of a prison record. Not surprisingly, most parolees fail, and rather quickly; rearrests are most common in the first six months after release. The latest government data on parole failure indicate the following:

- About two-thirds (68 percent) of released prisoners were arrested for a new crime within three years, and three-quarters (77 percent) were arrested within five years.
- Within five years of release, 82 percent of property offenders were arrested for a new crime, compared to 77 percent of drug offenders, 74 percent of public order offenders, and 71 percent of violent offenders.
- More than a third (37 percent) of all prisoners who were arrested within five years of release were arrested within the first six months after release, with more than half (57 percent) arrested by the end of the first year.
- A sixth (16 percent) of released prisoners were responsible for almost half (48 percent) of the nearly 1.2 million arrests that occurred in the five-year follow-up period.
- Within five years of release, 84 percent of inmates who were age 24 or younger at release were arrested, compared to 79 percent of inmates ages 25 to 39 and 69 percent of those age 40 or older.[144]

Figure 12.1 shows how a majority of inmates fail on parole and fail quickly.

A report by the influential Pew Foundation also found high recidivism rates but that not all states had the same failure rates. The more successful ones made important correctional decisions—such as the types of offenders sentenced to prison, how inmates are selected for release, how long they are under supervision—using carefully drawn empirical evidence. Which strategies were the most successful? States that made extensive use of probation for petty offenders had relatively higher inmate recidivism rates because only the most hard-core inmates were actually sent to prison. Parole was more successful in states that employed programs that target motivated offenders to stay crime- and drug-free through a combination of swift and certain sanctions for prison violations and rewards for obeying correctional rules.[145]

In deciding whether parole is effective, it is important to understand there are multiple outcome

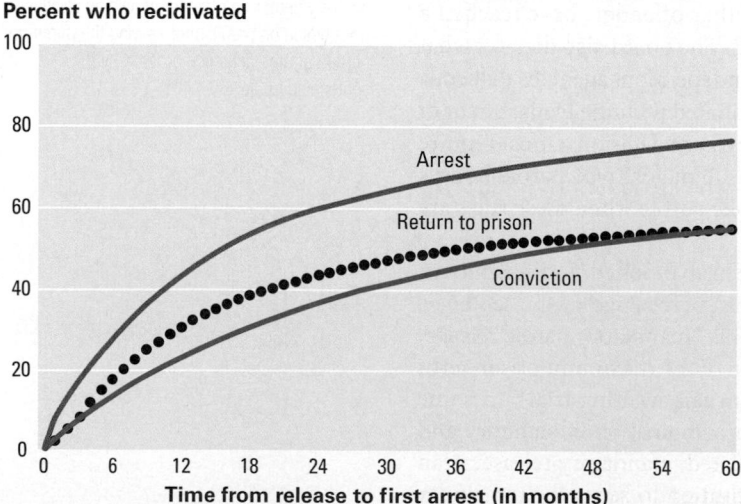

Percent who recidivated

Time from release to first arrest (in months)

FIGURE 12.1 Recidivism of Prisoners in 30 States by Time from Release to First Arrest that Led to Recidivating Event

Source: Matthew R. Durose, Alexia D. Cooper, and Howard N. Snyder, *Recidivism of Prisoners Released in 30 States in 2005: Patterns from 2005 to 2010*, Bureau of Justice Statistics, 2014.

Monitoring Parolees with GPS

Probationers aren't the only ones being monitored with GPS technology; parole agencies are now using GPS-based equipment to monitor and supervise offenders and maintain public safety.

For example, the California Department of Corrections and Rehabilitation Division of Adult Parole Operations runs one such GPS supervision program. Evaluations of efforts to monitor high-risk gang offenders who were placed on GPS monitoring found that when compared to subjects without GPS monitoring, those in GPS group were less likely to be arrested in general or for a violent offense. However, they were much more likely to commit technical and nontechnical violations of their parole.

High-Risk Sex Offenders

Another evaluation reviewed outcomes from all high-risk sex offenders released from California prisons between January 2006 and March 2009 who remained in the state of California. The one-year follow-up focused on a sample of 516 subjects that was divided equally into a treatment group, whose members were monitored by GPS, and a control group, whose members received traditional parole supervision.

The subjects in the GPS group demonstrated significantly better outcomes: Offenders who were monitored using GPS complied with the terms of their parole at higher rates than did offenders on traditional parole. Those placed on GPS monitoring had significantly lower recidivism rates than those who received traditional supervision. Cost analysis indicated that the GPS program expenses were roughly $35.96 per day per parolee, while the cost of traditional supervision is $27.45 per day per parolee. The GPS monitoring program was more expensive but more effective.

CRITICAL THINKING

Do you view the use of GPS monitoring and other technology as a panacea that can reduce crime at a relatively low cost, or the frightening start of government monitoring that will end up with all of us being tracked and watched to make sure we commit no wrongs? Has twenty-first century technology meant the end of personal privacy?

Sources: California Department of Corrections and Rehabilitation, "Electronic Monitoring," http://www.cdcr.ca.gov/parole/electronic-monitoring.html; National Institute of Justice, "Evaluating the Use of GPS Technology in the Community," https://nij.gov/topics/corrections/community/monitoring-technologies/Pages/gps-community.aspx. (URLs accessed May 2017.)

measures that can be used: rearrests, technical violations, re-incarcerations, additional convictions, and so on. Depending on the outcome measure used, parole may or may not look successful.[146]

Supervision on the Outside

After they are on the outside, parolees are supervised and monitored by parole officers, some of whom maintain a social work, treatment orientation, while others are more authoritative and rule oriented. Even though the difference in style and attitude may not determine parolee success, research does show that parole officers who hold more authoritative attitudes are more likely to pursue revocation hearings for offender noncompliance.[147] The Criminal Justice and Technology feature reviews new measures being used to monitor parolees in the community.

The Problem of Reentry

Parole failure is a significant problem, and a growing portion of the correctional population consists of parolees who failed on the outside. Why has the phenomenon of parole failure remained so stubborn and hard to control? Why is it so difficult to reenter society?

One reason may be the very nature of the prison experience itself. Being separated from family and friends takes a steep toll. As one 60-year-old male inmate put it:

Incarceration didn't teach me nothing except how to do some bad things better; only thing prison did, they separated me from my family for a long time; you miss your kids' birthdays and their basketball games; you miss family weddings, family members die and you don't get to say goodbye to them; you can't help your mother, it hurts.[148]

The psychological and economic problems that lead offenders to recidivism are rarely addressed by a stay in prison. Despite rehabilitation efforts, the typical ex-convict is still the same undereducated, unemployed, substance-abusing, lower-socioeconomic-status male he was when arrested. Being separated from friends and family, not sharing in conventional society, associating with dangerous people, and adapting to a volatile lifestyle probably have done little to improve the offender's personality or behavior. It seems naïve to think that incarceration alone can help someone overcome these lifelong disabilities. By their very nature, prisons seek to impose and maintain order and conformity rather than to help inmates develop skills such as independence and critical thinking—factors that may be essential after the inmate is forced to cope outside the prison walls.[149] Once outside, the ex-inmate faces a series of barriers that inhibits his adjustment to society; some of these are discussed next.

Why Do People Fail on Parole?

Why do so many inmates fail in the community? A number of social, economic, and personal factors interfere with reentry success. Reentry risks can be tied to legal changes in how people are released from prison. Changes in sentencing laws have resulted in the growth of mandatory release and limits on discretionary parole. Inmates may be discouraged from seeking involvement in rehabilitation programs because they no longer affect the chance of parole. The lack of incentive means that fewer inmates leaving prison have participated in programs to address deficiencies in the areas of employment, education, and substance use. Many of those being released have therefore not received adequate treatment and are unprepared for life in conventional society.[150]

Nor does the situation improve upon release. Many inmates are not assigned to supervision caseloads after they are back in the community. About 200,000 released inmates go unsupervised each year, three-quarters of whom have been released after completing their maximum sentence and are therefore not required to be supervised. A number of research efforts indicate that supervision can be valuable. When Michael Osterman looked at the records of those released from prison in New Jersey, he found that after three years those released with parole supervision were generally less involved in new crimes when compared with those who were released unconditionally.[151] Of course, inmates who "max out" or otherwise go unsupervised may be the more serious offenders whose survival in the community would be lower even if they were supervised. If these differences are controlled, the effect of supervision is neutralized.[152] So the actual effect of supervision after release is still open to debate.[153]

Regardless of how they are released, the risks the flood of newly released inmates present to the community include increases in child abuse, family violence, the spread of infectious diseases, homelessness, and community disorganization. Many have no way to cope and wind up in homeless shelters.[154] These problems take a heavy toll on communities and also limit reentry success.

PERSONAL PROBLEMS Reentry problems are related to the releasee's own lifelong personal deficits. They may have an antisocial personality and childhood experiences with family dysfunction; many have suffered from a lifetime of substance abuse or dependence disorder.[155] It is not surprising that releasees who maintain criminal peer

Recently released from prison on parole, 35-year-old Thomas Vescio is coping with being back in society, bipolar disorder, ADHD, and seizures. He is completely overwhelmed and sure he will be going back to prison. "Maybe it's easier to be locked up," he says.

associations, carry weapons, abuse alcohol, and harbor aggressive feelings are the most likely to fail upon reentry.[156]

Once outside, those who return to reoffending often suffer stigmatizing labels from both official (e.g., police) and nonofficial (e.g., neighbors, employers) sources that may reinforce their belief that they are outside the mainstream and that a criminal way of life is the only path left open. Stigma is especially hard on former sex offenders, who must register upon release so any efforts to remain anonymous are thwarted. As one parolee put it:

> You do your time (in prison) and don't want no more trouble in your life, but people look at you like you are a constant danger. They harassed me, followed me around and pinned stuff on my car with nasty words; one time guys followed me from a store and screamed "sex offender." I told the police, but they say there's nothing they can do. I've been chased and almost beaten; even cops follow me sometimes. I can't go anywhere without people that I know. I can't talk to kids; even if they ask me something, I'm supposed to walk away, and it makes you look mean always.[157]

Research also suggests that released inmates harbor cynicism toward the criminal justice system, especially when released to neighborhoods with a heavy concentration of formerly incarcerated persons.[158] Such attitudes do note bode well for successful reentry.

ECONOMIC PROBLEMS Prison takes a heavy economic toll on former inmates. Most people leave prison with no savings, no immediate entitlement to unemployment benefits, and few employment prospects, especially in this era of high unemployment.[159] The Pew Foundation found that serving time significantly reduces economic status and prospects:

- Serving time reduces hourly wages for men by approximately 11 percent, annual employment by nine weeks, and annual earnings by 40 percent.
- By age 48, the typical former inmate will have earned $179,000 less than if he had never been incarcerated.

A prison experience locks people onto the lowest rung of the economic ladder and significantly reduces their chances for upward economic mobility. A year after release, as many as 60 percent of former inmates are not employed in the regular labor market, and employers are increasingly reluctant to hire ex-offenders. Ex-offenders are commonly barred from working in the fields in which most jobs are being created, such as child care, education, security, nursing, and home health care. More jobs are also now unionized, and many unions exclude ex-offenders. Parolees who had a good employment record before their incarceration and who are able to find jobs after their release are the ones most likely to avoid recidivating. Another bit of good news comes from a four-state survey conducted by Paul Hirschfield and Alex Piquero, which found that though some people regard ex-offenders as dangerous and dishonest, many reject these stereotypes, and a majority say that they would be willing to work and associate with people who were previously incarcerated. Even people who believe in harsh punishment may be willing to work alongside people who paid their debt to society. If more people were acquainted with ex-offenders, the more willing they would be to hire them and give them the economic opportunities to succeed.[160]

FAMILY PROBLEMS Inmates with strong social support and close family ties have a better chance of making it on the outside.[161] But prison can take its toll on social relationships, and being a former inmate can devastate the economic and social functioning of a family. Poor inmates and their families may be no longer welcome in subsidized public housing complexes. Also, without government subsidies, former inmates' families may not have the economic means to find affordable housing. The Pew Foundation found that family income averaged over the years a father is incarcerated is 22 percent lower than family income was the year before the father was incarcerated. Even in the year after the father is released, family income remains 15 percent lower than it was the year before incarceration.[162]

Kids are hurt educationally, socially, and financially if a parent is a former inmate. The Pew Foundation found that children with fathers who have been incarcerated are significantly more likely than other children to be expelled or suspended from school (23 percent compared with 4 percent). Children of incarcerated and released parents may suffer confusion, sadness, and social stigma, and these feelings often result in difficulties in school, low self-esteem, aggressive behavior, and general emotional dysfunction. One reason is that mothers released from prison have difficulty finding services such as housing, employment, and child care, and this causes stress for them and their children.

Another problem is that if the parents are negative role models, children fail to develop positive attitudes about work and responsibility. Children of incarcerated parents are five times more likely to serve time in prison than children whose parents are not incarcerated.

COMMUNITY PROBLEMS Parole expert Richard Seiter notes that when there were only a few hundred thousand prisoners and a few thousand releasees per year, the issues surrounding the release of offenders did not overwhelm communities.[163] Families could house ex-inmates, job-search organizations could find them jobs, and community social service agencies could respond to their individual needs for mental health or substance abuse treatment. Today, the sheer number of reentering inmates has taxed the communities to which they are returning.[164]

Community characteristics can also influence the way parole violations are handled. Parolees returning to communities with high unemployment rates—a factor considered by parole board members to be an unstable environment—are more likely to have their parole revoked.[165] Similarly, parolees living in areas with concentrated disadvantage and social disorder, where bars are plentiful and liquor stores abundant, also suffer higher rates of recidivism.[166] Clearly, the neighborhood plays a significant role in parole success. Communities that can provide social and mental health services also influence parole success. For example, many former inmates need mental and psychological services that some communities simply cannot provide. Even when public mental health services are available, many mentally ill individuals fail to use them because they fear institutionalization, deny they are mentally ill, or distrust the mental health system. The situation will become more serious as more and more parolees are released into the same disorganized communities where deteriorated conditions may have motivated their original crimes. Having mental health services nearby seems to have a significant effect on parole board decision making.[167] The further parolees live from social service providers, the more likely they will be returned to prison.

Recognizing that some communities experience high rates of incarceration and reentry, some have created coalitions of community organizations to interact with every person returning home from prison. In New York City, the NYC Justice Corps provides transitional employment for young adults returning home from prison and jail in two neighborhoods most impacted by incarceration and reentry. In each location, a local organization brings together young people with their community to identify community improvement projects that the NYC Justice Corps members can execute while developing hard skills that ready them for the labor market.[168]

LEGAL PROBLEMS Ex-inmates may also find that going straight is an economic impossibility. Many employers are reluctant to hire people who have served time. Even if a criminal record does not automatically prohibit employment, why would an employer hire an ex-con when other applicants are available? If ex-offenders lie about their prison experience and are later found out, they will be dismissed for misrepresentation. Research shows that former inmates who gain and keep meaningful employment are more likely to succeed on parole than those who are unemployed or underemployed.[169] One reason why ex-inmates find it so difficult to make it on the outside is the legal restrictions they are forced to endure. These may include prohibitions on certain kinds of employment, limits on obtaining licenses, and restrictions on their freedom of movement (see the Contemporary Issues in Criminal Justice box).[170]

Improving Chances on Reentry

Can something be done to ease reentry? Now that the scope of the problem has been recognized, both the federal and state governments have devoted energy to improving success at reentry. On April 9, 2008, the Second Chance Act was signed into law. This federal legislation authorized various grants to government agencies and nonprofit

Criminal Records and Reentry Success

I am writing this letter ... out of desperation and to tell you a little about the struggles of reentering society as a convicted felon. I have worked hard to turn my life around. I have remained clean for nearly eight years, I am succeeding in college, and I continue to share my story in schools, treatment facilities, and correctional institutions, yet I have nothing to show for it.... I have had numerous interviews and sent out more than 200 résumés for jobs for which I am more than qualified. I have had denial after denial because of my felony. I do understand that you are not responsible for the choices that have brought me to this point. Furthermore, I recognize that if I was not abiding by the law, if I was not clean, and if I was not focusing my efforts toward a successful future, I would have no claim to make.

So writes Jay, a man convicted of involuntary vehicular manslaughter and sentenced to 38 months in state prison nine years before. He is not alone: a criminal label can haunt people for the rest of their lives, well beyond their offending years and despite the fact that they have stayed "clean" for quite some time.

Many people with records suffer stigma that prevents them from getting jobs. A recent study shows that nearly one-third of American adults have been arrested by age 23. This record will keep many people from obtaining employment, even if they have paid their dues, are qualified for the job, and are unlikely to reoffend.

Criminal records run the gamut from one-time arrests where charges are dropped, to lengthy, serious, and violent criminal histories. Many people who have been arrested—and, therefore, technically have a criminal record that shows up on a background check—were never convicted of a crime. This is true not only among those charged with minor crimes but also for many individuals arrested for serious offenses.

The impact of having a criminal record is most often felt among African Americans, who may already experience racial discrimination in the labor market and are more likely than whites to have a criminal record. Research shows that a criminal record reduces the likelihood of a job callback or offer by approximately 50 percent. This criminal record "penalty" is substantially greater for African Americans than for white applicants. Latinos suffer similar penalties in the employment market.

In addition to these significant and often overlapping challenges, an extra set of punishments, or "collateral consequences," is imposed on individuals as a direct result of their criminal convictions. These legal restrictions create barriers to jobs, housing, benefits, and voting. More than 80 percent of the statutes that place restrictions on people convicted of crime operate as denial of employment opportunities. Although some of these consequences serve important public safety purposes, others may be antiquated and create unnecessary barriers to legitimate work opportunities. A commonly cited example is that, in some states, formerly incarcerated people who were trained as barbers cannot hold those jobs after release because state laws prohibit felons from practicing the trade, presumably because their access to sharp objects makes them a threat to the public.

Regardless of the legal restrictions, the majority of employers indicate they would "probably" or "definitely" not be willing to hire an applicant with a criminal record. A recent report by the National Employment Law Project found frequent use of blanket "no-hire" policies among major corporations. Employers do not want to hire individuals who might commit future crimes and who may be a risk to their employees' and customers' safety. The assumption, of course, is that a prior record signals higher odds that the individual will commit more crimes in the future.

CRITICAL THINKING

1. What can be done to reduce the effect of labels and stigma placed on people who have paid their debt?
2. Should records be expunged within a certain time frame if a person does not reoffend? Or should knowledge of a prior criminal record be available because employers have a right to know about the background of the people they are considering hiring?

Sources: Mike Vuolo, Sarah Lageson, and Christopher Uggen, "Criminal Record Questions in the Era of 'Ban the Box,'" *Criminology and Public Policy* 16 (2017): 139–165; Amy Solomon, "In Search of a Job: Criminal Records as Barriers to Employment," *NIJ Journal* 270 (2012), http://www.nij.gov/nij/journals/270/criminal -records.htm (accessed May 2017).

AP Images/Melanie Stetson Freeman

Inmates serving time at San Quentin prison in California learn how to code as part of the Last Mile program. The program teaches them skills that can ensure they will get good-paying jobs when they are released. Prisoners who have been in the program longer help newcomers.

groups to provide a variety of services (including employment assistance, housing, substance abuse treatment, and family programming) that can help reduce reoffending and decrease violations of probation and parole. In response, a number of correctional authorities have created reentry programs. Some start preparing inmates for release almost as soon as their sentence begins. Others provide postrelease counseling and support.

What reentry programs are most successful? A recent study by Christy Visher and her colleagues examined the impact of 12 reentry-related, prerelease services commonly used by corrections agencies.[171] The findings were rather interesting and even counterintuitive. First, services that address "criminal attitudes, personal relationships, anger management, and education deficits" are important—and should be implemented prior to release and to the provision of post-release services. In other words, programming that focused on "individual change" were among the most effective. Second, services that provide practical skills (e.g., life skills programs and employment services) are unlikely to improve post-release outcomes. How is this possible? This explanation was offered: "Life skills programs, and other services focused on practical reentry strategies, including many employment services (e.g., preparing a resume or interviewing skills), may give the impression to individuals receiving these services that they are prepared for reentry and that returning home will not be difficult." Instead, fundamental cognitive changes are necessary, otherwise when inmates are released and hit obstacles on the outside, they may become frustrated and resort to their old ways.

ETHICALREFLECTION

A New Jersey state trooper pulled over Albert Florence's pregnant wife as she was driving with him and their four-year-old son in the car. Because Albert Florence owned the vehicle, the officer ran his license and discovered an outstanding warrant for a noncriminal traffic fine. Despite the fact that Florence had already paid the fine and carried an official letter proving it, the police officer arrested him and placed him in a local jail where he was incarcerated for six days and subjected to two invasive strip searches. A judge then freed Florence, confirming that he had in fact paid his fine. Florence filed suit, claiming the degrading searches violated his Fourth Amendment rights.

In *Florence v. Board of Chosen Freeholders*, the Supreme Court, in a 5–4 decision, ruled that county jails can routinely strip search all new detainees, including those, like Albert Florence, who had been arrested for minor offenses and were unlikely to spend more than one night in jail. The Court concluded that a prisoner's likelihood of possessing contraband based on the severity of the current offense or an arrestee's criminal history is too difficult to determine effectively. The Court pointed out instances, such as the arrest of Timothy McVeigh, in which an individual who commits a minor traffic offense is capable of extreme violence. Correctional facilities have a strong interest in keeping their employees and inmates safe. A general strip search policy adequately and effectively protects that interest. The Court did note that there may be an exception to this rule when the arrestees are not entering the general population and will not have substantial contact with other inmates. In his dissent, Justice Stephen Breyer, along with Justices Ruth Bader Ginsburg, Sonia Sotomayor, and Elena Kagan, opined that strip searches of individuals arrested for minor offenses are unreasonable unless the prison official has a reasonable suspicion that the individual possesses drugs or other contraband.

Writing Challenge: Reread this chapter's section on prisoners' rights, then write an essay addressing the ethics of correctional authorities having the right to strip search all people entering a detention facility, whether it be jail or prison. Is it fair to subject people to this indignity, as the Supreme Court ruled, to maintain security? Would it be unethical to spare some but not others this indignity? Before you answer, remember to consider whether people should be spared such treatment merely because of their age, status, religion, or gender. For example, should an elderly nun, arrested at an antiwar demonstration, be stripped searched if she is to be held in detention?

SUMMARY

L01 *Discuss the male prison experience* A significant number of facilities are old and in ill repair. Institutions are overcrowded, and meaningful treatment efforts are often a matter of wishful thinking. The typical prison is often described as a "school for crime." Recidivism rates are shockingly high. Prisons in the United States are total institutions that limit individuality and demand obedience. Inmates locked within their walls are segregated from the outside world. They have to learn to cope with their new environment or risk injury or even death. Young males may be raped and kept as sexual slaves by older, more aggressive inmates. However, many inmates refuse to report rape, and others may misunderstand what constitutes a rape, so the true extent of prison rape may never be known.

LO2 *Describe the inmate social code and inmate culture* Part of living in prison involves learning to protect oneself and developing survival instincts. The inmate social code refers to unwritten guidelines that express the values, attitudes, and type of behavior that older inmates demanded of younger ones. Inmates form their own world, with a unique set of norms and rules, known as the inmate subculture. Those who become the most "prisonized" will be the least likely to avoid criminal activity on the outside.

LO3 *Summarize the female prison experience* Women's prisons tend to be smaller than those housing male inmates, but female inmates may suffer from a lack of adequate job training and from inferior health, treatment, and educational facilities. Unlike male inmates, women usually do not present an immediate physical danger to staff and fellow inmates. Make-believe family groups contain masculine and feminine figures acting as fathers and mothers; some even act as children and take on the role of brother or sister.

LO4 *Discuss the different forms of correctional treatment* Counseling programs help inmates control their emotions, communicate with others, deal with legal concerns, manage general life issues, control substance abuse, and develop and maintain social relationships. Inmate rehabilitation is also pursued through vocational and educational training.

LO5 *Describe the world of correctional officers* Correctional officers are now viewed as dedicated public servants. Most are in favor of rehabilitation efforts, so that the typical correctional officer has been characterized as a "people worker." There are few gender differences in the behavior of correctional officers.

LO6 *Discuss the causes of prison violence* Violence can involve both collective and individual conflict: inmate versus inmate, inmate versus staff, or staff versus inmate. Prison violence is associated with overcrowding, lack of effective dispute-resolution mechanisms, individual history of violence, and poor prison conditions.

LO7 *Explain what is meant by prisoners' rights, and discuss some key privileges that have been granted to inmates* Today, inmates have the right to medical care, freedom from cruel and unusual treatment, the right to an attorney, and the right to practice their religion. Inmates can sue the prison administration if their rights have been violated—for example, if they are denied proper medical care.

LO8 *Discuss the parole process and the problems of prisoner reentry* Most inmates are paroled either by mandatory release or parole board vote. Parole is generally viewed as a privilege granted to deserving inmates on the basis of their good behavior while in prison. More than half of all parolees return to prison shortly after their release. Recidivism may be a by-product of the disruptive effect a prison experience has on personal relationships.

KEY TERMS

total institutions, p. 296

inmate subculture, p. 300

inmate social code, p. 300

prisonization, p. 300

make-believe family, also known as a play family, p. 303

cognitive-behavioral therapy (CBT), p. 304

therapeutic communities, p, 305

work release, p. 308

furlough, p. 308

hands-off doctrine, p. 312

substantive rights, p. 313

jailhouse lawyers, p. 313

cruel and unusual punishment, p. 314

parole, p. 317

parole board, p. 317

REVIEW QUESTIONS

1. Considering the dangers that men face during their prison stay, should nonviolent inmates be placed in separate institutions to protect them from harm?

2. Should women be allowed to work as guards in men's prisons? What about male guards in women's prisons?

3. Should prison inmates be allowed a free college education while noncriminals are forced to pay tuition?

4. Which would be more effective: telling inmates that they have to earn the right to be paroled, or giving inmates their parole date in advance and telling them they will lose it for misbehavior?

5. What is the role of the parole board?

6. Should a former prisoner enjoy all the civil rights afforded to the average citizen?

7. Should former inmates lose their right to vote?

RUSSIAN TOOLBOX IN THE 2016
AGANDA, FAKE NEWS, TROLLS, AND BOTS
ING AND THEFT OF POLITICAL INFORMATION
D LEAKS OF DAMAGING MATERIAL
ASSINATION AND POLITICAL VIOLEN
ESTMENT CONTROL IN KEY ECONOM
ADY BUSINESS/FINANCIAL

Contemporary Issues in American Criminal Justice

In a declassified version of a classified document, the US intelligence community concluded that "Vladimir Putin ordered an influence campaign in 2016 aimed at the US presidential election," with the specific goal of harming Hillary Clinton's "electability and potential presidency."[1] The report went on to state: "We further assess Putin and the Russian Government developed a clear preference for President-elect Donald Trump," and it even claimed "Russia has sought to influence elections across Europe."

Did Russia hack the US presidential election or otherwise influence it? It is probably impossible to know with absolute certainty. At the time of this writing, the matter was anything but resolved. The Federal Bureau of Investigation was pursuing at least three separate probes related to the alleged hack.[2] One of the investigations was looking into the people behind the 2015 breaches of the Democratic National Committee's computer systems. Another was examining financial transactions by Russian individuals and companies that were alleged to have had connections with President Trump.

Assuming a campaign of influence did play out, how did it happen? One allegation is that hackers from Russia have a track recording of accessing servers belonging to the government and political parties of rival countries. More plausible is the explanation that it's all part of a covert plan to manipulate rivals. In an opinion column for the *Washington Post*, David Ignatius wrote that "The Kremlin's attempt to meddle in the 2016 US presidential election is part of a much bigger tale of Russian covert action—in which Trump's campaign was perhaps a tool, witting or unwitting."[3] And as the intelligence community report noted, "Moscow will apply lessons learned from its campaign aimed at the US presidential election to future influence efforts in the United States and worldwide, including against US allies and their election processes." It will be interesting to continue following this case.

Part 5 contains two chapters that cover special issues in criminal justice. Chapter 13 looks at the history of juvenile justice and current issues such as transfer to the adult court and juvenile sentencing issues. Chapter 14 looks at emerging issues the justice system must learn to confront: cyber crime, global crime, green crime, and corporate crime. To the extent allegations of Russian election hacking prove true, the conduct could rise to the level of transnational criminal activity—the kinds of crime that offend the core values of the international community.

Anadolu Agency/Getty Images

13 Juvenile Justice in the Twenty-First Century

Recent research on adolescent development has generated concern about our nation's treatment of young people in the juvenile justice system. Much of what has happened in juvenile justice in the past 15 years has not been informed by—and in some cases has ignored—what we now know about the adolescent brain. In response to this "disconnect," the Office of Juvenile Justice and Delinquency Prevention (OJJDP) in the US Justice Department asked the National Academy of Sciences (NAS) to "take stock" of changes in juvenile justice in light of current knowledge concerning adolescent development. The NAS empaneled the Committee on Assessing Juvenile Justice Reform, which in 2013 released a report summarizing its findings.[4] The news was not very good. Much needs to be done to bring juvenile justice in line with scientific findings concerning brain development.

We know juveniles differ from adults. They have a harder time controlling themselves in emotionally charged situations. They are more subject to peer pressure than adults. They also exhibit less of a future orientation. According to the NAS, "The combination of these three cognitive patterns accounts for the tendency of adolescents to prefer and engage in risk behaviors that have a high probability of immediate reward but can have harmful consequences." Also, the NAS noted that "adolescents lack mature capacity for self-regulation because the brain system that influences pleasure-seeking and emotional reactivity develops more rapidly than the brain system that supports self-control." The result? Juveniles are *programmed* to more easily resort to crime. The juvenile justice system, however, does not readily acknowledge this. Indeed, it seems to *ignore* it almost completely.

It gets worse. The typical juvenile offender is not a hardened violent criminal; most commit relatively minor offenses. Nearly half of all juvenile offenders enter the system just once. Only about one-third of arrested juveniles go on to commit an adult offense. In response to the perception that juvenile delinquency is on the rise, and in response to the perception that juveniles are committing more serious offenses with greater frequency, strict policies have been enacted to address what is primarily a problem of perception. Zero-tolerance approaches are popular.

Joseph Rodriguez/Redux

LEARNING OBJECTIVES

LO1 Describe the history of juvenile justice

LO2 Discuss the establishment of the juvenile court

LO3 Describe the changes in juvenile justice that began in the 1960s and continue today

LO4 Summarize police processing of juvenile offenders

LO5 Describe the juvenile court process

LO6 Explain the concept of waiver

LO7 Explain the importance of *In re Gault*

LO8 Describe the juvenile correctional process

Long sentences are imposed. Some have been so severe the Supreme Court has had to step in (e.g., *Miller v. Alabama* in 2012). Confinement is used with surprising frequency. More and more juveniles are being prosecuted as adults. States have even changed the legal definition of juvenile in the case of certain crimes. The list goes on.

The NAS also reminds us that there are three critical conditions necessary for healthy development in young people: "(1) the presence of a parent or parent figure who is involved with the adolescent and concerned about his or her successful development, (2) inclusion in a peer group that values and models prosocial behavior and academic success, and (3) activities that contribute to autonomous decision making and critical thinking." Unfortunately, though, the juvenile justice system's reliance on "containment, confinement, and control" threatens juveniles' life chances. Regardless of whether the punishment in question is "justified," and regardless of the seriousness of a young person's misdeeds, punishments that threaten family bonds, remove people from prosocial society, and strip them of constructive decision making are bound to threaten them in the long run.

Independent of (yet interrelated with) the adult criminal justice system, the juvenile justice system is primarily responsible for dealing with juvenile and youth crime, as well as with incorrigible and truant children and runaways. Conceived at the turn of the twentieth century, the juvenile justice system was viewed as a quasi-social welfare agency that was to act as a surrogate parent in the interests of the child; this is referred to as the *parens patriae* philosophy. Many people who work in the system still hold to the original social welfare principles of the juvenile justice system. In contrast, those who adopt a crime control orientation suggest that the juvenile justice system's *parens patriae* philosophy is outdated. They point to nationally publicized incidents of juvenile violence, such as the shootings at Columbine High School in Colorado, as indicators that serious juvenile offenders should be punished and disciplined rather than treated and rehabilitated. "Why should we give special treatment to violent young juveniles?" they ask.

It remains to be seen whether the juvenile justice system will continue on its path toward deterrence, punishment, and control or return to its former role as a treatment-dispensing agency. This chapter reviews the history of juvenile justice and discusses the justice system's processing of youthful offenders.

The History of Juvenile Justice

LO1 Describe the history of juvenile justice

The modern practice of legally separating adult criminals and juvenile offenders can be traced back to two developments in English custom and law that occurred centuries ago: the development of Elizabethan-era poor laws and the creation of the English chancery court. Both of these innovations were designed to allow the state to take control of the lives of needy but not necessarily criminal children.[5]

- *Poor laws.* As early as 1535, the English passed statutes known as poor laws, which (among other things) mandated the appointment of overseers who placed destitute or neglected children with families who then trained them in agricultural, trade, or domestic services; this practice was referred to as *indenture*. The Elizabethan poor laws of 1601 created a system of churchwardens and overseers who, with the consent of the justices of the peace, identified vagrant, delinquent, and neglected children and took measures to put them to work. Often this meant placing them in poorhouses or workhouses or, more commonly, apprenticing them until their adulthood.
- *Chancery courts.* English chancery courts provided judicial relief to those who had no legal standing or could expect no legal relief because of the corruption and

parens patriae Latin term meaning "father of his country." According to this legal philosophy, the government is the guardian of everyone who has a disability, especially children, and has a legal duty to act in their best interests until they reach the age of majority.

poor laws Seventeenth-century laws in England that bound out vagrants and abandoned children as indentured servants to masters.

inadequacy of other common-law courts. People who felt their rights were being violated could take their cases to the chancery court for review. In this capacity, the chancery court protected the property rights and welfare of more minor children who could not care for themselves—children whose position and property were of direct concern to the monarch. The courts dealt with issues of guardianship and the use and control of property. Thus, if the guardian of an orphaned child wanted to sell off his ward's inheritance, the chancery court might be asked to review the proceedings and determine whether the sale was in the child's best interest.

Care of Children in Early America

Poor laws and chancery courts were brought from England to colonial America. Poor laws were passed in Virginia in 1646 and in Connecticut and Massachusetts in 1678, and they continued in force until the early nineteenth century. They mandated care for wayward and destitute children. However, those youths who committed serious criminal offenses continued to be tried in the same courts as adults.

To accommodate dependent youths, local jurisdictions developed almshouses, poorhouses, and workhouses. Crowded and unhealthy, these shelters accepted the poor, the insane, the diseased, and vagrant and destitute children. Middle-class civic leaders, who referred to themselves as child savers, began to develop organizations and groups to help alleviate the burdens of the poor and immigrants by sponsoring shelter care for youths, educational and social activities, and the development of settlement houses. In retrospect, their main focus seems to have been on extending governmental control over a whole range of youthful activities that previously had been left to private or family control, including idleness, drinking, vagrancy, and delinquency.[6]

The Child-Saving Movement

The child savers were responsible for creating a number of programs for indigent youths, including the New York House of Refuge, which began operations in 1825.[7] Its charter was to protect indigent youths who were at risk of crime by taking them off the streets and reforming them in a family-like environment.[8]

The New York House of Refuge, actually a reformatory, opened on January 1, 1825, with only six boys and three girls, but within the first decade of its operation,

child savers Late nineteenth-century reformers in America who developed programs for troubled youths and influenced legislation creating the juvenile justice system.

The Granger Collection, NYC

Boys on the steps of an abandoned tenement building in New York City, about 1889. The child savers were concerned that, if left alone, children like these would enter a life of crime. They created the House of Refuge to care for poor and neglected kids. Critics accused them of class and race bias.

Duties and Characteristics of the Job

- Social workers aid individuals or families who are disadvantaged or face particular challenges.

- Social workers pick an area of specialization within one of several larger categories.

- Child, family, and health social workers aid families dealing with issues of social functioning, such as child abuse and truancy.

- Social work is a demanding profession both intellectually and emotionally.

Job Outlook

- The prospects for employment as a social worker are good because jobs are expected to grow faster than average in the near future.

- Due to the impending retirement of the baby boom generation, many job opportunities are available in hospices and nursing homes for social workers specializing in elder care.

- The employment of school and private social service agencies will also increase.

Salary

- Recent median annual earnings of child, family, and school social workers are $45,900.

- The lowest 10 percent earn less than $28,530, and the top 10 percent earn more than $76,820.

- Social workers' salaries vary according to their specialization.

Qualifications

- The ability to meet the challenging education requirements and certification are the primary qualifications necessary to become a social worker.

- Personal characteristics, such as sensitivity, responsibility, and the ability to work independently are also very important.

- Potential social workers must have at least a bachelor's degree in social work to start at entry-level positions, and additional education for higher degrees will prepare them for more advanced duties.

Education and Training

- For entry-level positions, a bachelor's degree in social work (BSW) or in a similar field, such as sociology, is necessary.

- Those who want to advance further should earn a master's degree in social work (MSW) or a doctorate (PhD or DSW).

- Those who want to ascend to the highest-level positions in an organization employing social workers or design new social work policies or programs should pursue a PhD.

Reality Check

- Social workers' education is never truly complete. They must keep up on recent development through attending conferences, reading the literature, and possibly participating in in-service training.

- Social workers must be empathetic and willing to tackle difficult problems.

- People who cannot work well on their own will not make good social workers.

- The highest-level positions require extensive education and training.

Source: Bureau of Labor Statistics, US Department of Labor, "Social Workers," *Occupational Outlook Handbook*, http://www.bls.gov/ooh/Community-and-Social-Service/Social-workers.htm (accessed May 2017).

1,678 children were sent there because of vagrancy and petty crimes. As a resident, an adolescent's daily schedule was devoted for the most part to supervised labor, which was regarded as beneficial to education and discipline. Male inmates worked in shops that produced brushes, cane chairs, brass nails, and shoes. The female inmates sewed uniforms, did laundry, and carried out other domestic work. The reformatory had the authority to bind out inmates through indenture agreements to private employers; most males so bound out were farm workers, and most females were domestic laborers.

The Refuge Movement Spreads

When the House of Refuge opened, critics complained that the institution was run like a prison, with strict discipline and absolute separation of the sexes. Such a harsh program drove many children to run away, and the House of Refuge was forced to take a more lenient approach. Despite criticism, the concept enjoyed expanding popularity. In 1826, for example, the Boston City Council founded the House of Reformation for juvenile offenders.[9]

The child savers also influenced state and local governments to create independent correctional institutions to house minors. The first of these reform schools opened in Westboro, Massachusetts, in 1848 and in Rochester, New York, in 1849. Children lived in congregate conditions and spent their days working at institutional jobs, learning a trade where possible, and receiving some basic education. They were racially and sexually segregated, discipline was harsh and often involved whipping and isolation, and the physical care was of poor quality.

In 1853, New York philanthropist Charles Loring Brace helped develop the **Children's Aid Society** as an alternative for dealing with neglected and delinquent youths. Brace proposed rescuing wayward youths from the harsh environment of the city and providing them with temporary shelter and care. He then sought to place them in private homes in rural communities where they could engage in farming and agricultural work beyond the influence of the city. Although some placements proved successful, others resulted in the exploitation of children in a strange environment with few avenues of escape.

Children's Aid Society A child-saving organization begun by Charles Loring Brace; it took children from the streets in large cities and placed them with farm families on the prairie.

Establishment of the Juvenile Court

As the nation expanded, it became evident that private charities and public organizations were not caring adequately for the growing number of troubled youths. The child savers lobbied for an independent, state-supported juvenile court, and their efforts prompted the development of the first comprehensive juvenile court in Illinois in 1899. The Illinois Juvenile Court Act set up an independent court to handle criminal law violations by children under 16 years of age, as well as to care for neglected, dependent, and wayward youths. The act also created a probation department to monitor youths in the community and to direct juvenile court judges to place serious offenders in secure schools for boys and industrial schools for girls. The ostensible purpose of the act was to separate juveniles from adult offenders and to provide a legal framework in which juveniles could get adequate care and custody. By 1925, most states had developed juvenile courts.

LO2 Discuss the establishment of the juvenile court

juvenile court A court that has original jurisdiction over persons defined by statute as juveniles and alleged to be delinquents or status offenders.

The Development of Juvenile Justice

The juvenile court movement quickly spread across the United States. In its early form, it provided youths with quasi-legal, quasi-therapeutic, personalized justice. The main concern was the "best interests of the child," not strict adherence to legal doctrine, constitutional rights, or due process of law. The court was paternalistic, rather than adversarial. Attorneys were not required; hearsay evidence, inadmissible in criminal trials, was commonly employed in the adjudication of juvenile offenders. Children were encouraged to admit their "guilt" in open court (in violation of their Fifth Amendment rights). Verdicts were based on a "preponderance of the evidence," instead of being "beyond a reasonable doubt." Juvenile courts then functioned as quasi-social service agencies.

REFORM SCHOOLS Youngsters who were found delinquent in juvenile court could spend years in a state training school. Although they prided themselves on being non-punitive, these early reform schools attempted to exercise control based on the concept of reform through hard work and discipline. In the second half of the nineteenth century, the emphasis shifted from massive industrial schools to the cottage system. Juvenile offenders were housed in a series of small cabins, each one holding 20 to 40 children, run by "cottage parents," who attempted to create a homelike atmosphere. The first cottage system was established in Massachusetts, the second in Ohio. The system was generally applauded for being a great improvement over the industrial training schools.[10] By the 1950s, psychological treatment was introduced in juvenile corrections. Group counseling techniques became standard procedure in most juvenile institutions.

LEGAL CHANGE In the 1960s and 1970s, the US Supreme Court radically altered the juvenile justice system when it issued a series of decisions that established the right of juveniles to due process of law. The Court established that juveniles had the same rights as adults in important areas of trial process, including the right to confront witnesses, notice of charges, and the right to counsel. Exhibit 13.1 lists some of the legal cases that were most important in bringing procedural due process to the juvenile justice process.

WEB APP 13.1 Visit the website of the Office of Juvenile Justice and Delinquency Prevention in the US Justice Department at **http://www.ojjdp.gov**. Follow the "Research and Statistics" link, and answer this question: Was juvenile delinquency more of a problem in years past? Why or why not?

EXHIBIT 13.1 Important Juvenile Justice Cases

- *Kent v. United States* (1966) determined that a child has the right to an attorney at any hearing to decide whether his or her case should be transferred to juvenile court (waiver hearings).[11]

- *In re Gault* (1967) ruled that a minor has basic due process rights at trial, including the following: (1) notice of the charges, (2) right to counsel, (3) right to confront and cross-examine witnesses, (4) privilege against self-incrimination, and (5) the right to a transcript of the trial record.[12]

- *In re Winship* (1970) determined that the level of evidence for a finding of "juvenile delinquency" is proof beyond a reasonable doubt.[13]

- *McKeiver v. Pennsylvania* (1971) held that trial by jury in a juvenile court's adjudicative stage is not a constitutional requirement.[14]

- *Breed v. Jones* (1975) ruled that a child has the protection of the double-jeopardy clause of the Fifth Amendment and cannot be tried twice for the same crime.[15]

- *Fare v. Michael C.* (1979) held that a child has the protection of the *Miranda* decision: the right to remain silent during a police interrogation and to request that a lawyer be provided to protect his or her interests.[16]

- *Schall v. Martin* (1984) allowed for the placement of children in preventive detention before their adjudication.[17]

- *New Jersey v. T.L.O.* (1985) determined that although the Fourth Amendment protection against unreasonable search and seizure applies to children, school officials can legally search kids who violate school rules (e.g., smoking on campus), even when there is no evidence that the student violated the law.[18]

- *Vernonia School District v. Acton* (1995) held that the Fourth Amendment's guarantee against unreasonable searches is not violated by drug testing all students choosing to participate in interscholastic athletics.[19]

- *Roper v. Simmons* (2005) determined that juveniles who commit murder before they turn 18 cannot be sentenced to death.[20]

- *Graham v. Florida* (2010) prohibited life imprisonment for juveniles convicted for nonhomicide offenses.[21]

- *Miller v. Alabama* (2012) held that mandatory sentences of life without parole are unconstitutional for juveniles regardless of the underlying offense.[22]

- *Montgomery v. Louisiana* (2016) held that *Miller v. Alabama* should be applied retroactively, meaning juveniles sentenced to life prior to the Court's 2012 decision should also benefit from it.[23]

REALITYCHECK

Myth or Reality?

All juveniles fall under the jurisdiction of the adult court at age 18.

MYTH. There is considerable variation from state to state in terms of who is considered an adult for purposes of criminal prosecution. In Connecticut, New York, and North Carolina, the oldest age for juvenile court jurisdiction in delinquency matters is 15. This means that youths 16 or older are tried as adults in those states. And there are exceptions to these rules. Sometimes younger individuals can be "waived" to adult court—a topic taken up later in the chapter.

At what age should a person be considered an adult for purposes of criminal prosecution? Can you conceive of a situation in which someone who is 10 years old or younger should be prosecuted for a crime?

Besides the legal revolution brought about by the Supreme Court, Congress passed the Juvenile Justice and Delinquency Prevention Act of 1974 (JJDP Act) and established the federal Office of Juvenile Justice and Delinquency Prevention (OJJDP).[24] This legislation was enacted to identify the needs of youths and to fund programs in the juvenile justice system. Its main goal was to separate wayward, nondangerous youths from institutions housing delinquents and to remove adolescents from institutions housing adult offenders. In 1988, the act was amended to address the issue of minority overrepresentation in the juvenile justice system, and, in 1996, in a move reflecting the growing national frustration with serious delinquent offenders, the act was again amended to make it easier to hold delinquents in adult penal institutions. The various stages in the history of juvenile justice are set out in Concept Summary 13.1.

CONCEPT SUMMARY 13.1 Shifting Philosophies of Juvenile Justice

- **Before 1899:** Juveniles treated similarly to adult offenders. No distinction by age or capacity to commit criminal acts.

- **1899–1950s:** Children treated differently beginning with the Illinois Juvenile Court Act of 1899. By 1925, juvenile court acts had been established in virtually every state. *Parens patriae* philosophy dominates.

- **1950–1970:** Recognition by experts that the rehabilitation model and the protective nature of *parens patriae* had failed to prevent delinquency.

- **1970–1980:** Introduction of constitutional due process into the juvenile justice system. Experimentation with diversion and concern about stigma and labeling. Juvenile Justice and Delinquency Prevention Act of 1974 enacted.

- **1980–2000:** Rising juvenile crime rates, coupled with the perceived failure of rehabilitation to control delinquency, lead to a shift to a crime control and punishment philosophy similar to that of the adult criminal justice system. Focus on expanding the crime control capabilities of the juvenile justice system so that it resembles the adult system.

- **2000–today:** Balanced approach. Attempt to provide treatment to needy youths and get tough with dangerous repeat offenders.

Juvenile Justice Today

Today, the juvenile justice system has jurisdiction over two distinct categories of offenders: delinquents and status offenders.[25] **Juvenile delinquency** is a term applied to children who fall under a jurisdictional age limit, which varies from state to state, and who commit an act in violation of the penal code. **Status offenders** commit acts forbidden to minors, which include truancy and being a habitually disobedient and ungovernable child (see Figure 13.1). They are commonly characterized in state statutes as persons or children in need of supervision (PINS or CHINS). Most states distinguish such behavior from delinquent conduct to reduce the effect of any stigma on children, although in most jurisdictions, status offenders can be placed on probation much as delinquent offenders can. They are, however, in most instances barred from being placed in secure facilities that hold delinquent offenders. In addition, juvenile courts generally have jurisdiction over situations involving conduct directed at (rather than committed by) juveniles, such as parental neglect, deprivation, abandonment, and abuse.

The states have also set different maximum ages below which children fall under the jurisdiction of the juvenile court. Many states include all children under 18, others set the limit at 17, and still others at 16.

Some states exclude certain classes of offenders or offenses from the juvenile justice system. Those youths who commit serious violent offenses such as rape or murder may be automatically excluded from the juvenile justice system and treated as adults on the premise that they stand little chance of rehabilitation within the confines of the juvenile system. Juvenile court judges may also transfer, or waive, to adult court repeat offenders whom they deem untreatable by the juvenile authorities.

Another trend has been to create family courts, which include a broad range of family- and child-related issues within their jurisdictions. Family courts are in use or are being considered in more than half of all states. They are designed to provide more individualized, client-focused treatment than traditional juvenile courts and to bring a holistic approach to helping kids and their families, rather than focusing on punishing and/or controlling delinquency.[26]

L03 Describe the changes in juvenile justice that began in the 1960s and continue today

juvenile delinquency Participation in illegal behavior by a minor who falls under a statutory age limit.

status offenders Juveniles who engage in behavior legally forbidden to minors, such as running away, truancy, or incorrigibility.

WEB APP 13.2 Visit the website of the Center for Court Innovation at **http://www.courtinnovation.org**. Follow the link to "Youth Court." What is a youth court? How does it differ from traditional court? Are youth courts more effective than traditional courts? Why or why not?

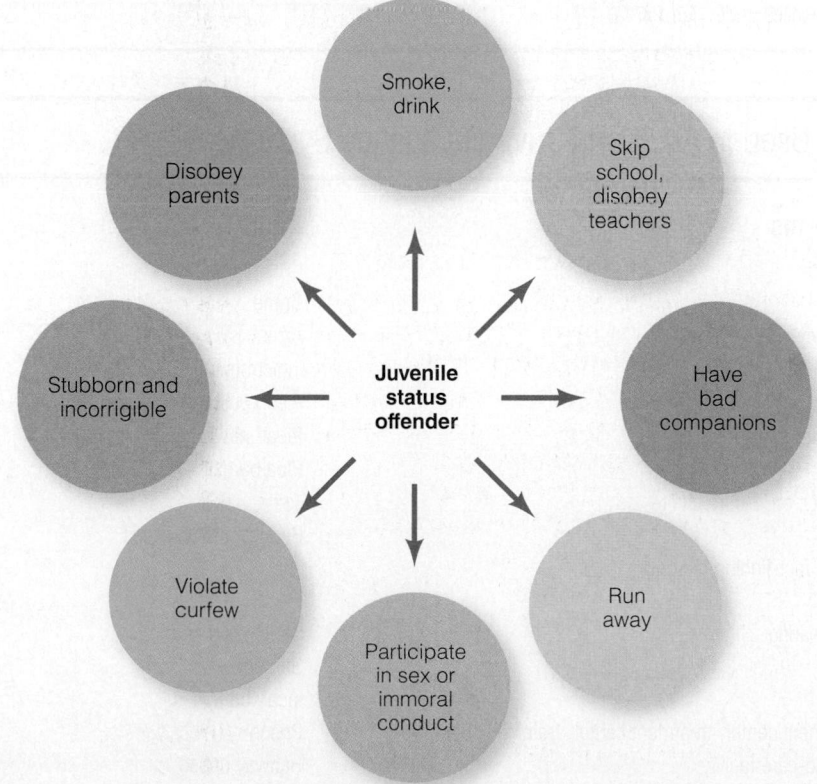

FIGURE 13.1 Examples of Status Offenses

The juvenile justice system has evolved into a parallel yet independent system of justice with its own terminology and rules of procedure. Exhibit 13.2 describes the basic similarities and differences between the juvenile and adult justice systems. Exhibit 13.3 points out how the language used in the juvenile court differs from that used in the adult system.

EXHIBIT 13.2 Similarities and Differences Between Juvenile and Adult Justice Systems

Similarities	Differences
Discretion used by police officers, judges, and correctional personnel	The primary purpose of juvenile procedures is protection and treatment; with adults, the aim is to punish the guilty.
Right to receive *Miranda* warning	Jurisdiction is determined by age in the juvenile system, but by the nature of the offense in the adult system.
Protection from prejudicial lineups or other identification procedures	Juveniles can be apprehended for acts that would not be criminal if committed by an adult (status offenses).
Procedural safeguards when making an admission of guilt	Juvenile proceedings are not considered criminal; adult proceedings are.
Advocacy roles of prosecutors and defense attorneys	Juvenile court proceedings are generally informal and private; adult court proceedings are more formal and are open to the public.
Right to counsel at most key stages of the court process	Courts cannot release to the press identifying information about a juvenile, but they must release information about an adult.
Availability of pretrial motions	Parents are highly involved in the juvenile process but not in the adult process.
Plea negotiation/plea bargaining	The standard of arrest is more stringent for adults than for juveniles.
Right to a hearing and an appeal	Juveniles are released into parental custody; adults are generally given bail.
Standard of proof beyond a reasonable doubt	Juveniles have no constitutional right to a jury trial; adults do. Some states extend this right to juveniles by statute.
Pretrial detention possible	Juveniles can be searched in school without probable cause or a warrant.
Detention without bail if considered dangerous	A juvenile's record is generally sealed when the age of majority is reached; an adult's record is permanent
Probation as a sentencing option	A juvenile court cannot sentence juveniles to county jails or state prisons, which are reserved for adults.
Community treatment as a sentencing option	The US Supreme Court has declared that the Eighth Amendment prohibits the death penalty for juveniles under age 18.

EXHIBIT 13.3 Comparison of Terms Used in Adult and Juvenile Justice Systems

	Juvenile Terms	Adult Terms
The person and the act	Delinquent child	Criminal
	Delinquent act	Crime
Preadjudicatory stage	Take into custody	Arrest
	Petition	Indictment
	Agree to a finding	Plead guilty
	Deny the petition	Plead not guilty
	Adjustment	Plea bargain
	Detention facility; child-care shelter	Jail
Adjudicatory stage	Substitution	Reduction of charges
	Adjudicatory or fact-finding hearing	Trial
	Adjudication	
Postadjudicatory stage	Dispositional hearing	Sentencing hearing
	Disposition	Sentence
	Commitment	Incarceration
	Youth development center; treatment center; training school	Prison
	Residential child-care facility	Halfway house
	Aftercare	Parole

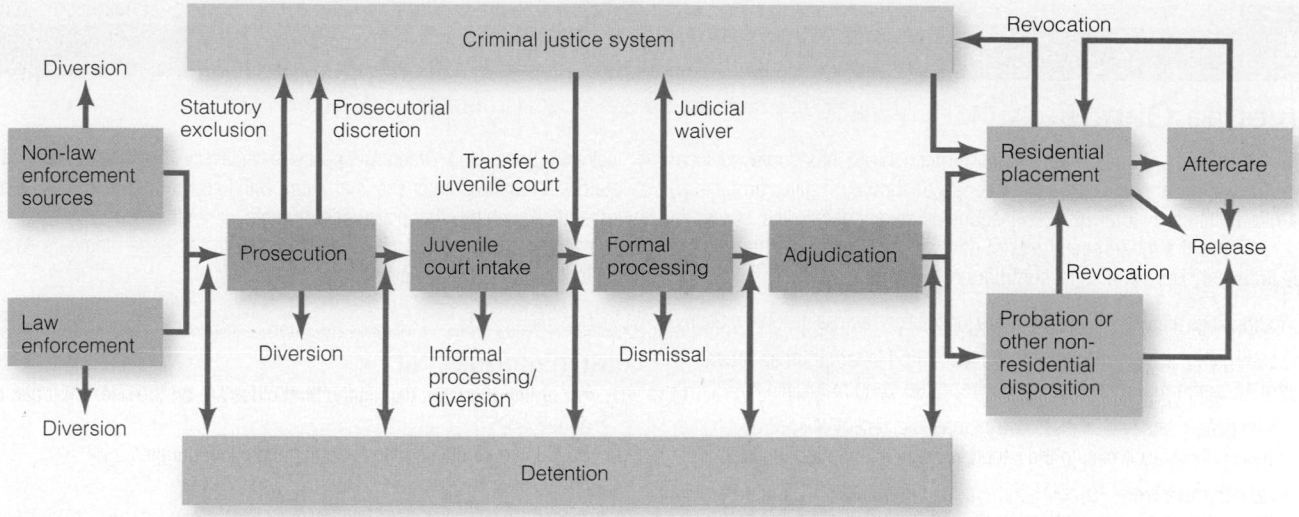

FIGURE 13.2 Case Flow Through the Juvenile Justice System

Source: Office of Juvenile Justice and Delinquency Prevention, *Statistical Briefing Book*, https://www.ojjdp.gov/ojstatbb/structure_process/case.html (accessed March 2017).

Today, the juvenile justice system is responsible for processing and treating almost 2 million cases of youthful misbehavior annually. Each state's system is unique, so it is difficult to give a precise accounting of the justice process. Moreover, depending on local practice and tradition, case processing often varies from community to community within a single state. Keeping this in mind, the following sections provide a general description of some key processes and decision points in juvenile justice. Figure 13.2 presents a model of the juvenile justice process.

Police Processing of the Juvenile Offender

According to the Uniform Crime Reports, police officers arrested 709,000 juveniles in 2015 (most recent numbers as of this writing), down from a high of over 1.2 million in 2004.[77] Most large police departments have detectives who handle only juvenile delinquency cases and focus their attention on the problems of youth (such as youth gangs—see the accompanying Contemporary Issues in Criminal Justice box). In addition to conducting their own investigations, they typically take control of cases after an arrest is made by a uniformed officer.

Most states do not have specific statutory provisions distinguishing the arrest process for children from that for adults. Some jurisdictions, however, give broad arrest powers to the police in juvenile cases by authorizing the officer to make an arrest whenever he or she believes the child's behavior falls within the jurisdiction of the juvenile court. Consequently, police may arrest youths for behavior considered legal for adults, including running away, curfew violations, and being in possession of alcohol.

L04 Summarize police processing of juvenile offenders

Use of Discretion

When a juvenile is found to have engaged in delinquent or incorrigible behavior, police agencies are charged with the decision to release or to detain the child and refer her to juvenile court. Because of the state's interest in the child, the police generally have more discretion in the investigatory and arrest stages of the juvenile process than they do when dealing with adult offenders.

This discretionary decision—to release or to detain—is based not only on the nature of the offense but also on police attitudes and the child's social and personal conditions

Juvenile Gangs

Since 1996, the National Youth Gang Center (NYGS) has surveyed local law enforcement agencies to gain a sense of the youth gang problem in the United States. A total of 2,199 agencies responded to the survey in 2012, which is the most recent year of data as of this writing. What did the surveys reveal? Here is a short summary of the findings:

- Youth gangs are active in about 3,000 jurisdictions across the United States.

- Youth gangs are overwhelmingly concentrated in larger urban areas, but 15 percent of rural jurisdictions reported gang problems.

- Youth gang-related homicides have increased in recent years (2,363 homicides in 2012, according to the Federal Bureau of Investigation [FBI]).

- In 2012, there were 30,700 youth gangs operating in the United States, with a total membership (estimated) of 850,000.

How do law enforcement agencies distinguish between gang members and nongang members? Six common practices are employed. The most successful and common strategy is to focus on specific displays and symbols (colors, tattoos, etc.). Otherwise, police may classify someone as being affiliated with a gang if he or she is arrested with known gang members, is designated as such by other police departments, or is identified by informants. A number, surprisingly, willingly identify themselves as gang members, in both custodial and noncustodial settings.

CRITICAL THINKING
1. According to recent data, gang homicides are on the rise. What can be done?
2. Why do you think so many young people join gangs?

Sources: National Gang Center, *National Gang Center Newsletter*, Fall 2016, https://www.nationalgangcenter.gov/Content/Newsletters/NGC-Newsletter-2016-Fall.pdf; Arlen Egley Jr., James C. Howell, and Meena Harris, *Highlights of the 2012 National Youth Gang Survey*, Office of Juvenile Justice and Delinquency Prevention, 2014, http://www.ojjdp.gov/pubs/248025.pdf. (URLs accessed May 2017.)

at the time of the arrest. The following is a partial list of factors believed to be significant in police decision making about juvenile offenders:

- The type and seriousness of the child's offense
- The ability of the parents to be of assistance in disciplining the child
- The child's past contacts with police
- The degree of cooperation obtained from the child and parents, along with their demeanor, attitude, and personal characteristics
- Whether the child denies the allegations in the petition and insists on a court hearing[28]

Legal Rights

After a juvenile has been taken into custody, the child has the same right to be free from unreasonable searches and seizures as an adult does. Children in police custody can be detained prior to trial, interrogated, and placed in lineups. Because of their youth and

Derrik Pannesi shows tattoos on his hands during a break in his job training with the jail alternative program at Roca Inc. in Somerville, Massachusetts. Pannesi credited Roca, whose mission is to disrupt the cycle of incarceration by helping young people transform their lives, with getting him on track after an adolescence filled with gang activity and multiple stints behind bars. In spite of the message tattooed on the back of his hands, he acknowledged Roca was beginning to gain his trust. Soon, though, Pannesi was back in jail, rearrested after police lodged gun- and drug-related charges against him.

AP Images/Charles Krupa

inexperience, children are generally afforded more protections than adults. Even though the Supreme Court has given juveniles the same *Miranda* rights as adults, police must ensure that the juvenile suspect understands his constitutional rights and, if there is some question, must provide access to a parent or guardian to protect the child's legal interests. Police should interrogate a juvenile without an adult present only if they are sure that the youth is unquestionably mature and experienced enough to understand his legal rights.[29]

The Juvenile Court Process

After the police have determined that a case warrants further attention, they will bind it over to the prosecutor's office, which then has the responsibility for channeling the case through the juvenile court. In addition, cases may be petitioned to the court from nonlaw enforcement sources, such as when educational authorities ask the court to intervene in cases of truancy or when parents directly petition the court asking that their child be considered a status offender. The juvenile court plays a major role in controlling juvenile behavior and delivering social services to children in need.

US juvenile courts process an estimated 1.6 million delinquency cases each year. The juvenile court delinquency caseload today is four times as large as it was in 1960.

The Intake Process

After police processing, the juvenile offender is usually remanded to the local juvenile court's intake division. At this juncture, court intake officers or probation personnel review and initially screen the child and the family to determine whether the child needs to be handled formally or the case can be settled without the need for costly and intrusive official intervention. Their report helps the prosecutor decide whether to handle the case informally or bind it over for trial. The intake stage represents an opportunity to place a child in informal programs both within the court and in the community. The intake process also is critically important because more than half of the referrals to the juvenile courts never go beyond this stage.

The Detention Process

After a juvenile is formally taken into custody, either as a delinquent or as a status offender, the prosecutor usually makes a decision to release the child to the parent or guardian or to detain the child in a secure shelter pending trial.

Detention has always been a controversial area of juvenile justice. Far too many children have been routinely placed in detention while awaiting court appearances. Status offenders and delinquents have been held in the same facility, and in many parts of the country, adult county jails were used to detain juvenile offenders. The Juvenile Justice Act of 1974 emphasized reducing the number of children placed in inappropriate detention facilities. Although the act was largely effective, the practice continues in some places.

Despite such measures, hundreds of thousands of youths, most of whom are already living under difficult circumstances, are placed in pretrial detention each year. Many have suffered long histories of abuse and mental health problems.[30] The detention decision may reflect a child's personal characteristics and the quality of his or her home life rather than dangerousness or flight risk.[31] Detention is widely misapplied, according to the report by the Justice Policy Institute, a Washington, DC–based group, because even though detention facilities are meant to temporarily house those youths who are likely to reoffend before their trial or who are unlikely to appear for their court date, many of the youths in this country's detention centers do not meet these criteria. Of youths in detention, 70 percent are held for nonviolent charges. More than two-thirds are charged with property offenses, public order offenses, technical probation violations, or status offenses (such as running away or breaking curfew).[32]

LO5 Describe the juvenile court process

REALITYCHECK

Myth or Reality?

Juveniles enjoy different rights than adults.

REALITY. The Supreme Court has over the years extended more and more protections to juveniles (see Exhibit 13.1), but there are still rights that juveniles do not enjoy. One is the right to a jury trial.

Should juveniles have access to trial by jury? Why or why not? Juvenile proceedings are also usually closed to the public, unlike adult criminal trials. Is this advantageous or disadvantageous to the juvenile?

detention The temporary care of a child alleged to be a delinquent or status offender who requires secure custody, pending court disposition.

14 Crime and Justice in the New Millennium

REALITYCHECK

Myth or Reality?

- Corporate criminals rarely go to jail.
- Worries about illegal logging are the overblown fantasies of a group of troublemaking tree huggers.
- A cyber attack against Iran derailed its nuclear program.
- There are more drug users in the world than the populations of England, Italy, and France combined.

During a holiday event on December 2, 2015, Syed Rizwan Farook and his wife, Tashfeen Malik, entered the San Bernardino (California) Inland Regional Center and opened fire on those in attendance. The couple killed 14 and wounded 22.[1] A health inspector for the county, Farook had been in the building earlier that day for a meeting, but left before the party. He came back later, this time with Malik. Both donned ski masks and tactical gear and were armed with semi-automatic pistols, rifles, and explosives. They fired upward of 75 bullets over a four-minute period and left before police could arrive at the scene. Farook and Malik also left three explosive devices behind, which authorities believe they were designed to target first responders, but fortunately they did not detonate.

Police arrived shortly after the couple fled. Having recognized his voice and build, a witness identified Farook. Thereafter, officers learned that Farook had rented a black Ford Expedition SUV with Utah plates four days before. A few hours into the investigation, and based on a tip from a neighbor, police went to Farook's home in nearby Redlands. The Expedition was seen leaving the area, and officers gave chase. Farook and Malik were soon stopped, whereupon they exchanged gunfire with police and were killed.[2]

In the aftermath of the shooting, speculation abounded as to the causes. Some said a workplace dispute prompted the shooting. Others said the motive was terrorism. Unfortunately, the latter was true; the investigation revealed that both Farook and Malik were "homegrown violent extremists" who had been inspired by foreign terror groups.[3] They had been radicalized as early as 2013 and, according to (then) FBI Director James Comey, "were talking to each other about jihad and martyrdom" even before they were engaged.[4] The couple used social media to pledge allegiance to the Islamic State shortly before they were killed by police. Neither Farook nor Malik had criminal records and were not on any terror watch list, making it especially difficult to predict that they would perpetrate such an atrocious act.

Handout/FBI/Getty Images News/Getty Images; Handout/Getty Images News/Getty Images; Patrick T. Fallon/Getty Images

LEARNING OBJECTIVES

LO1 List the various forms of terrorism and their goals

LO2 Discuss the impact of corporate enterprise crime

LO3 Evaluate the various forms of green crime

LO4 Describe the various forms of cybercrime

LO5 Summarize methods used to control cybercrime

LO6 Explain the relationship between globalization and transnational organized crime

LO7 Discuss various types of transnational crime

LO8 List some of the most important transnational crime groups

LO9 Explain the methods law enforcement is now using to thwart transnational criminal syndicates

CORPORATE CRIME LAW ENFORCEMENT The detection and enforcement of large-scale corporate crime are primarily in the hands of administrative departments and agencies with investigation arms to police the areas of commerce that are their responsibility. The Securities and Exchange Commission (SEC) has been given the responsibility for overseeing the nation's capital markets. It is assigned the task of protecting investors, facilitating capital formation, and maintaining fair, orderly, and efficient markets.

If SEC investigators detect inappropriate behavior in the financial system, they may decide to bring a case in federal court or before an administrative law judge, depending on the type of sanction or relief that is being sought. For example, if the commission seeks to bar or remove someone from acting as a corporate officer, they must take the case to a federal district court. During the proceeding, the SEC will ask the judge to issue a court order, called an injunction, prohibiting any further acts or practices that violate the law or commission rules. An injunction can also require audits and accounting for frauds. In addition to barring or suspending the individual from serving as a corporate officer or director, the SEC can seek civil monetary penalties or the return of illegal profits (called disgorgement). A person who violates the court's order may be found in contempt and be subject to additional fines or imprisonment.

The decision to pursue criminal rather than civil violations usually is based on both the seriousness of the case and the perpetrator's intent, actions to conceal the violation, and prior record. Any evidence of criminal activity is then sent to the Department of Justice or the FBI for investigation. Some other federal agencies, such as the EPA and the US Postal Service, have their own investigative arms. Enforcement generally is reactive (generated by complaints) rather than proactive (involving ongoing investigations or the monitoring of activities). Investigations are carried out by the various federal agencies and the FBI. If criminal prosecution is called for, the case will be handled by attorneys from the criminal, tax, antitrust, and civil rights divisions of the Justice Department. If insufficient evidence is available to warrant a criminal prosecution, the case will be handled civilly or administratively by some other federal agency. For example, the Federal Trade Commission can issue a cease and desist order in antitrust or merchandising fraud cases.

STATE LEVEL ENFORCEMENT Responding to the threat of large-scale corporate fraud, a number of states have created special task forces and prosecution teams to crack down on fraudulent schemes and bring perpetrators to justice. In addition, state legislatures have passed a spate of new laws aimed directly at easing prosecution for corporate crimes. For example, the Mortgage Fraud Task Force in Dade County, Florida (Miami) was created to address the issues of mortgage and foreclosure rescue fraud. The task force investigates cases in which false or misleading documents are filed to fool lenders into making mortgage loans to people who cannot hope to pay them back or on properties whose values have been grossly inflated.[38]

Green Crime

On April 20, 2010, an explosion occurred on the *Deepwater Horizon* oil rig, killing 11 platform workers and injuring 17 others.[39] The rig was built by Hyundai Heavy Industries of Korea, owned by the Transocean Drilling Corporation, the drilling overseen by Halliburton, and leased by BP (formerly British Petroleum), to drill a deep water (5,000 feet below the surface) rig in the Gulf of Mexico. At first, estimates of the spill were 5,000 barrels a day, but they quickly rose to 60,000. While company officials frantically tried to stem the flow with a variety of failed schemes, millions of barrels of escaping oil created a slick that covered thousands of square miles, devastating wildlife, and causing one of the greatest environmental disasters in the nation's history. BP, facing civil fines, offered to place $20 billion in an escrow account to cover damages. The leak was finally stopped in August 2010.

On June 1, 2010, the federal government announced that it had launched a criminal probe to "prosecute to the fullest extent of the law" any persons or companies that broke the law in the time leading up to the spill.[40] Under federal environmental laws, a company may be charged with a misdemeanor for negligent conduct or a felony if there is evidence that company personnel knowingly engaged in conduct risking injury. It would be a criminal act if, for example, employees of BP or its subcontractors Transocean and Halliburton did any of the following:

- Lied in the permit process for obtaining a drilling license
- Tried to cover up the severity of the spill
- Knowing of negligence in construction, chose to ignore the danger it imposed
- Engaged in or approved of unsafe, risky, or dangerous methods to remove the drill, knowing that such methods could injure those on board

In the aftermath of the case, BP agreed to pay $4.5 billion in fines and other penalties and to plead guilty to 14 criminal charges related to the rig explosion. Then, on January 3, 2013, Transocean agreed to plead guilty to violating the Clean Water Act (CWA) and to pay a total of $1.4 billion in civil and criminal fines and penalties for its conduct in relation to the *Deepwater Horizon* disaster.[41]

Oil spills are just part of the growing **green crime** problem that is facing the justice system. Green crimes are violations of existing criminal laws designed to protect people, the environment, or both. They include crimes against workers such as occupational health and safety crimes, as well as laws designed to protect nature and the environment (the Clean Air Act, Clean Water Act, etc.). Green crimes involve a wide range of actions and outcomes that harm the environment and that stem from decisions about what is produced, where it is produced, and how it is produced.[42] Global warming, overdevelopment, population growth, and other changes will continue to bring these issues front and center, and they will soon become a major focus of the criminal justice system.[43]

green crime Criminal activity that involves violation of rules and laws designed to protect the environment, including illegal dumping, polluting, fishing, logging, and so on.

Forms of Green Crime

Green crime can take many different forms, ranging from deforestation and illegal logging to violations of worker safety. A few of the most damaging green crimes are set out next.

LO3 Evaluate the various forms of green crime

ILLEGAL LOGGING Illegal logging involves harvesting, processing, and transporting timber or wood products in violation of existing laws and treaties.[44] It is a universal phenomenon, occurring in major timber-producing countries, especially in the third world where enforcement is lax. Logging violations include taking trees in protected areas such as national parks, going over legally prescribed logging quotas, processing logs without acquiring licenses, and exporting logs without paying export duties. By sidestepping the law, loggers can create greater profits than those generated through legal methods. The situation is serious because illegal logging can have severe environmental and social impact: illegal logging exhausts forests, destroys wildlife, and damages its habitats. It causes ruinous damage to the forests, including deforestation and forest degradation worldwide. The destruction of forest cover can cause flash floods and landslides that have killed thousands of people.[45]

While the scale of illegal logging is difficult to estimate, it is believed that more than half of all logging activities in the most vulnerable forest regions—Southeast Asia, central Africa, South America, and Russia—may be conducted illegally. Worldwide estimates suggest that illegal activities may account for over a tenth of the total global timber trade, representing products worth at least $15 billion per year.

ILLEGAL FISHING Unlicensed and illegal fishing practices are another billion-dollar green crime. It can take on many forms and involve highly different parties, ranging from huge factory ships operating on the high seas that catch thousands of tons of fish on each voyage, to smaller, locally operating ships that confine themselves to national waters. Illegal fishing occurs when these ships sign on to their home nation's rules but then choose to ignore their scope and boundary, or operate in a country's waters without permission or on the high seas without a flag. Because catches remain clandestine and are not reported, their illegal fishing can have a detrimental effect on some species as government regulators have no idea how many are being caught. As a result, stocks become depleted and species endangered. Illegal fishing reduces the number of new adults that can replace those lost from fishing, and the ability of populations to replenish themselves is quickly lost.[46]

ILLEGAL POLLUTING Some green-criminals want to skirt local, state, and federal restrictions on dumping dangerous substances in the environment. Rather than pay expensive processing fees, they may secretly dispose of hazardous wastes in illegal dump sites. Illegally dumped wastes can be hazardous or nonhazardous materials that are discarded in an effort to avoid disposal fees or the time and effort required for proper disposal. Materials dumped range from used motor oil to waste from construction sites.

Criminal environmental pollution is defined as the intentional or negligent discharge of a toxic or contaminating substance into the biosystem that is known to have an adverse effect on the natural environment or life. Individuals and companies may commit this crime to save processing and dumping fees, thereby adding to profits. Illegal pollution schemes may involve the ground release of toxic chemicals such as Kepone, vinyl chloride, mercury, PCBs, and asbestos. Illegal and/or controlled air pollutants include hydrochlorofluorocarbons (HCFCs), aerosols, asbestos, carbon monoxide, chlorofluorocarbons (CFCs), criteria air pollutants, lead, mercury, methane, nitrogen oxides (NO_x), radon, refrigerants, and sulfur oxides (SO_2). Water pollution is defined as the dumping of a substance that degrades or alters the quality of the waters to an extent that is detrimental to their use by humans or by an animal or a plant that is useful to humans. This includes the disposal into rivers, lakes, and streams of toxic chemicals.[47]

Environmental crimes can range from widespread pollution caused by industrial waste to individuals illegally dumping in a neighborhood environment. Denver City Councilman Paul Lopez examines an illegal dumpsite where a fence had been torched in the Westwood neighborhood of Denver, Colorado. Lopez is pushing for a tougher ordinance in the city. "We have to get people to realize this neighborhood is not a dumping ground. We refuse to be treated like this," Lopez said.

Craig F. Walker/Getty Images

Enforcing Environmental Laws

The United States and most sovereign nations have passed laws making it a crime to pollute or damage the environment. For example, among environmental laws in the United States are the following:

- *Clean Water Act (1972)*. Establishes and maintains goals and standards for US water quality and purity. It was amended in 1987 to increase controls on toxic pollutants, and in 1990 to more effectively address the hazard of oil spills.
- *Emergency Planning and Community Right-to-Know Act (1986)*. Requires companies to disclose information about toxic chemicals they release into the air and water and dispose of on land.
- *Endangered Species Act (1973)*. Designed to protect and recover endangered and threatened species of fish, wildlife, and plants in the United States and beyond. The law works in part by protecting species habitats.
- *Oil Pollution Act (1990)*. Enacted in the aftermath of the *Exxon Valdez* oil spill in Alaska's Prince William Sound, this law streamlines federal response to oil spills by requiring oil storage facilities and vessels to prepare spill-response plans and provide for their rapid implementation. The law also increases polluters' liability for cleanup costs and damage to natural resources.

The major enforcement arm against environmental crimes is the Environmental Protection Agency, which was given full law enforcement authority in 1988. The EPA has successfully prosecuted significant violations across all major environmental statutes, including data fraud cases (e.g., private laboratories submitting false environmental data to state and federal environmental agencies); indiscriminate hazardous waste dumping that resulted in serious injuries and death; industry-wide ocean dumping by cruise ships; oil spills that caused significant damage to waterways, wetlands, and beaches; international smuggling of CFC refrigerants that damage the ozone layer and increase skin cancer risk; and illegal handling of hazardous substances such as pesticides and asbestos that exposed children, the poor, and other especially vulnerable groups to potentially serious illness.[48] Its Criminal Investigation Division (EPA CID) investigates allegations of criminal wrongdoing prohibited by various environmental statutes.

Cybercrime

Cybercrime typically involves the theft and/or destruction of information, resources, or funds via computer networks and/or the Internet. This relatively new category of crimes presents a compelling challenge for the justice system and the law enforcement community because (1) it is rapidly evolving, with new schemes being created daily; (2) it is difficult to detect through traditional law enforcement channels; and (3) to control it, agents of the justice system must develop technical skills that match those of the perpetrators.[49] It is even possible that the recent decline in crime is actually a result of cybercrime replacing traditional street crime. Instead of robbing a bank at gunpoint, a new group of contemporary thieves finds it easier to hack into accounts and transfer funds to offshore banks. Instead of shoplifting from a brick-and-mortar store, the contemporary cyberthief devises clever schemes to steal from e-tailers.

There are at least three main forms of cybercrime (summarized in Concept Summary 14.1). Some cybercriminals use modern technology to accumulate goods and services. Cybertheft schemes range from illegally copying material under copyright protection to using technology to commit traditional theft-based offenses such as larceny and fraud. Other cybercriminals are motivated less by profit and more by the urge to commit cybervandalism, or technological destruction. They aim their malicious attacks at disrupting, defacing, and destroying technology they find offensive. Finally, cyberwarfare consists of acts aimed at undermining the social, economic, and political system of an enemy nation by destroying its electronic infrastructure and disrupting its economy. This can range from stealing secrets from foreign nations (cyberespionage) to destroying an enemy's Web-based infrastructure.

LO4 Describe the various forms of cybercrime

cybercrime Illegal activity that uses a computer as its primary means of commission. Common forms of cybercrime include theft and destruction of information, resources, and funds.

WEB APP 14.2 The FBI maintains a comprehensive site that has a lot of information and stories on cybercrime at **https://www.fbi .gov/investigate/cyber**. Do you think a separate federal agency should be created to enforce cyber laws?

A specialist works at the **Defense Computer Forensics Laboratory (DCFL)** in Linthicum, Maryland. The lab is ground zero in the nation's fight against cybercrime. Government computer scientists work to combat cyber attacks by thieves, hostile states, and hackers. Since its creation in 1998, the DCFL has provided the Defense Department with investigative services, digital search assistance, and expert testimony in court.

CONCEPT SUMMARY 14 .1 Typology of Cybercrimes

Crime	Definition	Examples
Cybertheft	Use of cyberspace to distribute illegal goods and services or to defraud people for quick profits	Illegal copyright infringement, identity theft, Internet securities fraud, warez
Cybervandalism	Use of cyberspace for revenge, for destruction, or to achieve malicious ends	Website defacement, worms, viruses, cyberstalking, cyberbullying
Cyberwar	An effort by enemy forces to disrupt the intersection where the virtual electronic reality of computers meets the physical world	Use of logic bombs to disrupt or destroy "secure" systems or networks, use of the Internet to communicate covertly with agents around the world

Cybertheft: Cybercrimes for Profit

The Internet enables criminals to operate in a more efficient and effective manner. Cyberthieves now have the luxury of remaining anonymous, living almost anywhere on the planet, conducting their business during the day or at night, and working alone or in a group, while at the same time reaching a much greater number of potential victims than ever before. No longer are con artists and criminal entrepreneurs limited to fleecing victims in a particular geographic locale; the whole world can be their target. And the technology revolution has opened up novel avenues of attack for **cybertheft**—ranging from the unlawful distribution of computer software to Internet security fraud—that heretofore were nonexistent.

Cyberthieves conspire to use cyberspace either to distribute illegal goods and services or to defraud people for quick profits. Some of the most common methods are described next.

cybertheft The use of computer networks for criminal profits. Illegal copyright infringement, identity theft, and Internet securities fraud are examples of cybertheft.

COMPUTER FRAUD Computer fraud is not a unique offense but rather a common-law crime committed using contemporary technology. Consequently, many computer crimes are prosecuted under such traditional criminal statutes as those prohibiting larceny and fraud. However, not all computer crimes fall under common-law statutes because the property stolen may be intangible—that is, electronic and/or magnetic impulse. Two examples of such crimes are:

- *Theft of information*. This is the unauthorized obtaining of information from a computer (e.g., hacking), including software that is copied for profit.
- *Software theft*. The comparative ease of making copies of computer software has led to a huge illegal market, depriving authors of very significant revenues.

INTERNET PORNOGRAPHY The IT revolution has revitalized the porn industry. The Internet is an ideal venue for selling and distributing adult material; the computer is an ideal device for storing and viewing it. Although it is difficult to estimate the extent of the industry, it is estimated that the revenue generated from adult sites each year is greater than all movie box office sales. The number of visits to pornographic sites (mostly by men, though women make up about 30 percent of the viewers) surpasses those made to Internet search engines; some individual sites report as many as 50 million hits per year.[50] Revenue from Internet porn comes from a number of sources: paid subscriptions, advertisements for other porn sites, fees for diverting web traffic to other sites, sale of sex-related products, and providing auxiliary services such as age verification services. Nonetheless, industry sales are in decline: free Internet content has cut into paid services. As a result, producers, actors, and actresses in the domestic adult film industry have found their income substantially declining.

Because many porn sites are located in foreign lands, enforcement has proven difficult. However, law enforcement agencies here and abroad are now cracking down on the distribution of sexual material involving juveniles (kiddie porn).

COPYRIGHT INFRINGEMENT It is now common for groups of individuals to plan and work together to obtain software illegally and then "crack" or "rip" its copyright protections before posting it on the Internet for use by other members of the group. Its criminal purveyors refer to this pirated material as **warez** (pronounced like "wares," as in "software"). Frequently, these new pirated copies reach the Internet days or weeks before the legitimate product is commercially available.

warez Copyrighted software illegally downloaded and sold by organized groups without license to do so.

INTERNET SECURITIES FRAUD Internet securities fraud involves using the Internet to intentionally manipulate the securities marketplace for profit. Three major types of Internet securities fraud are common today:

- *Market manipulation*. Stock market manipulation occurs when an individual tries to control the price of stock by interfering with the natural forces of supply and demand. There are two principal forms of this crime: the "pump and dump" and the "cyber smear." In a pump and dump scheme, erroneous and deceptive information is posted online to get unsuspecting investors interested in a stock while those spreading the information sell previously purchased stock at an inflated price. The cyber smear is a reverse pump and dump: negative information is spread online about a stock, driving down its price and enabling people to buy it at an artificially low price before rebuttals by the company's officers reestablish the legitimate price.
- *Fraudulent offerings of securities*. Some cybercriminals create websites specifically designed to sell securities fraudulently. To make the offerings look more attractive than they are, assets may be inflated, expected returns overstated, and risks understated. In these schemes, investors are promised abnormally high profits on their investments. No investment is actually made. Early investors are paid returns with the investment money received from the later investors. The system usually collapses, and the later investors do not receive dividends and lose their initial investment.
- *Illegal touting*. This crime occurs when individuals make securities recommendations and fail to disclose that they are being paid to disseminate their favorable opinions.

IDENTITY THEFT These thieves use the Internet to steal someone's identity and/or impersonate the victim to open a new credit card account or conduct some other financial transaction. Identity theft can destroy a person's life by manipulating credit records or depleting bank accounts. Some identity thieves create false emails and/or websites that look legitimate but are designed to gain illegal access to a victims' personal information; this is known as phishing (and also as *carding* and *spoofing*).

Phishing emails and websites have become even more of a problem now that cyber-criminals can easily copy brand names, the names of corporate personnel, and their insignia directly into the email. The look is so authentic that victims believe the email comes from the advertised company. Most phishers send out spam emails to a large number of recipients, knowing that some of those recipients will have accounts with the company they are impersonating. Some phishing schemes involve job offers. After the unsuspecting victims fill out the "application," answering personal questions and including their Social Security number, the phisher has them in his grasp.[51]

E-TAILING FRAUD New fraud schemes are evolving to exploit the fact that billions of dollars of goods are sold on the Internet each year. E-tailing fraud can involve both illegally buying and selling merchandise on the Internet. Some e-tailing scams involve failure to deliver on promised purchases or services, and others involve the substitution of cheaper or used material for higher-quality purchases.

ILLEGAL DRUG DISTRIBUTION The Internet has become a prime purveyor of prescription drugs, some of which can be quite dangerous when they are used to excess or fall into the hands of minors. Thousands of websites advertise or offer controlled prescription drugs for sale. Many require no prescription from a patient's physician, while others simply ask that the prescription be faxed—increasing the risk of multiple use of one prescription or other fraud.[52] Beyond the "visible" Internet lies a huge marketplace for all manner of legal and illegal drugs—the "dark web," whose sites are not accessed via conventional search engines.[53]

Cybervandalism: Cybercrime with Malicious Intent

Some cybercriminals may be motivated not by greed or profit but by the desire for revenge, to inflict wanton destruction, and/or to achieve a malicious intent. Cybervandalism involves such crimes as sending destructive viruses and worms to attack important computer networks. Cybervandals are motivated more by malice than by greed:

- Some cybervandals target computers and networks, seeking revenge for some perceived wrong.
- Some desire to exhibit their technical prowess and superiority.
- Some want to highlight the vulnerability of computer security systems.
- Some want to spy on other people's private financial and personal information ("computer voyeurism").
- Some want to destroy computer security because they believe in open access to all systems and programs.[54]

Some of the most common forms of cybervandalism are discussed in detail next.

VIRUSES AND WORMS A computer virus is one type of malicious software program (also called *malware*) that disrupts or destroys existing programs and networks, causing them to perform the task for which the virus was designed.[55] The virus is then spread from one computer to another when a user sends out an infected file through email or may even hack into a network. Computer worms are similar to viruses, but they use computer networks or the Internet to self-replicate and "send themselves" to other users, generally via email without the aid of the operator.

TROJAN HORSES Some hackers may introduce a Trojan horse program into a computer system. The Trojan horse looks like a benign application, but it contains illicit

---

identity theft Using the Internet to steal someone's identity and/or impersonate the victim to conduct illicit transactions, such as committing fraud using the victim's name and identity.

phishing Also known as carding and spoofing, phishing consists of illegally acquiring personal information, such as bank passwords and credit card numbers, by masquerading as a trustworthy person or business in what appears to be an official electronic communication, such as an email or an instant message. The term *phishing* comes from the lures used to "fish" for financial information and passwords.

e-tailing fraud Using the Internet to illegally buy or sell merchandise.

cybervandalism Malicious attacks aimed at disrupting, defacing, and destroying technology.

---

codes that can damage the system operations. Sometimes hackers with a sense of irony will install a Trojan horse and claim that it is an antivirus program. When it is opened, it spreads viruses in the computer system. Trojan horses do not replicate themselves as viruses do, but they can be just as destructive. They continue to afflict computers around the world.[56]

DENIAL-OF-SERVICE ATTACK A denial-of-service attack is an attempt to extort money from legitimate users of an Internet service by threatening to interfere with the user's access to that service.[57] Examples include attempts to "flood" a computer network, thereby preventing access by legitimate network traffic; attempts to disrupt connections within a computer network, thereby interrupting access to a service; attempts to prevent a particular individual from accessing a service; and attempts to disrupt service to a specific system or person.

WEB DEFACEMENT Cybervandals may target the websites of their victims. Web defacement is a type of cybervandalism that occurs when a computer hacker intrudes on another person's website by inserting or substituting codes that expose visitors to the site to misleading or provocative information.

CYBERSTALKING AND CYBER HARASSMENT Traditional stalking involves repeated harassing or threatening behavior, such as following a person, appearing at a person's home or place of business, making harassing phone calls, leaving written messages or objects, or vandalizing a person's property. Cyberstalking is the use of the Internet, email, or other electronic communications to stalk, and it generally refers to a pattern of threatening or malicious behaviors. Cyber harassment usually pertains to threatening or harassing email messages, instant messages, or blog entries or websites dedicated solely to tormenting an individual. It typically involves less threat of force and violence than cyberstalking.[58] Some cyberstalkers pursue minors through online chat rooms, establish a relationship with a child, and later ask to make contact. Today, Internet predators are more likely to meet, develop relationships with, and beguile at-risk adolescents and underage teenagers, rather than using coercion and violence.[59]

Cyberbullying

Experts define bullying among children as repeated negative acts committed by one or more children against another.[60] These negative acts may be physical or verbal in nature—for example, hitting or kicking, teasing or taunting—or they may involve indirect actions such as manipulating friendships or purposely excluding other children from activities. Bullying is a problem that remains to be solved, and it has now expanded from the physical environment to the virtual.

Because of the availability of cyberspace, physical distance is no longer a refuge from the frequency and depth of harm doled out by a bully to his or her victim.[61] Cyberbullying is willful and repeated harm inflicted through the medium of electronic text. Like their real-world counterparts, cyberbullies are malicious and cowardly aggressors who seek pleasure or profit through the mistreatment of other individuals. Although power in traditional bullying might derive from physical (stature) or social (competency or popularity) advantage, online power may simply stem from proficiency on the Net. Cyberbullies who are able to navigate the Internet and utilize technology in a way that enables them to harass others are in a position of power relative to their victims. There are four major approaches that cyberbullies employ to harass their victims:

- Bullies can send harassing emails or instant messages.
- They can post obscene, insulting, and slanderous messages on social networking sites.
- They can develop websites to promote and disseminate defamatory content.
- They can send harassing text messages to the victim via cell phones.[62]

denial-of-service attack Extorting money from an Internet service user by threatening to prevent the user having access to the service.

cyberstalking Using the Internet, email, or other electronic communications devices to stalk or harass another person.

cyberbullying Willful and repeated harm done through the medium of electronic text.

cyberwarfare Politically motivated attacks designed to compromise the electronic infrastructure of an enemy nation and disrupt its economy.

REALITYCHECK

Myth or Reality?

A cyber attack against Iran derailed its nuclear program.

REALITY. The Stuxnet worm wiped out a fifth of the centrifuges Iran was using to make fissionable material.

Think of ways cyberwar can be waged against a nation's infrastructure.

L05 Summarize methods used to control cybercrime

Cyberwarfare

The justice system must now also be on guard against attacks of cyberwarfare that are aimed at the United States by overseas adversaries. Although the term may be difficult to define, **cyberwarfare** can be viewed as an effort by covert forces to disrupt the points where the virtual electronic reality of computers intersects the physical world.[63]

Cyberwarfare has been defined as "premeditated, politically motivated attack[s] against information, computer systems, computer programs, and data which result in violence against noncombatant targets by sub-national groups or clandestine agents."[64] Cyberwarfare may involve the use of computer network tools to shut down critical national infrastructures or to coerce or intimidate a government or civilian population.[65]

Even though they may come from a region where computer databases and the Internet are not widely used, terrorist organizations are beginning to understand the damage that cybercrime can inflict on their targets. Terrorist organizations are now adapting information technology into their arsenal, and agencies of the justice system have to be ready for a sustained attack on the nation's electronic infrastructure.

One form of attack is cyberespionage. This involves hacking into secure computer networks at the target nation's most sensitive military bases, defense contractors, and aerospace companies in order to steal important data or to assess their defenses. Infrastructure attacks can also be aimed at water treatment plants, electric plants, dams, oil refineries, and nuclear power plants. These industries all provide vital services to society by allowing people to go about their daily lives. Terrorist computer hackers could make a dam overflow or cause real property damage to oil refineries or nuclear plants by shutting down safeguards in the system designed to prevent catastrophic meltdowns.

Controlling Cybercrime

The proliferation of cybercrime has created the need for new laws and enforcement processes. Because technology evolves so rapidly, enforcement presents challenges that are particularly vexing. Numerous organizations have been set up to provide training and support for law enforcement agents. In addition, federal and state laws have been aimed at particular areas of high-tech crimes.[66] What are some of the legislative initiatives designed to limit or control cybercrime?

SOFTWARE PIRACY The government has actively pursued members of the warez community, and some have been charged and convicted under the Computer Fraud and Abuse Act (CFAA), which criminalizes accessing computer systems without authorization to obtain information.[67] The Digital Millennium Copyright Act (DMCA) makes it a crime to circumvent antipiracy measures built into most commercial software and also outlaws the manufacture, sale, or distribution of code-cracking devices used to copy software illegally.[68]

COPYRIGHT INFRINGEMENT The US Criminal Code provides penalties for a first-time illegal copyright offender of five years of incarceration and a fine of $250,000.[69] Infringing copies and all equipment used to make those copies are also subject to forfeiture and destruction.[70]

IDENTITY THEFT To meet this increasing threat, Congress passed the Identity Theft and Assumption Deterrence Act of 1998 (the Identity Theft Act) to make it a federal crime when anyone knowingly transfers or uses, without lawful authority, a means of identification of another person with the intent to commit, or to aid or abet, any unlawful activity that constitutes a violation of federal law, or that constitutes a felony under any applicable state or local law.[71] Violations of the act are investigated by federal investigative agencies such as the US Secret Service, the FBI, and the US Postal Inspection Service.

In 2004, the Identity Theft Penalty Enhancement Act was signed into law. The act increases existing penalties for the crime of identity theft, establishes aggravated identity theft as a criminal offense, and establishes mandatory penalties for aggravated identity theft. According to this law, anyone who knowingly "transfers, possesses, or uses, without lawful authority" someone else's identification will be sentenced to an extra prison term of two years with no possibility of parole. Individuals committing identity fraud while engaged in crimes associated with terrorism—such as aircraft destruction, arson, airport violence, or kidnapping top government officials—will receive a mandatory sentence enhancement of five years.

INTERNET PORNOGRAPHY It is difficult to detect and control Internet pornography. Opponents of any controls warn that the right of free speech may be violated. Congress has struggled to create legislation that will restrict objectionable use without violating First Amendment freedoms. Fearing the proliferation of kiddie porn over the Internet, Congress enacted the Child Pornography Prevention Act of 1996 (CPPA), which outlawed sexually related material that used or *appeared to use* children under 18 engaging in sexual conduct. In *Ashcroft v. The Free Speech Coalition*, the Supreme Court ruled that sexually related material in which an actual child appears is illegal, but possessing "virtual" pornography is legal. The Court reasoned that real children are not harmed by pornography that depicts a virtual child.[72] In response to the Court's decision, Congress passed the PROTECT (Prosecutorial Remedies and Other Tools to end the Exploitation of Children Today) Act of 2003, which outlawed virtual kiddie porn that makes it almost impossible to distinguish the difference between a real child and a morphed or created image.[73] The Supreme Court reviewed this law in a 2009 case, *United States v. Williams*, which held that the government can legitimately outlaw the sale of child pornography even if the images are computer generated, if those purchasing the images *thought they were buying images of real children*. The Court noted that offers to engage in illegal transactions are excluded from First Amendment protection, so that the "speech" of an individual claiming to be in possession of child pornography is therefore not protected by the First Amendment.[74] So possessing virtual child pornography may be legal, but selling it may be a crime.

COMPUTER CRIMES Congress has treated computer-related crimes as distinct federal offenses since passage of the Counterfeit Access Device and Computer Fraud and Abuse Law in 1984.[75] The 1984 act protected classified US defense and foreign relations information, financial institution and consumer reporting agency files, and access to computers operated for the government. The act was supplemented in 1996 by the National Information Infrastructure Protection Act (NIIPA), which significantly broadens the scope of the law.

Enforcing Cyber Laws

How has the justice system responded to cybercrime? Most of the efforts are being made at the federal level. The government is now operating a number of organizations that are coordinating efforts to control cyberfraud. One approach is to create working groups that coordinate the activities of numerous agencies involved in investigating cybercrime. The Interagency Telemarketing and Internet Fraud Working Group brings together representatives of numerous US Attorneys' offices, the FBI, the Secret Service, the Postal Inspection Service, the Federal Trade Commission, the Securities and Exchange Commission, and other law enforcement and regulatory agencies to share information about trends and patterns in Internet fraud schemes. One of the most successful federal efforts is the New York Electronic Crimes Task Force (NYECTF), a partnership between the Secret Service and a host of other public safety agencies and private corporations. Its success has prompted Boston, Miami, Charlotte, Chicago, Las Vegas, San Francisco, Los Angeles, and Washington, DC, to set up similar task forces.[76]

Globalization and Transnational Organized Crime

LO6 Explain the relationship between globalization and transnational organized crime

globalization The process of creating a global economy through transnational markets and political and legal systems.

WEB APP 14.3 Read more about the pros and cons of globalization here: **https://www.forbes.com/sites/mikecollins/2015/05/06/the-pros-and-cons-of-globalization/**.

transnational organized crime Use of illegal tactics to gain profit in the global marketplace, typically involving the cross-border sale and distribution of illegal commodities.

The new global economy is a particular vexing development for agents of the criminal justice system because it vastly expands the reach of criminal organizations while at the same time creating new opportunities for criminal conspiracies. Globalization refers to the process of creating transnational markets and political and legal systems and has shifted the focus of crime from a local to a world perspective.

Globalization began when large companies decided to establish themselves in foreign markets by adapting their products or services to the local culture. The process took off with the fall of the Soviet Union, which opened new European markets. The development of China into an industrial superpower encouraged foreign investors to take advantage of China's huge supply of workers. As the Internet and communication revolution unfolded, companies were able to establish instant communications with their far-flung corporate empires, a technological breakthrough that further aided trade and foreign investments.

While globalization can improve the standard of living in third-world nations by providing jobs and training, it can also be a device for criminal cartels to avoid prosecution and regulation, while expanding their markets and profits.[77]

Transnational Organized Crime

It is not surprising that globalization has created a fertile ground for contemporary criminal organizations. By expanding the reach of both criminal and noncriminal organizations, globalization also increases the vulnerability of indigenous people with a traditional way of life.[78] With money and power to spare, organized crime groups can recruit new members, bribe government officials, and even fund private armies. Transnational organized crime has globalized its activities for the same reasons that legitimate multinational corporations have expanded around the world: new markets bring new sources of profits. Illicit enterprises are able to expand to take advantage of these new economic circumstances thanks to the communications and international transportation revolution.[79] Technological advances such as efficient and widespread commercial airline traffic, improvements in telecommunications (ranging from global cell phone connectivity to the Internet), and the growth of international trade have all aided the growth in illicit transnational activities. These changes have facilitated the

US law enforcement officials escort Joaquin "El Chapo" Guzman, center, from a plane to a waiting caravan of SUVs at Long Island MacArthur Airport, in Ronkonkoma, New York. Prosecutors and lawyers for the infamous drug lord sparred over his tough jail conditions. The government argued the restrictions were appropriate for someone known for escaping twice from prison in Mexico.

AP Images/Uncredited

cross-border movement of goods and people, conditions exploited by criminals who now use Internet chat rooms to plan their activities. On a cultural level, globalization brings with it an ideology of free markets and free trade. Local officials may exploit their position and demand bribes from multinational companies to do business in their country. To limit bribing of foreign officials, Congress in 1977 passed the Foreign Corrupt Practices Act (FCPA), which made it a criminal offense to bribe foreign officials or to make other questionable overseas payments.[80]

Despite the penalties imposed by the FCPA, corporations that deal in global trade are still being forced to give bribes to secure favorable trade agreements. For example, Pfizer, one of the world's largest drug companies, paid a $60 million fine to settle a government probe of the use of illegal payments to win business in China. Pfizer is not alone. Rival Johnson & Johnson agreed to pay $70 million to settle charges that it paid bribes and kickbacks to win business in Greece, Iraq, Poland, and Romania.[81]

The cultural shift produced by globalization often means less local government intervention and regulation, conditions exploited by crime groups to cross unpatrolled borders and to expand their activities to new regions of the world. Transnational organized crime groups freely exploit this new freedom to travel to regions where they cannot be extradited, base their operations in countries with ineffective or corrupt law enforcement, and launder their money in countries with bank secrecy or few effective controls. Globalization has allowed both individual offenders and criminal gangs to gain tremendous operational benefits while reducing risks of apprehension and punishment. In other words, crime has gone global.

Types of Transnational Crimes

The globalization of crime involves traditional crimes such as the distribution of pornography and developing criminal activities such as cybercrime. Other criminal activities with a global reach include human trafficking, migrant smuggling, drug smuggling, arms dealing, maritime piracy, and trafficking in environmental resources and counterfeit goods.[82]

The global gangs exploit instability to set up operations in areas that are beyond the reach of the law. Criminal gangs then create even more instability so that the local population becomes dependent on criminal activity for their economic survival. Would a local farmer involved in drug production in a rural area of Bolivia dare to take on the criminal gang—which he not only depends on for his livelihood but which promises deadly reprisals for disloyalty—knowing that he is beyond the protection of the law?

Global gangs take advantage of the latest technological developments to distribute illegal materials. An example of a traditional crime that has been revolutionized by global communications is child pornography. The Internet has enabled cheap and instant global distribution to millions of customers from concealed origins, usually situated in countries where prosecution is unlikely. In the past, the images would have had to be processed, printed, and the hard copies distributed via mail or retail outlets.[83]

The trade in human organs—especially kidneys—is substantial, and demand appears to be growing. Desperate victims in developing countries are exploited as their kidneys are purchased for low prices; others sell their body parts when traffickers use coercive means, such as force or threats of force, to secure the removal of the victim's organs. These crimes would not be possible without global transportation means available today.[84]

The profits from transnational criminal enterprise can be immense. The United Nations estimates that immigrant smugglers earn about $7 billion per year smuggling an estimated 3 million people (though some may be smuggled more than once). Of the between 170 and 250 million drug users in the world, up to 38 million may be routine or problem users, and more than 4 million are in treatment. The illegal drug trade brings in about $350 billion per year. Human trafficking, another activity of transnational gangs, is discussed in the Contemporary Issues in Criminal Justice feature.

LO7 Discuss various types of transnational crime

REALITYCHECK

Myth or Reality?

There are more drug users in the world than the populations of England, Italy, and France combined.

REALITY. And you can throw in Spain and Holland as well.

With an estimated 250 million users, the profits from illegal drug trafficking are immense.

Global Trafficking in Persons

Human trafficking has become a global problem. How great a problem? The United Nations estimates that at least 12 million adults and children are in forced labor, bonded labor, and commercial sexual servitude at any given time. Of these victims, more than half are female, many forced into sexual slavery. A disturbing trend is an increase in the share of children among the victims. Globally, children now comprise nearly one-third of all detected trafficking victims. Out of every three child victims, two are girls. In Africa and the Middle East, children comprise a majority of the detected victims; in Europe and central Asia, however, children are vastly outnumbered by adults.

Every year, hundreds of thousands of women and children—primarily from Southeast Asia and eastern Europe—are lured by the promise of good jobs and then end up forced into brothels or as circuit travelers in labor camps. Most go to wealthy industrialized countries. Japan now has more than 10,000 commercial sex establishments with 150,000 to 200,000 foreign girls trafficked into the country each year. India has experienced a large influx of foreign sex workers who are believed to be the source of the HIV epidemic that is sweeping the country. Traffickers import up to 50,000 women and children every year into the United States despite legal prohibitions (in addition to prostitution, some are brought in to work in sweatshops).

Global trafficking gangs use force, fraud, or coercion to exploit a person for profit. Victims are subjected to labor and/or sexual exploitation. Gangs prey on the weak, targeting vulnerable men, women, and children. They use creative and ruthless ploys designed to trick, coerce, and win the confidence of potential victims. Very often, these ruses involve promises of a better life through employment, educational opportunities, or marriage.

Trafficking for labor exploitation—the form of trafficking claiming the greatest number of victims—includes traditional slavery, forced labor, and holding people in bondage until they can pay off debts. Trafficking for sexual exploitation may include involvement in prostitution or pornographic films. The use of force or coercion can be direct and violent or psychological. Women may be kidnapped, beaten, raped, and led to believe they can never return home. If they still won't cooperate, their families and friends may be threatened or attacked.

Trafficking gangs are located in Latin America, Asia, and eastern European nations such as Bulgaria and Russia. The UN report found that sex traffickers are often women, many of whom began as sex workers themselves. They are encouraged by their recruiter/trafficker to return home and recruit other women, often under the scrutiny of people working for the trafficker to make sure they don't try to escape.

Because it is a global enterprise, there is a great deal of cooperation in trafficking, so that in eastern Europe a single gang may include Russians, Moldavians, Egyptians, and Syrians. Cooperation allows sex slaves to be trafficked not only to neighboring countries but all around the globe. The United Nations found that victims from east Asia were detected in more than 20 countries in regions throughout the world, including Europe, the Americas, the Middle East, central Asia, and Africa.

Combating Trafficking

The United States has made stopping the trafficking of women a top priority. More than 15 years ago, the "Memorandum on Steps to Combat Violence Against Women and the Trafficking of Women and Girls" was issued, directing the secretary of state, the attorney general, and the president's Interagency Council on Women to expand their work against violence against women to include work against the trafficking of women. Since then, a variety of government agencies have worked together to develop trainings to provide federal, state, and local law enforcement with the tools and strategies they need to identify human trafficking victims and prosecute offenders. Agencies that are cooperating include the Federal Law Enforcement Training Center, US Immigration and Customs Enforcement (ICE), the FBI, the Human Trafficking Prosecution Unit of the US Department of Justice, and the Department of Labor. There are now multi-agency specialized task forces called Anti-Trafficking Coordination Teams that focus primarily on the eradication of human trafficking gangs. The United States is not alone in its efforts. In the former Soviet Union, prevention education projects are aimed at potential victims of trafficking, and nongovernmental organizations have established hotlines for victims or women seeking information about the risks of accepting job offers abroad.

Despite increased awareness of the problem and increased efforts by law enforcement agencies, there are still very few convictions for trafficking in persons. About 40 percent of all affected countries report having 10 or more yearly convictions, and 15 percent report having no convictions at all. Fewer countries are reporting increases in the numbers of convictions, which remain very low. This may reflect the difficulties of the criminal justice systems to appropriately respond to trafficking in persons.

CRITICAL THINKING

1. If put in charge, what would you do to slow or end the international sex trade? Before you answer, remember the saying that prostitution is the oldest profession, which implies that curbing it may prove quite difficult.

2. Should men who hire prostitutes who are obviously involved in the sex trade against their will be punished more severely to deter them from contributing to the exploitation of these vulnerable young women? Or is it unfair to expect someone to know the reasons their sex partner was involved in prostitution?

Sources: United Nations Office on Drugs and Crime, *Global Report on Trafficking in Persons, 2015*, http://www.unodc.org/documents/data-and-analysis/glotip /2016_Global_Report_on_Trafficking_in_Persons.pdf; Department of Homeland Security, *Human Trafficking*, https://www.dhs.gov/topic/human-trafficking (URLs accessed March 2017); Mark Lusk and Faith Lucas, "The Challenge of Human Trafficking and Contemporary Slavery," *Journal of Comparative Social Welfare* 25 (2009): 49–57.

Transnational Crime Groups

LO8 List some of the most important transnational crime groups

Transnational crime networks may locate themselves in nations whose governments are too weak to present effective opposition. If they believe that the government may be interfering with their illegal activities that bring them immense profits, such as drug trafficking, they will carry out a terror campaign, killing police officials and using bribery, violence, or terror to achieve their goals. The political turmoil of the twenty-first century coupled with advances in telecommunications and computer technology have had the unintended effect of providing avenues for the rapid expansion of transnational organized crime activities.

ASIAN GANGS Asian groups are involved in a number of global criminal conspiracies ranging from extortion and smuggling to arms dealing and human trafficking.[85] Demand for drugs by wealth urban residents of east Asia has also fueled and revitalized organized crime in that part of the world. The United Nations Office of Drugs and Crime (UNODC) estimates that Asian organized crime groups earn about $90 to $100 billion each year from illegal activities. Critics of the surge in criminal activity have alleged that Asian governments are prioritizing economic development over threats to public safety.[86]

AFRICAN GANGS Nigerian criminal enterprises are the most significant of these groups and operate in more than 80 other countries.[87] Highly aggressive, they primarily engage in drug trafficking and financial frauds. Nigerian gangs deliver heroin from Southeast and western Asia into Europe and the United States and cocaine from South America into Europe and South Africa. Large populations of ethnic Nigerians in India, Pakistan, and Thailand have given these enterprises direct access to 90 percent of the world's heroin production. The associated money laundering has helped establish Nigerian criminal enterprises on every populated continent of the world.

RUSSIAN TRANSNATIONAL CRIME GROUPS Since the collapse of the Soviet Union in 1991, criminal organizations in Russia and other former Soviet republics such as Ukraine have engaged in a variety of crimes: drugs and arms trafficking, stolen automobiles, trafficking in women and children, and money laundering.[88] No area of the world seems immune to this menace, especially not the United States. America is the land of opportunity for unloading criminal goods and laundering dirty money.

Russian criminals make extensive use of the state governmental apparatus to protect and promote their criminal activities. For example, most businesses in Russia—legal, quasi-legal, and illegal—must operate with the protection of a *krysha* (roof). The protection is often provided by police or security officials employed outside their "official" capacities for this purpose. In other cases, officials are "silent partners" in criminal enterprises that they, in turn, protect. The criminalization of the privatization process has resulted in the massive use of state funds for criminal gain. Valuable properties are purchased through insider deals for much less than their true value and then resold for lucrative profits. Criminals have been able to directly influence the state's domestic and foreign policy to promote the interests of organized crime either by attaining public office themselves or by buying public officials.

In the United States, Russian criminal groups are extensively engaged in a broad array of frauds and scams, including health care fraud, insurance scams, stock frauds, antiquities swindles, forgery, and fuel tax evasion schemes.[89] Russians are believed to be the main purveyors of credit card fraud in the United States. Legitimate businesses, such as the movie business and textile industry, have become targets of criminals from the former Soviet Union, and they are often used for money laundering and extortion.

MEXICAN DRUG CARTELS Mexican drug cartels have become large-scale suppliers of narcotics, marijuana, and methamphetamines to the United States. Mexican drug gangs routinely use violence, and fighting for control of the border regions has affected US citizens: large numbers of Americans have been kidnapped, and Mexican drug cartel members have threatened to kill US journalists covering drug violence in the border region. And, as a result of their immense profits, Mexican cartels are the leading wholesale launderers of drug money from the United States.[90] By some estimates they take in between $19 and $29 billion annually from the United States.[91]

Of the numerous drug cartels operating in Mexico, the main ones are the Sinaloa Federation, which controls 40 to 60 percent of the country's drug trade (it was formerly

WEB APP 14.4 US Immigration and Customs Enforcement is the principal investigative arm of the US Department of Homeland Security (DHS) and the second largest investigative agency in the federal government, with more than 20,000 employees in offices in all 50 states and 47 foreign countries. To read about some of their antitransnational gang initiatives, go to **https://www.ice.gov/national-gang-unit**.

headed by Joaquin "El Chapo" Guzman, who is now in US custody); Jalisco New Generation, which burst onto the scene in 2011 with its public display of 35 corpses of alleged Los Zetas members; Los Zetas, which consists of former elite military personnel from Mexico; the Gulf Cartel, Sinaloa's main competitor; Beltran Leyva; the Juarez cartel; and the Tijuana/Arellan Felix group.[92] In recent years, new cartels have formed, and others have become allies in a constantly shifting landscape of drug activity. It is nearly impossible to keep tabs on all the groups' movements and composition.

Controlling Transnational Crime

Efforts to combat transnational organized crime are typically in the hands of federal agencies. One approach is to form international working groups to collect intelligence, share information, and plot unified strategies among member nations. The FBI belongs to several international working groups aimed at combating transnational gangs in various parts of the world. For example, to combat the influence and reach of Eurasian organized crime, the FBI is involved in the following groups and activities:

- *Eurasian Organized Crime Working Group.* Established in 1994, it meets to discuss and jointly address the transnational aspects of Eurasian organized crime that impact member countries and the international community in general. The member countries are Canada, Great Britain, Germany, France, Italy, Japan, the United States, and Russia.
- *Central European Working Group.* This group is part of a project that brings together the FBI and central European law enforcement agencies to discuss cooperative investigative matters covering the broad spectrum of Eurasian organized crime. A principal concern is the growing presence of Russian and other Eurasian organized criminals in Central Europe and the United States. The initiative works on practical interaction between the participating agencies to establish lines of communication and working relationships, to develop strategies and tactics to address transnational organized crime matters impacting the region, and to identify potential common targets.
- *Southeast European Cooperative Initiative.* This is an international organization intended to coordinate police and customs regional actions for preventing and combating transborder crime. It is headquartered in Bucharest, Romania, and has 12 fully participating member countries. The United States has been one of 14 countries with observer status since 1998. The initiative's center serves as a clearinghouse for information and intelligence sharing, allowing the quick exchange of information in a professional and trustworthy environment. The initiative also supports specialized task forces for countering serious transborder crime such as smuggling, financial crimes, terrorism, and the trafficking of people, drugs, and cars.

ORGANIZED CRIME LAWS Congress has passed a number of laws that have made it easier for agencies to bring transnational gangs to justice. One of the first measures aimed directly at organized crime was the Interstate and Foreign Travel or Transportation in Aid of Racketeering Enterprises Act (Travel Act).[93] The Travel Act prohibits travel in interstate commerce or use of interstate facilities with the intent to promote, manage, establish, carry on, or facilitate an unlawful activity; it also prohibits the actual or attempted engagement in these activities. In 1970, Congress passed the Organized Crime Control Act. Title IX of the act, probably its most effective measure, is the Racketeer Influenced and Corrupt Organization Act (RICO).[94] RICO did not create new categories of crimes but rather new categories of offenses in racketeering activity, which it defined as involvement in two or more acts prohibited by 24 existing federal and 8 state statutes. The offenses listed in RICO include state-defined crimes, such as murder, kidnapping, gambling, arson, robbery, bribery, extortion, and narcotic violations; and federally defined crimes, such as bribery, counterfeiting, transmission of gambling information, prostitution, and mail fraud. RICO is designed to limit patterns of organized criminal activity by prohibiting involvement in acts intended to do the following:

- Derive income from racketeering or the unlawful collection of debts and use or investment of such income.

Racketeer Influenced and Corrupt Organization Act (RICO)
Federal legislation that enables prosecutors to bring additional criminal or civil charges against people engaged in two or more acts prohibited by 24 existing federal and 8 state laws. RICO features monetary penalties that allow the government to confiscate all profits derived from criminal activities. Originally intended to be used against organized criminals, RICO has also been used against white-collar criminals.

- Acquire through racketeering an interest in or control over any enterprise engaged in interstate or foreign commerce.
- Conduct business through a pattern of racketeering.
- Conspire to use racketeering as a means of making income, collecting loans, or conducting business.

An individual convicted under RICO is subject to 20 years in prison and a $25,000 fine. Additionally, the accused must forfeit to the US government any interest in a business in violation of RICO. These penalties are much more potent than simple conviction and imprisonment.[95]

Why Is It So Difficult to Eradicate Global Crime?

While international cooperation is now common, and law enforcement agencies are willing to work together to fight transnational gangs, these criminal organizations are extremely hard to eradicate. The gangs are ready to use violence and are well equipped to carry out threats. Take for example the so-called war on drugs. One reason it has proven so difficult for law enforcement to combat the drug cartels is that the cartels can use their firepower to intimidate police, judges, and potential witnesses. The shifting alliances and changes of location can confound law enforcement efforts. For example, the Los Zetas gang, whose core members are former members of the Mexican military's elite Special Air Mobile Force Group (*Grupo Aeromovil de Fuerzas Especiales*, GAFES) are able to carry out complex operations using their military training and sophisticated weaponry.[96] The Zetas began as enforcers for the Gulf cartel and are now their rivals. From their base in Nuevo Laredo, their sphere of influence extends across Mexico and deep into Central America, trafficking in arms, kidnapping, and competing for control of trafficking routes along the eastern half of the US–Mexican border. And when they feel threatened, they are quite willing to fight the law. It is estimated that more than 80,000 people have been killed by the drug gangs since 2006.[97]

Adding to control problems is the fact that the drug trade is an important source of foreign revenue, and destroying the drug trade undermines the economies of third-world nations. Even if the government of one nation was willing to cooperate in vigorous drug suppression efforts, suppliers in other nations, eager to cash in on the sellers' market, would be encouraged to turn more acreage over to coca or poppy production. Today, almost every Caribbean country is involved with narcotrafficking; illicit drug shipments in the region are worth more money than the top five legitimate exports combined. Drug gangs are able to corrupt the political structure and destabilize countries. Drug addiction and violent crime are now common in Jamaica, Puerto Rico, and even

AP Images/Anja Niedringhaus

It is difficult to control the international drug trade since enemy states prevent US law enforcement agents from entry. Here, Afghan poppy farmers prepare the soil for their poppy seeds in the fields of Cham Kalai, a village located in Afghanistan's eastern Nangarhar province, a Taliban stronghold. Poppy cultivation in Nangarhar province has skyrocketed and profits have been used to fund terrorist activities.

Although most people loathe the thought of torturing anyone, some experts argue that torture can sometimes be justified in what they call the ticking bomb scenario. Suppose the government found out that a captured terrorist knew the whereabouts of a dangerous explosive device that was set to go off and kill thousands of innocent people. Consider the fact that opponents of torture believe that even imminent danger does not justify state violence. There is also a danger that torture would then become calculated and premeditated; torturers would have to be trained and be in place, ready to take action. Because torturers would be part of the government bureaucracy, there is no way to ensure that they would use their skills only in certain morally justifiable cases.

Writing Challenge: Reflecting back on this chapter's terrorism discussion, write an essay that presents an ethical argument for both sides of this issue. Answer the following questions: Would the torture of a suspected terrorist determined to destroy the government and harm innocent civilians ever be ethical? Under the circumstances presented above, would it be ethical to waterboard or otherwise torture this single suspect if it would save the population of a city?

small islands such as St. Kitts. The corruption of the police and other security forces has reached a crisis point, where an officer can earn the equivalent of half a year's salary by simply looking the other way on a drug deal.[98]

Another problem is that the United States has little influence in some key drug-producing areas such as Helmon Province in Afghanistan—an area still controlled by the Taliban—and in rebel-held areas of Myanmar (formerly Burma).[99] War and terrorism also may make gang control strategies problematic. After the United States toppled Afghanistan's Taliban government, the remnants began to grow and sell poppy to support their insurgency; Afghanistan now supplies a significant percentage of the world's opium.[100] And while the Colombian guerillas may not be interested in joining or colluding with crime cartels, they finance their war against the government by aiding drug traffickers and "taxing" crops and sales.[101] Considering these problems, it is not surprising that transnational gangs continue to flourish.

SUMMARY

LO1 *List the various forms of terrorism and their goals* There are a number of different forms of terrorism. Revolutionary terrorists use violence to frighten those in power and their supporters to replace the existing government with a regime that holds acceptable political or religious views. Political terrorists attack people or groups who oppose the terrorists' political ideology or whom the terrorists define as "outsiders" who must be destroyed. Nationalist terrorists promote the interests of a minority ethnic or religious group who believes it has been persecuted under majority rule and wants to carve out its own independent homeland. Retributive terrorists use violence as a method of influence, persuasion, or intimidation to get people to accept their social, religious, or political views. State-sponsored terrorists are part of a repressive government regime that forces its citizens into obedience, oppresses minorities, and stifles political dissent. Some cults may be classified as terror groups because their leaders demand that followers prove their loyalty through violence or intimidation. Sometimes terrorist groups become involved in common-law crimes such as drug dealing and kidnapping, or even selling nuclear materials. This is known as criminal terrorism.

LO2 *Discuss the impact of corporate enterprise crime* The crimes of the rich and powerful have the most significant impact on society. Experts place their total monetary value in the hundreds of billions of dollars, far outstripping the expense of any other type of crime. Large-scale investment growth has led to significant increases in the amount of fraud and misconduct on Wall Street. Investment firms

have engaged in deceptive securities sales that have cost investors billions.

LO3 *Evaluate the various forms of green crime* The United States and most sovereign nations have passed laws making it a crime to pollute or damage the environment. Green crimes involve the environment and include such activities as illegal logging, illegal fishing, illegal polluting, and the like. In some instances, environmental criminals conduct activities overseas to avoid legal controls and enforcement.

LO4 *Describe the various forms of cybercrime* Cybercrime typically involves the theft and/or destruction of information, resources, or funds via computers, computer networks, and the Internet. Cybertheft is the use of computer networks for criminal profits. It includes computer fraud, certain forms of Internet pornography, copyright infringement, Internet securities fraud, identity theft, e-tailing fraud, and illegal drug distribution, among other activities. Cybervandalism, or technological destruction, involves malicious attacks aimed at disrupting, defacing, and destroying technology. Cyberbullying is willful and repeated harm inflicted through the medium of electronic text. Cyberwarfare consists of politically motivated attacks designed to compromise the electronic infrastructure of the enemy and to disrupt its economy.

LO5 *Summarize methods used to control cybercrime* Numerous organizations have been set up to provide training and support for law enforcement agents. In addition, new federal and state laws have been enacted to help discourage particular types of high-tech crimes. In the future, technological prowess may make it possible to identify cybercriminals and bring them to justice before they can carry out their attacks.

L06 *Explain the relationship between globalization and transnational organized crime* Globalization is the process of creating a global economy through transnational markets and political and legal systems. It has shifted the focus of crime from a local to a world perspective. With money and power to spare, criminal enterprise groups can recruit new members, bribe government officials, and even fund private armies. Transnational organized crime involves ongoing international criminal enterprise groups whose purpose is personal economic gain through illegitimate means.

L07 *Discuss various types of transnational crime* Transnational gangs are involved in money laundering, human smuggling, cybercrime, and trafficking of humans, drugs, weapons, body parts, and nuclear material. There is also a troubling overseas trade in prostitution. Transnational gangs export women from third-world nations for the purposes of prostitution. Some may be kidnapped or forced into prostitution against their will through violence and threats.

L08 *List some of the most important transnational crime groups* Eastern gangs trace their origin to countries spanning the Baltics, the Balkans, central/eastern Europe, Russia, the Caucasus, and central Asia. Russian organized crime is active in Europe, Africa, Asia, and North and South America. Asian gangs include the Yakuza Japanese criminal group, often involved in multinational criminal activities such as human trafficking, gambling, prostitution, and undermining licit businesses. Chinese groups are also involved in human trafficking—bringing large numbers of Chinese migrants to North America and essentially enslaving them for profit. A number of powerful Mexican drug cartels now dominate the cross-border drug trade into the United States.

L09 *Explain the methods law enforcement is now using to thwart transnational criminal syndicates* Efforts to combat transnational organized crime are typically in the hands of federal agencies. One approach is for them to form international working groups to collect intelligence, share information, and plot unified strategies among member nations. US law enforcement agencies have cooperated in cross-border operations to eradicate gang activity.

KEY TERMS

terrorism, p. 355

USA Patriot Act (USAPA), p. 359

corporate enterprise crime, p. 360

Ponzi scheme, p. 361

green crime, p. 363

cybercrime, p. 365

cybertheft, p. 366

warez, p. 367

identity theft, p. 368

phishing, p. 368

e-tailing fraud, p. 368

cybervandalism, p. 368

denial-of-service attack, p. 369

cyberstalking, p. 369

cyberbullying, p. 369

cyberwarfare, p. 370

globalization, p. 372

transnational organized crime, p. 372

Racketeer Influenced and Corrupt Organization Act (RICO), p. 376

REVIEW QUESTIONS

1. Should the US government use drones to spy on suspected terrorists on American soil?

2. Would you allow federal agents to use intense interrogation techniques such as waterboarding to pry information from terror suspects?

3. Should people who illegally download movies be prosecuted for theft?

4. How can Internet pornography be controlled considering that a great deal of adult content is available on foreign websites?

5. Considering the threat of transnational drug trafficking, should drugs be legalized and controlled by the government?

6. Should the Internet be more closely monitored and controlled to prevent the threat of cyberwar?

7. Is there any point to placing economic sanctions on billion-dollar corporations? Should corporate executives be put in prison? Put another way, what is the purpose of incarcerating someone like 72-year-old Bernard Madoff? Is he really a threat to society?

Glossary

actus reus An illegal act. The *actus reus* can be an affirmative act, such as taking money or shooting someone, or a failure to act, such as failing to take proper precautions while driving a car.

adjudication The determination of guilt or innocence; a judgment concerning criminal charges. The majority of offenders charged plead guilty; of the remainder, some cases are adjudicated by a judge and a jury, some are adjudicated by a judge without a jury, and others are dismissed.

adversarial procedure The process of publicly pitting the prosecution and the defense against one another in pursuit of the truth.

aggravated assault An unlawful attack by one person upon another, accompanied by the use of a weapon, for the purpose of inflicting severe or aggravated bodily injury.

antisocial (sociopathic, psychopathic) personality Individuals who are always in trouble and do not learn from either experience or punishment. They are loners who engage in frequent callous and hedonistic behaviors, are emotionally immature, and lack responsibility, judgment, and empathy.

appeal A request for an appellate court to examine a lower court's decision to determine whether proper procedures were followed.

appellate court A court that reconsiders a case that has already been tried to determine whether the measures used complied with accepted rules of criminal procedure and were in accordance with constitutional doctrines.

arson Any willful or malicious burning or attempting to burn, with or without intent to defraud, a dwelling house, public building, motor vehicle or aircraft, or personal property of another.

assigned counsel A lawyer appointed by the court to represent a defendant in a criminal case because the person is too poor to hire counsel.

B

bail The monetary amount for or condition of pretrial release, normally set by a judge at the initial appearance. The purpose of bail is to ensure the return of the accused at subsequent proceedings.

Bail Reform Act of 1984 Federal legislation that provides for both greater emphasis on release on recognizance for nondangerous offenders and preventive detention for those who present a menace to the community.

bench trial The trial of a criminal matter by a judge only. The accused waives any constitutional right to trial by jury.

Bill of Rights The first 10 amendments to the US Constitution that spell out specific freedoms granted to citizens and limit the power of the federal government to conduct criminal prosecutions.

biometrics Automated methods of recognizing a person based on a physiological or behavioral characteristic.

biosocial theory Human behavior is a function of the interaction of biochemical, neurological, and genetic factors with environmental stimuli.

bipolar disorder A psychological condition marked by mood swings between periods of wild elation and deep depression.

blameworthy Culpable or guilty of participating in a particular criminal offense.

blue curtain The secretive, insulated police culture that isolates officers from the rest of society.

boot camp A short-term militaristic correctional facility in which inmates undergo intensive physical conditioning and discipline.

broken windows hypothesis The view that deteriorated communities serve as a magnet for criminals and attract criminal activity.

broken windows model A term used to describe the role of the police as maintainers of community order and safety.

brutalization effect An outcome of capital punishment that enhances, rather than deters, the level of violence in society. The death penalty reinforces the view that violence is an appropriate response to provocation.

Bureau of Alcohol, Tobacco, Firearms, and Explosives (ATF) Federal agency with jurisdiction over the illegal sale, importation, and criminal misuse of firearms and explosives and the distribution of untaxed liquor and cigarettes.

burglary The unlawful entry of a structure to commit a felony or a theft.

C

challenge for cause A request that a prospective juror be removed because he or she is biased or has prior knowledge about a case, or for other reasons that demonstrate the individual's inability to render a fair and impartial judgment in a particular case.

child savers Late nineteenth-century reformers in America who developed programs for troubled youths and influenced legislation creating the juvenile justice system.

Children's Aid Society A child-saving organization begun by Charles Loring Brace; it took children from the streets in large cities and placed them with farm families on the prairie.

chivalry hypothesis The view that the low rates of female crime and delinquency are a reflection of the leniency with which police and judges treat female offenders.

chronic offender A delinquent offender who is arrested five or more times before he or she is 18 and who stands a good chance of becoming an adult criminal; these offenders are responsible for more than half of all serious crimes.

civil law All law that is not criminal, including the law of torts (personal wrongs) and contract, property, maritime, and commercial law.

cognitive-behavioral therapy (CBT) A treatment approach that focuses on patterns of thinking and beliefs to help people become conscious of their own thoughts and behaviors so they can make positive changes.

commitment Decision of judge ordering an adjudicated and sentenced juvenile offender to be placed in a correctional facility.

common law Early English law, developed by judges, that incorporated Anglo-Saxon tribal custom, feudal rules and practices, and the everyday rules of behavior of local villages. Common law became the standardized law of the land in England and eventually formed the basis of criminal law in the United States.

community service restitution An alternative sanction that requires an offender to work in the community at such tasks as cleaning public parks or working with disabled children in lieu of an incarceration sentence.

community-oriented policing (COP) Programs and strategies designed to bring police and the public closer together and create a more cooperative working environment between them.

CompStat A program originated by the New York City police that used carefully collected and analyzed crime data to shape policy and evaluate police effectiveness.

compulsory process Compelling the production of witnesses via a subpoena.

concurrent sentences Prison sentences for two or more criminal acts, served simultaneously and run together.

conduct disorder (CD) A pattern of repetitive behavior in which the rights of others or social norms are violated.

conflict view of crime The law is controlled by the rich and powerful who shape its content to ensure their continued economic domination of society. The criminal justice system is an instrument of social and economic repression.

confrontation clause A part of the Sixth Amendment that establishes the right of a criminal defendant to see and cross-examine all the witnesses against him or her.

congregate system Prison system first used in New York that allowed inmates to engage in group activities such as work, meals, and recreation.

consecutive sentence A prison sentence for two or more criminal acts, served one after the other.

consensus view of crime The majority of citizens in a society share common ideals and work toward a common good. Crimes are acts that are outlawed because they conflict with the rules of the majority and are harmful to society.

constable In medieval England, an appointed official who administered and supervised the legal affairs of a small community.

contract system The practice of correctional officials selling the labor of inmates to private businesses.

contract system (attorney) Providing counsel to indigent offenders by having attorneys under contract to the county handle all (or some) such cases.

convict-lease system The practice of leasing inmates to a business for a fixed annual fee.

corporate enterprise crime Illegal activities of people and organizations whose acknowledged purpose is to profit through illegitimate business enterprise.

corruption Exercising legitimate discretion for improper reasons or using illegal means to achieve approved goals.

court of last resort A court that handles the final appeal on a matter. The US Supreme Court is the official court of last resort for criminal matters.

courtroom work group The phrase used to indicate that all parties in the adversary process work together cooperatively to settle cases with the least amount of effort and conflict.

courts of general jurisdiction State or federal courts that have jurisdiction over felony offenses and more serious civil cases (i.e., cases involving more than a dollar amount set by the legislature).

crime A violation of societal rules of behavior as interpreted and expressed by a criminal legal code created by people holding social and political power. Individuals who violate these rules are subject to sanctions by state authority, social stigma, and loss of status.

crime control perspective A model of criminal justice that emphasizes the control of dangerous offenders and the protection of society. Its advocates call for harsh punishments as a deterrent to crime and support availability of the death penalty.

criminal justice process The decision-making points, from the initial investigation or arrest by police to the eventual release of the offender and his or her reentry into society; the various sequential criminal justice stages through which the offender passes.

criminal justice system The law enforcement, court, and correctional agencies that work together to effect the apprehension, prosecution, and control of criminal offenders. They are charged with maintaining order, enforcing the law, identifying transgressors, bringing the guilty to justice, and treating criminal behavior.

criminal procedure The rules and laws that define the operation of criminal proceedings. Procedural law describes the methods that must be followed in obtaining warrants, investigating offenses, effecting lawful arrests, conducting trials, introducing evidence, sentencing convicted offenders, and reviewing cases by appellate courts.

cross-examination The process in which the defense and the prosecution interrogate witnesses for the other side during a trial.

cruel and unusual punishment Physical punishment or punishment that is far in excess of that given to people under similar circumstances and is therefore banned by the Eighth Amendment. The death penalty has so far not been considered cruel and unusual if it is administered in a fair and nondiscriminatory fashion.

cultural transmission The passing of cultural values from one generation to the next.

culture of poverty The crushing lifestyle of slum areas produces a culture of poverty, passed from one generation to the next, marked by apathy, cynicism, feelings of helplessness, and mistrust of social institutions, such as schools, government agencies, and the police.

cumulative disadvantage The tendency of prior social problems to produce future ones that accumulate and undermine success.

Customs and Border Protection (CBP) Federal agency responsible for the control and protection of America's borders and ports of entry. Its first priority is keeping terrorists and their weapons out of the United States.

cyberbullying Willful and repeated harm done through the medium of electronic text.

cybercrime Illegal activity that uses a computer as its primary means of commission. Common forms of cybercrime include theft and destruction of information, resources, and funds.

cyberstalking Using the Internet, email, or other electronic communications devices to stalk or harass another person.

cybertheft The use of computer networks for criminal profits. Illegal copyright infringement, identity theft, and Internet securities fraud are examples of cybertheft.

cybervandalism Malicious attacks aimed at disrupting, defacing, and destroying technology.

cyberwarfare Politically motivated attacks designed to compromise the electronic infrastructure of an enemy nation and disrupt its economy.

cynicism The belief that most people's actions are motivated solely by personal needs and selfishness.

D

data mining Using computer software to conduct analysis of behavior patterns in an effort to identify crime patterns and link them to suspects.

day fees A program requiring probationers to pay some of the costs of their treatment.

day fines Fines geared to the average daily income of the convicted offender in an effort to bring equity to the sentencing process.

day reporting centers (DRCs) Nonresidential community-based treatment programs.

deadly force Force that is likely to cause death or bodily harm.

decriminalization Reducing the penalty for a criminal act but not actually legalizing it.

deinstitutionalization The policy of removing as many offenders as possible from secure confinement and treating them in the community.

demeanor The way in which a person outwardly manifests his or her personality.

denial-of-service attack Extorting money from an Internet service user by threatening to prevent the user having access to the service.

Department of Homeland Security (DHS) Federal agency responsible for preventing terrorist attacks within the United States, reducing America's vulnerability to terrorism, and minimizing the damage and assisting in recovery from attacks that do occur.

deposit bail The monetary amount set by a judge at a hearing as a condition of pretrial release; the percentage of the total bond required to be paid by the defendant.

detention The temporary care of a child alleged to be a delinquent or status offender who requires secure custody, pending court disposition.

determinate sentences Fixed terms of incarceration, such as three years imprisonment. Many people consider determinate sentences too restrictive for rehabilitative purposes; the advantage is that offenders know how much time they have to serve—that is, when they will be released.

deterrent effect Stopping or reducing crime by convincing would-be criminals that they stand a significant risk of being apprehended and punished for their crimes.

developmental theory Social interactions that are developed over the life course shape behavior. Some interactions, such as involvement with deviant peers, encourage law violations whereas others, such as marriage and military service, may help people desist from crime.

directed patrol A patrol strategy that involves concentrating police resources in areas where certain crimes are a significant problem.

directed verdict The right of a judge to direct a jury to acquit a defendant because the state has not proved the elements of the crime or otherwise has not established guilt according to law.

direct examination The questioning of one's own (prosecution or defense) witness during a trial.

discretion The use of personal decision making and choice in carrying out operations in the criminal justice system. For example, police discretion can involve deciding whether to make an arrest; prosecutorial discretion can involve deciding whether to accept a plea bargain.

dispositions For juvenile offenders, the equivalent of sentencing for adult offenders. The theory is that disposition is more rehabilitative than retributive. Possible dispositions include dismissing the case, releasing the youth to the custody of his or her parents, placing the offender on probation, or sending him or her to a state correctional institution.

diversion A noncriminal alternative to trial, usually featuring counseling, job training, and educational opportunities.

DNA profiling The identification of criminal suspects by matching DNA samples taken from their person with specimens found at the crime scene.

double marginality The social burden African American police officers carry by virtue of being both minority group members and law enforcement officers.

Drug Enforcement Administration (DEA) The federal agency that enforces federal drug control laws.

due process perspective Due process provides the basic rights of a defendant in criminal proceedings and the requirements for a fair trial.

E

electronic monitoring (EM) Requiring convicted offenders to wear a monitoring device as part of their community sentence. Typically part of a house arrest order, this enables the probation department to ensure that offenders are complying with court-ordered limitations on their freedom.

emotional intelligence The capability of monitoring one's own feelings and actions in order to guide action.

entrapment A criminal defense that maintains the police originated the criminal idea or initiated the criminal action.

equal justice perspective The view that all people should be treated equally before the law. Equality may best be achieved through individual discretion in the justice process.

equity The action or practice of awarding each person what is due him or her; sanctions based on equity seek to compensate individual victims and society in general for their losses due to crime.

e-tailing fraud Using the Internet to illegally buy or sell merchandise.

evidence-based justice Determining through the use of the scientific method whether criminal justice programs actually reduce crime rates and offender recidivism.

ex post facto laws Acts that retroactively change the legal status of actions that were committed before the enactment of a law and/or change the consequences after it was enacted.

exclusionary rule Evidence seized in violation of the Fourth Amendment cannot be used in a court of law.

excuse defenses A defense in which a person states that his or her mental state was so impaired that he or she lacked the capacity to form sufficient intent to be held criminally responsible.

Federal Bureau of Investigation (FBI) The arm of the US Justice Department that investigates violations of federal law, seeks to protect America from terrorist attacks, gathers crime statistics, runs a comprehensive crime laboratory, and helps train local law enforcement officers.

F

felony A more serious offense that carries a penalty of incarceration in a state prison, usually for one year or more. Persons convicted of felony offenses lose certain rights, such as the right to vote, to hold elective office, or to maintain certain licenses.

fines Money payments levied on offenders to compensate society for their misdeeds.

foot patrol Police patrols that take officers out of cars and put them on a walking beat to strengthen ties with the community.

forcible rape Under common law, the carnal knowledge of a female forcibly and against her will. Many states have made rape a gender-neutral crime. The FBI has created a new definition of rape for its UCR program: "The penetration, no matter how slight, of the vagina or anus with any body part or object, or oral penetration by a sex organ of another person, without the consent of the victim."

forensic science The use of scientific techniques to investigate questions of interest to the justice system and to solve crimes.

forfeiture The seizure of personal property by the state as a civil or criminal penalty.

furlough A correctional policy that allows inmates to leave the institution for vocational or educational training, for employment, or to maintain family ties.

fusion centers Mechanisms to exchange information and intelligence, maximize resources, streamline operations, and improve the ability to fight crime and terrorism by analyzing data from a variety of sources.

G

general deterrence The theory that crime rates are influenced and controlled by the threat of criminal punishment. If people fear being apprehended and punished, they will not risk breaking the law.

Gideon v. Wainwright The 1963 US Supreme Court case that granted counsel to indigent defendants in felony prosecutions.

globalization The process of creating a global economy through transnational markets and political and legal systems.

good faith exception The principle that evidence may be used in a criminal trial, even though the search warrant used to obtain it is technically faulty, if the police acted in good faith and to the best of their ability when they sought to obtain it from a judge.

grand jury A type of jury responsible for investigating alleged crimes, examining evidence, and issuing indictments.

grass eaters A term for police officers who accept payoffs when everyday duties place them in a position to "look the other way."

green crime Criminal activity that involves violation of rules and laws designed to protect the environment, including illegal dumping, polluting, fishing, logging, and so on.

H

halfway houses Community-based correctional facilities that house inmates before their outright release so they can become gradually acclimated to conventional society.

hands-off doctrine The legal practice of allowing prison administrators a free hand to run the institution, even if correctional practices violate inmates' constitutional rights; ended with the onset of the prisoners' rights movement in the 1960s.

hearsay evidence Testimony that is not firsthand but, rather, relates information told by a second party.

hot spots of crime Places from which a significant portion of all police calls originate. These hot spots include taverns and housing projects.

house arrest A form of intermediate sanction that requires the convicted offender to spend a designated amount of time per week in his or her own home—such as from 6 P.M. Friday until 8 A.M. Monday.

hue and cry In medieval England, a call for assistance. The policy of self-help that prevailed in villages demanded that everyone respond if a citizen raised a hue and cry to get their aid.

hulks Abandoned ships anchored in harbors and used in eighteenth-century England to house prisoners.

hundred In medieval England, a group of 100 families responsible for maintaining order and trying minor offenses.

I

identity theft Using the Internet to steal someone's identity and/or impersonate the victim to conduct illicit transactions, such as committing fraud using the victim's name and identity.

incapacitation The policy of keeping dangerous criminals in confinement to eliminate the risk of their repeating their offense in society.

indeterminate sentences Terms of incarceration with a stated minimum and maximum length, such as a sentence to prison for a period of 3 to 10 years. The prisoner would be eligible for parole after the minimum sentence has been served. Based on the belief that sentences should fit the crime, indeterminate sentences allow individualized sentences and provide for sentencing flexibility. Judges can set a high minimum to override the purpose of the indeterminate sentence.

indictment The action by a grand jury when it finds that probable cause exists for prosecution of an accused suspect.

information Charging document filed by the prosecution that forms the basis of the preliminary hearing.

initial appearance A juvenile's first appearance before the juvenile court judge, in which the charges are reviewed and an effort is made to settle the case without a trial. If the child does not have legal counsel, an attorney is appointed.

inmate social code An unwritten code of behavior, passed from older inmates to younger ones, that serves as a guideline to appropriate inmate behavior within the correctional institution.

inmate subculture The loosely defined culture that pervades prisons and has its own norms, rules, and language.

in-presence requirement With a few exceptions, in order to make an arrest in a misdemeanor, a police officer must have witnessed the crime personally.

insanity A legal defense that maintains a defendant was incapable of forming criminal intent because he or she suffers from a defect of reason or mental illness.

intake The process in which a probation officer settles cases at the initial appearance before the onset of formal criminal proceedings; also, the process in which a juvenile referral is received and a decision is made to file a petition in the juvenile court, release the juvenile, or refer the juvenile elsewhere.

intelligence-led policing (ILP) The collection and analysis of information to generate an "intelligence end product" designed to inform police decision making at both the tactical and the strategic level.

intensive probation supervision (IPS) A type of intermediate sanction involving small probation caseloads and strict monitoring on a daily or weekly basis.

interactionist view of crime Criminal law reflects the values of people who use their social and political power to shape the legal system.

intermediate sanctions Punishments that fall between probation and prison ("probation plus"). Community-based sanctions, including house arrest and intensive supervision, serve as alternatives to incarceration.

internal affairs The branch of the police department that investigates charges of corruption or misconduct on the part of police officers.

J

jails Places to detain people awaiting trial, to serve as a lockup for drunks and disorderly individuals, and to confine convicted misdemeanants serving sentences of less than one year.

jailhouse lawyers Inmates trained in law or otherwise educated who help other inmates prepare legal briefs and appeals.

judicial reprieve The common-law practice that allowed judges to suspend punishment so that convicted offenders could seek a pardon, gather new evidence, or demonstrate that they had reformed their behavior.

jury nullification A defense tactic that consists of suggesting that the jury acquit a defendant, despite evidence that he actually violated the law, by maintaining that the law was unjust or not applicable to the case.

jury trial The process of deciding a case by a group of persons selected and sworn in to serve as jurors at a criminal trial, often as a 6- or 12-person jury.

just desert The philosophy of justice asserting that those who violate the rights of others deserve to be punished. The severity of punishment should be commensurate with the seriousness of the crime.

justice of the peace Established in 1326 England, the office was created to help the shire reeve in controlling the county; it later took on judicial functions.

justification defense A defense for a criminal act claiming that the criminal act was reasonable or necessary under the circumstances.

juvenile court A court that has original jurisdiction over persons defined by statute as juveniles and alleged to be delinquents or status offenders.

juvenile delinquency Participation in illegal behavior by a minor who falls under a statutory age limit.

K

Knapp Commission A public body that led an investigation into police corruption in New York and uncovered a widespread network of payoffs and bribes.

L

landmark decision A decision handed down by the US Supreme Court that becomes the law of the land and serves as a precedent for resolving similar legal issues.

larceny The unlawful taking, carrying, leading, or riding away of property from the possession or constructive possession of another.

latent trait A hidden trait that guides human behavior.

Law Enforcement Assistance Administration (LEAA) Funded by the federal government's Safe Streets Act, this agency provided technical assistance and hundreds of millions of dollars in aid to local and state justice agencies between 1969 and 1982.

legalization The removal of all criminal penalties from a previously outlawed act.

less-lethal weapons Weapons designed to disable or immobilize rather than kill criminal suspects.

lex talionis Latin for "law as retaliation." From Hammurabi's ancient legal code, the belief that the purpose of the law is to provide retaliation for an offended party and that the punishment should fit the crime.

life course theory Theory that focuses on changes in criminality over the life course brought about by shifts in experience and life events.

M

make-believe family, also known as a play family In female institutions, the substitute family group—including faux father, mother, and siblings—created by some inmates.

mala in se Refers to acts that society considers inherently evil, such as murder and rape.

mala prohibitum Crimes created by legislative bodies that reflect prevailing moral beliefs and practices.

mandatory sentence A statutory requirement that a certain penalty shall be set and carried out in all cases upon conviction for a specified offense or series of offenses.

Manhattan Bail Project The innovative experiment in bail reform that introduced and successfully tested the concept of release on recognizance.

maximum-security prisons Correctional institutions that houses dangerous felons and maintains strict security measures, high walls, and limited contact with the outside world.

meat eaters A term for police officers who actively solicit bribes and vigorously engage in corrupt practices.

medical model A correctional philosophy grounded on the belief that inmates are sick people who need treatment rather than punishment to help them reform.

medium-security prisons Less secure institutions that house nonviolent offenders and provides more opportunities for contact with the outside world.

mens rea Guilty mind. The mental element of a crime or the intent to commit a criminal act.

minimum-security prisons The least secure institutions, which house white-collar and nonviolent offenders, maintain few security measures, and have liberal furlough and visitation policies.

Miranda **warning** The requirement that police officers inform suspects subjected to custodial interrogation that they have a constitutional right to remain silent, that their statements can later be used against them in court, that they can have an attorney present to help them, and that the state will pay for an attorney if they cannot afford to hire one.

misdemeanor A minor crime usually punished by less than one year's imprisonment in a local institution, such as a county jail.

Missouri Plan A method of picking judges through nonpartisan elections as a way to ensure that judges adhere to high standards of judicial performance.

monetary restitution A sanction requiring that convicted offenders compensate crime victims by reimbursing them for out-of-pocket losses caused by the crime. Losses can include property damage, lost wages, and medical costs.

moral entrepreneurs People who wage moral crusades to control criminal law so that it reflects their own personal values.

motivational interviewing A technique that increases the probationers' awareness of their potential problems by asking them to visualize a better future and learn strategies to reach their goals.

motor vehicle theft The theft of a motor vehicle.

murder and nonnegligent manslaughter The willful (nonnegligent) killing of one human being by another.

N

National Crime Victimization Survey (NCVS) A national survey of approximately 90,000 households, used to estimate the frequency of crime victimization, as well as characteristics of victims.

National Criminal Intelligence Sharing Plan (NCISP) A formal intelligence-sharing initiative that identifies the security and intelligence-sharing needs recognized in the wake of the 9/11 terrorist attacks.

National Incident-Based Reporting System (NIBRS) Program that requires local police agencies to provide a brief account of each incident and arrest within 22 crime patterns, including incident, victim, and offender information.

neighborhood-oriented policing (NOP) Community-oriented policing efforts aimed at individual neighborhoods.

no bill The action by a grand jury when it votes not to indict an accused suspect.

nolle prosequi The term used when a prosecutor decides to drop a case after a complaint has been formally made. Reasons for a *nolle prosequi* include evidence insufficiency, reluctance of witnesses to testify, police error, and office policy.

nondeadly force Force that is unlikely to cause death or significant bodily harm.

nonintervention perspective A view of criminal justice that emphasizes the least intrusive treatment possible. Among its central policies are decarceration, diversion, and decriminalization. In other words, less is better.

O

obitiatry Helping people take their own lives.

official crime statistics Compiled by the FBI in its Uniform Crime Reports, these are a tally of serious crimes reported to police agencies each year.

order maintenance (peacekeeping) The order-maintenance aspect of the police role involves peacekeeping, maintaining order and authority without the need for formal arrest, "handling the situation," and keeping things under control by using threats, persuasion, and understanding.

P

parens patriae Latin term meaning "father of his country." According to this legal philosophy, the government is the guardian of everyone who has a disability, especially children, and has a legal duty to act in their best interests until they reach the age of majority.

parole The early release of a prisoner from imprisonment, subject to conditions set by a parole board.

parole board A panel of people who decide whether an offender should be released from prison on parole after serving the minimum portion of their sentence ordered by the sentencing judge.

Part I crimes The eight crimes for which, because of their seriousness and frequency, the FBI reports their incidence in its annual Uniform Crime Reports. The Part I crimes are murder and nonnegligent manslaughter, forcible rape, robbery, aggravated assault, burglary, larceny, motor vehicle theft, and arson.

Part II crimes All other crimes except the eight Part I crimes. The FBI records all arrests made for Part II crimes, including race, gender, and age information.

penal harm A philosophy based on the belief that harsh treatment while serving a correctional sentence will convince offenders that crime does not pay, thereby lowering the chances of recidivism

penitentiaries State or federal correctional institutions for the incarceration of felony offenders for terms of one year or more.

penitentiary house Term used for early prisons, so named because inmates were supposed to feel penitence for their sins.

Pennsylvania system The correctional model used in Pennsylvania that isolated inmates from one another to prevent them from planning escapes, to make them easy to manage, and to give them time to experience penitence.

peremptory challenge The dismissal of a potential juror by either the prosecution or the defense for unexplained, discretionary reasons.

phishing Also known as carding and spoofing, phishing consists of illegally acquiring personal information, such as bank passwords and credit card numbers, by masquerading as a trustworthy person or business in what appears to be an official electronic communication, such as an email or an instant message. The term *phishing* comes from the lures used to "fish" for financial information and passwords.

plea bargaining Nonjudicial settlement of a case in which the defendant exchanges a guilty plea for some consideration, such as a reduced sentence.

police brutality Usually involves such actions as the use of abusive language, the unnecessary use of force or coercion, threats, prodding with nightsticks, stopping and searching people to harass them, and so on.

police chief The top administrator of the police department who sets policy and has general control over departmental practices. The chief is typically a political rather than a civil service appointee and serves at the pleasure of the mayor.

Ponzi scheme An investment fraud that involves the payment of purported returns to existing investors from funds contributed by new investors.

poor laws Seventeenth-century laws in England that bound out vagrants and abandoned children as indentured servants to masters.

predictive policing Application of advanced analytics to criminal justice data for the purpose of predicting where and when crime will occur.

preliminary hearing A hearing that occurs in lieu of a grand jury hearing, when the prosecutor charges via information. Three issues are decided: whether a crime was committed, whether the court has jurisdiction over the case, and whether there is sufficient probable cause to believe the defendant committed the alleged crime.

preponderance of the evidence The level of proof in civil cases; more than half the evidence supports the allegations of one side.

presentence investigation An investigation performed by a probation officer attached to a trial court after the conviction of a defendant.

presentment The report of a grand jury investigation, which usually includes a recommendation of indictment.

pretrial detention Holding an offender in secure confinement before trial.

pretrial diversion A program that provides nonpunitive, community-based alternatives to more intrusive forms of punishment such as jail or prison.

pretrial procedures Critical pretrial processes and decisions, including bail, arraignment, and plea negotiation.

preventive detention The practice of holding dangerous suspects before trial without bail.

prisons State or federal correctional institutions for incarceration of felony offenders for terms of one year or more.

prisonization Assimilation into the separate culture in the prison that has its own set of rewards and behaviors, as well as its own norms, rules, and language. The traditional prison culture is now being replaced by a violent gang culture.

private policing Crime prevention, detection, and the apprehension of criminals carried out by private organizations or individuals for commercial purposes.

pro se "For oneself"; presenting one's own defense in a criminal trial; self-representation.

proactive policing A police department policy that emphasizes stopping crimes before they occur, rather than reacting to crimes that have already occurred.

probable cause The evidentiary criterion necessary to sustain an arrest or the issuance of an arrest or search warrant; less than absolute certainty or "beyond a reasonable doubt," but greater than mere suspicion or "hunch."

probable cause hearing Term used in some jurisdictions for a preliminary hearing to show cause to bring a case to trial.

probation A sentence entailing the conditional release of a convicted offender into the community under the supervision of the court (in the person of a probation officer), subject to certain conditions for a specified time.

probation rules Conditions or restrictions mandated by the court that must be obeyed by a probationer.

problem-oriented policing (POP) A style of police operations that stresses proactive problem solving, rather than reactive crime fighting.

proof beyond a reasonable doubt The standard of proof needed to convict in a criminal case. The evidence offered in court does not have to amount to absolute certainty, but it should leave no reasonable doubt that the defendant committed the alleged crime.

propensity theory The view that a stable unchanging feature, characteristic, property, or condition, such as defective intelligence or impulsive personality, makes some people crime prone.

prosecutor Representative of the state (executive branch) in criminal proceedings; advocate for the state's case—the charge—in the adversary trial. Examples include the attorney general of the United States, US attorneys, the attorneys general of the states, district attorneys, and police prosecutors.

psychodynamic view Criminals are driven by unconscious thought patterns, developed in early childhood, that control behaviors over the life course.

public defender An attorney usually employed (at no cost to the accused) by the government to represent poor persons accused of a crime.

public law The branch of law that deals with the state or government and its relationships with individuals or other governments.

R

racial profiling The practice of police targeting minority groups because of a belief that they are more likely to be engaged in criminal activity.

racial threat hypothesis The view that the percentage of minorities in the population shapes the level of police activity.

Racketeer Influenced and Corrupt Organization Act (RICO) Federal legislation that enables prosecutors to bring additional criminal or civil charges against people engaged in two or more acts prohibited by 24 existing federal and 8 state laws. RICO features monetary penalties that allow the government to confiscate all profits derived from criminal activities. Originally intended to be used against organized criminals, RICO has also been used against white-collar criminals.

rational choice theory People will engage in delinquent and criminal behavior after weighing the consequences and benefits of their actions. Delinquent behavior is a rational choice made by a motivated offender who perceives the chances of gain as outweighing any perceived punishment or loss.

recognizance The medieval practice of allowing convicted offenders to go unpunished if they agreed to refrain from any further criminal behavior.

rehabilitation The strategy of applying proper treatment so an offender will present no further threat to society.

rehabilitation perspective The view that the primary purpose of criminal justice is helping to care for people who cannot manage themselves. Crime is an expression of frustration and anger created by social inequality and can be controlled by giving people the means to improve their lifestyle through conventional endeavors.

relative deprivation The view that extreme social and economic differences among people living in the same community exacerbate criminal activity.

release on recognizance (ROR) A nonmonetary condition for the pretrial release of an accused individual; an alternative to monetary bail that is granted after the court determines that the accused has ties in the community, has no prior record of default, and is likely to appear at subsequent proceedings.

residential community corrections (RCC) A nonsecure facility, located in the community, that houses probationers who need a more secure environment. Typically, residents are free during the day to go to work, school, or treatment, and they return in the evening for counseling sessions and meals.

restitution A condition of probation in which the offender repays society or the victim of crime for the trouble and expense the offender caused.

restorative justice A view of criminal justice that advocates peaceful solutions and mediation rather than coercive punishments.

revocation An administrative act performed by a parole authority that removes a person from parole, or a judicial order by a court removing a person from parole or probation, in response to a violation on the part of the parolee or probationer.

risk classification Classifying probationers so that they may receive an appropriate level of treatment and control.

robbery The taking or attempting to take anything of value from the care, custody, or control of a person or persons by force or threat of force or violence and/or by putting the victim in fear.

S

search warrant An order issued by a judge, directing officers to conduct a search of specified premises for specified objects or persons and bring them before the court.

Secret Service Federal agency responsible for executive protection and for investigation of counterfeiting and various forms of financial fraud.

self-defense A legal defense in which defendants claim that their behavior was legally justified by the necessity to protect their own life and property, or that of another victim, from potential harm.

self-report surveys A research approach that requires subjects to reveal their own participation in delinquent or criminal acts.

sentencing circle A type of sentencing in which victims, family members, community members, and the offender participate in an effort to devise fair and reasonable sanctions that are ultimately aimed at reintegrating the offender into the community.

sentencing guidelines A set of standards that define parameters for trial judges to follow in their sentencing decisions.

sheriff The chief law enforcement officer in a county.

shire reeve In medieval England, the senior law enforcement figure in a county; the forerunner of today's sheriff.

shock probation A sentence in which offenders serve a short prison term before they begin probation to impress them with the pains of imprisonment.

Sixth Amendment The US constitutional amendment containing various criminal trial rights, such as the right to public trial, the right to trial by jury, and the right to confrontation of witnesses.

social bonds The ties people have to family, peers, social institutions, and significant others.

social conflict theory Human behavior is shaped by interpersonal conflict, and those who maintain social power use it to further their own interests.

social control The control of an individual's behavior by social and institutional forces in society.

social learning theory Behavior patterns are modeled and learned in interactions with others.

social process theory An individual's behavior is shaped by interactions with key social institutions—family, school, peer group, and the like.

social structure theory A person's position in the social structure controls his or her behavior. Those in the lowest socioeconomic tier are more likely to succumb to crime-promoting elements in their environment, whereas those in the highest tier enjoy social and economic advantages that insulate them from crime-producing forces.

specific deterrence A crime control policy suggesting that punishment should be severe enough to convince convicted offenders never to repeat their criminal activity.

split sentences A practice that requires convicted criminals to spend a portion of their sentence behind bars and the remainder in the community.

stalking The willful, malicious, and repeated following and harassing of another person.

stare decisis Latin for "to stand by decided cases." The legal principle by which the decision or holding in an earlier case becomes the standard by which subsequent similar cases are judged.

state courts of limited jurisdiction Courts that have jurisdiction over misdemeanors and conduct preliminary investigations of felony charges.

state (organized) crime Criminal acts committed by state officials within the context of their jobs as government representatives.

status offenders Juveniles who engage in behavior legally forbidden to minors, such as running away, truancy, or incorrigibility.

stigmatize To characterize or brand someone as disgraceful in order to make them feel shameful and ruin their reputation.

sting operation An undercover police operation in which police pose as criminals to trap law violators.

stop and frisk The situation when police officers who are suspicious of an individual run their hands lightly over the suspect's outer garments to determine whether the person is carrying a concealed weapon. Also called a patdown or threshold inquiry, a stop and frisk is intended to stop short of any activity that could be considered a violation of Fourth Amendment rights.

strict liability crimes Illegal acts whose elements do not contain the need for intent, or *mens rea*; usually, an act that endangers the public welfare, such as illegal dumping of toxic wastes.

subcultures A substratum of society that maintains a unique set of values and beliefs.

substantive criminal law A body of specific rules that declare what conduct is criminal and that prescribe the punishment to be imposed for such conduct.

substantive rights A number of civil rights that the courts, through a slow process of legal review, have established for inmates, including the rights to receive mail and medical benefits and to practice their religion.

suicide by cop A form of suicide in which a person acts in an aggressive manner with police officers in order to induce them to shoot to kill.

super-maximum-security prisons The newest form of a maximum-security prisons that uses high-level security measures to incapacitate the nation's most dangerous criminals. Most inmates are in lockdown 23 hours a day.

sureties During the Middle Ages, people responsible for the behavior of an offender released before trial.

suspended sentence A prison term that is delayed while the defendant undergoes a period of community treatment. If the treatment is successful, the prison sentence is terminated.

T

terrorism Premeditated, politically motivated violence perpetrated by subnational groups or clandestine agents against noncombatant targets, usually intended to influence an audience.

therapeutic communities Institutions that rely on positive peer pressure within a highly structured social environment to create positive inmate change.

time-in-rank system For police officers to advance in rank, they must spend an appropriate amount of time, usually years, in the preceding rank; for example, to become a captain, an officer must first spend time as a lieutenant.

tithings In medieval England, a group of 10 families who collectively dealt with minor disturbances and breaches of the peace.

tort A personal injury or wrong for which an action for damages may be brought.

total institutions Regimented, dehumanizing institutions such as a prison, in which inmates are kept in social isolation, cut off from the world at large.

trajectory theory The view that there are multiple independent paths to a criminal career and different types and classes of offenders.

transfer hearing The hearing in which a decision is made to waive a juvenile to the criminal court. Waiver decisions are based on such criteria as the child's age, her or his prior offense history, and the nature of the offense.

transnational organized crime Use of illegal tactics to gain profit in the global marketplace, typically involving the cross-border sale and distribution of illegal commodities.

treatment The rehabilitative method used to effect a change of behavior in the juvenile offender, in the form of therapy, or educational or vocational programs.

true bill of indictment A written statement charging a defendant with the commission of a crime, drawn up by a prosecuting attorney and considered by a grand jury. If the grand jury finds sufficient evidence to support the indictment, it will issue a true bill of indictment.

U

Uniform Crime Reports (UCR) The FBI's yearly publication of where, when, and how much serious crime occurred in the prior year.

US magistrate judge A federal trial judge who is appointed by a district court judge and who presides over various civil cases with the consent of the parties and over certain misdemeanor cases.

US Marshals Service Federal agency whose jurisdiction includes protecting federal officials, transporting criminal defendants, and tracking down fugitives.

USA Patriot Act (USAPA) A law designed to grant new powers to domestic law enforcement and international intelligence agencies in an effort to fight terrorism.

V

venire The group called for jury duty from which jury panels are selected.

vice squads Police officers assigned to enforce morality-based laws, such as those on prostitution, gambling, and pornography.

victim impact statement A postconviction statement by the victim of crime that may be used to guide sentencing decisions.

vigilantes Groups of citizens who tracked down wanted criminals in the Old West.

voir dire The process in which a potential jury panel is questioned by the prosecution and the defense to select jurors who are unbiased and objective.

W

waiver A practice in which the juvenile court waives its jurisdiction over a juvenile and transfers the case to adult criminal court for trial. In some states, a waiver hearing is held to determine jurisdiction, whereas in others, juveniles may be automatically waived if they are accused of committing a serious crime such as murder.

Walnut Street Jail An eighteenth-century institution that housed convicted criminals in Philadelphia.

warez Copyrighted software illegally downloaded and sold by organized groups without license to do so.

watch system During the Middle Ages in England, men were organized in church parishes to guard at night against disturbances and breaches of the peace under the direction of the local constable.

widening the net of justice The view that programs designed to divert offenders from the justice system actually enmesh them further in the process by substituting more intrusive treatment programs for less intrusive punishment-oriented outcomes.

work release A prison treatment program that allows inmates to be released during the day to work in the community and then return to prison at night.

writ of certiorari An order of a superior court requesting that the record of an inferior court (or administrative body) be brought forward for review or inspection.

writ of *habeas corpus* A judicial order requesting that a person who detains another person produce the body of the prisoner and give reasons for his or her capture and detention. *Habeas corpus* is a legal device used to request that a judicial body review the reasons for a person's confinement and the conditions of confinement. *Habeas corpus* is known as "the great writ."

Z

zero tolerance The practice of seizing all instrumentalities of a crime, including homes, boats, and cars. It is an extreme example of the law of forfeiture.

Notes

All URLs accessed in 2017

Chapter 1, Crime and Criminal Justice

1. Kevin Sack and Alan Blinder, "No Regrets From Dylann Roof in Jailhouse Manifesto," *New York Times*, January 5, 2017, https://www.nytimes.com/2017/01/05/us/no-regrets-from-dylann-roof-in-jailhouse-manifesto.html.

2. Alan Blinder and Kevin Sack, "Dylann Roof Is Sentenced to Death in Charleston Church Massacre," *New York Times*, January 10, 2017, https://www.nytimes.com/2017/01/10/us/dylann-roof-trial-charleston.html.

3. Ibid.

4. Samuel Walker, *Popular Justice* (New York: Oxford University Press, 1980).

5. Ibid.

6. For an insightful analysis of this effort, see Samuel Walker, "Origins of the Contemporary Criminal Justice Paradigm: The American Bar Foundation Survey, 1953–1969," *Justice Quarterly* 9 (1992): 47–76.

7. President's Commission on Law Enforcement and the Administration of Justice, *The Challenge of Crime in a Free Society* (Washington, DC: Government Printing Office, 1967).

8. See Public Law No. 90–351, Title I-Omnibus Crime Control Safe Streets Act of 1968, 90th Congress, June 19, 1968.

9. For a review, see Kevin Wright, "Twenty-Two Years of Federal Investment in Criminal Justice Research: The National Institute of Justice, 1968–1989," *Journal of Criminal Justice* 22 (1994): 27–40.

10. Lawrence Sherman, Denise Gottfredson, Doris MacKenzie, John Eck, Peter Reuter, and Shawn Bushway, *Preventing Crime: What Works, What Doesn't, What's Promising* (Washington, DC: US Department of Justice, Office of Justice Programs, 1997).

11. See, generally, Brandon Welsh and David Farrington, *Preventing Crime: What Works for Children, Offenders, Victims and Places* (London: Springer-Verlag, 2006).

12. Dennis Rosenbaum and Gordon Hanson, "Assessing the Effects of School-Based Drug Education: A Six-Year Multilevel Analysis of Project D.A.R.E.," *Journal of Research in Crime and Delinquency* 35 (1998): 381–412.

13. Bureau of Justice Statistics, *Justice Expenditure and Employment Extracts, 2012* (Washington, DC: Bureau of Justice Statistics, 2015), https://www.bjs.gov/index.cfm?ty=pbdetail&iid=5239.

14. Brian A. Reaves, *Local Police Departments, 2013: Personnel, Policies, and Practices* (Washington, DC: Bureau of Justice Statistics, 2015), p. 2.

15. Brian A. Reaves, *Federal Law Enforcement Officers, 2008* (Washington, DC: Bureau of Justice Statistics, 2012). Though dated, this is the most recent report available as of this writing.

16. Federal Bureau of Investigation, *Crime in the United States, 2015* (Washington, DC: Federal Bureau of Investigation, 2015), https://ucr.fbi.gov/crime-in-the-u.s/2015/crime-in-the-u.s.-2015.

17. Robert C. LaFountain, Shauna M. Strickland, Richard Y. Schauffler, Kathryn A. Holt, and Kathryn J. Lewis, *Examining the Work of State Courts: An Overview of 2013 State Court Caseload Trends* (Williamsburg, VA: National Center for State Courts, 2015).

18. Danielle Kaeble and Lauren Glaze, *Correctional Populations in the United States, 2015* (Washington, DC: Bureau of Justice Statistics, 2016), https://www.bjs.gov/content/pub/pdf/cpus15.pdf.

19. Tracey Kyckelhahn, *State Corrections Expenditures, FY 1982–2010* (Washington, DC: Bureau of Justice Statistics, 2012). Though dated, this is the most recent report available as of this writing.

20. For an analysis of this issue, see Samuel Walker, Cassia Spohn, and Miriam DeLone, *The Color of Justice: Race, Ethnicity, and Crime in America*, 6th ed. (Boston: Cengage, 2017).

21. See Dennis Rader biography, available at http://www.biography.com/people/dennis-rader-241487.

22. Herbert L. Packer, *The Limits of the Criminal Sanction* (Stanford, CA: Stanford University Press, 1975), p. 21.

23. Thomas Cohen and Tracey Kyckelhahn, *Felony Defendants in Large Urban Counties, 2006* (Washington, DC: Bureau of Justice Statistics, 2010), https://www.bjs.gov/content/pub/pdf/fdluc06.pdf. Though dated, this is the most recent report available as of this writing.

24. James Eisenstein and Herbert Jacob, *Felony Justice* (Boston: Little, Brown, 1977); Peter Nardulli, *The Courtroom Elite* (Cambridge, MA: Ballinger, 1978); Paul Wice, *Chaos in the Courthouse* (New York: Praeger, 1985); Marcia Lipetz, *Routine Justice: Processing Cases in Women's Court* (New Brunswick, NJ: Transaction Books, 1983).

25. Samuel Walker, *Sense and Nonsense About Crime, Drugs, and Communities*, 8th edition (Boston: Cengage, 2015).

26. Malcolm Feeley, *The Process Is the Punishment* (New York: Russell Sage, 1979).

27. John DiLulio, *No Escape: The Future of American Corrections* (New York: Basic Books, 1991).

28. Thomas Loughran, Alex Piquero, Jeffrey Fagan, and Edward Mulvey, "Differential Deterrence: Studying Heterogeneity and Changes in Perceptual Deterrence Among Serious Youthful Offenders," *Crime and Delinquency* 58 (2012): 3–27.

29. Raymond Paternoster, "How Much Do We Really Know About Criminal Deterrence?" *Journal of Criminal Law and Criminology* 100 (2010): 765–823.

30. Francis Cullen, John Paul Wright, and Mitchell Chamlin, "Social Support and Social Reform: A Progressive Crime Control Agenda," *Crime and Delinquency* 45 (1999): 188–207.

31. Jane Sprott, "Are Members of the Public Tough on Crime? The Dimensions of Public 'Punitiveness,'" *Journal of Criminal Justice* 27 (1999): 467–474.

32. Packer, *The Limits of the Criminal Sanction*, p. 175.

33. Eric Stewart, Ronald Simons, Rand Conger, and Laura Scaramella, "Beyond the Interactional Relationship Between Delinquency and Parenting Practices: The Contribution of Legal Sanctions," *Journal of Research in Crime and Delinquency* 39 (2002): 36–60.

34. Cassia Spohn and David Holleran, "The Effect of Imprisonment on Recidivism Rates of Felony Offenders: A Focus on Drug Offenders," *Criminology* 40 (2002): 329–359.

35. See, for example, Jill S. Levenson and Kristen M. Zgoba, "Community Protection Policies and Repeat Sexual Offenses in Florida," *International Journal of Offender Therapy and Comparative Criminology* 60 (2016): 1140–1158; Kristen Zgoba and Karen Bachar, "Sex Offender Registration and Notification: Research Finds Limited Effects in New Jersey," National Institute of Justice, April 2009, https://www.ncjrs.gov/pdffiles1/nij/225402.pdf.

36. *Doe v. Pryor*, 61 F. Supp. 2d 1235 (M.D. Ala. 1999).

37. Howard Zehr, *Changing Lenses: Restorative Justice for Our Times*, 25th anniversary edition (Herald Press, 2015).

38. Larry Tifft, foreword to *The Mask of Love*, Dennis Sullivan (Port Washington, NY: Kennikat Press, 1980), p. 6.

39. Christopher Cooper, "Patrol Police Officer Conflict Resolution Processes," *Journal of Criminal Justice* 25 (1997): 87–101.

40. Robert Coates, Mark Umbreit, and Betty Vos, "Responding to Hate Crimes Through Restorative Justice Dialogue," *Contemporary Justice Review* 9 (2006): 7–21; Kathleen Daly and Julie Stubbs, "Feminist Engagement with Restorative Justice," *Theoretical Criminology* 10 (2006): 9–28.

41. This section relies heavily on Joycelyn M. Pollock, *Ethical Dilemmas and Decisions in Criminal Justice*, 9th ed. (Boston: Cengage, 2017).

Chapter 2, The Nature of Crime and Victimization

1. Centers for Disease Control and Prevention, *Increases in Drug and Opioid Overdose Deaths – United States, 2000–2014*, January 1, 2016, http://www.cdc.gov/mmwr/preview/mmwrhtml/mm6450a3.htm.

2. Miles E. Johnson, "Heroin's Death Toll Reaches Another Gruesome Landmark," *Mother Jones*, October 16, 2015, http://www.motherjones.com/politics/2015/10/heroin-kills-more-people-car-crashes-most-america.

3. Theodore J. Cicero, Matthew S. Ellis, Hilary L. Surratt, and Steven P. Kurtz, "The Changing Face of Heroin Use in the United States: A Retrospective Analysis of the Past 50 Years," *JAMA Psychiatry* 71 (2014): 821–826.

4. Ian Tuttle, "America's Heroin Crisis Was Birthed by the Law of Unintended Consequences," *National Review*, January 25, 2016.

5. Nick Miroff, "Tracing the U.S. Heroin Surge Back South of the Border as Mexican Cannabis Output Falls," *Washington Post*, April 6, 2014, https://www.washingtonpost.com/world/tracing-the-us-heroin-surge-back-south-of-the-border-as-mexican-cannabis-output-falls/2014/04/06/58dfc590-2123-4cc6-b664-1e5948960576_story.html.

6. For a general discussion of Marxist thought on criminal law, see Michael Lynch, Raymond Michalowski, and W. Byron Groves, *The New Primer in Radical Criminology: Critical Perspectives on Crime, Power, and Identity*, 3rd ed. (Monsey, NY: Criminal Justice Press, 2000).

7. Howard Becker, *Outsiders, Studies in the Sociology of Deviance* (New York: Macmillan, 1963).

8. The National Council on Alcoholism and Drug Dependence, https://www.ncadd.org/.

9. Federal Bureau of Investigation, *Crime in the United States, 2015*, https://ucr.fbi.gov/crime-in-the-u.s/2015/crime-in-the-u.s.-2015.

10. Federal Bureau of Investigation, *Crime in the United States, 2015*, Table 1, https://ucr.fbi.gov/crime-in-the-u.s/2015/crime-in-the-u.s.-2015/tables/table-1.

11. Min Xie, "Area Differences and Time Trends in Crime Reporting: Comparing New York with Other Metropolitan Areas," *Justice Quarterly* 31 (2014): 43–73.

12. Federal Bureau of Investigation, *The Expansion of NIBRS*, https://ucr.fbi.gov/nibrs/2015.

13. Data in this section come from Jennifer L. Truman and Rachel E. Morgan, *Criminal Victimization, 2015* (Washington, DC: Bureau of Justice Statistics, 2016), https://www.bjs.gov/content/pub/pdf/cv15.pdf.

14. Stephen Cernkovich, Peggy Giordano, and Meredith Pugh, "Chronic Offenders: The Missing Cases in Self-Report Delinquency," *Criminology* 76 (1985): 705–732.

15. Alfred Blumstein, Jacqueline Cohen, and Richard Rosenfeld, "Trend and Deviation in Crime Rates: A Comparison of UCR and NCVS Data for Burglary and Robbery," *Criminology* 29 (1991): 237–248.

16. Clarence Schrag, *Crime and Justice: American Style* (Washington, DC: US Government Printing Office, 1971), p. 17.

17. Federal Bureau of Investigation, *Crime in the United States, 2015*.

18. Data in this section are from Truman and Morgan, *Criminal Victimization, 2015*.

19. Ibid.

20. Data used in this section are from Jerald G. Bachman, Lloyd D. Johnston, and Patrick M. O'Malley, *Monitoring the Future: Questionnaire Responses from the Nation's High School Seniors, 2012* (Ann Arbor: University of Michigan, 2014), http://www.monitoringthefuture.org/datavolumes/2012/2012dv.pdf. Though dated, this is the most recent report available as of this writing.

21. National Center for Education Statistics, *Fast Facts*, http://nces.ed.gov/fastfacts/display.asp?id=372.

22. Federal Bureau of Investigation, *Crime in the United States, 2015*, "Robbery," https://ucr.fbi.gov/crime-in-the-u.s/2015/crime-in-the-u.s.-2015/offenses-known-to-law-enforcement/robbery.

23. Federal Bureau of Investigation, *Crime in the United States, 2015*, Table 35, https://ucr.fbi.gov/crime-in-the-u.s/2015/crime-in-the-u.s.-2015/tables/table-35.

24. Paul Tracy, Kimberly Kempf-Leonard, and Stephanie Abramoske-James, "Gender Differences in Delinquency and Juvenile Justice Processing: Evidence from National Data," *Crime and Delinquency* 55 (2009): 171–215.

25. Federal Bureau of Investigation, *Crime in the United States, 2015*, Table 33, https://ucr.fbi.gov/crime-in-the-u.s/2015/crime-in-the-u.s.-2015/tables/table-33.

26. Daniel Mears, Matthew Ploeger, and Mark Warr, "Explaining the Gender Gap in Delinquency: Peer Influence and Moral Evaluations of Behavior," *Journal of Research in Crime and Delinquency* 35 (1998): 251–266.

27. Federal Bureau of Investigation, *Crime in the United States, 2015*, Table 43, https://ucr.fbi.gov/crime-in-the-u.s/2015/crime-in-the-u.s.-2015/tables/table-43.

28. Robert Brame, Shawn Bushway, Ray Paternoster, and Michael G. Turner "Demographic Patterns of Cumulative Arrest Prevalence by Ages 18 and 23," *Crime and Delinquency* 60 (2014): 471–486.

29. Tammy Rinehart Kochel, David B. Wilson, and Stephen D. Mastrofski, "Effect of Suspect Race on Officers' Arrest Decisions," *Criminology* 49 (2011): 473–512.

30. Rob Tillyer, "Opening the Black Box of Officer Decision-Making: An Examination of Race, Criminal History, and Discretionary Searches," *Justice Quarterly* 31 (2014): 961–986.

31. Leo Carroll and M. Lilliana Gonzalez. "Out of Place: Racial Stereotypes and the Ecology of Frisks and Searches Following Traffic Stops," *Journal of Research in Crime and Delinquency* 51 (2014): 559–584; Kenneth Novak and Mitchell Chamlin, "Racial Threat, Suspicion, and Police Behavior: The Impact of Race and Place in Traffic Enforcement," *Crime and Delinquency* 58 (2012): 275–300.

32. Andres F. Rengifo and Don Stemen, "The Unintended Effects of Penal Reform: African American Presence, Incarceration, and the Abolition of Discretionary Parole in the United States," *Crime and Delinquency*, first published online May 25, 2012.

33. Robin Shepard Engel and Jennifer M. Calnon, "Examining the Influence of Drivers' Characteristics During Traffic Stops with Police," *Justice Quarterly* 21 (2004).

34. Malcolm D. Holmes, Brad Smith, Adrienne Freng, and Ed Munoz, "Minority Threat, Crime Control, and Police Resource Allocation in the Southwestern United States," *Crime and Delinquency* 54 (2008): 128–152; Bradley Keen and David Jacobs, "Racial Threat, Partisan Politics, and Racial Disparities in Prison Admissions," *Criminology* 47 (2009): 209–238.

35. Robert Agnew, "A General Strain Theory of Community Differences in Crime Rates," *Journal of Research in Crime and Delinquency* 36 (1999): 123–155.

36. Bonita Veysey and Steven Messner, "Further Testing of Social Disorganization Theory: An Elaboration of Sampson and Groves's Community Structure and Crime," *Journal of Research in Crime and Delinquency* 36 (1999): 156–174.

37. Judith Blau and Peter Blau, "The Cost of Inequality: Metropolitan Structure and Violent Crime," *American Sociological Review* 47 (1982): 114–129.

38. Nancy Rodriguez, "Concentrated Disadvantage and the Incarceration of Youth: Examining How Context Affects Juvenile Justice," *Journal of Research in Crime and Delinquency*, first published online December 13, 2011.

39. Herman Schwendinger and Julia Schwendinger, "The Paradigmatic Crisis in Delinquency Theory," *Crime and Social Justice* 18 (1982): 70–78.

40. Michael Gottfredson and Travis Hirschi, "The True Value of Lambda Would Appear to Be Zero: An Essay on Career Criminals, Criminal Careers, Selective Incapacitation, Cohort Studies and Related Topics," *Criminology* 24 (1986): 213–234. Further support for their position can be found in Lawrence Cohen and Kenneth Land, "Age Structure and Crime," *American Sociological Review* 52 (1987): 170–183.

41. Marvin Wolfgang, Robert Figlio, and Thorsten Sellin, *Delinquency in a Birth Cohort* (Chicago: University of Chicago Press, 1972).

42. Marvin Wolfgang, Terence Thornberry, and Robert Figlio, *From Boy to Man, from Delinquency to Crime* (Chicago: University of Chicago Press, 1996).

43. Truman and Morgan, *Criminal Victimization, 2015*, p. 9.

44. Ibid., p. 13.

45. Ibid., p. 5.

46. Janet Lauritsen and Kenna Davis Quinet, "Repeat Victimizations Among Adolescents and Young Adults," *Journal of Quantitative Criminology* 11 (1995): 143–163.

47. Denise Osborn, Dan Ellingworth, Tim Hope, and Alan Trickett, "Are Repeatedly Victimized Households Different?" *Journal of Quantitative Criminology* 12 (1996): 223–245.

48. Terry Buss and Rashid Abdu, "Repeat Victims of Violence in an Urban Trauma Center," *Violence and Victims* 10 (1995): 183–187.

49. David A. Ward, Mark C. Stafford, and Louis N. Gray, "Rational Choice, Deterrence, and Theoretical Integration," *Journal of Applied Social Psychology* 36 (2000): 571–585.

50. Thomas A. Loughran, Ray Paternoster, and Aaron Chalfin, "Can Rational Choice Be Considered a General Theory of Crime? Evidence from Individual-Level Panel Data," *Criminology* 54 (2016): 86–112.

51. Ross Matsueda, Derek Kreager, and David Huizinga, "Deterring Delinquents: A Rational Choice Model of Theft and Violence," *American Sociological Review* 71 (2006): 95–122.

52. Alicia Sitren and Brandon Applegate, "Testing the Deterrent Effects of Personal and Vicarious Experience with Punishment and Punishment Avoidance," *Deviant Behavior* 28 (2007): 29–55.

53. Andrew Klein and Terri Tobin, "A Longitudinal Study of Arrested Batterers, 1995–2005: Career Criminals," *Violence Against Women* 14 (2008): 136–157.

54. Rudy Haapanen, Lee Britton, and Tim Croisdale, "Persistent Criminality and Career Length," *Crime and Delinquency* 53 (2007): 133–155.

55. Daniel Nagin and Greg Pogarsky, "Integrating Celerity, Impulsivity, and Extralegal Sanction Threats into a Model of General Deterrence: Theory and Evidence," *Criminology* 39 (2001): 865–892.

56. Cheryl L. Maxson, Kristy N. Matsuda, and Karen Hennigan, "Deterrability Among Gang and Nongang Juvenile Offenders: Are Gang Members More (or Less) Deterrable Than Other Juvenile Offenders?" *Crime and Delinquency* 57 (2011): 516–543.

57. Douglas S. Massey, "The Brave New World of Biosocial Science," *Criminology* 53 (2015): 127–131; John Paul Wright and Francis T. Cullen, "The

Future of Biosocial Criminology: Beyond Scholars' Professional Ideology," *Journal of Contemporary Criminal Justice* 28 (2012): 237–253.

58. Todd A. Jusko, Charles R. Henderson Jr., Bruce P. Lanphear, Deborah A. Cory-Slechta, Patrick J. Parsons, and Richard L. Canfield, "Blood Lead Concentrations < 10 µg/dL and Child Intelligence at 6 Years of Age," *Environmental Health Perspectives* 116 (2008): 243–248; Joel Nigg, G. Mark Knottnerus, Michelle Martel, Molly Nikolas, Kevin Cavanagh, Wilfried Karmaus, and Marsha D. Rappley, "Low Blood Lead Levels Associated with Clinically Diagnosed Attention-Deficit/Hyperactivity Disorder and Mediated by Weak Cognitive Control," *Biological Psychiatry* 63 (2008): 325–331.

59. Lauren Wakschlag, Kate Pickett, Kristen Kasza, and Rolf Loeber, "Is Prenatal Smoking Associated with a Developmental Pattern of Conduct Problems in Young Boys?" *Journal of the American Academy of Child and Adolescent Psychiatry* 45 (2006): 461–467; "Diet and the Unborn Child: The Omega Point," *The Economist*, January 19, 2006.

60. Cody Jorgensen, Nathaniel Anderson, and J. C. Barnes, "Bad Brains: Crime and Drug Abuse from a Neurocriminological Perspective," *American Journal of Criminal Justice* 41 (2016): 291–312.

61. Alice Jones, Kristin Laurens, Catherine Herba, Gareth Barker, and Essi Viding, "Amygdala Hypoactivity to Fearful Faces in Boys with Conduct Problems and Callous-Unemotional Traits," *American Journal of Psychiatry* 166 (2009): 95–102.

62. Thomas Crowley, Manish S. Dalwani, Susan K. Mikulich-Gilbertson, Yiping P. Du, Carl W. Lejuez, Kristen M. Raymond, and Marie T. Banich, "Risky Decisions and Their Consequences: Neural Processing by Boys with Antisocial Substance Disorder," *PLoS One*, September 22, 2010, http://journals.plos.org/plosone/article?id=10.1371/journal.pone.0012835.

63. Anita Thapar, Kate Langley, Tom Fowler, Frances Rice, Darko Turic, Naureen Whittinger, John Aggleton, Marianne Van den Bree, Michael Owen, and Michael O'Donovan, "Catechol O-methyltransferase Gene Variant and Birth Weight Predict Early-Onset Antisocial Behavior in Children with Attention-Deficit/ Hyperactivity

Disorder," *Archives of General Psychiatry* 62 (2005): 1275–1278.

64. Ronald L. Simons, Man Kit Lei, Eric A. Stewart, Steven R. H. Beach, Gene H. Brody, Robert A. Philibert, and Frederick X. Gibbons, "Social Adversity, Genetic Variation, Street Code, and Aggression: A Genetically Informed Model of Violent Behavior," *Youth Violence and Juvenile Justice* 10 (2012): 3–24; Kevin Beaver, John Paul Wright, and Matt DeLisi, "Delinquent Peer Group Formation: Evidence of a Gene X Environment Correlation," *Journal of Genetic Psychology* 169 (2008): 227–244.

65. See, for example, Callie H. Burt and Ronald L. Simons, "Pulling Back the Curtain on Heritability Studies: Biosocial Criminology in the Postgenomic Era," *Criminology* 52 (2014): 223–262; J. C. Barnes, John Paul Wright, Brian B. Boutwell, et al., "Demonstrating the Validity of Twin Research in Criminology," *Criminology* 52 (2014): 588–626.

66. Paige Crosby Ouimette, "Psychopathology and Sexual Aggression in Nonincarcerated Men," *Violence and Victimization* 12 (1997): 389–397.

67. Robert Krueger, Avshalom Caspi, Phil Silva, and Rob McGee, "Personality Traits Are Differentially Linked to Mental Disorders: A Multitrait-Multidiagnosis Study of an Adolescent Birth Cohort," *Journal of Abnormal Psychology* 105 (1996): 299–312.

68. See, for example, Michael Ostermann and Jason Matejkowski, "Estimating the Impact of Mental Illness on Costs of Crimes," *Criminal Justice and Behavior* 41 (2014): 20–40. CBC News, "Ohio School Shooter Wears 'Killer' T-Shirt to Court," March 19, 2013, http://www.cbc.ca/news/world/story/2013/03/19/us-ohio-school-shooting-sentencing.html; Thomas O'Hare, Ce Shen, and Margaret Sherrer, "High-Risk Behaviors and Drinking-to-Cope as Mediators of Lifetime Abuse and PTSD Symptoms in Clients with Severe Mental Illness," *Journal of Traumatic Stress* 23 (2010): 255–263; Tamsin B. R. Short, Stuart Thomas, Stefan Luebbers, Paul Mullen, and James Ogloff, "A Case-Linkage Study of Crime Victimisation in Schizophrenia-Spectrum Disorders over a Period of Deinstitutionalization," *BMC Psychiatry* 13 (2013): 1–9; Tamar Mendelson, Alezandria Turner, and Darius Tandon, "Violence Exposure and Depressive Symptoms Among Adolescents and Young Adults

Disconnected from School and Work," *Journal of Community Psychology* 38 (2010): 607–621.

69. Travis C. Pratt, Francis T. Cullen, Christine S. Sellers, et al., "The Empirical Status of Social Learning Theory: A Meta-Analysis," *Justice Quarterly* 27 (2010): 765–802.

70. David Eitle and R. Jay Turner, "Exposure to Community Violence and Young Adult Crime: The Effects of Witnessing Violence, Traumatic Victimization, and Other Stressful Life Events," *Journal of Research in Crime and Delinquency* 39 (2002): 214–238. See also Albert Bandura, *Aggression: A Social Learning Analysis* (Englewood Cliffs, NJ: Prentice Hall, 1973); Albert Bandura, *Social Learning Theory* (Englewood Cliffs, NJ: Prentice Hall, 1977).

71. Elizabeth Cauffman, Laurence Steinberg, and Alex Piquero, "Psychological, Neuropsychological, and Physiological Correlates of Serious Antisocial Behavior in Adolescence: The Role of Self-Control," *Criminology* 43 (2005): 133–176.

72. Shadd Maruna, "Desistance from Crime and Explanatory Style: A New Direction in the Psychology of Reform," *Journal of Contemporary Criminal Justice* 20 (2004): 184–200.

73. Tony Ward and Claire Stewart, "The Relationship Between Human Needs and Criminogenic Needs," *Psychology, Crime and Law* 9 (2003): 219–225.

74. See, for example, Jeremy Staff, Corey Whichard, Sonja E. Siennick, and Jennifer Maggs, "Early Life Risks, Antisocial Tendencies, and Preteen Delinquency," *Criminology* 53 (2015): 677–701.

75. Rolf Holmqvist, "Psychopathy and Affect Consciousness in Young Criminal Offenders," *Journal of Interpersonal Violence* 23 (2008): 209–224.

76. US Census Bureau, *Poverty Thresholds*, http://www.census.gov/data/tables/time-series/demo/income-poverty/historical-poverty-thresholds.html.

77. Sara Thompson and Rosemary Gartner, "The Spatial Distribution and Social Context of Homicide in Toronto's Neighborhoods," *Journal of Research in Crime and Delinquency* 51 (2014): 88–118.

78. Oscar Lewis, "The Culture of Poverty," *Scientific American* 215 (1966): 19–25.

79. William Julius Wilson, *The Truly Disadvantaged* (Chicago: University of Chicago Press, 1987).

80. C. L. Storr, C. Y. Chen, and J. C. Anthony, "'Unequal Opportunity': Neighbourhood Disadvantage and the Chance to Buy Illegal Drugs," *Journal of Epidemiology and Community Health* 58 (2004): 231–238.

81. David Pyrooz, "Structural Covariates of Gang Homicide in Large U.S. Cities," *Journal of Research in Crime and Delinquency* 49 (2012): 489–515.

82. Steven Messner and Richard Rosenfeld, *Crime and the American Dream* (Belmont, CA: Wadsworth, 1994), p. 11.

83. See, for example, Anthony A. Braga and Ronald V. Clarke, "Explaining High-Risk Concentrations of Crime in the City: Social Disorganization, Crime Opportunities, and Important Next Steps," *Journal of Research in Crime and Delinquency* 51 (2014): 480–497; Stacy De Coster, Karen Heimer, and Stacy Wittrock, "Neighborhood Disadvantage, Social Capital, Street Context, and Youth Violence," *Sociological Quarterly* (2006): 723–753.

84. Lisa Mufti, "Advancing Institutional Anomie Theory," *International Journal of Offender Therapy and Comparative Criminology* 50 (2006): 630–653.

85. Ibid.

86. Callie H. Burt and Carter Rees, "Behavioral Heterogeneity in Adolescent Friendship Networks," *Justice Quarterly* 32 (2015): 872–899.

87. Travis Hirschi, *Causes of Delinquency* (Berkeley: University of California Press, 1969).

88. Travis C. Pratt and Francis T. Cullen, "The Empirical Status of Gottfredson and Hirschi's General Theory of Crime: A Meta-Analysis," *Criminology* 38 (2000): 931–964.

89. See, for example, Emily Restivo and Mark M. Lanier, "Measuring the Contextual Effects and Mitigating Factors of Labeling Theory," *Justice Quarterly* 32 (2015): 116–141; Robert G. Morris and Alex R. Piquero, "For Whom Do Sanctions Deter and Label?" *Justice Quarterly* 30 (2013): 837–868.

90. John Braithwaite, "Retributivism, Punishment, and Privilege," in *Punishment and Privilege*, ed. W. Byron Groves and Graeme Newman (Albany, NY: Harrow & Heston, 1986), pp. 55–66.

91. Michael Hallett, "Reentry to What? Theorizing Prisoner Reentry in the Jobless Future," *Critical Criminology* 20 (2012): 213–228.

92. Scott A. Bonn, *Mass Deception: Moral Panic and the U.S. War on Iraq* (New Brunswick, NJ: Rutgers University Press, 2010).

93. Marvin Krohn, Alan Lizotte, and Cynthia Perez, "The Interrelationship Between Substance Use and Precocious Transitions to Adult Sexuality," *Journal of Health and Social Behavior* 38 (1997): 88.

94. Peggy Giordano, Stephen Cernkovich, and Jennifer Rudolph, "Gender, Crime, and Desistance: Toward a Theory of Cognitive Transformation?" *American Journal of Sociology* 107 (2002): 990–1064.

95. Gerald Patterson, Barbara DeBaryshe, and Elizabeth Ramsey, "A Developmental Perspective on Antisocial Behavior," *American Psychologist* 44 (1989): 329–335.

96. Robert Sampson and John Laub, "Crime and Deviance in the Life Course," *American Review of Sociology* 18 (1992): 63–84.

97. David Farrington, Darrick Jolliffe, Rolf Loeber, Magda Stouthamer-Loeber, and Larry Kalb, "The Concentration of Offenders in Families, and Family Criminality in the Prediction of Boys' Criminality," *Journal of Adolescence* 24 (2001): 579–596.

98. Matt DeLisi and Kevin M. Beaver, *Criminological Theory: A Life-Course Approach*, 2nd ed. (Burlington, MA: Jones & Bartlett Learning, 2014).

99. Lara DePadilla, Molly Perkins, Kirk Elifson, and Claire Sterk, "Adult Criminal Involvement: A Cross-Sectional Inquiry into Correlates and Mechanisms over the Life Course," *Criminal Justice Review* 37 (2012): 110–126.

100. Shawn Bushway, Marvin Krohn, Alan Lizotte, Matthew Phillips, and Nicole Schmidt, "Are Risky Youth Less Protectable as They Age? The Dynamics of Protection During Adolescence and Young Adulthood," *Justice Quarterly* 30 (2013): 84–116.

101. Alex Piquero, David Farrington, Jonathan Shepherd, and Katherine Auty, "Offending and Early Death in the Cambridge Study in Delinquent Development," *Justice Quarterly* 31 (2014): 445–472.

102. T. E. Moffitt, "Adolescence-Limited and Life-Course Persistent Antisocial Behavior: A Developmental Taxonomy," *Psychological Review* 100 (1993): 674–701; Turgut Ozkan and John L. Worrall, "A Psychosocial Test of the Maturity Gap Thesis," *Criminal Justice and Behavior*, forthcoming in 2017.

103. Alex Piquero, "Taking Stock of Developmental Trajectories of Criminal Activity over the Life Course," in *The Long View of Crime: A Synthesis of Longitudinal Research*, ed. Akiva Liberman (New York: Springer, 2008), pp. 23–78.

Chapter 3, Criminal Law: Substance and Procedure

1. Christopher Ingraham, "America's $6.7 Billion Marijuana Habit, Mapped," *Washington Post*, January 6, 2017, https://www.washingtonpost.com /news/wonk/wp/2017/01/06 /americas-6-7-billion-marijuana -habit-mapped/.

2. Arcview Market Research, https:// www.arcviewmarketresearch.com/.

3. Ibid.

4. Substance Abuse and Mental Health Services Administration, *2015 National Survey on Drug Use and Health*, Table 1.1B, https://www.samhsa.gov /data/sites/default/files/NSDUH -DetTabs-2015/NSDUH-DetTabs -2015/NSDUH-DetTabs-2015.htm #tab1-1b.

5. Code of Hammurabi, available online at http://avalon.law.yale.edu/ancient /hamframe.asp.

6. See John Weaver, *Warren—The Man, the Court, the Era* (Boston: Little, Brown, 1967); see also "We the People," *Time*, July 6, 1987, p. 6.

7. *Kansas v. Hendricks*, 521 U.S. 346 (1997); *Chicago v. Morales*, 527 U.S. 41 (1999).

8. *Chicago v. Morales*, 527 U.S. 41 (1999).

9. Daniel Suleiman, "The Capital Punishment Exception: A Case for Constitutionalizing the Substantive Criminal Law," *Columbia Law Review* 104 (2004): 426–458.

10. *Calder v. Bull*, 3 U.S. 386 (1798).

11. See, for example, *General Laws of Massachusetts, Part II: Real and Personal Property and Domestic Relations. Title III. Domestic Relations*, Section 209 (June 30, 2002).

12. Sheldon Krantz, *Law of Corrections and Prisoners' Rights, Cases and Materials*, 3rd ed. (St. Paul, MN: West, 1986), p. 702; Barbara Knight and Stephen Early Jr., *Prisoners' Rights in America* (Chicago: Nelson-Hall, 1986), Ch. 1; see also Fred Cohen, "The Law of Prisoners' Rights—An Overview," *Criminal Law Bulletin* 24 (1988): 321–349.

13. William Blackstone, *Commentaries on the Law of England*, Vol. 1, ed. Thomas

Cooley (Chicago: Callaghan, 1899), pp. 4, 26. Blackstone was an English barrister who lectured on the English common law at Oxford University in 1753.

14. See *United States v. Balint*, 258 U.S. 250 (1922); see also *Morissette v. United States*, 342 U.S. (1952).

15. *Regina v. Dudley and Stephens*, 14 Q.B.D. 273 (1884).

16. For a history and analysis of these types of defenses, see Eugene Milhizer, "Justification and Excuse: What They Were, What They Are, and What They Ought to Be," *St. John's Law Review* 78 (1012): 725–895.

17. Henry Fradella, *From Insanity to Diminished Capacity: Mental Illness and Criminal Defenses of Excuse in Contemporary American Law* (Bethesda, MD: Academic Press, 2007).

18. Samuel M. Davis, *Rights of Juveniles: The Juvenile Justice System* (New York: Boardman, 1974; updated 1993), Ch. 2; Larry Siegel and Joseph Senna, *Juvenile Delinquency: Theory, Practice, and Law* (St. Paul, MN: West, 1996).

19. *Sherman v. United States*, 356 US 369 (1958); see also *Jacobson v. United States*, 503 US 540 (1992).

20. "Criminal Law—Mutual Combat Mitigation—Appellate Court of Illinois Holds that Disproportionate Reaction to Provocation Negates Mutual Combat Mitigation—*People v. Thompson*, 821 N.E. 2d 664 (Ii. App. Ct. 2004)," *Harvard Law Review* 118 (2005): 2437–2444.

21. Florida Statutes, Justifiable Use of Force, http://www.leg.state.fl.us /statutes/index.cfm?App_mode =Display_Statute&URL=0700-0799 /0776/0776.html.

22. Patrik Jonsson, "Is Self-Defense Law Vigilante Justice? Some Say Proposed Laws Can Help Deter Gun Violence. Others Worry about Deadly Confrontations," *Christian Science Monitor*, February 24, 2006.

23. Associated Press, "Conn. Officer Charged in Fatal Crash Drove 94 MPH," November 18, 2009, http:// www.newsday.com/news/nation/conn -officer-charged-in-fatal-crash-drove -94-mph-1.1603847.

24. Rick Callahan, "Prosecutor Expects Others to Try Executed Vet's Gulf Illness Defense," Associated Press, March 18, 2003, http://www.myplainview.com /news/article/Prosecutor-expects -others-to-try-executed-vet-s-8996236 .php; Deborah W. Denno, "Gender,

Crime, and the Criminal Law Defenses," *Journal of Criminal Law and Criminology* 85 (1994): 80–180.

25. *Lawrence v. Texas*, 539 U.S. 558 (2003).

26. Marvin Zalman, John Strate, Denis Hunter, and James Sellars, "Michigan Assisted Suicide Three Ring Circus: The Intersection of Law and Politics," *Ohio Northern Law Review* 23 (1997): 230–276.

27. 1992 P.A. 270 as amended by 1993 P.A.3, M.C. L. ss. 752.1021 to 752.1027.

28. ProCon.org, "State-by-State Guide to Physician-Assisted Suicide," http:// euthanasia.procon.org/view.resource .php?resourceID=000132; see also Michigan Code of Criminal Procedure, *Assisting a Suicide*, Section 750.329a.

29. National Center for Victims of Crime, "Criminal Stalking Laws," https:// victimsofcrime.org/our-programs /stalking-resource-center/stalking -laws/criminal-stalking-laws-by -state; see also National Institute of Justice, *Project to Develop a Model Anti-Stalking Statute* (Washington, DC: National Institute of Justice, 1994).

30. See, for example, Matthew Lyon, "No Means No? Withdrawal of Consent During Intercourse and the Continuing Evolution of the Definition of Rape," *Journal of Criminal Law and Criminology* 95 (2004): 277–314.

31. National Conference of State Legislators, "Identity Theft," http://www.ncsl .org/issues-research/banking/identity -theft-state-statutes.aspx.

32. Environmental Protection Agency, Criminal Enforcement Division, https://www.epa.gov/enforcement /criminal-enforcement.

33. For a full list of such states and their laws, visit http://medicalmarijuana .procon.org/view.resource.php? resourceID=000881.

34. Seattle Police Department, http:// spdblotter.seattle.gov/2012/12/05 /officers-shall-not-take-any-enforcement -action-other-than-to-issue-a-verbal -warning-for-a-violation-of-i-502.

35. Public Law No. 107-56 (October 26, 2001).

36. "President Signs USA PATRIOT Improvement and Reauthorization Act," http://georgewbush-whitehouse .archives.gov/infocus/patriotact/.

37. Tom Cohen, "Obama Approves Extension of Expiring Patriot Act Provisions," *CNN Politics*, May 27, 2011, http://www .cnn.com/2011/POLITICS/05/27 /congress.patriot.act/.

38. Public Law No. 114-23 (June 2, 2015).

39. 384 US 436, 86 S.Ct. 1602, 16 L.Ed.2d 694 (1966).

40. Daniel Suleiman, "The Capital Punishment Exception: A Case for Constitutionalizing the Substantive Criminal Law," *Columbia Law Review* 104 (2004): 426–458.

41. *Baze and Bowling v. Rees*, 553 U.S. 35 (2008).

42. See "Essay," *Time*, February 26, 1973, p. 95; also, for a tribute to the Bill of Rights and due process, see James MacGregor Burns and Stewart Burns, *The Pursuit of Rights in America* (New York: Knopf, 1991).

43. *Griswold v. Connecticut*, 381 U.S. 479 (1965).

44. *Rochin v. California*, 342 U.S. 165 (1952).

45. *Herring v. United States*, 555, U.S. 135 (2009).

Chapter 4, Police in Society: History and Organization

1. Karl Vick, "What Cops Say About Policing Today," *Time*, August 13, 2015, http://time.com/3996100/cops-policing -america-ferguson/.

2. Heather MacDonald, "The New Nationwide Crime Wave," *Wall Street Journal*, May 29, 2015, http://www .wsj.com/articles/the-new-nationwide -crime-wave-1432938425.

3. Karl Vick, "What It's Like Being a Cop Now," *Time*, August 24, 2015, pp. 32–41.

4. Richard Rosenfeld, "Was There a 'Ferguson Effect' on Crime in St. Louis?" http://sentencingproject.org/doc /publications/inc_Ferguson_Effect.pdf.

5. Matthew Friedman, Nicole Fortier, and James Cullen, *Crime in 2015: A Preliminary Analysis* (New York: Brennan Center, 2015).

6. See, for example, David C. Pyrooz, Scott H. Decker, Scott E. Wolfe, and John A. Shjarback, "Was There a Ferguson Effect on Crime Rates in Large U.S. Cities?" *Journal of Criminal Justice* 46 (2016): 1–8; Scott E. Wolfe and Justin Nix, "The Alleged 'Ferguson Effect' and Police Willingness to Engage in Community Partnership," *Law and Human Behavior* 40 (2016): 1–10.

7. Steve Visser, "Baton Rouge Shooting: 3 Officers Dead; Shooter Was Missouri Man, Sources Say," *CNN.com*, http:// www.cnn.com/2016/07/17/us/baton -route-police-shooting/.

8. Kathy A. Bolten, "Police 'Heartbroken' After Ambush leaves 2 Des Moines – Area Officers Dead," http://www.desmoinesregister.com/story/news/2016/11/02/2-police-officers-killed-ambush-attacks/93155012/; Mark Berman, "San Antonio Police Arrest Man Wanted in Killing of Officer Targeted for 'the Uniform,'" *Washington Post*, November 22, 2016, https://www.washingtonpost.com/news/post-nation/wp/2016/11/21/san-antonio-police-say-attacker-who-ambushed-officer-was-targeting-the-uniform/.

9. National Law Enforcement Officers Memorial Fund, *2016 Preliminary End-of-Year Law Enforcement Officer Fatalities Report*, http://www.nleomf.org/facts/research-bulletins/.

10. See, for example, Bureau of Justice Statistics, "Census of Fatal Occupational Injuries," https://www.bls.gov/iif/oshcfoi1.htm.

11. This section relies heavily on such sources as Malcolm Sparrow, Mark Moore, and David Kennedy, *Beyond 911: A New Era for Policing* (New York: Basic Books, 1990); Daniel Devlin, *Police Procedure, Administration, and Organization* (London: Butterworth, 1966); Robert Fogelson, *Big City Police* (Cambridge, MA: Harvard University Press, 1977); Roger Lane, *Policing the City, Boston 1822–1885* (Cambridge, MA: Harvard University Press, 1967); J. J. Tobias, *Crime and Industrial Society in the Nineteenth Century* (New York: Schocken Books, 1967); Samuel Walker, *A Critical History of Police Reform: The Emergence of Professionalism* (Lexington, MA: Lexington Books, 1977); Samuel Walker, *Popular Justice* (New York: Oxford University Press, 1980); John McMullan, "The New Improved Monied Police: Reform Crime Control and Commodification of Policing in London," *British Journal of Criminology* 36 (1996): 85–108.

12. Devlin, *Police Procedure, Administration, and Organization*.

13. McMullan, "The New Improved Monied Police," p. 92.

14. Phillip Reichel, "Southern Slave Patrols as a Transitional Type," *American Journal of Police* 7 (1988): 51–78.

15. Walker, *Popular Justice*, 61.

16. Christopher Thale, "Assigned to Patrol: Neighborhoods, Police, and Changing Deployment Practices in New York City Before 1930," *Journal of Social History* 37 (2004): 1037–1064.

17. Walker, *Popular Justice*, 8.

18. Dennis Rousey, "Cops and Guns: Police Use of Deadly Force in Nineteenth-Century New Orleans," *American Journal of Legal History* 28 (1984): 41–66.

19. Law Enforcement Assistance Administration, *Two Hundred Years of American Criminal Justice* (Washington, DC: Government Printing Office, 1976).

20. National Commission on Law Observance and Enforcement, *Report on the Police* (Washington, DC: Government Printing Office, 1931), pp. 5–7.

21. Pamela Irving Jackson, *Minority Group Threat, Crime, and Policing* (New York: Praeger, 1989).

22. James Q. Wilson and George Kelling, "Broken Windows," *Atlantic Monthly* 249 (1982): 29–38.

23. Frank Tippett, "It Looks Just Like a War Zone," *Time*, May 27, 1985, pp. 16–22; "San Francisco, New York Police Troubled by Series of Scandals," *Criminal Justice Newsletter* 16 (1985): 2–4; Karen Polk, "New York Police: Caught in the Middle and Losing Faith," *Boston Globe*, December 28, 1988, p. 3.

24. Staff of the *Los Angeles Times*, *Understanding the Riots: Los Angeles Before and After the Rodney King Case* (Los Angeles: *Los Angeles Times*, 1992).

25. David H. Bayley, "Policing in America," *Society* 36 (1998).

26. *Final Report of the President's Task Force on 21st Century Policing* (Washington, DC: Office of Community Oriented Policing Services, 2015).

27. Ibid.

28. Julian A. Cook III, "Police Culture in the Twenty-First Century: A Critique of the President's Task Force's Final Report," *Notre Dame Law Review* 92 (2016): 106–114.

29. Brian A. Reaves, *Local Police Departments, 2013: Personnel, Policies, and Practices* (Washington, DC: Bureau of Justice Statistics, 2015).

30. Brian A. Reaves, *Federal Law Enforcement Officers, 2008* (Washington, DC: Bureau of Justice Statistics, 2012). Though dated, this report contains the most recent data available as of this writing.

31. https://www.fbi.gov/about/faqs.

32. https://www.usmarshals.gov/duties/factsheets/overview.pdf.

33. https://www.cbp.gov/about.

34. Bruce Smith, *Police Systems in the United States* (New York: Harper & Row, 1960).

35. Reaves, *Local Police Departments, 2013*.

36. *Texas Homeland Security Strategic Plan, 2015–2020*, https://www.preparingtexas.org/Resources/documents/Texas%20HS%20Strategic%20Plan%202015-2020.pdf.

37. Reaves, *Local Police Departments, 2013*.

38. Harris County Regional Joint Information Center, http://www.readyharris.org/.

39. Montgomery County, Maryland, Office of Emergency Management and Homeland Security, https://www.montgomerycountymd.gov/oemhs/.

40. Reaves, *Local Police Departments, 2013*.

41. For an overview of the department's many counterterrorism initiatives, see http://www.nyc.gov/html/nypd/html/administration/counterterrorism_units.shtml.

42. ASIS International, *The United States Security Industry: Size and Scope, Insights, Trends, and Data, 2014–2017* (Alexandria, VA: ASIS International, 2014).

43. Elizabeth E. Joh, "The Paradox of Private Policing," *Journal of Criminal Law and Criminology* 95 (2004): 49–131.

44. David A. Sklansky, "The Private Police," *UCLA Law Review* 46 (1999): 1165–1287.

45. Elizabeth E. Joh, "Conceptualizing the Private Police," *Utah Law Review* (2005): 573–617, at 588–593.

46. Ibid., 588.

47. Clifford Shearing and Philip Stenning, "Say 'Cheese'? The Disney Order That Is Not So Mickey Mouse," in *Private Policing* (Thousand Oaks, CA: Sage, 1987).

48. Andrea Elliott, "In Stores, Private Handcuffs for Sticky Fingers," *New York Times*, June 17, 2003, A1.

49. See, for example, *Wade v. Byles*, 83 F.3d 902 (7th Cir. 1996); *Gallagher v. Neil Young Freedom Concert*, 49 F.3d 1442 (10th Cir. 1995); *United States v. Francoeur*, 547 F.2d 891 (5th Cir. 1977); *People v. Taylor*, 271 Cal. Rptr. 785 (Ct. App. 1990); *United States v. Lima*, 424 A.2d 113 (DC 1980) (en banc); *People v. Toliver*, 377 N.E.2d 207 (Ill. App. Ct. 1978); *People v. Holloway*, 267 N.W.2d 454 (Mich. Ct. App. 1978); *State v. Buswell*, 460 N.W.2d 614 (Minn. 1990).

50. See, for example, *United States v. Antonelli*, 434 F.2d 335 (2d Cir. 1970);

City of Grand Rapids v. Impens, 327 N.W.2d 278 (Mich. 1982).

51. See, for example, *United States v. Cruz*, 783 F.2d 1470, 1473 (9th Cir. 1986); *State v. Garcia*, 528 So. 2d 76 (Fla. Dist. Ct. App. 1988); *Perez v. State*, 517 So. 2d 106 (Fla. Dist. Ct. App. 1987); *People v. Gorski*, 494 N.E.2d 246 (Ill. App. Ct. 1986); *State v. Farmer*, 510 P.2d 180 (Kan. 1973); *Commonwealth v. Lindenmuth*, 554 A.2d 62 (Pa. Super. Ct. 1989).

52. Joh, "The Paradox of Private Policing," p. 64.

53. James Byrne and Gary Marx, "Technological Innovations in Crime Prevention and Policing: A Review of the Research on Implementation and Impact," *Cahiers Politiestudies Jaargang* 20 (2011): 17–40, at 20.

54. Rebecca Kanable, "Dig into Data Mining," *Law Enforcement Technology* 34 (2007): 62, 64–68, 70.

55. Oak Ridge National Laboratory, http://infohouse.p2ric.org/ref/16 /15985.htm.

56. Brad Heath, "New Police Radars Can 'See' Inside Homes," *USA Today*, January 20, 2015, http://www.usatoday .com/story/news/2015/01/19/police -radar-see-through-walls/22007615/.

57. This section is based on Derek Paulsen, "To Map or Not to Map: Assessing the Impact of Crime Maps on Police Officer Perceptions of Crime," *International Journal of Police Science and Management* 6 (2004): 234–246; William W. Bratton and Peter Knobler, *Turnaround: How America's Top Cop Reversed the Crime Epidemic* (New York: Random House, 1998), p. 289; Jeremy Travis, "Computerized Crime Mapping," *NIJ News*, January 1999.

58. US Department of Homeland Security, "Introduction to Biometrics," http://www.biometrics.gov /ReferenceRoom/Introduction.aspx; Fernando L. Podio, "Biometrics— Technologies for Highly Secure Personal Authentication," *ITL Bulletin* (National Institute of Standards and Technology).

59. Ibid.

60. Frederick Bieber, Charles Brenner, and David Lazer, "Finding Criminals Through DNA of Their Relatives," *Science* 312 (2006): 1315–1316.

61. "FBI's DNA Profile Clearinghouse Announces First 'Cold Hit,'" *Criminal Justice Newsletter* 16 (1999): 5.

62. "South Side Strangler's Execution Cited as DNA Evidence Landmark," *Criminal Justice Newsletter* 2 (1994): 3.

63. Federal Bureau of Investigation, "CODIS: Combined DNA Index System," https://www.fbi.gov/services /laboratory/biometric-analysis/codis.

64. Karen Norrgard, "Forensics, DNA Fingerprinting, and CODIS," *Nature Education* 1 (2008): 1.

65. Kevin. J. Strom and Matthew J. Hickman, "Unanalyzed Evidence in Law-Enforcement Agencies: A National Examination of Forensic Processing in Police Departments," *Criminology and Public Policy* 9 (2010): 381–404.

66. Valerie Hans, David Kay, Michael Dann, Erin Farley, and Stephanie Albertson, "Science in the Jury Box: Jurors' Comprehension of Mitochondrial DNA Evidence," *Law and Human Behavior* 35 (2011): 60–71.

67. Police Executive Research Forum, *Future Trends in Policing* (Washington, DC: Office of Community Oriented Policing Services, 2014).

68. Shumuriel Ratliff, "Hartselle Police Use Social Networking to Catch Crooks," http://www.waff.com /story/17316642/hartselle-police-use -social-networking-to-crack-down -on-crooks.

69. Meredith Broussard, "When Cops Check Facebook," *The Atlantic*, April 15, 2015, http://www.theatlantic .com/politics/archive/2015/04/when -cops-check-facebook/390882/.

70. W. L. Perry, B. McInnis, C. C. Price, S. C. Smith, and J. S. Hollywood, *Predictive Policing: The Role of Crime Forecasting in Law Enforcement Operations* (Santa Monica, CA: RAND Corporation, 2013), p. xiv.

71. G. O. Mohler, M. B. Short, S. Malinowski, M. Johnson, G. E. Tita, A. L. Bertozzi, and P. J. Brantingham, "Randomized Controlled Field Trials of Predictive Policing," *Journal of the American Statistical Association* 110 (2015): 1399–1411.

72. S. Wolpert, "Predictive Policing Substantially Reduces Crime in Los Angeles During Months-Long Test," *UCLA Newsroom*, October 7, 2015, http://newsroom.ucla.edu/releases /predictive-policing-substantially -reduces-crime-in-los-angeles-during -months-long-test.

73. Sklansky, "The Private Police," p. 1168.

74. *Griffin v. Maryland*, 378 US 130 (1964).

Chapter 5, The Police: Role and Function

1. W. L. Perry, B. McInnis, C. C. Price, S.C. Smith, and J. S. Hollywood, *Predictive Policing: The Role of Crime Forecasting in Law Enforcement Operations* (Santa Monica, CA: RAND Corporation, 2013), p. xiv.

2. G. O. Mohler, M. B. Short, S. Malinowski, M. Johnson, G. E. Tita, A. L. Bertozzi, and P. J. Brantingham, "Randomized Controlled Field Trials of Predictive Policing," *Journal of the American Statistical Association* 110 (2015): 1399–1411.

3. S. Wolpert, "Predictive Policing Substantially Reduces Crime in Los Angeles During Months-Long Test," *UCLA Newsroom*, October 7, 2015, http://newsroom.ucla.edu/releases /predictive-policing-substantially -reduces-crime-in-los-angeles-during -months-long-test.

4. James Willis, Stephen Mastrofski, and David Weisburd, "Making Sense of COMPSTAT: A Theory-Based Analysis of Organizational Change in Three Police Departments," *Law and Society Review* 41 (2007): 147–188.

5. Christine Eith and Matthew R. Durose, *Contacts Between Police and the Public, 2008* (Washington, DC: Bureau of Justice Statistics, 2011).

6. Federal Bureau of Investigation, *Uniform Crime Reports, 2015*, https:// ucr.fbi.gov/crime-in-the.u.s/2015 /crime-in-the.u.s.-2015; Brian A. Reaves, *Local Police Departments, 2013: Personnel, Policies, and Practices* (Washington, DC: Bureau of Justice Statistics, 2015), p. 2.

7. Brian A. Reaves and Pheny Smith, *Law Enforcement Management and Administrative Statistics, 1993: Data for Individual State and Local Agencies with 100 or More Officers* (Washington, DC: Bureau of Justice Statistics, 1995).

8. American Bar Association, *Standards Relating to Urban Police Function* (New York: Institute of Judicial Administration, 1974), standard 2.2.

9. Albert J. Reiss, *The Police and the Public* (New Haven, CT: Yale University Press, 1971), p. 19.

10. James Q. Wilson, *Varieties of Police Behavior: The Management of Law and Order in Eight Communities* (Cambridge, MA: Harvard University Press, 1968).

11. James Q. Wilson and Barbara Boland, "The Effect of Police on Crime," *Law and Society Review* 12 (1978): 367–384.
12. Robert Sampson, "Deterrent Effects of the Police on Crime: A Replication and Theoretical Extension," *Law and Society Review* 22 (1988): 163–191.
13. Richard Timothy Coupe and Laurence Blake, "The Effects of Patrol Workloads and Response Strength on Arrests at Burglary Emergencies," *Journal of Criminal Justice* 33 (2005): 239–255.
14. Lawrence Sherman, James Shaw, and Dennis Rogan, *The Kansas City Gun Experiment* (Washington, DC: National Institute of Justice, 1994).
15. For a review of the literature, see Anthony A. Braga, Brandon C. Welsh, and Cory Schnell, "Can Policing Disorder Reduce Crime? A Systematic Review and Meta-Analysis," *Journal of Research in Crime and Delinquency* 52 (2015): 567–588.
16. For a thorough review of this issue, see Andrew Karmen, *Why Is New York City's Murder Rate Dropping So Sharply?* (New York: John Jay College, 1996).
17. Robert Davis, Pedro Mateu-Gelabert, and Joel Miller, "Can Effective Policing Also Be Respectful? Two Examples in the South Bronx," *Police Quarterly* 8 (2005): 229–247.
18. Mitchell Chamlin, "Crime and Arrests: An Autoregressive Integrated Moving Average (ARIMA) Approach," *Journal of Quantitative Criminology* 4 (1988) 247–255.
19. Stewart D'Alessio and Lisa Stolzenberg, "Crime, Arrests, and Pretrial Jail Incarceration: An Examination of the Deterrence Thesis," *Criminology* 36 (1998): 735–761.
20. Perry Shapiro and Harold Votey, "Deterrence and Subjective Probabilities of Arrest: Modeling Individual Decisions to Drink and Drive in Sweden," *Law and Society Review* 18 (1984): 111–149.
21. William Spelman and Dale K. William, *Calling the Police: A Replication of the Citizen Reporting Component of the Kansas City Response Time Analysis* (Washington, DC: Police Foundation, 1976).
22. Jae-Seung Lee, Jonathan Lee, and Larry T. Hoover, "What Conditions Affect Police Response Time? Examining Situational and Neighborhood Factors," *Police Quarterly* 20 (2017):

61–80; Abdullah Cihan, Yan Zhang, and Larry Hoover, "Police Response Time to In-Progress Burglary," *Police Quarterly* 15 (2012): 308–327.
23. George Kelling and James Q. Wilson, "Broken Windows: The Police and Neighborhood Safety," *Atlantic Monthly* 249 (1982): 29–38.
24. Catherine Coles and George Kelling, *Fixing Broken Windows: Restoring Order and Reducing Crime in Our Communities* (New York: Free Press, 1998).
25. Anthony A. Braga and Brenda J. Bond, "Policing Crime and Disorder Hot Spots: A Randomized Controlled Trial," *Criminology* 46 (2008): 577–606; but see David Weisburd, Joshua C. Hinkle, Anthony A. Braga, and Alese Wooditch, "Understanding the Mechanisms Underlying Broken Windows Policing: The Need for Evaluation Evidence," *Journal of Research in Crime and Delinquency* 52 (2015): 589–608.
26. Vincent Henry, *The Compstat Paradigm: Management Accountability in Policing, Business and the Public Sector* (New York: Looseleaf Law Publications, 2002).
27. For a view of the modern detective, see William Sanders, *Detective Work: A Study of Criminal Investigations* (New York: Free Press, 1977).
28. Mark Pogrebin and Eric Poole, "Vice Isn't Nice: A Look at the Effects of Working Undercover," *Journal of Criminal Justice* 21 (1993): 385–396; Gary Marx, *Undercover: Police Surveillance in America* (Berkeley: University of California Press, 1988).
29. Martin Innes, *Investigating Murder: Detective Work and the Police Response to Criminal Homicide* (Clarendon Studies in Criminology) (London: Oxford University Press, 2003).
30. John B. Edwards, "Homicide Investigative Strategies," *FBI Law Enforcement Bulletin* 74 (2005): 11–21.
31. Robert Langworthy, "Do Stings Control Crime? An Evaluation of a Police Fencing Operation," *Justice Quarterly* 6 (1989): 27–45.
32. Mary Dodge, Donna Starr-Gimeno, and Thomas Williams, "Puttin' on the Sting: Women Police Officers' Perspectives on Reverse Prostitution Assignment," *International Journal of Police Science and Management* 7 (2005): 71–85.

33. Peter Greenwood and Joan Petersilia, *Summary and Policy Implications,* Vol. 1, *The Criminal Investigation Process* (Santa Monica, CA: RAND, 1975).
34. Mark Willman and John Snortum, "Detective Work: The Criminal Investigation Process in a Medium-Size Police Department," *Criminal Justice Review* 9 (1984): 33–39.
35. John L. Worrall, "Investigative Resources and Crime Clearances: A Group-Based Trajectory Approach," *Criminal Justice Policy Review,* forthcoming.
36. Janice Puckett and Richard Lundman, "Factors Affecting Homicide Clearances: Multivariate Analysis of a More Complete Conceptual Framework," *Journal of Research in Crime and Delinquency* 40 (2003): 171–194.
37. Police Executive Research Forum, *Calling the Police: Citizen Reporting of Serious Crime* (Washington, DC: Police Executive Research Forum, 1981).
38. John Eck, *Solving Crimes: The Investigation of Burglary and Robbery* (Washington, DC: Police Executive Research Forum, 1984).
39. A. Fischer, "CopLink Nabs Criminals Faster," *Arizona Daily Star,* January 7, 2001; A. Robbins, *PC Magazine* 22 (2003); M. Sink, "An Electronic Cop that Plays Hunches," *New York Times,* November 2, 2002.
40. Paul Johnson and Robin Williams, "Internationalizing New Technologies of Crime Control: Forensic DNA Databasing and Datasharing in the European Union," *Policing and Society* 17 (2007): 103–118.
41. For a general review, see Robert Trojanowicz and Bonnie Bucqueroux, *Community Policing: A Contemporary Perspective* (Cincinnati: Anderson, 1990).
42. Police Foundation, *The Newark Foot Patrol Experiment* (Washington, DC: Police Foundation, 1981).
43. John Worrall and Jihong Zhao. "The Role of the COPS Office in Community Policing," *Policing: An International Journal of Police Strategies and Management* 26 (2003), 64–87.
44. Jihong Zhao, Nicholas Lovrich, and Quint Thurman, "The Status of Community Policing in American Cities," *Policing* 22 (1999): 74–92.
45. Albert Cardarelli, Jack McDevitt, and Katrina Baum, "The Rhetoric and Reality of Community Policing in Small and Medium-Sized Cities and Towns," *Policing* 21 (1998): 397–415.

46. Brian Renauer, "Reducing Fear of Crime," *Police Quarterly* 10 (2007): 41–62.

47. Susan Sadd and Randolph Grinc, *Implementation Challenges in Community Policing* (Washington, DC: National Institute of Justice, 1996).

48. Donald Green, Dara Strolovitch, and Janelle Wong, "Defended Neighborhoods: Integration and Racially Motivated Crime," *American Journal of Sociology* 104 (1998): 372–403.

49. Robin Shepard Engel, *How Police Supervisory Styles Influence Patrol Officer Behavior* (Washington, DC: National Institute of Justice, 2003).

50. Amy Halsted, Max Bromley, and John Cochran, "The Effects of Work Orientations on Job Satisfaction among Sheriffs' Deputies Practicing Community-Oriented Policing," *Policing: An International Journal of Police Strategies and Management* 23 (2000): 82–104.

51. Venessa Garcia, "Constructing the 'Other' within Police Culture: An Analysis of a Deviant Unit Within the Police Organization," *Police Practice and Research* 6 (2005): 65–80.

52. Kevin Ford, Daniel Weissbein, and Kevin Plamondon, "Distinguishing Organizational from Strategy Commitment: Linking Officers' Commitment to Community Policing to Job Behaviors and Satisfaction," *Justice Quarterly* 20 (2003): 159–186.

53. Michael Palmiotto, Michael Birzer, and N. Prabha Unnithan, "Training in Community Policing: A Suggested Curriculum," *Policing: An International Journal of Police Strategies and Management* 23 (2000): 8–21.

54. Lisa Riechers and Roy Roberg, "Community Policing: A Critical Review of Underlying Assumptions," *Journal of Police Science and Administration* 17 (1990): 112–113.

55. See, for example, Chapter 5 in John L. Worrall, *Crime Control in America: What Works*, 3 ed. (Columbus, OH: Pearson, 2015).

56. Ling Ren, Liqun Cao, Nicholas Lovrich, and Michael Gaffney, "Linking Confidence in the Police with the Performance of the Police: Community Policing Can Make a Difference," *Journal of Criminal Justice* 33 (2005): 55–66.

57. Jihong Zhao, Ni He, and Nicholas Lovrich, "Value Change Among Police Officers at a Time of Organizational Reform: A Follow-Up Study of Rokeach Values," *Policing* 22 (1999): 152–170.

58. Herman Goldstein, "Improving Policing: A Problem-Oriented Approach," *Crime and Delinquency* 25 (1979): 236–258.

59. Jerome Skolnick and David Bayley, *Community Policing: Issues and Practices Around the World* (Washington, DC: National Institute of Justice, 1988), p. 12.

60. Lawrence Sherman, Patrick Gartin, and Michael Buerger, "Hot Spots of Predatory Crime: Routine Activities and the Criminology of Place," *Criminology* 27 (1989): 27–55.

61. Ibid., 45.

62. See, for example, Roberto G. Santos and Rachel Boba Santos, "An Ex Post Facto Evaluation of Tactical Police Response in Residential Theft from Vehicle Micro-time Hot Spots," *Journal of Quantitative Criminology* 31 (2015): 679–698; Anthony Braga and David Weisburd, "The Effects of Focused Deterrence Strategies on Crime: A Systematic Review and Meta-Analysis of the Empirical Evidence," *Journal of Research in Crime and Delinquency* 49 (2012): 323–358.

63. Sherry Plaster Carter, Stanley Carter, and Andrew Dannenberg, "Zoning Out Crime and Improving Community Health in Sarasota, Florida: 'Crime Prevention Through Environmental Design,'" *American Journal of Public Health* 93 (2003): 1442–1445.

64. Anthony Braga, David Kennedy, Elin Waring, and Anne Morrison Piehl, "Problem-Oriented Policing, Deterrence, and Youth Violence: An Evaluation of Boston's Operation Ceasefire," *Journal of Research in Crime and Delinquency* 38 (2001): 195–225; see also Anthony A. Braga, David M. Hureau, and Andrew V. Papachristos, "Deterring Gang-Involved Gun Violence: Measuring the Impact of Boston's Operation Ceasefire on Street Gang Behavior," *Journal of Quantitative Criminology* 30 (2014): 113–139.

65. Andrew M. Fox, Charles M. Katz, David E. Choate, and E. C. Hedberg, "Evaluation of the Phoenix TRUCE Project: A Replication of Chicago Ceasefire," *Justice Quarterly* 32 (2015): 85–115.

66. Bureau of Justice Assistance, *Problem-Oriented Drug Enforcement: A Community-Based Approach for Effective Policing* (Washington, DC: National Institute of Justice, 1993).

67. Ibid., pp. 64–65.

68. David L. Carter and Jeremy G. Carter, "Intelligence-Led Policing: Conceptual and Functional Considerations for Public Police," *Criminal Justice Policy Review* 20 (2009): 310–325.

69. Global Intelligence Working Group, *National Criminal Intelligence Sharing Plan* (Washington, DC: Office of Justice Programs, 2003), p. 6.

70. Jerry Ratcliffe, *Intelligence-Led Policing* (New York: Willan, 2008).

71. Carter and Carter, p. 310.

72. Ibid., p. 312.

73. Ratcliffe, *Intelligence-Led Policing*.

74. Marilyn B. Peterson, "Toward a Model for Intelligence-Led Policing in the United States," in *Turnkey Intelligence: Unlocking Your Agency's Intelligence Capability* (Lawrenceville, NJ: International Association of Law Enforcement Intelligence Analysts, Law Enforcement Intelligence Unit, and National White Collar Crime Center, 2002), p. 5.

75. National Criminal Intelligence Sharing Plan, https://it.ojp.gov/documents/ncisp/.

76. *Fusion Center Guidelines: Developing and Sharing Information and Intelligence in a New Era*, https://it.ojp.gov/documents/fusion_center_guidelines_law_enforcement.pdfhttps://it.ojp.gov/documents/fusion_center_guidelines_law_enforcement.pdf.

77. Charles R. Swanson, Leonard Territo, and Robert W. Taylor, *Police Administration: Structures, Processes, and Behavior*, 7th ed. (Upper Saddle River, NJ: Prentice Hall, 2008), pp. 77–78.

78. http://www.bpad.com/; William Doerner and Terry Nowell, "The Reliability of the Behavioral-Personnel Assessment Device (BPAD) in Selecting Police Recruits," *Policing* 22 (1999): 343–352.

79. Brian A. Reaves, *Local Police Departments, 2007* (Washington, DC: Bureau of Justice Statistics, 2010).

80. See, for example, http://www.dallaspolice.net/training-academy.

81. Philip Ash, Karen Slora, and Cynthia Britton, "Police Agency Officer Selection Practices," *Journal of Police Science and Administration* 17 (1990): 258–269.

82. See, for example, http://www.sjpd.org/BFO/Community/TeamKids/.

Chapter 6, Issues in Policing: Professional, Social, and Legal

1. Rich Morin, Kim Parker, Renee Stepler, and Andrew Mercer, *Behind the Badge*, January 11, 2017, http://www.pewsocialtrends.org/2017/01/11/behind-the-badge/.

2. Ibid.

3. Jihong Zhao and Nicholas Lovrich, "Determinants of Minority Employment in American Municipal Police Agencies: The Representation of African American Officers," *Journal of Criminal Justice* 26 (1998): 267–278.

4. Brian A. Reaves, *Local Police Departments, 2013: Personnel, Policies, and Practices* (Washington, DC: Bureau of Justice Statistics, 2015).

5. T. David Murphy and John Worrall, "Residency Requirements and Public Perceptions of the Police in Large Municipalities," *Policing* 22 (1999): 327–342.

6. Jack Kuykendall and David Burns, "The African American Police Officer: An Historical Perspective," *Journal of Contemporary Criminal Justice* 1 (1980): 4–13.

7. Ibid.

8. Nicholas Alex, *Black in Blue: A Study of the Negro Policeman* (New York: Appleton-Century-Crofts, 1969).

9. Joseph Gustafson, "Diversity in Municipal Police Agencies: A National Examination of Minority Hiring and Promotion," *Policing: An International Journal of Police Strategies and Management* 36 (2013): 719–736.

10. Stephen Leinen, *African American Police, White Society* (New York: New York University Press, 1984).

11. Ni He, Jihong Zhao, and Ling Ren, "Do Race and Gender Matter in Police Stress? A Preliminary Assessment of the Interactive Effects," *Journal of Criminal Justice* 33 (2005): 535–547.

12. Joseph L. Gustafson, "Tokenism in Policing: An Empirical Test of Kanter's Hypothesis," *Journal of Criminal Justice* 36 (2008): 1–10.

13. For a review of the history of women in policing, see Dorothy Moses Schulz, "From Policewoman to Police Officer: An Unfinished Revolution," *Police Studies* 16 (1993): 90–99; Cathryn House, "The Changing Role of Women in Law Enforcement," *Police Chief* 60 (1993): 139–144.

14. Susan Martin, "Female Officers on the Move? A Status Report on Women in Policing," in *Critical Issues in Policing*, ed. Roger Dunham and Geoffrey Alpert (Grove Park, IL: Waveland Press, 1988), pp. 312–331.

15. *LeBoeuf v. Ramsey*, 503 F.Supp. 747 (D. Mass 1980).

16. Michael Birzer and Delores Craig, "Gender Differences in Police Physical Ability Test Performance," *American Journal of Police* 15 (1996): 93–106.

17. Reaves, *Local Police Departments, 2013*.

18. Jill Harrison, "Women in Law Enforcement: Subverting Sexual Harassment with Social Bonds," *Women and Criminal Justice* 22 (2012): 226–238; James Daum and Cindy Johns, "Police Work from a Woman's Perspective," *Police Chief* 61 (1994): 46–49.

19. Mary Brown, "The Plight of Female Police: A Survey of NW Patrolmen," *Police Chief* 61 (1994): 50–53.

20. Matthew Hickman, Alex Piquero, and Jack Greene, "Discretion and Gender Disproportionality in Police Disciplinary Systems," *Policing: An International Journal of Police Strategies and Management* 23 (2000): 105–116.

21. Robin Haarr and Merry Morash, "Gender, Race, and Strategies of Coping with Occupational Stress in Policing," *Justice Quarterly* 16 (1999): 303–336.

22. Ibid.

23. Eric Poole and Mark Pogrebin, "Factors Affecting the Decision to Remain in Policing: A Study of Women Officers," *Journal of Police Science and Administration* 16 (1988): 49–55.

24. See, for example, Gary Cordner and AnnMarie Cordner, "Stuck on a Plateau? Obstacles to Recruitment, Selection, and Retention of Women Police," *Police Quarterly* 14 (2011): 207–226.

25. Reaves, *Local Police Departments, 2013*.

26. Bruce Berg, "Who Should Teach Police? A Typology and Assessment of Police Academy Instructors," *American Journal of Police* 9 (1990): 79–100.

27. David Carter and Allen Sapp, *The State of Police Education: Critical Findings* (Washington, DC: Police Executive Research Forum, 1988), p. 6.

28. John Krimmel, "The Performance of College-Educated Police: A Study of Self-Rated Police Performance Measures," *American Journal of Police* 15 (1996): 85–95.

29. See, for example, Richard Harris, *The Police Academy: An Inside View* (New York: Wiley, 1973); John Van Maanen, "Observations on the Making of a Policeman," in *Order Under Law*, ed. R. Culbertson and M. Tezak (Prospect Heights, IL: Waveland Press, 1981), pp. 111–126; Jonathan Rubenstein, *City Police* (New York: Ballantine Books, 1973); John Broderick, *Police in a Time of Change* (Morristown, NJ: General Learning Press, 1977).

30. Gary R. Rothwell, "Whistle-Blowing and the Code of Silence in Police Agencies: Policy and Structural Predictors," *Crime and Delinquency* 53 (2007): 605–632; Louise Westmarland, "Police Ethics and Integrity: Breaking the Blue Code of Silence," *Policing and Society* 15 (2005): 145–165.

31. Malcolm Sparrow, Mark Moore, and David Kennedy, *Beyond 911: A New Era for Policing* (New York: Basic Books, 1992), p. 51.

32. M. Steven Meagher and Nancy Yentes, "Choosing a Career in Policing: A Comparison of Male and Female Perceptions," *Journal of Police Science and Administration* 16 (1986): 320–327.

33. Venessa Garcia, "Constructing the 'Other' Within Police Culture: An Analysis of a Deviant Unit Within the Police Organization," *Police Practice and Research* 6 (2005): 65–80.

34. Michael K. Brown, *Working the Street* (New York: Russell Sage, 1981), p. 82.

35. Stan Shernock, "An Empirical Examination of the Relationship Between Police Solidarity and Community Orientation," *Journal of Police Science and Administration* 18 (1988): 182–198.

36. John Crank, *Understanding Police Culture*, 2nd ed. (Cincinnati: Anderson, 2003).

37. Eugene Paoline, "Taking Stock: Toward a Richer Understanding of Police Culture," *Journal of Criminal Justice* 31 (2003): 199–214.

38. Crank, *Understanding Police Culture*, pp. 359–363.

39. Egon Bittner, *The Functions of Police in Modern Society* (Cambridge, MA: Oelgeschlager, Gunn & Hain, 1980), p. 63.

40. Richard Lundman, *Police and Policing* (New York: Holt, Rinehart & Winston, 1980); see also Jerome Skolnick, *Justice Without Trial* (New York: Wiley, 1966).

41. Robert Regoli, Robert Culbertson, John Crank, and James Powell, "Career Stage and Cynicism Among

Police Chiefs," *Justice Quarterly* 7 (1990): 592–614.

42. William Westly, *Violence and the Police: A Sociological Study of Law, Custom, and Morality* (Cambridge, MA: MIT Press, 1970).

43. Skolnick, *Justice Without Trial*, pp. 42–68.

44. Milton Rokeach, Martin Miller, and John Snyder, "The Value Gap Between Police and Policed," *Journal of Social Issues* 27 (1971): 155–171.

45. Wallace Graves, "Police Cynicism: Causes and Cures," *FBI Law Enforcement Bulletin* 65 (1996): 16–21.

46. Larry Tifft, "The 'Cop Personality' Reconsidered," *Journal of Police Science and Administration* 2 (1974): 268; David Bayley and Harold Mendelsohn, *Minorities and the Police* (New York: Free Press, 1969); Robert Balch, "The Police Personality: Fact or Fiction?" *Journal of Criminal Law, Criminology, and Police Science* 63 (1972): 117.

47. Lowell Storms, Nolan Penn, and James Tenzell, "Policemen's Perception of Real and Ideal Policemen," *Journal of Police Science and Administration* 17 (1990): 40–43.

48. Skolnick, *Justice Without Trial*.

49. Carroll Seron, Joseph Pereira, and Jean Kovath, "Judging Police Misconduct: 'Street-Level' versus Professional Policing," *Law and Society Review* 38 (2004): 665–710.

50. Peter Salovey and John D. Mayer, "Emotional Intelligence," *Imagination, Cognition, and Personality* 9 (1990): 185–211.

51. Michael E. Burnette, *Emotional Intelligence and the Police* (Germany: VDM Verlag, 2008).

52. Ivan Y. Sun, Brian K. Payne, and Yuning Wu, "The Impact of Situational Factors, Officer Characteristics, and Neighborhood Context on Police Behavior: A Multilevel Analysis," *Journal of Criminal Justice* 36 (2008): 22–32.

53. Kenneth Litwin, "A Multilevel Multivariate Analysis of Factors Affecting Homicide Clearances," *Journal of Research in Crime and Delinquency* 41 (2004): 327–351.

54. Robert Kane, "Patterns of Arrest in Domestic Violence Encounters: Identifying a Police Decision-Making Model," *Journal of Criminal Justice* 27 (1999): 65–79.

55. Gregory Howard Williams, *The Law and Politics of Police Discretion* (Westport, CT: Greenwood Press, 1984).

56. Dana Jones and Joanne Belknap, "Police Responses to Battering in a Progressive Pro-Arrest Jurisdiction," *Justice Quarterly* 16 (1999): 249–273.

57. Allison Chappell, John Macdonald, and Patrick Manz, "The Organizational Determinants of Police Arrest Decisions," *Crime and Delinquency* 52 (2006): 287–306.

58. Richard R. Johnson and Mengyan Dai, "Police Enforcement of Domestic Violence Laws: Supervisory Control or Officer Prerogatives?" *Justice Quarterly* 33 (2016): 185–208.

59. Westly, *Violence and the Police*.

60. Peter Liu and Thomas Cook, "Speeding Violation Dispositions in Relation to Police Officers' Perception of the Offenders," *Policing and Society* (March 15, 2005): 83–88.

61. Joseph Schafer and Stephen Mastrofski, "Police Leniency in Traffic Enforcement Encounters: Exploratory Findings from Observations and Interviews," *Journal of Criminal Justice* 33 (2005): 225–238; Richard Lundman, "Demeanor or Crime? The Midwest City Police-Citizen Encounters Study," *Criminology* 32 (1994): 631–653; Nathan Goldman, *The Differential Selection of Juvenile Offenders for Court Appearance* (New York: National Council on Crime and Delinquency, 1963).

62. David Klinger, "Bringing Crime Back In: Toward a Better Understanding of Police Arrest Decisions," *Journal of Research in Crime and Delinquency* 33 (1996): 333–336; "More on Demeanor and Arrest in Dade County," *Criminology* 34 (1996): 61–79; "Demeanor or Crime? Why 'Hostile' Citizens Are More Likely to Be Arrested," *Criminology* 32 (1994): 475–493.

63. Ambrose Leung, Frances Woolley, Richard Tremblay, and Frank Vitaro, "Who Gets Caught? Statistical Discrimination in Law Enforcement," *Journal of Socio-Economics* 34 (2005): 289–309.

64. Jennifer Schwartz and Bryan D. Rookey, "The Narrowing Gender Gap in Arrests: Assessing Competing Explanations Using Self-Report, Traffic Fatality, and Official Data on Drunk Driving, 1980–2004," *Criminology* 46 (2008): 637–671.

65. R. Steven Daniels, Lorin Baum-hover, William Formby, and Carolyn Clark-Daniels, "Police Discretion and Elder Mistreatment: A Nested Model of Observation, Reporting, and Satisfaction," *Journal of Criminal Justice* 27 (1999): 209–225.

66. For a review, see Frank Schmalleger and John L. Worrall, *Policing Today* (Upper Saddle River, NJ: Pearson, 2010), p. 319.

67. Brian Withrow, "Race-Based Policing: A Descriptive Analysis of the Wichita Stop Study," *Police Practice and Research* 5 (2004): 223–240; Brian Withrow, "A Comparative Analysis of Commonly Used Benchmarks in Racial Profiling: A Research Note," *Justice Research and Policy* 6 (2004): 71–92; Amy Farrell, Jack McDevitt, Lisa Bailey, Carsten Andresen, and Erica Pierce, "Massachusetts Racial and Gender Profiling Final Report" (Boston: Northeastern University, 2004), http://masspolicereform.com/wp-content/uploads/2015/04/profiling_finalreport.pdf; Richard Lundman, "Driver Race, Ethnicity, and Gender and Citizen Reports of Vehicle Searches by Police and Vehicle Search Hits," *Journal of Criminal Law and Criminology* 94 (2004): 309–350; Michael Smith and Geoffrey Alpert, "Explaining Police Bias: A Theory of Social Conditioning and Illusory Correlation," *Criminal Justice and Behavior* 34 (2007): 1262–1283; *Interim Report of the State Police Review Team Regarding Allegations of Racial Profiling* (Trenton, NJ: Office of the Attorney General, 1999).

68. David Eitle, Lisa Stolzenberg, and Stewart J. D'Alessio, "Police Organizational Factors, the Racial Composition of the Police, and the Probability of Arrest," *Justice Quarterly* 22 (2005): 30–57; Matt DeLisi and Robert Regoli, "Race, Conventional Crime, and Criminal Justice: The Declining Importance of Skin Color," *Journal of Criminal Justice* 27 (1999): 549–557; Jon Gould and Stephen Mastrofski, "Suspect Searches: Assessing Police Behavior Under the US Constitution," *Criminology and Public Policy* 3 (2004): 315–362; Joseph Schafer, David Carter, and Andra Katz-Bannister, "Studying Traffic Stop Encounters," *Journal of Criminal Justice* 32 (2004): 159–170; James Lange, Mark Johnson, and Robert Voas, "Testing the Racial Profiling Hypothesis for Seemingly Disparate Traffic Stops on the New Jersey Turnpike," *Justice Quarterly* 22 (2005): 193–223; Geoffrey P. Alpert, Roger G. Dunham, and Michael R. Smith,

"Investigating Racial Profiling by the Miami-Dade Police Department: A Multimethod Approach," *Criminology and Public Policy* 6 (2007): 25–56.

69. Mathias Risse and Richard Zeckhauser, "Racial Profiling," *Philosophy and Public Affairs* 32 (2004): 131–170.

70. Karen Kruger and Nicholas Valltos, "Dealing with Domestic Violence in Law Enforcement Relationships," *FBI Law Enforcement Bulletin* 71 (2002): 1–7.

71. Richard C. Lumb and Ronald Breazeale, "Police Officer Attitudes and Community Policing Implementation," *Policing and Society* 13 (2003): 91–106.

72. Donald Yates and Vijayan Pillai, "Frustration and Strain Among Fort Worth Police Officers," *Sociology and Social Research: An International Journal* 76 (1992): 145–149.

73. For an impressive review, see Richard Farmer, "Clinical and Managerial Implications of Stress Research on the Police," *Journal of Police Science and Administration* 17 (1990): 205–217.

74. Lawrence Travis III and Craig Winston, "Dissension in the Ranks: Officer Resistance to Community Policing and Support for the Organization," *Journal of Crime and Justice* 21 (1998): 139–155.

75. Francis Cullen, Terrence Lemming, Bruce Link, and John Wozniak, "The Impact of Social Supports on Police Stress," *Criminology* 23 (1985): 503–522.

76. Merry Morash, Robin Haarr, and Dae-Hoon Kwak, "Multilevel Influences on Police Stress," *Journal of Contemporary Criminal Justice* 22 (2006): 26–43.

77. Farmer, "Clinical and Managerial Implications"; Nancy Norvell, Dale Belles, and Holly Hills, "Perceived Stress Levels and Physical Symptoms in Supervisory Law Enforcement Personnel," *Journal of Police Science and Administration* 16 (1988): 75–79.

78. Donald Yates and Vijayan Pillai, "Attitudes Toward Community Policing: A Causal Analysis," *Social Science Journal* 33 (1996): 193–209.

79. Harvey McMurray, "Attitudes of Assaulted Police Officers and Their Policy Implications," *Journal of Police Science and Administration* 17 (1990): 44–48.

80. Lawrence Blum, *Force Under Pressure: How Cops Live and Why They Die* (New York: Lantern Books, 2000).

81. Rose Lee Josephson and Martin Reiser, "Officer Suicide in the Los Angeles Police Department: A Twelve-Year Follow-Up," *Journal of Police Science and Administration* 17 (1990): 227–230.

82. Yates and Pillai, "Attitudes Toward Community Policing," pp. 205–206.

83. Ibid.

84. Rosanna Church and Naomi Robertson, "How State Police Agencies Are Addressing the Issue of Wellness," *Policing* 22 (1999): 304–312.

85. Farmer, "Clinical and Managerial Implications," p. 215.

86. Peter Hart, Alexander Wearing, and Bruce Headey, "Assessing Police Work Experiences: Development of the Police Daily Hassles and Uplifts Scales," *Journal of Criminal Justice* 21 (1993): 553–573.

87. Scott R. Senjo and Karla Dhungana, "A Field Data Examination of Policy Constructs Related to Fatigue Conditions in Law Enforcement Personnel," *Police Quarterly* 12 (2009): 123–136.

88. Bryan Vila and Dennis J. Kenney, "Tired Cops: The Prevalence and Potential Consequences of Police Fatigue," *NIJ Journal* 248 (2002): 16–21.

89. Luenda E. Charles, Cecil M. Burchfiel, Desta Fekedulegn, Bryan Vila, Tara A. Hartley, James Slaven, Anna Mnatsakanova, and John M. Violanti, "Shift Work and Sleep: The Buffalo Police Health Study," *Policing* 30 (2007): 215–227.

90. Sean Griffin and Thomas Bernard, "Angry Aggression Among Police Officers," *Police Quarterly* 6 (2003): 3–21.

91. Kim Michelle Lersch and Tom Mieczkowski, "Who Are the Problem-Prone Officers? An Analysis of Citizen Complaints," *American Journal of Police* 15 (1996): 23–42.

92. Samuel Walker, Geoffrey P. Alpert, and Dennis J. Kenney, *Early Warning Systems: Responding to the Problem Police Officer, Research in Brief* (Washington, DC: National Institute of Justice, 2001).

93. Michael D. White, "Controlling Police Decisions to Use Deadly Force: Reexamining the Importance of Administrative Policy," *Crime and Delinquency* 47 (2001): 131.

94. Samuel Walker, *Popular Justice*, 2nd ed. (New York: Oxford University Press, 1997), pp. 48–64.

95. Herman Goldstein, *Police Corruption* (Washington, DC: Police Foundation, 1975), p. 3.

96. Lawrence Sherman, *Scandal and Reform: Controlling Police Corruption* (Berkeley: University of California Press, 1978), p. 194.

97. Barbara Gelb, *Tarnished Brass: The Decade After Serpico* (New York: Putnam, 1983); Candace McCoy, "Lawsuits Against Police: What Impact Do They Have?" *Criminal Law Bulletin* 20 (1984): 49–56.

98. Samuel Walker, *Police Accountability: The Role of Citizen Oversight* (Belmont, CA: Wadsworth, 2001); Liqun Cao and Bu Huang, "Determinants of Citizen Complaints Against Police Abuse of Power," *Journal of Criminal Justice* 28 (2000): 203–213; Peter Finn, "Getting Along with Citizen Oversight," *FBI Law Enforcement Bulletin* 69 (2000): 22–27.

99. Christine Eith and Matthew R. Durose, *Contacts Between the Police and the Public, 2008* (Washington, DC: Bureau of Justice Statistics, 2011).

100. Ibid.

101. Lawrence Sherman and Robert Langworthy, "Measuring Homicide by Police Officers," *Journal of Criminal Law and Criminology* 4 (1979): 546–560.

102. Ibid.

103. Federal Bureau of Investigation, *Crime in the United States, 2015*, "Expanded Homicide Data," https://ucr.fbi.gov/crime-in-the-u.s/2015/crime-in-the-u.s.-2015/tables/expanded_homicide_data_table_14_justifiable_homicide_by_weapon_law_enforcement_2011-2015.xls.

104. Richard Parent and Simon Verdun-Jones, "Victim-Precipitated Homicide: Police Use of Deadly Force in British Columbia," *Policing* 21 (1998): 432–449.

105. Anthony J. Pinizzotto, Edward F. Davis, and Charles E. Miller III, "Suicide by Cop: Defining a Devastating Dilemma," *FBI Law Enforcement Bulletin* 74 (2005): 8–20.

106. *Tennessee v. Garner*, 471 US 1 (1985).

107. Frank Zarb, "Police Liability for Creating the Need to Use Deadly Force in Self-Defense," *Michigan Law Review* 86 (1988): 1982–2009.

108. Brian A. Lawton, "Levels of Nonlethal Force: An Examination of Individual, Situational, and Contextual Factors," *Journal of Research in Crime and Delinquency* 44 (2007): 163–184.

109. Matthew J. Hickman, Alex R. Piquero, and Joel H. Garner, "Toward a National Estimate of Police Use of Nonlethal Force," *Criminology and Public Policy* 7 (2008): 563–604.

110. *Graham v. Connor*, 490 US 386 (1989).

111. Richard Lumb and Paul Friday, "Impact of Pepper Spray Availability on Police Officer Use-of-Force Decisions," *Policing* 20 (1997): 136–149.

112. Michael D. White and Justin Ready, "The Impact of the Taser on Suspect Resistance: Identifying Predictors of Effectiveness," *Crime and Delinquency* 56 (2010): 70–102.

113. *Miranda v. Arizona*, 384 US 436 (1966).

114. *Colorado v. Connelly*, 479 US 157 (1986).

115. Marvin Zalman and Brad W. Smith, "Attitudes of Police Executives Toward *Miranda* and Interrogation Policies," *Journal of Criminal Law and Criminology* 97 (2007): 873–942; Victoria Time and Brian Payne, "Police Chiefs' Perceptions About *Miranda*: An Analysis of Survey Data," *Journal of Criminal Justice* 30 (2002): 77–86.

116. Ronald Allen, "*Miranda*'s Hollow Core," *Northwestern University Law Review* 100 (2006): 71–85.

117. G. Daniel Lassiter, Jennifer Ratcliff, Lezlee Ware, and Clinton Irvin, "Videotaped Confessions: Panacea or Pandora's Box?" *Law and Policy* 28 (2006): 192–210.

118. *Fare v. Michael C.*, 439 US 1310 (1978).

119. *New York v. Quarles*, 467 US 649 (1984).

120. *Oregon v. Elstad*, 470 US 298 (1985).

121. *Colorado v. Connelly*, 479 US 157 (1986).

122. *Moran v. Burbine*, 475 US 412 (1986).

123. *Colorado v. Spring*, 479 US 564 (1987).

124. *Minnick v. Mississippi*, 498 US 146

125. *Arizona v. Fulminante*, 499 US 279

126. *Davis v. United States*, 512 US 452 (1994).

127. *Chavez v. Martinez*, 538 US 760 (2003)

128. *United States v. Patane*, 542 US 630 (2004)

129. *Missouri v. Seibert*, 542 US 600 (2004).

130. *Maryland v. Shatzer*, 559 US 98 (2010).

131. *Florida v. Powell*, 559 US ____ (2010).

132. *Berghuis v. Thompkins*, 560 US 370 (2010).

133. *J.D.B. v. North Carolina*, 564 US ____ (2011).

134. *Howes v. Fields*, 565 US ____ (2012).

135. *Chimel v. California*, 395 US 752 (1969).

136. *Riley v. California*, 573 US 2 ____ (2014).

137. *Terry v. Ohio*, 392 US 1 (1968).

138. *Illinois v. Wardlow*, 528 US 119 (2000).

139. Carroll v. United States, 267 US 132 (1925).

140. *United States v. Ross*, 456 US 798 (1982).

141. Drivers, *Pennsylvania v. Mimms*, 434 US 106 (1977); passengers, *Maryland v. Wilson*, 117 US 882 (1997) and *Arizona v. Johnson*, 555 US 323 (2009).

142. Mark Hansen, "Rousting Miss Daisy?" *American Bar Association Journal* 83 (1997): 22; *Knowles v. Iowa*, 525 US 113 (1998); *Wyoming v. Houghton*, 526 US 295 (1999).

143. *Arizona v. Gant*, 556 US 332 (2009); see also *Davis v. United States*, 564 US ____ (2011).

144. *Bumper v. North Carolina*, 391 US 543 (1960).

145. *Ohio v. Robinette*, 519 US 33 (1996).

146. Limitations on the plain-view doctrine have been defined in *Arizona v. Hicks*, 480 US 321 (1987); the recording of serial numbers from stereo components in a suspect's apartment could not be justified as being in plain view.

147. *Warden v. Hayden*, 387 US 294 (1967); *Minnesota v. Olson*, 495 US 91 (1990); *Breithaupt v. Abram*, 352 US 432 (1957).

148. *Kentucky v. King*, 563 US ____ (2011).

149. *Plumhoff v. Rickard*, 572 US 2 ____ (2014).

150. *Weeks v. United States*, 232 US 383 (1914).

151. *Mapp v. Ohio*, 367 US 643 (1961).

152. William Greenhalgh, *The Fourth Amendment Handbook: A Chronological Survey of Supreme Court Decisions* (Chicago: American Bar Association Section on Criminal Justice, 1995).

153. *United States v. Leon*, 468 US 897 (1984).

154. Eugene Paoline, William Terrill, and Jason Ingram, "Police Use of Force and Officer Injuries: Comparing Conducted Energy Devices (CEDs) to Hands- and Weapons-Based Tactics," *Police Quarterly* 15 (2012): 115–136.

155. Michael D. White and Justin Ready, "Examining Fatal and Nonfatal Incidents Involving the Taser," *Criminology and Public Policy* 8 (2009): 865–891.

Chapter 7, Courts, Prosecution, and the Defense

1. N. Totenberg, "Justice Antonin Scalia, Known for Biting Dissents, Dies at 79," *NPR*, February 16, 2016, http://www.npr.org/2016/02/13/140647230/justice-antonin-scalia-known-for-biting-dissents-dies-at-79.

2. Maybell Romero, "Profit-Driving Prosecution and the Competitive Bidding Process," *Journal of Criminal Law and Criminology* 107, forthcoming, https://papers.ssrn.com/sol3/papers.cfm?abstract_id=2820312.

3. Sean Rosenmerkel and Donald Farole, Jr., *Felony Sentences in State Courts, 2006—Statistical Tables* (Washington, DC: Bureau of Justice Statistics, 2009), Table 4.4.

4. Greg Berman and John Feinblatt, *Problem-Solving Courts: A Brief Primer* (New York: Center for Court Innovation, 2001).

5. Ibid.

6. R. LaFountain, S. Strickland, R. Schauffler, K. Holt, and K. Lewis, *Examining the Work of State Courts: An Overview of 2013 State Court Caseloads* (National Center for State Courts, 2015).

7. US Constitution, Art. 3, Secs. 1 and 2.

8. See, for example, http://www.judicialselection.com.

9. Sari Escovitz with Fred Kurland and Nan Gold, *Judicial Selection and Tenure* (Chicago: American Judicature Society, 1974), pp. 3–16.

10. Judith McFarlane, Ann Malecha, Julia Gist, Kathy Watson, Elizabeth Batten, Iva Hall, and Sheila Smith, "Protection Orders and Intimate Partner Violence: An 18-Month Study of 150 Black, Hispanic, and White Women," *American Journal of Public Health* 94 (2004): 613–618.

11. Steven W. Perry and Duren Banks, *Prosecutors in State Courts, 2007* (Washington, DC: Bureau of Justice Statistics, 2011). Though dated, this study contains the most recent data available as of this writing.

12. Ibid.

13. Jessie Larson, "Unequal Justice: The Supreme Court's Failure to Curtail Selective Prosecution for the Death Penalty," *Journal of Criminal Law and Criminology* 93 (2003): 1009–1031.

14. Kenneth C. Davis, *Discretionary Justice* (Baton Rouge: Louisiana State University Press, 1969), p. 180; see also James B. Stewart, *The Prosecutor* (New York: Simon & Schuster, 1987).

15. Barbara Boland, *The Prosecution of Felony Arrests* (Washington, DC: Government Printing Office, 1983).

16. Jeffrey Spears and Cassia Spohn, "The Effect of Evidence Factors and Victim Characteristics on Prosecutors'

NOTES **N-15**

Charging Decisions in Sexual Assault Cases," *Justice Quarterly* 14 (1997): 501–524.

17. Ibid.

18. Myrna Dawson and Ronit Dinovitzer, "Victim Cooperation and the Prosecution of Domestic Violence in a Specialized Court," *Justice Quarterly* 18 (2001): 593–622.

19. Rodney Kingsworth, John Lopez, Jennifer Wentworth, and Debra Cummings, "Adult Sexual Assault: The Role of Racial/Ethnic Composition in Prosecution and Sentence," *Journal of Criminal Justice* 26 (1998): 359–372.

20. Michael Edmund O'Neill, "Understanding Federal Prosecutorial Declinations: An Empirical Analysis of Predictive Factors," *American Criminal Law Review* 41 (2004): 1439–1533.

21. Shaila Dewan, "Prosecutors Say Cuts Force Plea Bargains," *The New York Times*, March 10, 2003, p. B3.

22. Charles D. Breitel, "Controls in Criminal Law Enforcement," *University of Chicago Law Review* 27 (1960): 427.

23. Cassia Spohn, Dawn Beichner, and Erika Davis-Frenzel, "Prosecutorial Justifications for Sexual Assault Case Rejection: Guarding the 'Gateway to Justice,'" *Social Problems* 48 (2001): 206–235.

24. "Prosecutor Conduct," editorial, *USA Today*, April 1, 1999, p. 14A.

25. *North Carolina v. Pearce*, 395 US 711 (1969).

26. *Blackledge v. Perry*, 417 US 21 (1974).

27. *Bordenkircher v. Hayes*, 434 US 357 (1978).

28. *Gideon v. Wainwright*, 372 US 335 (1963).

29. *Argersinger v. Hamlin*, 407 US 25 (1972).

30. *Douglas v. California*, 372 US 353 (1963).

31. *In re Gault*, 387 US 1 (1967).

32. *Coleman v. Alabama*, 399 US 1 (1970).

33. *Argersinger v. Hamlin*, 407 US 25 (1972).

34. *Morrissey v. Brewer*, 408 US 471.

35. *Gagnon v. Scarpelli*, 411 US 778.

36. *Ross v. Moffitt*, 417 US 600 (1974).

37. *Scott v. Illinois*, 440 US 367 (1979).

38. *Morris v. Slappy*, 461 US 1 (1983).

39. *Wheat v. United States*, 486 US 153.

40. *United States v. Monsanto*, 491 US 600.

41. *United States v. Gonzalez-Lopez*, 548 US 140 (2006).

42. *Rothgery v. Gillespie County*, 554 US 191 (2008).

43. Stephen D. Owens, Elizabeth Accetta, Jennifer J. Charles, and Samantha E. Shoemaker, *Indigent Defense Services in the United States, FY 2008–2012—Updated* (Washington, DC: Bureau of Justice Statistics, 2014).

44. Caroline Wolf Harlow, *Defense Counsel in Criminal Cases* (Washington, DC: Bureau of Justice Statistics, 2000); see also Arye Rattner, Hagit Turjeman, and Gideon Fishman, "Public versus Private Defense: Can Money Buy Justice?" *Journal of Criminal Justice* 36 (2008): 43–49.

45. *Strickland v. Washington*, 466 US 668 (1984).

46. *Florida v. Nixon*, 543 US 175 (2004).

47. The following sections are based on National Center for State Courts, *The Evolution of a High-Technology Courtroom*, http://www.ncsc.org/sitecore /content/microsites/future-trends -2011/home/technology/1-4-evolution -of-high-tech-courtroom.aspx; Jessica Moyeda, "Courtroom Technology," *Cornell Law School Graduate Student Papers*, Paper 30, http://scholarship .law.cornell.edu/cgi/viewcontent.cgi ?article=1046&context=lps_papers; Patrick Michael, "Technology in the Courtroom," *Law Technology Today*, July 9, 2013, http://www .lawtechnologytoday.org/2013/07 /technology-in-the-courtroom/.

48. *United States v. Cammisano*, 413 F.Supp. 886 (1976).

49. *Imbler v. Pachtman*, 424 US 409 (1976); also see *Burns v. Reed*, 500 US 478 (1991) and *Kalina v. Fletcher*, 522 US 118 (1997).

Chapter 8, Pretrial and Trial Procedures

1. Philip Matthew Stinson, John Liederbach, Steven P. Lab, and Steven L. Brewer, Jr., *Police Integrity Lost: A Study of Law Enforcement Officers Arrested* (Washington, DC: National Institute of Justice, 2016), p. 239.

2. Jack Leonard and James Queally, "Convicting a Police Officer in an On-Duty Shooting Is an Uphill Climb," *Los Angeles Times*, January 11, 2016, http://www.latimes.com/local /lanow/la-me-ln-police-shooting -prosecutions-20160111-story.html.

3. Kimberly Kindy and Kimbriell Kelly, "Thousands Dead, Few Prosecuted," *The Washington Post*, http://www.washingtonpost.com /sf/investigative/2015/04/11 /thousands-dead-few-prosecuted/.

4. Patrick Semansky, "What It's So Hard to Convict Officers Accused of Serious Crimes," *Associated Press*, May 24, 2016, http://www.cbsnews.com/news /difficulty-of-convicting-cops -baltimore-police-officer-edward -nero-acquittal-freddie-gray/.

5. Kindy and Kelly, "Thousands Dead, Few Prosecuted."

6. Ibid.

7. *Stack v. Boyle*, 342 US 1 (1951).

8. Data in this section come from Brian A. Reaves, *Felony Defendants in Large Urban Counties, 2009 – Statistical Tables* (Washington, DC: Bureau of Justice Statistics, 2013) and Thomas Cohen and Tracey Kyckelhahn, *Felony Defendants in Large Urban Counties, 2006* (Washington, DC: Bureau of Justice Statistics, 2010).

9. Traci Schlesinger, "Racial and Ethnic Disparity in Pretrial Criminal Processing," *Justice Quarterly* 22 (2005): 170–192.

10. Cohen and Kyckelhahn, *Felony Defendants in Large Urban Counties*.

11. Vera Institute of Justice, *1961–1971: Programs in Criminal Justice* (New York: Vera Institute of Justice, 1972).

12. Public Law No. 89-465, 18 USC., sec. 3146 (1966).

13. 18 USC., sec. 3142 (1984).

14. See, generally, Fred Cohen, "The New Federal Crime Control Act," *Criminal Law Bulletin* 21 (1985): 330–337.

15. This section leans on John Clark and D. Alan Henry, *Pretrial Services Programming at the Start of the 21st Century: A Survey of Pretrial Services Programs* (Washington, DC: Bureau of Justice Assistance, 2003).

16. Ric Simmons, "Reexamining the Grand Jury: Is There Room for Democracy in the Criminal Justice System?" *Boston University Law Review* 82 (2002): 1–76.

17. John Gibeaut, "Indictment of a System," *ABA Journal* 87 (2001): 34.

18. Kirke D. Weaver, "A Change of Heart or a Change of Law? Withdrawing a Guilty Plea Under Federal Rule of Criminal Procedure 32(e)," *Journal of Criminal Law and Criminology* 92 (2001): 273–306.

19. Anne Piehl and Shawn Bushway, "Measuring and Explaining Charge Bargaining," *Journal of Quantitative Criminology* 23 (2007): 105–125.

20. Shawn D. Bushway, Allison Redlich, and Robert J. Norris, "An Explicit Test of Plea Bargaining in the 'Shadow of the Trial,'" *Criminology* 52 (2014): 723–754.

21. George Fisher, "Plea Bargaining's Triumph," *Yale Law Journal* 109 (2000): 857–1058.

22. Fred Zacharis, "Justice in Plea Bargaining," *William and Mary Law Review* 39 (1998): 1121–1189.

23. Nathaniel J. Pallone, "Without Plea-Bargaining, Megan Kanka Would Be Alive Today," *Criminology and Public Policy* 3 (2003): 83–96.

24. William Stuntz, "Plea Bargaining and Criminal Law's Disappearing Shadow," *Harvard Law Review* 117 (2004): 2548–2569.

25. Mike McConville, "Plea Bargaining: Ethics and Politics," *Journal of Law and Society* 25 (1998): 526–555.

26. *Hill v. Lockhart*, 474 US 52 (1985).

27. *Boykin v. Alabama*, 395 US 238 (1969); *Brady v. United States*, 397 US 742 (1970).

28. *Santobello v. New York*, 404 US 257 (1971).

29. *Ricketts v. Adamson*, 483 US 1 (1987).

30. *Bordenkircher v. Hayes*, 434 US 357 (1978).

31. *North Carolina v. Alford*, 400 US 25 (1970).

32. *United States v. Mezzanatto*, 513 US 196 (1995).

33. Jeremy Ball, "Is It a Prosecutor's World? Determinants of Court Bargaining Decisions," *Journal of Contemporary Criminal Justice* 22 (2006): 241–260.

34. Deirdre M. Bowen, "Calling Your Bluff: How Prosecutors and Defense Attorneys Adapt to Plea Bargaining Strategies to Increase Formalization," *Justice Quarterly* 26 (2009): 2–29.

35. Stephen P. Lagoy, Joseph J. Senna, and Larry J. Siegel, "An Empirical Study on Information Usage for Prosecutorial Decision Making in Plea Negotiations," *American Criminal Law Review* 13 (1976): 435–471.

36. Besiki Luka Kutateladze, Nancy R. Andiloro, and Brian D. Johnson, "Opening Pandora's Box: How Does Defendant Race Influence Plea Bargaining?" *Justice Quarterly* 33 (2016): 398–426.

37. Keith Bystrom, "Communicating Plea Offers to the Client," in *Ethical Problems Facing the Criminal Defense Lawyer*, ed. Rodney Uphoff (Chicago: American Bar Association Section on Criminal Justice, 1995), p. 84.

38. American Bar Association, *Standards Relating to Pleas of Guilty*, standard 3.3; National Advisory Commission on Criminal Justice Standards and Goals, Task Force Report on Courts (Washington, DC: Government Printing Office, 1973), p. 42.

39. American Bar Association, *Standards Relating to Pleas of Guilty*, p. 73; see also Alan Alschuler, "The Trial Judge's Role in Plea Bargaining," *Columbia Law Review* 76 (1976): 1059.

40. Barbara Boland and Brian Forst, *The Prevalence of Guilty Pleas* (Washington, DC: Bureau of Justice Statistics, 1984), p. 3; see also Gary Hengstler, "The Troubled Justice System," *American Bar Association Journal* 80 (1994): 44.

41. National Institute of Law Enforcement and Criminal Justice, *Plea Bargaining in the United States*, pp. 37–40.

42. For a discussion of this issue, see Michael Tonry, "Plea Bargaining Bans and Rules," in *Sentencing Reform Impacts* (Washington, DC: Government Printing Office, 1987).

43. Franklyn Dunford, D. Wayne Osgood, and Hart Weichselbaum, *National Evaluation of Diversion Programs* (Washington, DC: Government Printing Office, 1982).

44. Sharla Rausch and Charles Logan, "Diversion from Juvenile Court: Panacea or Pandora's Box?" in *Evaluating Juvenile Justice*, ed. James Kleugel (Beverly Hills, CA: Sage, 1983), pp. 19–30.

45. John Hepburn, "Recidivism Among Drug Offenders Following Exposure to Treatment," *Criminal Justice Policy Review* 16 (2005): 237–259.

46. *Tumey v. Ohio*, 273 US 510 (1927), at 523.

47. See, for example, Minn. R. Crim. P. 26.03, subd. 13(4).

48. *Riggins v. Nevada*, 504 US 127 (1992).

49. *Diaz v. United States*, 223 US 442 (1912); *Taylor v. Illinois*, 484 US 400 (1988).

50. *Illinois v. Allen*, 397 US 337 (1970).

51. *Maryland v. Craig*, 497 US 836 (1990).

52. *Washington v. Texas*, 388 US 14 (1967).

53. *Baldwin v. New York*, 399 US 66 (1970).

54. *Scott v. Illinois*, 440 US 367 (1979).

55. *Shelton v. Alabama*, 122 US 1764 (2002).

56. *Faretta v. California*, 422 US 806 (1975).

57. See American Bar Association, *Standards Relating to Speedy Trial* (Chicago: ABA, 1995).

58. *Klopfer v. North Carolina*, 386 US 213 (1967).

59. *Wilson v. Layne*, 526 US 603 (1999).

60. See *Brinegar v. United States*, 338 US 160 (1949); *In re Winship*, 397 US 358, 90 (1970).

61. *Brinegar v. United States*, at 174.

62. See *In re Winship*, at 397.

63. Ibid., at 371, 90 S. Ct. at 1076.

64. Brian Kalt, "The Exclusion of Felons from Jury Service," *American University Law Review* 53 (2003): 65–189.

65. George Hayden, Joseph Senna, and Larry Siegel, "Prosecutorial Discretion in Peremptory Challenges: An Empirical Investigation of Information Use in the Massachusetts Jury Selection Process," *New England Law Review* 13 (1978): 768.

66. *Batson v. Kentucky*, 476 US 79 (1986); see also Alan Alschuler and Randall Kennedy, "Equal Justice—Would Color-Conscious Jury Selection Help?" *American Bar Association Journal* 81 (1995): 36–37.

67. John Schwartz, "As Jurors Turn to Web, Mistrials Are Popping Up," *The New York Times*, March 17, 2009, http://www.nytimes.com/2009/03/18/us/18juries.html.

68. Arie Rubenstein, "Verdicts of Conscience: Nullification and the Modern Jury Trial," *Columbia Law Review* 106 (2006): 959–993.

69. David Pepper, "Nullifying History: Modern-Day Misuse of the Right to Decide the Law," *Case Western Reserve Law Review* 50 (2000): 599–643.

70. *Chapman v. California*, 386 US 18 (1967).

71. *Douglas v. California*, 372 US 353 (1963).

Chapter 9, Punishment and Sentencing

1. Data are drawn from http://www.deathpenaltyinfo.org/; 2017 data are not yet available as of this writing.

2. Pew Research Center, *Less Support for Death Penalty, Especially Among Democrats*, April 16, 2015, http://www.people-press.org/2015/04/16/less-support-for-death-penalty-especially-among-democrats/.

3. Death Penalty Information Center, http://www.deathpenaltyinfo.org/abolitionist-and-retentionist-countries.

4. Among the most helpful sources for this section were Benedict Alper, *Prisons Inside-Out* (Cambridge, MA: Ballinger, 1974); Gustave de Beaumont and Alexis de Tocqueville, *On the Penitentiary System in the United States and Its Applications in France* (Carbondale: Southern Illinois University Press, 1964); Orlando Lewis, *The Development of American Prisons and Prison Customs, 1776–1845* (Montclair, NJ: Patterson-Smith, 1967); Leonard Orland, ed., *Justice, Punishment, and Treatment* (New York: Free Press, 1973); J. Goebel, *Felony and Misdemeanor* (Philadelphia: University of Pennsylvania Press, 1976); Georg Rusche and Otto Kircheimer, *Punishment and Social Structure* (New York: Russell & Russell, 1939); Samuel Walker, *Popular Justice* (New York: Oxford University Press, 1980); Graeme R. Newman, *The Punishment Response* (Piscataway, NJ: Transaction Publishers, 2008); David Rothman, *Conscience and Convenience* (Boston: Little, Brown, 1980); George Ives, *A History of Penal Methods* (Montclair, NJ: Patterson-Smith, 1970); Robert Hughes, *The Fatal Shore* (New York: Knopf, 1986); Leon Radzinowicz, *A History of English Criminal Law*, Vol. 1 (London: Stevens, 1943), p. 5.

5. *Crime and Punishment in America, 1999*, Report 229 (Washington, DC: National Center for Policy Analysis, 1999).

6. Sean Rosenmerkel, Matthew Durose, and Patrick Langan, *Felony Sentences in State Courts, 2006* (Washington, DC: Bureau of Justice Statistics, 2009), p. 6.

7. Matthew R. Durose, Alexia D. Cooper, and Howard N. Snyder, *Recidivism of Prisoners Released in 30 States in 2005: Patterns from 2005 to 2010* (Washington, DC: Bureau of Justice Statistics, 2014).

8. Faith Lutze, "The Influence of Shock Incarceration Program on Inmate Adjustment and Attitudinal Change," *Journal of Criminal Justice* 29 (2001): 255–266.

9. E. Ann Carson, *Prisoners in 2015* (Washington, DC: Bureau of Justice Statistics, 2016).

10. Tomislav Kovandzic and Lynne Vieraitis, "The Effect of County-Level Prison Population Growth on Crime Rates," *Criminology and Public Policy* 5 (2006): 213–244.

11. Raymond Liedka, Anne Morrison Piehl, and Bert Useem, "The Crime-Control Effect of Incarceration: Does Scale Matter?" *Criminology and Public Policy* 5 (2006): 245–276.

12. Ibid.

13. Charles Logan, *Criminal Justice Performance Measures for Prisons* (Washington, DC: Bureau of Justice Statistics, 1993), p. 3.

14. Alexis Durham, "The Justice Model in Historical Context: Early Law, the Emergence of Science, and the Rise of Incarceration," *Journal of Criminal Justice* 16 (1988): 331–346.

15. Andrew von Hirsh, *Doing Justice: The Choice of Punishments* (New York: Hill and Wang, 1976).

16. Shawn Bushway, "The Impact of an Arrest on the Job Stability of Young White American Men," *Journal of Research in Crime and Delinquency* 35 (1998): 454–479.

17. Lawrence W. Sherman, David P. Farrington, Doris Layton MacKenzie, Brandon Walsh, Denise Gottfredson, John Eck, Shawn Bushway, and Peter Reuter, *Evidence-Based Crime Prevention* (London: Routledge and Kegan Paul, 2002); see also Arnulf Kolstad, "Imprisonment as Rehabilitation: Offenders' Assessment of Why It Does Not Work," *Journal of Criminal Justice* 24 (1996): 323–335.

18. Francis Cullen, John Paul Wright, Shayna Brown, Melissa Moon, and Brandon Applegate, "Public Support for Early Intervention Programs: Implications for a Progressive Policy Agenda," *Crime and Delinquency* 44 (1998): 187–204; Richard McCorkle, "Research Note: Punish and Rehabilitate? Public Attitudes Toward Six Common Crimes," *Crime and Delinquency* 39 (1993): 240–252; D. A. Andrews, Ivan Zinger, Robert Hoge, James Bonta, Paul Gendreau, and Francis Cullen, "Does Correctional Treatment Work? A Clinically Relevant and Psychologically Informed Meta-Analysis," *Criminology* 28 (1990): 369–404.

19. Paula Ditton and Doris James Wilson, *Truth in Sentencing in State Prisons* (Washington, DC: Bureau of Justice Statistics, 1999).

20. Jo Dixon, "The Organizational Context of Criminal Sentencing," *American Journal of Sociology* 100 (1995): 1157–1198.

21. Michael Tonry, *Reconsidering Indeterminate and Structured Sentencing Series: Sentencing and Corrections: Issues for the 21st Century* (Washington, DC: National Institute of Justice, 1999).

22. *Blakely v. Washington*, 542 US 296 (2004).

23. *United States v. Booker*, 543 US 220 (2005).

24. Michael Tonry, "The Failure of the US Sentencing Commission's Guidelines," *Crime and Delinquency* 39 (1993): 131–149.

25. Sean Nicholson-Crotty, "The Impact of Sentencing Guidelines on State-Level Sanctions: An Analysis over Time," *Crime and Delinquency* 50 (2004): 395–410.

26. United States Sentencing Commission, "Final Report on the Impact of *United States v. Booker* on Federal Sentencing," March 2006, http://www.ussc.gov/sites/default/files/pdf/news/congressional-testimony-and-reports/submissions/200603-booker/Booker_Report.pdf.

27. Jeffrey T. Ulmer, Megan C. Kurlychek, and John H. Kramer, "Prosecutorial Discretion and the Imposition of Mandatory Minimum Sentences," *Journal of Research in Crime and Delinquency* 44 (2007): 427–458.

28. See, for example, John L. Worrall, *Crime Control in America: What Works?* (Boston: Allyn & Bacon, 2008), pp. 193–199.

29. Marc Mauer, *Americans Behind Bars: The International Use of Incarceration, 1992–93: Part II* (Washington, DC: The Sentencing Project, 1994).

30. For a review of the literature, see John L. Worrall, *Crime Control in America: What Works?* 2nd ed. (Boston: Allyn & Bacon, 2008), pp. 198–199.

31. Thomas B. Marvell and Carlisle E. Moody, "The Lethal Effects of Three-Strikes Laws," *Journal of Legal Studies* 30 (2001): 89–106; Thomas Kovandzic, John J. Sloan, III, and Lynne M. Vieraitis, "Unintended Consequences of Politically Popular Sentencing Policy: The Homicide-Promoting Effects of 'Three Strikes' in US Cities (1980–1999)," *Criminology and Public Policy* 1 (2002): 159–201.

32. *Lockyer v. Andrade*, 538 US 63 (2003).

33. *Ewing v. California*, 538 US 11 (2003).

34. The most recent data as of this writing are found in Matthew Durose and Patrick Langan, *Felony Sentences in State Courts, 2006* (Washington, DC: Bureau of Justice Statistics, 2009), https://www.bjs.gov/content/pub/pdf/fssc06st.pdf.

35. Ibid.

36. Brent Smith and Kelly Damphouse, "Terrorism, Politics, and Punishment: A Test of Structural-Contextual Theory and the Liberation Hypothesis," *Criminology* 36 (1998): 67–92.

37. Stewart D'Alessio and Lisa Stolzenberg, "Socioeconomic Status and the Sentencing of the Traditional Offender," *Journal of Criminal Justice* 21 (1993): 61–77.

38. Travis W. Franklin, "Sentencing Outcomes in US District Courts: Can Offenders' Educational Attainment Guard Against Prevalent Criminal Stereotypes?" *Crime and Delinquency* 63 (2017): 137–165.

39. Cecilia Saulters-Tubbs, "Prosecutorial and Judicial Treatment of Female Offenders," *Federal Probation* 57 (1993): 37–41.

40. See, for example, Janet Johnston, Thomas Kennedy, and I. Gayle Shuman, "Gender Differences in the Sentencing of Felony Offenders," *Federal Probation* 87 (1987): 49–56; Cassia Spohn and Susan Welch, "The Effect of Prior Record in Sentencing Research: An Examination of the Assumption that Any Measure Is Adequate," *Justice Quarterly* 4 (1987): 286–302; David Willison, "The Effects of Counsel on the Severity of Criminal Sentences. A Statistical Assessment," *Justice System Journal* 9 (1984): 87–101.

41. Cassia Spohn, Miriam DeLone, and Jeffrey Spears, "Race/Ethnicity, Gender, and Sentence Severity in Dade County, Florida: An Examination of the Decision to Withhold Adjudication," *Journal of Crime and Justice* 21 (1998): 111–132.

42. Ellen Hochstedler Steury and Nancy Frank, "Gender Bias and Pretrial Release: More Pieces of the Puzzle," *Journal of Criminal Justice* 18 (1990): 417–432.

43. Shimica Gaskins, "Women of Circumstance—The Effects of Mandatory Minimum Sentencing on Women Minimally Involved in Drug Crimes," *American Criminal Law Review* 41 (2004): 1533–1563.

44. Stephanie Bontrager, Kelle Barrick, and Elizabeth Stupi, "Gender and Sentencing: A Meta-Analysis of Contemporary Research," *Journal of Gender, Race, and Justice* 26 (2013): 349–367.

45. Shawn Bushway and Anne Morrison Piehl, "The Inextricable Link Between Age and Criminal History in Sentencing," *Crime and Delinquency* 53 (2007): 156–183.

46. Dean Champion, "Elderly Felons and Sentencing Severity: Interregional Variations in Leniency and Sentencing Trends," *Criminal Justice Review* 12 (1987): 7–15.

47. Darrell Steffensmeier, John Kramer, and Jeffery Ulmer, "Age Differences in Sentencing," *Justice Quarterly* 12 (1995): 583–601.

48. Darrell Steffensmeier, Jeffery Ulmer, and John Kramer, "The Interaction of Race, Gender, and Age in Criminal Sentencing: The Punishment Cost of Being Young, Black, and Male," *Criminology* 36 (1998): 763–798.

49. Tracy Nobiling, Cassia Spohn, and Miriam DeLone, "A Tale of Two Counties: Unemployment and Sentence Severity," *Justice Quarterly* 15 (1998): 459–486.

50. Shawn Bushway and Anne Morrison Piehl, "Judging Judicial Discretion: Legal Factors and Racial Discrimination in Sentencing," *Law and Society Review* 35 (2001): 733–765.

51. Michael Tonry, *Malign Neglect: Race, Crime, and Punishment in America* (New York: Oxford University Press, 1995), pp. 105–109.

52. Travis W. Franklin, "Race and Ethnicity Effects in Federal Sentencing: A Propensity Score Analysis," *Justice Quarterly* 32 (2015): 653–679.

53. John Wooldredge, "Neighborhood Effects on Felony Sentencing," *Journal of Research in Crime and Delinquency* 44 (2007): 238–263.

54. Cassia Spohn, "Thirty Years of Sentencing Reform: A Quest for a Racially Neutral Sentencing Process," in *Policies, Processes, and Decisions of the Criminal Justice System*, Vol. 3, *Criminal Justice 2000* (Washington, DC: US Department of Justice, 2000), pp. 455–456.

55. Ibid.

56. Rhys Hester and Todd K. Hartman, "Conditional Race Disparities in Criminal Sentencing: A Test of the Liberation Hypothesis from a Non-guidelines State," *Journal of Quantitative Criminology* 33 (2017): 77–100.

57. Eric P. Baumer, "Reassessing and Redirecting Research on Race and Sentencing," *Justice Quarterly* 30 (2013): 231–261.

58. Bruce Western, *Punishment and Inequality in America* (New York: Russell Sage Foundation, 2006).

59. See, for example, Tara N. Richards, Wesley G. Jennings, M. Dwayne Smith, et al., "Explaining the 'Female Victim Effect' in Capital Punishment: An Examination of Victim Sex-Specific Models of Juror Sentence Decision-Making," *Crime and Delinquency* 62 (2016): 875–898.

60. *Payne v. Tennessee*, 501 US 808 (1991).

61. Robert Davis and Barbara Smith, "The Effects of Victim Impact Statements on Sentencing Decisions: A Test in an Urban Setting," *Justice Quarterly* 11 (1994): 453–469; Edna Erez and Pamela Tontodonato, "The Effect of Victim Participation in Sentencing on Sentence Outcome," *Criminology* 28 (1990): 451–474.

62. Rodney Kingsworth, Randall MacIntosh, and Jennifer Wentworth, "Sexual Assault: The Role of Prior Relationship and Victim Characteristics in Case Processing," *Justice Quarterly* 16 (1999): 276–302.

63. *Coker v. Georgia*, 433 US 584 (1977); see also *Lockett v. Ohio*, 438 US 586 (1978).

64. For more on this issue, read Hugo Adam and Paul Cassell, *Debating the Death Penalty: Should America Have Capital Punishment? The Experts on Both Sides Make Their Best Case* (London: Oxford University Press, 2003).

65. Stephen Layson, "United States Time-Series Homicide Regressions with Adaptive Expectations," *Bulletin of the New York Academy of Medicine* 62 (1986): 589–619.

66. James Galliher and John Galliher, "A 'Commonsense' Theory of Deterrence and the 'Ideology' of Science: The New York State Death Penalty Debate," *Journal of Criminal Law and Criminology* 92 (2002): 307.

67. Steven Stack, "The Effect of Well-Publicized Executions on Homicide in California," *Journal of Crime and Justice* 21 (1998): 1–12.

68. David Friedrichs, "Comment—Humanism and the Death Penalty: An Alternative Perspective," *Justice Quarterly* 6 (1989): 197–209.

69. Alexis Durham, H. Preston Elrod, and Patrick Kinkade, "Public Support to the Death Penalty: Beyond Gallup," *Justice Quarterly* 13 (1996): 705–736.

70. Marvin Zalman, "Qualitatively Estimating the Incidence of Wrongful Convictions," *Criminal Law Bulletin* 48 (2012): 221–279.

NOTES   **N-19**

71. The Innocence Project, http://www.innocenceproject.org.

72. Samuel R. Gross, Barbara O'Brien, and Edward H. Kennedy, "Rate of False Conviction of Criminal Defendants Who Are Sentenced to Death," *Proceedings of the National Academy of Sciences*, http://www.pnas.org/content/111/20/7230.full.

73. Baxter Oliphant, *Support for Death Penalty Lowest in More than Four Decades*, http://www.pewresearch.org/fact-tank/2016/09/29/support-for-death-penalty-lowest-in-more-than-four-decades/.

74. *Sourcebook of Criminal Justice Statistics*, "Attitudes Toward the Better Penalty for Murder," http://www.albany.edu/sourcebook/pdf/t2492010.pdf.

75. James Unnever and Francis Cullen, "Executing the Innocent and Support for Capital Punishment: Implications for Public Policy," *Criminology and Public Policy* 4 (2005): 3–37.

76. Scott Vollum, Dennis Longmire, and Jacqueline Buffington-Vollum, "Confidence in the Death Penalty and Support for Its Use: Exploring the Value-Expressive Dimension of Death Penalty Attitudes," *Justice Quarterly* 21 (2004): 521–546.

77. Gennaro Vito and Thomas Keil, "Elements of Support for Capital Punishment: An Examination of Changing Attitudes," *Journal of Crime and Justice* 21 (1998): 17–25.

78. Denise Paquette Boots, Kathleen Heide, and John Cochran, "Death Penalty Support for Special Offender Populations of Legally Convicted Murderers: Juveniles, the Mentally Retarded, and the Mentally Incompetent," *Behavioral Sciences and the Law* 22 (2004): 223–238.

79. James Unnever and Francis Cullen, "The Racial Divide in Support for the Death Penalty: Does White Racism Matter?" *Social Forces* 85 (2007): 1281–1301.

80. D. Nagin and J. Petter, *Deterrence and the Death Penalty*, Committee on Law and Justice at the National Research Council, April 2012, http://www.nap.edu/catalog/13363/deterrence-and-the-death-penalty.

81. Isaac Ehrlich, "The Deterrent Effect of Capital Punishment: A Question of Life or Death," *American Economic Review* 65 (1975): 397.

82. For a review, see William Bailey, "The General Prevention Effect of Capital Punishment for Noncapital Felonies," in *The Death Penalty in America: Current Research*, ed. Robert Bohm (Cincinnati: Anderson, 1991), pp. 21–38.

83. Bijou Yang and David Lester, "The Deterrent Effect of Executions: A Meta-Analysis of Thirty Years After Ehrlich," *Journal of Criminal Justice* 36 (2008): 453–460.

84. Rick Ruddell and Martin Urbina, "Minority Threat and Punishment: A Cross-National Analysis," *Justice Quarterly* 21 (2004): 903–931.

85. Marian Williams and Jefferson Holcomb, "Racial Disparity and Death Sentences in Ohio," *Journal of Criminal Justice* 29 (2001): 207–218.

86. Jon Sorenson and Donald Wallace, "Prosecutorial Discretion in Seeking Death: An Analysis of Racial Disparity in the Pretrial Stages of Case Processing in a Midwestern County," *Justice Quarterly* 16 (1999): 559–578.

87. Marian R. Williams, "Understanding the Influence of Victim Gender in Death Penalty Cases: The Importance of Victim Race, Sex-Related Victimization, and Jury Decision Making," *Criminology* 45 (2007): 865–891; Catherine Lee, "Hispanics and the Death Penalty: Discriminatory Charging Practices in San Joaquin County, California," *Journal of Criminal Justice* 35 (2007): 17–27.

88. Jefferson Holcomb, Marian Williams, and Stephen Demuth, "White Female Victims and Death Penalty Disparity Research," *Justice Quarterly* 21 (2004): 877–902.

89. Lawrence Greenfield and David Hinners, *Capital Punishment, 1984* (Washington, DC: Bureau of Justice Statistics, 1985).

90. Death Penalty Information Center, *Facts about the Death Penalty*, http://www.deathpenaltyinfo.org/documents/FactSheet.pdf.

91. Gennaro Vito and Thomas Keil, "Capital Sentencing in Kentucky: An Analysis of the Factors Influencing Decision Making in the Post-*Gregg* Period," *Journal of Criminal Law and Criminology* 79 (1988): 483–508.

92. Geoffrey Rapp, "The Economics of Shootouts: Does the Passage of Capital Punishment Laws Protect or Endanger Police Officers?" *Albany Law Review* 65 (2002): 1051–1084.

93. William Bailey, "Disaggregation in Deterrence and Death Penalty Research: The Case of Murder in Chicago," *Journal of Criminal Law and Criminology* 74 (1986): 827–859.

94. Gennaro Vito, Pat Koester, and Deborah Wilson, "Return of the Dead: An Update on the Status of Furman-Commuted Death Row Inmates," in *The Death Penalty in America*, ed. Bohm, pp. 89–100; Gennaro Vito, Deborah Wilson, and Edward Latessa, "Comparison of the Dead: Attributes and Outcomes of Furman-Commuted Death Row Inmates in Kentucky and Ohio," in *The Death Penalty in America*, ed. Bohm, pp. 101–112.

95. John Cochran, Mitchell Chamlin, and Mark Seth, "Deterrence or Brutalization? An Impact Assessment of Oklahoma's Return to Capital Punishment," *Criminology* 32 (1994): 107–134.

96. William Bailey, "Deterrence, Brutalization, and the Death Penalty: Another Examination of Oklahoma's Return to Capital Punishment," *Justice Quarterly* 36 (1998): 711–734.

97. *Hill v. McDonough*, 547 US 573 (2006).

98. Robert Johnson, *Death Work: A Study of the Modern Execution Process* (Pacific Grove, CA: Brooks/Cole, 1990).

99. Death Penalty Information Center, *Abolitionist and Retionist Countries*, http://www.deathpenaltyinfo.org/abolitionist-and-retentionist-countries.

100. LiYing Li, "The Tainted Milk Scandal: Punishing Economic Criminals in China," unpublished paper (Denver: Metropolitan College of Denver, 2011).

101. Tracy L. Snell, *Capital Punishment, 2011* (Washington, DC: Bureau of Justice Statistics, 2011), p. 12.

102. See, for example, Ernest Van Den Haag, *Punishing Criminals: Concerning a Very Old and Painful Question* (New York: Basic Books, 1975), pp. 209–211; Walter Berns, "Defending the Death Penalty," *Crime and Delinquency* 26 (1980): 503–511.

103. Thoroddur Bjarnason and Michael Welch, "Father Knows Best: Parishes, Priests, and American Catholic Parishioners' Attitudes Toward Capital Punishment," *Journal for the Scientific Study of Religion* 43 (2004): 103–118.

104. Franklin Zimring, *The Contradictions of American Capital Punishment* (London: Oxford University Press, 2003).

105. Vance McLaughlin and Paul Blackman, "Mass Legal Executions in Georgia," *Georgia Historical Quarterly* 88 (2004): 66–84.

106. Austin Sarat, "Innocence, Error, and the 'New Abolitionism': A Commentary," *Criminology and Public Policy* 4 (2005): 45–53.

107. *Furman v. Georgia*, 408 US 238 (1972).

108. *Gregg v. Georgia*, 428 US 153 (1976).

109. Ibid., at pp. 205–207.

110. *Ring v. Arizona*, 536 US 584 (2002).

111. *Furman v. Georgia*, 408 US 238 (1972).

112. *Gregg v. Georgia*, 428 US 153 (1976).

113. *Woodson v. North Carolina*, 428 US 280 (1976).

114. *Coker v. Georgia*, 430 US 349 (1977).

115. *Lockett v. Ohio*, 438 US 586 (1978).

116. *Enmund v. Florida*, 458 US 782 (1982).

117. *Glass v. Louisiana*, 471 US 1080 (1985).

118. *Cubana v. Bullock*, 474 US 376 (1986).

119. *Ford v. Wainwright*, 477 US 399 (1986).

120. *Atkins v. Virginia*, 536 US 304 (2002).

121. *Ring v. Arizona*, 536 US 584 (2002).

122. *Roper v. Simmons*, 543 US 551 (2005).

123. *Deck v. Missouri*, 544 US 622 (2005).

124. *Oregon v. Guzek*, 546 US 517 (2006).

125. *Baze v. Rees*, 553 US 35 (2008).

126. *Kennedy v. Louisiana*, 554 US 407 (2008).

127. *Glossip v. Gross*, 576 US ___ (2015).

128. Larry Welborn, "Relatives of Woman Slain in 1988 Offer Victim-Impact Statements," *Orange County Register*, March 14, 2012, p. 8.
Chapter 10, Community Sentences: Probation, Intermediate Sanctions, and Restorative Justice

1. Allie Gross, "In Georgia, a Traffic Ticket Can Land You in the Slammer," *Motherjones*, February 26, 2015, http://www.motherjones.com/politics/2015/02/georgia-probation-misdemeanor-poor-jail.

2. Robina Institute of Criminal Law and Criminal Justice, *American Exceptionalism in Probation Supervision* (Minneapolis, MN: Robina Institute, February 2, 2016), https://robinainstitute.umn.edu/publications/data-brief-american-exceptionalism-probation-supervision.

3. Data were drawn from the United Nations Office on Drugs and Crime, https://data.unodc.org/.

4. Brandon Applegate, Hayden Smith, Alicia Sitren, and Nicolette Fariello Springer, "From the Inside: The Meaning of Probation to Probationers," *Criminal Justice Review* 34 (2009): 80–95.

5. Christopher Krebs, Kevin Strom, Willem Koetse, and Pamela Lattimore, "The Impact of Residential and Nonresidential Drug Treatment on Recidivism Among Drug-Involved Probationers: A Survival Analysis," *Crime and Delinquency* 55 (2009): 442–471.

6. Applegate, Smith, Sitren, and Springer, "From the Inside: The Meaning of Probation to Probationers"; for a history of probation, see Edward Sieh, "From Augustus to the Progressives: A Study of Probation's Formative Years," *Federal Probation* 57 (1993): 67–72.

7. Sieh, "From Augustus to the Progressives."

8. David Rothman, *Conscience and Convenience* (Boston: Little, Brown, 1980), pp. 82–117.

9. Ibid.

10. Danielle Kaeble and Thomas P. Bonczar, *Probation and Parole in the United States, 2015* (Washington, DC: Bureau of Justice Statistics, 2016).

11. *Gall v. United States*, 552 US 38 (2007).

12. Sean Rosenmerkel, Matthew Durose, and Donald Farole, Jr., *Felony Sentences in State Courts, 2006* (Washington, DC: Bureau of Justice Statistics, 2009), http://bjs.ojp.usdoj.gov/content/pub/ascii/fssc06st.txt.

13. Ibid.

14. Heather Barklage, Dane Miller, and Gene Bonham Jr., "Probation Conditions vs. Probation Officer Directives," *Federal Probation* 70 (2006), http://www.uscourts.gov/statistics-reports/publications/federal-probation-journal.

15. Karl Hanson and Suzanne Wallace-Carpretta, "Predictors of Criminal Recidivism among Male Batterers," *Psychology, Crime and Law* 10 (2004): 413–427.

16. *Higdon v. United States*, 627 F.2d 893 (9th Cir., 1980).

17. *United States v. Lee*, No. 01-4485 01/07/03, *United States v. Lee*, PICS N. 03-0023.

18. *United States v. Gallo*, 20 F.3d 7 (1st Cir., 1994).

19. Todd Clear and Edward Latessa, "Probation Officers' Roles in Intensive Supervision: Surveillance versus Treatment," *Justice Quarterly* 10 (1993): 441–462.

20. Jay Whetzel, Mario Paparozzi, Melissa Alexander, and Christopher Lowenkamp, "Goodbye to a Worn-Out Dichotomy: Law Enforcement, Social Work, and a Balanced Approach," *Federal Probation* 75 (2011): 7–12.

21. Joel Miller, "Contemporary Modes of Probation Officer Supervision: The Triumph of the 'Synthetic' Officer?" *Justice Quarterly.* 32 (2015): 314–336.

22. Jeffrey Lin, Joel Miller, and Mayumi Fukushima, "Juvenile Probation Officers' Dispositional Recommendations: Predictive Factors and Their Alignment with Predictors of Recidivism," *Journal of Crime and Justice* 31 (2008): 1–34.

23. Jill Viglione, Danielle Rudes, and Faye Taxman, "Misalignment in Supervision: Implementing Risk/Needs Assessment Instruments in Probation," *Criminal Justice and Behavior* 42 (2015): 263–285.

24. Lawrence Sherman, "Use Probation to Prevent Murder," *Criminology and Public Policy* 6 (2007): 843–849.

25. Melinda Schlager, "Validity of the Level of Service Inventory-Revised (LSI-R) Among African American and Hispanic Male Offenders," *Criminal Justice and Behavior* 34 (2007): 545–554; Carolin Kroner, Cornelis Stadtland, Matthias Eidt, and Norbert Nedopil, "The Validity of the Violence Risk Appraisal Guide (VRAG) in Predicting Criminal Recidivism," *Criminal Behaviour and Mental Health* 17 (2007): 89–100.

26. Melissa Alexander, Bradley Whitley, and Christopher Bersch, "Driving Evidence-Based Supervision to the Next Level: Utilizing PCRA, 'Drivers,' and Effective Supervision Techniques," *Federal Probation* 78 (2014), http://www.uscourts.gov/statistics-reports/publications/federal-probation-journal.

27. Diana Wendy Fitzgibbon, "Deconstructing Probation: Risk and Developments in Practice," *Journal of Social Work Practice* 22 (2008): 85–101.

28. Nancy Ritter, "Predicting Recidivism Risk: New Tool in Philadelphia Shows Great Promise," *NIJ Journal* 271 (2013): 4–10, http://www.nij.gov/journals/271/Pages/predicting-recidivism.aspx.

29. "Rape Victim's Mom Sues Attacker and Probation Chief," CBS Chicago, January 26, 2011, http://chicago.cbslocal.com/2011/01/26/rape-victims-family-sues-county-probation-dept/.
NOTES   N-21

30. Mary McMurran, "Motivational Interviewing with Offenders: A Systematic Review," *Legal and Criminological Psychology* 14 (2009): 83–100; Scott Walters, Amanda Vader, Norma Nguyen, Robert Harris, and Jennifer Eells, "Motivational Interviewing as a Supervision Strategy in Probation: A Randomized Effectiveness Trial," *Journal of Offender Rehabilitation* 49 (2010): 309–323.

31. *Minnesota v. Murphy*, 465 US 420 (1984).

32. *Griffin v. Wisconsin*, 483 US 868 (1987).

33. *United States v. Knights*, 534 US 112 (2001).

34. *Mempa v. Rhay*, 389 US 128 (1967).

35. *Morrissey v. Brewer*, 408 US 471 (1972).

36. *Gagnon v. Scarpelli*, 411 US 778 (1973).

37. *Beardon v. Georgia*, 461 US 660 (1983).

38. *United States v. Granderson*, 511 US 39 (1994).

39. See, for example, Christian Henrichson, Joshua Rinaldi, and Ruth Delaney, *The Price of Jails: Measuring the Taxpayer Cost of Local Incarceration* (New York: Vera Institute of Justice, 2015).

40. M. Kevin Gray, Monique Fields, and Sheila Royo Maxwell, "Examining Probation Violations: Who, What, and When," *Crime and Delinquency* 47 (2001): 537–557.

41. Kelli Stevens-Martin, Olusegun Oyewole, and Cynthia Hipolito, "Technical Revocations of Probation in One Jurisdiction: Uncovering the Hidden Realities" *Federal Probation* 78 (2014), http://www.uscourts.gov/statistics-reports/publications/federal-probation-journal; Nancy Rodriguez and Vincent Webb, "Probation Violations, Revocations, and Imprisonment: The Decisions of Probation Officers, Prosecutors, and Judges Pre- and Post-Mandatory Drug Treatment," *Criminal Justice Policy Review* 18 (2007): 3–30.

42. Krebs, Strom, Koetse, and Lattimore, "The Impact of Residential and Nonresidential Drug Treatment on Recidivism Among Drug-Involved Probationers."

43. Eladio Castillo and Leanne Alarid Fiftal, "Factors Associated with Recidivism Among Offenders with Mental Illness," *International Journal of Offender Therapy and Comparative Criminology* 55 (2011): 98–117.

44. Joan Petersilia, Susan Turner, James Kahan, and Joyce Peterson, *Granting Felons Probation: Public Risks and Alternatives* (Santa Monica, CA: Rand, 1985).

45. Cassia Spohn and David Holleran, "The Effect of Imprisonment on Recidivism Rates of Felony Offenders: A Focus on Drug Offenders," *Criminology* 40 (2002): 329–359.

46. Daniel Mears, Joshua Cochran, and William Bales, "Gender Differences in the Effects of Prison on Recidivism," *Journal of Criminal Justice* 50 (2012): 370–378.

47. Paula M. Ditton, *Mental Health and Treatment of Inmates and Probationers* (Washington, DC: Bureau of Justice Statistics, 1999).

48. Kathryn Morgan, "Factors Associated with Probation Outcome," *Journal of Criminal Justice* 22 (1994): 341–353.

49. Naomi Freeman, "Predictors of Rearrest for Rapists and Child Molesters on Probation," *Criminal Justice and Behavior* 34 (2007): 752–768.

50. Kathryn Morgan, "Factors Influencing Probation Outcome: A Review of the Literature," *Federal Probation* 57 (1993): 23–29.

51. Fitzgibbon, "Deconstructing Probation."

52. Joan Petersilia, "Probation in the United States," in *Crime and Justice: A Review of Research* 21 (Chicago: University of Chicago Press, 1997), p. 185.

53. "Law in Massachusetts Requires Probationers to Pay 'Day Fees,'" *Criminal Justice Newsletter*, September 15, 1988, p. 1.

54. Peter Finn and Dale Parent, *Making the Offender Foot the Bill: A Texas Program* (Washington, DC: National Institute of Justice, 1992).

55. State of Arizona, Senate Bill 1476 (2008), http://www.azleg.gov/legtext/48leg/2r/bills/sb1476p.pdf.

56. Nicole Leeper Piquero, "A Recidivism Analysis of Maryland's Community Probation Program," *Journal of Criminal Justice* 31 (2003): 295–308.

57. Todd R. Clear, "Places Not Cases: Rethinking the Probation Focus," *Howard Journal of Criminal Justice* 44 (2005): 172–184.

58. Andrew Klein and Ann Crowe, "Findings from an Outcome Examination of Rhode Island's Specialized Domestic Violence Probation Supervision Program," *Violence Against Women* 14 (2008): 226–246.

59. Roberto Hugh Potter and Timothy Akers, "Improving the Health of Minority Communities Through Probation-Public Health Collaborations: An Application of the Epidemiological Criminology Framework," *Journal of Offender Rehabilitation* 49 (2010): 595–609.

60. Private Probation Services, http://www.privateprobationservices.com/(accessed March 2017).

61. Christine Schloss and Leanne Alarid, "Standards in the Privatization of Probation Services: A Statutory Analysis," *Criminal Justice Review* 32 (2007): 233–245.

62. "HOPE in Hawaii: Swift and Sure Changes in Probation," National Institute of Justice, 2008, http://www.ncjrs.gov/pdffiles1/nij/222758.pdf.

63. "Evaluating Delaware's Decide Your Time Program for Drug-Using Offenders Under Community Supervision," National Institute of Justice, 2011, https://www.nij.gov/topics/corrections/community/drug-offenders/Pages/decide-your-time.aspx.

64. Todd Clear and Patricia Hardyman, "The New Intensive Supervision Movement," *Crime and Delinquency* 36 (1990): 42–60.

65. Norval Morris and Michael Tonry, *Between Prison and Probation: Intermediate Punishments in a Rational Sentencing System* (New York: Oxford University Press, 1990).

66. Ibid., p. 8.

67. For a thorough review of these programs, see James Byrne, Arthur Lurigio, and Joan Petersilia, eds., *Smart Sentencing: The Emergence of Intermediate Sanctions* (Newbury Park, CA: Sage, 1993). Hereinafter cited as *Smart Sentencing*.

68. Michael Tonry and Richard Will, *Intermediate Sanctions* (Washington, DC: National Institute of Justice, 1990).

69. Sally Hillsman and Judith Greene, "Tailoring Fines to the Financial Means of Offenders," *Judicature* 72 (1988): 38–45.

70. George Cole, "Monetary Sanctions: The Problem of Compliance," in *Smart Sentencing*, pp. 51–64.

71. *Tate v. Short*, 401 US 395, 91 S.Ct. 668, 28 L.Ed.2d 130 (1971).

72. Doris Layton MacKenzie, "Evidence-Based Corrections: Identifying What Works," *Crime and Delinquency* 46 (2000): 457–472.

73. John L. Worrall, "Addicted to the Drug War: The Role of Civil Asset Forfeiture as a Budgetary Necessity in Contemporary Law Enforcement," *Journal of Criminal Justice* 29 (2001): 171–187.

N-22 NOTES

74. C. Yorke, *Some Consideration on the Law of Forfeiture for High Treason*, 2nd ed. (1746), p. 26, cited in David Fried, "Rationalizing Criminal Forfeiture," *Journal of Criminal Law and Criminology* 79 (1988): 328–436.

75. Fried, "Rationalizing Criminal Forfeiture," p. 436.

76. James B. Jacobs, Coleen Friel, and Edward O'Callaghan, "Pension Forfeiture: A Problematic Sanction for Public Corruption," *American Criminal Law Review* 35 (1997): 57–92.

77. Worrall, "Addicted to the Drug War."

78. For a general review, see Burt Galaway and Joe Hudson, *Criminal Justice, Restitution, and Reconciliation* (New York: Criminal Justice Press, 1990); Robert Carter, Jay Cocks, and Daniel Glazer, "Community Service: A Review of the Basic Issues," *Federal Probation* 51 (1987): 4–11.

79. Frederick Allen and Harvey Treger, "Community Service Orders in Federal Probation: Perceptions of Probationers and Host Agencies," *Federal Probation* 54 (1990): 8–14.

80. Gail Caputo, "Community Service in Texas: Results of a Probation Survey," *Corrections Compendium* 30 (2005): 8–12.

81. Sudipto Roy, "Two Types of Juvenile Restitution Programs in Two Midwestern Counties: A Comparative Study," *Federal Probation* 57 (1993): 48–53.

82. Ibid.

83. Jordan Hyatt and Geoffrey C. Barnes, "An Experimental Evaluation of the Impact of Intensive Supervision on the Recidivism of High-Risk Probationers," *Crime and Delinquency* 63 (2017): 3–38.

84. Jodi Lane, Susan Turner, Terry Fain, and Amber Sehgal, "Evaluating an Experimental Intensive Juvenile Probation Program: Supervision and Official Outcomes," *Crime and Delinquency* 51 (2005): 26–52.

85. Sarah Kuck Jalbert, William Rhodes, Michael Kane, Elyse Clawson, Bradford Bogue, Chris Flygare, Ryan Kling, and Meaghan Guevara, "A Multi-Site Evaluation of Reduced Probation Caseload Size in an Evidence-Based Practice Setting," National Institute of Justice, Office of Justice Programs, 2010, https://www.ncjrs.gov/pdffiles1/nij/grants/234596.pdf.

86. Greg Warchol, "Intensive Supervision Probation: An Impact Evaluation," *Justice Professional* 13 (2000): 219–232.

87. James Byrne and Linda Kelly, "Restructuring Probation as an Intermediate Sanction: An Evaluation of the Massachusetts Intensive Probation Supervision Program," final report to the National Institute of Justice, Research Program on the Punishment and Control of Offenders, Washington, DC, 1989.

88. James Ryan, "Who Gets Revoked? A Comparison of Intensive Supervision Successes and Failures in Vermont," *Crime and Delinquency* 43 (1997): 104–118.

89. Angela Robertson, Paul Grimes, and Kevin Rogers, "A Short-Run Cost-Benefit Analysis of Community-Based Interventions for Juvenile Offenders," *Crime and Delinquency* 47 (2001): 265–284.

90. Linda Smith and Ronald Akers, "A Comparison of Recidivism of Florida's Community Control and Prison: A Five-Year Survival Analysis," *Journal of Research in Crime and Delinquency* 30 (1993): 267–292.

91. Robert N. Altman, Robert E. Murray, and Evey B. Wooten, "Home Confinement: A 90s Approach to Community Supervision," *Federal Probation* 61 (1997): 30–32.

92. Matthew DeMichele, Brian Payne, and Deeanna Button, "Electronic Monitoring of Sex Offenders: Identifying Unanticipated Consequences and Implications," *Journal of Offender Rehabilitation* 46 (2008): 119–135.

93. William Burrell and Robert Gable, "From B. F. Skinner to Spiderman to Martha Stewart: The Past, Present and Future of Electronic Monitoring of Offenders," *Journal of Offender Rehabilitation* 46 (2008): 101–118; Hugh Downing, "Emergence of Global Positioning Satellite (GPS) Systems in Correctional Applications," *Corrections Today* 68 (2006): 42–45.

94. Edna Erez and Peter Ibarra, "Making Your Home a Shelter: Electronic Monitoring and Victim Re-Entry in Domestic Violence Cases," *British Journal of Criminology* 47 (2007): 100–120.

95. Stephen Gies, Randy Gainey, Marcia Cohen, Eoin Healy, Martha Yeide, Alan Bekelman, et al., *Monitoring High-Risk Gang Offenders with GPS Technology: An Evaluation of the California Supervision Program Final Report* (Washington, DC: Office of Justice Programs, US Department of Justice, National Institute of Justice, 2013).

96. Kathy Padgett, William Bales, and Thomas Blomberg, "Under Surveillance: An Empirical Test of the Effectiveness and Consequences of Electronic Monitoring," *Criminology and Public Policy* 5 (2006): 61–91.

97. William Bales, Karen Mann, Thomas Blomberg, Gerry Gaes, Kelle Barrick, Karla Dhungana, and Brian McManus, *A Quantitative and Qualitative Assessment of Electronic Monitoring* (Washington, DC: National Institute of Justice, 2010), http://www.ncjrs.gov/pdffiles1/nij/grants/230530.pdf.

98. Avdi Avdija and JiHee Lee, "Does Electronic Monitoring Home Detention Program Work? Evaluating Program Suitability Based on Offenders' Post-Program Recidivism Status," *Justice Policy Journal* 11 (2014): 1–15.

99. Numerex, http://numerex.com/solutions/safety-security/electronicmonitoring/solution-components/.

100. National Institute of Justice, *Evaluating a Location-Based Offender Monitoring System*, https://www.nij.gov/topics/corrections/community/monitoring-technologies/pages/location-based-monitoring.aspx.

101. See, generally, Edward Latessa and Lawrence Travis III, "Residential Community Correctional Programs," in *Smart Sentencing*, pp. 65–79.

102. Dale Parent, *Day Reporting Centers for Criminal Offenders: A Descriptive Analysis of Existing Programs* (Washington, DC: National Institute of Justice, 1990); Jack McDevitt and Robyn Miliano, "Day Reporting Centers: An Innovative Concept in Intermediate Sanctions," in *Smart Sentencing*, pp. 80–105.

103. David Diggs and Stephen Pieper, "Using Day Reporting Centers as an Alternative to Jail," *Federal Probation* 58 (1994): 9–12.

104. Michael Ostermann, "An Analysis of New Jersey's Day Reporting Center and Halfway Back Programs: Embracing the Rehabilitative Ideal Through Evidence Based Practices," *Journal of Offender Rehabilitation* 48 (2009): 139–153.

105. Dae-Young Kim, Hee-Jong Joo, and William McCarty, "Risk Assessment and Classification of Day Reporting Center Clients: An Actuarial Approach," *Criminal Justice and Behavior* 35 (2008): 792–812.

106. Amy Craddock, "Day Reporting Center Completion: Comparison of

Individual and Multilevel Models," *Crime and Delinquency* 55 (2009): 105–133; Sudipto Roy and Shannon Barton, "Convicted Drunk Drivers in Electronic Monitoring Home Detention and Day Reporting Centers," *Federal Probation* 70 (2006), http://www.uscourts.gov/statistics -reports/publications/federal -probation-journal.

107. Kathleen Daly and Russ Immarigeon, "The Past, Present, and Future of Restorative Justice: Some Critical Reflections," *Contemporary Justice Review* 1 (1998): 21–45.

108. John Braithwaite, *Crime, Shame, and Reintegration* (Melbourne, Australia: Cambridge University Press, 1989).

109. Gene Stephens, "The Future of Policing: From a War Model to a Peace Model," in *The Past, Present and Future of American Criminal Justice*, ed. Brendan Maguire and Polly Radosh (Dix Hills, NY: General Hall, 1996), pp. 77–93.

110. Kay Pranis, "Peacemaking Circles: Restorative Justice in Practice Allows Victims and Offenders to Begin Repairing the Harm," *Corrections Today* 59 (1997): 74.

111. Carol LaPrairie, "The 'New' Justice: Some Implications for Aboriginal Communities," *Canadian Journal of Criminology* 40 (1998): 61–79.

112. David R. Karp and Beau Breslin, "Restorative Justice in School Communities," *Youth and Society* 33 (2001): 249–272.

113. Paul Jesilow and Deborah Parsons, "Community Policing as Peacemaking," *Policing and Society* 10 (2000): 163–183.

114. Centre for Justice and Reconciliation, *Police Cautioning*, http:// restorativejustice.org/restorative -justice/rj-in-the-criminal-justice -system/law-enforcement/police -cautioning/; Aidan Wilcox, Richard Young, and Carolyn Hoyle, "Two-Year Re-sanctioning Study: A Comparison of Restorative and Traditional Cautions," *British Home Office*, 2004, http://webarchive.nationalarchives .gov.uk/20110220105210/rds .homeoffice.gov.uk/rds/pdfs04 /rdsolr5704.pdf; Aidan Wilcox and Richard Young, "How Green Was Thames Valley? Policing the Image of Restorative Justice Cautions," *Policing and Society* 17 (2007): 141–163.

115. Natalie Kroovand Hipple, Jeff Gruenewald, and Edmund F. McGarrell, "Restorativeness, Procedural Justice, and Defiance as Predictors of Re-offending of Participants in Family Group Conferences," *Crime and Delinquency* 60 (2014): 1131–1157.

116. See, for example, Lawrence W. Sherman, Heather Strang, Evan Mayo-Wilson, Daniel J. Woods, and Barak Ariel, "Are Restorative Justice Conferences Effective in Reducing Repeat Offending? Findings from a Campbell Systematic Review," *Journal of Quantitative Criminology* 31 (2015): 1–24.

117. Gordon Bazemore and Curt Taylor Griffiths, "Conferences, Circles, Boards, and Mediations: The 'New Wave' of Community Justice Decision Making," *Federal Probation* 61 (1997): 25–37.

118. Mark Umbreit and Rina Ritter, "Arab Offenders Meet Jewish Victim: Restorative Family Dialogue in Israel," *Conflict Resolution Quarterly* 24 (2006): 99–109.

119. John Braithwaite, "Setting Standards for Restorative Justice," *British Journal of Criminology* 42 (2002): 563–577.

120. Nancy Rodriguez, "Restorative Justice, Communities, and Delinquency: Whom Do We Reintegrate?" *Criminology and Public Policy* 4 (2005): 103–130.

121. Braithwaite, "Setting Standards for Restorative Justice."

122. David Altschuler, "Community Justice Initiatives: Issues and Challenges in the US Context," *Federal Probation* 65 (2001): 28–33.

123. Lois Presser and Patricia Van Voorhis, "Values and Evaluation: Assessing Processes and Outcomes of Restorative Justice Programs," *Crime and Delinquency* 48 (2002): 162–189.

124. Sharon Levrant, Francis Cullen, Betsy Fulton, and John Wozniak, "Reconsidering Restorative Justice: The Corruption of Benevolence Revisited?" *Crime and Delinquency* 45 (1999): 3–28.

125. Dean Gromet and John Darley, "Restoration and Retribution: How Including Retributive Components Affects the Acceptability of Restorative Justice Procedures," *Social Justice Research* 19 (2006): 395–432.

126. Michael E. Smith, *What Future for "Public Safety" and "Restorative Justice" in Community Corrections?* (Washington, DC: National Institute of Justice, 2001).

Chapter 11, Corrections: History, Institutions, and Populations

1. Associated Press, "Attica Corrections Officers Plead Guilty to 2011 Inmate Beating Just as Trial Begins," March 2, 2015, http://www.nydailynews.com /news/crime/attica-corrections -officers-plead-guilty-inmate-beating -article-1.2134374; Tom Robbins, "A Brutal Beating Wakes Attica's Ghosts: A Prison, Infamous for Bloodshed, Faces a Reckoning as Guards Go on Trial," *The New York Times*, February 28, 2015, http://www .nytimes.com/2015/03/01/nyregion /attica-prison-infamous-for -bloodshed-faces-a-reckoning-as -guards-go-on-trial.html.

2. E. Ann Carson, *Prisoners in 2015*, Bureau of Justice Statistics, https://www .bjs.gov/content/pub/pdf/p15.pdf.

3. See David Fogel, *We Are the Living Proof*, 2nd ed. (Cincinnati: Anderson, 1978); Andrew von Hirsch, *Doing Justice: The Choice of Punishments* (New York: Hill and Wang, 1976).

4. Francis Cullen, "The Twelve People Who Saved Rehabilitation: How the Science of Criminology Made a Difference," *Criminology* 43 (2005): 1–42.

5. Malcolm Feeley and Jonathan Simon, "The New Penology: Notes on the Emerging Strategy of Corrections and Its Implications," *Criminology* 30 (2006): 449–474.

6. Carson, *Prisoners in 2015*; World Prison Brief, http://www.prisonstudies .org/highest-to-lowest/prison _population_rate?field_region _taxonomy_tid=All.

7. Paul Schupp and Craig Rivera, "Identifying Imprisonment Patterns and Their Relation to Crime Among New York Counties 1990–2000," *Criminal Justice Policy Review* 21 (2010): 50–75.

8. Ernest Drucker, *A Plague of Prisons: The Epidemiology of Mass Incarceration in America*, reprint ed. (New York: New Press, 2013).

9. Michelle Alexander, *The New Jim Crow: Mass Incarceration in the Age of Color Blindness* (New York: New Press, 2012).

10. Among the most helpful sources in developing this section were Mark Colvin, *Penitentiaries, Reformatories, and Chain Gangs* (New York: St. Martin's Press, 1997); Benedict

Alper, *Prisons Inside-Out* (Cambridge, MA: Ballinger, 1974); Harry Elmer Barnes, *The Story of Punishment*, 2nd ed. (Montclair, NJ: Patterson-Smith, 1972); Gustave de Beaumont and Alexis de Tocqueville, *On the Penitentiary System in the United States and Its Applications in France* (Carbondale: Southern Illinois University Press, 1964); Orlando Lewis, *The Development of American Prisons and Prison Customs, 1776–1845* (Montclair, NJ: Patterson-Smith, 1967); Georg Rusche and Otto Kircheimer, *Punishment and Social Structure* (New York: Russell and Russell, 1939); Samuel Walker, *Popular Justice* (New York: Oxford University Press, 1980); Graeme Newman, *The Punishment Response* (Philadelphia, PA: J. B. Lippincott, 1978); David Rothman, *Conscience and Convenience* (Boston: Little, Brown, 1980).

11. Frederick Pollock and Frederick Maitland, *History of English Law* (London: Cambridge University Press, 1952).

12. Marvin Wolfgang, "Crime and Punishment in Renaissance Florence," *Journal of Criminal Law and Criminology* 81 (1990): 567–584

13. John Howard, *The State of Prisons*, 4th ed. (Montclair, NJ: Patterson-Smith, 1972; reprint 1973).

14. Alexis Durham III, "Newgate of Connecticut: Origins and Early Days of an Early American Prison," *Justice Quarterly* 6 (1989): 89–116.

15. Dario Melossi and Massimo Pavarini, *The Prison and the Factory: Origins of the Penitentiary System* (Totowa, NJ: Barnes and Noble, 1981).

16. Lewis, *Development of American Prisons and Prison Customs*, p. 17.

17. See, generally, David Rothman, *The Discovery of the Asylum* (Boston: Little, Brown, 1970).

18. Ibid., p. 144.

19. Walker, *Popular Justice*, p. 70.

20. Ibid., p. 71.

21. Beverly Smith, "Military Training at New York's Elmira Reformatory, 1880–1920," *Federal Probation* 52 (1988): 33–41.

22. William Parker, *Parole: Origins, Development, Current Practices, and Statutes* (College Park, MD: American Correctional Association, 1972); Walker, *Popular Justice*.

23. This section leans heavily on David Rothman, *Conscience and Convenience*.

24. Ibid., p. 23.

25. Ibid., p. 133.

26. 18 USC. 1761.

27. Barbara Auerbach, George Sexton, Franklin Farrow, and Robert Lawson, *Work in American Prisons: The Private Sector Gets Involved* (Washington, DC: National Institute of Justice, 1988), p. 72.

28. See, generally, Jameson Doig, *Criminal Corrections: Ideals and Realities* (Lexington, MA: Lexington Books, 1983).

29. James Stephan and Georgette Walsh, *Census of Jail Facilities, 2006* (Washington, DC: Bureau of Justice Statistics, 2011). This is the most recent report available at the time of this writing.

30. Data in this section come from Danielle Kaeble and Lauren Glaze, *Correctional Populations in the United States, 2015*, Bureau of Justice Statistics, 2016, https://www.bjs.gov /content/pub/pdf/cpus15.pdf; Todd Minton and Zhen Zeng, *Jail Inmates at Midyear 2014*, Bureau of Justice Statistics, 2015, https://www.bjs.gov /content/pub/pdf/jim14.pdf.

31. Minton and Zeng, *Jail Inmates at Midyear 2014*.

32. Tina Freiburger and Carly Hilinski, "An Examination of the Interactions of Race and Gender on Sentencing Decisions Using a Trichotomous Dependent Variable," *Crime and Delinquency* 59 (2013): 59–86.

33. Ibid.

34. National Institute of Corrections and the National Center on Institutions and Alternatives (NCIA), *National Study of Jail Suicide: 20 Years Later* (2010), http://static.nicic.gov/Library /024308.pdf.

35. Brandon Applegate, Ray Surette, and Bernard McCarthy, "Detention and Desistance from Crime: Evaluating the Influence of a New Generation of Jail on Recidivism," *Journal of Criminal Justice* 27 (1999): 539–548.

36. James J. Stephan, *Census of State and Federal Correctional Facilities, 2005*, Bureau of Justice Statistics, 2008. This report is the most recent available at the time of this writing.

37. Human Rights Watch, *Prison Conditions in the United States*, https://www .hrw.org/sites/default/files/reports /US91N.pdf.

38. "Suit Alleges Violations in California's 'Super-Max' Prison," *Criminal Justice Newsletter*, September 1, 1993, p. 2.

39. Jeffrey Ian Ross, ed., *The Globalization of Supermax Prisons* (New Brunswick, NJ: Rutgers University Press, 2013).

40. Jody Sundt, Thomas Castellano, and Chad Briggs, "The Sociopolitical Context of Prison Violence and Its Control: A Case Study of Supermax and Its Effect in Illinois," *Prison Journal* 88 (2008): 94–122.

41. Keramet Reiter, "Parole, Snitch, or Die: California's Supermax Prisons and Prisoners, 1997–2007," *Punishment and Society* 14 (2012): 530–563.

42. Keramet Reiter, "The Supermax Prison: A Blunt Means of Control, or a Subtle Form of Violence?" *Radical Philosophy Review*, first published online September 20, 2014.

43. Daniel P. Mears and Jamie Watson, "Towards a Fair and Balanced Assessment of Supermax Prisons," *Justice Quarterly* 23 (2006): 232–270.

44. Daniel P. Mears and William Bales, "Supermax Incarceration and Recidivism," *Criminology* 47 (2009). 801–836.

45. Daniel P. Mears and Jennifer Castro, "Wardens' Views on the Wisdom of Supermax Prisons," *Crime and Delinquency* 52 (2006): 398–431.

46. Carson, *Prisoners in 2015*.

47. Sean Nicholson-Crotty, "The Impact of Sentencing Guidelines on State-Level Sanctions: An Analysis Over Time," *Crime and Delinquency* 50 (2004): 395–411.

48. Pew Foundation Report, "Max Out: The Rise in Prison Inmates Released Without Supervision," June 2014, http://www.pewtrusts.org/en /research-and-analysis/reports/2014 /06/04/max-out.

49. Benjamin Steiner and John Wooldredge, "Comparing State-versus Facility-Level Effects on Crowding in US Correctional Facilities," *Crime and Delinquency* 54 (2008): 259–290.

50. Data in this and the next subsections are drawn from Carson, *Prisoners in 2015*.

51. Greg Greenberg and Robert Rosenheck, "Homelessness in the State and Federal Prison Population," *Criminal Behaviour and Mental Health* 18 (2008): 88–103.

52. Seena Fazel and John Danesh, "Serious Mental Disorder in 23,000 Prisoners: A Systematic Review of Sixty-Two Surveys," *Lancet* 359 (2002): 545–561.

53. James Anderson, Laronistine Dyson, and Jerald Burns, *Boot Camps: An Intermediate Sanction* (Lanham, MD: University Press of America, 1999), pp. 1–17.

54. Ibid., 328–329.

55. Doris Layton Mackenzie and James Shaw, "The Impact of Shock Incarceration on Technical Violations and New Criminal Activities," *Justice Quarterly* 10 (1993): 463–487.

56. Vanessa St. Gerard, "Federal Prisons to Eliminate Boot Camps," *Corrections Today* 67 (2005): 13–16.

57. Correctional Research Associates, *Treating Youthful Offenders in the Community: An Evaluation Conducted by A. J. Reiss* (Washington, DC: Correctional Research Associates, 1966).

58. Corrections Corporation of America, http://www.cca.com.

59. GEO Corporation, https://www.geogroup.com/LOCATIONS.

60. Richard Harding, "Private Prisons," in *Crime and Justice: An Annual Edition*, ed. Michael Tonry (Chicago: University of Chicago Press, 2001), pp. 265–347.

61. Carson, *Prisoners in 2015*.

62. William Bales, Laura Bedard, Susan Quinn, David Ensley, and Glen Holley, "Recidivism of Public and Private State Prison Inmates in Florida," *Criminology and Public Policy* 4 (2005): 57–82; Lonn Lanza-Kaduce, Karen Parker, and Charles Thomas, "A Comparative Recidivism Analysis of Releases from Private and Public Prisons," *Crime and Delinquency* 45 (1999): 28–47.

63. Charles Thomas, "Recidivism of Public and Private State Prison Inmates in Florida: Issues and Unanswered Questions," *Criminology and Public Policy* 4 (2005): 89–99.

64. *Minneci v. Pollard*, 565 US ___ (2012).

Chapter 12, Prison Life: Living in and Leaving Prison

1. Families Against Mandatory Minimums, "Orville Lee Wollard," http://famm.org/orville-lee-wollard/.

2. S. Bousquet, "Blown Away: The Warning Shot That Condemned a Man and Changed a State," *Miami Herald*, February 8, 2016, http://www.miamiherald.com/news/politics-government/state-politics/article58719808.html.

3. Families Against Mandatory Minimums, "Orville Lee Wollard."

4. Florida Senate, "CS/HB 135: Mandatory Minimum Sentences," https://www.flsenate.gov/Session/Bill/2016/0135.

5. Bousquet, "Blown Away."

6. Ibid.

7. E. Ann Carson, *Prisoners in 2015*, Bureau of Justice Statistics, 2016.

8. James J. Stephan, *Census of State and Federal Correctional Facilities, 2005*, Bureau of Justice Statistics, 2008. Unfortunately, these are the most recent statistics available as of this writing.

9. Ibid.

10. Richard Berk, Heather Ladd, Heidi Graziano, and Jong-Ho Baek, "A Randomized Experiment Testing Inmate Classification Systems," *Criminology and Public Policy* 2 (2003): 215–242.

11. James A. Paluch Jr., *A Life for a Life: Life Imprisonment (America's Other Death Penalty)* (Los Angeles: Roxbury Press, 2004), p. 4.

12. Margaret Leigey, "For the Longest Time: The Adjustment of Inmates to a Sentence of Life Without Parole," *Prison Journal* 90 (2010): 247–268.

13. Manop Kanato, "Drug Use and Health Among Prison Inmates," *Current Opinion in Psychiatry* 21 (2008): 252–254.

14. Gresham Sykes, *The Society of Captives* (Princeton, NJ: Princeton University Press, 1958).

15. Karen Lahm, "Inmate-on-Inmate Assault: A Multilevel Examination of Prison Violence," *Criminal Justice and Behavior* 35 (2008): 120–137.

16. Robert Johnson, *Hard Time: Understanding and Reforming the Prison* (Monterey, CA: Brooks/Cole, 1987), p. 115.

17. John D. Wooldredge, "Inmate Lifestyles and Opportunities for Victimization," *Journal of Research in Crime and Delinquency* 35 (1998): 480–502.

18. Attapol Kuanliang, Jon Sorensen, and Mark Cunningham, "Juvenile Inmates in an Adult Prison System: Rates of Disciplinary Misconduct and Violence," *Criminal Justice and Behavior* 35 (2008): 1186–1201.

19. Mark Kellar and Hsiao-Ming Wang, "Inmate Assaults in Texas County Jails," *Prison Journal* 85 (2005): 515–534.

20. Benjamin Steiner and John Wooldredge, "Inmate versus Environmental Effects on Prison Rule Violations," *Criminal Justice and Behavior* 35 (2008): 438–456.

21. Alan Prendergast, "Raped and Extorted by a Prison Gang, Scott Howard Was Called a 'Drama Queen' by Corrections Officials," *Denver Westword News* (February 2, 2011), http://www.westword.com/news/raped-and-extorted-by-a-prison-gang-scott-howard-was-called-a-drama-queen-by-corrections-officials-5111568.

22. T. J. Parsell, *Fish: A Memoir of a Boy in a Man's Prison* (Cambridge, MA: Da Capo Press, 2007).

23. Christopher Hensley, Mary Koscheski, and Richard Tewksbury, "Examining the Characteristics of Male Sexual Assault Targets in a Southern Maximum-Security Prison," *Journal of Interpersonal Violence* 20 (2005): 667–679.

24. Wilbert Rideau and Ron Wikberg, *Life Sentences: Rage and Survival Behind Bars* (New York: Times Books, 1992), pp. 78–80.

25. Hensley, Koscheski, and Tewksbury, "Examining the Characteristics of Male Sexual Assault Targets in a Southern Maximum-Security Prison."

26. Mark Fleisher and Jessie Krienert, *The Myth of Prison Rape: Sexual Culture in American Prisons* (Lanham, MD: Rowman & Littlefield, 2009).

27. Allen Beck, Marcus Berzofsky, Rachel Caspar, and Christopher Krebs, *Sexual Victimization in Prisons and Jails Reported by Inmates, 2011–12 Update*, Bureau of Justice Statistics, 2014.

28. Kristine Levan Miller, "The Darkest Figure of Crime: Perceptions of Reasons for Male Inmates to Not Report Sexual Assault," *Justice Quarterly* 27 (2010): 692–712.

29. Tonisha Jones and Travis Pratt, "The Prevalence of Sexual Violence in Prison," *International Journal of Offender Therapy and Comparative Criminology* 52 (2008): 280–295.

30. Allen Beck and Candace Johnson, *Sexual Victimization Reported by Former State Prisoners, 2008*, Bureau of Justice Statistics, 2012.

31. Nancy Wolff and Jing Shi, "Patterns of Victimization and Feelings of Safety Inside Prison: The Experience of Male and Female Inmates," *Crime and Delinquency* 57 (2011): 29–55.

32. Mark Fleisher and Jessie Krienert, *The Culture of Prison Sexual Violence*, US Department of Justice, National Institute of Justice, 2006.

33. S. 1435[108]: Prison Rape Elimination Act of 2003; Public Law No: 108-79.

34. John Irwin, "Adaptation to Being Corrected: Corrections from the Convict's Perspective," in *Handbook of Criminology*, ed. Daniel Glazer

(Chicago: Rand McNally, 1974), pp. 971–993.

35. Donald Clemmer, *The Prison Community* (New York: Holt, Rinehart & Winston, 1958).

36. Gresham Sykes and Sheldon Messinger, "The Inmate Social Code," in *The Sociology of Punishment and Corrections*, ed. Norman Johnston, Leonard Savitz, and Marvin Wolfgang (New York: Wiley, 1970), pp. 401–408.

37. Ibid., p. 439.

38. James B. Jacobs, ed., *New Perspectives on Prisons and Imprisonment* (Ithaca, NY: Cornell University Press, 1983); James B. Jacobs, "Street Gangs Behind Bars," *Social Problems* 21 (1974): 395–409; James B. Jacobs, "Race Relations and the Prison Subculture," in *Crime and Justice*, Vol. 1, ed. Norval Morris and Michael Tonry (Chicago: University of Chicago Press, 1979), pp. 1–28.

39. Matt DeLisi, Chad Trulson, James Marquart, Alan Drury, and Anna Kosloski, "Inside the Prison Black Box: Toward a Life Course Importation Model of Inmate Behavior," *International Journal of Offender Therapy and Comparative Criminology* 55 (2011): 1186–1207.

40. Nicole Hahn Rafter, *Partial Justice* (New Brunswick, NJ: Transaction Books, 1990), pp. 181–182.

41. Kathryn Watterson and Meda Chesney-Lind, *Women in Prison: Inside the Concrete Womb* (Boston: Northeastern University Press, 1996).

42. Pamela Schram, "Stereotypes About Vocational Programming for Female Inmates," *Prison Journal* 78 (1998): 244–271.

43. Morash, Harr, and Rucker, "A Comparison of Programming for Women and Men in US Prisons in the 1980s."

44. Shawn M. Flower, *Gender-Responsive Strategies for Women Offenders*, Bureau of Justice Statistics, 2010.

45. Ibid., p. 4.

46. Vernetta Young and Rebecca Reviere, *Women Behind Bars: Gender and Race in US Prisons* (Boulder, CO: Lynne Rienner Publishers, 2006).

47. Margaret Leigey and Katie Reed, "A Woman's Life Before Serving Life: Examining the Negative Pre-incarceration Life Events of Female Life-Sentenced Inmates," *Women and Criminal Justice* 20 (2010): 302–322.

48. Lauren Sharkey, "Does Overcrowding in Prisons Exacerbate the Risk of Suicide Among Women Prisoners?" *Howard Journal of Criminal Justice* 49 (2010): 111–124.

49. Amanda Noblet, "Women in Prison: A Review of the Current Female Prison System: Future Directions and Alternatives," *Internet Journal of Criminology 2008*, https://media.wix.com/ugd/b93dd4_e9db5c003c6e4b9c95145e088960c501.pdf.

50. Seena Fazel and John Danesh, "Serious Mental Disorder in 23,000 Prisoners: A Systematic Review of 62 Surveys," *Lancet* 359 (2002): 545–561.

51. Gary Michael McClelland, Linda Teplin, Karen Abram, and Naomi Jacobs, "HIV and AIDS Risk Behaviors Among Female Jail Detainees: Implications for Public Health Policy," *American Journal of Public Health* 92 (2002): 818–826.

52. Breea Willingham, "Black Women's Prison Narratives and the Intersection of Race, Gender, and Sexuality in US Prisons," *Critical Survey* 23 (2011): 55–66.

53. Paula C. Johnson, *Inner Lives: Voices of African American Women in Prison* (New York: New York University Press, 2003), p. 203.

54. Christine Grella and Lisa Greenwell, "Correlates of Parental Status and Attitudes Toward Parenting Among Substance-Abusing Women Offenders," *Prison Journal* 86 (2006): 89–113.

55. Lee Ann Slocum, Sally Simpson, and Douglas Smith, "Strained Lives and Crime: Examining Intra-Individual Variation in Strain and Offending in a Sample of Incarcerated Women," *Criminology* 43 (2005): 1067–1110.

56. Beck, Berzofsky, Caspar, and Krebs, *Sexual Victimization in Prisons and Jails Reported by Inmates, 2011–12 Update*.

57. Meda Chesney-Lind, "Vengeful Equity: Sentencing Women to Prison," in *The Female Offender: Girls, Women, and Crime*, ed. Meda Chesney-Lind and Lisa J. Pasko (Thousand Oaks, CA: Sage, 1997).

58. Rebecca Trammell, "Relational Violence in Women's Prison: How Women Describe Interpersonal Violence and Gender," *Women and Criminal Justice* 19 (2009): 267–285.

59. Nancy Wolff, Cynthia Blitz, and Jing Shi, "Rates of Sexual Victimization in Prison for Inmates With and Without Mental Disorders," *Psychiatric Services* 58 (2007): 1087–1094; see also Candace Kruttschnitt and Sharon Krmpotich, "Aggressive Behavior Among Female Inmates: An Exploratory Study," *Justice Quarterly* 7 (1990): 370–389.

60. Candace Kruttschnitt, Rosemary Gartner, and Amy Miller, "Doing Her Own Time? Women's Responses to Prison in the Context of the Old and New Penology," *Criminology* 38 (2000): 681–718.

61. Mark Pogrebin and Mary Dodge, "Women's Accounts of Their Prison Experiences: A Retrospective View of Their Subjective Realities," *Journal of Criminal Justice* 29 (2001): 531–541.

62. Shanhe Jiang and L. Thomas Winfree Jr., "Social Support, Gender, and Inmate Adjustment to Prison Life," *Prison Journal* 86 (2006): 32–55.

63. Kimberly Collica, *Female Prisoners, AIDS, and Peer Programs* (New York: Springer, 2013), pp. 26–29.

64. Alyssa Whitby Chamberlain, "Offender Rehabilitation: Examining Changes in Inmate Treatment Characteristics, Program Participation, and Institutional Behavior," *Justice Quarterly* 29 (2012): 183–228.

65. Dianna Newbern, Donald Dansereau, and Urvashi Pitre, "Positive Effects on Life Skills Motivation and Self-Efficacy: Node-Link Maps in a Modified Therapeutic Community," *American Journal of Drug and Alcohol Abuse* 25 (1999): 407–410.

66. Anouk Bosma, Maarten Kunst, Joni Reef, Anja Dirkzwager, and Paul Nieuwbeerta, "Prison-Based Rehabilitation: Predictors of Offender Treatment Participation and Completion," *Crime and Delinquency* 62 (2016): 1095–1120.

67. Steven D. Vannoy and William T. Hoyt, "Evaluation of an Anger Therapy Intervention for Incarcerated Adult Males," *Journal of Offender Rehabilitation* 39 (2004): 40.

68. Sesha Kethineni and Jeremy Braithwaite, "The Effects of a Cognitive-Behavioral Program for At-Risk Youth: Changes in Attitudes, Social Skills, Family, and Community and Peer Relationships," *Victims and Offenders* 6 (2011): 93–116; Patrick Clark, "Preventing Future Crime with Cognitive Behavioral Therapy," *National Institute of Justice Journal* 265 (2010), http://www.ojp.usdoj.gov/nij/journals/265/therapy.htm.

69. Mark Lipsey, Nana Landenberger, and Sandra Wilson, "Effects of Cognitive-Behavioral Programs for Criminal Offenders," *Campbell Systematic*

Reviews (2007): 6, https://www .campbellcollaboration.org/media /k2/attachments/1028_R.pdf.

70. Byron R. Johnson, "Religious Programming, Institutional Adjustment and Recidivism Among Former Inmates in Prison Fellowship Programs," *Justice Quarterly* 21 (2004): 329–354.

71. Charles McDaniel, Derek Davis, and Sabrina Neff, "Charitable Choice and Prison Ministries: Constitutional and Institutional Challenges to Rehabilitating the American Penal System," *Criminal Justice Policy Review* 16 (2005): 164–189.

72. Lawrence T. Jablecki, "A Critique of Faith-Based Prison Programs," *The Humanist* 65 (2005): 11–16.

73. Corrections Corporation of America, *Faith-Based Programs*, http://www.cca .com/inmate-services/inmate-reentry -preparation/faith-based-programs.

74. Janeen Buck Willison, Diana Brazzell, and KiDeuk Kim, *Faith-Based Corrections and Reentry Programs: Advancing a Conceptual Framework for Research and Evaluation* (Washington, DC: Urban Institute, 2010), https://www.ncjrs.gov/pdffiles1 /nij/grants/234058.pdf.

75. Dawn Daggett, Scott Camp, and Okyun Kwon, "Faith-Based Correctional Programming in Federal Prisons: Factors Affecting Program Completion," *Criminal Justice and Behavior* 35 (2008): 848–862.

76. Philip Magaletta, Pamela Diamond, Beth Weinman, Ashley Burnell, and Carl Leukefeld, "Preentry Substance Abuse Services: The Heterogeneity of Offender Experiences," *Crime and Delinquency* 60 (2014): 193–215; CASAColumbia, "New CASA Report Finds: 65% of All US Inmates Meet Medical Criteria for Substance Abuse Addiction, Only 11% Receive Any Treatment," February 26, 2010, http://www.centeronaddiction.org /newsroom/press-releases/2010 -behind-bars-II.

77. Federal Bureau of Prisons, "Substance Abuse Treatment," https://www.bop .gov/inmates/custody_and_care /substance_abuse_treatment.jsp.

78. Kate Dolan, James Shearer, Bethany White, Zhou Jialun, John Kaldor, and Alex Wodak, "Four-Year Follow-up of Imprisoned Male Heroin Users and Methadone Treatment: Mortality, Re-Incarceration and Hepatitis C Infection," *Addiction* 100 (2005): 820–828.

79. Clayton Mosher and Dretha Phillips, "The Dynamics of a Prison-Based Therapeutic Community for Women Offenders: Retention, Completion, and Outcomes," *Prison Journal* 86 (2006): 6–31.

80. Sheldon X. Zhang, Robert E. L. Roberts, and Kathryn E. McCollister, "Therapeutic Community in a California Prison: Treatment Outcomes after 5 Years," *Crime and Delinquency* 57 (2011): 82–101; J. Mitchell Miller and Holly Ventura Miller, "Considering the Effectiveness of Drug Treatment Behind Bars: Findings from the South Carolina RSAT Evaluation," *Justice Quarterly* 28 (2011): 70–86.

81. Wayne Welsh, "A Multisite Evaluation of Prison-Based Therapeutic Community Drug Treatment," *Criminal Justice and Behavior* 34 (2007): 1481–1498.

82. Daniel Werb, Thomas Kerr, Will Small, Kathy Li, Julio Montaner, and Evan Wood, "HIV Risks Associated with Incarceration Among Injection Drug Users: Implications for Prison-Based Public Health Strategies," *Journal of Public Health* 30 (2008): 126–132.

83. Karen Lahm, "Educational Participation and Inmate Misconduct," *Journal of Offender Rehabilitation* 48 (2009): 37–52.

84. Rosa Minhyo Cho and John H. Tyler, "Does Prison-Based Adult Basic Education Improve Postrelease Outcomes for Male Prisoners in Florida?" *Crime and Delinquency*, first published online November 30, 2010.

85. Bill Conlon, Scott Harris, Jeffrey Nagel, Mike Hillman, and Rick Hanson, "Education: Don't Leave Prison without It," *Corrections Today* 70 (2008): 48–52; David Wilson, Catherine Gallagher, and Doris MacKensie, "A Meta-Analysis of Corrections-Based Education, Vocation, and Work Programs for Adult Offenders," *Journal of Research in Crime and Delinquency* 37 (2000): 347–368.

86. Howard Skolnik and John Slansky, "A First Step in Helping Inmates Get Good Jobs After Release," *Corrections Today* 53 (1991): 92.

87. Federal Bureau of Prisons web page concerning UNICOR Federal Prison Industries, http://www.UNICOR.gov /Contracting.aspx.

88. Courtesy of the Prison Industry Authority, 560 East Natoma St., Folsom, CA, 95630-2200.

89. Douglas Lipton, Robert Martinson, and Judith Wilks, *The Effectiveness of Correctional Treatment: A Survey of Treatment Evaluation Studies* (New York: Praeger, 1975).

90. James Wilson and Robert Davis, "Good Intentions Meet Hard Realities: An Evaluation of the Project Greenlight Reentry Program," *Criminology and Public Policy* 5 (2006): 303–338.

91. Paula Smith, Paul Gendreau, and Kristin Swartz, "Validating the Principles of Effective Intervention: A Systematic Review of the Contributions of Meta-Analysis in the Field of Corrections," *Victims and Offenders* 4 (2009): 148–169.

92. Paul Gendreau and Robert Ross, "Effective Correctional Treatment: Bibliotherapy for Cynics," *Crime and Delinquency* 27 (1979): 463–489.

93. Mark W. Lipsey and Francis T. Cullen, "The Effectiveness of Correctional Rehabilitation: A Review of Systematic Reviews," *Annual Review of Law and Social Science* 3 (2007): 297–320.

94. Lucien X. Lombardo, *Guards Imprisoned* (New York: Elsevier, 1981); James Jacobs and Norma Crotty, "The Guard's World," in *New Perspectives on Prisons and Imprisonment*, ed. James Jacobs (Ithaca, NY: Cornell University Press, 1983), pp. 133–141.

95. Richard Tewksbury and Elizabeth Mustaine, "Correctional Orientations of Prison Staff," *Prison Journal* 88 (2008): 207–233.

96. Brie Williams, Marc Stern, Jeff Mellow, Meredith Safer, and Robert Greifinger, "Aging in Correctional Custody: Setting a Policy Agenda for Older Prisoner Health Care," *American Journal of Public Health* 102 (2012): 1475–1481.

97. Joseph Martin, Bronwen Lichtenstein, Robert Jenkot, and David Forde, "They Can Take Us Over Any Time They Want: Correctional Officers' Responses to Prison Crowding," *Prison Journal* 92 (2012): 88–105.

98. Eric Lambert, Nancy Hogan, Kelly Cheeseman Dial, Irshad Altheimer, and Shannon Barton-Bellessa, "Examining the Effects of Stressors on Organizational Citizenship Behaviors Among Private Correctional Staff: A Preliminary Study," *Security Journal* 25 (2012): 152–172.

99. Eric Lambert, Nancy Hogan, and Irshad Altheimer, "An Exploratory Examination of the Consequences of Burnout in Terms of Life Satisfaction, Turnover Intent, and Absenteeism

Among Private Correctional Staff," *Prison Journal* 90 (2010): 94–114.

100. Stephen Owen, "Occupational Stress Among Correctional Supervisors," *Prison Journal* 86 (2006): 164–181; Eugene Paoline, Eric Lambert, and Nancy Hogan, "A Calm and Happy Keeper of the Keys: The Impact of ACA Views, Relations with Coworkers, and Policy Views on the Job Stress and Job Satisfaction of Jail Staff," *Prison Journal* 86 (2006): 182–205.

101. Mike Vuolo and Candace Kruttschnitt, "Prisoners' Adjustment, Correctional Officers, and Context: The Foreground and Background of Punishment in Late Modernity," *Law and Society Review* 42 (2008): 307–335.

102. Dana Britton, *At Work in the Iron Cage: The Prison as Gendered Organization* (New York: New York University Press, 2003), Ch. 6.

103. Associated Press, "Delaware Guards 'Severely' Beaten by Prisoners During Riot that Left 1 Dead," February 2, 2017, http://www.wbaltv.com/article /1-hostage-dead-another-rescued-at -delaware-prison/8666961.

104. David Duffee, *Corrections, Practice and Policy* (New York: Random House, 1989), p. 305.

105. Randy Martin and Sherwood Zimmerman, "A Typology of the Causes of Prison Riots and an Analytical Extension to the 1986 West Virginia Riot," *Justice Quarterly* 7 (1990): 711–737.

106. Benjamin Steiner, "Assessing Static and Dynamic Influences on Inmate Violence Levels," *Crime and Delinquency* 55 (2009): 134–161.

107. David Allender and Frank Marcell, "Career Criminals, Security Threat Groups, and Prison Gangs," *FBI Law Enforcement Bulletin* 72 (2003): 8–12.

108. Terri Compton and Mike Meacham, "Prison Gangs: Descriptions and Selected Intervention," *Forensic Examiner* 14 (2005): 26–31.

109. Jon Sorensen and Mark Cunningham, "Conviction Offense and Prison Violence: A Comparative Study of Murderers and Other Offenders," *Crime and Delinquency* 56 (2010): 103–125.

110. Steiner and Wooldredge, "Inmate versus Environmental Effects on Prison Rule Violations."

111. Kuanliang, Sorensen, and Cunningham, "Juvenile Inmates in an Adult Prison System: Rates of Disciplinary Misconduct and Violence."

112. Sorensen and Cunningham, "Conviction Offense and Prison Violence."

113. Grant Harris, Tracey Skilling, and Marnie Rice, "The Construct of Psychopathy," in *Crime and Justice: An Annual Edition*, ed. Michael Tonry (Chicago: University of Chicago Press, 2001), pp. 197–265.

114. For a series of papers on the position, see A. Cohen, G. Cole, and R. Baily, eds. *Prison Violence* (Lexington, MA: Lexington Books, 1976).

115. Lahm, "Inmate-on-Inmate Assault."

116. David M. Bierie, "Is Tougher Better? The Impact of Physical Prison Conditions on Inmate Violence," *International Journal of Offender Therapy and Comparative Criminology* 56 (2012): 338–355.

117. Scott Camp and Gerald Gaes, "Criminogenic Effects of the Prison Environment on Inmate Behavior: Some Experimental Evidence," *Crime and Delinquency* 51 (2005): 425–442.

118. Hans Toch, "Cumulative Default: The Cost of Disruptive Prison Careers," *Criminal Justice and Behavior* 35 (2008): 943–955.

119. Bert Useem and Michael Resig, "Collective Action in Prisons: Protests, Disturbances, and Riots," *Criminology* 37 (1999): 735–760.

120. Prison Litigation Reform Act P.L. 104-134, 110 Stat. 1321 (2006); 42 U.S.C. § 1997e (1994 ed. and Supp. II).

121. *Booth v. Churner*, 532 U.S. 731 (2001); *Porter v. Nussle*, 534 U.S. 516 (2002).

122. ACLU, "Know Your Rights: The Prison Litigation Reform Act (PLRA)," https://www.aclu.org/files/assets/kyr _plra_aug2011_1.pdf.

123. *Shaw v. Murphy*, 532 U.S. 223 (2001).

124. *Cutter v. Wilkinson*, 544 U.S. 709 (2005).

125. *Newman v. Alabama*, 405 U.S. 319 (1972).

126. *Estelle v. Gamble*, 429 U.S. 97 (1976).

127. Ibid.

128. Lester Wright, "Health Care in Prison Thirty Years after *Estelle v. Gamble*," *Journal of Correctional Health Care* 14 (2008): 31–35.

129. *Trop v. Dulles*, 356 U.S. 86 (1958); see also *Furman v. Georgia*, 408 U.S. 238 (1972).

130. *Weems v. United States*, 217 U.S. 349 (1910).

131. *Lee v. Tahash*, 352 F.2d 970 (8th Cir., 1965).

132. *Estelle v. Gamble*, 429 U.S. 97 (1976).

133. *Robinson v. California*, 370 U.S. 660 (1962).

134. *Gregg v. Georgia*, 428 U.S. 153 (1976).

135. *Jackson v. Bishop*, 404 F.2d 571 (8th Cir. 1968).

136. *Johnson v. California*, 543 U.S. 499 (2005).

137. *Bell v. Wolfish*, 441 U.S. 520 (1979); also see "*Bell v. Wolfish*: The Rights of Pretrial Detainees," *New England Journal of Prison Law* 6 (1979): 134.

138. *Farmer v. Brennan*, 511 U.S. 825 (1994).

139. *Rhodes v. Chapman*, 452 U.S. 337 (1981); for further analysis of *Rhodes*, see Randall Pooler, "Prison Overcrowding and the Eighth Amendment: The Rhodes Not Taken," *New England Journal on Criminal and Civil Confinement* 8 (1983): 1–28.

140. Kristin Preston, "Right Place, Right Time: GPS Monitoring in Pinellas County," *Geography and Public Safety* 2 (2009): 3–5, https://www.nij.gov /topics/technology/maps/Documents /gps-bulletin-v2i1.pdf.

141. Joel Caplan and Susan Kinnevy, "National Surveys of State Paroling Authorities: Models of Service," *Federal Probation* 74 (2010): 34–42.

142. Danielle Kaeble and Thomas P. Bonczar, *Probation and Parole in the United States, 2015*, Bureau of Justice Statistics, 2016.

143. *Swarthout v. Cooke* and *Cate v. Clay* 562 U.S. ___ (2011).

144. Alexia Cooper, Matthew Durose, and Howard Snyder, "Recidivism of Prisoners Released in 30 States in 2005: Patterns from 2005 to 2010," Bureau of Justice Statistics, 2014.

145. Pew Center on the States, *State of Recidivism: The Revolving Door of America's Prisons* (Washington, DC: Pew Charitable Trusts, 2011).

146. Michael Ostermann, Laura Salerno, and Jordan M. Hyatt, "How Different Operationalizations of Recidivism Impact Conclusions of Effectiveness of Parole Supervision," *Journal of Research in Crime and Delinquency* 52 (2015): 771–796.

147. Benjamin Steiner, Lawrence Travis, Matthew Makarios, and Taylor Brickley, "The Influence of Parole Officers' Attitudes on Supervision Practices," *Justice Quarterly* 28 (2011): 903–927.

148. Jospeter Mbuba, "Lethal Rejection: Recounting Offenders' Experience in Prison and Societal Reaction Post Release," *Prison Journal* 92 (2012): 231–252.

149. Stephen Duguid, *Can Prisons Work? The Prisoner as Object and Subject in Modern Corrections* (Toronto: University of Toronto Press, 2000).

150. Joan Petersilia, *When Prisoners Come Home: Parole and Prisoner Reentry* (New York: Oxford University Press, 2003); Joan Petersilia, "Hard Time Ex-Offenders Returning Home After Prison," *Corrections Today* 67 (2005): 66–72; Joan Petersilia, "When Prisoners Return to Communities: Political, Economic, and Social Consequences," *Federal Probation* 65 (2001): 3–9.

151. Michael Ostermann, "How Do Former Inmates Perform in the Community? A Survival Analysis of Rearrests, Reconvictions, and Technical Parole Violations," *Crime and Delinquency* 61 (2015): 163–187; also see Michael Ostermann and Jordan M. Hyatt, "Is Something Better Than Nothing? The Effect of Short Terms of Mandatory Parole Supervision," *Justice Quarterly* 33 (2016): 785–810.

152. Michael Ostermann, "Parole? Nope, Not for Me: Voluntarily Maxing Out of Prison," *Crime and Delinquency* 57 (2011): 686–708.

153. Megan Kurlychek, Andrew Wheeler, Leigh Tinik, and Cynthia Kempinen, "How Long After? A Natural Experiment Assessing the Length of Aftercare Service Delivery on Recidivism," *Crime and Delinquency* 57 (2011): 778–800.

154. Stephen Metraux and Dennis P. Culhane, "Recent Incarceration History Among a Sheltered Homeless Population," *Crime and Delinquency* 52 (2006): 504–517, http://repository.upenn.edu/spp_papers/61/.

155. Catherine Hamilton, Louise Falshaw, and Kevin D. Browne, "The Link Between Recurrent Maltreatment and Offending Behavior," *International Journal of Offender Therapy and Comparative Criminology* 46 (2002): 75–95.

156. Brent Benda, "Gender Differences in Life-Course Theory of Recidivism: A Survival Analysis," *International Journal of Offender Therapy and Comparative Criminology* 49 (2005): 325–342.

157. Mbuba, "Lethal Rejection: Recounting Offenders' Experience in Prison and Societal Reaction Post Release."

158. David S. Kirk, "Prisoner Reentry and the Reproduction of Legal Cynicism," *Social Problems* 63 (2016): 222–243.

159. Petersilia, "Hard Time Ex-Offenders Returning Home After Prison."

160. Paul Hirschfield and Alex Piquero, "Normalization and Legitimation: Modeling Stigmatizing Attitudes Toward Ex-Offenders," *Criminology* 48 (2010): 27–55.

161. Mark Berg and Beth Huebner, "Reentry and the Ties that Bind: An Examination of Social Ties, Employment, and Recidivism," *Justice Quarterly* 28 (2011) 382–410; Andy Hochstetler, Matt DeLisi, and Travis C. Pratt, "Social Support and Feelings of Hostility Among Released Inmates," *Crime and Delinquency* 56 (2010): 588–607.

162. Pew Charitable Trusts, *Collateral Costs: Incarceration's Effect on Economic Mobility* (Washington, DC: Pew Charitable Trusts, 2010).

163. Richard Seiter, "Prisoner Reentry and the Role of Parole Officers," *Federal Probation* 66 (2002): 50–54.

164. Charis Kubrin and Eric Stewart, "Predicting Who Reoffends: The Neglected Role of Neighborhood Context in Recidivism Studies," *Criminology* 44 (2006): 165–197.

165. Ryken Grattet, Joan Petersilia, and Jeffery Lin, *Parole Violations and Revocations in California* (Washington, DC: National Institute of Justice, 2008).

166. Alyssa W. Chamberlain and Danielle Wallace, "Mass Reentry Neighborhood Context and Recidivism: Examining How the Distribution of Parolees Within and Across Neighborhoods Impacts Recidivism," *Justice Quarterly* 35 (2016): 912–941.

167. John Hipp, Joan Petersilia, and Susan Turner, "Parolee Recidivism in California: The Effect of Neighborhood Context and Social Service Agency Characteristics," *Criminology* 48 (2010): 947–979.

168. Jeremy Travis, Anna Crayton, and Debbie Mukamal, "A New Era in Inmate Reentry," *Corrections Today* 71 (2009): 38–41.

169. Thomas Hanlon, David Nurco, Richard Bateman, and Kevin O'Grady, "The Response of Drug Abuser Parolees to a Combination of Treatment and Intensive Supervision," *Prison Journal* 78 (1998): 31–44.

170. Kathleen Olivares, Velmer Burton, and Francis Cullen, "The Collateral Consequences of a Felony Conviction: A National Study of State Legal Codes Ten Years Later," *Federal Probation* 60 (1996): 10–17.

171. Christy A. Visher, Pamela K. Lattimore, Kelle Barrick, and Stephen Tueller, "Evaluating the Long-Term Effects of Prisoner Reentry Services on Recidivism: What Types of Services Matter?" *Justice Quarterly* 34 (2017): 136–165.

Chapter 13, Juvenile Justice in the Twenty-First Century

1. Office of the Director of National Intelligence, https://www.dni.gov/files/documents/ICA_2017_01.pdf.

2. Reuters, "U.S. Inquiries Into Russian Election Hacking Include Three FBI Probes," February 18, 2017, http://fortune.com/2017/02/18/russia-election-hack-3-fbi-probes/.

3. David Ignatius, "Russia's Assault on America's Elections Is Just One Example of a Global Threat," *The Washington Post*, February 23, 2017, https://www.washingtonpost.com/opinions/global-opinions/russias-assault-on-americas-elections-is-just-one-example-of-a-global-threat/2017/02/23/3a3dca7e-fa16-11e6-9845-576c69081518_story.html.

4. National Research Council, Committee on Assessing Juvenile Justice Reform, *Reforming Juvenile Justice: A Developmental Approach* (Washington, DC: The National Academies Press, 2013).

5. David S. Tanenhaus, *Juvenile Justice in the Making* (New York: Oxford University Press, 2004); Lawrence Stone, *The Family, Sex, and Marriage in England: 1500–1800* (New York: Harper & Row, 1977); Philippe Aries, *Century of Childhood: A Social History of Family Life* (New York: Vintage Press, 1962); Douglas R. Rendleman, "*Parens Patriae*: From Chancery to the Juvenile Court," *South Carolina Law Review* 23 (1971): 205–229; Anthony M. Platt, "The Rise of the Child-Saving Movement: A Study in Social Policy and Correctional Reform," *Annals of the American Academy of Political and Social Science* 381 (1979): 21–38; Robert S. Pickett, *House of Refuge: Origins of Juvenile Reform in New York State, 1815–1857* (Syracuse, NY: Syracuse University Press, 1969).

6. Anthony Platt, *The Child Savers: The Invention of Delinquency* (Chicago: University of Chicago Press, 1969), pp. 11–38.

7. See, generally, Anne Meis Knupfer, *Reform and Resistance: Gender, Delinquency, and America's First Juvenile Court* (London: Routledge, 2001).

8. This section is based on material from the New York State Archives, *The Greatest Reform School in the World: A Guide to the Records of the*

New York House of Refuge: A Brief History 1824–1857 (Albany: New York State Archives, 2001); Sanford J. Fox, "Juvenile Justice Reform: A Historical Perspective," *Stanford Law Review* 22 (1970): 1187.

9. Pickett, *House of Refuge.*

10. LaMar T. Empey, *American Delinquency: Its Meaning and Construction* (Homewood, IL: Dorsey Press, 1978), p. 515.

11. *Kent. v. United States*, 383 US 541 (1966).

12. *In re Gault*, 387 US 1 (1967).

13. *In re Winship*, 397 US 358 (1970).

14. *McKeiver v. Pennsylvania*, 403 US 528 (1971).

15. *Breed v. Jones*, 421 US 519 (1975).

16. *Fare v. Michael C.*, 442 US 707 (1979).

17. *Schull v. Martin*, 467 US 253 (1984).

18. *New Jersey v. T.L.O.*, 469 US 325 (1985).

19. *Vernonia School District v. Acton*, 515 US 646 (1995).

20. *Roper v. Simmons*, 543 US 551 (2005).

21. *Graham v. Florida*, 560 US ___ (2010).

22. *Miller v. Alabama*, 567 US ___ (2012).

23. *Montgomery v. Louisiana*, 577 US ___ (2016).

24. Public Law 93-415 (1974).

25. For a comprehensive view of juvenile law, see, generally, Joseph J. Senna and Larry J. Siegel, *Juvenile Law: Cases and Comments*, 2nd ed. (St. Paul, MN: West, 1992).

26. Erika Gebo, "Do Family Courts Administer Individualized Justice in Delinquency Cases?" *Criminal Justice Policy Review* 16 (2005): 190–210.

27. Federal Bureau of Investigation, *Crime in the United States, 2015*, https://ucr.fbi.gov/crime-in-the-u.s/2015/crime-in-the-u.s.-2015/tables/table-38.

28. Richard J. Lundman, "Routine Police Arrest Practices," *Social Problems* 22 (1974): 127–141; Robert E. Worden and Stephanie M. Myers, *Police Encounters with Juvenile Suspects* (Albany: Handling Criminal Justice Research Center and School of Criminal Justice, State University of New York, 2001).

29. *Fare v. Michael C.*, 442 US 707 (1979).

30. Ana Abates, Norman Hoffmann, and Ronald Anton, "Prevalence of Co-occurring Disorders Among Juveniles Committed to Detention Centers," *International Journal of Offender Therapy and Comparative Criminology* 49 (2005): 179–194.

31. Nancy Rodriquez, "Juvenile Court Context and Detention Decisions: Reconsidering the Role of Race, Ethnicity, and Community Characteristics in Juvenile Court Processes," *Justice Quarterly* 24 (2007): 629–656.

32. Barry Holman and Jason Seidenberg, *The Dangers of Detention: the Impact of Incarcerating Youth in Detention and Other Secure Facilities* (Washington, DC: Justice Policy Institute, 2006), http://www.justicepolicy.org/images/upload/06-11_rep_dangersofdetention_jj.pdf.

33. *Schell v. Martin*, 467 US 253 (1984).

34. See Juvenile Justice and Delinquency Prevention Act of 1974, 42 U.S.C., sec. 5633.

35. Catherine Van Dijk, An Nuytiens, and Christian Eliaerts, "The Referral of Juvenile Offenders to the Adult Court in Belgium: Theory and Practice," *Howard Journal of Criminal Justice* 44 (2005): 151–166.

36. *Kent v. United States*, 383 US 541 (1966).

37. *Breed v. Jones*, 421 US 519 (1975).

38. John Burrow, "Reverse Waiver and the Effects of Legal, Statutory, and Secondary Legal Factors on Sentencing Outcomes for Juvenile Offenders," *Crime and Delinquency* 54 (2008): 34–64.

39. Julie Furdella and Charles Puzzanchera, *Delinquency Cases in Juvenile Court, 2013* (Washington, DC: Office of Juvenile Justice and Delinquency Prevention, 2015), https://www.ojjdp.gov/pubs/248899.pdf.

40. Howard N. Snyder, Melissa Sickmund, and Eileen Poe-Yamagata, *Juvenile Transfers to Criminal Court in the 1990s: Lessons Learned from Four Studies* (Washington, DC: Office of Juvenile Justice and Delinquency Prevention, 2000).

41. For a summary of the research, see Charles E. Loeffler and Aaron Chalfin, "Estimating the Crime Effects of Raising the Age of Majority: Evidence from Connecticut," *Criminology and Public Policy* 16 (2017): 45–71.

42. James Austin, Kelly Dedel Johnson, and Maria Gregoriou, *Juveniles in Adult Prisons and Jails* (Washington, DC: Bureau of Justice Assistance, 2000).

43. Ibid.

44. Aaron Kupchik, "The Correctional Experiences of Youth in Adult and Juvenile Prisons," *Justice Quarterly* 24 (2007): 247–270.

45. Benjamin Steiner and Emily Wright, "Assessing the Relative Effects of State Direct File Waiver Laws on Violent Juvenile Crime: Deterrence or Irrelevance?" *Journal of Criminal Law and Criminology* 96 (2006): 1451–1477.

46. Loeffler and Chalfin, "Estimating the Crime Effects of Raising the Age of Majority."

47. Benjamin Steiner, "The Effects of Juvenile Transfer to Criminal Court on Incarceration Decisions," *Justice Quarterly* 26 (2009): 77–106; Megan Kurlychek and Brian Johnson, "The Juvenile Penalty: A Comparison of Juvenile and Young Adult Sentencing Outcomes in Criminal Court," *Criminology* 42 (2004): 485–517.

48. Barry Feld, "The Juvenile Court Meets the Principle of the Offense: Legislative Changes in Juvenile Waiver Statutes," *Journal of Criminal Law and Criminology* 78 (1987): 471–533. See also John Kramer, Henry Sontheimer, and John Lemmon, "Pennsylvania Waiver to Adult Court," paper presented at the annual meeting of the American Society of Criminology, San Francisco, November 1991; authors confirm that juveniles tried in adult courts are generally male, age 17 or older, and disproportionately minorities.

49. Jeffrey Fagan, Martin Forst, and T. Scott Vivona, "Racial Determinants of the Judicial Transfer Decision: Prosecuting Violent Youth in Criminal Court," *Crime and Delinquency* 33 (1987): 359–386; J. Fagan, E. Slaughter, and E. Hartstone, "Blind Justice: The Impact of Race on the Juvenile Justice Process," *Crime and Delinquency* 53 (1987): 224–258; J. Fagan and E. P. Deschenes, "Determinants of Judicial Waiver Decisions for Violent Juvenile Offenders," *Journal of Criminal Law and Criminology* 81 (1990): 314–347; see also James Howell, "Juvenile Transfers to Criminal Court," *Juvenile and Family Justice Journal* 6 (1997): 12–14.

50. Sarah Hockenberry and Charles Puzzanchera, *Delinquency Cases Waived to Criminal Court, 2011* (Washington, DC: Office of Juvenile Justice and Delinquency Prevention, 2014), https://www.ojjdp.gov/pubs/248410.pdf.

51. *In re Gault*, 387 US 1 (1967).

52. Melissa Sickmund and Charles Puzzanchera, *Juvenile Offenders and Victims: 2014 National Report* (Washington, DC: National Center for Juvenile Justice, 2014), p. 96.

53. Ibid.

54. See Joseph Goldstein, Anna Freud, and Albert Solnit, *Beyond the Best Interest of the Child* (New York: Free Press, 1973).

55. See Michael Serrill, "Police Write a New Law on Juvenile Crime," *Police Magazine* (September 1979): 47; see also A. Schneider and D. Schram, *Assessment of Juvenile Justice Reform in Washington State*, Vols. 1–4 (Washington, DC: Department of Justice, Institute of Policy Analysis, 1983); T. Castellano, "Justice Model in the Juvenile Justice System— Washington State's Experience," *Law and Policy* 8 (1986): 479.

56. Emily Gaarder, Nancy Rodriguez, and Marjorie Zatz, "Criers, Liars, and Manipulators: Probation Officers' Views of Girls," *Justice Quarterly* 21 (2004): 547–578.

57. Office of Juvenile Justice and Delinquency Prevention, *Juveniles in Corrections*, https://www.ojjdp.gov/ojstatbb/corrections/qa08201.asp.

58. David Smith, "The Effectiveness of the Juvenile Justice System," *Criminal Justice: International Journal of Policy and Practice* 5 (2005): 181–195.

59. Barry C. Feld, *Bad Kids: Race and the Transformation of the Juvenile Court* (New York: Oxford University Press, 1999).

60. Alexes Harris, "Diverting and Abdicating Judicial Discretion: Cultural, Political, and Procedural Dynamics in California Juvenile Justice," *Law and Society Review* 41 (2007): 387–428.

61. John Johnson Kerbs, "(Un)equal Justice: Juvenile Court Abolition and African Americans," *Annals, AAPSS* 564 (1999): 109–125.

62. Melissa Sickmund and Charles Puzzanchere, eds., *Juvenile Offenders and Victims: 2014 National Report* (Pittsburgh: National Center for Juvenile Justice, 2014), p. 176

63. National Council on Crime and Delinquency, *And Justice for Some: Differential Treatment of Minority Youth in the Justice System*, January 2007, http://www.nccdglobal.org/sites/default/files/publication_pdf/justice-for-some.pdf; see also The Sentencing Project, *Disproportionate Minority Contact in the Juvenile Justice System* (Washington, DC: The Sentencing Project, 2015), http://www.sentencingproject.org/wp-content/uploads/2015/11/Disproportionate-Minority-Contact-in-the-Juvenile-Justice-System.pdf.

Chapter 14, Crime and Justice in the New Millennium

1. Los Angeles Times, "San Bernardino Terror Attack," http://www.latimes.com/topic/crime-law-justice/crime/shootings/san-bernardino-terror-attack-EVCAL00077-topic.html.

2. R. Lin II and R. Winton, "San Bernardino Suspects 'Sprayed the Room with Bullets,' Police Chief Says," *Los Angeles Times*, December 4, 2015, http://www.latimes.com/local/lanow/la-me-ln-san-bernardino-suspects-sprayed-the-room-with-bullets-20151203-story.html.

3. J. T. DeSocio and G. Graciette, "FBI: San Bernardino Shooters Were Radicalized at Least 2 Years Ago," Fox LA, December 9, 2015, http://www.foxla.com/news/local-news/56610235-story.

4. P. Williams and H. Abdullah, "FBI: San Bernardino Shooters Radicalized Before They Met," NBC News, December 9, 2016, http://www.nbcnews.com/storyline/san-bernardino-shooting/fbi-san-bernardino-shooters-radicalized-they-met-n476971.

5. Nikos Passas and David Nelken, "The Thin Line Between Legitimate and Criminal Enterprises: Subsidy Frauds in the European Community," *Crime, Law, and Social Change* 19 (1993): 223–243.

6. Mark Haller, "Illegal Enterprise: A Theoretical and Historical Interpretation," *Criminology* 28 (1990): 207–235.

7. For a thorough review, see David Friedrichs, *Trusted Criminals* (Belmont, CA: Wadsworth, 1996).

8. Kitty Calavita and Henry Pontell, "Savings and Loan Fraud as Organized Crime: Toward a Conceptual Typology of Corporate Illegality," *Criminology* 31 (1993): 519–548.

9. Walter Laqueur, *The New Terrorism: Fanaticism and the Arms of Mass Destruction Terrorism and History* (New York: Oxford University Press, 1999).

10. Edmund Burke, *Reflections on the Revolution in France, 1790* (New York: Penguin Classics; reprint edition 1982).

11. Lindsay Clutterbuck, "The Progenitors of Terrorism: Russian Revolutionaries or Extreme Irish Republicans?" *Terrorism and Political Violence* 16 (2004): 154–181.

12. Title 22 of the United States Code section 2656f (d) (1999).

13. Jack Gibbs, "Conceptualization of Terrorism," *American Sociological Review* 54 (1989): 329–340, at 330.

14. Ibid.

15. CNN, "Wisconsin Sikh Temple Shooting," http://www.cnn.com/specials/us/sikh-temple-shooting/.

16. Clark McCauley and Sophia Moskalenko, "Two Possible Profiles of Lone-Actor Terrorists," National Consortium for the Study of Terrorism and Responses to Terrorism (START), 2013, http://www.start.umd.edu/publication/two-possible-profiles-lone-actor-terrorists.

17. Lawrence Miller, "The Terrorist Mind: A Psychological and Political Analysis, Part I," *International Journal of Offender Therapy and Comparative Criminology* 50 (2006): 121–138.

18. Gabriela Fried, "Piecing Memories Together After State Terror and Policies of Oblivion in Uruguay: The Female Political Prisoner's Testimonial Project (1997–2004)," *Social Identities* 12 (2006): 543–562.

19. Martin Miller, "Ordinary Terrorism in Historical Perspective," *Journal for the Study of Radicalism* 2 (2008): 125–154.

20. Lawrence Miller, "The Terrorist Mind: A Psychological and Political Analysis, Part II," *International Journal of Offender Therapy and Comparative Criminology* 50 (2006): 255–268.

21. Ibid.

22. Chris Dishman, "Terrorism, Crime, and Transformation," *Studies in Conflict and Terrorism* 24 (2001): 43–56.

23. Stevan Weine, Chloe Polutnik, and Ahmed Younis, "The Role of Community Policing in Countering Violent Extremism," National Consortium for the Study of Terrorism and Responses to Terrorism (START), February 2015, http://www.start.umd.edu/pubs/STARTResearchBrief_CommunityPolicing_Feb2015.pdf.

24. Jeremy Diamond, "NSA Surveillance Bill Passes After Weeks-Long Showdown," CNN, June 2, 2015, http://www.cnn.com/2015/06/02/politics/senate-usa-freedom-act-vote-patriot-act-nsa/.

25. H.R. 3361 – USA FREEDOM Act, 113th Congress (2013–2014), https://www.congress.gov/bill/113th-congress/house-bill/3361.

26. Edwin Sutherland, *White-Collar Crime: The Uncut Version* (New Haven, CT: Yale University Press, 1983).

27. Ronald Kramer and Raymond Michalowski, "State-Corporate Crime,"

paper presented at the annual meeting of the American Society of Criminology, Baltimore, November 1990.

28. Edwin Sutherland, "White-Collar Criminality," *American Sociological Review* 5 (1940): 2–10.

29. Natalie Taylor, "Under-Reporting of Crime Against Small Business: Attitudes Towards Police and Reporting Practices," *Policing and Society* 13 (2003): 79–90.

30. Federal Bureau of Investigation, "Volkswagen AG Agrees to Plead Guilty and Pay $4.3 Billion in Criminal and Civil Penalties," https://www.justice.gov/opa/pr/volkswagen-ag-agrees-plead-guilty-and-pay-43-billion-criminal-and-civil-penalties-six.

31. Chris Isidore, "Three Former Executives of Japanese Airbag Maker Takata Were Indicted Over the Company's Exploding Airbags Friday," CNN Money, January 16, 2017, http://money.cnn.com/2017/01/13/news/companies/takata-criminal-settlement/.

32. Brent Snavely, "Takata Agrees to $1B Plea Deal to Settle Airbag Case," *Detroit Free Press*, February 27, 2017, http://www.usatoday.com/story/money/cars/2017/02/27/takata-agrees-1b-plea-deal-settle-airbag-case/98502552/.

33. Securities and Exchange Commission, "SEC Charges Bernard L. Madoff for Multi-Billion Dollar Ponzi Scheme," December 11, 2008, https://www.sec.gov/news/press/2008/2008-293.htm; Joe Lauria, "Life Inside the Weird World of Bernard Madoff," *The Times*, March 22, 2009, http://www.thesundaytimes.co.uk/sto/business/article157099.ece.

34. Securities and Exchange Commission, "SEC Charges Bernard L. Madoff for Multi-Billion Dollar Ponzi Scheme"; Report of Investigation, US Securities and Exchange Commission Office of Inspector General, Case No. OIG-509, *Investigation of Failure of the SEC to Uncover Bernard Madoff's Ponzi Scheme*, https://www.sec.gov/news/studies/2009/oig-509.pdf.

35. Sean Rosenmerkel, "Wrongfulness and Harmfulness as Components of Seriousness of White-Collar Offenses," *Journal of Contemporary Criminal Justice* 17 (2001): 308–328.

36. Jonathan Lechter, Daniel Posner, and George Morris, "Antitrust Violations," *American Criminal Law Review* 39 (2002): 225–273.

37. Mark Cohen, "Environmental Crime and Punishment: Legal/Economic Theory and Empirical Evidence on Enforcement of Federal Environmental Statutes," *Journal of Criminal Law and Criminology* 82 (1992): 1054–1109.

38. Miami-Dade Mortgage Fraud Task Force, http://www.miamidade.gov/police/prevention-mortgage-fraud.asp.

39. Thomas Catan and Guy Chazan, "Spill Draws Criminal Probe," *The Wall Street Journal*, June 2, 2010, https://www.wsj.com/articles/SB10001424052748704875604575280983140254458.

40. Helene Cooper and Peter Baker, "US Opens Criminal Inquiry into Oil Spill," *The New York Times*, June 1, 2010, http://www.nytimes.com/2010/06/02/us/02spill.html.

41. Department of Justice, "Transocean Agrees to Plead Guilty to Environmental Crime and Enter Civil Settlement to Resolve US Clean Water Act Penalty Claims from Deepwater Horizon Incident, Transocean to Pay Record $1 Billion in Civil Penalties and $400 Million in Criminal Fines," January 3, 2012, https://www.justice.gov/opa/pr/transocean-agrees-plead-guilty-environmental-crime-and-enter-civil-settlement-resolve-us.

42. Michael J. Lynch and Paul Stretesky, "Green Criminology in the United States," in *Issues in Green Criminology*, ed. Piers Beirne and Nigel South (Portland, OR: Willan, 2008), pp. 248–269, at 249.

43. Michael O'Hear, "Sentencing the Green-Collar Offender: Punishment, Culpability, and Environmental Crime," *Journal of Criminal Law and Criminology* 95 (2004): 133–276.

44. This section relies on Duncan Brack, *Illegal Logging* (London: Chatham House, 2007).

45. Ibid.

46. World Wildlife Fund, "Illegal Fishing," http://www.worldwildlife.org/threats/illegal-fishing.

47. Andrew Oliveira, Christopher Schenck, Christopher Cole, and Nicole Janes, "Environmental Crimes (Annual Survey of White-Collar Crime)," *American Criminal Law Review* 42 (2005): 347–380.

48. Environmental Protection Agency, "Criminal Enforcement," https://www.epa.gov/enforcement/criminal-enforcement.

49. Statement of Michael A. Vatis, director, National Infrastructure Protection Center, Federal Bureau of Investigation, on cyber crime before the Senate Judiciary Committee, Criminal Justice Oversight Subcommittee, and House Judiciary Committee, Crime Subcommittee, February 29, 2000.

50. Daily Infographic, "The Stats on Internet Pornography," http://www.dailyinfographic.com/the-stats-on-internet-pornography-infographic.

51. Identity Theft Resource Center (ITRC), "Scams and Consumer Alerts," http://www.idtheftcenter.org/.

52. National Center on Addiction and Substance Abuse at Columbia University, "'You've Got Drugs!' V: Prescription Drug Pushers on the Internet," May 2008, http://www.centeronaddiction.org/addiction-research/reports/youve-got-drugs-perscription-drug-pushers-internet-2008.

53. *The Economist*, "Shedding Light on the Dark Web," July 16, 2016, http://www.economist.com/news/international/21702176-drug-trade-moving-street-online-cryptomarkets-forced-compete.

54. Anne Branscomb, "Rogue Computer Programs and Computer Rogues: Tailoring Punishment to Fit the Crime," *Rutgers Computer and Technology Law Journal* 16 (1990): 24–26.

55. Heather Jacobson and Rebecca Green, "Computer Crimes," *American Criminal Law Review* 39 (2002): 272–326.

56. Joan E. Solsman and Richard Nieva, "Google Accounts Hit with Malware – A Million and Growing," November 30, 2016, https://www.cnet.com/news/google-gooligan-accounts-hacked-malware-trojan-horse-gmail-play-drive-photos-docs/.

57. This section relies heavily on United States Computer Emergency Readiness Team, "Understanding Denial-of-Service Attacks," https://www.us-cert.gov/ncas/tips/ST04-015.

58. See, for example, Working to Halt Online Abuse, http://www.haltabuse.org/resources/laws/.

59. Janis Wolak, David Finkelhor, Kimberly Mitchell, and Michele Ybarra, "Online 'Predators' and Their Victims: Myths, Realities, and Implications for Prevention and Treatment," *American Psychologist* 63 (2008): 111–128.

60. Jane Ireland and Rachel Monaghan, "Behaviours Indicative of Bullying Among Young and Juvenile Male Offenders: A Study of Perpetrator and Victim Characteristics," *Aggressive Behavior* 32 (2006): 172–180.

61. This section relies heavily on Justin Patchin and Sameer Hinduja, "Bullies Move Beyond the Schoolyard: A Preliminary Look at Cyberbullying," *Youth Violence and Juvenile Justice* 4 (2006): 148–169.

62. Ibid.

63. Barry C. Collin, "The Future of Cyber-Terrorism: Where the Physical and Virtual Worlds Converge," http://www.crime-research.org/library/Cyberter.htm.

64. Mark Pollitt, "Cyberterrorism—Fact or Fancy?" *Computer Fraud and Security* 2 (1998): 8–10.

65. James Lewis, "Assessing the Risks of Cyberterrorism, Cyber War, and Other Cyber Threats," report submitted to the Center for Strategic and International Studies, Washington, DC, 2002, p. 1.

66. Heather Jacobson and Rebecca Green, "Computer Crime," *American Criminal Law Review* 39 (2002): 273–326; Identity Theft and Assumption Act of 1998 (18 U.S.C. S 1028(a)(7)); Bruce Swartz, Deputy Assistant General, Criminal Division, "Justice Department Internet Fraud Testimony Before the House Energy and Commerce Committee, May 23, 2001"; Comprehensive Crime Control Act of 1984, PL 98-473, 2101-03, 98 Stat. 1837, 2190 (1984), adding 18 U.S.C. 1030 (1984); Counterfeit Active Device and Computer Fraud and Abuse Act Amended by PL 99-474, 100 Stat. 1213 (1986) codified at 18 U.S.C. 1030 (Supp. V 1987); Computer Abuse Amendments Act 18 U.S.C. section 1030 (1994); Copyright Infringement Act 17 U.S.C. section 506(a) 1994; Electronic Communications Privacy Act of 1986, 18 U.S.C. 2510-2520 (1988 and Supp. II 1990).

67. Computer Fraud and Abuse Act (CFAA), 18 U.S.C. section 1030 (1998).

68. Digital Millennium Copyright Act, Public Law 105-304 (1998).

69. Title 18, U.S.C., section 2319.

70. Title 17, U.S.C., section 506.

71. Identity Theft and Assumption Deterrence Act, as amended by Public Law 105-318, 112 Stat. 3007 (October 30, 1998).

72. *Ashcroft v. Free Speech Coalition*, 535 US 234 (2002).

73. The Prosecutorial Remedies and Other Tools to End the Exploitation of Children, 18 U.S.C. 1466A (2003).

74. *United States v. Williams*, 553 US 285 (2008).

75. PL 98-473, Title H, Chapter XXI, [sections] 2102(a), 98 Stat. 1837, 2190 (1984).

76. Statement of Mr. Bob Weaver, Deputy Special Agent in Charge, New York Field Office, United States Secret Service, Before the House Financial Services Committee, the Subcommittee on Financial Institutions and Consumer Credit, and the Subcommittee on Oversight and Investigations, US House of Representatives, April 3, 2003.

77. Andrew Nikiforuk, *Pandemonium: How Globalization and Trade Are Putting the World at Risk* (Queensland, NZ: University of Queensland Press, 2007).

78. David Friedrichs and Jessica Friedrichs, "The World Bank and Crimes of Globalization: A Case Study," *Social Justice* 29 (2002): 13–36.

79. United Nations Office on Drugs and Crime, *The Globalization of Crime: A Transnational Organized Crime Threat Assessment*, https://www.unodc.org/documents/data-and-analysis/tocta/TOCTA_Report_2010_low_res.pdf.

80. Public Law No. 95-213, 101-104, 91 Stat. 1494.

81. Reuters, "Pfizer Settles Foreign Bribery Case with US Government," August 7, 2012, http://www.reuters.com/article/us-pfizer-settlement-idUSBRE8760WM20120807.

82. United Nations Office on Drugs and Crime, *The Globalization of Crime: A Transnational Organized Crime Threat Assessment*.

83. Ibid.

84. US Department of State, *Trafficking in Persons Report, 2016*, https://www.state.gov/documents/organization/258876.pdf.

85. FBI, "Asian Criminal Enterprises," https://www2.fbi.gov/hq/cid/orgcrime/asiancrim.htm.

86. Roderic Broadhurst, "Of Triads, Yakuza, and the Gangs of Asia," December 6, 2016, *U.S. News and World Report*, https://www.usnews.com/news/best-countries/articles/2016-12-06/governments-ignore-organized-crime-crisis-across-asia.

87. See, for example, Stephen Ellis, *This Present Darkness: A History of Nigerian Organized Crime* (Oxford, UK: Oxford University Press, 2016).

88. Chaim Shinar, "Organized Crime in Russia," *European Review* 24 (2016): 631–640.

89. For a recent example, see John Marzulli, "Feds Arrest Nine Members of a Brooklyn-Based Russian Criminal Enterprise," *New York Daily News*, November 9, 2016, http://www.nydailynews.com/new-york/brooklyn/feds-bust-9-members-brooklyn-based-russian-criminal-enterprise-article-1.2865940.

90. Christina Sterbenz, "These Are the 2 Classic Ways Mexican Cartels Launder Money," *Business Insider*, February 20, 2015, http://www.businessinsider.com/how-mexican-cartels-launder-their-money-2015-2.

91. Department of Homeland Security, "United States – Mexico Bi-National Criminal Proceeds Study," https://www.ice.gov/doclib/cornerstone/pdf/cps-study.pdf.

92. Madison Park, "Mexico's Most Notorious Drug Cartels," CNN, August 18, 2016, http://www.cnn.com/2016/08/18/americas/mexican-drug-cartels/.

93. 18 U.S.C. 1952 (1976).

94. Public Law 91-452, Title IX, 84 Stat. 922 (1970) (codified at 18 U.S.C. 1961-68, 1976).

95. Ibid.

96. William Booth, "Mexican Azteca Gang Leader Arrested in Killings of 3 Tied to US," *Washington Post*, March 30, 2010, http://www.washingtonpost.com/wp-dyn/content/article/2010/03/29/AR2010032903373.html.

97. CNN Library, "Mexico Drug War Fast Facts," December 19, 2016, http://www.cnn.com/2013/09/02/world/americas/mexico-drug-war-fast-facts/.

98. Orlando Patterson, "The Other Losing War," *The New York Times*, January 13, 2007.

99. Declan Walsh, "Afghan Province to Provide One-Third of World's Heroin," *The Guardian*, June 14, 2006, https://www.theguardian.com/world/2006/jun/14/afghanistan.drugstrade.

100. "Afghanistan's Opium Production Soaring, Says UN," October 23, 2016, *The Guardian*, https://www.theguardian.com/world/2016/oct/23/afghanistan-opium-production-soaring-un-office-on-drugs-and-crime.

101. Francisco Gutierrez, "Institutionalizing Global Wars: State Transformations in Colombia, 1978–2002: Colombian Policy Directed at Its Wars, Paradoxically, Narrows the Government's Margin of Maneuver Even as It Tries to Expand It," *Journal of International Affairs* 57 (2003): 135–152.

Case Index

Name Index

Garrett, Pat, 6
Geier, William, 290
Gendreau, Paul, 309
Gherle, Emily, 340
Gibbons, Kent, 237
Gibbons, Malinda, 237
Giffords, Gabrielle, 16, 179
Gilbert, Kristen, 179
Gillespie, Edward, 88
Goodall, Martin, 97
Gordon, Steven Dean, 229, 236
Gorsuch, Marie Louise, 169
Gorsuch, Neil, 169
Graham, Melvin, 4
Greaves, Theresa Rose, 119
Griffen, Jim, 125
Gross, Samuel, 232
Grunwald, Meagan, 342
Gunter, Cortney, 255
Guzman, Joaquin "El Chapo," 372, 376

H

Hamilton, Zachary, 256
Hammond, Dwight and Steve, 355
Harris, Joseph, 102
Harris, Ross, 206
Hatch, Orrin, 75
Hayes, Cardell, 66
Hemenway, David, 67
Henry II, 57, 274
Henson, Scott, 115
Hernandez, Aaron, 16
Hickenlooper, John, 317
Hiniger, Damon, 290
Hirschfield, Paul, 321
Hirschi, Travis, 49
Hochman, Nathan, 260
Hoffman, Philip Seymour, 28
Holmes, James, 16, 18, 63
Hoose, David, 179
Hoover, Herbert, 7
Horton, Willie, 279
Houser, Lowell, 143
Howard, John, 218, 274
Howard, Scott, 298
Hribal, Alex, 342
Hurd, Cynthia, 4

I

Ignatius, David, 327
Innes, Martin, 117

J

Jackall, Robert, 117
Jackson, Kianna, 229

James, Jesse, 6
Joh, Elizabeth, 95
Johnson, Lyndon, 7
Johnson, Micah Xavier, 80
Johnson, Robert, 234
Jones, Joshua, 97
Jorgensen, Jennifer, 58

K

Kaczynski, Ted, 179
Kane, Robert, 148
Kanger, Ken, 348
Kanka, Megan, 69, 198
Kelling, George, 114
Kelly, Robert and Mary, 58
Kendall, George, 229
Kennedy, Aaron, 191
Kennedy, Anthony, 169
Kerbs, John, 347
Kevorkian, Jack, 69
King, Daniel, 63
King, Rodney, 87
Kleiman, Mark A., 256
Klinger, David, 139
Koetters, Joseph, 198
Kohn, Sally, 355
Krebs, Christopher, 245, 253

L

Labrie, Owen, 257
Lahm, Karen, 307
Lambert, Eric, 309
Land, Precious, 44
Lane, T. J., 47
LaPierre, Wayne, 67
Lattimore, Pamela, 256
Levine, Leonard, 198
Lewinski, Shari, 163
Li, LiYing, 235
Lima-Marin, Rene, 317
Lipsey, Mark, 309
Liu, Wenjian, 141
Lofstrom, Magnus, 287
Long, Gavin, 80
Lopez, Paul, 364
Loughner, Jared Lee, 16, 179
Low, Sabina, 349

M

Maass, Dave, 115
MacDonald, Heather, 79
Macomber, Joshua, 315
Madoff, Bernard, 16, 353, 360–361
Malik, Tashfeen, 352

Mann, Teresa, 177
Markovsky, Jennifer, 202
Mars, Bruno, 257
Martin, Trayvon, 66
Martin, Wade, 75
Martinez, Gilbert, 202
Martinson, Robert, 308
Masterson, Bat, 6
Mateen, Omar, 3, 358
Mauer, Marc, 223
McClain, William, 222
McDonald, Laquan, 186
McGuire, Rachel, 102
McReynolds, Jim, 11
McVeigh, Tim, 23
Mears, Daniel, 284
Menzies, Diane, 229
Merritt, Erin, 250
Miles, Linda, 39
Miller, F. Glenn, Jr., 172
Miller, Joel, 249
Miller, Lindsay, 97
Mockaitis, tom, 355
Mohamed, Mohamed, 120
Moran, Jason, 101
Morissette, Alanis, 260
Morris, Robert, 315

N

Neithercut, Geoffrey L., 221
Nieves, Jose, 143
Noble, Dylan, 145
Nomura, Yoichiro, 360
Norton, Kayla Rae, 222

O

Obama, Barack, 71, 87, 146, 316
O'Connell, Daniel, 256
O'Hara, Austin, 294
Osborne, Thomas Mott, 278
Osterman, Michael, 320

P

Packer, Herbert, 13
Padget, Kathy, 262
Page, Wade Michael, 357
Paluch, James A., Jr., 297
Pannesi, Derrik, 338
Parsell, T. J., 298
Peel, Robert, 83
Penn, William, 274, 275
Piehl, Anne Morrison, 228
Piquero, Alex, 321
Putin, Vladimir, 327

Subject Index

deadly force, 144–146

Deadspin, 146

Death in Custody Reporting Act (2013), 146

death penalty. *See* capital punishment

Death Penalty Information Center, 235

Death penalty quiz, 235

death penalty statute, 60

decriminalization, 20, 68

Deepwater Horizon oil spill, 70, 362–363

defense attorney, 176–181

    competence, 180–181

    defending the despised, 179

    effectiveness of private counsel, 180

    ethics, 24

    indigent defendants, 178–179

    myth vs. reality, 25

    plea bargaining, 199

    private bar, 179–180

    right to counsel, 177

    role, 176–177

    trial, 208

Defense Computer Forensics Laboratory (DCFL), 366

defense-of-life shooting, 67

defenses. *See* criminal defenses

deinstitutionalization, 20

Delinquency in a Birth Cohort (Wolfgang et al.), 42

demeanor, 139

denial-of-service attack, 369

Department of Homeland Security (DHS), 90, 358

deposit bail, 189, 191

desert/incapacitation model, 272

detectives, 116, 117. *See also* investigation function

detention, 339–340

determinate sentence, 221–222

deterrence

    capital punishment, 230–231, 232–233

    goal of sentencing, as, 218–219

deterrent effect, 111

Deuel Vocational Institution, 287

developmental theory, 50, 51

DHS (Department of Homeland Security), 90, 358

Digital Millennium Copyright Act (DMCA), 370

direct appeal, 211

direct examination, 207

direct file waiver, 342

direct-supervision jail, 281–282

directed patrol, 113

discretion

    correctional officers, 25

    defined, 138

juvenile justice, 337–338

    police, 138–140

    prosecutor, 174–175

discretionary appeal, 211

discretionary parole, 317

Disneyland, 95

district attorney, 173. *See also* prosecutor

district courts, 160, 164f, 165–166

diversion, 200–201

DMCA (Digital Millennium Copyright Act), 370

DNA exonerees, 232

DNA profiling, 100, 119

DNA testing, 100–101

documentary evidence, 207

domestic relations court, 164f

domestic violence court, 162

double-blind lineup administration, 233

double jeopardy, 72

double marginality, 133

DRC (day reporting center), 264

drones, 116

drug cartels, 375

drug court, 162

Drug Enforcement Administration (DEA), 90

drug overdose, 28

Drug Policy Alliance, 25

drug treatment, 305–306

due process clause, 72

due process of law, 73–74

due process perspective, 18–19

dumping, illegal, 364

duress, 63

Durham rule, 64

E

e-tailing fraud, 368

early correctional institutions, 275

early jails, 274

Eastern State Penitentiary, 275, 276

educational programs, 306–307

Eighth Amendment, 72–73, 188, 314

elderly inmates, 288

electronic monitoring (EM), 262, 264

electronic offender tracking, 263

Elmira Reformatory, 277, 278, 306

EM (electronic monitoring), 262, 264

Emergency Planning and Community Right-to-Know Act, 365

emotional intelligence, 138

enclosed space detection system (ESDS), 99

Endangered Species Act, 365

English Penal Servitude Act, 277

entrapment, 65

environmental contaminants, 45

environmental crime. *See* green crime

environmental laws, 69

Environmental Protection Agency (EPA), 69, 362, 365

equal justice perspective, 20

equity, 220

Ethical Reflection boxes

    crime report manipulation, 52

    heavy-handed approaches to law enforcement, 128

    incarceration vs. house arrest, 268

    juvenile transfer to adult court, 350

    mens rea reform, 75

    overcriminalization, 25

    plea bargaining, 211

    prison vouchers, 291

    private police, 103

    prosecutorial misconduct, 183

    strip search of all people entering detention facility, 324

    tasers, 153

    torture, 378

    victim impact statement, 235

ethics, 22–25

    corrections, 24–25

    courts, 24

    defense attorney, 24

    law enforcement, 23

    prosecution, 24, 176

Eurasian Organized Crime Working Group, 376

evidence at trial, 207

evidence-based justice, 8

evidence-based programming, 8

evidentiary standards of proof, 204, 205

ex post facto laws, 58, 59

exceptional circumstances doctrine, 314

excessive bail, 72

excluded offense waiver, 342

exclusionary rule, 72, 75, 153

excuse defenses, 63–65

exigent circumstances, 152–153

Eyman Prison, 279

F

Facebook, 102

facial recognition software, 100

fact-finding hearing, 343

failure or omission to act, 60

fairness, 19

faith-based programs, 305

Families Against Mandatory Minimums, 223

family court, 164f, 335

family group conference, 266–267

high-definition surveying (HDS), 99–100
Hispanics. *See* race and ethnicity
historical overview
    ancient legal codes, 57
    Auburn system, 275, 276
    Cincinnati National Congress (1870), 277
    colonial America, 83
    community-oriented policing, 120
    contract system, 276
    convict-lease system, 276, 278
    correctional institutions, 273–280
    early police agencies, 6, 83–85
    English system, 82–83
    hulks, 274
    juvenile justice, 330–334
    medical model, 279
    New York (Auburn) system, 275, 276
    parole, 277–278
    Pennsylvania system, 276
    post-1960s policing, 86–87
    President's Task Force on 21st Century Policing, 87–89
    probation, 246
    professionalism, 85
    punishment, 214–216
    stare decisis, 57
    thief takers, 82–83
HIV-infected inmates, 306
Holocaust survivor syndrome, 68
Homeland Security agencies, 90–91
HOPE program, 256
hormone imbalance, 45
hot spots of crime, 100, 123
HotSpot probation, 255
house arrest, 261–262, 264
House of Corrections (Detroit), 306
House of Reformation (Boston), 332
Hudson Dusters, 6
hue and cry, 82
hulks, 274
human organs, trade in, 373
human trafficking, 374
hundred, 82
hung jury, 209
hydrocodone, 28
Hyundai Heavy Industries, 362

I

IACP (International Association of Chiefs of Police), 24, 85
identity theft, 69, 368, 370–371
Identity Theft and Assumption Deterrence Act, 370
Identity Theft Penalty Enhancement Act, 371

ignorance of the law, 62, 75
illegal drug abuse, 28
illegal drug distribution, 368
illegal drug trade, 373
illegal fishing, 363–364
illegal logging, 363
illegal polluting, 364
illegal touting, 367
Illinois Juvenile Court Act, 333
ILP (intelligence-led policing), 123–126
immigrant smuggling, 373
immigration and crime, 37, 38
Immigration and Customs Enforcement (ICE), 100, 375
immunity, 68, 183
in-presence requirement, 12
inadequacy of counsel, 180–181
incapacitation, 219
incarceration rate, 242
indenture, 330
indeterminate sentence, 220–221
indictment, 194
indictment process, 193–194
indigent defendants, 178–179
indirect-supervision jail, 282
inferior courts, 164f
information, 12, 194
information process, 194–195
information technology (IT), 118–119
infraction, 59
infrastructure attacks, 370
initial appearance, 343
initial contact, 11
inmate-balance theory, 312
inmate social code, 300
inmate subculture, 300–301
Innocence Project, 232
insanity, 64
Insanity Defense Reform Act, 64
institutional racism, 40
instructions to jury, 208–209
insurgent, 356
intake, 250
intelligence-led policing (ILP), 123–126
Intelligence Working Group, 125
intensive probation supervision (IPS), 261, 264
interactionist view of crime, 30–31
Interagency Telemarketing and Internet Fraud Working Group, 371
intermediate appellate courts, 163–164, 164f
intermediate sanctions, 257–264
    advantages, 257–258
    concept summary, 264
    day reporting center (DRC), 264
    defined, 257

    electronic monitoring (EM), 262, 264
    fine, 258, 264
    forfeiture, 258–259, 264
    GPS monitoring, 262–263
    house arrest, 261–262, 264
    intensive probation supervision (IPS), 261, 264
    residential community corrections (RCC), 263–264
    restitution, 259–260, 264
    shock probation, 260, 264
    split sentence, 260, 264
internal affairs, 126
International Association of Chiefs of Police (IACP), 24, 85
international terrorism, 355
Internet pornography, 367, 371
Internet predators, 369
Internet securities fraud, 367
interrogation and confessions, 148–149
Interstate and Foreign Travel or Transportation in aid of Racketeering Enterprises Act (Travel Act), 376
intoxication, 64
investigation, 11–12
investigation function, 116–120
    effectiveness, 118
    forensic science, 119–120
    information technology (IT), 118–119
    length of investigation, 118
    sources of information, 118
    sting operation, 117–118
    three-pronged approach, 117
    unsolved cases, 118
IPS (intensive probation supervision), 261, 264
irresistible impulse test, 64
Islamic State of Iraq and the Levant (ISIL), 357

J

J-Net, 182
jail
    defined, 272
    gender, 280, 280t
    historical overview, 274
    juveniles in adult facilities, 281, 340
    new-generation, 281–283
    population trends, 280
    purposes, 280
    race and ethnicity, 280–281
    suicide, 281
jail incarceration rate, 280
jailhouse lawyer, 313
Jalisco New Generation, 376

National Information Infrastructure
 Protection Act (NIIPA), 371
National Institute of Bail Enforcement, 191
National Institute of Justice (NIJ), 7, 128,
 148
National Institute of Law Enforcement and
 Criminal Justice (NILECJ), 7
National Prison Project, 313
National Research Council, 232
National Survey on Drug Use and
 Health, 54
National Youth Gang Center (NYGS),
 338
nationalist terrorism, 356–357
Native Americans, 266
NCVS. *See* National Crime Victimization
 Survey (NCVS)
necessity, 66
neighborhood-oriented policing (NOP),
 121
neurological factors and crime, 45, 51
new crimes and legal categories, 68–72
new-generation jail, 281–283
New Jim Crow, The (Alexander), 272
New Mexico State Penitentiary riot, 279,
 311
new penology, 272
New York (Auburn) system, 275, 276
New York City Police Department
 (NYCPD)
 CompStat, 114–115
 Counterterrorism Bureau, 94
 crime report manipulation, 52
 internal investigation every time
  officer's weapon is discharge,
  145–146
 size, 93
 stop, question, and frisk (SQF), 111
New York House of Refuge, 331–332
Newgate Prison, 274
NIBRS (National Incident-Based Reporting
 System), 33
NIIPA (National Information
 Infrastructure Protection Act), 371
NIJ (National Institute of Justice), 7, 128,
 148
911 calls, 113
Nixle, 102
no bill, 194
nolle prosequi, 12, 174, 218
nolo contendere, 196
nondeadly force, 147
nonintervention perspective, 19–20
nonnegligent manslaughter, 31
nonreporting of crime, 32
NOP (neighborhood-oriented policing),
 121

North End Gang, 6
not-guilty plea, 196
"nothing works" philosophy, 308–309
NYC Justice Corps, 322
NYECTF (New York Electronic Crimes
 Task Force), 371
"NYPD's Compstat: Compare Statistics or
 Compose Statistics, The" (Eterno/
 Silverman), 52

O

obitiatry, 69
objective reasonableness standard, 145, 147
occupation of headquarters of Malheur
 National Wildlife Refuge, 355
ocean dumping by cruise ships, 69
Office of Community Oriented Policing
 Services (COPS) program, 121
Office of Homeland Security and
 Emergency Management (OHSEM -
 Harris County, Texas), 92–93
Office of Juvenile Justice and Delinquency
 Prevention (OJJDP), 7, 128, 328, 333,
 334, 340
official crime statistics, 31
Oil Pollution Act, 365
oil spills, 362–363
OJJDP (Office of Juvenile Justice and
 Delinquency Prevention), 7, 128,
 328, 333, 334, 340
Oklahoma Department of Corrections, 263
opening statements, 207
Operation Ceasefire, 123
opium, 377, 378
Orange Is the New Black (TV), 303
ordeal, 57
order maintenance, 110, 112
Organized Crime Control Act (1970), 90,
 376
organized crime laws, 376–377
outsourcing prosecution, 158–160
overcriminalization, 25
Overcriminalization Task Force, 25
overview/review. *See* concept summary
OxyContin, 28

P

Panasonic, 97
paper and pencil interviewing (PAPI), 34
paralegal, 173
parens patriae, 330, 331
parole
 defined, 317
 discretionary/mandatory release, 317
 effectiveness, 318–319
 historical overview, 277–278

 juvenile justice, 347
 legal right to, 318
 monitoring parolees with GPS, 319
 problem of reentry. *See* reentry into the
  community
 reasons for parole failure, 320–321
 recidivism, 318, 318f
 supervision, 319
parole board, 317
Part I crimes, 31
Part II crimes, 32
Patriot Act, 70, 71
patrol function
 arrests, 113
 broken windows policing, 114
 CompStat, 114–115, 124t
 directed patrol, 113
 effectiveness, 112
 order maintenance, 110, 112
 proactive policing, 111–113
 purposes, 110
 rapid response, 114
 technology, 114–115
PCRA (Post-Conviction Risk Assessment),
 251
peacekeeping, 110, 112
penal harm, 280
penitentiary, 218
Penitentiary Act, 274
penitentiary house, 275
Pennsylvania system, 276
peremptory challenge, 206
PERF (Police Executive Research Forum),
 97, 102
permanent underclass, 48
personal alarm location system, 283
personality theory, 47
persons in need of supervision (PINS), 335
Pew Charitable Trusts, 7, 263
Pew Foundation, 321
Pew Research Center, 67, 130
Pfizer, 373
Philadelphia Society for Alleviating the
 Miseries of Public Prisons, 275, 277
phishing, 368
Phoenix Police Department, 98
physician-assisted suicide, 69
PINS (persons in need of supervision),
 335
plain view search, 152
planning and research functions, 128
play family, 303
plea, 196
plea bargaining, 13, 196–200
 ad hoc, 197
 defense counsel, 199
 defined, 196

range controlled radar (RCR), 283
Range-R, 151
rank system, 109
rape, 69
rational choice theory, 44–45, 51
RCC (residential community corrections),
   263–264
RDAP (residential drug abuse program),
   305
real evidence, 207
realitycheck. *See* myth vs. reality
reasonable doubt standard, 204
reasonable suspicion, 205, 252
recidivism
   bail release, 190
   HOPE program, 256
   parole, 318, 318f
   patrol, 112
   supermax incarceration, 284
   tasers, 148
recognizance, 246
recoupment, 178
reentry into the community, 319–324
   community problems, 322
   criminal record "penalty," 323
   economic problems, 321
   family problems, 321–322
   improving chances on reentry,
     322–324
   legal problems, 322
   personal problems, 320–321
   postrelease programs, 308
reform school, 333
reforming, reinvesting, and restructuring,
   254
rehabilitation, 220
rehabilitation perspective, 18
reintegrative shaming, 264–265
relational rehabilitation programs, 266
relative deprivation, 41
release on recognizance (ROR), 190
religious freedom, 314
repeat victimization, 43–44
residential community corrections (RCC),
   263–264
residential drug abuse program (RDAP),
   305
restitution, 220, 259–260, 264
restorative cautioning, 266
restorative conference, 266
restorative justice, 264–268
   awareness of cultural and social
     differences, 267–268
   balancing needs of offenders and
     victims, 268
   basic principles, 265
   court programs, 267

defined, 264
family group conference, 266–267
Native Americans, 266
police programs, 266
pretrial programs, 266–267
race, 267
reintegrative shaming, 264–265
restoration programs, 266
schools, 266
Restorative Justice Online, 265
restorative justice perspective, 21
retribution, 219–220
retributive terrorism, 356–357
reverse waiver, 342
review boards, 144, 145, 146
revocation
   defined, 247
   probation, 252–253
revolutionary, 356
Revolutionary Armed Forces of Colombia
   (FARC), 358
revolutionary terrorists, 356
RICO (Racketeer Influenced and Corrupt
   Organization Act), 259, 376–377
right to be competent at trial, 202
right to compulsory process, 203
right to confront witnesses, 202–203
right to counsel, 72, 74, 177, 203
right to impartial judge, 202
right to impartial jury, 203
right to public trial, 72, 204
right to reasonable care, 316–317
right to speedy trial, 72, 204
risk classification, 251
robbery, 31, 32
Roca Inc., 338
ROR (release on recognizance), 190
roving wiretaps, 71, 72
Russian election hacking, 327
Russian transnational crime groups, 375

S

Safe Streets and Crime Control Act, 7
San Francisco Pretrial Diversion Project,
   102
San Quentin prison, 278, 323
schizophrenia, 46
school vouchers, 291
scientific research, 8
search and seizure, 72
   automobile search, 152
   consent search, 152
   exclusionary rule, 153
   exigent circumstances, 152–153
   good faith exception, 153
   plain view search, 152

private police, 103
probable cause, 151
search incident to valid arrest, 151–152
search warrant, 149–151
stop and frisk, 152
strip search of inmates entering
   detention facility, 324
warrantless search, 151–153
search incident to valid arrest, 151–152
search warrant, 149–151
SEC (Securities and Exchange
   Commission), 362
Second Amendment, 67
Second Chance Act, 322
Second Chances program, 289
Secret Service, 91, 370
Section 1983 lawsuits, 313
Securities and Exchange Commission
   (SEC), 362
selection effect, 161
self-control theory, 51
self-defense, 65–66
self-defense gun use, 67
self-incrimination, 72, 74
self-report trends, 36
Senior Salute, 257
sentence discount, 198
sentencing, 13, 210–211
   age, 227
   concurrent/consecutive sentence, 224,
     224f
   determinate sentence, 221–222
   education, 227
   factors to consider, 226
   gender, 227
   goals, 218–220
   good time, 224–225
   guidelines, 222–223
   indeterminate sentence, 220–221
   juvenile justice, 344–345
   mandatory sentence, 223
   mean/median sentence length, 225t
   race, 228–229
   social class, 227
   three-strikes law, 223–224
   victim characteristics, 229
sentencing circle, 266
sentencing enhancement laws, 286
sentencing guidelines, 222–223
Sentencing Project, 228, 344
September 11, 2001 terrorist attacks, 61, 70
sex offender registration, 20, 69
sexual violence in prison, 298–299, 303
shaming and stigmatizing offenders, 264
sheriff, 82, 92
shire reeve, 82
shock incarceration, 289

shock probation, 260, 264

Sinaloa Federation, 375

Sing Sing prison, 277, 278

Sixth Amendment, 72, 177, 202, 204

skip tracers, 191

SMART (Supervision Motivation Accountable Responsibility and Treatment) probation, 252

"So Far, So Good: What We Know About Marijuana Legalization in Colorado, Washington, Alaska, Oregon and Washington, DC," 25

social agent policing style, 137

social bonds, 49

social class

    crime, 40–41

    sentencing, 227

social conflict theory, 49–50

social control, 9

social control theory, 49, 51

social learning theory, 46, 49, 51

social media, 102

social process theory, 49

social reaction (labeling) theory, 49

social structure theory, 47–49, 51

social worker, 332

Society for Alleviating the Miseries of Public Prisons, 275, 277

sociopathic personality, 47

sodomy statutes, 68

software piracy, 69, 367, 370

software theft, 367

solitary confinement, 315–316

sources of crime data. See measuring crime

Southeast European Cooperative Initiative, 376

specialized courts, 161–163

specialized probation, 255

specific deterrence, 219

split sentence, 247, 260, 264

spoofing, 368

SQF (stop, question, and frisk), 111

staff-on-inmate sexual misconduct, 303

stalking, 69, 369

stand-your-ground laws, 66

Standards Relating to Speedy Trial, 204

stare decisis, 56, 57

state courts

    appellate courts, 163–164

    courts of general jurisdiction, 163

    courts of limited jurisdiction, 160–163

    model of state judicial system, 164f

    specialized courts, 161–163

state courts of limited jurisdiction, 160–163

state criminal appeals, 164

state law enforcement agencies, 91–92

State of the Prisons, The (Howard), 274

State of the Prisons in England and Wales, The (Howard), 218

state (organized) crime, 50

state-sponsored terrorism, 356–357

state supreme court, 164f

states and constitutional restrictions, 73

status offenders, 335, 335f

statute of limitations, 11

statutory rape, 65

Step'n Out program, 256

Steps to Respect, 349

stigma, 20

stigmatize, 49

sting operation, 117–118

stock market manipulation, 367

stop, question, and frisk (SQF), 111

stop and frisk, 152

strain theory, 48, 51

strict liability crime, 62, 63

strict scrutiny standard, 316

strip search of inmates, 324

Stuxnet worm, 370

subculture, 49

substantial capacity test, 64

substantive criminal law, 56

substantive due process, 59, 74

substantive rights, 313–317

sufficient evidence, 205

suicide by cop, 144, 145

suicide in jails, 281

suicide warning system, 283

Sumners-Ashurst Act, 278

super-maximum-security prison (supermax prison), 284

superior court, 164f

Supervision Motivation Accountable Responsibility and Treatment program (SMART probation), 252

support functions, 126–128

Supreme Court of the United States. See US Supreme Court

sureties, 246

surety bail, 190

suspended sentence, 247

T

Takata Corporation, 360

taser, 148, 153

TASER International, 97

"tax on poverty," 241

TC (therapeutic communities), 305–306

technocorrections, 283

technology, 96–103. See also Criminal Justice and Technology boxes

    biometrics, 100

body cameras, 97–98

court management, 181–183

crime mapping, 100

crime scene investigation, 99–100

DNA testing, 100–101

hard/soft, 96, 98

identifying criminals, 99

investigation function, 118–119

locating criminals, 99

patrol function, 114–115

predictive analytics, 102–103

social media and networking, 102

Ten Commandments, 57

terrorism, 3, 354–359

    common aims of terror groups, 356–358

    computer hackers, 370

    county law enforcement agencies, 92–93

    definitions, 71, 355, 356

    Homeland Security agencies, 90–91

    law enforcement agencies, 94, 358

    metropolitan law enforcement agencies, 94

    prosecutor, 174

    September 11, 2001 terrorist attacks, 61, 70

    state law enforcement agencies, 91–92

    USA Freedom Act, 71–72, 359

    USA Patriot Act, 71, 359

testimonial evidence, 207

Texas Homeland Security office, 91

Texas Rangers, 91

"The Jungle," 48

theft of access numbers, 69

theft of information, 367

therapeutic communities (TC), 305–306

thief takers, 82–83

"thin blue line," 137

three-strikes law, 223–224

through-wall radar, 99, 151

ticket-of-leave, 277

Tijuana/Arellan Felix group, 376

time-in-rank system, 109

Tired Cops: The Prevalence and Potential Consequences of Police Fatigue, 142

tithing, 82

tort, 56

torture, 378

total institution, 296

town court judge, 170

trafficking in persons, 374

training, 121, 126–127

trajectory theory, 51

transfer hearing, 341

transfer to adult court (waiver), 341–343, 350

transnational crime groups, 374–376
transnational organized crime, 372–378
    controlling transnational crime, 376–377
    defined, 372
    difficulty in eradicating global crime, 377–378
    organized crime laws, 376–377
    Russian election hacking, 327
    transnational crime groups, 374–376
    types of transnational crimes, 373
Transocean Drilling Corporation, 362, 363
Travel Act (Interstate and Foreign Travel or Transportation in aid of Racketeering Enterprises Act), 376
treatment, 344
"Treatment of Youth of Color in the Justice System," 347–348
trial, 13
    bench, 201
    competence to stand trial, 202
    jury. *See* jury trial
    reasonable doubt standard, 204
    right to compulsory process, 203
    right to confront witnesses, 202–203
    right to counsel, 203
    right to impartial judge, 202
    right to impartial jury, 203
    right to public trial, 204
    right to speedy trial, 204
Trojan horse, 368–369
true bill of indictment, 12
"truly disadvantaged," 48
truth-in-sentencing laws, 286
Twitter, 102
211 Crew, 298

U

UCR. *See* Uniform Crime Reports (UCR)
UK National DNA Database, 119
UK National Drugs Intelligence Unit, 123
unborn fetus, 58
Unborn Victims of Violence Act, 58
unemployment and crime, 37, 41
unequal and inconsistent treatment, 20
UNICOR, 307
Uniform Crime Reports (UCR)
    accuracy, 32
    defined, 31
    hierarchy rule, 33

    interjurisdictional differences in crime, 33
    methods of expressing crime data, 32
    official crime statistics, 31
    replacement of UCR by NIBRS, 33
    trends, 35
United Nations Office of Drugs and Crime (UNODC), 375
unsecured bail, 190
unsolved cases, 118
urban poverty, 48
US Constitution. *See* constitutional criminal procedure
US courts of appeal, 165f, 166
US Department of Education, 36
US Department of Justice, 71, 299, 328, 362
US district courts, 165–166
US Justice Department agencies, 89–90
US magistrate judge, 170
US Marshals Service, 90
US Postal Inspection Service, 370
US Postal Service, 362
US State Department, 355
US Supreme Court
    case conference, 166
    majority/minority opinion, 167
    overview (flowchart), 167f
    writ of certiorari, 166
USA Freedom Act, 71–72, 359
USA Patriot Act (USAPA), 70, 71, 359
use of force, 144–147
    deadly force, 144–146
    less-lethal weapons, 147, 148
    nondeadly force, 147
    objective reasonableness standard, 145, 147
    relative ranking of force types, 145f

V

venire, 206
Vera Institute of Justice, 191
verdict, 209
Vestal, New York, Police Department, 108f
Vice Lords, 301
vice squad, 116
Vicodin, 28
victim. *See also* crime victimization
    plea bargaining, 200
    sentencing, 229
victim impact statement, 229, 235

victim-offender relationships, 43
Vigilant Solutions, 115
vigilantes, 83, 84
violation, 59
Virginia Emergency Operations Center, 125
viruses and worms, 368
vitamin and mineral deficiencies, 45
vocational programs, 307–308
vocational training centers, 289
voir dire, 206
Volkswagen, 360

W

waiver (juvenile), 341–343, 350
Wallkill Correctional Institute, 289
Walnut Street Jail, 275, 306
war on drugs, 377
warez, 367
warrantless search, 151–153
Washington Post, 146
watch system, 82
WatchGuard, 97
watchman policing style, 137
water pollution, 364
web defacement, 369
wedding cake model of justice, 16–17, 16f
wergild, 57, 216
white-collar crime, 359
Wickersham Commission, 7
widening the net of justice, 20, 201
women. *See also* gender
    chivalry hypothesis, 227
    correctional officers, 309–310
    police officers, 133–135
    prison inmates, 301–303
work release, 308
work-release programs, 279
worms, 368
writ of certiorari, 166
writ of *habeas corpus,* 211
wrongful conviction, 232, 233

Y

youth crime. *See* juvenile justice

Z

zealots, 349
zero tolerance, 259